John Winthrop
America's Forgotten Founding Father

FRANCIS J. BREMER

OXFORD
UNIVERSITY PRESS

OXFORD

UNIVERSITY PRESS

Auckland   Bangkok   Buenos Aires   Cape Town   Chennai
Dar es Salaam   Delhi   Hong Kong   Istanbul   Karachi   Kolkata
Kuala Lumpur   Madrid   Melbourne   Mexico City   Mumbai   Nairobi
São Paulo   Shanghai   Taipei   Tokyo   Toronto

Copyright © 2003 by Oxford University Press, Inc.

Published by Oxford University Press, Inc., 2003
198 Madison Avenue, New York, New York 10016
www.oup.com

First issued as an Oxford University Press paperback, 2005
ISBN-13: 978-0-19-517981-1
ISBN-10: 0-19-517981-1

Oxford is a registered trademark of Oxford University Press

The Library of Congress has cataloged the cloth edition as follows:
Bremer, Francis J.
John Winthrop: America's forgotten founding father /
Francis J. Bremer.
p.   cm.
Includes bibliographical references and index.
ISBN-13: 978-0-19-514913-5
ISBN-10: 0-19-514913-0
1. Winthrop, John, 1588–1649. 2. Governors—Massachusetts—Biography.
3. Puritans—Massachusetts—Biography.
4. Massachusetts—History—Colonial period, ca. 1600–1775.
5. Puritans—Massachusetts—History—17th century.
6. Great Britain—History—Tudors, 1485–1603.
7. Great Britain—History—Early Stuarts, 1603–1649.
8. England—Church history—16th century.
9. England—Church history—17th century.
I. Title
F67.W79 B74   2003   974.4'02'092—dc21   2002038143

1 3 5 7 9 8 6 4 2
Printed in the United States of America
on acid-free paper

for Bobbi

as John to Margaret,
"My only beloved spouse, my most sweet friend,
and faithful companion of my pilgrimage"

Contents

Acknowledgments and Thanks

O VER THE YEARS I have come to feel a strong connection between the stories of the past and places of the past, so it seemed natural to seek out the English places where the Winthrops had lived, attended school, served on the commission, and raised their families. I was fortunate to meet and befriend Martin and Jane Wood. Living a few hundred yards from St. Bartholomew's Church in Groton, Martin is himself an avid student of the early modern history of the parish and the region. Our families became friends, and over the past decade it has been a rare visit to England that did not find me spending time as a guest of the Woods. Together Martin and I explored towns, churches, and graveyards, walked the fields to gain an idea of the bounds of Winthrop's manor, and peered at microfilm in the record offices at Bury and Ipswich. Through the Woods I came to know and appreciate other members of the Boxford and Groton communities. Edgar and Jean Elliott once lived in what had been the Winthrop mansion house, where Edgar had himself been raised. During a massive rehabilitation preparatory to its division into three separate households, they took extensive photographs, which reveal the structure and decorations of the Tudor building. Their loan of those pictures proved invaluable in establishing Groton Place as the mansion house and in understanding its layout. Ron Partridge and his wife, Gladys, lived in Groton Hall, the original hall of the pre-Reformation manor, which came to house Winthrops as well in the late sixteenth and early seventeenth centuries. Their generosity in showing me the Hall and discussing its evolution likewise proved of great use. These and other residents of Groton, such as Mary Every, encouraged my work and shared generously of themselves. I was entered on the parish rolls as a nonresident member and allowed to read lessons during worship—a privilege I much value. John Taylor of nearby Newton discussed with me farming in Groton in Winthrop's times and today. In nearby Boxford, Jenny Robinson, a dedicated local historian of that community, was equally unstinting in her support and encouragement, allowing me to see and use some of the products of her own research and inviting my wife and me to relax in the splendors of the garden behind the Tudor coach house, across from St. Mary's church, that is her home.

IN A MORE traditional vein I have also profited from numerous scholars on both sides of the Atlantic. My greatest debts are perhaps to those who helped me to find my way through the thickets of English history, religion, and law. There was no Tudor-Stuart historian at Columbia University when I did my graduate work there, so my education in the field has come from reading books and asking questions. Among the many English-based scholars who patiently responded were Simon Adams, Ian Archer, J. H. Baker, Michael Braddick, Susan Brigden, Nicholas Canny, John Coffey, John Craig, Pauline Croft, Colin Davis, David Dymond, Lori Anne Ferrell, Ken Fincham, Frank Grace, Steve Gunn, Susan Hardman-Moore, Simon Healey, Steve Hindle, Ralph Houlbrooke, Judith Maltby, Peter Northeast, Jane Ohlmeyer, Glynn Parry, Andrew Petteggree, Wilfred Prest, Michael Questier, Steven Rappaport, John Schofield, Roger Thomson, Nicholas Tyacke, Susan Wabuda, Tim Wales, and John Walter. In this country I have benefited from the advice of Bob Anderson, Sarge Bush, Charles Cohen, Richard Dunn, David H. Fischer, Stephen Foster, Chris Fritsch, Richard Gildrie, David Hall, Stephen Innes, Rolf Loeber, Robert Middlekauff, Carol Miller, Mark Peterson, Richard Rath, and Hal Worthly.

At Millersville University I have benefited from the collegial atmosphere and the support of faculty colleagues, administrators, and students. Among those I would especially like to thank are Dennis Downey, John Osborne, Linda Clark-Newman, Jack Fischel, John Thornton, Chris Dahl, Susan Ortmann, Monica Spiese, John MacDonald, Richard Rath, Glen McCaskey, Jill Kress, and Terry Sales. The Faculty Grants Committee of Millersville University has been generous in supporting my research trips.

Other debts are more specific. Sue Sadler conducted the original research into John Winthrop's tenure on the Commission of the Peace. Tom Freeman showed me the Emmanuel College manuscripts relating to William Winthrop and assisted me on numerous occasions as I labored to identify Winthrop connections to the early English Reformation. Brett Usher pointed me to the Exchequer's composition books for first fruits, sharing with me his own findings in that treasure trove and saving me from errors on many occasions. Christopher Thompson not only shared with me his insights into the Forth family and their connections with the Riches but chauffered me around southeast Essex to examine Great Stambridge and the other places of Winthrop interest in that area. I have learned much from Tom Webster, who is one of the most brilliant of the younger generation of puritan scholars. At a National Endowment for the Humanities seminar in 1975 Tim Breen helped me to understand the broader cultural forces that are a key to understanding the past, and he has since been a valued friend and source of encouragement.

It is always a blessing when academic contacts lead to personal friendship, and I have been fortunate in this many times over. I still remember the wonderful humanity of Christopher Hill, holding the hands of my young daughters Heather and Kristin and skipping along the streets of Cincinnati, Ohio, in 1975. Christopher was there to speak at a conference I had organized at Thomas More College, "Puritanism in Old and New England"; we had corresponded, but it was the first time we had met. Though his advice was of more direct relevance to *Congregational Communion*, his enthusiasm for the early modern period remains an inspiration, and I have valued his friendship and my visits with him and Bridget.

I first met Pat Collinson when I was a Fulbright Fellow at Cambridge University. His Tudor-Stuart seminar introduced me to issues I would spend many more years considering and to fellow investigators whose friendship I have valued. Over the past decade Pat has come to Millersville University to speak, visited my family, played with our pet ferret, and shared his warmth, wit, and vast knowledge of the English world of John Winthrop.

That same year at Cambridge I came to know John Morrill, who has become a cherished friend, and his family friends of my family. We have collaborated in teaching a National Endowment for the Humanities summer seminar, "Two Faces of Puritanism: Oliver Cromwell and John Winthrop," at Millersville University; offered a pair of coordinated courses on seventeenth-century England and New England at Selwyn College, Cambridge; and cochaired a Liberty Fund seminar on the political thought of Winthrop and Cromwell in Lavenham, Suffolk. These opportunities have done much to shape my understanding of Winthrop and his place in the broader puritan movement.

Diarmaid MacCulloch arranged for me to be a visiting fellow at St. Cross College, Oxford, in 1997, giving me an opportunity to use the wonderful resources of the Bodleian Library and to discuss my interests with the brilliant collection of early modern English historians at Oxford. In the intervening years we have visited and corresponded, and I have profited from Diarmaid's exhaustive knowledge of the early English Reformation and of his home county of Suffolk. He has generously read the early chapters of this book and offered advice.

Mike McGiffert has long been a friend and supporter of my work. He read the first chapters of the book in early drafts, when encouragement was particularly important. Then he read the entire manuscript before it went into production. While I have not taken all his advice, I know that this is a better book where I have followed his suggestions.

My studies in the doctoral program at Columbia University were supervised by Alden Vaughan. At the time I did not appreciate how lucky I was to work with someone who encouraged his students to find their own topics and reach their own conclusions, who cared for them as individuals, and who would always be willing to offer advice and help. From him I learned not only how to be a historian but also how to be a teacher. Though

I never came to fully share his particular interests in early American history, he has always shown an interest in my work, and his advice has always been valuable.

I taught Dan Richter when he was an undergraduate at Thomas More College in Kentucky, but he has never held that against me. I take pride in having played a small role in helping this outstanding historian and appreciate the time he took to read and critique portions of this book in manuscript.

Lynn Botelho was part of a group of young and promising scholars at Cambridge when I spent time there in the early 1990s and now is a colleague in Pennsylvania's State System of Higher Education, teaching in the History Department at Indiana University of Pennsylvania. We worked together in organizing a 1999 conference, "The Worlds of John Winthrop: England and New England, 1588–1649," team-taught a course on the period via teleconferencing, and are collaborating on editing the book of essays developed from the conference.

NONE OF MY WORK on Winthrop would have been possible without the support of the Massachusetts Historical Society. I remember more than a decade ago calling Conrad Wright, whom I knew casually, when I wanted to find out where I could access a microfilm of John Winthrop's sermon notebook, which potentially had value for the project I was then working on, *Congregational Communion*. That conversation led to an offer that I assume the duties of editing the Winthrop Papers as a volunteer editor taking over after the retirement of Malcolm Frieburg, who had begun working on the project in his capacity as the society's editor of publications. Little did I know how much Winthrop material there remained to discover and publish, and as I gathered more and more of it the need for a new biography became evident. The tasks of editor and biographer were often indistinguishable, and much time was spent on Boylston Street. Conrad and Malcolm, Director Len Tucker and his successor, Bill Fowler, editorial staff members Don Yacovone and Ed Hansen, librarian Peter Drummy and his staff, and others who worked at the MHS were essential to the project.

As editor of the Winthrop Papers I have come to know members of the Winthrop family living today: John and Libby, Frederick, Nathaniel, Robert, and others have encouraged my investigations into their ancestor and searched their basements and attics with me in the quest for missing manuscripts, unfortunately without success.

MY WORK on England and New England in this period has been assisted by grants from the National Endowment for the Humanities, the American Philosophical Society, the Fulbright Foundation, the American Council of Learned Societies, and Millersville University. My experience of cochairing a seminar on Winthrop and Cromwell supported by the Liberty Fund helped to refine my understanding of Winthrop and his ideas.

Research has been conducted in numerous libraries and archival collections, and I would like to thank the professional staff of the following for their courtesy and assistance: Dr. Williams's Library in London, the Bodleian Library, the British Library, the National Library of Ireland, the Irish National Archives, the Inner Temple, Gray's Inn, the archives of the Clothworkers Company, the Guildhall Library, the Greater London Record Office, Cambridge University, the English College at Rome, the Folger Shakespeare Library, the Suffolk Record Office in Bury St. Edmunds, the Suffolk Record Office in Ipswich, the Public Record Office, the Essex Record Office in Colchester, the Essex Record Office in Chelmsford, the Essex Record Office in Southend, Allegheny College, the New York Society Library, the Massachusetts Historical Society, the American Antiquarian Society, the Harvard University Libraries, the Boston Athenæum, the Boston Public Library, and the New England Historical and Genealogical Society. I owe a special thanks to the Interlibrary Loan Service of Millersville University, and in particular Kay Fouts, for obtaining copies of books, theses and microfilm.

I would like to thank the staff at Oxford University Press for their support in making this book a reality. I am particularly grateful to Susan Ferber, who heard me speak on John Winthrop at a small conference in Cambridge, England, encouraged me to bring the project to the press, and has offered the right balance of support and advice throughout the processes of composition and revision.

As JOHN WINTHROP knew the value of family, so do I. The dedication of this book to my wife, Bobbi, is a small gesture of appreciation for all the love and support she has offered throughout our life together. We have been blessed by three wonderful children—Heather, Kristin, and Megan—of whom I am extremely proud. Megan deserves special thanks for her nonspecialist reading of the manuscript and the advice she gave. Our grandchildren—Keegan, Taylor, Ryan, and Lucy—have helped me to see the world anew. Telling them stories, taking them on trips, and watching them play baseball, soccer, and other sports have provided my life the balance that we all need. My brother-in-law, Larry Woodlock, helped me with translating material from Latin when I stumbled on my own. I would also like to thank my mother, Marie Bremer. And, finally, I wish to take this opportunity to thank my father, Francis Bremer, and my mother-in-law, Alice Woodlock, both of whom passed away during the preparations for this book.

Introduction

JOHN WINTHROP'S NAME is familiar to many who have studied American history. Countless college students have been assigned Edmund Morgan's short and fascinating study *The Puritan Dilemma: The Story of John Winthrop*. Readers of *Time* magazine may recollect that in that publication's listing of millennial landmarks the Reverend Peter Gomes identified Winthrop's "Model of Christian Charity" as the greatest sermon of the past thousand years. Numerous presidents and presidential candidates, including those as diverse as Ronald Reagan and Michael Dukakis, have quoted that 1630 address of the Massachusetts governor to try to reinspire Americans of our time to recognize that we are as a "city on a hill" and to urge upon us the duties of community. Yet Reagan and Dukakis rarely mentioned Winthrop's name while quoting his words, and most Americans are unfamiliar with his story and his significance. In this sense, John Winthrop is, indeed, America's forgotten Founding Father.

Those who have written about Winthrop have focused on his career in America to the extent that the first forty-two years of his life, with all they meant for the shaping of his identity and values, have been merely sketched or entirely ignored. In part this is because many authors have been less interested in the man and more concerned with using his life and writings to support their own interpretations of colonial life in general and puritanism in particular. His usefulness for such purposes derives from his undoubted centrality to early New England's history and the extensiveness of his surviving writings, through which much of that history is filtered. Thus we have had the Winthrop used to dispel the images of dour steeple-hatted zealots and humanize the early colonists. We have had the tolerant Winthrop, who resisted the bigotry of his more zealous contemporaries, but also the intolerant Winthrop, who drove Roger Williams and Anne Hutchinson into the howling American wilderness. Winthrop has also been used to demonstrate both the misogyny of early New Englanders and their loving marriages. Some, seeking to portray the native Americans as victims of an invasion of America, have interpreted Winthrop and his writings to advance their views. In these and other such cases the Winthrop of modern histories has been constructed to suit particular agendas. It is time for a biography that is interested primarily in John Winthrop himself.

In approaching this study I assumed that the making of John Winthrop was a process that involved the interaction of his own efforts at self-fashioning and the circumstances with which the broader forces of history confronted him. To understand the man properly requires not only examining his accomplishments in directing the Massachusetts Bay Colony in the 1630s and 1640s but looking back to his life, thoughts, and experiences before he came to the New World in 1630. Who was the man who led the great migration to New England in 1630, and how did he become the man that he was? What were the forces and experiences that shaped his sense of identity, destiny, and responsibility to others? This is, then, a study of the life and times of John Winthrop.

The possibilities of self-fashioning in the early modern era were set by the social, economic, geographic, and other circumstances in which one was born. The materials out of which one shaped an identity included family heritage, the cultural currents and countercurrents of the time, and the influence of friends as well as the core personality of the individual. To understand Winthrop requires examining the Tudor world into which he was born and the world of the early Stuart monarchs in which he matured. In recovering that context we are aided by the enormous outpouring of studies on the politics, society, economy, and religion of Tudor-Stuart England in the last quarter century. In placing Winthrop in that setting I have also been fortunate to identify numerous manuscript materials that had been overlooked by those interested primarily in the American Winthrop. My understanding of Winthrop's American career has been similarly enriched by the labors of countless scholars who have followed in the footsteps of Perry Miller in examining and deciphering the meaning of colonial New England.

PART ONE OF THIS STUDY follows the lives of Winthrop's grandfather, father, and uncles, not only for insight into his family heritage but as a means of understanding the economic, social, and religious transformation of early modern England in which they all played roles. Part Two focuses on his youth, education, and rise to a position of responsibility in the government of his county. It also examines his domestic life, struggles for religious assurance, and the factors that led him to emigrate. Part Three traces the more familiar story of Winthrop's role in the founding and shaping of Massachusetts and interprets his actions and positions by reference to his English experience and values.

No one who has written about John Winthrop would deny that he was a "puritan," yet students of the era find it impossible to agree on what exactly a "puritan" was. This is due in large measure to the fact that there was never—at least not prior to the settlement of New England—an institution, membership in which classified one as a puritan. Rather, we need to talk of a puritan character, or an orientation of consciousness and commitment toward certain religious beliefs and practice. In the broadest sense, it emerged as the response of the "hotter sort" of English Protestants who found Henry VIII's reformation incomplete and sought to purge the English church and society of remnants of Roman Catholic faith and practice. Referring to these reformers in the mid-sixteenth century I follow the lead of Diarmaid MacCulloch and other recent scholars in calling them "evangelicals," seeking to evoke their concern with spreading the reformed message through the purification of church institutions and the provision of a preaching ministry to serve all parishes. As the story progresses I will also occasionally refer to them as "the godly," a term they used to recognize the sense they had of the presence of God's spirit in one another. I do not use the word to suggest that others, who did not adopt it, were in any way less dedicated to their faith and their God. During the period of the sixteenth and early seventeenth centuries the godly, or evangelicals, can best be understood as representing a band that is located toward one end of the English religious spectrum. Looked at from afar, it seems a band of a single color. Examining it more closely, one can detect many different shadings. Furthermore, viewed from inside, the religious identity of any one individual was perceived differently depending on the observer's position on the spectrum. Their enemies sought to make puritans appear more extreme by stressing their distance from the center of the spectrum. The godly themselves often staked a claim to being part of the religious mainstream by lashing out against those further toward their end of the spectrum. As a result, who was and was not a member of the godly was largely in the eye of the beholder.

By the 1610s, in part because of episcopal efforts to precisely define what was and was not acceptable practice, the identification of the self-proclaimed godly as "puritan" became more common (some had used it earlier), and I begin to use the term to refer to Winthrop and others at that point in the story. At the same time, these efforts by the hierarchy resulted in puritans becoming more self-aware of their differences from "carnal gospellers" and other churchgoers who denied the need of further reform. But while the distinctions between puritans and others on the spectrum may have become clearer, there still was no single "puritan" way, and that has led me to adopt the practice of English historians in declining to capitalize the word. To me, "Puritan" suggests a fixed and defined entity, whereas "puritan" implies an orientation rather than a platform.

With apologies to those who would prefer things more tidy, I therefore employ "hotter sort of Protestant," "evangelical," "reformed," "godly," and "puritan" as being roughly synonymous. Each term evokes the image of a person who had a sense of being a sinner redeemed by God's grace and called to be a soldier of the Lord promoting true doctrine (generally some form of Calvinism), preaching, Scripture reading, love (albeit often a form of tough love), and the changes in church and society needed to advance those goals. Not all who shared this mission saw eye to eye, and that is another reason why John Winthrop's story, and that of puritanism in general, are so fascinating.

IN JOHN WINTHROP'S WORLD the new year was dated as beginning on March 25. I have imposed the modern convention of making January 1 the start of the new year. I have not adjusted the months and days recorded in the sources to reflect the other changes that would be made with the transition from the Julian to the Gregorian calendar in the British world in the eighteenth century. I have also modernized all quotations. Since some sources exist only in partially or completely modernized forms, this is the only way to achieve consistency. And I believe that it is the words used by Winthrop and his contemporaries that provide a flavor of their personalities, not the peculiarities of their spelling.

The prologue and the vignettes that open each chapter are intended to evoke something of the texture of Winthrop's life and times. Most of the details—even the name of the Winthrop family dog—are verifiable, but I have used my imagination to shape known facts into patterns that are plausible but not provable. They are set off from the main text, where I have labored to provide traditional documentation for my interpretations. Throughout the volume I have strived to bring readers to an appreciation of John Winthrop as he and others of his time saw him.

Prologue

━━━━━━━━

☙

Prologue

*W*INTER 1606. The winds blow hard over the marshes of south-east Essex at this time of year, bringing the piercing cold from Siberia and Scandinavia across the North Sea. The cold cuts through woolen clothes and cloaks, and its effects are intensified with the damp that is a year-round feature of this bleak landscape. The sun offers little comfort, rising late and setting early. Even today, when piers and beaches might draw crowds in summertime, the winter is a hard season in towns like Southend-on-Sea, Great Stambridge, and Rochford. In the seventeenth century, with no electricity to bring comfort or entertainment, it was an even bleaker place. As night closed in, the hearth became a center of sociability, with members of each household gathering around the light and heat of a roaring fire. In some dwellings, laboring men repaired their farm implements while their wives spun and their children played games. In the halls of the upper class, the focus was more on sociability. Around the fires of both the humble and the well-to-do, the time was passed by storytelling.[1]

For the gentry in this part of Essex, one such gathering place was Rochford Hall, the home of the Rich family. Both the community and the family were noted for zealous Protestantism. Rochford had been the scene of the burning of the reformer John Simson during the reign of the Catholic Queen Mary.[2] And, as if those flames had not killed but rather kindled a renewed dedication to Protestant reform, Rochford Hall under Queen Elizabeth had become a center for those who fought for the further purification of the Church of England. Lord Rich, the brother-in-law of the earl of Essex, the queen's favorite, named Robert Wright as his domestic chaplain at Rochford Hall. Wright, who had sought ordination in Amsterdam because of his disapproval of some of the unreformed practices of the Church of England, organized members of the Rich household into a gathered congregation, a set of believers meeting apart from the parish church. Members of the local parish were drawn away from the official services to listen to Wright preach at the Hall. This violated the canons of the church and led to the bishop of London prosecuting Wright and members of his flock. Among the charges was the claim that Wright had referred to "preachers that followed the Book of Common Prayer as 'dumb dogs.'"[3] The result had been the brief imprisonment of both Lord Rich and Wright, as well as the confirmation of their reputation for godliness. The zeal for reform that characterized the two men remained the hallmark of Rochford Hall in the early 1600s.

GIVEN THE CONCERN of members of the Rich family to do God's will, puritan clergy from the area such as Ezekiel Culverwell and Arthur Dent would have been frequent guests. Samuel Purchas, the rector of the nearby parish of Eastwood, would have been welcomed to Rochford Hall. He was a conscientious pastor such as the Rich family approved of; his brother and successor would later be deprived of his church living for puritan practices. Purchas had other links to the Rich family as well. The Rich family owned the manor of Eastwood, and Samuel Vassal, a friend of Purchas, farmed land there.

Purchas was more than just a country rector. He had taken upon himself the mantle of Richard Hakluyt, the famous promoter of English colonization, and at this time was involved in gathering the stories of English and other voyagers to the New World that he would publish as *Hakluyt Posthumus; or Purchas His Pilgrimes*.[4] So, as he joined with his neighbors, the clergyman would take advantage of the long winter evenings to share tales of new worlds and exciting adventures of the sort that would fire the imaginations of his listeners, especially the younger members of the group. Among those who would have gathered in the great hall to hear him was Nathaniel Rich, the son of Lord Rich. His cousins, Robert and Henry Rich, would be present on occasion. As a matter of course John Forth, the Rich family's bailiff, their agent in dealing with tenants and collecting rents, would be there. Also mingling with this company to listen to the exotic tales of Samuel Purchas would have been Forth's young son-in-law, John Winthrop.

Purchas told tales of Columbus and the explorer's encounters with "certain Caribs, which used inhumane huntings for human game, to take men to eat them."[5] He recounted the wonders discovered by the Cabots in northern climes, where the "inhabitants wear bear skins" and there were "white bears and stags far greater than ours."[6] He described Cortés's conquest of Mexico and the explorations of the Isthmus of Panama, of Peru, and of Africa. If asked about English adventurers, he would have regaled his audience with tales of wonder and danger featuring explorers such as Sir Martin Frobisher, Sir Humfry Gilbert, and John Smith.[7] On the voyage of Stephen Burrough along the coast of Newfoundland, the ship was lost and the mariners forced to winter on the ice, where "their shoes did freeze as hard as horns on their feet, and as they sat within doors before a great fire . . . , putting their feet to the fire they burned their hose, and discerned that by the smell before they could feel the heat."[8] Purchas told of the sufferings of the lost colony of Roanoke and the early Jamestown colonists. His interpretation of these adventures would have resonated with his godly audience, for whereas Hakluyt's compilations carried a more secular argument for England's expansion, Purchas expressed the conviction that God was waiting for England to take up the task of spreading the gospel to these new lands.[9] Riveting in themselves, Purchas's tales were thus wrapped in a call to religious service, which would make them especially alluring to his audience at Rochford Hall.

JOHN WINTHROP HAD BEEN four months past his seventeenth birthday in April of 1605 when the Reverend Ezekiel Culverwell joined him in marriage to Mary Forth in the parish church of Great Stambridge. Winthrop had been raised in the Stour Valley, which formed the border between north Essex and the county of Suffolk, but following his marriage he settled in Great Stambridge on lands provided by his father-in-law, John Forth. It was a difficult move for the young man. His bride was neither as well educated as the women of his own family nor as committed to godliness as Winthrop had expected. His relationship with his father-in-law was strained. Besides, coming from a region where proponents of a reformed evangelical faith, such as Winthrop himself, dominated the cultural scene, the young man would have been uncomfortable in this area of southeast Essex where religion was more contested and where godly men and women were often scorned and derided.

Equally troubling for the young man were his poor prospects. The only son of a younger son, John had few expectations. The Suffolk manor on which he had been raised belonged to his uncle, and prospects of it eventually passing to his father and then to him were uncertain at best. His father, Adam, was a well-respected barrister who handled legal matters for his brother and other landlords, and he was well connected with the godly elite, both clerical and lay, in the Stour Valley. But Adam's wealth and landholdings were modest and would have been stretched to provide for John and his three surviving daughters as well. John had aspired to a career in the ministry and had studied briefly at Trinity College, Cambridge, but family and friends had dissuaded him from that course, and his strong attraction to Mary Forth had led him to abandon the university. His future now appeared to depend on how he could fit in with and impress the leaders of southeast Essex who were his new neighbors. For John Winthrop the winter nights must have seemed bleak indeed.

The years at Great Stambridge would, however, prove to be a time not only of testing but of great fruitfulness. Ezekiel Culverwell had himself spent many years in the Stour Valley and was a friend to many of the clergy whom Winthrop had met and befriended when growing up. Culverwell became an important support to Winthrop and a strong influence on the young man's piety as he struggled to learn how to remain godly in an ungodly world. Despite what differences may have existed between them, as bailiff for the Rich family John's father-in-law provided the young man with an entrée into that powerful circle. At Rochford Hall Winthrop would have mingled with both members of the gentry, including Robert Rich, later to be the second earl of Warwick, his brother, Henry Rich, later to be the earl of Holland, and the local intelligentsia, including clergy like Culverwell, Dent, and Purchas.

IN THE EARLY MODERN WORLD the character of men and women was shaped in part by the circumstances in which they were born but in part also by their own efforts of self-fashioning, though this was less common at the extreme ends of the social spectrum. Those who inherited titles were burdened by long family traditions that set rigid expectations and virtually determined their life courses.[10] Members of the lower class were generally condemned by circumstance to lives of grinding poverty and desperation. On the other hand, those who were part of the rising middling classes, profiting from the fluctuating market and the expansion of opportunities in education and the professions, were more likely to have options to choose from. This was particularly true for younger sons and the sons of younger sons, men unlikely to inherit an estate or a business. Protestantism played a part in this process as well, emphasizing as it did the need to reject one's natural and sinful self. Conversion, which was so great a concern for those who aspired to God's grace, brought about a rebirth and set an agenda for refashioning the new self in a godly manner.[11]

The John Winthrop who listened to the tales of Purchas in the early 1600s and who came to America in 1630 was the product of such a process. His background certainly helped to shape him, but it also presented him with choices. Unlike many Englishmen, whose background and status as heirs almost determined their futures, John Winthrop—young, married, with little land and few prospects—could have chosen from any number of paths. His own family provided him different models to emulate. His grandfather had risen from obscurity to be a leading figure in the London business community. His own father, Adam, was a barrister, an estate manager, and a college officer. His uncle John was a brawler and scoundrel who was excommunicated and sought a new life on the Irish frontier. His other uncle, William, was a leading supporter of religious reform. In leaving his home along the Stour Valley to attend Cambridge University, John had entered a world of new ideas and new experiences. His marriage and move to Great Stambridge had been another epiphany.

Granted, John had been raised by his parents in a way designed to set him on a certain path and to instill in him certain values. Still, the efforts of parents are but one influence in determining the life and character of the man. One had only to look as far as the very different lives of John's father and two uncles to see that. John would draw on the world he grew up in, the family tales he was told, the people who moved through his youth, and the ideas that he was exposed to in order to shape himself into a humble Christian prepared to follow whatever path God set him on. As he listened to Purchas in 1606, he could not have imagined that his pilgrimage would make him a central figure in later chronicles of English exploits in the New World.

Part One

Heritage

☙

The Winthrop Family

Adam Winthrop (?–?) m Jane Burton (?–?)

Alice Hunne (?–1533) m Adam Winthrop (1498–1562) m (2) Agnes Sharpe (c1516–1565)

William (1529–1582)
m
Elizabeth Norwood (?–1578)
Children:
Joshua (1559–1626)
Adam (1561–1631)
Elizabeth (1569–1631)

Alice (1539–1607)
m
Thomas Mildmay

Bridget (1543–1614)
m
Roger Alabaster

Mary (1545–c1605)
m (1)
William Cely
m (2)
Abraham Vesey

John (1547–1613)
m
Elizabeth Rysby
m (?)
Elizabeth Powlden

Adam (1548–1623)
m (1) 1574
Alice Still
no issue
m (2)
Anne Browne (?–1629)

Susannah (1552–1604)
m
John Cotta

Anne (1586–1619)
m
Thomas Fones

John (1588–1649)
m (1) 1605
Mary Forth (1583–1615)
m (2) 1615
Thomasine Clopton (1583–1616)
m (3) 1618
Margaret Tyndal (?–1647)
m (4) 1647
Martha Rainsborow Coytmore

Jane (1592–1666?)
m
Thomas Gostlin

Lucy (1601–1679)
m
Emmanuel Downing

John (s of 1) (1606–1676)

Henry (s of 1) (1608–1630)

Forth (s of 1) (1610–1630)

Mary (d of 1) (1612–1643)

Stephen (s of 3) (1619–1658)

Adam (s of 3) (1620–1652)

Deane (s of 3) (1623–1704)

Samuel (s of 3) (1627–1674)

1

Lavenham to London

OCTOBER 1498. Adam Winthrop was carrying his infant son, the next Adam, from his home to the church of Saints Peter and Paul sitting on the hill overlooking the prosperous town of Lavenham. There he would present the baby to the parish priest, Thomas Appleton, to be baptized according to the rites of the Catholic Church.[1] Accompanying Adam were some of his friends from the parish, perhaps including members of the prominent Lavenham families, the Springs, the Risbys, and the Ponders. Jane Burton Winthrop, young Adam's mother, was left lying in at home, denied entry into the holy precincts of the church until she was purified in a rite that usually came about a month after the childbirth.

A booming regional economy, a strong sense of piety, and a desire to create monuments to that piety that would stand them in good stead when they went to their last judgment had recently prompted the Christians of Suffolk to expand and beautify the churches of the region, and nowhere was that more evident than in Lavenham.[2] Just four years earlier the base of a new church tower had been laid, and plans were also under way to add a new chapel, dedicated to the Holy Trinity, on the north side of the chancel.[3] Building supplies cluttered the church precincts, and the dust of construction floated in the air as the senior Winthrop and the friends he had chosen as sponsors, or godparents, met the priest at the south door of the church. Custom dictated two godfathers and one godmother for a boy.[4] The priest made "a sign of the cross on the infant's forehead, breast, and right hand. He placed some salt in the baby's mouth according to custom; then the priest exorcized the devil from its body with a number of prayers, and pronounced baptism as the sole means 'to obtain eternal grace by spiritual regeneration.'" The preliminary ritual completed, the baptismal party made their way to the fourteenth-century font. The font in Lavenham was made of Purbeck marble, adorned with the shields of Saints Peter and Paul and carved panels, one of which depicted a mother and child with a satanic angel turning away. That image was deliberate, for the rite of baptism was intended to symbolize both renunciation of Satan and incorporation into the communion of saints.[5] The church interior was dark, illuminated primarily by the light shining through the stained glass windows, the colored beams bearing moving motes of dust generated by the construction. Each of the various altars in the church was lit with candles, and where the believers gathered around the font other candles created a small island of light around the Winthrop infant as the priest "divided the water with his right hand and cast it in the four directions of the cross. He breathed three times upon it and then spilled wax in a cruciform pattern. He divided the holy water with a candle, before returning the taper to the cleric beside him. Oil and chrism were added with a long rod or spoon."[6] The rite continued with a reminder that all men are born in sin but that through the sacrament of baptism the child might be regenerated. The sponsors were questioned; then they asked for baptism on behalf of the infant. Dipping him three times into the waters of the font, the priest proclaimed, in Latin, "Adam, I baptize thee in the name of the Father, the Son, and the Holy Ghost." He anointed the infant with chrism, making a cross on Adam's forehead, signifying that "hereafter he shall not be ashamed to confess the faith of Christ crucified." The babe was wrapped in a chrismal robe, and a candle was lit and placed in his hand.

The ceremony of baptism evoked the sense of union between natural and supernatural that was so much a part of the early modern world of the Winthrops. In receiving the sacrament the infant Adam entered the Christian community. All knew that his future health, physical and spiritual, would be constantly tested. The devil who was exorcized from the infant would try again to seize his soul. The communion of saints to which he had been admitted would help Adam to resist those assaults. Sin was inevitable, but forgiveness was promised to those who followed the path set out by God and employed the means of grace, such as the sacraments, which were provided by God's church. Religion was not merely a part of life; it was the center of existence and permeated all other aspects. Although the fourteenth-century heresy of Lollardy had struck a chord with many in Suffolk, the faith of Adam Winthrop's neighbors in 1498, nineteen years before Martin Luther's challenge, was that of the Catholic Church governed from Rome.

The centrality of this faith was illustrated not only by the magnificent church and its new additions but by the prosperous religious guilds of the town. Lavenham had four such fraternities, dedicated to the Holy Trinity, Our Lady, Corpus Christi, and Saints Peter and Paul.[7] Each provided candles and other accoutrements of worship, procured prayers and alms for the repose of the souls of departed members, and promoted charity and a sense of community.[8] The impressive Corpus Christi guildhall still stands on the square in Lavenham as testimony to the support that such fraternities commanded. Clergymen such as Thomas Appleton directed the laity in how to best serve God, their authority derived from a chain of authority that went back to St. Peter. They were empowered by the sacrament of Holy Orders to perform the miracle of the mass, to administer grace through other sacraments, and to forgive sins. Their literacy, dress, and use of Latin in the rituals of worship were all badges of their superior nature.

☙

*T*HE ELDER ADAM WINTHROP, who sought baptism for his young son, is the first forebear of John Winthrop whom we can identify with any certainty. Even here we do not know where he came from, when he married, if he had other children, or even when he died. He is simply identified as a clothier. His wife, Jane Burton Winthrop, is almost equally hidden from our inquiries. No registration of births, marriages, or deaths was required in England at this time, and only those of gentle birth or pretensions had reason to preserve their genealogies. It is believed that the couple lived in a building that still stands, on what is now called Barn Street in Lavenham. Transformed over the centuries—for a time it was a grammar school in which the artist John Constable learned his early lessons—portions of the fifteenth-century home survive, most notably a carved wooden frieze, dating from the time of the Winthrops, on which are carved shields embossed with the letter *W*, angels, an image of Christ crucified, and a figure thought to represent St. Edward the Confessor.[9] Perhaps it was there that the Winthrops joined with friends and neighbors to celebrate the baptism of young Adam.

East Anglia in general, and this area of south Suffolk in particular, had prospered from the cloth trade in the fifteenth century, and Lavenham was one of the centers of that industry. Those who succeeded as craftsmen in the surrounding villages gravitated to such towns in the hope of achieving greater success as clothiers; this makes a family tradition that says Adam and Jane both came to Lavenham from the area around Groton at least plausible. As a clothier, Adam would have been an organizer and financier, providing capital for the purchase of wool, generally from Lincolnshire, Northamptonshire, or elsewhere, because Suffolk wool was not rated highly. He would have recruited and paid dyers, weavers, fullers, and other craftsmen who produced the broad cloths for which the region was noted, and then sold them, often at London's Blackwell Hall, to members of the city trade guilds who would export them abroad. The clothiers, especially the Springs, Risbys, Braunches, and Ponders, were important men in Lavenham—prosperous, influencing town affairs, and contributing to the beautification of the church.

Adam Winthrop, the Lavenham clothier, died when his son was still young. His widow married John Ponder, a clothier of greater stature than her first husband. Ponder would be credited with contributing four marks to the building of the church tower in 1520, and when he died he was buried in a tomb substantial enough that it could much later be moved into the church itself.[10] John Ponder had four sons of his own; two of them would become clothiers, one a clergyman, and another a member of the Pewterers Company of London.[11] Even so, he did not neglect his stepson. On one of his trips to Blackwell Hall he arranged for the young Adam to be apprenticed to Edward Altham, a member of the Fullers Company of London. The Fullers, like the Pewterers Company, was one of the great self-regulating guilds of London that controlled the manufacture and distribution of goods. John Ponder would have paid a fee for apprenticing his stepson, and, though the records do not survive, that fee would have been registered by the company. Altham on his part would have been looking for a young man who had some education and polish and, most important, was of good character, for Adam would live in his house and potentially become a fellow guild member. Under Altham young Adam would learn the skills of cleansing and thickening cloth to prepare it for finishing.

On arriving in London in 1515 Adam would have been examined by the wardens of the guild, who, dressed in the livery of the Fullers, would then have administered an oath to the young man. Within a year Altham was also required to bring the apprentice before the municipal officials, perhaps on one of the set guild days, to have his contract officially enrolled. Each of these ceremonies had its own rituals and was designed to underline the importance of the occasion as the young man was launched on the path to company membership and city citizenship.[12]

LAVENHAM WAS A MAJOR market town, but nothing he had experienced there could have prepared Adam Winthrop for London. Fueled by peace, by a respite from epidemic diseases, and by an expanding prosperity, England's population grew rapidly in the sixteenth century, and nowhere was the growth more evident than in London. Adam was but one drop in a stream of young men that flooded the neighborhoods of the metropolis before forcing expansion beyond the old medieval walls. Over one thousand young men arrived in London annually to apprentice at this time, and still the demand for labor exceeded the supply.[13] In the course of the sixteenth century the population of London rose from around 50,000 to over 200,000.[14] By contrast, the total population of Lavenham at this time was about 1,100.[15] Most Londoners lived within the square mile outlined by the city walls, portions of which remained from Roman days but had been regularly repaired, most recently in 1477, so as to provide the city with protection against dynastic challengers and peasant rebels.[16] As he explored his new home Adam could have walked from the Tower in the east to Ludgate, the western gate, in about a half hour. Exiting Ludgate he could have walked westward toward the Inns of Court, the training ground for lawyers, and then on a short distance to Westminster, the seat of the kingdom's central courts and government.

The City of London comprised numerous neighborhoods and divided for purposes of civil government into wards—twenty-five at the time of Adam's arrival—and into more than one hundred parishes for purposes of worship. The city as a whole was governed by a mayor, a sheriff, and a council of aldermen, but most affairs that concerned the inhabitants were handled on the local level. Parishes, which usually contained fewer than a hundred households, were run by vestries that chose church wardens to handle everyday matters. In each ward, householders (occupants of dwelling places who were entitled to vote) gathered annually in what was called the wardmote. Presided over by the ward's city alderman, the wardmote elected juries; licensed bakers, brewers, and innkeepers; chose local officers such as constable, beadle, and scavenger; and entertained complaints from citizens. The guilds, or livery companies, also played a role in government, not only by regulating their own trades but also by carrying out government edicts. Merchants, artisans, and tradesmen tended to congregate together with others of their profession. Bread Street, Ironmonger Lane, Fish Market, and Wood Street were but some of the names that designated urban markets, and members of livery companies often lived near the company hall where they conducted their business and regulated their trade. Scattered throughout the city were pockets of foreign nationals—strangers, as they were known—who had been allowed to settle and pursue their trades in the city.

Dominating the urban landscape was the cathedral dedicated to St. Paul. Citizens gathered there for worship on major feast days, but it was a hub for business transactions as well since its many altars provided ample opportunities for swearing to contracts. Nearby was the Folkmoot, where London's citizens gathered to conduct civic business. Cheapside, a major market street, together with the nearby Guildhall, formed another civic center, the site for processions and parades as well as trade.[17] But while Adam would have become familiar with these neighborhoods, most of his time was spent in the confines of Altham's home and the streets around it.

A prosperous member of the Fullers such as Edward Altham would have owned property with perhaps thirty or forty feet of street frontage containing a range of shopfronts, which he might use to sell his own goods or rent out to other merchants. These typically three-story structures, each with its overhanging upper stories and shop signs, crowded the light from the canyonlike streets and trapped the smells of food, sweat, and human as well as animal waste. The burning of sea coal in countless hearths not only added its distinctive smell but also contributed to the foglike haze in which

the city was often cloaked. Extending along one or both sides of a courtyard behind the shops was the hall where the family and servants lived.

Adam would have lived with Altham's other apprentices, either above
the shops or in the hall. He would have taken his meals with the family,
received his clothing from Altham, and been subject to his master's discipline just as if he were Altham's own son.[18] His master's status would have
assured Adam of accommodation and diet superior to that of many apprentices, not to mention most other Londoners. Most of his daylight hours
would have been spent learning the mysteries of his new vocation. His
future prospects depended on mastering his trade, and success was by no
means guaranteed. During the period from 1510 to 1529 barely one in three
apprentices actually finished their terms.[19]

Winthrop's contract prohibited him from marrying during his appren-
ticeship, as well as from gambling, frequenting taverns, and haunting play-
houses.[20] Living with their master's family made avoiding these prohibitions
more difficult for youngsters and inhibited the easy development of a youthful apprentice culture. Nevertheless, young men would cross the Thames
to Southwark to watch bear baiting or walk to Smithfield for horse racing.
Executions at Tyburn and the pillorying of false traders at the Tun on
Cornhill Street were spectacles that drew crowds. Various civic occasions
were marked by pageants and processions, with the members of the city
livery companies parading in all their finery. The celebration of Midsummer Eve saw homes decked out in greenery, bonfires set in the streets, and
a parade led by representations of the giants Gog and Magog. Christmastime
also saw celebrations. Events such as these were part of the London life in
which Adam immersed himself. Routines were also occasionally broken by
random violence, often inflicted on foreigners by youthful mobs that included apprentices. A chronicle of the times recorded one such outbreak in
Adam's first year in the city when, on May Day 1516, "the commons of the
city and the apprentices did rob and spoil strangers, and was in divers places
of the city gallows set up" where many were "hanged and quartered."[21]

As overwhelming to Adam as the city's many neighborhoods and activities were its sounds, a tumultuous cacophony that would have confused
him until he gradually adapted to the metropolis and was able to sort out
its many different notes. Heard throughout the day and throughout the
city was the melody of the bells of the parish churches—bells to summon
believers to services, bells to mark the hour of the day, bells to note the
approaching death of a parishioner (but never for the dead), and bells rung
by exuberant youth or others for no reason at all. Near the northern wall
one could hear the lowing of cattle and the sounds of pigs, sheep, and
other livestock at Smithfield. In other parts of the city one heard tapping
from the shops of shoemakers, thumps from the coopers, clinking sounds
from the workshops of pot makers, the pounding noise of hammers and

anvils from the smiths, and countless other distinctive noises of trade. Near the baiting arena could be heard the spine-chilling roars of the bears and the snarl of dogs during performances, and at other times the yelps and growls of the hundreds of animals penned in the kennels. From the play-houses came the cheers and jeers of the crowds, as well as the drums, trum-pets, and other noises of the performances. Everywhere shopkeepers called to passersby as they hawked their wares, their cries interrupted by the shouts of itinerant peddlers competing for the same business. The crowded streets were filled with conversation in most of the languages of Europe. Gather-ing places like the Exchange and the area around St. Paul's gave off a par-ticularly busy buzz of talk. Carts rumbled over the cobbled streets, their clattering passage marked by the jingling of bells on the horse harnesses and the shouts of the drivers to clear their way. In most areas of the city there would have been the background sound of rushing water—water moving through the conduits along Cornhill and other streets, and the sound of the Thames rushing through the narrow arches of the bridges that spanned the river as it shifted with the tides. Processions, pageants, and other spe-cial events broke through the everyday noise with notes of their own.[22]

One link of continuity between life in Lavenham and London was re-ligion, for the services Adam attended in London were the same as in the Suffolk market town. Indeed, the ritual rhythms and sounds of the Latin liturgy were the same throughout Christendom and gave worshipers a sense of being connected to a wider community than the parish or even the na-tion. Yet the spiritual realm was not without tensions, and friction between laymen and the clergy was also a part of the London scene. A short time before Adam's journey to the city, Richard Hunne had dramatically chal-lenged church officials. In 1511 Hunne, a member of the Merchant Tailors Company, had angered church officials by defending a fellow merchant's wife who had been accused of heresy. Within a year his son died, and Hunne refused to hand over to the parish priest the boy's winding sheet, which was the traditional fee for performing a funeral. He maintained his posi-tion despite the judgment of church courts, and his resistance to the un-popular fee garnered considerable popular support. Hunne was charged with heresy and imprisoned. Shortly thereafter he was found hanging in his cell. Many concluded that he had been murdered on the order of church officials, and he became something of a martyr in the eyes of those who were discontented with the church.[23]

Because he was contracted to a prominent company man, Adam's ap-prenticeship lasted longer than average, eleven rather than seven years, but in return he would have expected to benefit from Altham's patronage. In September 1526 Adam accompanied Altham to the Fullers Company Hall on Fenchurch Street, where he swore an oath before the master and wardens and was admitted a member of the company.[24] A few days later

Altham and one of the company wardens went with Winthrop to the Guildhall, where he took the oath of a freeman and was enrolled as a citizen of
London.[25] With the assistance of Altham or of his Ponder kin, Adam soon
set himself up as a householder of the Company in the Cornhill ward,
meaning that he could operate his own business. His feet firmly planted on
the path to success, he was now able to wed, and on November 16, 1527,
he married Alice Hunne.[26] Alice was the daughter of Richard Hunne, and
by marrying her Adam identified himself with the movement for church
reform. In the year following Adam's marriage the Fullers merged with
the Shearsmen, another company involved in the manufacture of cloth (cutting and trimming the fulled cloth), to form a larger and wealthier association, the Clothworkers Company, which immediately became one of the
elite livery companies of the city.[27]

All of the guilds were hierarchical organizations, and Adam's business
acumen was reflected in his rapid rise from journeyman, or yeoman, to
householder before 1531 and to member of the livery (entitled to wear the
elaborate garb of the company) in 1536, a privilege extended to only one in
four members of the company. Like other ambitious men of the time, he
was not above bending the rules to achieve advantage. Among the functions of each guild was to ensure the quality of the goods produced by its
members. In 1530 Winthrop was fined fifteen shillings for resisting a search
of his goods by company inspectors and for two cloths that failed to meet
set standards. Similar fines would be assessed on him in 1537, 1542, and
1543, but this did not block his growing success. He was authorized to take
on apprentices of his own, the first in 1531, another two years later, and
still others in the 1540s. In 1537, with Altham as master of the Clothworkers,
Adam began his climb to power in the company when he was chosen one
of the stewards.[28] This would have involved him in various guild activities,
including making preparations for the company's great annual feast.[29] In
1543 he was elected renter warden, an office that required him to collect
and account for rents on company property, disburse charitable gifts, and
otherwise manage financial accounts. As one of the wardens he also met
regularly with other officers to judge disputes, approve apprenticeships
and entries into the company, and deal with matters regarding the Hall
and other company property, as well as planning business, social, and charitable activities of the company. In 1546 Adam Winthrop was elected prime
warden and then, in 1551, was elected master, the highest office in the company and a position that gave him significant status in the city. In these
offices he was a key figure in the major rebuilding of the Clothworkers
Hall in 1549.[30] Entering the new complex from Mincing Lane, he would
have taken pride in a large hall, flanked by a courtyard on the left and
formal gardens on the right. In the range that crossed the back of the hall
were kitchens, a warehouse, and a buttery.[31]

As he rose through the ranks of the Clothworkers, Adam kept his eye on his own business as well. He was primarily engaged in the export of cloths to the continent, an enterprise that required him to pay attention to the political and economic trends that influenced the nation's trade.[32] Henry VIII had been crowned in 1509, much to the delight of Englishmen who viewed his youth, polish, education, and gregariousness as a refreshing change from the dour personality and controversial policies of his father. Henry's marriage to Catherine of Aragon reinforced a positive relationship not only with Spain but also with the lands of the Holy Roman Empire governed by her nephew Charles V. Henry demonstrated his learning and commitment to the Catholic faith when he published *Assertio Septem Sacramentorum* (1521) refuting Martin Luther's views on the sacraments; he was rewarded by the pope with the title "Defender of the Faith."

By the mid-1520s, however, Henry was expressing concerns about Catherine's failure to deliver a son and heir, concerns that led him to question the legitimacy of a marriage that had only been made possible by a special dispensation permitting him to marry his brother's widow. He embarked on a path that would lead to both a personal marriage annulment and England's separation from the Catholic Church, a course that held serious implications for the nation's political and economic relations with other European powers. English merchants, including Adam Winthrop, found their trade interfered with as unfriendly powers failed to protect it.[33] A list of grievances that English diplomats presented to imperial representatives at a Diet in 1545 included a complaint filed in 1542 by "John Towson of Plymouth and Adam Wintrop of London" who charged that they had been robbed of £176 of merchandise "by one Stephen Barbere and his accomplices of Montegro in the Bay of Biscay."[34] At this time Adam clearly was one of the smaller number of English cloth merchants who were trading to the south as opposed to in the Baltic.

As his business grew, Winthrop came to own at least one ship, the *Mary Flower*, and a three-quarter interest in another, the *John* of London. As a shipowner he also dealt with cargoes other than cloth, such as lead. Between 1540 and 1550 he appeared before the High Court of Admiralty six times as a defendant and another seven times as a plaintiff in cases involving disputes over loss of goods, debts, and failures to pay for the transit of freight.[35] One measure of his prosperity is found in the subsidy returns for 1541. At this time Winthrop lived in the parish of St. Peter's Cornhill. Assessed for this tax on the basis of £200 of property, he was the third wealthiest listed individual in the parish.[36] At a time when most Englishmen's horizon extended no further than the spires of churches in neighboring communities, and their worlds reached only as far as the nearest market town or shire hall, the Winthrops were engaging with the world beyond England.[37]

While jostling his way to business success, Adam was presiding over a growing family. A year after his marriage to Alice Hunne she bore a son, Thomas, who died six months later. In November 1529 she gave birth to another boy, christened William at the church of St. Peter's in Cornhill. A daughter and two more sons quickly followed, but all these died very young. Alice herself passed away, probably from complications of childbirth, in 1533. Adam, as was then customary, wasted little time in finding a new wife. In July 1534 he wed Agnes Sharpe, the daughter of Robert Sharpe of Islington, just outside of London in the county of Middlesex. Not until November 1539 would she deliver a child, christened Alice at St. Peter's Cornhill. Other children soon followed: Bridget in 1543; Mary in 1545; twins John and Adam in 1547 (Adam died six months later); another Adam in 1548; and two more daughters, Catherine in 1549 and Susannah in 1550.[38]

With a little imagination it is possible to gain an idea of the family's domestic circumstances. Years later, in 1577, William Winthrop would sell a property on Finkes Lane in Cornhill that he had obtained from his father. At the time he sold it William had divided it into two houses and rented them out, but its location and size make it likely that at some time this had served as the family home. Though the details provided in the deed of sale are sparse, they enable us to relate it to other, better-documented homes in the ward and thus to reasonably speculate on what it might have been like when the Winthrops lived there.[39] The property had a thirty-seven-foot frontage along Finkes Lane and extended fifty-four feet to the rear. This was a substantial building, which fits with everything we know of Adam's status in the ward. It was a timber-framed structure of four and a half stories resting on a cellar. On the ground floor was a shop on the street side, behind which was a storeroom for cloths and an open yard. Beyond the yard was a kitchen, a separate element of the property connected to the front by a first-floor gallery. The first floor above the ground level would have contained a hall and most likely a buttery or pantry for storage of kitchen utensils, linens, and other equipment necessary for running a household.

The living quarters for family, servants, and apprentices would have been on the upper levels. Exposed beams and joists would have been carved in a decorative fashion, and the walls of the hall would have been adorned with painted cloths or tapestries, depicting legendary or biblical stories. Ground floors were likely tiled. Furnishings are harder to estimate but would have probably included a table with at least one chair and some forms (benches) or stools in the hall, as well as beds and chests. There was a privy on the third floor consisting of a seat built over the joists with a wood-lined "pipe" connecting it to a cesspit below, which would have to be regularly cleaned out. A brick chimney would have served a large fireplace in the kitchen and some fireplaces in the living quarters. Coal was the fuel used most often, though turves (slabs of peat) and wood were sometimes employed.[40] Despite this heating the Winthrops would have learned to deal with cold, especially during those winter months when the River Thames froze over. Windows were more common and larger (and therefore more drafty) in London than elsewhere in England, reflecting a foreign influence. Light would have come from the fire and from torches or tallow candles. Water may have come from a brick-lined well in the yard; otherwise it would have been carried by water bearers from the conduit on Cornhill, which had been enlarged in 1475.

The family's life would not have been without the opportunity for recreation. Some sports, such as football, were played in the streets of London at this time. Archery was possible, as butts were laid out north of the city. The Clothworkers had a tennis court on Fenchurch Street as early as 1535 and, despite criticisms of the sport, owned two bowling alleys as of 1612.[41] Pageantry broke the rhythms of the ordinary. In 1547 Adam in his livery would have joined with the other liveried members of the Clothworkers in the ceremonies marking the official entry of King Edward VI to the city—along Gracechurch Street to Cornhill, to Cheapside, to St. Paul's. At various spots along the route, including (in the Winthrop neighborhood) the conduit on Cornhill and the porch of St. Peter's, the procession would halt for pageants, speeches, and songs. Similar processions marked the installation of the city's lord mayor and other such occasions.[42] This was all part of Adam Winthrop's world. The young man from Lavenham grew accustomed to life in the city and reveled in the intensity of that life.

SHORTLY AFTER BEING ELECTED master of the Clothworkers in 1552, Adam sat for his portrait. He had successfully navigated his course at a time when market fluctuations, religious revolution, and political upheavals had entangled and defeated many ambitious men. The portrait shows a man of influence and wealth who is accustomed to success, adorned in his company livery and wearing the type of velvet flat cap popularized by Henry VIII.[43] He appears friendly if determined, and his face shows little sign of strain or troubles. Adam had traveled far from his origins in terms of status as well as geography. He was fortunate in presiding over a household filled with a wife and children, servants, and apprentices. His oldest son, William, had been admitted to the Clothworkers by right of patrimony in 1544 and joined Adam in business. If precedent followed, Adam, as master of one of the great livery companies, would have anticipated being chosen for positions of civic leadership. If he could have seen the future, he would not have been so assured.

2

Reformation

AROUND THE CORNER from where the Winthrops lived in the parish of St. Peter's Cornhill was the church of St. Michael's. Neighborhood lore told of how, years before, "upon St. James' night, certain men in the loft next under the Bells, ringing of a Peal, a Tempest of lightning and thunder did arise, [and] an ugly shaped sight appeared to them, coming in the north window, and lighted on the North, for fear whereof they all fell down, and lay as dead for the time, letting the Bells ring and cease of their own accord. When the ringers came to themselves, they found certain stones of the North window to be raised and scratched, as if they had been [made of] so much butter, printed with a Lion's claw. The same stones were fastened there again, and so remain to this day." Young boys in the parish such as William Winthrop and his young brothers, John and Adam, often climbed to the steeple to stare at the impress of the demon's feet and trace with their fingers those marks of Satan.[1]

☙

*T*HE DISTINCTION WE NOW MAKE between the supernatural and the natural was not one that the Winthrops would have understood. There were no clear boundaries separating the spheres inhabited by men, angels, and devils. Like his father and like all other Englishmen of the time, William Winthrop saw the supernatural reflected in every action of every day. God's power not only sustained the universe but also directed it. Things that later generations would explain in natural terms were seen in the sixteenth and seventeenth centuries as attributable to supernatural forces. Though people disagreed over the proper shaping of the church, none questioned the presence of God and the devil in their midst. Lightning was fire hurled down by evil spirits that lurked everywhere. Disease was a judgment used by God to punish individuals or to test them. Sudden deaths, earthquakes, eclipses, strange lights in the night sky, and countless other phenomena were believed to be providential signs or warnings whereby the divine will was revealed. The story of a man selling his soul to the devil for power, which would be dramatized by Christopher Marlowe in *Dr. Faustus*, was a familiar one in Winthrop's world.[2] It was a commonplace that many, denied God's saving grace, turn to the forces of evil and sell themselves to Satan to become witches and warlocks. For the audiences of Tudor England, this was not a mere literary fancy employed by playwrights such as Shakespeare, it was a fact of life, reinforced by occasional trials, confessions, and executions.[3]

None of this would change between the birth of the elder Adam Winthrop in Lavenham in 1498 and the death of his grandson John in Boston, Massachusetts, in 1649, but some aspects of the religious worldview would. When Adam Winthrop, the son and namesake of the babe christened in Lavenham, was brought to be baptized at St. Peter's Cornhill in 1548, the ceremony differed significantly from his own initiation into the Christian community a half century earlier. Much of the ritual of that earlier time had been called into question by Protestant reformers.[4] The subsequent religious struggles that divided England in his grandfather's time and raged during his father's lifetime would play a considerable part in shaping the choices that John Winthrop would face in his life.

THE UNITY OF CHRISTENDOM was shattered by Martin Luther in 1517, and the ideas of the German reformer fed the dissatisfaction of many English reformers with the Catholic Church. At the heart of this dispute were quarrels over different understandings of man's relationship with God that would come to dominate English history for more than a century and do much to shape the lives of future generations of Winthrops and spur the settlement of New England.

All Christians agreed that man was born corrupted by the effects of Adam's original sin and that as a result it was impossible to earn salvation by absolute adherence to the covenant of works, wherein God had guaranteed men salvation for total obedience. With faculties impaired by original sin, each individual would inevitably commit actual sins and become addicted to the habit of sin, spurning God and seeking self-gratification. God alone could effect an individual's liberation from this thralldom. By the Middle Ages the church emphasized the role it played as God's surrogate in forgiving sins: Christ had told Peter that "whatsoever ye shall bind on earth shall be bound in heaven: and whatsoever ye shall loose on earth shall be loosed also in heaven." Along with this development, and with little scriptural justification, the church had adopted the doctrine of purgatory as a place where sinners whose offenses did not deserve eternal damnation but equally did not merit heaven would suffer for a time until they were brought to the celestial kingdom. The institutional church could act on behalf of God not only in remitting sins but in offering a reprieve from time in purgatory. Going back to the days of the early church fathers, there had been disagreement as to what role, if any, man still had to play in the drama of salvation. In the Middle Ages the church chose to emphasize the importance of good behavior and tied its own judgments of men to human actions. Furthermore, complementing the role of the church, those who had already gone to eternal rest with God, whether acclaimed saints or family ancestors, could intercede with God on the behalf of sinners on earth and in purgatory. Christians on earth, using the means set forth by the church, could offer prayers and apply earned indulgences to their departed in purgatory in the confidence that when those loved ones reached heaven they would in turn intercede with God for their earthly kin. Through the church the individual was made to feel part of a communion of saints—those in heaven, those in purgatory, and those in the contemporary Christian community.

Two elements of these teachings raised concern among some Christians. One was the emphasis on actions that the church contended produced grace and earned spiritual indulgence. Though the fine theological print asserted that action could only be meritorious if inspired by God-given grace (thus, it was God that enabled the reward, not fallen man), the common understanding was that human works could earn supernatural merit. The second complaint was that the emphasis on the institution of the church, its ministers and sacraments, and the saints as intercessors led many to wrongly conclude that those men and means were efficacious and powerful in themselves, generating confidence in the intermediaries as opposed to God and substituting a connection with the means for a connection between the individual and God. To prevent such a false sense of man's empowerment some theologians, Augustine being the most well known, had chosen to stress man's absolute inability (without God's grace) to achieve any good thing or to moderate the damnation deserved for sin.

In the early sixteenth century the church's financial needs led to fundraising campaigns that seemed to connect the granting of indulgences to the actual payment of a fee, as opposed to indulgences being granted for the God-generated charitable impulse behind such donations. Troubled by this, an Augustinian monk, Martin Luther, attacked what he saw as the church's overemphasis on man's potential. Denying that any human works could be the cause of salvation, Luther preached that salvation was based on God-given faith alone. He was not the first to target these abuses in church practice, nor the first to question official teachings on these matters, but the recent invention of the printing press enabled his ideas to spread more rapidly than had been the case with earlier critics such as John Wycliffe and John Huss. Furthermore, political conditions in Germany provided Luther protection from the first efforts of church leaders to silence what they viewed as his impertinence. Because the papacy was not willing to consider reform from the top down (though many loyal Catholics agreed with the need), the protest became a popular one, and Luther's ideas rapidly spread and mutated as they were considered and revised by contemporary reformers such as Ulrich Zwingli and later ones such as John Calvin.[5]

In the doctrinal debates that followed, the beliefs of the reformers led them to strike a number of positions that had consequences for the actual practice of faith, though of course not all Protestants reached all of the same conclusions. The "cult" of the saints was attacked as leading to idolatrous worship of those saints as distributors of material benefits. Demands were made to repudiate such beliefs and to remove all images and relics of saints from churches. Some went further, attacking images of God, including the cross, believing that on the one hand these came to be viewed as powerful talismans in their own right and that on the other hand they limited understanding of God by fixing the divinity in a particular form. In general, reformers wished to make the Bible the primary means of contact between God and man, in contrast to the visual presentations of Christianity featured in medieval churches. This meant a new emphasis on the sermon but also an insistence that the Scriptures be translated into vernacular languages and made readily available to individuals. The special empowerment of the priest through the sacrament of Holy Orders was rejected and the priesthood of all believers asserted. Reformers demanded that symbols of special priestly status, such as ecclesiastical vestments, be discarded. Elements that separated the believers from equal participation in religious services were attacked: the reformers argued that rood screens separating the priest from the congregation should be torn down, altars renamed "communion tables" and moved from the chancel to the aisle, where they would be closer to the congregation, the Latin liturgy replaced with a vernacular worship, and choral music in worship prohibited. The doctrine of purgatory was rejected, and with this there was no longer a rationale for prayers for the dead, whether by individuals for their departed family or friends, or by hireling priests offering prayers and chanted masses for the dead, paid for by testamentary gifts.

Henry VIII's initial opposition to Lutheran views kept the impetus for reform in England under wraps until his own quarrel with the papacy led him to break with Rome. The genesis of the English Reformation was Henry VIII's conclusion that the failure of his wife, Catherine, to produce a son was God's punishment for the couple having entered a marriage that, though approved by the pope, was forbidden by God's will as revealed in Scripture. The reluctance of the papacy to grant Henry an annulment led to what began as efforts to pressure the church and resulted in a new Church of England. The attack on Rome began in earnest with the so-called Reformation Parliament, which assembled in 1529. Acts were passed to regulate burial and probate fees such as Richard Hunne had protested. Over the next few years additional church privileges were stripped away as Henry sought to use such pressure to convince the pope to grant his annulment. A royal commission to study the need for an English Bible reported favorably. A Supplication Against the Ordinaries objected to the number of holy days, oppression of the church courts, and other aspects of church practice. The crisis truly came in 1533. In that year Henry secretly married Anne Boleyn, Parliament passed an Act in Restraint of Appeals to Rome, Archbishop Thomas Cranmer passed judgment that Henry's marriage to Catherine had been invalid, and the pope excommunicated the king. The following year saw passage of an Act of Succession privileging the offspring of Henry and Anne over his daughter by Catherine, as well as passage of the Act of Supremacy and other laws that effectively institutionalized the new national church with the monarch as its head.

This new church was, however, without a clear identity, its character being contested between the Catholic doctrinal and liturgical propensities of the king and the reform vision of the men whom he needed to run his new Protestant church. Whereas Lutheranism, Calvinism, and other reform movements were based on a religious vision and subsequently developed institutional identities, the English church had a structure before it had a platform. The fortunes of the various factions in the church waxed and waned as the king sought to counter foreign threats and domestic unrest. On the whole, during the reign of Henry and his successor, Edward VI, Archbishop Thomas Cranmer was able to move the church incrementally toward a stance more in keeping with what was often referred to as "the best reformed churches of Christendom," but its character would change often and remain contested until well into the seventeenth century.

No one at this time on either side of Europe's religious divide believed in pluralism or tolerance of opposition religious views. Uniformity within kingdoms was sought and enforced. Henry's government began to move against those who opposed the changes and refused to take an Oath of Supremacy, leading eventually to the execution for treason of recalcitrant monks and of notables such as Sir Thomas More and Bishop John Fisher. Thomas Cromwell was named vice-gerent in spiritual matters and ordered a visitation of the monastic houses of all religious orders such as the Benedictines, Augustinians, and Carthusians (orders that were not under the direct control of the bishops) with a view to suppressing them. In 1536 Henry approved the Ten Articles, which were perceived as shifting the doctrinal basis of the new church in a Lutheran direction. In 1537 the larger monasteries began to be closed, a fate that would gradually be imposed on all of them. The next year vice-gerential injunctions instructed clergy to preach quarterly sermons and to discourage pilgrimages to shrines and superstitious use of images. Further measures to close the remaining major shrines were taken in 1541. After earlier unofficial but popular English translations of the Scriptures, such as that by William Tyndale, in 1539 the Great Bible was officially published, and in the following year each English parish was ordered to own and display the English Bible.

Underlying the debates over whether such reforms went too far or not far enough was the question of the authority from which they derived their legitimacy. In rejecting the authority of the pope, Henry VIII had asserted control over the Church of England. His legitimacy was never universally accepted, however, even by those who applauded his actions. From the very start of the English Reformation it proved impossible for any person, group, or institution to gain acceptance as authorized to establish the principles of true religion and the religious practices that reflected God's will, as the pope had been accepted. The reformers likewise rejected the notion that the individual clergyman was imbued by the sacrament of Holy Orders with special powers and insight and strove to deconstruct those elements of liturgy and ceremony that implied that the minister possessed such gifts. But if authority was not vested in the pope nor his clerical representatives, where were Englishmen such as the Winthrops to turn for an understanding of God's will and for spiritual guidance? Like other Protestants, they believed that God's will was to be found in the Scriptures and that the Bible must be made accessible to all in the printed vernacular editions, but it was one thing to assert that the Scripture was the word of God and another to agree on the meaning of that word. Did the priesthood of all believers imply that each individual Christian was to determine God's meaning for himself or herself? The dangerous consequences of such a radical decentralization of authority became quickly apparent, but it was not easy to find another alternative, and the effort to do so would divide Englishmen for over a century.

The legislation of Henry VIII's Reformation Parliament placed the monarch at the head of the church in England, but few were ready to trust the king with the authority claimed by the pope. If the monarch was not to be regarded as Christ's vicar, then neither was any individual bishop or archbishop to be regarded as infallible. Such princes of the church were mere men, appointed by the king, whose judgments were to be considered but not blindly accepted. The root problem with authority was found throughout the church, right down to the level of the parish. While some parishioners, perhaps a majority, might accept the authority of any individual legally instituted as their pastor, the hotter sort of Protestants were not willing to uncritically accept the supervision of the men they found looking down at them from the pulpit. In the long run those churchmen who were readily followed at every level were those whose authority was achieved by virtue of their learning, an aura of godliness, and acceptance by other godly men with whom they were associated. Such authority was often found in the reputation of a particular man (or church or community) that led to designation as one of "God's candlesticks" or as "a city upon a hill." Such reputations generally emerged in the context of communities of believers, whether they be gatherings of fellows and students at Cambridge, conferences of clerical colleagues, or prayer groups of godly laymen.

WHEN HENRY DIED in 1547, to be succeeded by his nine-year-old son, Edward VI, reformers such as Archbishop Cranmer still saw their objectives largely unrealized. But the young king would throw his support behind the reformers, and under Cranmer's leadership the church continued to redefine itself doctrinally in accord with the patterns established on the continent. The new king quickly authorized Cranmer to proceed with additional reforms—notably, issuance in 1547 of the *Book of Homilies*, scripted sermons to be read by all clergy at Sunday worship. Though the pace of reform was not fast enough to satisfy some of the more zealous evangelicals (as the hotter Protestants were also known), such as John Hooper, significant steps were taken, the most significant being the issuance of the Book of Common Prayer in 1549 and its revision in 1552. While certain remnants of Catholicism remained—most controversially the use of clerical vestments—other items on the reformed agenda were adopted, such as orders for destruction of all remaining images and shrines, replacement of altars with communion tables, and abolition of the traditional mass, chantries and other forms of prayers for the dead, and private confession. Those who disagreed with these policies, of course, questioned Cranmer's authority to make them. If Catholics, they sought to slow the process of reform; if advanced Protestants, they worked to accelerate it.

ADAM WINTHROP OF THE CLOTHWORKERS and other Londoners experienced the consequences of these religious changes in their churches every Sunday. St. Peter's Cornhill, where the Winthrops worshiped, had been typical of the richly adorned churches of pre-Reformation London, embellished with banners depicting saints such as St. Peter and biblical scenes such as the baptizing of Christ by John the Baptist. A rood screen with elaborately carved figures of Christ, the Virgin Mary, and St. John the Evangelist separated the congregation from the elevated chancel where the priest presided over the sacrifice of the mass at the altar. There were two organs for the accompaniment of the choir. The church was further enriched with candlesticks, communion chalices and patens. Relics of saints were objects of devotion. Elaborate altar cloths were changed to reflect the different liturgical seasons. Richly embroidered vestments were available for the priests. Painted veils covered the statues and the rood during the period of Lent. Throughout the church there were numerous screened off chapels for religious guilds (associations of believers dedicated to a particular saint) and chantries (where priests sang masses for departed souls), each decorated with its own statues of saints.[6]

English reformers saw all of this as symbolic of false doctrines. They rejected the rood screen's separation of the laity from the eucharistic ceremony, believed that painted and carved images encouraged idolatry, and challenged the use of traditional music. As the reform movement spread in the early 1530s, so did popular attacks on images, which received official sanction in 1534. Rood screens were torn down and in some cases burned. While such incidents occurred throughout England, London was the center of the outbreaks of iconoclasm.[7]

What did Adam Winthrop think of these changes? Unfortunately, no writings of his survive, and we can only speculate on how his surroundings and interests may have led him to adopt an outward posture of support for the new religious world. East Anglia, from which he had come, had a tradition of supporting religious reform and would become a center of the new ideas, which flowed into Essex and Suffolk from across the North Sea. London, with its own trade links with continental centers of Protestantism, also became noted for evangelical strength. His marriage to a daughter of Richard Hunne at a time when Henry VIII was fighting Protestant influence in England suggests a radical orientation. And the Clothworkers as a company was more identified with support of reformed preachers and ideas than many of the city's other guilds.

Government-ordered religious reform began as Adam was starting his climb to power in the Clothworkers, and if for any reason he had his doubts about the course his nation's leaders were pursuing, he did not express them. Furthermore, he was certainly willing to profit from the changes being made. The dissolution of the monasteries led to government sale of those properties, and Adam took advantage of this in 1544 when he purchased the Suffolk manor of Groton, which had formerly belonged to the Abbey of St. Edmund at Bury.[8] He also had no qualms about exercising the right that he acquired by this purchase to choose the new rector of Groton's parish church, naming his stepbrother Roger Ponder. Under the new regime clergy inducted into livings had to pay the Exchequer a tax referred to as "first fruits," which would be paid in installments; they often arranged for others to serve as sureties for the payment. Adam Winthrop took the unusual step for a patron of joining with Thomas Borowe of St. Peter's to guarantee the first fruits for Ponder.[9]

Equally indicative of his sentiments is his election as a churchwarden of St. Peter's Cornhill in 1546—a position that he could have avoided—which made him responsible for carrying out ordinances of reform.[10] When some of the ornaments of the church were sold off in the further cleansing of the churches in Edward's reign, he purchased "two great green sarcenet streamers and two small green sarcenet streamers with red crosses," helping to raise funds for reform and perhaps planning to use the cloth for other purposes.[11] In 1552 John Pulleyne, a recent graduate of Christ Church, Oxford, was installed as the new rector at St. Peter's. He was already known as a strong advocate of reform and especially as an opponent of ceremonies, but at this point such reformers were in the ascendant, as indicated by the fact that he also served as chaplain to the prominent duchess of Suffolk.[12]

Adam Winthrop was a prominent Londoner by virtue of his position in the Clothworkers and was at a stage in his career when he would have been on the verge of even greater responsibilities in the city. In 1548 he had been granted a coat of arms and the rank of gentleman.[13] He had certainly taken enough steps to identify himself with the new reform and, like others in that situation, would have been threatened when Edward VI died in 1553. Efforts to place the Protestant Lady Jane Grey on the throne quickly failed, and the Catholic daughter of Henry VIII and Catherine of Aragon, Mary Tudor, was proclaimed queen in July of that year. Any Protestants who may have felt inclined to trust the monarch to make all decisions in matters of religion were shown the danger of that course when Mary took steps to restore Catholicism. Many prominent churchmen and lay patrons of reform were imprisoned (including Archbishop Cranmer and Bishops Hugh Latimer and John Hooper) and would suffer martyrdom by being burned alive in public spectacles in London, Oxford, Colchester, and elsewhere. Over eight hundred men and women fled to the continent rather than risk arrest and execution, taking up residence in centers of reform such as Zurich, Frankfurt, Strasbourg, and Geneva.

The sympathies of men such as the Winthrops were closely watched. At St. Peter's, Pulleyne was replaced by a John Hodgkins, a priest who became an eager participant in the efforts of London's Catholic Bishop William Bonner to root out Protestantism.[14] As a leader of one of the great city companies, Adam had a role to play in civic ceremonies and was looked to to provide leadership. Should Hodgkins have reported him as a nonparticipant in the restored Catholic worship, he would likely have ended in prison with other godly merchants. So Adam decided at this time to leave London and retire to his country manor at Groton, where royal and episcopal scrutiny was less likely to extend, and where the incumbent in the parish rectory was his own appointee. His move can only be viewed as an attempt to avoid the choices that the queen was seeking to force on the leaders of state and church.

While the rest of the family accompanied Adam to Suffolk, William Winthrop, Adam's oldest son, remained in the city to manage the family business affairs. Born in 1529, he had been educated at the grammar school in the parish of St. Peter's.[15] William grew up against the background of reform, and his Christian beliefs were shaped by the evangelical cause to which he would devote his life. His own strategy to avoid being reported by the new rector of St. Peter's for nonattendance was merely to move a few blocks, taking up residence in the next-door parish of St. Michael's Cornhill. Freed from the close scrutiny of the rector of St. Peter's, and not informing the priests of his new parish of his presence, William worshiped instead in various places as part of a Protestant underground congregation in the city.[16] On the first two Easters of Mary's reign, Winthrop likely joined Christopher Goodman and Michael Reniger at the communion services Pulleyne conducted in his own home.[17] While private homes were often the places for such services, other venues, including ships in port, were also used. Joining this underground community was the course chosen by many who sought to continue the practice of their reformed faith while escaping both martyrdom and the option of exile. It would be a mistake to give too much credit to the ability of the Marian authorities to root out all dissent, and William's relative lack of prominence made it possible for him and others like him to elude detection. Another Londoner who evaded the authorities was Edward Underhill, who wrote that "there was no such [better] place to shift in in this realm as London, notwithstanding the great spying and search." Underhill reported that he got a bricklayer to seal his Protestant books "in a brick wall by the chimney side of my chamber, where they were preserved from mold or mice until the first year of our most gracious queen Elizabeth."[18]

Like other Protestant merchants and shipowners, Winthrop was able to aid the cause in various ways, secretly moving books and funds between the exile community abroad and the reformed underground in England. A letter from the imprisoned Bishop Hooper to an unnamed merchant giving thanks for his assistance was likely written to Winthrop, whose name appears on the back of the letter.[19] His ships may have been among those used as sites for secret worship. His contacts with those in London jails enabled him to gather and preserve some of the papers of those who would be martyred.

William occasionally visited his father and siblings in Groton, and these trips to Suffolk provided opportunities to make contact with reformers in that county and, en route between London and Groton, to visit other reformers in Essex, where his friend Pulleyne was actively nurturing the Protestant underground in Colchester. The Stour River Valley separating the two counties of Essex and Suffolk was a hotbed of evangelicalism. Stratford St. Mary and Hadleigh had been among the first parishes to experiment with English-language liturgy, doing so in 1538, ten years before it was legal.[20] The burning of the popular evangelical preacher Rowland Taylor in a field outside of Hadleigh was one of the dramatic incidents narrated by John Foxe in the *Book of Martyrs*, the monumental narrative of the Marian persecutions that placed those sufferings in a historical perspective and used them to shape English identity. Foxe also claimed that three years after the accession of Mary only two members of the parish of Stoke-by-Nayland were willing to receive communion in the Catholic fashion.[21] More people from Colchester were burned in the Marian fires than from any other town except London. William would have been heartened by these signs of steadfastness and carried the stories of rural nonconformity back to his fellow London Protestants.

Catholics' hopes for a permanent restoration of their faith ended with the death of Queen Mary on November 17, 1558. She and her Spanish husband, Phillip II, had not produced an heir, so the throne passed to the last surviving daughter of Henry VIII, Elizabeth. The daughter of Henry VIII and Anne Boleyn, Elizabeth was considered illegitimate by Catholics, since they did not recognize the annulment of Henry's first marriage. This alone would have pushed Elizabeth towards the restoration of Protestantism she instituted. The Elizabethan settlement, however, did not satisfy all reformers, some of whom felt that the new church was not sufficiently purged of Catholic remnants. Indeed, in some respects it was not as reformed as men like the Winthrops remembered it to have been in the last days of Edward VI. They objected to what they saw as inadequate steps to ensure a preaching ministry for all parishes and were offended by the retention of practices that they identified with Catholicism in the liturgy set out in the Book of Common Prayer. The result was a renewed struggle within English Protestantism between those willing to accept Elizabeth's position as authoritative and advocates of further reform.

The supporters of further reform, previously identified as the "hotter sort of Protestants" and as "evangelicals," now began to identify themselves as "the godly" and to occasionally be accused by establishment churchmen as "puritans" or "precisians." Historians have long found it difficult to define these terms precisely, but for men and women of the time the distinction between those content with the Elizabethan settlement and those who sought further reform was as clear (and also as imprecise) as that made between political liberals and conservatives in our own time. Yet all of these Protestants agreed on the dangers posed by Rome, and anti-Catholicism became one of the principal ties binding these divided English Protestants together.

William Winthrop played an important if relatively quiet role in the struggle to achieve greater reform. Much of his effort was focused on his own parish of St. Michael's Cornhill. He first appears in the records of the church in July 1559 when his son Joshua was baptized—an apt name for the first Winthrop to enter the promised land of Protestant England following the accession of Elizabeth.[22] In 1562 John Philpott became the new rector of St. Michael's following his ordination two years earlier by Bishop Edmund Grindal. He was likely the nephew of the Marian martyr of the same name, who had been known to Winthrop. Philpott showed an active interest in the London churches of foreign Protestants, called the "stranger churches," which many hot reformers saw as models for further reform. Along with John Gough of St. Peter's Cornhill and Robert Crowley, Philpott was a lecturer at St. Antholin's parish. The three were also leaders of the "most fruitfull and comfortable exercise named prophesying used once a week at St. Peter's, where 2 or 3 hundred were assembled."[23] In 1567 the three clergymen were suspended for their strenuous opposition to the wearing of ecclesiastical vestments, which they viewed as one of the Catholic remnants that needed to be purged from church practice.[24]

As a supporter of Philpott, and as a sermon gadder—one who traveled to other parishes to listen to additional preaching—Winthrop was esteemed as one of the godly and soon rose to hold office in the parish of St. Michael's. In 1564 he was chosen one of the collectors for the poor. The parish took its responsibility to its less fortunate members seriously. After the closure of chantries the parish had converted a range of residences in the church-yard, formerly used for choir members, to houses for the poor, and then, much to the annoyance of John Stowe, "had greatly blemished [the church] by the building of lower tenements on the north side thereof towards the high street, in place of a green churchyard, whereby the church is dark-ened and otherwise annoyed."[25] Four years after becoming collector for the poor, Winthrop was elected to be one of the churchwardens, the lay governors of the parish church. During his tenure the wardens took a num-ber of steps to move the parish along the path of reform. They sold the old organs and used the proceeds to order copies of Foxe's *Book of Martyrs* and a copy of Calvin's *Institutes of the Christian Religion* to be kept in the church.[26] Having purged the church of organ music, Winthrop and his fellow parish leaders purchased eight "Geneve Books" and began the custom of congre-gational singing of metrical psalms.[27]

As a churchwarden William was on the lookout for opposition to re-form within the parish, and on one occasion this involved him in a clash with John Stowe, the antiquarian and author of *A Survey of London*. Stowe was alienated from his own brother and mother, in part because they sup-ported reform, whereas Stowe was sympathetic to Catholicism and had been a sharp critic of Winthrop's friends Robert Crowley and John Philpott. As a result Mrs. Stowe favored her son Thomas in her will. The two broth-ers quarreled often, and at one point in 1568 Thomas entered John's home and removed a book from his library, claiming that it proved that John was dabbling in magic. William Winthrop intervened, and John Stowe, deny-ing the charges, suggested that Winthrop show the book to "some learned men" for their judgment, suggesting among others Bishop Grindal and John Foxe, both of whom were known to Winthrop.[28] Nothing came of this incident directly, but it may have had a role in a later search of Stowe's library conducted by Grindal's agents.[29]

Winthrop continued to serve the parish as churchwarden in 1570, 1573, and 1576, and also as a feoffee, or trustee, for parish lands. During his last term as churchwarden the parish paid for a visiting Scottish preacher.[30] Though the clergyman cannot be identified, Scots were viewed by most English reformers as representing the more advanced Protestantism that they were themselves striving for; hiring such a preacher was another means of promoting reform views in the parish. Winthrop contributed to the cause of reform in other ways as well. He had had frequent contacts with fellow reformers during the Marian persecutions and was able to provide John Foxe with some of the material for his *Book of Martyrs*. His assistance to Foxe would be a matter of pride to William's brother Adam and Adam's son John, who would carry the tale with him to New England and pass it on to his own children. Eventually, Cotton Mather would write of William that he was "a memorable favorer of the reformed religion in the days of Queen Mary, into whose hands the famous martyr, Philpott, committed his papers."[31] In 1560 William wrote to John Foxe urging him to remember a "few names which have not bowed their knees to Baal," men whose views had been authorized by their lives and sufferings. Among those whom Winthrop brought to the attention of Foxe were Henry Bull, James Yonge, William Playfere, William Fawset, and Peter Forman.[32] Each of these was firmly in the evangelical movement, and Winthrop's intervention on their behalf was additional evidence of his involvement with the Marian Protestant underground.[33]

In the same letter to Foxe, Winthrop also referred to his and his wife's "brother" Thomas Upcher. Whether this was a blood relation or a sign of spiritual closeness is unclear. Upcher had been arrested in Bocking, Essex, in 1553 for hosting a secret gathering, or conventicle, of reformers, who had been engaged in discussions of prayer without forms and ceremonies. Spared imprisonment, Upcher had been in contact with those who were in jail until he and his wife fled to the reformed city of Arau. On returning to England he would play a key role in spreading reformed ideas in Colchester, where he would have further contacts with the Winthrops and their friends.[34]

Hearing his brother discuss these men and their efforts, William's younger and admiring brother Adam was drawn to the cause. In terms of practice, the evangelicals at this time sought the elimination of vestments, suspect images, and symbols such as the use of rings in matrimony and signing with the cross in baptism. In terms of governance they were drawn to continental, especially Genevan, models that placed less emphasis on national leaders and more on the laity and the parish clergy. The stranger

churches in London—the congregations of foreign Protestants—were fascinating to the reformers because they were free to shape their own affairs
in a way that made them, in the view of one historian, "a Trojan horse,
bringing Reformed worship and discipline fully armed into the midst of
the Anglican camp."[35] Winthrop's involvement with these churches began
shortly after the start of Elizabeth's reign when he solicited his fellow merchants for funds to support a group of Spanish Protestants who were seeking to organize under the leadership of Casiodoro de Reina, and he may
have been one of those who helped persuade Bishop Grindal to allow the
Spanish to use the church of St. Mary Axe for their services.[36] Shortly after
its formation, however, the Spanish church splintered after de Reina was
accused of heresy and then sexual impropriety. Though the charges may
have been manufactured by agents working for the Spanish government or
Inquisition, they could not be ignored. The consistory of the French church
on Threadneedle Street, which acted as an informal governing body for all
the stranger churches, called da Reina before them. He denied the charges
but was urged to place the dispute before Bishop Grindal, who appointed a
fact-finding body with some members chosen by the Spaniard, including
William Wittingham, Miles Coverdale, and a "Mr. Withemme" who might
very well have been Winthrop. Following the hearing, de Reina fled; his
supporters joined the Italian stranger church, while the majority of the
Spanish joined the larger French church.

    Winthrop was involved in both of these churches as well. Indeed, one
scholar has claimed that Winthrop "had in 1561 complete oversight and
responsibility as the coordinator of the English sponsors of the poor foreign Protestants in London."[37] Twice he was called upon by the leaders of
the French congregation to raise funds for their assistance, the first time in
1564 when the congregation was ravaged by plague, and then again in 1572
when they were seeking to help alleviate the sufferings resultant from the
St. Bartholomew's Day massacre of Protestants in France. But he was trusted
as more than a fund-raiser, as demonstrated when Pierre Fouet, a disgruntled member of the congregation, sought his advice.[38]

    In 1570 William Winthrop was elected one of the elders of the Italian
Protestant church in London. It was unusual for an Englishman to serve in
such a capacity in one of the stranger churches, but serve Winthrop did,
and his name appears in the congregation's records through 1573.[39] It was
through his contact with this church that he became fascinated with the
story of Olympia Morata. Morata was a wellborn and well-educated young
woman who had been converted to Protestantism by reading the works of
Luther. Forced to flee Italy, she married and moved throughout Europe
before dying of plague in 1554. Her trials and death elicited testimonials
from Theodore Beza and other leading reformers, and her legend was fueled by the publication of her writings. Her tale was of particular interest

to the Italian Protestants in London. From them William obtained copies of Morata's letters, which he shared with his brother Adam in Groton.[40]

The stranger churches were of particular interest to those advocating further reform in the Church of England. Their practices were admired by Englishmen looking for ways to bring their own religious practice into closer approximation to God's will. Winthrop was a link between those congregations and the leaders of English godly reform such as John Field and Thomas Wilcox, whose 1572 *Admonition to Parliament* unsuccessfully urged Parliament to initiate reforms that the queen had been unwilling to undertake. Winthrop first came to know Field when the latter was awarded a university exhibition by the Clothworkers in 1566, the same year that Field was ordained by Bishop Grindal. Over the next few years Field preached frequently to the company.[41] Winthrop may have recruited Field for the task of gathering materials for his friend Foxe, and it has been suggested that Field came to serve as Foxe's curate in the London parish of St. Giles Cripplegate. When Field was imprisoned following publication of the *Admonition*, Winthrop's friend James Yonge served as a conduit between Field and Foxe. The execution of perceived heretics was not a monopoly of Queen Mary, and in 1575 Winthrop, Field, and Foxe accompanied each other to witness the burning of Anabaptists in London. Though having little sympathy with those who denied infant baptism, they did not approve of the penalty; Foxe is reported to have said, "I would not countenance their errors but I would spare their lives."[42]

Unable to persuade the authorities to institute changes, the reformers sought to build from the foundations by working to place godly ministers in the nation's parishes. This involved promoting proper evangelical training at Oxford and Cambridge, persuading patrons to appoint such men to livings, and making sure that those appointed could afford to accept the posts. A 1535 statute required all inductees to clerical livings worth more than eight marks to pay the first-fruits tax. William Winthrop and other godly laymen assisted in this task by standing as sureties for the payments of men whose views of reform agreed with theirs.[43] By supporting such clergymen financially, they also sought to enhance the ministers' reputations and thus their authority within their parishes.[44] Winthrop was active in this regard both in London and in East Anglia. He was one of the guarantors for Robert Cole in the parish of All Hallow's Bread Street and for Richard Porder at St. Peter's Cornhill, who received that living in 1568 when John Gough was deprived for refusing to wear the prescribed vestments. But Winthrop's concerns extended beyond London. He recommended his friend Peter Forman to his father, Adam, for installation in Groton and then guaranteed the first fruits. After Forman's death he guaranteed the first fruits for Henry Browne to be rector of Groton. He did the same to assist Marcelline Outread in Essex and Roger Kelke and George Still in Suffolk livings.[45]

William's energetic support of religious reform detracted from his attention to his business, and he never achieved the success that his father had in the Clothworkers, though he continued to trade with northern Europe and the Bay of Biscay and was a member of the Spanish Company chartered in 1577.[46] He was not admitted to the livery of the Clothworkers until 1570 and failed to hold any office other than steward, administering some of the internal affairs of the company, to which he was elected in 1574 when he was forty-five years old.[47]

His reputation as a reformer helped William in the Cornhill ward, where local affairs were managed by the gathering of citizens known as the wardmote. In 1571 he was chosen one of the speakers of the wardmote inquest. The following two years he served on the grand jury, and he would serve again as speaker in 1575 and 1577.[48] That latter year, however, saw Winthrop's fortunes collapse. He was forced to sell property on Finkes Lane and dispatch his wife to live with her relations in Kent, where she died in 1578.[49] Having managed to provide apprenticeships for his sons, Adam and Joshua, William applied for assistance from the parish, and in November 1577 the churchwardens of St. Michael's voted that he should have the next house available in the churchyard. The following June he was assigned one of the poor houses which had so exercised John Stowe. There he lived till his death in March 1582.[50] His younger brother Adam remembered him as "a good man, without harm, and a lover of piety," and his principal legacy would be the efforts of his brother Adam and Adam's son John in promoting religious reform.[51] For them, at least, William's exemplary life would be a light that would guide their own lives.

3

John and Adam

SIX-YEAR-OLD ADAM WINTHROP was entranced with the new world in which he found himself following his father's move to Groton, Suffolk, in 1554. The air was free of the coal-smoke miasma of London but filled with the smells of the open fields of the countryside. Cattle and sheep grazed along the local streams, and hares were a common sight. The sounds also differed from those of Cornhill, but, more important, sounds in the countryside were distinct, striking against a general quietness as opposed to the backdrop of constant noise that characterized the urban soundscape. Walking the local lanes, Adam and his brother and sisters could hear the rustling of leaves as the wind blew through the trees, the chirping of birds, the gurgle of brooks. Birds in the trees, frogs in ponds, dogs barking on nearby farms, and the grunts of pigs, lowing of cattle, and neighing of horses all put their stamp on life in Groton. Mixed with these, of course, were some familiar sounds, such as the peal of church bells marking the time, calling to worship, tolling the passing of a neighbor. Men in the fields talked and argued, shouted and sang.[1]

ⱽ

THOUGH WILLIAM WINTHROP was an important part of John Winthrop's heritage, it was in the area of Groton, Suffolk, where the first governor of Massachusetts was born and where he, his father, and his grandfather worshiped. Adam Winthrop of the Clothworkers purchased Groton Manor in 1544, but it was not until a decade later, when he was already fifty-six years old, that he abandoned London and moved to Suffolk. In 1533, before the Abbey of St. Edmund at Bury had been closed and its properties seized by the crown, Groton Manor had been leased to three local residents, John Gale, William Gooche, and Richard Bonde, for twenty years.[2] As the new landlord, Adam inherited the terms and the rents provided for in that lease and was not able to make the traditional manor house, Groton Hall, his place of residence until it expired. Consequently, shortly after purchasing the manor, he acquired a ninety-nine-year lease of the existing rectory and glebe land, an arrangement facilitated by the fact that as lord of the manor he was also patron of the church living.[3] He took steps to expand the existing rectory, turning it into "a large and stately house which is called by the name of Groton Place where the old parsonage formerly stood."[4] Though currently covered by a Georgian facade, Groton Place, which Adam would refer to as his "mansion house," is a stately structure of two stories with two wings extending away from the central unit on each side of it to form a U. A diagram of the house from the time of the Winthrops indicates a series of outbuildings, which closed the U to form an interior courtyard.[5] Even when these improvements were completed, however, Adam initially showed no interest in settling on the country estate, pursuing instead his rise in the Clothworkers. He did take an interest in Groton affairs, as indicated by his appointment of his stepbrother Roger Ponder as rector of St. Bartholomew's parish in 1547.[6]

With the accession of Mary and the reimposition of Catholic practice, Adam moved to Groton, one of a collection of three small villages that included Boxford and Edwardston, in the administrative district (called a hundred) of Babergh for purposes of civil government, and part of the archdeaconry of Sudbury for religious supervision. Growing up in Lavenham, Adam may very well have traveled as a boy through the neighboring countryside with his father or with his stepfather as they dealt with local craftsmen in their clothworking business. Groton and the surrounding towns would not have been new to him as they were to his children, who had been raised in London. Assuming that he moved in 1554—the date of his last recorded attendance at the Clothworkers Court—his oldest daughter, Alice, would have been about fifteen; Bridget was eleven; Mary nine; John seven; Adam six; and Susannah two. The change for them would have been dramatic as they traded the narrow canyons of London's streets for the rolling hills and high, open skies of the East Anglian landscape.

More important to everyday life than the nearby county border separating Essex and Suffolk was the reality of the region's geography. Groton was in a broad valley that was formed by the River Stour as it flowed eastward toward the North Sea. The beautiful skies, the green fields, and the meandering river will be familiar to anyone who has admired the paintings of John Constable, for Dedham Vale, Gunn Hill, Stoke-by-Nayland, and other scenes that he immortalized in the nineteenth century were aspects of the Stour Valley. "Constable Country" was little changed from when John Winthrop's contemporary, the antiquary Robert Reyce of nearby Preston, wrote that the region was one of a "continual evenness and plainness . . . , void of any great hills, high mountains, or steep rocks, notwithstanding which it is not always so low or flat but that in every place it is severed and divided with little hills easy for ascent, and pleasant rivers watering the low valleys, with a most beautiful prospect which ministers unto the inhabitants a full choice of healthful and pleasant situations for their seemly houses."[7] Throughout the Stour Valley, villages were scattered every three to five miles. Then as now someone walking the bounds of Groton would have a clear view of the flint-faced church towers marking the presence of those nearby towns.

The soil along the valley was a clay loam, with a richer loamy character closer to the Stour and along the rivers such as the Box that flowed into it. Interspersed through the region were ancient woodlands.[8] This land, on the Suffolk side part of what was regarded as High Suffolk, was best suited to pastoral agriculture, particularly dairy farming. The author of the *Chorography of Suffolk* at the end of the sixteenth century wrote that it was "exceeding fruitful, comparable to any part of England for pasture for oxen and kine," and that "in this part of the country are made butter and cheese in exceeding great quantity, of wonderful goodness comparable to any in the realm."[9] Much of the land in this area of the Stour Valley had long been enclosed, and the parcels of land were often marked with hedges. Manorial lords such as Adam Winthrop leased portions of their holdings to local farmers, whose families supplemented their meager living with earnings from weaving and other tasks associated with the cloth industry.

The roads of the area were considered by Robert Reyce "so straightened and narrowed in many places, what with the foulness of the ways, which in the clay woodland soil is ever increased, especially in winter season, that the ordinary passage one from another during that time is made most difficult."[10] Reyce was no more complimentary of the bridges over the Stour at Wixoe, Clare, Melford, Sudbury, Bures, Nayland, Stratford, and Cattawade that connected the two sides of the valley, spans that were often in a condition of decay "through the continual violence of the floods."[11]

The climate was generally praised by contemporaries as "healthful and temperate." Suffolk tended to be one of the drier parts of the country. Because of the region's eastern location in England, "this shire . . . saluteth the gladsome spring, [which] visiteth these parts somewhat more timely than in other western parts," borne on sharp and prevalent winds from the northwest. "The welcome summer . . . with a most mild course lovingly nourisheth and kindly ripens all sorts of fruits." The winter, according to Reyce, "though it is often sharp and enduring, yet it is never so violent and stormy as in other places," though the frosts were often severe.[12]

WE HAVE NO IDEA how the Winthrops were viewed by their neighbors, and little information on their life in the 1550s. It is even difficult to establish the degree to which this reformed Protestant family used their power over the local church to shape religion in the community. The elder Adam's stepbrother Roger Ponder had vacated the church living to which Adam had named him before the Winthrops moved to Groton and had been replaced by John Gryffyth in October 1553, but we know little of Gryffyth's religious persuasion or anything else about him.[13] Late in 1557 or early the next year Gryffyth resigned, and Adam named James Barwick, whose views and practices are also elusive, as the new rector.[14] While William Winthrop had emerged as a strong proponent of reform, his involvement with Groton was marginal. He had remained in London through the Marian persecutions, and during that period Adam had taken steps to transfer his London property to William. Adam then obtained a license to alienate that would enable him to pass ownership of Groton Manor to his and Agnes's oldest son, John.[15] Adam did not anticipate returning to London. Further evidence of his new focus on Suffolk is found in his will, which indicates that he acquired additional land in Groton and Boxford by purchase and consolidated holdings by exchanges with local landowners such as the Cloptons.

Clearly Adam and Agnes planned on raising their younger children, including their sons John and Adam, in Groton. There had long been a school of sorts in Boxford, the market town just down the hill from Groton, and perhaps young John and his brother Adam began their education there.[16] Following the death of Queen Mary and Elizabeth's restoration of a Protestant Church of England, young Adam was sent to Ipswich to study in a grammar school run by John Dawes. There he would learn Latin and Greek and prepare for possible college admission. For John a more basic education would be sufficient, but as the youngest son Adam would inherit little land, so his opportunities would depend more on his learning and the connections he could make.[17] John Dawes had received his BA and MA from St. John's College, Cambridge, and had spent the Marian years on the continent. He was a zealous religious reformer like William Winthrop and had connections with many fellow reformers such as John Foxe and Roger Kelke. The decision to send young Adam to school at Ipswich may have been influenced by William, whose Hunne relations were connected with Richard Byrd, alderman of Ipswich, though another consideration was likely the presence there of Ponder kin who could also provide family support for the youngster.[18]

Dawes's school was a private academy that would be transformed into a chartered grammar school by Queen Elizabeth in 1566.[19] Dawes himself was instrumental in the first translation into English of John Calvin's *Institutes of the Christian Religion* (1561).[20] He also published a translation of Henry Bullinger's *Hundred Sermons upon the Apocalypse* (1561), which in the original Latin had been dedicated by the Zurich pastor in 1557 to the English exiles with the assurance that Christ would never fail his true church on earth.[21] Years later, his onetime student Adam Winthrop attested that

Dawes was "well learned in the Latin and Greek tongues," and that student's later writings show that he learned well from his master.

While young Adam was still at school in Ipswich, his family circumstances dramatically changed. In November 1562 his father died at Groton and was buried on the twelfth of that month. William, who had been largely provided for earlier, obtained some small parcels of land in Suffolk, his father's clothing, including his company livery, and all of the furnishings and work implements in the Winthrop property in London.[22] Adam also received some small parcels of land. Groton Manor along with the bulk of the estate, was bestowed on Agnes for use until her death, when it would pass to John Winthrop and his heirs, with Adam designated to inherit if John died without issue. John also received the lease to the Groton "mansion house." Adam bequeathed Alice and Bridget £66 13s. 4d. each to be paid on their marriage or when they reached the age of twenty-three, and to Mary and Susanna £50 each to be paid on their marriage or their twenty-first birthday.[23] Richard Byrd of Ipswich was named the executor of the will.

A number of events of later significance occurred in the years following Adam's passing. This was a time when the tide of reform was beginning to surge in the Stour Valley, and the next few decades would see a growing number of pulpits held by godly preachers. The rector of St. Bartholomew's, Peter Forman, died, and Adam's widow, Agnes, inducted Henry Browne as the new incumbent.[24] Payment of the first fruits for Browne was guaranteed by William Winthrop and Roger Evans, a London skinner.[25] Around the same time, in 1563, William Bird was inducted as vicar of nearby Boxford. Both Browne and Bird were committed Calvinists, and both would be important friends to the younger Adam Winthrop.

In June 1563 the widowed Agnes Winthrop married William Mildmay of Springfield, Essex, at Groton church in a union that was to be very useful to the Winthrops.[26] One of Mildmay's brothers was Thomas Mildmay, who was an auditor of the Court of Augmentations, which sold off monastic lands.[27] Another brother was Walter Mildmay, who began his rise to power working for Thomas at the Court of Augmentations and rose to be Queen Elizabeth's chancellor of the Exchequer and founder of Emmanuel College, Cambridge. It would have been to Thomas Mildmay that Adam Winthrop would have gone to seek the purchase of Groton Manor, and this perhaps initiated family contacts that later led to William's rapid courtship of Adam's widow.[28]

The marriage of Agnes and William Mildmay was followed five days later by the marriage, also at St. Bartholomew's, of William's son Thomas to Agnes's daughter Alice.[29] Both couples settled on William's manor at Springfield Barnes, Essex, which had once belonged to Coggeshall Abbey and had been acquired in the reign of Edward VI. John Winthrop was fifteen when his father died and sixteen when his mother remarried. While his brother Adam continued at school in Ipswich, it is likely that John relocated at Springfield Barnes. Given his later penchant for crossing the lines of acceptable behavior, it is tempting to raise the question of how these events affected him and what type of supervision he was getting in his mid-teens. The strong adult guidance that young Adam would receive through his adolescence is nowhere suggested in what we know of John's life. It is perhaps not surprising, therefore, that the subsequent stories of these two brothers would be one of stark contrast.

A MERE TWO YEARS LATER, with Agnes Winthrop Mildmay's death in May 1565, ownership of Groton Manor passed to the eighteen-year-old John Winthrop. On February 6, 1567, he married Elizabeth Risby of Thorpe Morieux, a town about ten miles north of Groton.[30] The Risbys were an established family in the area. There had been Risbys in Lavenham when John's father was a boy, and they owned land in Cockfield, Felsham, Edwardstone, and Groton as well as other towns in the region.[31] George Risby, Elizabeth's uncle, was the lord of Coddenham Hall Manor in Boxford in the early 1560s.[32] While Elizabeth's birth date is not preserved it has been estimated at 1552. Her father had died in 1557, leaving a substantial £100 to each of his daughters upon their marriage.[33] Elizabeth's mother had subsequently married John Wincoll of Little Waldingfield, and Elizabeth assumed the responsibility but also the burden for the "tuition and custody" of Wincoll's daughter, Amy.[34] Marriage offered Elizabeth both her father's monetary bequest and a chance to run her own household. But the marriage to John Winthrop proved to be a difficult one, due in part to the youth of the couple and the fact that neither had a surviving parent to turn to for advice. Depositions from a much later lawsuit contain John's charges that "Elizabeth his wife had eloped from him, and lived a most lewd and wicked life to his great grief and discontent," while Elizabeth maintained in the suit that "he did neglect and cast [her] off by reason that his affections were set upon other women."[35] Some of their dissatisfaction might have been fueled by their failure to have children through the early years of their marriage.

In 1582, when they had all but broken up, Elizabeth gave birth to a son, Benjamin. The boy was christened in the parish of St. Andrew Undershaft in London, perhaps indicating that Elizabeth spent the last part of her pregnancy with family or friends in the city.[36] Within two years the marriage had fallen apart. On June 14, 1584, John signed an agreement whereby he undertook to pay Elizabeth £24 per quarter of the year for the remainder of her life.[37] This indicates that a formal decree of separation had been granted to them. Since annulment was extremely rare and granted on very specific grounds—and never when there had been cohabitation and a child—and since divorce with the possibility of remarriage was not recognized in English law, this is the most that the couple could have achieved. Such a judicial separation "from bed and board" granted by the church courts was the only way that a couple could legally live apart in England.[38] Separation did not ease the relations between the Winthrops, however, and three years later Elizabeth had to file suit in Chancery to get John to live up to his agreement.[39]

DURING THIS PERIOD John's brother's path was quite different. Following the death of his father, young Adam had continued his schooling in Ipswich, where he not only won the approval of John Dawes but also attracted the attention of Roger Kelke, the town preacher.[40] Kelke was also master of Magdalene College, Cambridge, and in 1567 Adam Winthrop matriculated there, moving onto one of the principal stages where the struggle for the nature of the English church was being fought. With his older brother William guiding his course and providing a model, Adam would himself become an advocate of godly reformation.

Cambridge at the time consisted of fourteen residential colleges where students lived and received most of their instruction.[41] Each of the colleges was largely governed by a master and fellows, who also served as the instructional faculty. At the heart of each college was a hall, where the fellows and undergraduates dined and where lectures, disputations, and the occasional play might be staged. Joined to the hall to form a quadrangle was a chapel and ranges of chambers. The size of the colleges varied. The combined number of fellows and scholars (undergraduates) at most colleges was below one hundred, and in 1573 Magdalene was listed as having forty-nine.[42]

Instruction was conducted by lectures, which could be performed in the public schools of the university (available to undergraduates of all colleges) or within the college. Disputations in which students debated set propositions were another form of instruction, while college tutors supervised the independent reading and learning of their pupils as well as their private lives. Reformers of the time insisted on the importance of an educated ministry, and great emphasis was placed upon candidates for holy orders receiving a university degree, which would normally be accomplished in three years. For those students not intending a ministerial career, a degree was not necessary, and the university experience could be curtailed.

Cambridge itself was described at a slightly later date as a "town situated in a low, dirty, unpleasant place, the streets ill-paved, the air thick, as infested by the fens."[43] The River Cam wound past the backs of most of the colleges. Magdalene was on the opposite side of the river, connected to the town and the other colleges by the "great bridge." One of the smaller colleges, it had been refounded with new statutes little more than a decade before. Physically the quadrangle was not yet completed when Adam matriculated. It was noted for a rose garden and the close proximity of a brewhouse.[44]

Roger Kelke had an established reputation for supporting further reformation of the church. He had himself studied under Thomas Lever at St. John's College and followed Lever into exile during the Marian persecutions. Through the efforts of William Cecil, Elizabeth's chief advisor and chancellor of the university, Kelke had been appointed master of Magdalene at the accession of Elizabeth. The quarrel over the queen's insistence that clergy wear the surplice (an ecclesiastical vestment which most Protestants saw as a remnant of Catholicism) became the symbol of the struggle for further reform. In 1565 Kelke was one of the signatories of a letter to Cecil urging that the queen's directive requiring the wearing of surplices and other ecclesiastical vestments might be stayed at Cambridge since "here were a multitude of pious and learned men who thought in their consciences all using of such garments was unlawful for them."[45] One of Kelke's protégés had been Stephen Limbert, who following his studies at Magdalene led an attack on the organ at Norwich Cathedral in a protest against choral music in church services in 1569.[46] Limbert was gone when Adam entered the college, but among those who were in the small community were Henry Ussher, Hugh Broughton, and Thomas Gataker, all of whom made their marks as reformers. Ussher became the effective founder and vice provost of Trinity College, Dublin. After receiving his BA in 1570, Broughton moved on to fellowships at St. John's and Christ's colleges and became known as a sharp critic of popery and its remnants in the Book of Common Prayer.[47] Gataker, who probably left Magdalene soon after Adam's arrival, became domestic chaplain to the earl of Leicester.[48]

Equally important were those fellows and undergraduates Adam would have encountered in university settings, in the town, and listening to sermons in various Cambridge churches and chapels, some of whom would figure in his later life as allies in the godly reform of England. William Fulke was the university preacher as well as a fellow of St. John's. William Whitaker was master of Trinity, and Thomas Cartwright a fellow of that college. Richard Rogers matriculated at Christ's a year before Adam entered the university, and George Gifford was there as well. John Still was a fellow of Christ's at that time, as was Edward Derring, who also served as Lady Margaret Preacher in 1567. Laurence Chaderton received his BA from Christ's in 1567 and became a fellow of that college. At St. John's, the nearest college to Magdalene, Robert Some and John Knewstub were fellows in addition to Fulke; in 1568 George Still matriculated, followed by Henry Sandes in 1569.[49] Adam, at the age of nineteen, was more mature than most students when he began his college studies, and so it is not surprising that some of the strongest friendships he made were not with undergraduates but with fellows such as Still, Knewstub, and Sandes.

The early years of Elizabeth's reign had seen a concerted effort to purge the university and the town of the remnants of popery. The university cross was sold, along with copes, surplices, altar cloths, mass books, and chalices, the raw materials of which could be refashioned. Geneva psalters—the psalm books used to sing God's worship in Calvin's Geneva—were employed. Still, controversies over the further progress of reform were common during Adam's tenure at Cambridge. As he began his studies a feud erupted between John Whitgift and Thomas Cartwright, two men who would come to epitomize the church establishment and the puritan opposition to it. In 1567 Whitgift was elected master of Trinity College, where Cartwright was a fellow. Whitgift served as Queen's Professor of Divinity at the university, while Cartwright held the equally prestigious post of Lady Margaret Professor of Divinity. According to Thomas Fuller's account, in August, during Whitgift's absence from the college, Cartwright preached "three sermons on one day in the chapel, so vehemently inveighing against the ceremonies of the church that at evening prayer all the scholars, save three . . . cast off their surplices as an abominable relic of superstition."[50] Over the succeeding months Cartwright's following grew. When he preached at the university church of Great St. Mary's, the clerk had to take the windows out so that those crowded outside could hear.

Cartwright's influence spread to other colleges, and it was reported that in defiance of church law "one in Christ's College and sundry in St. John's will be very hardly brought to wear surplices."[51] At St. John's, William Fulke spearheaded an effort to replace Richard Longworth as master because he was deemed insufficiently supportive of reform. As the quarrel divided the college community Fulke was expelled, but he set up an academy in town at the Falcon Inn, where he lectured to students until he was restored to his fellowship. Longworth himself was also expelled. Fearing the election of either Fulke or Roger Kelke as the new master, the university officials steered the vote to the election of Nicholas Shephard in an effort to curb the spread of puritanism.[52] The establishment counteroffensive against the godly finally culminated in 1571 when Whitgift, then vice chancellor of the university, deprived Cartwright of his lectureship and banished him from the university despite petitions signed by numerous reformers, including John Still, on his behalf.

Despite such reverses, there is no question that Cambridge at this time was closely identified with the movement for further reform of the Church of England. Rejecting the finality of the queen's settlement and questioning the dictates of the bishops, reformers met together in college settings to establish the path to be followed to purify ceremonies and teachings. Such conferencing was not only seen as a way of reaching consensus on what was to be attempted but also served as a validating process because the positions reached were more highly regarded since they derived not from a single individual but from a group of godly men. Nowhere was this process of questioning and resolution more relied on than at Christ's College, where Lawrence Chaderton was most closely identified with it. And when Chaderton became master of Emmanuel College he introduced there the practice of sharing one's religious gifts through regular conferencing sessions.[53]

Paralleling these gatherings within particular colleges were similar conferences uniting members of different colleges. In Adam Winthrop's day John Carter, later a godly preacher in the Stour Valley, participated "in weekly conferences with Chaderton, Lancelot Andrewes of Pembroke, Mr. Culverwell (presumably Ezekiel Culverwell), John Knewstub of St. John's . . . and others, 'whom God raised up and fitted to send forth into his Harvest, to gather his Corn, then ripe for the Sickle, into his Barn.'"[54] College tutors held regular conferences for prayer and discussion with their students, and Adam Winthrop likely participated in such meetings. At the heart of all such gatherings was the attempt to assist one another to find the answers to questions about doctrine and its interpretation. Sometimes agreement was impossible, so some questions were left unresolved. When a consensus did emerge, it was expected that all would accept it, though the formulation was often loose enough to allow room for some individual interpretation. The goal was to achieve unity while not demanding absolute uniformity on exact formulations of agreed-on conclusions. Adam Winthrop learned to combine a communal search for truth with respect for the views of fellow seekers. It was a lesson he would pass on to his son.

It is not clear how long Adam stayed at Cambridge, and there is no evidence that he took a degree, but there is ample evidence of his adherence to the reformist cause during his time at the university. His friends—especially John Still and John Knewstub—were clearly supporters of Cartwright. Over the years Adam would purchase for his library books by Cartwright, Fulke, Whitaker, and other reformers from his Cambridge days, and mention the deaths of Robert Some and Whitaker in his diary.[55] Adam had become a member of a network of godly clergy and laymen that would serve him well throughout his life and strongly influence the shape of his son's.

On December 16, 1574, Adam Winthrop married Alice Still, the sister of his Cambridge friend John Still. In the same year Still married Anne Alabaster, Adam's niece, the daughter of his sister Bridget Winthrop Alabaster. Still had been appointed to the benefice of Hadleigh, near Groton, in 1571, which appointment also made him dean of Bocking (Essex). Both of these positions gave him an important presence in the Stour Valley. In July 1574 he had been elected master of St. John's, and in that capacity he would assist his friend and new brother-in-law, appointing Adam on March 13, 1575, to the stewardship of the college's manors in Kent and Berkshire and to the office of receiver for Berkshire with a yearly stipend of five marks.[56]

His brother William would have approved of Adam's godly connections and appears not only to have guided and helped him directly but also to have assisted those who helped Adam. In 1568 William had served as one of the guarantors of first fruits for Roger Kelke when the latter was inducted rector of Sproughton, Suffolk.[57] And in 1574 he was one of the guarantors for John Still's brother, George, when the latter was inducted as rector of Whatfield, Suffolk.[58]

At some point Adam may have considered a career in the ministry, either as a preacher or university fellow. But it was about this time that he embarked on a different course, being admitted in 1574 to the Inner Temple, one of the Inns of Court in London that were the training schools for the nation's lawyers. The sixteenth century was an age of growth and increasing importance for the legal profession, and this was reflected in the physical expansion and beautification of the Inns. Legal training would offer a younger son such as Adam Winthrop an opportunity to achieve distinction and would also provide opportunities to assist the cause of reformation.[59]

Education at the Inns was most intense during the law terms, when the central courts met at Westminster Hall, though residence and study were required in some vacations between terms. The routine was similar in many respects to college life. Members of the Inner Temple lived together in chambers, attended daily chapel, and took dinner and supper in a common dining hall during terms. They learned the law from lectures or readings that followed the meals in hall, from attendance in the morning at the sessions of the courts in Westminster, and from their own readings of law reports and early published compilations.[60]

TRAGEDY INTERRUPTED ADAM'S STUDIES on Christmas Eve in 1577 when his wife, Alice, died during childbirth along with their stillborn son. "Send both forward to eternity and to god" was his later diary reference to the sad event.[61] Fourteen months later he married Anne Browne, whom he had known for many years, since her father Henry Browne had served briefly as rector of Groton and was an established landowner in Edwardstone. By 1580 Henry Browne had left Edwardstone for his lands in Prittewell, Essex, and Adam and Anne moved into the house that he had vacated. In January 1581 Anne entered labor, which must have caused Adam considerable anxiety. She gave birth to a daughter, whom they named Anne, but the infant died two weeks later.[62] The following year Adam suffered another grievous loss with the death of his beloved brother William.

Despite this turmoil in his domestic life, Adam persevered with his studies, and on February 9, 1584, he was admitted to the bar in the status of an utter barrister on the recommendation of Robert Dudley, the earl of Leicester.[63] This meant that he was entitled to plead cases before the courts of the kingdom as well as to handle other legal business. Leicester's sponsorship was another product of Adam's success in forging a network of influential friends. Leicester, one of Elizabeth's favorites, had emerged as a major court patron of puritans.[64] Any one of three clergymen who served the earl as chaplains in this period—William Fulke, John Still, and John Knewstub—may have introduced Adam to Leicester.[65] The earl had served as a governor of the Inner Temple since 1561 and in 1570 had purchased the property immediately to the west of the Inn, which became known as Leicester House. However the introduction had been made, Leicester's letter to the benchers of the Temple makes it clear that Adam was known to Dudley, who claimed to be "specially moved through a desire of his well doing."[66] Later that year Adam was one of the sixty barristers of the Inner Temple who signed a Declaration of Loyalty and Oath of Association submitted to the queen, who at that time faced renewed threats from Catholics who challenged her legitimacy.[67] The large number of Catholic recusants at the Inns of Court, including perhaps as much as one third of the membership of the Inner Temple, had been a constant source of concern for zealous Protestants and made them one of the groups targeted to sign the loyalty oath.[68]

As an utter barrister Adam would have been expected to continue his studies and to participate in the exercises of the Inner Temple for at least another three years. In 1574 the judges had stipulated that a five-year probationary period subsequent to being called to the bar was necessary for a barrister to appear at the bar in Westminster, but before that Adam would have been allowed to give counsel, plead cases in the circuits, keep manorial courts, and draw up conveyances and other legal documents. This latter seems to have been the course that Adam chose to follow, though he performed enough of the duties of Inn membership to retain his good standing for the next decade. But in June 1595 it was ordered that four other barristers "and Mr. Wintrop, because they have not taken upon them to be stewards of the readers' dinner, as by order of the House they ought to have done, shall be from henceforth put out of this House and be disadmitted thereof for ever."[69] While the Inns were in some respects like colleges, they were in other respects like guilds such as the Clothworkers, and Adam paid the penalty for failing to perform one of the tasks that went with his position. Though it precluded any further rise in the profession, his expulsion from the Inn would not have affected his local practice of the law. The fact is that by that time Adam had put aside any dreams of a career in the high courts of the realm and settled securely in the Groton area. He added to the land he inherited from his father and provided legal counsel for his brother John, including being John's agent in making payments of £20 annually to Elizabeth Risby during her coverture. Though the brothers were never close, they appear to have forged a working relationship at this time.

Returning home was made more attractive by the close proximity of friends and the dawn of a period of godly religious ascendancy. In 1573 George Gifford had complained that "the carelessness in feeding the Lord's flock hath been so great, that in most places either ravening wolves or else such lewd, unskillful, blind guides as are not able to govern themselves, instead of true pastors, are made governors in the church and have the rule over the flock of Christ."[70] But this was already changing due to the influence of godly ministers and magistrates. In 1577 John Still was collated to the position of archdeacon of Sudbury, the local authority in the church for most of the western half of the county of Suffolk, a position in which he would perform significant service to the godly cause.[71] In 1578 Adam's friend Henry Sandes became vicar of Preston, and the following year John Knewstub was inducted into the rectory of Cockfield, both villages a half-day's journey to the north of Groton.[72] During the last quarter of the sixteenth century, religious reformers achieved the greatest success they would have in the region along the Stour Valley, making it "a closer approximation to the type of a godly commonwealth than in any part of England at any time."[73]

To call the region of the Stour Valley a "godly kingdom" does not mean that everyone within the region accepted the more advanced religious views of the evangelicals, nor that the "kingdom" had clearly delineated boundaries. Rather, I am suggesting that this became a region where godly magistrates controlled most of the institutions of local authority and where a greater percentage of church livings were held by evangelical preachers than was the case anywhere else in England. The result was a cultural climate in which reformers were in the ascendant rather than on the margins. They were able to advance their agenda openly and were free to promote a social gospel that stressed the needs of community over the interests of individuals. The dawn of this new day of reform in the Stour Valley was one of the things that drew Adam home. He would make his own contributions to building the kingdom, and his son John would be raised in it. And though it will take us away from our focus on the Winthrops for a time, it is essential that we examine the rise and character of that "kingdom," for it would be that model which John Winthrop sought to recreate in New England.

THE FOUNDATIONS OF THIS EFFORT to undo the religious remnants of the Marian regime in the Stour Valley were undertaken by two godly bishops with a reputation for evangelicalism. Edmund Grindal was the first Elizabethan bishop of the diocese of London, which included Essex. Grindal had supported the London stranger churches and encouraged prophesyings. He labored to place evangelical preaching ministers throughout his diocese and had some success, even when it meant cutting ceremonial corners. A good example of this is to be found in the case of Thomas Upcher, William Winthrop's friend and possible relative, to whom Grindal gave a dispensation to conduct services in St. Leonard's Colchester without wearing the prescribed surplice. The first Elizabethan bishop of Norfolk, whose jurisdiction included Suffolk, was John Parkhurst, another Marian exile and convinced evangelical. As time went on Parkhurst advanced the careers of numerous ministers later cited for nonconformity and did more to advance the cause of godly reform than anyone else in the diocese. His strong sympathy for those attacked as puritans set him apart from his fellow bishops and made him suspect in the eyes of many of the queen's counselors.[74]

Neither Grindal nor Parkhurst was able to do all that he might have wished in the 1560s. They had to contend with powerful conservative forces in their dioceses (this was especially true in the case of Parkhurst). Their ability to transform local religion was also hindered by a shortage of qualified candidates for parish preaching posts. Soon that would change, as Cambridge contemporaries of Adam received their degrees and were ordained, and many gravitated to the Stour Valley, where godly lay patrons were eager to appoint them to livings. It is true that episcopal support for reform would not always be as strong as it was in the 1560s. But if few of their successors were as energetic in promoting reform, few would seek to curtail it.[75] Essentially, qualified subscription to the official articles of faith and partial conformity to prescribed liturgical practices was accepted by these bishops, from the beginning of Elizabeth's reign until the 1610s.[76]

The seeds were planted by Grindal and Parkhurst. During the episcopates of less evangelical bishops those seeds were free to mature because the Stour Valley was as far from the diocesan seats of the cities of London and of Norwich as one could be in those two dioceses. That frontier was easily neglected by bishops who were content to leave matters of local discipline to their archdeacons. And the men who held those posts from the 1570s through the 1610s were more often than not promoters and supporters of reform. The first archdeacon of Colchester was John Pulleyne, the Winthrops' rector at St. Peter's Cornhill before Queen Mary's accession, with whom William Winthrop had worshiped in the London Marian underground. In 1572 Pulleyne was succeeded by George Withers, who had previously attracted notice and censure for his reformist preaching in Bury St. Edmunds and who as archdeacon would support godly preachers. Another key figure was Adam Winthrop's brother-in-law John Still, who was archdeacon of Sudbury from 1576 to 1593 and would use his office to favor the cause of reform.

This is not to say that in the godly kingdom no reformer was brought before the archidiaconal courts, but the records show that clergy subjected to scrutiny for overzealousness were treated gently. Some ministers cited in the visitations of church officials for failure to perform the ceremonies as prescribed were never called to account. For many who were summoned to appear before church courts, promises to reconsider their nonconformity were often sufficient to gain their release. Even formal admonitions were rarely handed out. Occasionally pressures from above did require harsher measures against nonconformity, even suspension from the ministry. However, before 1620, in the Stour Valley, episcopal appreciation of the good done by reformist ministers in preaching Protestant doctrines and raising the standards of public morality more than overcame any worries the bishops had about local nonconformity.

Equally critical to the forging of the godly kingdom of John Winthrop's youth was the fact that in the 1570s more and more of the lay powers based in the region became noted patrons of reform and were able to temper episcopal harshness on the rare occasions when it reached out against the evangelical clergy. Ultimately the foundation that sustained this godly kingdom was cooperation between godly magistrates and godly ministers, which the Reverend Samuel Ward spoke of as "two optic pieces" both of which needed to be in proper focus for the good of the society.[77] The region was rich in godly laymen: the Highams, Jermyns, Bacons, Springs, Barnardistons, Riches, and others who shared reformed sympathies came to dominate the commission of the peace, the county bench of justices, in both Essex and Suffolk. These men used their patronage to appoint godly clergy to livings through the region. In the critical decades of the 1570s and 1580s these local figures could call for support on national leaders such as Burghley, Leicester, Walsingham, and Mildmay at the queen's court. It was in the decade prior to John Winthrop's birth that this transformation of the bench had been effected in Suffolk, a change solidified with the appointments of Sir John Higham and Sir Robert Jermyn, whom Adam Winthrop referred to as "a pious man and a lover of true religion."[78] By the end of the 1570s John Knewstub, in dedicating his *Answeare unto Certaine Assertions* (1579) to the members of the bench, could refer to them as "those gentlemen in Suffolk whom the true worshiping God hath made right worshipful."[79] They would provide the examples that John Winthrop would eventually try to model himself on.

While episcopal and lay patronage and support provided a foundation upon which the godly kingdom could be erected, in the Stour Valley the walls were built and the rooms furnished by the evangelical efforts of the godly clergy laboring individually and in their various forms of clerical association. Educated clergy were to regularly prepare and preach sermons designed to uproot from their parishioners' minds the false doctrines of

Rome and to guide those men and women to a true faith and moral practice. To assist each minister's ability to advance this agenda, and to keep uniformity in what was preached, collegial consultation and aid were essential. The initial form that this took was prophesyings, exercises in which clergy gathered to listen to one of their colleagues preach and to shape a religious consensus for their parishes. Bishop Edwin Sandys wrote that they had existed in the diocese of London "almost since the beginning of her Majesty's reign" and were "thought very necessary for the increase of knowledge to all ministers."[80] The archdeacon of Essex, John Walker, described six such exercises in his archdeaconry, including two in the area of the Stour Valley, and reported that there had been "increase of learning, and edifying of the people to have grown thereby." Citing earlier precedents, Walker argued that "Paul was not ashamed to go to Jerusalem after he had long preached the Gospel to confer with the rest of the apostles, and divers times to decide and debate controversies."[81] While the situation in the diocese of Norwich is less clear since there are no episcopal statements comparable to that of Sandys, nor reports from the archdeacons of Sudbury or Suffolk, there is evidence that prophesying had been established in the city of Norwich as early as 1564.[82] Directives for the proper ordering of such exercises throughout the diocese were issued in 1575.[83]

Prophesyings were not the only occasions for ministers to assist one another. Clergy found other ways of enhancing their friends' reputation among the laity. Epistles to the reader were employed by ministers to enhance the authority of sermons published by their friends, and on occasion a minister would preach in a friend's town to bolster his position with his parishioners. An interesting early example of this is to be found in Colchester in the late 1570s when the reformed clergyman at St. Leonard's, William Winthrop's "brother" Thomas Upcher, was the target of printed libels circulated by his enemies to undermine his standing in the community. Preachers from both sides of the Stour came to Colchester to offer their support, including Oliver Pigge of Abberton, John Wilton of Aldham, and Robert Welche of Great Waldingfield. Welche, in particular, "preached against the abuse of libeling [and] said in his Sermon that if the like abuse were in Geneva the offender should be hanged."[84]

When the prophesyings were halted on the directives of Queen Elizabeth, whose attitude toward a preaching ministry was at best ambivalent, other forms of association were advanced to achieve the same goals of establishing clerical unity and enhancing the authority of the clergy among the laity. The conference movement in the godly kingdom of the Stour in the 1580s is generally seen as an effort to establish a presbyterian church within the church. However, since these clerical conferences had no institutional authority over the parishes from which their ministers came as they would have in a presbyterian system, they should be seen more as associations serving the needs of godly clergymen and the advance of reform among the laity. Conferences provided forums in which ministers could discuss and reach conclusions about issues that were troubling them and acted as authorizing mechanisms whereby the clergy could return to their parishes with the reputation of the group reinforcing the positions they would advance. The most famous of all these was in the heart of the Stour Valley, at Dedham, and drew its membership from both sides of the river. But the conference movement in the region had begun slightly earlier, when John Knewstub convened a gathering of "three-score ministers, appointed out of Essex, Cambridgeshire, and Norfolk," and undoubtedly Suffolk itself, in Cockfield, Suffolk, on May 16, 1582, "to confer of the Common Booke what might be tolerated, and what necessarily to be refused in every point of it; apparel, matter, form, days, fastings, injunctions etc."[85] It is generally believed that it was this Cockfield meeting that gave rise to the local conferences that grew up throughout the region over the following years, in Cockfield itself, in Dedham, in Braintree, and elsewhere.

These East Anglian conferences were clearly part of a national movement, and on several occasions representatives from regional conferences gathered in London or at Stourbridge Fair, outside of Cambridge. There were informal links as well. Thomas Crooke, who was a fellow at Trinity College, Cambridge, when Adam Winthrop, Knewstub, and others were at the university, became rector of Great Waldingfield, next to Groton, in 1574. He then moved on to London, where he was a preacher at Gray's Inn and a member of the London clerical conference. But what is most significant in examining the heritage of John Winthrop is the role of the conferences in shaping the religion of the Stour Valley. To enhance their work, there seems to have been some effort to link the regional conferences. Henry Sandes of Boxford, who was a member of the Dedham conference, was not only a close friend of John Knewstub but was also part of the group that met at Cockfield. In June 1587 "Sandes delivered a message from the brethren of another company, who desired that some things might be communicated from these meetings one to another."[86] When members of the Braintree conference requested in July 1587 that Lawrence Newman of Coggeshall be allowed to leave the Dedham meeting and join himself to the Braintree group, the Dedham conference concluded that "if he thought he could be of both meetings, and hold out, they would be glad in it."[87]

Occasionally these gatherings are portrayed as elements in an underground movement. While those involved clearly were not interested in advertising their efforts to those at Lambeth Palace, the home of the archbishop of Canterbury, the nature and purpose of the clerical gatherings make the idea that they were secret untenable. Anyone who has visited such small towns as Cockfield, Boxford, or Braintree knows how impossible it would have been for a dozen or more clergy to gather in such a place unbeknown to the local parishioners. And while the deliberations themselves were likely closed in whole or part to the laity, the fact that a parochial minister was involved in such an effort had to be known if it was to enhance his authority with his people.

What these godly clergy were attempting to create was a model of how life might be under a reformed episcopal system. Rather than discount the formal organization of the church, they sought to work with it. Rather than hide from the local authorities, they sought their help. A few examples from the records of the Dedham conference suggest this. Some of the members of the conference proposed to George Withers, the archdeacon of Colchester, that he transform his archidiaconal visitations "to be as Synods were in the old time, where we may use our freedom in conference and determining of ecclesiastical matters with him as fellow laborers and brethren."[88] When the conference was asked by one of the members how to deal with fractious members of his parish, he was advised that if his own admonitions failed, he should bring the offenders to the attention of the local justice or the appropriate court leet, or should "complain of them to the Bishop for redress."[89] Also, on more than one occasion the conference turned for help to the archdeacon, as when, following "an ungodly sermon" preached in Hadleigh, it was proposed that notes of the sermon be sent to "Mr. Doctor Still to be dealt with," Still being archdeacon of Sudbury.[90]

The view from Groton was that such efforts were central to the completion of England's reform and the perfecting of the godly kingdom. From the perspective of Lambeth Palace, the outlook was different. Clerical conferencing was feared as representing a challenge to the hierarchical system of church government, which vested power in the bishops. It was easy to perceive in the conference movement an attempt to push England toward a presbyterian system such as existed in Scotland, where elected presbyteries rather than bishops governed the national church. Indeed, some of the national leaders of reform, particularly Thomas Cartwright and John Field, did seek some such changes in the constitution of the church. While godly control was being consolidated in the Stour Valley, the quarrel over the church had become more divisive in the nation's highest councils. In 1581 Peter Wentworth had introduced a bill in Parliament calling for the replacement of episcopacy with a presbyterian church government, but the queen forbade it being taken up. Consecrated archbishop of Canterbury in 1583, Cartwright's old foe John Whitgift initiated a new campaign that required clergy to subscribe to the Three Articles, which accepted the royal supremacy, recognized the Thirty-nine Articles of the church as agreeable to the word of God, and—most troublesome—demanded that the cler-gyman would use the forms of the Prayer Book, including those ceremo-nies the godly sought to avoid as remnants of Catholicism. The demand for formal subscription caused dismay among reformers and led to the sus-pension of many nonconforming ministers who refused to subscribe. Throughout the country protests were mobilized against these suspensions. In 1584 reformed members of Parliament supported an effort to replace the Book of Common Prayer with a liturgy devoid of Catholic practice, such as the one Calvin had instituted in Geneva. Again the queen pre-vented the bill from having a reading. Thomas Cartwright's return from abroad to take a position in the household of the earl of Leicester encour-aged reformers but only stiffened Whitgift's fears of the movement.[91]

The dispute between Protestant supporters of the church was played out against a rising fear of Spain and concern that English Catholics might flock to aid a Spanish invasion. While the church authorities were fending off demands for further reform, they were also cooperating with parlia-mentary reformers in striking out against Catholics. English Protestants disagreed over the need to purge every vestige of Catholic practice from church worship, but all were united in loathing the central teachings of Rome, and their hostility was reinforced by the merger of Spanish plots with papal efforts to restore that faith in England. Death sentences for priests caught celebrating the mass and harsh fines on those who recused themselves from Church of England worship were legislated in 1581. Three priests, including Edmund Campion, were executed in that year. In 1584 Burghley and Walsingham drafted the Oath of Loyalty for people like Adam Winthrop and his fellow barristers of the Inner Temple to sign, pledging themselves to protect Elizabeth and overthrow her enemies. In 1586, as rumors of Spain's gathering of an immense armada grew in intensity, twelve Catholic priests and three laymen were executed. Having ignored earlier evidence of Mary Stuart's complicity in plots against her, Elizabeth was finally persuaded to allow the trial in 1586 and execution in 1587 of the exiled Queen of Scots. In 1588, the year of Spain's attempted invasion, thirty-one Catholic priests were executed.[92]

Despite these efforts, and despite the fact that historians have often listed "anti-Catholicism" as one of the hallmarks of what they call "puritanism," the fact is that in the Stour Valley the godly could on occasion be found interacting with local Catholics.[93] This was certainly true of the Winthrops and may explain the absence of strong anti-Catholic statements in the writ-ings of the future governor of Massachusetts. Adam Winthrop was friendly with William Mannock, who was one of the prominent Catholics in the Stour Valley. The two dined at each other's homes. In 1602 Mannock sent Adam three yards of satin as a New Year's token of his friendship.[94] Later, in 1622, Henry Sandes would ask John Winthrop to intercede with the

Mannock family to secure their appointment of a godly minister in the family-held living at Stoke-by-Nayland.[95]

William Alabaster, Adam's nephew, was another Catholic who was a frequent visitor to Groton. In 1597 Alabaster had seemed launched on a brilliant career in the Protestant English church. He was catechist at Trinity College, Cambridge. He had secured the patronage of the earl of Essex, accompanying the earl on a military expedition against Cádiz and receiving from Essex the living of Landulf, Cornwall.[96] But an encounter in London with an imprisoned Catholic priest led to his conversion. He visited his uncle Adam at Groton in the summer of 1597 and made "himself known to be a papist."[97] Alabaster was soon imprisoned for attempting to convert others to Catholicism, escaped, and fled to Rome, where he took up residence at the English College in the papal city. In his responses to the questions put him on admission there he stated, "My mother is descended from the Winthrops, a distinguished stock."[98] Alabaster would become notorious, first by recanting his conversion, then by converting to Rome again, and finally when he returned to England, impressed the king with his learning, and ended his life as rector of the parish of Little Shelford in Cambridgeshire. Yet his orthodoxy was always in question, and Oliver Cromwell recounted suspicions about Alabaster's preaching during his maiden speech to the Parliament of 1629.[99] Despite all this, Adam Winthrop followed his nephew's career, continued to welcome him to Groton, and discussed his situation with him on numerous occasions. Perhaps the fact that the godly felt secure in their control of the Stour Valley and confident of their eventual triumph allowed them to combine a hatred of Catholicism in principle with a tolerance of individual Catholic friends and kin.

Concerned about Rome, Whitgift and his episcopal colleagues also perceived a threat from outside the church on the other end of the spectrum. As early as the 1560s the impatience of some reformers had led them to abandon the broader cause of transforming the Church of England and to choose a path of separation and the creation of independent congregations of believers following a path they believed to be that set forth in Scripture. In 1567 such a separatist congregation had been detected in London. With the heightened tensions of the 1580s the movement appeared more threatening. In 1582 Robert Browne published *A Treatise of Reformation Without Tarrying for Anie*, which was a call for godly men and women to take matters into their own hands rather than waiting for the queen and her bishops to see the light. Two separatist leaders, Henry Barrow and John Greenwood, were arrested in 1587 and would be executed in 1593. It was effective for the defenders of orthodoxy to argue that separatism was the inevitable result of principled nonconformity.

The reformers were zealous in joining the government in efforts to root out Catholicism and indeed argued that the persistence of Catholic practices in the Church of England was the major justification for further reform. They worked hard to differentiate themselves from the separatists and other Protestant extremists. Adam Winthrop's friend John Knewstub achieved fame in the 1570s as the hammer of the familists, a fringe group that followed the teachings of the Dutch mystic Hendrik Niclaes. By preaching and working against this perfectionist heresy, Knewstub secured a reputation that made questions about his own loyalty to the church unthinkable.[100]

Despite their setbacks in the Parliaments of the early 1580s, while fighting Catholics and sectaries the reformers continued their struggle to perfect the Church of England. In the Parliament of 1586 Peter Wentworth again moved to change the liturgy, and in 1587 Anthony Cope renewed that effort, while Wentworth argued for the right of Parliament to debate religious matters. Elizabeth saw this as an infringement on her authority and ordered Wentworth, Cope, and Edward Lewknor imprisoned for their impertinence while her officials persuaded Parliament to cease deliberations on the disputed matters. Outside of Westminster, reformers read and considered Walter Traver's *Disciplina Ecclesiae* (1574) and manuscript copies of the *Book of Discipline*, which is believed to have been Thomas Cartwright's argument for presbyterian reform. Frustrated by setbacks, a segment of the reformers published a series of bitter anti-episcopal propaganda under the pseudonym Martin Marprelate in 1588. More *Marprelate Tracts* appeared in the following year and spurred Whitgift to a full assault. Charges were brought against John Penry, the suspected printer of the *Marprelate Tracts*, and he was executed in 1593. The search for the elusive Martin Marprelate turned into an effort to uproot the so-called presbyterian movement. Reformers hauled before the High Commission—a church court with extensive powers—revealed the workings of the conference movement in the Stour Valley and elsewhere. Thomas Cartwright and others were interrogated before the Star Chamber, and under the weight of this assault the conference movement per se ceased to exist.[101]

It is clear from the records of the Dedham conference that the ministers of the Stour Valley had often disagreed with their London allies and others labeled "presbyterian." Historians have been too willing to assume that because Bancroft charged a uniformity among the regional "presbyterians" he attacked, there was indeed such a uniformity. The fortunate position of the reformers in the Stour Valley, where they still in essence had the power to define orthodoxy in their small godly kingdom, gave them a different perspective than that of more embattled evangelicals elsewhere. Be that as it may, however, the conferences in the Stour Valley region were forced to disband as such under the weight of Bancroft's attack.[102]

Just as after the suppression of the prophesyings reformers had organized conferences, after the collapse of the conference movement the drive to associate merely took new forms, this time as combination lectureships, fasts, and similar gatherings. All of these had existed in the past, but they now took on new importance as they became the primary means for facilitating clerical gathering. It was these forms of association that provided the largest role for the laity. The Catholic priest William Weston observed such a gathering outside the walls of Wisbech castle where he was confined: the justices and the clergy and the laity "flocking from all quarters to be present at their exercises. These they used to begin with three or four sermons, preached one after the other. Then they went to communion. . . . They all had their Bibles, and looked diligently for the texts that were quoted by their preachers, comparing different passages to see if they had been brought forward truly and to the point. . . . When the congregation was dismissed, after the long fast that had been imposed upon them all, and after the whole day had been consumed in these exercises, they ended . . . with a plentiful supper."[103] Such holy fairs were essential to the establishment of a public culture of reform in the Stour Valley.[104]

There were other ways, more personal ways, in which the authority of the clergy and their agenda were established in this period through the interaction of godly clergy with each other, and godly clergy with pious lay men and women in more domestic types of forums. Richard Rogers wrote in his diary of conferences with Ezekiel Culverwell, some while they rode through the countryside.[105] Giles Firmin recalled John Knewstub and John Rogers riding through the countryside together and sharing their faith and views on evangelical strategies.[106] Godly communion could involve laity along with the clergy. In his *Seven Treatises*, Richard Rogers called on believers to engage with fellow saints in godly communion and to covenant with them.[107] He also gave an example of a group that joined in such communion, "fasted betwixt ourselves, to the stirring up ourselves to greater godliness . . . and then we determined to bring into writing a direction for our lives, which might be both for our selves and others."[108] Such covenanted groups were the leaven that helped the cause of the godly on the parish level to rise. Prayers for the dying could reflect webs of support that united layman and cleric, and gatherings of the faithful to repeat and discuss sermons heard in church were occasions where the spirit and authority of the clergy could act in a lay environment.[109]

At the time John Winthrop was born and during the years he was growing up, in most parishes in the Stour Valley the majority of the laity accepted their clergyman just as they would have accepted anyone placed before them by lay patrons and accepted by the local church officialdom. These were the parishioners whom many clergy would label disdainfully "carnal gospellers."[110] They accepted clerical teachings and tried to live by them but never internalized the values of godliness, never experienced a spiritual rebirth. Others in the parish, like Adam Winthrop, accepted the clergy because as saints themselves such laymen recognized in men like Knewstub, Sandes, and Rogers fellow saints who were authorized to lead by virtue of education and grace—and whose qualifications were recognized and promoted through word of mouth and by published endorsements by fellow members of godly conferences. Those few lay parishioners in the region who might have found an alternative, perhaps more ceremonial version of faith more congenial for the most part accepted what they had, because they found themselves in a minority and because the lay magistrates and local church officials to whom they could protest were deaf to their complaints. Even clergy in the region who found themselves in the minority found complaining to be for the most part futile; when the Reverend Thomas Rogers complained to Archdeacon Still about his removal from the godly combination lecture at Bury St. Edmunds, he was ignored.[111]

THE EXISTENCE OF A GODLY KINGDOM in the Stour manifested itself in various forms and in all ways of life. It was reflected in the prevalence of a culture of social reform in the towns and villages of the region. Braintree and Finchingfield are among the towns that historians have singled out where vestries, with the clergy in attendance, acted as town meetings regulating affairs so as to achieve godly neighborhoods.[112] The "godly orders" of Dedham's ancients reflect a social policy spurred by godliness.[113] In Boxford, where Adam Winthrop and his son John would frequently attend the sermons of preachers such as their friend Henry Sandes, an agreement "was concluded by the chief inhabitants of the parish" in 1608 whereby trade was regulated, the Sabbath was improved, inhabitants were required to post bond before taking in servants or laborers who might become a public charge, and other similar policies set for the good ordering of the community.[114] The reformation of manners in the Essex town of Terling "provided a strong base of godliness among the parishioners" that led to the suppression of Sunday dancing and alehouse disorders and a curtailing of swearing.[115] To these examples could be added Colchester, Sudbury, and Bury St. Edmunds. Perhaps the success of the godly in reforming particular local communities was made easier in this region because of the overall climate of support for reform.

Another, related reflection of the transformation of the Stour Valley into a godly kingdom was the attention paid to education. Writing of Suffolk, Robert Reyce said that "no good town" was without a school, and "for free schools here be sundry, well founded and endowed, whom I beseech the Lord so to bless that they may still more and more bring forth many good members for the state and commonwealth, and of these free schools I find to be at Ipswich, St. Edmunds Bury, Hadleigh, Boxford."[116] These were supported by alliances of godly gentlemen and clergy. The members of the board of governors of the Boxford school, founded in 1595, which stood on land granted by Adam Winthrop, included the clergymen John Knewstub, Henry Sandes, and Thomas Lovell and the gentlemen Adam Winthrop, Sir William Waldegrave, Brampton Gurdon, William Clopton, and John Peyton.[117] On the other side of the valley were important free schools that were founded or rechartered in Elizabeth's reign, including those at Colchester, Dedham, and Halstead. Other schools emerged from old chantry foundations, such as those at Sudbury, Braintree, Long Melford, and Stoke-by-Clare. Though not established by royal charter, the school at Felsted was otherwise identical in its goals and operation. It was well endowed by the Rich family and was the school where Oliver Cromwell would send his children. Many of these schools had links to the godly colleges at Cambridge.[118]

As godly as the kingdom of the Stour was, it was not a fairy-tale kingdom. In 1604 the Reverend Nicholas Bownde complained that some parishes were still plagued by "idle shepherds and hirelings who seek the fleece and not the flock."[119] And there were strains in the social fabric of this kingdom as one would find in any other. Conflict occasionally erupted between townsmen and gentry in places such as Bury St. Edmunds and Ipswich.[120] In times of economic stress the clergy often had to take a prophetic stance in exhorting the well-off to perform their duties of Christian charity, as, for example, in Thomas Carew's Bildeston *Caveat for Clothiers* and Bezaleel Carter's denunciation of "some even of our greatest professors" in the Clare combination lecture.[121]

None of this diminishes the fact that for a time the godly in the Stour Valley were in control.[122] They felt no sense of alienation, because they held the local seats of authority. It was there, in the Suffolk-Essex borderland, through the efforts of sympathetic religious officials and godly magistrates, along with the ministry of evangelical clergy associated with each other and with the zealous lay men and women in their parishes, that it could be claimed that a godly commonwealth had been erected.

Certainly those who lived on both sides of the river took pride in the godliness of their land. Robert Reyce wrote in his account of Suffolk that "the Lord hath vouchsafed many singular benefits as proper to this country among which this one is not the least, the great number of religious, grave, reverend, and learned ministers of God's holy word, which are planted in this shire, traveling in the Lord's harvest, with sound doctrine and upright life."[123] An even stronger statement is found regarding the region on the Essex side of the river in Richard Sibbes's dedication of a work of Ezekiel Culverwell to their common friend Mrs. More. Referring to her upbringing as a youth in the area of Felsted, Essex, where Culverwell preached in the 1580s, Sibbes stated that "[i]n those times those parts were in regard of the air unhealthful, yet that air was so sweetened with the savory breath of the Gospel, that they were termed the holy land."[124] The region's reputation for godly preachers drew Cambridge students and others to the churches of the valley to hear sermons. Thomas Goodwin later recalled how he and fellow students, including William Bridge and Jeremiah Burroughes, would ride to Dedham "to get a little fire."[125] The region was considered an ideal location by aspiring preachers. Henry Jessey, on leaving Cambridge, "begged the Lord to place him in Essex, near Suffolk, or in Suffolk, near Essex."[126] From the perspective of the godly, John Winthrop was fortunate to be born and raised in the Stour Valley. It was, in retrospect, the most important ingredient of his heritage.

Part Two

Struggle

&

4

Youth

WITH A LITTLE IMAGINATION we can see the young John Winthrop, aged eight, on a hot August morning in 1596, climbing Pitches Mount, the ancient earthwork about a half mile from his home. Together with some friends he was pretending to be living in a time when Saxon warriors built such fortifications to defend their settlements. On the Mount, away from the view of their parents, the youngsters could transport themselves back into those distant days and engage in playful recreations of battles, just as boys seem to have always done. On this day they approached the Mount from the east, having earlier in the day explored Groton Wood, the dense forest that brooded over the open fields of the region. Carrying bows and arrows, they were always alert for hares, a common feature of the landscape. But John also kept track of the passing of time, as marked by the sun's journey across the clear Suffolk sky. His father was expecting a visit from John Knewstub, the pastor of nearby Cockfield, and young John—fashioning himself in his mind as a clergyman—tried never to miss a chance to observe and listen to his father's clerical friends.

C3

ADAM AND ANNE WINTHROP were living in Edwardstone when John was born in 1588.[1] During the boy's youth Adam was a modest landholder with property in Edwardstone, Boxford, and other nearby communities, including Polstead and Hadleigh.[2] Some of these lands were rented, but others he farmed with the assistance of his own servants and additional hands hired to help at harvest. Like others in the region Adam was interested in new forms of husbandry. He owned a copy of Barnaby Googe's *Foure Bookes of Husbandry* (1577) and other books on the subject.[3] He grew grain crops—rye, barley, wheat, bullimong (a mixture of various grains grown together for cattle feed)—as well as peas.[4] He also hired laborers to mow, and to ditch and hedge, a sign that the Winthrop fields were marked by some of the hedges that are still a commonplace in the Stour

Valley.[5] Hedging did not always serve its purpose however, as in June of 1596 his neighbor Pardey's cattle crossed into one of Adam's fields and destroyed the grain, and on another occasion he found "Alcocke's beasts were in my barley."[6]

Some of the Winthrop holdings were woodland, and the sale of timber was a source of income—ash for poles, oak for housing, chestnut for a variety of uses. There were other sources of wealth as well. A 1595 list Adam made recorded livestock that included twenty-nine sheep, twelve lambs, ten milk cows and a bull, two heifers and two yearling bullocks, four weanlings, two sucking calves, two sows, five barrow hogs, and ten pigs.[7] He owned beehives and looked for the swarming of the bees, since honey would have been used in the household as a sweetener.[8] Adam also owned a plough and a cart, which he not only used on his own land but rented to neighbors for an additional source of income.[9] Following the guidance of Janus Dubravius's *A New Booke of Good Husbandry . . . conteining the order and maner of making fish ponds*, Adam stocked various ponds on his property with fish, largely carp, pike, and tench.[10] Not only did this supplement the family diet, but the annual cleansing of the ponds also provided muck that was used as manure.[11] In 1596 he dragged the "great pond" by his Edwardstone home and took out thirty-five carp.[12]

BUT ADAM WAS ALSO a lawyer, with his livery as a member of the bar kept in a specially built walnut cupboard in his home.[13] The world of books and discussions of law were also a part of young John's environment. Adam conducted manorial courts for his brother as well as for other area landowners. His expertise was in demand when legal instruments had to be drawn up or witnessed. In a list of his legal income in 1593 he included fees received from "Mr. John Forth for a pair of indentures (11s), Philip Gosling for a counsel (10s), John Bonde for a pair of indentures (10s), William Alston for a copy of a will (7s), Francis Pierce for 2 obligations (10d), and divers tenants of Groton for copies & entries (15s)."[14] But the largest item— £4 10s.—came from his work for John Still. In addition to providing legal advice, Adam handled Still's property in Hadleigh and likely performed similar services for others. When a member of the Inner Temple, he had been required to spend some time at the Inn, and he retained contacts with people of influence in the capital.[15]

In 1592 John Still, who had earlier been elected master of Trinity College, Cambridge, secured Adam's appointment as college auditor. Once a year Adam would journey to Cambridge to dine with the college fellows, review and sign the accounts, renew old acquaintances, meet with godly members of the university, and acquire books for his library. In addition to Still there were other members of the university community who were familiar to Adam from his own undergraduate days, including William

Whitaker, who was master of St. John's, and Robert Some, master of Peterhouse. His journeys to Cambridge provided him a chance to visit with William Alabaster, his nephew, who was a fellow of Trinity. Though some of the godly would later take a strong stand against play-acting, especially as found in the theaters of London, at this time there was no general objection to plays, and Adam may have very well attended a staging of Alabaster's verse drama *Roxanna*, which was performed at the college in the early 1590s. He developed new friendships and often invited students to his Suffolk home. Among the undergraduates at Trinity in the early 1590s were John Cotta, who would marry Adam's youngest sister, Susannah, and Robert Hawes and Thomas Newton, both of whom would later be part of the lectureship at Boxford supported by Adam. Two other members of that lectureship, Thomas Garthwayte and Humphry Morgan, were undergraduates at St. John's in the later 1590s.

Whether inspecting his fields, journeying to Cambridge to audit accounts, or going to London for legal business, Adam traveled on horseback. Travel routes were often dictated by the location of friends and family who would provide hospitality on multiple day trips. His accounts in the 1590s show him owning a bay trotting gelding as well as another gelding, a two-year-old colt, and a young mare in addition to various cart horses.[16] Adam had undoubtedly learned to ride as a youth and would have taught his son horsemanship, but he was a man who always tried to combine practical knowledge with the lessons of books, and he owned Thomas Blundeville's *The Foure Chiefest Offices Belonging to Horsemanship* (1580), which was dedicated to his own patron, the earl of Leicester.[17]

Over the years Adam built a modest library, but one that was impressive for someone of his status. Eighty-seven titles have been identified as having been in his possession at some point. The bulk of these are religious in nature, including a response of Thomas Cartwright to John Whitgift, two published sermons of William Fulke, and two tracts of William Whitaker. There are two tracts on witchcraft, his brother-in-law John Cotta's *The Trial of Witchcraft* (1616), and his friend George Gifford's *A Dialogue Concerning Witches and Witchcrafts* (1593), both of which took a moderate stand on the subject by setting a higher bar for prosecution and conviction of those suspected of the crime. Adam heavily annotated his copies of William Lambard's model local history, *The Perambulation of Kent* (1596), and Thomas Smith's treatise on English government, *De Republica Anglorum* (1584). He took notes on the flyleaf of his copy of John Stubb's criticism of Elizabeth's proposed marriage, *The Discoverie of a Gaping Gulf* (1579), for which, as Adam noted, Stubbs "was committed to the Tower, & from thence was brought to Westminster, and had judgment to have his right hand cut off, which was executed in King's street upon a scaffold, the third day of November anno D 1579." And, of course, there were legal works, including John Cowell's *The Interpreter* (1607), John Fortescue's *De Laudibus Legum Angliae* (1616), Lambard's *Eirenarcha, or, Of the Office of the Justices of the Peace* (1610), *Littleton's Tenures in English* (1592), and William Rastell's *Collection of the Statutes* (1557). The library was a resource not only for Adam and his household but also for friends and relatives to whom he lent books.[18]

LESS IS KNOWN of Adam's wife, Anne Browne Winthrop. Her father, Henry, had served for a brief time as rector of Groton.[19] Scattered notes, perhaps jotted down in preparation for his sermons, give hints as to the evangelical religious outlook that he inculcated in his daughters. The starting point of his faith was his commitment to God, "for my god is a great god and great king above all." He warned that "for the sins of the people God raiseth false prophets to deceive them," and insisted that "the minister and preacher must tell the people of their sins . . . and the people must seek knowledge at the minister." According to Browne, "the cause of error is the ignorance of God's word," and "preachers preaching the truth are not to be despised." He himself preached that "we must remember the law of God continually" and discussed the sin of "slandering, and who be slandered." He was outspoken "against idols and idolatry" at a time when the physical character of Stour Valley churches was being purged, stating that "Christ took not our nature upon him to be a patron to the carver or painter."[20] These views, reflecting a strong reformed commitment, were imbibed by his daughter Anne and passed on to her children.

Henry Browne was more than a clergyman, however. He owned considerable property in Essex as well as in Suffolk and a dye house in Boxford. Through his second marriage he owned a part interest in a ship. All this enabled him to provide well for his children and grandchildren in his will, including leaving the Edwardstone house to Anne.[21] But perhaps more important than these material legacies was the fact that he saw to the education of Anne and her sisters. Her surviving correspondence and copies of her books show John Winthrop's mother to have been very well educated for the time, fluent in a number of languages, and deeply interested in religious matters. She owned a copy of Philip Melancthon's Latin *Chronicon Carionis Expositum* (1581) and Jeronimo Osorio da Fonseca's *Vera Sapientia* (1582).[22] Her only surviving letter to her husband includes a postscript in French.[23]

That same letter to Adam, written in 1581, gives some sense of Anne's personality and the warmth of her relationship with her husband. Writing to him when he was at the Inner Temple, she refers to the "sweet and comfortable words, which always when you be present with me, are wont to flow most abundantly from your loving heart" and affirms her knowledge that "whether you be present with me, or absent from me, you are ever one towards me, and your heart remaineth always with me." Persuaded of this, she writes, "I will most assuredly, the lord assisting me by his grace, bear always the like loving heart unto you." In the meantime, "I will remain as one having a great inheritance, one rich treasure, and it being by force kept from him, or he being in a strange country and cannot enjoy it, longeth after it, sighing and sorrowing that he is so long bereft of it, yet rejoiceth that he hath so great a treasure pertaining to him, and hopeth that one day the time will come that he shall enjoy it, and have the whole benefit of it." With the letter she sent a shirt and five pairs of hose, and in it she asked Adam to send her a pound of starch and her Bible, "if it be ready," presumably referring to it being bound.[24]

During John's youth his father was often away from home, and, as was common in this period, Anne then assumed the responsibility of running the household. In 1593 Adam noted in his diary that "I departed from my house on Monday in Easter week, being the 16 of April 1593, and I left with my wife at my departing £12 in money, and I returned home on Friday the 19 of May."[25]

But there was another side to Anne Winthrop. She was a woman who took her faith seriously and expected other members of the family to do so as well. In 1603 the wife of Adam's nephew Joshua Winthrop came to Groton with her young son, retreating from London during a difficult period in her marriage. The daughter of Vincent Norrington, a prominent member of the Grocers Company, the young woman may have been frustrated by Joshua's more modest success, or perhaps she felt constrained by Joshua's efforts to follow in his father's footsteps as a supporter of godly reform. Arriving in Groton on a Saturday in late September, she took up lodgings with Paul Powle, an attorney who was a thorn in the side of the Winthrops. Hearing of her presence in Groton from others, Adam spoke with her and persuaded her to visit. When she did so after services on October 9, Anne Winthrop criticized the younger woman, also named Anne, for her costly apparel, and she stormed out in displeasure. Tongues were surely wagging in the small community, and all would have noticed when the young woman failed to attend the afternoon church services on the sixteenth. A few days afterward, Powle's home was broken into and Anne robbed, losing £3 of gold and most of her wearing linen. At this point she agreed to move in with her kin, but on the thirtieth Adam's wife "friendly reproved her" for failing to attend either Sabbath service. After an exchange of bitter words, the young Anne left to take up lodging elsewhere. A week later she sent for her possessions and returned to London.[26] A few years on, Joshua and Anne would migrate to Ireland, settling in the area of Bandon in the Munster Plantation.

ADAM AND ANNE'S FAMILY grew slowly, starting with the birth of a daughter, christened Anne after her mother, on January 16, 1586; John, the second surviving child, was born in 1588; another daughter, Jane, in 1592; she was followed in January 1600 by the couple's last child, Lucy.[27] The household also included various servants and guests. To take one period recorded in Adam's diary as a sample, in 1593 Frances Carpenter, age ten, came to dwell with the Winthrops. In the same year, Thomas Page and Mary Andrewe entered their service. Anne Page entered the Winthrops' service in July 1594.[28] A separate listing of servants wages indicated amounts paid in 1593 to Richard Edwards, Anne Manning, and Judith Baker.[29] Most of these were young people, who entered service to learn household and farming skills, acquire social polish, and put aside money for setting up their own households. One young man, the son of Thomas Appleton, whose sister Mary was to marry Robert Reyce, came to dwell with Adam to prepare for legal studies at the Inns of Court.[30] Hospitality also brought friends and family to stay for brief and longer periods. When John was four Justine Nicolson, the daughter of Edwardstone's rector, who also held the living at Groton, came to stay with the family for six months. While she was still there Humphrey Mildmay, the son of Sir Walter Mildmay, referred to by Adam as his "cousin," came to stay for two months.[31] A quite different member of the household when John was a boy was Adam's great mastiff, Grymble, who his master noted was "a gentle dog in the house."[32]

THE FAMILY FORTUNES CHANGED in the mid-1590s when the elder John Winthrop joined in the English colonization of Ireland. Following the suppression of the Desmond rebellion in Ireland in 1583, the English government undertook a major effort to colonize the south of that island, granting seignories in what was designated the Munster Plantation to men such as Walter Raleigh, Richard Grenville, and Edmund Spenser with the provision that they attract tenants to their lands.[33] On his visit to England to present his epic *The Faerie Queene* to Queen Elizabeth, Spenser visited old friends in Cambridge and was introduced to William Alabaster by William's uncle and Spenser's friend John Still.[34] Soon the Alabaster family and the Winthrops were talking of Ireland.[35] In July 1595 Adam Winthrop's brother-in-law Roger Alabaster, together with his wife and most of their children, departed for Munster. William Alabaster, having bid good-bye to his family in a heavy rain, returned to Cambridge the next day "malcontent."[36]

More important, Adam's brother John had determined to migrate. He was estranged from his wife, with no children nor prospects of any. He had further sullied his reputation by failing to observe the terms of the settlement he had made with Elizabeth. He was engaged in chronic quarrels with his Groton neighbors, the most recent leading to a court case in which the Groton churchwardens were suing him for having claimed and seized a cottage in the churchyard that had been built by the parish to house a poor man charged with ringing the church bells.[37] This was the type of case likely to stir up bitter local feelings. Ireland seemed to offer a chance at a new life and perhaps even a new marriage of sorts. Indeed, it was not uncommon for Englishmen prohibited from remarrying in England to cross the Irish Sea to start new families. By 1634 this had become so notorious that the Irish Parliament passed a law making bigamy a felony, "forasmuch as divers ill-disposed persons, being married, ran out of His Majesty's realms or dominions into this realm of Ireland . . . where they are not known, and there become to be married, having another husband or wife living."[38] Deciding to migrate, John left the management of Groton Manor in the hands of his brother.

For Adam Winthrop this meant the prospect of having to pay far more attention to the affairs of the estate. With these added obligations and with three young children, he decided to give up his membership in the Inner Temple. He settled his accounts with the chief butler and, shortly thereafter, having refused to serve as steward for a reader's dinner as was expected of him, was expelled from the Inner Temple.[39] A few years later, once his brother John had seemed to settle permanently in Ireland, it made sense for Adam and his family to move to the manor and dwell in Groton Place, the "mansion house."

MUCH OF YOUNG JOHN'S EXPERIENCE growing up in Edwardstone and Groton would have involved the natural world. He would have accompanied his father on rides through the countryside and become familiar with his father's lands as well as the fields that belonged to Groton Manor. Life flowed in rhythms set not by clocks but by the rising and setting of the sun and the turn of the seasons. There was a time to reap and a time to sow, a time when sheep lambed and horses foaled, a time when fishponds were dragged and cleaned and a time to restock them. With the turn of the seasons the fields changed from the pale greens or steel blues of sprouting barley, wheat, and rye to the yellows and golds of the maturing crops and the darker amber of the grain ready to harvest. Summer breezes stirred the shafts in a wavelike motion. Isolated clumps of trees—lime, oak, and ash—stood out like ships becalmed on the sea of grain.[40] Contrasting with the lighter colors of the crops were the darker greens of the hedges that marked off the field boundaries and the roads, thickly packed lines of blackthorn, hawthorn, holly, and willow interspersed with trees. The lines of these green walls of vegetation were brightened in the spring and summer with the wildflowers that sheltered along their base—the crimson of poppies, the purple mallow, and the yellows of oxlip and cowslip. While the higher ground was given to cultivation, in the bottomland along the streams were meadows where the Winthrops and other farmers grazed their cattle. Contrasting with the sweet fragrance of grasses and flowers in the higher ground, the bottoms were permeated with the dank, pungent smells of mud, beasts, and dung.

With the turn of the season in the fall, all of this changed. The harvested fields formed a bleak, dark landscape, occasionally but not often blanketed with snow. The hedges still marked the bounds, but now with dreary browns of exposed bark and branches. Only the green leaves of the holly and its bright red berries broke the gloom of the winter scene. And while at the height of the summer there were hardly five hours of darkness, in the depths of winter there were barely six hours of true light.

Weather was of concern for anyone whose family depended on the land, but it was also seen as evidence of supernatural interventions. Adam Winthrop noted extremes of weather in his diary. Snow and rain were recorded when they seemed abnormal. In 1602 "on the last day of June it thundered and lightened a great part of the night and set a tree on fire" in a park in Stoke-by-Nayland "which burned four days." On other occasions he noted that it "thundered and lightened" "exceedingly" or "wonderfully."[41] With strong summer storms there was danger of flooding, such as when the River Box flooded in August 1596. On December 23, 1601, the Winthrops felt the ground shake as much of England experienced an earthquake that Adam noted. Within weeks the London press put forth *The Wonders of the World. The Trembling of the Earth, and the warnings of the world before the Judgement Day.*[42]

This natural world was not bucolic and peaceful. John grew up witnessing violence in various forms. In February 1596 a dog killed one of Adam's lambs, and the following April another lamb was killed by "vermin." On another occasion Joseph Cole's dog bit one of Adam's rams in the neck. Hunting also involved violence, and the Winthrops indulged in it. Adam noted in 1595 that his brother John "killed a badger with his hounds," and in the following year John killed two badgers in the nearby parish of Semer.[43] Certain forms of hunting were illegal, however. On December 22, 1595, Adam was victimized by a poacher: John Jolly of nearby Polstead killed "two fat weathers" (castrated sheep) on Groton land, a felony for which Adam "caused him to be arrested."[44]

Violence between people and other crimes were also common. The Stour Valley may have been a godly kingdom, but it was not the Garden of Eden. If sermons about man's sinfulness would resonate with John Winthrop, it was at least in part because of what he witnessed and heard while growing up in the region. The year 1596 began with Adam noting that as he came from the market at Bury St. Edmunds "[t]he butcher of Wetherden Wood was cruelly murdered. His head was cut off and his body divided into four quarters, wrapped in a sheet, and laid upon his own horse . . . and so brought home to his wife"[45] In March Groton's rector, the Reverend Thomas Nicholson, was robbed. In May young Adam Cely, John's London cousin who was spending time with his Groton kin, stole fifteen shillings, for which, his uncle Adam noted, he was worthy to be fastened with a halter such as that used to control animals.[46] In September John Hawes tore Mary Pierce's petticoat, and when her sister Katherine sought to intervene he beat her with a crabtree staff. The following year, when John was nine, began with both Henry Sandes and the Winthrops themselves being robbed by "false knaves." In April Thomas Bond fled the region, having "gotten a maid with child." Toward the end of April Joan Browne Hilles, the sister of John's mother, came to the Winthrops "for that her husband had beaten her face and arms grievously."[47] In September the same John Hawes who had attempted to rape Mary Pierce killed Thomas Osborne on the road between Brantham and Thetford, for which he was later hanged. And the years that followed saw the litany of crimes continue. Thomas Hornby's daughter Bridget gave birth to an illegitimate child, which she destroyed. John Spenser of Groton stabbed John Penny of Hadleigh in the head with a dagger, killing him.

While these events all occurred close to home and involved people the Winthrops knew, Adam was often in attendance at the assizes, the regional courts for felony trials, and brought home reports of other crimes. A certain Criske was indicted for witchcraft. In 1605 at the assizes "Mistress Anne Browne was condemned of petit treason for procuring one Peter Goulding to murder her husband Mr. Browne, for the which fact the said Peter was hanged and she burned quick at Bury."[48] Some violence was self-inflicted. In his diary book Adam kept a "register of persons that have killed, hanged, or drowned themselves in Suffolk since the year of our Lord 1560." Among the locals contained in the list of fifteen were Joseph Bronde, who "killed himself with a pair of shears," William Gosnold, who "drowned himself in a pond," and Groton innkeeper Edward Couper, who "hanged himself in an upper chamber."[49] Lesser sins were taken in stride. When Adam found "one Scott, a butcher of Cockfield," lying drunk in his fields, he "took [him] home and laid him in a bed."[50] One of Adam's maids, Joan Betts, "did wound John Wailley my man in the head with her patten [sandal] for which she was very sorry."[51]

The life of a boy, of course, was filled with concerns that seemed more pressing than the affairs of the adult world. There were many other youths in the region; in Groton alone over thirty boys were born in the six years bracketing John's own birth. Not all of these would have been suitable playmates for a Winthrop, his family being of the gentry, but there were still plenty of peers to play and explore with. While the adventures of young boys were not the sort of things that people in the sixteenth century usually bothered to record, we can assume that play was an important part of youthful lives. John, in the company of Thomas Gostling and Lewis Kedby, would have often climbed Pitches Mount, perhaps accompanied by the genial mastiff Grymble, and walked to the neighboring parish of Lindsey to examine the remains of another ancient earthwork and an abandoned wooden castle. Though England was a largely deforested country, Groton Wood offered a landscape to explore that differed vastly from the open fields they were more used to. The boys would have learned to fish and hunt, mastering both archery and the use of guns. Rabbits abounded in the Stour Valley countryside and, along with birds, would have been prime targets for young marksmen. John, alas, according to his later testimony, was not a very good shot.

John would have also joined with the Gostling boys, Waldegrave Clopton, Richard Gale, and others in youthful games of football, imitating the fierce and occasionally bloody confrontations of the older youth and young men who represented the nearby villages in full pitched games. Adam Winthrop noted in 1617 that "Brand broke his leg at football."[52]

ADAM'S ABSENCE FOR LONG PERIODS during his son's youth meant that John was largely nurtured by the love of his mother and sisters, but when home Adam would have taken an interest in his children's early learning, including their religious instruction. A manuscript copy of "Principles of the Christian Religion" in one of Adam's commonplace books was the type of catechism that the youngsters would have been drilled at. The first principle concerned the importance of the Bible. "What sure ground have we to build our religion upon?" Adam or Anne would have asked, and the answer to be learned was "The word of God contained in the Scripture." Further questions and answers taught the children that the Scriptures were able to instruct them "in all points of faith that we are to believe and in all good duties that we are bound to practice." Later points that exist in the fragment dealt with the nature of God, "a spirit most perfect, most wise, almighty and most holy," the fact that "he did before all time by his unchangeable counsel ordain whatsoever afterward should come to pass," the nature of angels and devils, and the deserved fate of men for breaking the commandments—"His dreadful curse and everlasting death."[53]

Of course, these lessons were reinforced by the sermons that young John heard. On Sundays he would accompany his parents and siblings to Boxford or Groton to hear the two sermons customarily preached by Henry Sandes, the Reverend William Bird, or a visiting clergyman such as John Knewstub. Sometimes they might travel a little farther to hear Robert Welshe preach at Little Waldingfield. Clergymen were frequent guests at the Winthrop home. When Knewstub visited, young John would have listened to his father's old friend expound on the dangers posed by the heretical group called Family of Love, urge the need for social outreach, and bemoan the incomplete reformation of the church. He would have also been fascinated by the Cockfield minister's tales of his service to the earl of Leicester in the war in the Netherlands.

While religion permeated all aspects of life, it was not the only thing
that Adam would have imparted to his son. Although the Winthrops were
not on the top rung of county society, they were a privileged family. John
would not be sent to perform manual labor in the fields nor apprenticed to
learn a trade, but he did need to be taught how to ride. He learned how to
use a bow and arrow. It would have been his father who taught him how to
use a gun and to hunt. Adam would have taught the boy to fish in the
manor ponds and the local streams. John would have observed his father
conducting manorial courts and dealing with disputes among the manor's
tenants.[54]

As JOHN AND HIS SISTERS became older, more intense instruction would
have been called for. In 1595 Adam Winthrop first recorded payments to
John Chaplin for tutoring his children. Chaplin had received his BA from
Christ's College, Cambridge, in 1585 and his MA three years later; though
ordained in 1592, he had not yet found a clerical living. After a few years of
Chaplin's tutelage, it would have been time to enroll John in a grammar
school to prepare him for university. There is no record of which school
he attended, but two possibilities stand out.

Adam was involved in the affairs of the Boxford grammar school, having
been named one of the board of governors when the school was chartered by
the queen in 1596.[55] In 1602 he would donate land for the building of a new
schoolhouse.[56] Thomas Mildmay, the son of Adam's "cousin" William
Mildmay, who had been born in 1592, entered Boxford grammar school at
the age of eight.[57] All of this might suggest that John studied there.

However, as in the case of Mildmay, it was customary to send children
away to school. Another possibility is that John may have attended the
grammar school at Bury St. Edmunds, which was by the 1590s "already
distinguished, set in a strongly puritan town culturally dominated by a famous preaching exercise every Monday."[58] It was apart from Groton, but
not too far, and was within the godly kingdom of the Stour Valley. There
is circumstantial evidence suggesting that John attended Bury, including
the fact that he later sent his own sons Forth and John Jr. there; Forth went
to Bury after having been prepared by studies at Boxford, and this may
have been the case with his father as well.[59]

Since the regimens of most such schools were similar, an examination
of the Bury grammar school can give us an idea of John's experience at this
age. In 1586 the headmaster was Edmund Coote, followed in 1587 by
Nicholas Martyn.[60] The 1583 statutes of the school called for one hundred
students. No scholar was to be "admitted into the said school unless he can
read and write competently," and "[n]o scholar shall continue in the school
above five years, or six at the most, but shall depart wither to some university." Students were divided into five forms, with the school usher teaching

the lower two forms and the headmaster the older students. No scholar was to appear at school "with his head unkempt, his hands or face unwashed, his shoes unclean, his cap, hose, or vesture filthy, or seam rent." Each pupil was to have a supply of ink, paper, a pen, a knife to sharpen the quill, and books, which students were instructed to keep "fair, clean, and whole."[61] The entire student body was to be assembled at 6:00 A.M. for breakfast. At "half an hour after six of the clock in the morning, the scholars, kneeling devoutly and in their appointed places, shall say distinctly and in an audible voice" their prayers. Order was to be maintained, and any "as shall remove out of his place without reasonable cause, or shall make any din [or] noise, or pilfer, steal, lie, swear, or speak words of ribaldry shall be forthwith . . . sharply punished."

In the lowest form, or grade, students were taught the "rudiments and principles of the Latin tongue." Progressing to the second form they were exposed to Cato and other classic authors and to Aesop's fables. The third-form curriculum included works of Erasmus and Ovid, as well as some comedies of Plautus or Terence, and also called for instruction in the Greek alphabet. The next form progressed in learning Greek and continued to read classic works, including more Erasmus, Virgil, and Horace. The fifth form studied Cicero, Sallust, Caesar, and "some part of Socrates in Greek." The formal school day ended at five in the evening, but the usher or schoolmaster "shall every night teach [the] scholars three English words with their Latin significations, and three Latin words with their significations." On Saturday there was no instruction, but "the scholars shall make general repetition of all things taught them in the whole week before," and the schoolmaster's pupils would deliver "some epistle or epigram in verse that the said scholars have premeditated the forepart of the week, besides their ordinary lessons."

On Thursday afternoons, but only on "fair, sunny days," play was allowed for their health and as a reward for "good industry and pains taken in study," but "at such time as they shall have leave to play and sport themselves" they were allowed "only shooting in long bows or running at base." "Dice, cards, or any such unlawful gambling" were forbidden "upon pain of sharp punishment."

JOHN WINTHROP NEVER WROTE about his school days but did later reflect on other aspects of his youth. Although he was writing in contexts calculated to emphasize his struggles with sinful human nature, these memories nevertheless shed some light on his childhood. In his spiritual diary he reflected on how, "[w]hen I was a boy, I was at a house, where I spied 2 small books lying cast aside, so I stole them, & brought them away with me." Ever "since, when they have come to my mind I have grieved at it, & would gladly have made restitution, but that shame still letted me."[62] While

Winthrop does not share what the books were, the incident does speak to his love of books and also to the growth of a sense of conscience.

A different account, a spiritual autobiographical sketch composed at the time of his fiftieth birthday, also addresses his youthful struggle with temptations. "In my youth," he recalled, "I was very lewdly disposed, inclining unto and attempting (so far as my years enabled me) all kind of wickedness, except swearing and scorning religion, which I had no temptation unto in regard of my education. About ten years of age I had some notions of God, for in some great frighting or danger, I have prayed unto God, and have found manifest answer; the remembrance whereof many years after made me think that God did love me, but it made me no whit the better." This began to change, however. "After I was 12 years old, I began to have some more savor of Religion, and I thought I had more understanding in Divinity than many of my years, for in reading of some good books I conceived that I did know divers of those points before, though I knew not how I should come by such knowledge (but since I perceived it was out of some Logical principles, whereby out of some things I could conclude other). Yet I was still very wild, and dissolute, and as years came on my lusts grew stronger, but yet under some restraint of my natural reason; whereby I had the command of myself that I could turn into any form. I would, as occasion required, write letters etc. of mere vanity; and if occasion were, I could write others of savory and Godly counsel."[63] Experimenting with "turning into any form," he imagined himself perhaps as a boisterous and assertive landowner such as his uncle John, a lawyer such as his father, a soldier fighting alongside the earl of Leicester in the religious wars on the continent, a clergyman such as Knewstub, or perhaps a magistrate such as Sir Robert Jermyn.

Of course, Winthrop had been raised in a godly household, exposed to countless sermons, and catechized regularly, as well as witnessing numerous conversations between his father and godly clergy, so the fact that he had an advanced understanding of divinity for someone his age does not surprise us as much as his indication that he himself was surprised. His struggles with temptations and his confidence that he could master those impulses are typical of the vanity that clergy saw as all too common among their flocks.

At the age of fourteen John was deemed ready for university. It was time to begin the fashioning of his later life in earnest. He later indicated that he had been drawn to pursue a clerical career. Yet whether he chose to enter the ministry, to follow his father in the law, or to advance by other means, some university training was desirable. On December 2, 1602, Adam Winthrop rode to Cambridge to audit the Trinity College accounts. He was accompanied by his son, John, who was admitted to Trinity on December 8. This was toward the end of Michaelmas term, the fall term of the academic year. John may have begun his studies in Hilary or Lent term, which extended from January 13 to the second Friday before Easter, but it was not until the final segment of the Cambridge year, Easter term, which ran until July, that he officially matriculated in the university. John matriculated as a pensioner, which meant that his family paid his fees.

Though the number of undergraduates had increased, Cambridge itself was not very different from when Adam had matriculated at Magdalene. Perhaps the most significant change resulted from the foundation of Emmanuel College by Sir Walter Mildmay in 1584 for the purpose of providing the land with a reformed preaching ministry.[64] In some respects that would have been the logical school for John, especially if he was considering a ministerial career. Yet at this time Adam was most familiar with Trinity and as an officer of the college undoubtedly had some influence there.

Trinity, the largest Cambridge college, was in the process of considerable expansion under the leadership of the master, Dr. Thomas Neville.[65] Entering the Great Gate on the east side of the college, John would have noticed an empty niche where a statue of King Henry VIII was to be placed. Moving under the newly heightened entrance tower, he would have seen the area that was being transformed into the Great Court, one of Neville's major accomplishments. The chambers on the east side of the courtyard, pierced by the entrance, and the range of chambers on the south side had been completed a few years earlier. Another entrance, completed in 1597 and called the Queen's Gate for the statue of Queen Elizabeth affixed there, offered passage from the south side of the court to the schools of the university. Not yet begun was the new hall on the west side of the court. A study of possible models had led to the development of plans based on the hall of the Middle Temple, but construction would not begin until 1604. At the time of Winthrop's entrance the old and revered King Edward III gateway, which had occupied a position in the midst of the new Great Court, had been taken down and was being relocated on the north side between the newly completed library and the chapel.[66] At the time of Winthrop's first arrival workmen would have finished digging up the foundations of the old buildings that had been displaced to create the court, leveled the ground, and fenced in four rectangular areas that divided the large space. During his first year the large fountain that adorns the center of the court was begun.

The chapel, where John would have attended mandatory worship, was largely constructed in the 1560s and was much larger than the country churches of Edwardstone and Groton to which he was accustomed. Two hundred and five feet long and only thirty-three feet wide, the chapel was divided into twelve bays of equal size. The windows were simply decorated, with heraldic devices and coats of arms rather than images of the saints, but even this minimal adornment prompted some early acts of iconoclasm. Reflecting the reformed character of the college, the chapel was not consecrated, and the communion table was located in the body of the church rather than in the chancel.[67] As in other Cambridge chapels, the stalls for fellows and scholars were along the walls facing each other along the center aisle, which differed sharply from the organization of the seats facing the chancel in the congregations he had previously worshiped in.

Like all Cambridge colleges, Trinity was largely a self-sufficient community, with its own brewhouse, bakehouse, stables, wood yard, capon house, hen house, malt chamber, slaughter yard, "poundred meat house," swan house, and barber shop. There were also facilities for recreation. Outside the north wall but within the college precincts was a bowling green. A tennis court that had earlier existed had been torn down a few years earlier when the range of chambers on the east side of the Great Court claimed part of the site. A new tennis court was built, but not until 1611, after Winthrop's stay.

There is no record of where John Winthrop's rooms were in the college nor of the name of his tutor. Given the large-scale building program, it is likely he had a chamber that was more comfortable than those available at most colleges. Comfort, however, is a relative concept. Each of the building ranges had stairways off which there were two chambers per floor. A chamber had sleeping quarters for three or four, including a fellow or graduate student. Partitioned off from the sleeping area were small individual carrels for study. John would have been expected to provide his own coals or turves for heat, but no matter what efforts were made the chambers were cold and damp. On winter nights, with the fires banked up, the temperatures would be so cold that the ink in a scholar's ink pot could very easily freeze. Some sixteenth-century students at St. John's College had been known to run in the courtyard for a half hour before retiring "to get a heat on their feet when they go to bed."[68]

John's day would have begun at 5:00 A.M. when he gathered in the chapel with the rest of the collegiate community for morning prayer and a homily. Following breakfast in the hall he would commence his studies for the day, most often meeting with his college tutor to discuss his reading of an assigned text. After a midday dinner he would have participated in college or university disputations. A free period was followed by supper, then a review of the day's lessons before evening prayers at eight. The role of the tutor was central to the college experience. He was both teacher and guardian. As another Trinity student remembered his experience, his tutor was "careful of me, inquired of what company I was acquainted with, and sometimes read lectures to us, prayed with us in his chamber every night, and . . . was a generous savory Christian."[69] Prayer groups were common, bringing together fellows and undergraduates in shared spiritual communion. Winthrop, who we know participated in such groups in his later life, may have developed the habit at college. An observer of the practice wrote of students at Trinity a few decades later that their prayers in their tutors' rooms were "longer and louder by far at night than they are at chapel in the evening."[70]

The puritan influence at Cambridge at this time was perhaps not as strong as it had been when his father had studied there. As Regius Professor of Divinity, John Overall, who had been a fellow of Trinity until 1598, was promoting a more liberal theology of grace than was acceptable to most Calvinists.[71] Having left the godly kingdom of the Stour Valley, at Cambridge John would have come to appreciate that many of the ideas and values that he took for granted were actually contested in England as a whole, but there were nevertheless many godly influences that would have reinforced the lessons he had learned at home. The famous puritan spokesman William Perkins had preached at Great St. Andrew's in the town until his death in 1602, with Trinity students as well as others flocking to hear him. It had been the evangelical preaching of Perkins that was said to have contributed to the spiritual awakening of another Trinity undergraduate, John Cotton, who had matriculated at the college in 1598. The fact that Winthrop and Cotton were contemporaries at Trinity—Cotton received his BA in 1603—helps to explain the bond that would exist between them in New England.[72]

THIS IS NOT TO SUGGEST that Winthrop's time at Trinity was all study and prayer. Even godly undergraduates found ample opportunities for recreation of various sorts. Football was played by students in college courts and greens. Garret Island Green behind the college may have provided an ideal playing field; games may have also taken place on the college fields on the far side of the River Cam.[73] John Wheelwright, who would play a major part in Winthrop's New England career, played football and wrestled while an undergraduate at Cambridge. Though the tennis courts had been razed at Trinity, courts existed at other colleges and the bowling green remained. The field-like greens also offered space for running, jumping, and other exercise. Swimming in the River Cam was forbidden, but it was a prohibition often breached. Recreation of a different sort could be found dining or drinking with a friend or engaging in a game of chess, and there were seasonal occasions for entertainment or mischief at the midsummer games in the nearby Gogmagog Hills and at Stourbridge Fair in September.[74]

The godly never claimed to be perfect, and opportunities to stray from the path of godliness often tempted them at university. Some were attracted to the spectacle of bear-baiting in nearby Chesterton, but there were many occasions for excess within Cambridge itself. Thomas Shepard, later to be one of the leading lights of the New England clergy, recalled in his autobiography how when at Cambridge he "fell from God to loose and

lewd company, to lust and pride and gaming and bowling and drinking."
More graphically, he told of an occasion on which he "drank so much one
day that I was dead drunk, and that upon a Saturday night, and so was
carried from the place I had drink at and did feast at unto a scholar's chamber, one Basset of Christ's College, and knew not where I was until I awakened late on that Sabbath and sick with my beastly carriage."[75] Students
entered college at a time of life marked by sexual awakening, and so sexual
longings must also have tempted them in their almost cloistered lives.
Samuel Ward, later master of Sidney Sussex College and Lady Margaret
Professor of Divinity, recorded in his diary an "adulterous dream" when
he was a student in 1596, prompted by "the grievous sins in Trinity College, which had a woman which was [carried] from chamber to chamber in
the night time."[76]

Not all sexual feelings involved members of the opposite sex.[77]
Winthrop's contemporaries did not think of gender in the same way as we
do and did not use classifications such as heterosexual and homosexual.
Strong emotional bonds between individuals of the same sex were considered natural and were encouraged by both the classical tradition and the
Christian tradition of agape; as historian Donald Yacovone points out, "ver-
bal and physical expressions of affection, rather than calling one's 'manhood' into question, affirmed good character and, for Christians, provided
tangible evidence of saving grace."[78] Men, including Winthrop, recorded
dreams in which they were ravished by Christ. When departing from England in 1630 John Winthrop would write to his dear friend William Spring,
comparing their love to that between David and Jonathan. Lamenting how
his move would take him away from Spring, Winthrop wrote that "were I
now with you, I should bedew that sweet bosom with the tears of affection."[79] None of this is to say that such love was or would have been physically consummated. Just as having sexual relations with a woman outside
the bounds of marriage was a sin, so too acts of physical sex between men
were sinful. Yet the intense relationships formed by students at all-male
grammar schools and colleges presented their own particular forms of temptation, and sometimes individuals did act in ways that were considered sinful with members of their own sex, just as other individuals sinned with
members of the opposite sex.[80]

We should take care about assuming that Winthrop was referring to
sexual matters when he admitted in his diary "lusts . . . so masterly as no
good could fasten upon me." "Lust" was a term that covered all temptations of the flesh, including gluttony and drunkenness as well as those of a
sexual nature. It is likely, though, that at least some of Winthrop's anxiety
concerned his emergent sexuality. Writing in his diary a few years after he
left Cambridge, he recorded that he had made various "vows [and] promises to God" that he was unable to keep and had "great need to repent." He

found guidance in Thomas Cartwright's commentary on Acts 5:4 in that theologian's *Confutation of the Rhemists New Testament*. Cartwright approvingly quoted Augustine's "judgement . . . touching those that marry . . . after the vow of continency, and how he condemneth them that account the marriage of such persons adultery."[81] Winthrop had evidently made and then experienced trouble with having taken such a vow. His need to control his impulses may have contributed to his decision to cut short his education and enter marriage at a surprisingly early age.

As John set off from Groton for Cambridge in 1603, the countryside would have been abuzz. Elizabeth had died in March and been succeeded by her kinsman King James VI of Scotland, who became James I, king of England. Because he had reigned in a country with a Calvinist, presbyterian church, English reformers hoped that he would be sympathetic toward the reforms that the queen had resisted. Organized by the remnants of the conference movement, throughout the Stour Valley and elsewhere reformers put their signatures to what became known as the Millenary Petition, calling on the king to institute various reforms. Asserting that they were "neither . . . factious men affecting a popular parity in the Church, nor . . . schismatics aiming at the dissolution of the State ecclesiastical, but . . . faithful servants of Christ and loyal subjects to your majesty," the petitioners asked, among other things, "that the cross in baptism, interrogatories ministered to infants, [and] confirmation, as superfluous, may be taken away," that "none hereafter be admitted to the ministry but able and sufficient men, and those to preach diligently," and that "other abuses yet remaining and practiced in the Church of England" be reformed.[82] The Winthrops' friend Stephen Egerton was one of the more zealous supporters of the effort. The petition was presented to the king in April on his progress from Scotland to London, and he soon indicated a willingness to meet with spokesmen of the movement at Hampton Court Palace in January 1604.

At Trinity John Winthrop would have been caught up in the tensions of the moment. The bishops of the church, fearing the possibility that James might indeed be sympathetic to presbyterian-style reforms, had sent Trinity's Thomas Neville to Scotland to seek assurances that the king would not tamper with the structure of the church, his departure on April 4 being noted by Adam Winthrop in his diary.[83] Cambridge was divided over the issues. One group in the university issued a condemnation of the Millenary Petition, while Emmanuel's master, Laurence Chaderton, was chosen one of the delegates to present the reform case at the Hampton Court conference along with John Reynolds, Thomas Sparke, and the Winthrops' friend John Knewstub.[84]

In the months leading up to the meeting the Groton area, like much of the rest of the country, debated and prepared. Surveys were conducted to determine the quality of the clergy. A summary of the Essex results claimed that only 94 of the 344 incumbents were "good and faithful preachers," and pointed to the presence of gamblers, drunkards, and other unsuitable individuals in the ministry.[85] Adam Winthrop wrote for news to his friend John Still, now bishop of Bath and Wells. Nathaniel Still, the bishop's son, visited the Winthrops in the summer and brought messages from his father, then rode to Cambridge on a further mission. Fasts were held in Boxford and Groton in August and in Groton again in September. On the later occasion Thomas Newton, the clergyman of Stratford St. Mary, who had visited with Adam on August 2, preached on Amos 4:12—"Therefore thus will I do unto thee, O Israel: and because I will do this unto thee, prepare to meet thy God, O Israel." Humphrey Munning, Adam's cousin and also rector of Brettenham, visited and borrowed some works of theology. Toward the end of September Newton left for Cambridge as clergy traveled the countryside, meeting in conferences and gathering material to support their case for reform. In December Adam himself made his annual journey to audit the accounts of Trinity.[86]

Although bishops such as Whitgift and Bancroft mobilized opposition to reform, not all of the hierarchy were opposed. In the Townsend manuscripts in the British Library is a position paper that appears to have been drawn up for the Hampton Court conference. Among the points laid out were that men who were not well learned in the Scriptures should not be admitted to the ministry, that subscription as then used by the bishops of the church was unlawful, and that plural livings should be abolished. It was signed, as might be expected, by Knewstub, Chaderton, and Reynolds, but also by the bishops of Winchester, Durham, and Bath and Wells, the last being John Still.[87]

Anticipated as a possible start to the much delayed final reform of the church, the Hampton Court conference turned out to mark a negative turn of fortune. Though he agreed to a new translation of the Bible, made minor changes to the Prayer Book, ordered improvements in the official catechism, and urged the bishops to provide for learned clergy in every parish, King James refused the major points of the reformed petitions, warned against challenges to his authority, and threatened to harry out of the land those who opposed him. Some of this was rhetoric—James was always more concerned with having his right to impose ceremonies than with precise conformity to them—but he did agree to the request of the orthodox bishops that a new canon of the church require all clergy to subscribe to Archbishop Whitgift's Three Articles of 1583.[88] This meant that no one would be ordained or licensed to preach or lecture without swearing "assent to the thirty-nine articles of religion, and to the book of common prayer," and promising that "in public prayer and administration of the sacraments, I will use the form in the said book prescribed, and no other."[89] Richard Bancroft, the new archbishop of Canterbury, sent all the diocesan commissioners for his 1605 metropolitan visitation strict instructions that they "take care to see all the canons and constitutions published by his majesty's authority to be carefully and diligently observed."[90]

The effects of the new orthodox initiative were soon seen in the reports of episcopal visitations in the Stour Valley. John Knewstub was cited "for not wearing the surplice nor using the sign of the cross," though no action was immediately taken against him. Knewstub, seeking to find a new way to evade direct compliance with the new orders, evidently sought a curate who would wear the surplice, with the intent that that clergyman would perform the ceremonies requiring the vestment.[91] In Boxford in 1606 the churchwardens asked the visitors to excuse the Reverends Sandes and Bird for failing to wear the "surplice by reason they have not a convenient one."[92]

News from home was not only about religion, however. Adam was entangled in a number of disputes with neighbors and family members, some of which might have been part of the legacy left by the elder John Winthrop when he departed for Ireland. Adam had believed that the field called the "stone meadow" had been conveyed to him by his brother, but Groton's John Coe claimed that he had been admitted to the lease on the death of his father, leading to a suit that dragged on. Then, in May 1603, Coe seized some of Adam's "beasts in Stone meadow and would have driven them to Waldingfield," had Adam not stopped him.[93] In September Coe was arrested and carried to prison, but the dispute would continue into the following year. In July Adam paid Coe rent, perhaps indicating the latter's success in establishing his right. This was not the only time that Adam was embroiled in a dispute due to his brother's sloppiness. A similar dispute had led to a suit in the Court of Requests, with Paul Powle, often a thorn in the side of the Winthrops, suing in 1601 in regard to land and a house he had erected on property he claimed the elder John had leased to him that was also claimed by Adam.[94] And the dispute with Coe continued to simmer. Apparently there were still questions about the bounds of the land in question. Coe warned Adam in August to appear before the magistrates in the following month. A few days before the hearing, which was held by Sir William Waldegrave, Brampton Gurdon, and Sir Thomas Eden, Adam and his neighbor William Clopton walked the field and examined the markers. Though Adam seemed to have been vidicated, bad feelings continued, with Coe or one of his kin stabbing one of Adam's hogs the following January. As late as 1621 Adam would take satisfaction in noting that "Mr. Coe was arrested, and carried to prison."[95]

These disputes not only soured relationships between the Winthrops and some of their neighbors but also had implications for the future. Adam's estate was small enough that court costs and possible adverse judgments on land he considered his to use would jeopardize his son's future. Quarrels with other family members were also occupying Adam at this time. William Winthrop had died a pauper but had done what he could for his two sons, Adam and Joshua. Joshua was started in the Grocers Company and had achieved a modest status by 1578.[96] Adam was apprenticed to a widow of the Merchant Tailors Company and admitted freeman of that guild in 1588.[97] William had transferred the property he inherited in Boxford to the two young men. Both shared their father's concern with religious reform and stood as sureties for clergymen, notably for their brother-in-law Humphrey Munning when he received the living of Brettenham, Suffolk.[98] On various occasions Joshua and Adam visited the area, and they probably entrusted the management of their properties to their uncle John or their uncle Adam.

Like his uncle Adam, Joshua Winthrop was dragged into court through the machinations of the elder John Winthrop. In the 1601 suit lodged by Paul Powle against John and Adam Winthrop, Joshua was also named as a defendant. According to the affidavits filed with the Court of Requests, Powle had arrested Henry Vintener, a clothier of Groton, in the Sheriff's Court of London for failure to redeem a bill of obligation in the amount of £30. John Winthrop, who had earlier engaged Vintener in a performance bond for his own obligation to his estranged wife, Elizabeth, persuaded his nephew Joshua, as a citizen of London, to be one of Vintener's sureties in the case but offered Powle a guarantee if the latter promised not to execute a judgment against Joshua under any circumstances. Vintener lost but failed to pay, and when John failed to live up to his guarantee, Powle executed the judgment against Joshua, prompting a countersuit that got caught up in the Requests case as Powle sought vindication against the whole tribe of Winthrops.[99] William's son Adam also had complaints against his uncles, for the management of his Boxford property, and, John being absent in Ireland, initiated a series of actions against his uncle Adam.[100]

5

Turning Points

NOVEMBER 1604. John Winthrop rode with his friend William Forth of Nayland to visit the latter's kin at Great Stambridge, a parish in Rochford Hundred in southeast Essex. It was an odd time of year for such a journey since the days were short, the weather cold, and the roads poor. Their progress was slow, but they were in no hurry and passed the time talking about many things that interested them—their university studies, family news, the policies of the new king, James I. Being young men, they sympathized with each other over the constraints placed upon them by their age and circumstances. And they likely discussed young women they knew and their hopes for marriage.

The two broke their journey with a stay at Graces, the Chelmsford home of John Winthrop's Mildmay kin. There they were warmly entertained with food and drink. Family news was exchanged and national news discussed again, this time with their elders. The Mildmays had important connections at the royal court, and the young men were eager to hear what they had to say.

Refreshed by their stay at Graces, the travelers resumed their journey. As they continued to ride south the landscape flattened out. Eventually they reached the coastal marshlands in which Great Stambridge was located.

This was unlikely to have been John's first visit to the area. Henry Browne, his maternal grandfather, held property in Prittiwell and died there in 1597. The Forth family was scattered throughout Essex and Suffolk. Adam Winthrop had been engaged in a Great Stambridge land transaction with John Forth and his wife, Thomasine, in 1592.[1] Thomasine Forth was related to Adam's wife and to Joan Hilles, who married William Winthrop's son Adam. And there were other connections as well.[2] At Great Stambridge the two young men stayed with John Forth, who was a modest landholder but also the Rich family's bailiff for their lands in the hundred. Forth also had a reputation as a supporter of religious reform. During the visit Winthrop attended Sunday services at the church at Great Stambridge and was impressed by the sermons of the Reverend Ezekiel Culverwell, a clergyman who had earlier been forced from his Stour Valley ministry at Felsted. John was also impressed with Mary Forth, the daughter and sole heir of his host, four years his senior.

ᔓ

T HE TRIP JOHN WINTHROP TOOK to southeast Essex in 1604 unexpectedly became an important turning point in his life as he became involved with Mary Forth. The relationship between the two matured more rapidly than was customary. In early January John Forth traveled to Groton to meet with Adam and Anne Winthrop. Two months later Forth took Adam to view some of the lands that might figure in marriage negotiations, and those arrangements were rapidly concluded. On March 28 the betrothal of John Winthrop and Mary Forth was certified by Culverwell with the consent of their parents. The wedding took place at Great Stambridge on April 16 and would have been followed by a marriage feast that would include exchanges of gifts between the families. The couple journeyed to London for a brief stay and then traveled to Groton, where Adam and Anne hosted another marriage feast on May 8. Among the family guests was Adam's sister Alice and her husband, Sir Thomas Mildmay. John's sister Anne, who had herself married that February, attended with her husband, Thomas Fones.

Numerous questions about this marriage remain unanswered. At a time when men of his status usually did not wed until their late twenties, John was seventeen. Mary was also young, twenty-one rather than the average twenty-six.[3] By choosing marriage, John abandoned his Cambridge studies and thus any plans to enter the ministry. Later in life he would remember turning his back on that career more than once in ways that suggest his regret at the path not taken. The fact, mentioned earlier, that he had taken a vow of continency reinforces the impression that he had been fixed upon a ministerial career. He could have finished his studies, been ordained, and then married. Even if, as he suggested, friends (for unspecified reasons) had urged him not to become a clergyman, that does not explain his rush to marry, for rushing into marriage is exactly what he did.

Everything about the union seems rushed. The couple's courtship was very brief, and the parents' negotiations were conducted with surprising speed. A connection with the Forths was a step up for the Winthrops, especially given John's limited prospects at the time, though not a major one, since John Forth was one of the least eminent members of that family. And if social advancement was the goal, a more typical period of courtship would have been expected. The mystery is deepened by the fact that many of the normal signs of suitability that were looked for in marital unions at this time were absent. Judging from the very meager evidence we have about Mary, she was poorly educated in comparison to John's mother and sisters, and her piety did not run as deep as her new husband's. What is left is the speculation that the two were swept up by a strong physical attraction that forced their families to agree to the hasty march to the altar.

Whatever his expectations, the reality is that John's new life was filled with frustrations. Though it was assumed that the couple would live with Mary's father in Essex, following the wedding feast at Groton they lingered in Suffolk into the summer. Not until John Forth journeyed to Groton did the couple ride to Great Stambridge on July 25. But then John must have returned to Groton alone, for on August 15 Adam recorded in his diary that Mary and her father had come to visit. Two weeks later the young Winthrops set out again for Essex. By then they would have clearly known that Mary was pregnant. In September Adam made the journey to visit his son and daughter-in-law at Great Stambridge. Mary, whose mother had died when she was young, had no female kin at Great Stambridge, and this trip might have been for the purpose of accompanying the couple back to Groton, so that Anne Winthrop could supervise her lying-in. Beginning his spiritual diary on February 2, John recorded that worldly cares and a "secret desire after pleasures and itching after liberty and unlawful delights" had brought him to "wax weary of good duties . . . whence came much trouble and danger." He admitted that when Mary was ill he had not dealt with this "small trial" very well.[4] On the morning of February 12 Mary gave birth to a son, christened John Winthrop in Groton church on February 23. But all was not peaceful in the household. John recorded how during the week when Mary delivered he had felt ill and "gave myself to negligence and idleness, which I couldn't shake off a good while after," and that one morning he exploded in "a great fit of impatience for matter betwixt my wife and my mother, which I pray God forgive me."[5]

Friction between the two women continued. John confessed that while attending services at Groton on March 9, thoughts of moving back to Essex so "delighted me" that he was distracted from the sermon.[6] The appeal was not the salt marshes of Great Stambridge but escaping the tensions in the Groton household. Yet, torn between his mother and his wife, his old life and his new, he remained at Groton when John Forth escorted Mary and the baby back to Essex in April. John did not rejoin them until September, when he rode to Great Stambridge with his father and Henry Sandes. That trip was to arrange the transfer of some of John Forth's lands in Great Stambridge and also in Kersey, Suffolk, to John and Mary Winthrop. Adam looked out for his son's interests while Sandes served as a witness.[7] Though the family tensions gradually faded so that John and Mary would again spend time at Groton, for the most part their residence until 1613 was Great Stambridge.

This was a different environment than the one John had been raised in. The landscape was a flat salt marsh divided by numerous creeks that flowed into the sea. Flooding was common. It was far more damp than the Stour Valley and complaints about the air that moved off the marshes were commonplace. The region was notoriously unhealthy. If the roads and lanes of the Stour Valley were foul, they were still much better than the muddy tracks found in southeast Essex. It was said that the roads were so inundated with water that travelers journeying by night knew they were in the road by listening to the splash of their horse's hoofs.[8] Stock farming was the primary source of agricultural income in the region, with ewe flocks, whose milk was used to make Essex cheeses, and both dairy and beef cattle. Some land was also devoted to grain crops, with surpluses shipped to the London market by ship.[9]

Over the next few years John continued to confess to feelings of inadequacy in his diary, and this was no doubt due in large measure to the fact that his future was bleak. The couple probably lived with John Forth in a large farmhouse called Stewards. Forth would have set the tone and rules for the household.[10] There was little work for John Winthrop to do. He owned no property of his own. His college career had been abbreviated, and with it had gone any thoughts of the ministry. Visits to Rochford Hall would only have rubbed salt in his wounds by contrasting his meager prospects with those of the young men of the Rich family. Rochford Hall itself was an exception to the architectural drabness of the region. Surrounded by a wide moat, the Hall had massive towers in three of its four corners. The main ranges of buildings were three stories tall and encompassed three and possibly four internal courtyards.[11] There, in the company of his father-in-law, the Riches' steward, John would have met men of affairs in the county who had goals and the means to achieve them. He was able to listen in on discussions of the new king and what the godly might expect from him and to hear the tales related by Purchas of new worlds across the sea. The Virginia Company was forming at the time, and some of the men at Rochford Hall would be investors.

Among those John would have met there was the young Robert Rich. Rich was six months older than Winthrop, had also been raised in a godly household, and like John had studied briefly at Cambridge. The two had much in common, and both would become involved in the effort to establish puritan colonies abroad. Still, though they would see eye to eye on many things, one thing always divided them. John Winthrop was a gentleman; Robert Rich was an aristocrat. Pious lords like the Riches might recognize men like Winthrop as fellow members of a godly community and might join with them in various ventures, but the line that divided them would never disappear. As Winthrop would himself express it in his "Model of Christian Charity," "God Almighty in his most holy and wise providence hath so disposed of the condition of mankind, as in all times some must be rich, some poor; some high and eminent in power and dignity, others mean and in subjection."[12] Winthrop's place on the ladder of position and power was fairly low in the years immediately following his marriage. His status at this time was best expressed by his role at the Essex assizes of July 1612, held at Chelmsford. Among the justices on the bench were not only judges from Westminster such as Thomas Egerton, Lord Ellesmere, but members of the county commission such as Lord Rich, Winthrop's neighbor, and Sir Thomas Mildmay, Winthrop's kinsman. Though, as we shall see, his situation and status was changing by then, John Winthrop appears in the records as one of the more humble citizens called to serve on the grand jury.[13]

In choosing to marry, John had closed off at least some of the careers he could have contemplated, and so he struggled to identify a suitable role he could aspire to. Constrained in the choices available to him in his public life, John spent much of his time in Great Stambridge engaged in shaping his interior life. As he did so he was occasionally confused and troubled by the religious culture he found himself in. While his attendance at Cambridge would have disabused him of any lingering idea that the godly ascendancy in the Stour Valley was the norm throughout the kingdom, in the district of Rochford Hundred he found the reform cause embattled. Southeast Essex was not a godly kingdom. There were prominent evangelical preachers such as Culverwell and Arthur Dent, but there was also division in the area. The most notable example of this had come in the early 1580s, at the time when in the Stour Valley the godly were achieving cultural dominance.

The second Lord Rich, with whom Bishop Aylmer reported having had many "storms," and his brother, Richard Rich, were strong promoters of reform early in Elizabeth's reign, as was Robert Rich, who became the third Lord Rich in 1581. The latter took it upon himself to criticize local clergy for their shortcomings. Contention arose regarding a gathered congregation under the Reverend Robert Wright that Lord Rich allowed to meet in Rochford Hall, a stone's throw from the parish church. Wright and other members of the congregation, including John Forth, were imprisoned, though later released through the intercession of the Rich family. The controversy reached the Privy Council, but what was perhaps most notable was the number of local clergy, including Dent, who provided testimony against Wright. There were godly clergy and laity in this area, but their situation was much more contested than Winthrop was accustomed to. As a zealous minority, reformers advocated a more rigorously godly stance. To apply historian Patrick Collinson's evocative phrase, rather than experiencing the comfort that came from living in a city on a hill, they exhibited the defensiveness of those gathered in a holy huddle.[14]

Winthrop was exposed to a different model of godliness, and he found himself reconsidering things that he had taken for granted and wrestling with his new situation. Early on he hunted birds along the creeks and in the surrounding marshes, but he soon gave it up, having determined that it "could not stand with a good conscience in myself." His tortured reasoning in reaching that conclusion says volumes about a young man growing up and trying to determine who he would be. In the first place, he decided, such hunting was "simply prohibited by the law of the land, upon this ground amongst others, that it spoils more of the creatures than it gets." Furthermore, "it procures offence unto many," and he was finding the local godly particularly censorious. Third, he admitted, "it wastes great stores of time." The list goes on—"4 it toils a man's body overmuch . . . 5 it endangers a man's life . . . 6 it brings no profit, all things considered . . . 7 it hazards more of a man's estate by the penalty of it, than a man would willingly part with . . . 8 it brings a man of worth and godliness into some contempt." But there is more, an endearing confession to end the list—"lastly, for mine own part, I have ever been crossed in using it, for when I have gone about it, not without some wounds of conscience, and have taken much pains and hazarded my health, I have gotten sometime a very little, but most commonly nothing at all towards my cost and labor." And so young John Winthrop, self-confessed bad shot, hung up his fowling piece.[15]

Hunting was not the only behavior that he altered under the scrutiny of the local godly as he discovered the ways in which the religious culture of Rochford Hundred differed from that of the Stour Valley. "Finding that the variety of meats draws me on to eat more than standeth with my health," spiritual as well as physical, he "resolved not to eat of more than two dishes at any one meal, whether fish, flesh, fowl, or fruit, or white meats, etc., whether at home or abroad."[16] Some of his new neighbors were quick to challenge other practices. "Being admonished by a Christian friend that some good men were offended to hear of some gaming which was used in my house, by my servants, etc.," he "resolved that as for myself not to use any cardings, etc.," but the difficulties of living under his father-in-law's supervision and the friction that occasionally generated are evident in his concluding comment on card playing, that as it applied to others in the household he would "repress it as much as I could, during the continuance of my present state."[17]

Yet attention to such behavior did not bring the inner assurance that he hoped for. Charting his spiritual health in his diary, Winthrop demonstrated the difficulty that most godly men and women experienced as they dealt with the complex relationship between faith and works. The religion that has come to be identified as puritanism stressed the fact that man was by nature depraved and sinful. Each individual would follow in Adam and Eve's footsteps in breaking the covenant that God had made with man, promising eternal happiness in return for perfect obedience. God still required obedience to that Covenant of Works, and justice demanded that those who broke it be condemned. Nevertheless, God selected some to be saved despite their unworthiness, extending to them the Covenant of Grace and the experience of a conversion whereby they were born again through the application to them of the merits of Christ's sacrifice. The notion that the individual could in any way influence God's choice of the elect was rejected as limiting God's almighty power. Similarly, most English Protestants had followed the teachings of John Calvin in rejecting the notion that those whom God had decided to save could undo the divine decree by their actions.

Like all Christians, those who accepted these ideas—John Winthrop included—wished to know how they could determine that they were among those God had predestined to be saved. Ministers seeking to guide their congregations preached that the saints possessed an inner sense of God's love and of the Spirit's presence, and also that good works were fruit that grew from a regenerate being. Clergy who emphasized the Spirit's presence were in danger of drifting toward antinomianism and familism, beliefs that encouraged following the promptings of that Spirit, even if those promptings clashed with the teachings of the Bible, the church, or the state. On the other side, those who correlated external behavior and inner sanctity too closely, presenting sanctification as grounds for assurance, were in danger of the Arminian heresy that made the individual's salvation in part dependent on behavior. Late in the seventeenth century the puritan clergyman Stephen Lobb concluded that "it cannot be denied but many in their opposition to Antinomianism, etc. have fallen in with Arminian, etc. and that divers, in running from Arminianism, etc., have plunged themselves into the Antinomian gulf, and that they who lend their strength against the one error, are in danger of being accused of inclining too much towards the other."[18]

The Winthrops' friend John Knewstub was one of the most outspoken opponents of the sectarian group called the Family of Love, arguing that their teachings included familism (that men could achieve perfection in life) and antinomianism (that the moral law does not bind those predestined to salvation).[19] But in the early seventeenth century the greatest threat to the Calvinist foundations of English teachings seemed to come from those who wished to emphasize the importance of works and religious observance. Such individuals were labeled, not always fairly, as followers of the Dutchman Jacob Arminius—Arminians—whose views would be condemned by the international Calvinist Synod of Dort in 1619 but were very much contested by Protestants both before and after that date.[20]

Negotiating between Arminianism and antinomianism was difficult for ministers and laymen, and while the godly insisted on God's sovereignty, they recognized that the details of how God's will was enacted were mysteries that natural understanding could never precisely comprehend. Most were willing to allow a certain amount of freedom in explanations of the conversion process and its manifestations.[21] Still, anyone who speculated openly on these matters was likely to find his views subjected to criticism. Ezekiel Culverwell, whose preaching John Winthrop enthusiastically followed at Great Stambridge, would publish *A Treatise of Faith* (1623) intended especially for "the use of the weakest Christians," which was endorsed by the prominent ministers Richard Sibbes and William Gouge. But Culverwell was quickly taken to task for encouraging Arminianism, requiring the Essex clergyman to defend himself in *A Briefe Answere to Certaine Objections Against the Treatise of Faith . . . clearing him from the errors of Arminius, unjustly layd to his charge* (1626). Culverwell endorsed Richard Rogers's *Seven Treatises* (1603), the outstanding exposition of puritan practical divinity, which was subject to the same charge of overemphasizing behavior as a grounds of assurance. Ironically, the Reverend Francis Marbury also wrote a commendatory preface to Rogers's *Seven Treatises*; his daughter, Anne Marbury Hutchinson, would become famous for attacking all such approaches to faith. John Cotton, who would be closely affiliated with Hutchinson's brand of familism in Winthrop's Boston, had earlier been accused in England of the opposite, namely, embracing "the sour leaven of Arminianism" for his views on predestination.[22]

Like any layman's, John Winthrop's attempt to chart his way through these perilous waters was difficult, but necessary if he was to gain a sense of his true relationship with God. Listening to Culverwell and reflecting on his own "great desire of keeping peace & holding communion with God," he looked to his behavior for evidence of his inner state and was distressed when he failed to keep "divers vows, promises to God, or resolutions," as he had earlier when he took a vow of continency. He was determined to "reform these sins" by God's grace, specifically "pride, covetousness, love of this world, vanity of mind, unthankfulness, sloth (both in his service & in my calling), [and] not preparing myself with reverence & uprightness to come to his word," and prayed that God "would give me a new heart, joy in his spirit; that he would dwell with me, that he would strengthen me against the world, the flesh, & the Devil, [and] that he would forgive my sins & increase my faith." He felt that he had also displeased "my God by following idle & vain pastimes" and "omitting my family exercise." Though he "was much unsettled," "yet God (when I thought his anger was even hot against me) drew me to repentance & showed me sweet mercy." "A little after," however, "being out of order again through the force of a new temptation, & mine own rebellious wicked heart yielding itself to the slavery of sin, had brought me into the Lord's hands again." This cycle of sin, self-examination, repentance, receipt of divine mercy, and new failure is one commonly found in puritan diaries as the authors acknowledged an addiction to sin that they could not break on their own. Recording providences— such as a recovery from a "sore sickness"—that implied God had forgiven him, he diligently examined his behavior for what it said about his relationship with God.[23]

But Winthrop found more than circumstantial evidence of God's love. In early January 1612, having spent time visiting and comforting an elderly man in the community, Winthrop "dreamed that I was with Christ upon earth, & that being very insistent with him in many tears, for the assurance of the pardon of my sins, &c, I was so ravished with his love towards me, far exceeding the affection of the kindest husband, that being awakened it had made so deep [an] impression in my heart, as I was forced to unmeasurable weeping for a great while, & had a more lively feeling of the love of Christ than ever before."[24] Envisaging union with the divine in terms of conjugal intercourse with Christ was a common image among puritan authors, and this would not be the last time that Winthrop experienced God's love in this way.[25] While he would continue to chart the spiritual ups and downs of his life, it was this almost physical, ecstatic sense of God's love that gave him the confidence that would enable him to shape his character and path regardless of external opposition and occasional inner doubts.

As he sought assurance from his sense of a spiritual marriage with Christ, John was forced to deal with the fact that religion was at times a source of discord in his earthly marriage. There is no evidence that Mary Forth had a reputation for godliness, and John confided in his diary quarrels that came about as he attempted to bring her to his views. When he used spirited arguments, he could "not prevail, not so much as to make her to answer me, or to talk with me about any goodness." But this did seem to change. On one occasion, "when there were many things which justly made me fear a repulse," he asked her a question and was surprised "when it pleased God even then to so open her heart as that she became very ready and willing to lay open her heart to me in a very comfortable measure." Eventually, and after much prayer, "she proved after a right godly woman."[26] Here too, it was God that wrought change, not the unassisted efforts of men.

This was a time when men and women increasingly saw marriage not simply as a means of procreation and regulating sexual activity but also as a source of mutual support and comfort.[27] Clearly the marriage of John and Mary was successful by the first of these criteria. The birth of John Jr. in 1606 was followed by that of Henry, named after Henry Sandes, born in January 1608; Forth, named after his mother's family, born in December 1609; and Mary, born in 1612.[28] Two more daughters, both christened Anne, were born, in 1614 and 1615, but died almost immediately. However, one searches John's spiritual diary and correspondence in vain for any but the most perfunctory references to Mary herself. There are no surviving letters addressed to her. The one surviving letter of Mary's to John is rather brief and deals solely with household affairs, though she signs herself "thine ever loving wife till death."[29] John much later mentioned "looking over some letters of kindness that had passed between my first wife and me," but the phrase "letters of kindness" does not suggest deep emotional union, and while he recorded that, in reviewing these letters, he found his heart "accepting" the "scribbling hand, the mean congruity, the false orthography, & broken sentences,&c.," it seems clear that while Mary lived he held feelings of superiority that frayed their relationship.[30] One of the few glimpses of Mary's life that we get from her husband comes from when the three boys were very young. John recorded with thanks "a special providence of God, that my wife, taking up a mess of porridge before the children or anybody had eaten of it, she espied therein a great spider."[31]

During the early years of John and Mary's marriage, despite the uncertain nature of his worldly prospects, Winthrop experienced a growth in spiritual assurance and gained a reputation for godliness. His relationship with his wife did grow more settled. Then, as the first decade of the new century came to a close, new possibilities began to open. Most significant of these was the steps he and his father were able to take that would eventually gain him the possession of Groton Manor. What made that possible was his uncle John's troubles in England that led him to resettle in Ireland and eventually, and only after difficult negotiations, to sell his Groton estate to his nephew John.

IN THE YEARS AFTER HE SEPARATED from his wife in the early 1580s, the elder John Winthrop, lord of Groton Manor, had seen his reputation in the region steadily decline. He had no interest in the blossoming of religious reform. Indeed, his lifestyle was an affront to the values of the godly. On more than one occasion he failed to make maintenance payments to his wife, forcing her to petition the lord chancellor for relief.[32] He was sued by the Groton churchwardens in the Court of Requests when he seized a cottage in the churchyard which they claimed had been built by the parish and always let by the wardens to some poor man of the parish who would agree to ring the parish bells.[33] Other disputes over land titles also ended up in court. Seeking a new life and a greater estate, he emigrated to the Munster Plantation in June of 1596.

It is not clear where Winthrop first settled in Ireland. It may have been on Edmund Spenser's Kilcoman seignory, but it may have been on neighboring property belonging to Sir Walter Raleigh, since when Raleigh sold his land to Richard Boyle in 1602 Winthrop was a witness.[34] In any case, his lands would have been overrun in the Tyrone Rebellion in 1598 as Irish chieftains swept away many of the English settlements in the southwest. Spenser's Kilcoman Castle was burned, and refugees from throughout the region fled to the city of Cork.[35] A vivid contemporary account captures the speed with which the settlers were surprised and routed: "He that rode abroad could not get home to save himself but was intercepted; he that was in a thatched house had no leisure to shift himself into a castle for defense but was slain by the way. . . . In forty-eight hours was the mischief run all over the country."[36] Landowners of Winthrop's stature were expected to command local militia, but if he fought against the rebels it was not for long, since all of the contemporary accounts, such as that quoted above, attest to the total rout of the colonists. The struggle dragged on, merging with the English war against Spain.[37] As dispossessed colonists flooded penniless back to England, Spanish forces disembarked at the port of Kinsale in October 1601. But the English forces under the earl of Essex were able to turn the tide, and the defeat of Tyrone's army and his Spanish allies at Kinsale in December 1601 proved the decisive battle.

While the elder John Winthrop's whereabouts are unknown during the early period of the fighting, he was back in England early in 1601 when Adam's diary traces the development of a land dispute between his brother and Paul Powle. During the following year he made frequent visits to London, where he may have sold his existing interests in his Irish lands to his nephews Adam and Joshua. In August 1602 he departed for Ireland once again.[38] This time, however, he settled beyond the existing seignories. He thus participated in what historian Nicholas Canny has called "betterment migration," whereby settlers who became familiar with the region settled on more desirable lands outside the established plantation bounds. One such region identified by Canny was "along the west coast of County Cork, which gave access to rich sea-fishing and other natural resources."[39] Though for the next few years he would journey back and forth between Ireland and Groton, Winthrop joined with Sir John Skinner, Sir Thomas Brooke, Thomas Notte, James Salmon, and other English gentlemen in trying to establish a plantation in the West Carberry region of County Cork. He would settle there by the town of Aghadown. The ruins of Aghadown House, which may have been his home, still sit on an elevated site overlooking verdant fields.[40]

At some time before 1609 the elder John married in Ireland Elizabeth Powlden, the daughter of another English settler, thus committing himself to permanent settlement there. Because that marriage had no standing in English law, any children of the union would not be able to inherit Groton Manor, and under the terms of their father's will it would pass to his brother Adam if John died without issue.[41] As early as 1594 John had obtained a license to alienate the Groton estate (diverting it from the stipulated heirs) in order to profit by selling his life interest in it, though he had chosen not to at that time.[42] Had he exercised that right he would have eliminated his brother Adam's hopes to inherit. Keeping open the option of returning to and remaining in England, he instead guaranteed himself an income by leasing the estate to Adam. He also used the threat of a sale to extort funds from his brother. Then, as the decade came to a close, John used the leverage that he had by virtue of the license to alienate in order to pressure his brother into buying the manor. John was seeking a financial windfall that could help him advance the interests of his family in Ireland. Because from Adam's perspective a sale to another party would not only deny him his inheritance but also have a negative impact on his son, he labored to arrange a sale of the manor by his brother to his son.

One of the potential sticking points in the sale was the claims that Elizabeth Risby Winthrop had on the estate as a result of her marriage to the elder John. She was entitled to maintenance payments during his life regardless of who owned the manor, and she was also entitled to claim her dower rights following her husband's death. The elder John entered into an obligation for one thousand marks whereby he pledged to either secure a divorce that would bar Elizabeth from her dowry or to set aside a fund from which any such claim would be paid, thus protecting the purchasers. Wanting to conclude the deal, Adam and his son seemed willing to accept at face value the elder John's assertion that he had completed these steps.[43] But this was not the only obstacle to be surmounted. In order to effect the purchase Adam needed to arrange a number of things. In 1609 he acquired a license for himself and his brother to alienate their interests in the land and allow its passage to the young John Winthrop.[44] Because of this arrangement Adam would never own the manor, though many in the area believed that he did. His desire to have it sold to his son was undoubtedly due to his own age at the time, sixty-one. Adam sold lands in Edwardstone and elsewhere to raise some of the necessary funds, since his son did not personally have the resources to make the purchase.[45] In return for his aid young John pledged to pay him annually the sum that he would have realized from the rent of those lands. Adam also surrendered for a fee his offices at St. John's and Trinity colleges.[46] His son-in-law, Thomas Fones also invested in the purchase and gained a minor stake in the manor.[47] John and Mary sold some of the lands that she had inherited from her father in order to raise additional funds. All of this took time, and it is possible that the transfer was not finalized until 1612 or early 1613. But when it was completed the younger John Winthrop was the lord of Groton Manor, and a whole new set of opportunities were open to him.

MEANWHILE, OTHER CHANGES were occurring in the life of the younger John Winthrop. On September 25, 1609, he had presided for the first time over the Court Baron at Groton.[48] This was a manor court that met annually to deal with tenant rights and to register land transfers. It was customarily presided over by the lord of the manor or his steward. Adam Winthrop had served as steward for his brother, and would later do so for his son. It is likely that, with the sale of the estate proceeding, it was determined to give the younger John Winthrop the experience of presiding and at the same time to introduce him to the manor's tenants in his new capacity.

Some legal knowledge was useful for landowners as well as for paving one's way to advancement in Stuart England, and this presumably led to John's enrollment at Gray's Inn at about this time. While the admissions register of that Inn of Court shows him admitted on October 25, 1613, an earlier list of members of the Inn in 1611 includes Winthrop's name.[49] Interestingly, Nathaniel Rich was admitted to the same Inn in 1610. Unlike his father, John did not pursue his studies long enough to be called to the bar, but the legal training he received would stand him in good stead later in his career.

This was a difficult time for John. He was anxious about the sale of Groton Manor, dependent as it was on his unreliable uncle, on the one hand, and on the ability of his own family to raise the money for the purchase. Much of what would determine his future was beyond his control. He became seriously ill, and anxiety may have been a contributing factor. Then everything changed. On May 15, 1613, John Forth, Mary's father, died. Eight days later John Winthrop confided in his diary that he had felt his condition had been "much straightened," because of "my long sickness, partly through want of freedom, [and] partly through lack of outward things," and he had "prayed often to the Lord for deliverance, referring the means to himself." "Now," he wrote, the Lord "hath set me at great liberty, giving me a good end to my tedious quatrain, freedom from a superior will, & liberal maintenance by the death of my wife's father." Exulting in this new sense of freedom, he resolved "to give my life, my wit, my health, my wealth, to the service of my God & Savior" and enumerated eleven further resolutions on how he intended to live his life. He would live where it seemed God's will that he live. He resolved to faithfully "discharge that calling" which God pointed him to. He determined to avoid "vain & needless expenses, that I may be the more liberal to good uses." While he would be charitable to others, he would be careful to see that his charity "begin at home." His concern for his family was expressed in resolutions to engage the family in "morning prayers & evening [religious] exercises," to "have a special care for the education of my children," and to "banish profaneness from my family." Personally, he resolved to "diligently observe the Lord's Sabbath," to set aside his "morning[s] free for private prayer, meditation, & reading," to "flee Idleness," and to "pray & confer privately with my wife."[50]

By 1613 John decided that God had appointed that he leave the marshes of southeast Essex and move his family to Groton. He took possession of the mansion house that his grandfather had lived in, while his father and mother continued to reside at Groton Hall.[51] In July of that year the elder John Winthrop died at Aghadown, in Ireland. When word of his passing reached Groton, Adam Winthrop recorded the event and commented that his brother, who had led a notorious life and forced him to purchase the manor to prevent his inheritance being sold, "was neither useful to himself or me in his life; who was a hard brother to me at the time of his death."[52] His negative influence on his Groton kin would continue to be felt beyond the grave.

In returning to the Stour Valley John was able to reconnect with the clergy and laity who had helped shape his earliest religious impulses. On Friday, September 17, 1613, he met at Henry Sandes's house with a group of local clergy (including Sandes, Boxford's William Bird, and John Knewstub) and lay men and women to form a covenanted group to further their faith.[53] This practice had been recommended by Wethersfield's Richard Rogers in his *Seven Treatises* and was not uncommon in the region. Rogers held up as an example a group of men and women who had met "in a Christian man's house" in 1588 "for the continuance of love, and for the edifying one of another." Though they were generally regarded as godly by their neighbors, these men and women believed that they had not taken sufficient advantage of the opportunities they had by virtue of England's "long continued peace and liberty of the Gospel for the end for which God did send both, but that they had been dim lights." Seeking a "way to come out of this wearisome and unprofitable light," they "did covenant faithfully and seriously" to assist one another in getting more out of sermons by "godly conference" so that they would be "knit in that love, the bond of which could not be broken."[54] Imitating this effort, Winthrop, Sandes, Knewstub, and their friends pledged themselves to such mutual aid, to recall their covenant and communion every Friday, and to meet to renew the covenant on the Friday closest to September 17 the next year.[55] Winthrop might have felt in particular need of spiritual support, having become too sure of himself in light of the many blessings he had recently received, recording in his diary the sentiment that "[s]ecurity of heart ariseth of overmuch delight in the things of the world."[56]

But John's run of good fortune soon came to an end. In the summer of 1614 Mary gave birth to a daughter, baptized Anne, whom the Winthrops buried a little more than a week later.[57] The following June Mary prepared to give birth again. This time the delivery did not go well. Mary died on the twenty-sixth of the month, and the infant, again christened Anne, was buried with her three days later under the chancel of Groton church, as was the privilege for the lord of the manor and his immediate family. Their relationship had improved since the first days of their marriage, and one hesitates to read too much into his actions since remarriage itself was customary, but within only a few months he had arranged to marry again so as to provide a mother for his four young children. A marriage settlement was reached on September 15 and on December 6 John married Thomasine Clopton of Groton.[58] Like Mary, she was older than her new husband, having been born in 1583. John had played with her brothers and would have known her from the days of his youth. Her family was of a slightly higher status than the Winthrops. Her father, William Clopton, was lord of the manor of Castlins in Groton. Her mother, Margery, was a member of the prominent Waldegrave family of Essex.

His second marriage reflected John's new position in the county community. Despite the practical considerations that went into it, it became suffused with remarkable affection. John would remember Thomasine as "truly religious & industrious therein," unlike Mary. "She was sparing in outward show of zeal, &c, but her constant love to good Christians & the best things, with her reverent & careful attendance of God's ordinances, both public & private, with her care for avoiding of evil herself, & reproving it in others, did plainly show that truth, & the love of God, did lie at her heart."[59] She very likely influenced his decision to donate some manor waste land to the churchwardens and overseers of the poor for them to erect a parish poor house.[60] "Her loving & tender regard" of her family "was so amiable & observant," he wrote, that "I am not able to express it."[61]

But their union was short-lived. On "Saturday, being the last of November 1616, Thomasine, my dear & loved wife, was delivered of a daughter, which died the Monday following, in the morning." Thus begins John's long and moving account of two of the most difficult weeks of his life. On the day she gave birth Thomasine was taken with a high fever. On the following Wednesday John sent for his kinsman John Duke, a physician. Everyone feared for her life. On the Thursday night Henry Sandes was sent for, and Thomasine asked that the church bell toll to alert others of her imminent demise. She assured her husband that "God never bestows any blessing so great on his children but still he hath a greater in store," and reminded him how "God had dealt with Mr. Rogers before me in the like case" when he had lost a wife and remarried. Thomas Nicholson, Groton's rector, also came to pray with her, saying, "seeing her humbleness of mind & great comfort in God," that "her life had been so innocent & harmless as the Devil could find nothing to lay to her charge." Thomasine's fever came and went and with it her strength. Occasionally she was delusional. Despite Nicholson's assurances she felt assaulted with temptations, but she defied "Satan, & spitting at him, so as we might see by her setting of her teeth, & fixing her eyes, shaking her head & whole body, that she had a very great conflict with the adversary." She called for those close to her in order to give them last words. When her mother comforted her with the thought that she would soon be reunited with her father, who had recently died, she "replied that she should go to a better father than her earthly father." She exhorted her various sisters to "serve God & take heed of pride" and to bring up their children in the fear of God and expressed the hope that they should meet again in heaven. She thanked Adam and Anne Winthrop "for all their kindness & love towards her;" she called for her stepchildren and "blessed them severally, & would needs have Mary brought that she might kiss her, which she did." Her messages to her servants tended to be more pointed. While she commended Robert as having "many good things in you," and Mercy Smith as "a good woman," she called Anne Pold "a stubborn wench" and exhorted her to be obedient to Anne Winthrop. She warned Elizabeth Crouff to "take heed of pride," and "to Anne Addams she said, thou hast been in bad serving, long in an Alehouse, &c; thou makest no conscience of the Sabbath; when I would have had thee gone to Church thou wouldst not."

During the course of her decline she "prayed for the Church, &c, & for the ministry, that God would bless good ministers & convert such ill ones as did belong to him, & weed out the rest." John prayed with her and read to her from the Scriptures, especially the Gospel of John and the psalms. On the second Sunday of her illness, "when most of the company were gone down to dinner," John reminded her that the previous day was the anniversary of their marriage and talked with her of how she "should sup with Christ in Paradise that night" and of "the promises of the Gospel, & the happy estate that she was entering into." At five o'clock in the evening she "fell asleep in the Lord," and on the eleventh of December "she was buried in Groton chancel by my other wife, & her child was taken up, & laid with her."[62] They had been married just a year.

6

A Godly Magistrate

ON A WARM JULY DAY in 1615, John Winthrop sat nervously astride his horse on the road to Bury St. Edmunds. He was there with some of the country's leading citizens, awaiting the arrival of the king's justices who had been appointed to preside over the assize sessions. Just a month earlier he had been named to the Suffolk commission of the peace.[1] Accompanied by pikemen, and with trumpeters announcing their progress, Winthrop, his fellow county justices, the county sheriff, and the sheriff's bailiff were present to escort the assize judges to the town. All justices of the peace were required to attend the sessions, but the event was also one of the major social events of the year. For days Bury had been filling with men and women from throughout west Suffolk, some brought there by court business, others to take advantage of the sessions to buy or sell in the marketplace, and still others attracted by the spectacle and eager to witness the court proceedings.[2] Finally, the distinguished judges of the king's courts arrived, and the procession wound its way toward the town gates, where it was greeted by a large crowd. Bells rang and music was played as the magistrates, stopping first at their lodgings, proceeded to the church for prayer and a sermon.

The primary purpose of the assizes was to dispense the king's justice. England and Wales were divided into seven circuits, and commissions were issued by the king to groups of judges of the national courts at Westminster to ride the various circuits and try serious crimes. By the late sixteenth century virtually all felony offenses—burglary, homicide, witchcraft, rape, and arson—were being held over for the assizes rather than being dealt with by the county justices.[3]

Early the morning after their arrival, the assize judges convened for their business in a converted monastic schoolhouse next to the churchyard that had belonged to the former abbey.[4] Garbed in their robes of office, they sat in the middle of a raised bench at one end of a large hall while John Winthrop and the other county justices took their places to the side of the hall and on a lower tiered bench in front of the visiting justices. At a low table in front of and facing the benches sat the custos rotulorum—the justice who was keeper of rolls and president of the county commission of the peace—and the clerks of the court. Behind that group were the jury box and the prisoners' dock. Once the justices were seated, the clerk of the assizes read the royal commission whereby the judges were empowered. The business that the court would address was then presented—reports and referrals from constables, justices of the peace, and coroners. Thirteen to twenty-three citizens were called and sworn to sit on the grand jury.[5] Looking down from the bench as the grand jury was empaneled, Winthrop must have reflected on how far he had come in the mere three years since he had served on the grand jury at the Essex assizes. Once the presiding judge had read the charge to the court, the process of hearing and judging cases began.

While the center of attention would be the trials in the assize court, the members of the commission of the peace would hold other, separate meetings. On July 21, Winthrop and twenty-one of his fellow commissioners met and adopted various policies. They set out procedures for regulating the collection and distribution of money to the poor, decided that the nomination and selection of high constables would thereafter be done in open sessions rather than behind closed doors, required that the controversial matter of giving licenses to those who wished to keep alehouses be conducted in public, passed new regulations for the conduct of those alehouses, and took steps to better identify all householders eligible for jury service.[6]

CB

*W*INTHROP'S APPOINTMENT TO THE COMMISSION had given him an identity and a role to play in advancing God's kingdom. It had raised his status to the point where a marriage to Thomasine Clopton was considered an appropriate match, and it gave him a purpose to hold on to after her death. This experience would count more than any other as he would labor to govern the new colony of Massachusetts after 1630. Growing up at Groton, John had attended sessions of the commission in his father's company, and he had been taught to admire the magistrates who had helped to create a godly kingdom in the Stour Valley. Sir Robert Jermyn, whom Adam Winthrop referred to as "a pious man and a lover of true religion," and who served as custos rotulorum, was a man whom John particularly admired and would try to emulate.[7]

The commission was the chief administrative and judicial body in the county. Its members were substantial knights and gentry, and they were commissioned to inquire into, hear, and determine a long list of crimes. They also bore responsibility for administrative matters such as provision for the poor and orphans, licensing of alehouses, and maintenance of highways and bridges. Ideally, members would be chosen in such a way that no

Englishman would live more than seven miles from a justice. In Suffolk, during John Winthrop's tenure, the bench numbered almost seventy-five. By statute the entire commission was required to meet four times a year in what were known as quarter sessions, but rarely was even a majority present. The Suffolk justices met each quarter for a few days along the northern border, then a few days later held sessions at Woodbridge, then moved on to Ipswich, and finally ended their circuit at Bury St. Edmunds.[8] At each venue the bench was dominated by justices from the nearby hundreds, though some did travel distances to attend more than one meeting.[9]

In addition to their work at quarter sessions, the justices had individual policing responsibilities. They were empowered to arrest people and commit them to jail and to impose bonds on individuals as surety for their good behavior. Single justices who were designated as "of the quorum"—and John Winthrop never achieved that distinction—could handle minor matters by themselves, and a small group of justices, assuming at least one was of the quorum, had begun to meet in local petty sessions to handle cases that did not demand the attention of the full bench.[10] Winthrop did, on occasion, preside by himself over local disputes and the registration of land titles that involved his manorial land, his prerogative as lord of the manor and not as a justice of the peace.[11]

Service on the commission moved Winthrop onto the upper level of county leadership. During sessions he would join with his fellow justices in handing down decisions that shaped the character of the county. After sessions he would join them to dine and discuss the latest news from the court and abroad. But he was not entirely easy about his situation. Death had changed the face of the commission in recent years. In a sermon preached in Clare, along the Stour River, in 1621, Bezaleel Carter bemoaned the fact that many "merciful men" had "been taken away from us lately" and replaced by "oppressors, extortioners" who, "like the grasshoppers of Egypt, swarm amongst us."[12] In particular, the death of Sir Robert Jermyn in 1614 was an irreplaceable loss for those looking to the bench to promote godliness. Samuel Ward of Ipswich, called upon to preach the assize sermon in 1618, pointed out that the Suffolk commission was "a worthy bench, yet mingled with some dross, and not so refined as I have known and seen it." A bench that had been noted for its prosecution of a godly agenda now included "some whose skills & ability the Country doubts of, being conceived to be either so simple or so timorous that they dare not meddle with none that dare meddle with them, or else so popular they will displease none." Too many of the region's "[g]entry fear no more than to have a name that they fear God" rather than actually serving the Lord, and they "think when they have gotten an office they may swear by authority, oppress by license, drink and swill without control."[13] And with such a poor example and the lack of oversight that had been provided by the previous generation's godly magistracy, popular support for reformed practices was eroding. Looking back on this period the Reverend John Carter would recollect that "after many years the people were glutted with Manna and began to loath it" so that "there grew a great decay in their first love. About the year 1615 or something before there arose up a generation of malignant men, haters of a faithful and painful ministry, and of the power of Godliness."[14]

Ward's sermon expressed the godly perspective on the nature of the good magistrate, a view that Winthrop certainly shared and would carry to New England. According to Ward the "principal scope of magistracy in God's intention" was "to promote his glory, countenancing the Gospel and the professors of it, safeguarding the Church and Commonwealth, the first and second table."[15] The proper magistrate must have wisdom and experience, "strength of mind to govern and manage passion and unruly affections," and "that fortitude, valor, and magnanimity which we call courage and spirit."[16] After all, he asked, "had not the principal posts of an house need to be of heart of oak? Are rulers and standards that regulate other measures to be made of soft wood, or of lead, that will bend and bow at pleasure?"[17] The times demanded men of fortitude since magistrates would be called on to "encounter the Hydra of sin, [and] oppose the current of times and torrent of vice," and "must turn the wheel over the wicked, especially such roaring monsters and rebellious Choras, such lawless sons of Belial wherewith our times swarm."[18]

"Let the devil and the world storm and burst with envy," a godly magistrate "is worth a thousand of the common sort," Ward asserted.[19] In recent times too few had come into their "place by God's door and not by the Devil's window."[20] And Ward minced no words in standing before the judges and castigating some of their number, pointing out "[j]udges that judge for reward" and "such mercenary lawyers as sell both their tongues and their silence, their clients' causes and their own consciences," and in general those "muck-worms of the world, which . . . breed of putrefication, & beetles fed in the dung, relishing nothing else but earthly things, [who] think there is no other godliness but gain, no happiness but to scrape and gather, to have and to hold."[21] Addressing a specific concern, he urged them to "shake thy lap of bribes with Nehemiah" and complained that as for some of the magistrates, "the Devil himself they say may keep an Alehouse under their nose."[22]

Winthrop set down his own worries in his diary. He was concerned with exercising his authority to promote godliness. As the sessions approached in January 1617 he prepared himself "by earnest prayer," and riding to Bury he spent his time "as well as I could in good meditations." While there, he wrote, he refrained his "mouth, eyes, and ears from vanity" as well as he could. But in trying to follow the strict path that he thought appropriate to a godly magistrate, he was tempted by the "glory, wealth, pleasure & such like worldly felicity" that other magistrates looked for, and he thought that he heard some of his fellow judges saying of him that he "was a fool to set so light by honor, credit, wealth, [and] jollity," which others, who were esteemed "wise men," set out to gain. Whereas at one time men like Sir Robert Jermyn were respected for pursuing a godly path, now, Winthrop recorded, "all experience tells me, that in this way there is least company, & that those which do walk openly in this way shall be despised, pointed at, hated of the world, made a byword, reviled, slandered, rebuked, made a gazing stock, called puritans, nice fools, hypocrites, harebrained fellows, rash, indiscreet, vain glorious, & all that naught is." Yet, Winthrop reflected, "all this is nothing new to that which many of thine excellent servants have been tried with," and he prayed, "Teach me, O Lord, to put my trust in thee."[23] In writing this he perhaps was thinking of Richard Rogers's observation that "to be hated of the world, to be reviled, persecuted [and] slandered . . . is a sign that we are blessed."[24] And at last he recognized himself as one of those called puritans. Knowing that, as Thomas Carew had preached, "[h]ell is full of purposes, but heaven of performances," John was determined to act on his beliefs and to use his powers as a magistrate to patch the walls of the kingdom and maintain the threatened godly culture in the Stour Valley.[25]

Because the key characteristics of the godly magistrate as described by Ward and others were personal faith and integrity, Winthrop's effort to fashion himself for this role began with his need to master himself. No matter how sweet his early experience of God's love had been, Winthrop's assurance—like that of all puritans—was frequently challenged. He tried to structure his days properly, spending the mornings "wholly in the service of God & duties of my calling." After dinner he allowed an hour to "worldly affairs," visiting needy neighbors, and then spent more time in his study. But no sooner would he determine to structure his activities this way than he felt Satan begin to tempt him "with his wonted baits of worldly pleasures." While trying to follow the course he believed God demanded of the saints, he had to guard against any sense of personal pride and worth should he succeed in that venture. For a time "worldly delights which had held my heart in such slavery . . . began to be distasteful & of mean account with me," but then he would relapse, and confess that he "could not get at liberty from . . . vain pleasures." He would attend church and feel refreshed, then on retiring to his chamber for prayer "could not bring my mind to think seriously of any good thing, but it began to wander & be idle."[26]

He turned for counsel to Henry Sandes, who advised him to take time each day to reflect upon what he had acquired on the previous Sabbath, "for certainly the Sabbath is the market of our souls." He turned for guidance to the writings of Richard Rogers, William Perkins, and other godly authors. Trying again to shape his behavior, he found that "settling myself to walk uprightly with my God, & diligently in my calling, & having an heart willing to deny myself, I found the Godly life to be the only sweet life, & my peace with my God to be a true heaven upon earth." Once again he felt assured: "I found God ever present with me, in prayer & meditation, in the duties of my calling, &c. I could truly loath my former folly in preferring the love of earthly pleasures before the love of my heavenly father." Confident that he had left "fellowship with unfruitful works of darkness," he "was not then troubled with common cares & desires" such as his former longings for "food, apparel, credit, pleasure, &c., but was well contented with what God sent." However, as would always occur when he took pride in having changed his course, "before the week was gone I began to lose my former affections." He prayed as before but "could not find that comfort & feeling" he had previously enjoyed. He performed the duties of his magisterial calling but "not so cheerfully & fruitfully." The more he tried to control his inner state the worse he grew, "the more dull, unbelieving, vain in heart, &c." He became discontented and impatient with his failure, "sometimes ready to fret & storm against God because I found not that blessing upon my prayers & other means that I did expect." Only by surrendering, acknowledging his "unfaithfulness and pride of heart," and humbling himself before God did he receive a renewed assurance of God's love.[27]

Such episodes were common in Winthrop's life at this time, and common in the lives of many of his contemporaries. What was less common, or what we have less evidence of in the lives of others, was the ecstasy he would on occasion find as he surrendered to God. An account of one such experience is found in his diary at this time:

> O my lord, my love, how wholly delectable art thou! Let him kiss me with the kisses of his mouth, for his love is sweeter than wine. How lovely is thy countenance! How pleasant are thy embraces! My heart leaps within me for joy when I hear the voice of thee, my Lord, when thou say to my soul thou art her salvation. O my God, my king, what am I but dust!—a worm, a rebel, & thine enemy was I, wallowing in the blood & filth of my sins, when thou did cast the light of thy countenance upon me, when thou spreadest over me the lap of thy love, & say that I should live. Then did thou wash me in the ever flowing fountain of thy good. Thou did trim me as a bride prepared for her husband. . . . Wholly thine I am (my sweet Lord Jesus), unworthy (I acknowledge) so much honor as to wipe the dust off the feet of my Lord . . . , yet wilt thou honor me with the society of thy marriage chamber. Behold, all ye of the Lord, know & embrace with joy this unspeakable love of his towards you. God is love, assuredly.[28]

Fired by such moments, he would seek to respond to God's love by redoubled efforts to live a godly life. Then, invariably, "after a gleam of any special joy, whether in heavenly things or in earthly, there hath followed a storm of dumpishness and discomfort, that hath abolished the memory of the former joy."[29]

He wrote that he found that anyone who "would have surer peace and joy in Christianity must not aim at a condition retired from the world & free from temptations" but be engaged with his society. Though challenging, "the life which is most exercised with trials & temptations is the sweetest, & will prove the safest." As for those "trials as fall within compass of our callings, it is better to arm & withstand them than to avoid & shun them."[30] His life as a magistrate posed particular challenges because, as he acknowledged, he was particularly tempted by a desire to be well regarded by the men with whom he shared the bench. While some of his fellow magistrates disdained his unwillingness to indulge himself on social occasions, he was able to identify and befriend justices who shared his outlook. Brampton Gurdon of nearby Assington became a valued associate. Brampton's father, John, high sheriff of Suffolk in 1584, had been a supporter of godly clergy; he chose John Wincoll rector of Clopton in 1575, and William Winthrop guaranteed Wincoll's first fruits.[31] John Gurdon was also one of the overseers of Boxford school along with Adam Winthrop and John Knewstub.[32] The elder Gurdon was one of the godly magistrates Knewstub had extolled and John Winthrop had looked up to. In July of 1605 he was one of the seven justices who held sessions at Groton. When his wife, Amy, died in 1608, John Knewstub preached the funeral sermon. His son, Brampton, was older than John Winthrop, having been born in 1566. Brampton had studied law at Gray's Inn. He, too, was one of the original overseers of the Boxford school. Winthrop allied himself with the elder Gurdon but came to consider Brampton one of his closest friends. John formed another close friendship with William Spring, whose grandfather had been a member of the commission and whose father had died young. Thomas Jermyn, the son of Sir Robert, was another member of the commission whom Winthrop would have gravitated toward. Though Thomas had served with the earl of Essex in the siege of Rouen and again in Ireland, he never matched the high standard set by his father in the eyes of godly clergy and laymen. Nevertheless, Thomas Jermyn and Winthrop would become good friends, and at a future date Jermyn would use his influence in England to intercede on behalf of Winthrop's colony of Massachusetts.

Winthrop was somewhat overawed by the circles he was mixing in and confessed that "I find often times that coming out of good company I am sometimes more disquieted" than before. He speculated that because he was "taken up with too much regard for their persons" he neglected to make "that good use of such company as I ought." He later wrote to William Spring that during his early years on the commission he had admired and looked up to Spring "before you took any notice of me."[33] But he overcame this shyness and learned to benefit from godly friends, so that on another occasion he was able to record that "having occasion of conference with a Christian friend or 2, God so blessed it unto us, as we were all much quickened & refreshed by it." Such conferencing, an essential part of puritan piety, became an important part of Winthrop's life.[34]

John's relationship with his fellow justice Sir Robert Crane was a more complex matter. Crane had been raised in the household of Sir Robert Jermyn and as a protégé of Jermyn was supported by the godly. He was extolled by the Reverend Samuel Ward and others and by the late 1620s was seen as one of the leading puritan figures in the county. Yet rumors of his private life were disturbing, and he was reputed "a gentleman very prone to venery, and one that declined few that came into his way for that sport."[35] There is no evidence that Winthrop knew of or believed these rumors. While Winthrop's letters to Crane contain none of the warm sentiments that characterized his correspondence with Gurdon and Spring, he did ally himself with Crane, seeing in the rising figure someone who could perhaps advance his own career and the godly goals he espoused. Important as these political relationships were, however, none was to be as significant as the one he formed with Margaret Tyndal.

THERE IS NO DENYING THE GRIEF John experienced when Thomasine died, but he was also faced with the need to provide a replacement mother for his children, whom in the meantime he was raising with the help of his parents. This was especially important since he was often away from home, serving on the commission as well as still traveling to London to pursue his studies at Gray's Inn. As his thoughts turned to marrying again, John reflected on the varied marriages he was familiar with within his larger family circle. On the one extreme were those characterized by conflict. His aunt Joan Browne Hilles had been beaten by her husband and fled to her Groton kin for succor. There had been tensions between his cousin Joshua and his wife, who had also sought refuge for a time. Most vivid, perhaps, would have been the memories of his uncle John's bitter marriage with Elizabeth Risby and the later, illegal, marriage with Elizabeth Powlden in Ireland. His own marriage to Mary had not been without difficulties, though it had never reached the levels of discord of those other marriages. Yet balanced against these were the examples of his parents' union, the marriage of his godfather John Still, and his own marriage to his beloved Thomasine. In all cases the success or failure of the union was related to the character and compatibility of the spouses, and as he looked for a new wife John was seeking someone who, like Thomasine, was well read and pious.

Late in 1617 he began to court Margaret Tyndal of Great Maplestead, Essex, a town half a day's ride to the south of Groton. She was the daughter of Sir John Tyndal, a judge of Chancery who had been assassinated as he entered his chamber in Lincoln's Inn by a disgruntled litigant in 1616. Sir Francis Bacon, then attorney general, had investigated the incident and, referring to the case that had prompted the attack, wrote, "Sir John Tyndal, as to his cause, is a kind of martyr; for, if ever he made a just report in his life, this was it."[36] Sir John had left behind a wife, Anne Egerton, who had previously been married to William Deane; two sons, Deane and Arthur; his daughter, Margaret; and a stepson and two stepdaughters.

Winthrop had heard of the Tyndals from his father's friend Stephen Egerton, who was Anne Tyndal's brother. Egerton, who had often stayed with the Winthrops, had remained close to his sister, who would remember him generously in her will. The Deanes and Tyndals were also well known to Ezekiel Culverwell, whose early career had been spent in nearby Felsted and who was related to the Deanes by marriage. Culverwell strongly approved of Winthrop's courtship of Margaret Tyndal, as indicated in a letter he sent to Winthrop, but it is likely that the match was suggested to the Winthrops by Egerton, who visited Groton along with John Knewstub on September 11 and spent the night. One week later John set off on his first visit to the Tyndal home of Chelmsey House in Great Maplestead. Margaret was in her late twenties, a few years younger than John. She had been taught to read and write well and was noted for her piety.[37] The two quickly formed a strong attachment, and John confessed in his diary on November 22 that he had been having trouble concentrating on his regular course of work. But the road to the altar would not be a smooth one.

Some members of Margaret's family clearly saw Winthrop as an unworthy match. Foremost among these was Sir John Deane, Anne Tyndal's oldest son from her first marriage. Deane had been prepared for an eminent career with his education overseen by his uncle Alexander Nowell, the dean of St. Paul's, London, and by his cousin William Whitaker, the Regius Professor of Divinity at Cambridge. He received a knighthood in 1603 and was recognized as one of the leading figures in Essex. As such, he was chosen a member of every Parliament from 1607 until his death. He was appointed sheriff of Essex in 1610–1611 and served as deputy lieutenant of the Country of Essex from 1614 until his death. Presiding at Dynes Hall in Great Maplestead, he was an imposing figure and much involved in the affairs of his mother and his stepsiblings.

Deane's high opinion of his family's status was demonstrated by his paying to extend and transform the south transept of Great Maplestead church into a family mortuary chapel and arranging for the large funerary monument that was erected there in his memory. He considered the proposed match between his stepsister and John Winthrop as reflecting poorly on him and his family. One of Deane's concerns was the Winthrop finances. In one of his courtship letters to Margaret, John Winthrop addressed the issue of his modest resources and made an eloquent case for the importance of choosing spouses based on their piety rather than their material prosperity. But he also wrote of being able to assure her of an annual income of a modest £80 should he die before her. This was an indirect admission of problems with his title to Groton Manor. It is estimated that the annual income from Groton Manor was £120, but at this time John was committed to paying £40 annually to his aunt Elizabeth Risby Winthrop in satisfaction of her dower claim to one third of the estate. His uncle John had failed to deliver the promised protection against Elizabeth's dower rights, and following the elder John's death in 1613 she had appeared at Groton to make her claim. Unable to pay it, John agreed to annual payments for her lifetime, substantially reducing the income that he expected from lordship of the manor. While this would soon become an issue in lawsuits surrounding the title to the property, its effect in 1617 was to both raise questions about the Winthrops' land dealings, to rekindle memories of the elder John's mistreatment of his wife, and to highlight the meager resources of the family—all of which would have been of concern to Sir John Deane.

Two letters written to Margaret during their courtship by John, and another letter written to her by Adam Winthrop, hint at the struggle in the Tyndal household. John referred to "objections which thy friends have moved" and the "unequal conflict" she maintained against those who opposed the match. In another letter he referred to the "scars of such wounds" from the "conflict." It is likely that a visit of Sir Henry Mildmay and his wife to their Groton kin was designed to mobilize that family's considerable influence on behalf of the marriage. The influence of Egerton and Culverwell was also on the side of the couple and strengthened Margaret's resolve.[38] Adam was thankful that the couple had the support of Anne Tyndal, "the good lady, your dear mother."[39]

John portrayed his attraction to Margaret as one that was based on spiritual compatibility, and he was openly critical of those who "savor not the things of God" and seek only to "make sure of great portions with their wives, and large jointures from their husbands."[40] In his second letter, just a few weeks before the wedding, he regretted that her "uncle" and others arriving for the ceremony would be advising her to dress grandly. While he confessed "that there may be some ornaments which for virgins and knights' daughters, etc. may be comely and tolerable," and promised to "meddle with no particulars," he made it clear that he wished for little extravagance.[41]

The two long letters that John sent to Margaret before they wed can be characterized more as sermons than love letters. But then, their union was in large measure always to meld the spiritual with the physical, a combination captured in one of these letters that John sent his bride-to-be:

And now, my sweet Love, let me a while solace myself in the remembrance of our love, of which this spring time of our acquaintance can put forth as yet no more but the leaves and blossoms while the fruit lies wrapped up in the tender bud of hope. A little more patience will disclose this good fruit, and bring it to some maturity. Let it be our care and labor to preserve these hopeful buds from the beasts of the field, and from frosts, and other injuries of the air, lest our fruit fall off ere it be ripe, or lose ought in the beauty and pleasantness of it. Let us pluck up such nettles and thorns as would defraud our plants of their due nourishment. Let us not stick at some labor in watering, and manuring them. The plenty and goodness of our fruit shall recompense us abundantly. Our trees are planted in fruitful soil—the ground and pattern of our love is no other but that between Christ and his dear spouse, of whom she speaks as she finds, My well beloved is mine and I am his. . . . Love bred our fellowship, let love continue it. And love shall increase it until death dissolve it. The prime fruit of the spirit is love. Galatians: 5.22. Truth of spirit, and true love, abound with the spirit, and abound with love. Continue in the spirit and continue in love. Christ in his love, so fill our hearts with holy hunger and true appetite to eat and drink with him, and of him, in this his sweet love feast, which we are now preparing unto, that when our love feast shall come, Christ Jesus himself may come in unto us, and sup with us, and we with him—so shall we be merry indeed.[42]

The couple was married on April 29, 1618, in the church at Great Maplestead. They soon came to Groton to take up their residence.

A little less than a year later John must have thought that history was hideously repeating itself when Margaret entered a long and difficult labor. "She being above 40 hours in sore travail, . . . it began to be doubted of her life." Henry Sandes came and prayed with her, and John humbled himself in fasting and mourning and set himself "to prayer, & gave not over until God had sent her deliverance." But the completion of her labor with the birth of a son did not end her problems, for, like Thomasine only a few years earlier, "she was taken with a burning fever," and John Duke, who attended her as he had attended Thomasine on her deathbed, "made little reckoning of her life."[43] While she was still lingering, steps were taken for the baptism of her infant son. Stephen Winthrop was christened on March 31 in Groton church, with Lady Anne Tyndal as godmother and Stephen Egerton and Deane Tyndal as godfathers.[44] Then, a few days later, on "the 10th day of her sickness, diverse godly ministers meeting together did in their prayer remember her case in particular, & that very day & hour (as near as may be guessed) she found a sensible release of her disease," a recovery that Winthrop thanked God for.[45]

JOHN'S MARRIAGE TO MARGARET became one of the most significant relationships in his life. Indeed, next to his relationship with God it was rivaled only by the ties he had to his father. Traditional Christian teaching valued marriage for the procreation of children, the regulation of sexuality, and the provision of companionship. Within the union the husband's authority was recognized as primary. Women were weaker vessels and were expected to subject themselves to their husbands, though the one-sidedness of this was tempered somewhat by teachings on the duties husbands owed to their wives. Still, the basic theories left considerable room for interpretation. Many authors—and it has been argued that puritans were in the forefront of this development—had begun in the Tudor-Stuart period to stress the companionate elements of marriage and the need to find a spouse whom one could love and share responsibilities with.[46] In practice, of course, marriages differed greatly in quality, and the Winthrop family's experiences could be used to support any number of interpretations of what marriage at the time was all about.

Mature at the time of their marriage and well matched in their faith, John and Margaret were brought even closer together by their experiences, so that their marriage came to exemplify the strong companionate and affectionate unions urged on believers by godly clergy. They often attested that the love they had for each other helped them to better appreciate God's love. In one of her letters Margaret would write that "love liveth by love," and the love that existed and flourished between them contributed to John's belief in the centrality of love as an expression of Christian faith.[47] Frequently separated because of John's work, they reached out to one another in correspondence through which they shared ideas, responsibilities, and expressions of their mutual love. John would address her as his "sweet spouse," "loving friend," "most sweet heart," "very loving wife," "most loving and dear wife," and similar salutations. He wrote to her that "no distance of place or space of time can sever us in respect of our true and fervent affections to each other," that "the want of thy presence and amiable society makes me weary of all other accomplishments, so dear is thy Love to me," and that she was "more precious to me than any other thing in this world." He gave her "commission to conceive more of my Love than I can write" and ended letters with "the sweetest kisses and pure embracings of my kindest affection."[48]

Although not as many of Margaret's letters survive, they attest to the mutuality of love. Addressing him as her "most dear husband," on one occasion she wrote that "I have no way to manifest my love to you but by these unworthy lines, which I would entreat you to accept from her that loveth you with an unfeigned heart."[49] On another occasion she confessed that she missed his "beloved presence which I desire always to have with me" but accepted it as God's will. She had, she continued, "nothing more to write of to thee but my love, which is already known to thee, and it were needless for me to make relation of that which thou art so well assured."[50] His letters, she wrote, "did much refresh me," and elsewhere she referred to them as "tokens of your love and care of my good, now in your absence as well as when you are present; it makes me think that saying false, out of sight, out of mind."[51] On yet another occasion, addressing him as her "very loving husband," she expounded on the importance of their love. "Your love to me doth daily give me cause of comfort," she wrote, "and doth much increase my love to you."[52] In his response John spoke of her letter as "the true image of thy most loving heart, breathing out the faithful desires of thy sweet soul towards him that prizeth thee above all things in the world."[53]

Part of their married life involved the management of the Winthrop estate. Everyday life at Groton during the 1620s would not have differed much from what John's parents had experienced. The day began as early as four or five in the morning with what Winthrop referred to as the morning exercise, a gathering of the household for prayer and perhaps a Scripture reading. John relished leading his family congregation, and occasional neglect of the task was a cause for self-indictment in his diary. A similar evening exercise for the household marked the end of the day. Following the morning exercise John would have given the day's instructions to the farm laborers while Margaret would have set tasks for the maidservants whom she supervised. In his absence Margaret would have assumed all of these responsibilities. There is no clear indication of how many laborers and servants we are talking about in the 1620s. The account of Thomasine's death mentions nine servants in the household in 1617, and there may have been others. Eight servants may have emigrated with John to Massachusetts in 1630, and this would have been only a portion of the entire household. Tasks assigned, it was John's goal to spend the remainder of his morning in further prayer, meditation, and reading. Judging from the diaries of other godly women, it is likely that Margaret too retired for a time for private religious exercises. This would also have been a time for the religious training of the children. Though a concern of both parents, it would have been customary for Margaret to instruct the youngest children in their catechism. This did not mean that she would have neglected the older children, John's sons and daughters from his first marriage. Indeed, one of the striking testaments to her character is the evidence that correspondence reveals of how close John Jr. and Forth in particular came to revere her as their mother.

The labor in the fields of the manor that John oversaw varied with the seasons and required little hands-on supervision. The labor that Margaret supervised was extensive and more demanding of her time. This would have included instructing the dairymaid, who was expected to keep the dairy clean, milk the cows, and prepare butter and cheeses. Other tasks would have involved the mending and washing of clothes; cleaning the rooms and furniture of the mansion house, including the fireplace grates and implements; caring for the estate's swine and poultry; salting meat;

making malt and brewing beer and ale, which were the ordinary household drinks at all meals; and baking bread. Soap and candles may have been produced under her supervision or may have been purchased. Margaret was directly involved in cultivating the herbs and spices grown in the garden. She would have used some of these in preparing home remedies for the various ailments that afflicted members of the household. She also was engaged in preparing the family meals, and when John was away from home in London or elsewhere she enjoyed sending him food parcels that included turkeys, conserves, puddings, and other items from the Groton table. Some clothing for the household members was commissioned from tailors; other items were made by Margaret and the servants. Whenever he departed for London John carried lists of items to buy and send home, including pins, needles, stockings, and various fabrics. At Groton supervision of the beehives and the fishpond was John's responsibility but would have fallen to Margaret during his absences. She also would have assumed the responsibilities of keeping the household accounts, though primary responsibility for the manor accounts would have been assumed by a steward. Toward the end of the 1620s John Jr. helped with the management of affairs when he was resident at Groton.[54]

ANOTHER IMPORTANT PART of their life at Groton centered on the performance of their public religious responsibilities. This included attending sabbath services, fast days, and lectures. While John and Margaret would have attended lectures and occasional sermons in Boxford, they would have generally worshiped on the Sabbath at Groton.[55] That church was of modest size, accommodating fewer than a hundred and fifty worshipers. Any stained glass was long gone, as were wall paintings of saints or biblical stories that had typically adorned the region's churches in Catholic days. In place of these decorations would have been a set of boards on which were painted the Commandments. Queen Elizabeth had ordered these to be erected in the east end of every church chancel for purposes of instruction and ornamentation.[56] Other boards, with the Lord's Prayer and the Creed, were erected in some churches.

Church seating was relatively unknown before the Reformation, but with the advent of reform and the greater attention to preaching, seats and benches became common. By the seventeenth century such seating became fixed rather than movable and places were often assigned. In much of the Stour Valley it appears that seating was segregated, with women on the north side of the church and men on the south side. In most places, however, this gradually was modified to allow members of the parish gentry at least to sit together as a family. As patron of the living at Groton, John Winthrop would have had his own family pew in the prime space near the pulpit. This privileged position recognized the ranked social orders of the community while the involvement of all in the service spoke to their equality in the eyes of God.[57] The Winthrop pew would have likely been something between the elaborate box pews that were constructed in some wealthy parishes and a simple row pew. Certainly there would have been room for John to keep his quill and ink, and a platform on which to rest his commonplace book as he took his sermon notes.[58]

How far services in Groton and Boxford diverged from the prescribed forms of the Book of Common Prayer is impossible to know, particularly since it was in the interests of the congregations not to broadcast any innovations.[59] Furthermore, contemporary accounts of services make clear that it was common for clergy to mix and match worship from the order for public morning prayer and the order for receiving Holy Communion. At least the basic structure of the services would have been in keeping with the Prayer Book, beginning with an opening prayer by the clergyman, the congregants standing and joining in with their hands raised to heaven.[60] Next the minister would have led the congregation in an examination of the Commandments, reading them aloud while the parishioners followed each by asking for God's mercy and strength to keep that law. In the prescribed order of the liturgy the congregation next joined in a general confession in which they asked forgiveness for their transgressions. Next came the epistle, the gospel, and recitation of the Creed.

After the Creed came a psalm, followed by the morning sermon, the central element in the service in parishes like Groton, and another psalm. Whether recited or sung, it is likely that in Groton and Boxford the congregations used *The Whole Booke of Psalms, collected into English metre by T. Sternhold, J. Hopkins & others* (1562), which sought to make the verses memorable by translating them into English poetry. Next the minister would exhort the people to remember the poor. One of the suggested scriptural verses he was to use in urging this charity was from Matthew 5—"Let your light so shine before men, that they may see your good works, and glorify your Father which is in heaven." The churchwardens would then take a collection.

The communion liturgy and the sharing of the Lord's Supper would follow on specified Sundays. The Boxford churchwardens' accounts indicate that communion was celebrated once per month.[61] A week before that sacrament the minister would ask all who intended to receive to indicate their desire to do so and would remind them that any "open and notorious evil liver" who had offended the congregation or "done any wrong to his neighbors by word or deed" would be denied the sacrament until he had repented and amended his behavior. Likewise, any parishioners between whom "malice and hatred" reigned would be excluded.[62] This served the dual purpose of restricting the sacrament to those who were godly and encouraging the healing of community tensions and the exercise of Christian charity. In godly parishes such as Groton, recipients refused to kneel for the bread and wine and instead received sitting or standing. It is likely that a large silver communion cup decorated with a sea-monster motif, which John Winthrop donated for the use of the church in Boston, Massachusetts, in the early 1630s, was used in the services at Groton.[63] Included in that portion of the liturgy, but also used in services without communion, was a general confession. A passage that resonated strongly with Winthrop specified that "[w]e have left undone those things which we ought to have done, and we have done those things which we ought not to have done."[64]

The service would frequently conclude with the entire congregation reciting the Lord's Prayer, then being led by the minister in three collects, or short prayers, asking for God's blessing on the king, for peace, and for the grace to enable the members of the congregation to live righteously. Baptism of newborn infants would follow the worship service. In the afternoon the members of godly parishes would often reassemble for psalms, Scripture reading, and another sermon. As they gathered each Sunday, the members of the local community thus participated in services that prodded them to put aside their differences and to exercise Christian charity and reminded them of both their hierarchical responsibilities and their communal unity.[65]

IN WINTHROP'S UNDERSTANDING, the faith that grew from personal experience and public worship was meaningless unless it was manifested in his behavior. As he wrestled with his spiritual identity and family problems, John continued to function as a magistrate, coming to earn the respect of many of his peers. East Anglia, including Suffolk, was suffering from a decline in the cloth industry upon which the region's prosperity had been built. New types of cloth, particularly linens, were supplanting the traditional English woolens in the European marketplace, while wars on the continent also caused disruptions to trade. The result was growing unemployment, poverty, and crimes associated with dearth. In the 1610s and 1620s the Suffolk magistrates were increasingly occupied with the consequences of these developments.[66] Though the records are very scarce, the surviving fragments show Winthrop active with his fellow justices at quarter sessions and the assizes; settling disputes between the justices from Bury and other Suffolk justices; setting tax rates; regulating maltsters, who made beer and ales, innkeepers, and alehouse keepers; and insisting on proper attention to the needs of the "aged and impotent poor" while seeking to keep the able-bodied poor from becoming charges on their communities.[67]

Such problems could occur even in Winthrop's backyard. His own concern had been reflected in his 1618 donation of some of his manor land for the erection of a parish poor house.[68] However, the commission found that "the aged & impotent poor" of Boxford, Groton, and Edwardstone were "not relieved in such comfortable & sufficient means" as the law required and that "the other sort of poor, which are of able body to work, are in great distress & likely to perish for want of means to employ them" and ordered the churchwardens of the three parishes to provide succor for those unable to work and work opportunities for those who were able-bodied, warning that they would neglect this order at their peril.[69] Suffolk was unusual compared to other counties in that the militia was under the control of the commission as opposed to being commanded by a lord lieutenant. Consequently, as England reacted to the conflicts on the continent, John was involved in militia musters and impressment of troops. The commission also acted when Sudbury was visited by the plague, levying a rate on the other towns in the hundred to assist the suffering community.[70]

Not all of John's business as a justice was spent with the larger commission. He would be called upon by local residents to bind over those accused of petty crimes (requiring bonds to ensure their appearance at sessions), to settle minor disputes, and to intervene in breaches of the peace. In what was a typical action for a local justice of the peace, Winthrop, sitting with John Gurdon in Assington, bound over Groton butcher John Sugg to pay three shillings per month to the parish's overseers of the poor for the support of a bastard son he had fathered on the widow Colman.[71] It was on one such occasion that John experienced yet another sign of God's providential care of him:

> Riding through Boxford with Mr. Gurdon in his coach, my son Henry being with me, & one of Mr. Gurdon's men, entering the town the coachman was thrown off, & the horses ran through the town over logs & high stumps until they came to the causeway right against the church, & there were snarled in the logs, &c, & the coach being broken in pieces, top, bottom, & sides, yet by God's most wonderful providence we were all safe.[72]

John also served through this period on a Suffolk and Essex sewer commission. Despite what the name might imply, this was a commission charged by the king with supervising the repair of bridges, channels, and causeways—such as the one over the River Box next to Boxford church—and concerned with navigation of and passage over a region's waterways, passing orders for their repair and maintenance. The commission Winthrop was appointed to had jurisdiction over the hundreds of Suffolk and Essex "as doth adjoin to the River Stour."[73] Not only did this give him a further opportunity for public service, but it also brought him together with leaders from Essex in addition to those members of the Suffolk bench with whom he was in more regular contact.

DESPITE THE BLESSINGS of his marriage and his public success, Winthrop was not content in the 1610s. He struggled to discern God's plan for him and continued to wrestle with his faith. In August 1619 he confessed to having been drawn from his "steadfastness, & walked in an unsettled course for the space of a year & more." His "zeal was cooled," his "comfort in heavenly things was gone." Assurance that followed prayer, Sabbath observance, Scripture reading, or communion with fellow saints was transitory, "so soon gone as it was not to be regarded." Indeed, the things that he cherished most could lead him astray, for he found, referring to his pride in his marriage and public success, that he had "again embraced this present world, eagerly pursuing the delights & pleasures of it." As his "love of the world prevailed, so the love of God & all goodness decayed." Once again his initial reaction was to try harder, to put "religion in as familiar practice as our eating & drinking, dealings about earthly affairs, etc., & not to tie it only to the exercises of Divine worship."[74] Yet invariably, having been humbled by his failure to right his spiritual ship on his own, he would re-experience God's overwhelming love or receive a token of that divine love. Thus, in April 1620, when Margaret was again in a difficult labor, he humbled himself in prayer and, "being in the next chamber, as I arose from prayer I heard the child cry."[75] Even assured as he was of God's love, he continued to search for the destiny God had cast him for.

Reflecting on how his personal situation had changed over the previous decade, he could take satisfaction in having achieved considerable independence by becoming a substantial landowner. Though he had lost two wives, he was wedded to a woman who not only shared his bed but also matched his piety and concern to do God's will. His father and mother were still alive and strong supports to him, his wife, and his children. He was making a name for himself as a magistrate and forming alliances with some of the rising figures in the county. He was learning to better understand his spiritual dependence on God, yet he still experienced doubts about how to fashion himself to serve God's will. And while his personal future appeared bright, he was troubled by clouds he discerned on the broader horizon. Reformed religion had been increasingly embattled in the early years of the new century, even in the Stour Valley, where the walls of the godly kingdom had been breached by the death of many key protectors on both the national (Leicester, Burghley, Mildmay) and county (Robert Jermyn) levels and the departure from the region of others. Those who might once have accepted the godly culture because of the futility of complaining to local leaders of the church or state now spoke out more openly at the reformers, mocking them as puritans and disparaging their rejection of worldly pleasures. It was increasingly difficult for a magistrate of modest means to serve both king and faith. Looking at things in a broader perspective, the cause of reformed Protestantism was being challenged abroad as the Thirty Years War between Catholics and Protestants broke out on the continent in 1618. Fighting for God's cause would be more important than ever before but also more difficult. Not only was the future uncertain and threatening, but with those changing circumstances he was unsure of the role he was expected to play. And for John Winthrop, changes in his personal situation would heighten his doubt and insecurity.

7

The Godly Embattled

IT IS 1628, AND JOHN WINTHROP was considering purchasing a London home. He held a much coveted position as attorney of the Court of Wards and Liveries, an office that could well make him rich were he to bow to the importunities of friends and temper his high moral standards. John had achieved far more success than he would have expected in the days when he was a young guest at Rochford Hall, but with success came new demands and new temptations. He was troubled, for he needed a larger income. Not only was he burdened with the costs of a long-running lawsuit in the nearby Court of Chancery, but his family continued to grow, and providing for his children was increasingly costly. His eldest son, John, had recently run up bills on a tour of the Levant. His son Henry was begging for parental help to rescue a struggling venture growing tobacco in Barbados. Forth Winthrop was a student at Emmanuel College, Cambridge, and had written more than once to gently remind his father that college fees hadn't been paid. Then there was his daughter, Mary, for whom he would have to provide a dowry.

In addition, the post he held came with expectations that he live in a manner seen as appropriate for such an official. He had been urged to give up his practice of living with his Downing or Fones kin or in his law chambers and to buy a London house where he could live and entertain during the court sessions. He and Margaret could not afford two full households and considered selling Groton and settling in London, but John knew he would be unable to sell the Suffolk estate until the Chancery case challenging his title was decided. Besides, neither John nor Margaret was eager to abandon the Stour Valley. Nevertheless, he had begun to look at London property. His brother-in-law Emmanuel Downing had already dismissed one possibility as too small. And it wasn't only a house that people expected him to acquire. His sister Lucy Downing told him point-blank that the dinner service he was using was inappropriate and offered to help him purchase a more presentable set.[1] Winthrop had long bemoaned the fact that in England "we are grown to that height of intemperance in all excess of riot, that no man's estate will suffice to keep sail with his equals, and he that fails in it must live in scorn and contempt."[2] Now he faced that dilemma himself.

He was torn between his sense of duty and his ambition. If this was a crossroads type of choice, it was a recurring one. A puritan was made not by a single decision but by a life of choosing. John recognized the temptation to pursue worldly success over the health of his soul and asked God each day for strength to resist. At the same time, he was worried that England was also in danger of turning its back on God. He wondered how things could have come to this pass in the mere thirteen years since as a new justice of the peace he had nervously awaited the assize judges on the road to Bury St. Edmunds.

ॐ

*A*S HE FACED THESE and other problems in the 1620s, John would be without the strong and accustomed support of his father, for in 1623 Adam Winthrop passed away. Giving the news to his oldest son, John wrote that "your grandfather . . . hath finished his course and is gathered to his people in peace, as the ripe corn into the barn." Adam had "thought long for the day of his dissolution, and welcomed it most gladly. Thus is he gone before us, and we must go after in our time." Seeking consolation while expressing his own concern for the future, John wrote that "this advantage he hath of us, [that] he shall not see the evil which we may meet with ere we go hence. Happy [are] those who stand in good terms with God and their own conscience."[3] Never having been lord of the manor and patron of the living, Adam Winthrop could not be buried within the church, but on March 28, 1623, he was interred in a grave along the side of the church, next to the chancel door. A memorial was later placed over his resting place on which was inscribed his epitaph, "Heaven the Country: Christ the Way."[4] The love and advice of his father, which had always sustained him, would no longer be there as John faced some of the most difficult challenges of his life.

The death of Adam Winthrop seemed to give new urgency to a growing number of personal problems that challenged his ability to act in his domestic life as he deemed a loving husband and father should, while calling into question the rectitude that he had labored to make the foundation of his public life. Many of the problems had been triggered by the death of his uncle John in Ireland in 1613. Shortly thereafter Elizabeth Risby Winthrop had arrived in Groton armed with a writ and demanding one third of the estate according to her dower rights. In early January of 1614 John, "knowing no means to avoid the same, by mediation of friends on both parts, agreed to a composition with her, and for her right and title of dower" Elizabeth agreed to accept a rent charge of £40 yearly, to be paid in quarterly installments.[5] That meant one third of the normal income from the estate was going to his aunt, and he was still paying his father and mother for the income they had waived when they yielded their lease of the manor a few years earlier. Of course, John should have been protected by the obligation his uncle John had agreed to when he sold the manor, guaranteeing that he would either obtain a divorce decree barring Elizabeth's rights or else establish a fund to protect the purchasers against her claims, but the elder John had failed on both counts, prompting Adam to frequently complain about his "brother's unkind and unfaithful dealing with him."[6] The Groton Winthrops clearly knew that neither step had been accomplished, and in 1614 they investigated bringing suit against the elder Winthrop's Irish estate, which was in the hands of his Irish "wife," Elizabeth Powlden Winthrop. The following year one of the Powlden brothers initiated preliminary discussions of a settlement, but nothing came of this. Plans for a suit were deferred because John and his brother-in-law Thomas Fones had no contacts in Ireland whom they trusted and because of doubts about whether there were assets available to be seized and how much it would cost to prosecute the case.

John sorely needed money, since the Winthrop household placed increasing demands on his income. His children from his marriage to Mary Forth were growing up. John Jr. was sent to school at Bury, then in 1622 was enrolled at Trinity College in Dublin. Within two years, despite having been told by his father to "think not of seeing England till you may bring a hood at your back," he had abandoned his studies there and found a place at the Inner Temple.[7] His later accomplishments as a statesman, entrepreneur, medical consultant, and amateur scientist should not obscure the fact that as a young man John Jr. found it hard to settle on any course of action. Some of this, of course, may have been due to the circumstances of his youth. His mother, Mary, had died when he was only ten. Thomasine Clopton quickly won the affection of her stepchildren, only to be taken from them a year later. Young John was twelve when yet another mother entered his life in the form of Margaret Tyndal. There had been physical disruptions as well, with the move from Great Stambridge to Groton and then, just as he would have been adjusting to his new family, being sent off to school at Bury.[8] Recognizing this, his grandfather Adam sought to help the youngster develop a sense of roots. Adam used his copy of *Allestree's Almanack* for 1620 to record the passage of events that occurred in Groton—the daily comings and goings, sermons, weather, and other such events—which he then gave to the boy as a lasting chronicle of the year.[9]

Not entirely unlike his father, the youngster struggled to define himself and choose a direction for his life. Sensing that his son had not been blessed with a conversion experience, John wrote to him in Dublin that he hoped the young man would find "the sweet promises of God, and his free favor, whereby the soul hath a place of joy and refuge in all storms of adversity." Promising his prayers, he also assured him of his continuing material support, pledging that if the son avoided "baseness," the father would continue to "shorten myself to enlarge you."[10] A few years later, writing from Groton to John Jr. on the eve of the latter's entry to the Inner Temple, John said that he was "glad of your health, but should yet be more glad if I could hear that you were resolved upon any good course for the employment of your life and talents. I desire but that your judgement may be once rightly informed, and then let God dispose of you as you please."[11]

Following his son's admission to the Inner Temple, John arranged for him to share chambers there with Robert Gurdon, the second son of his friend Brampton, but the young man seems to have chosen instead to lodge first with his uncle and aunt Downing and then with his Fones kin. He seems not to have applied himself to his studies, and in 1626 he was considering marriage, his father having opened discussions with Edward Waldegrave of Lawford, Essex, concerning a possible union of young John with one of Waldegrave's younger daughters. He made clear that he sought "neither to persuade" his son "to that, nor dissuade you from this or any other [match] which you shall desire, that may be fitting to my estate, and hopeful of comfort to you," and implored him to consider that such comfort was "not to be judged of only by wealth and person, but by meet [proper] parts and godly education."[12] Though the Waldegraves were considered "a religious and worshipful family," the match was not concluded.[13]

In the spring of 1627 young John gave up his studies at the Inner Temple. Using family connections he obtained a berth as secretary to the captain of the ship *Due Repulse*, which carried the rear admiral's flag in a naval expedition to bring aid to the French Huguenot fortress of La Rochelle.[14] The duke of Buckingham, the king's favorite and leader of the expedition, proved inept both in the preparations he made for the expedition and in his execution of the plan. By November the English forces, battered by their struggles, withdrew home, and a few months later the Protestants of La Rochelle surrendered. Young John's taste for war may have been blunted by this experience, but his search for adventure was not. He considered joining one of the early expeditions to New England but chose not to on the advice of Emmanuel Downing, among others.[15] In June 1628, again through the intercession of family friends, he found a place on the *London*, a Levant Company merchant vessel sailing for the eastern Mediterranean. The cruise, for this is what it was for Winthrop, was a memorable experience. He marveled at the architectural splendors of Tuscany, strolled through botanical gardens at Pisa and Florence, wandered the streets and canals of Venice, and was amazed at the world of Constantinople. In the course of his travels he expended his credit, borrowed more from his father and uncle, and in July 1629 found himself in Amsterdam, again need-ing letters of credit to be able to complete his return home.[16] The experi-ence helped him to mature, but the costs—partially defrayed by his share of the sale of Great Stambridge lands he had inherited—were a burden on the family.[17]

Henry, young John's brother, posed an even greater challenge to his parents and their resources. There is no evidence that he was sent to gram-mar school and, while he was certainly taught to read and write, the poor quality of his spelling and grammar compared to his brothers' suggests that he either did not attend school or failed to apply himself. He accom-panied his father on trips to friends and relatives in London and elsewhere. References to him in his parents' correspondence suggest that he was lively and unruly. It was common for members of the gentry to send children out to live and learn in the households of friends, and Henry may have been placed for a time with the family of Sir Nathaniel Barnardiston in Kedington, Suffolk, in the hope that he would develop more disciplined habits.[18] In December 1626, at twenty years old, he accompanied an English expedi-tion to the West Indies, urged on by his family to "learn experience in maritime affairs."[19]

Having arrived at the island of Barbados in February 1627, Henry de-cided to stay on as one of "but three score of Christians and forty slaves of negroes and Indians." He settled on the island, committing himself to ad-venture for three years in return for the colonizing company paying him one hundred pounds per year plus payment for servants he would bring over.[20] In letters home Henry wrote that he found Barbados "the pleasantest island in all the West Indies," that he had "a crop of tobacco in the ground," and that after the harvest he hoped to send over five hundred pounds of tobacco, or even twice that.[21] He asked his father to send over two or three men as servants indentured for terms of three to five years, together with clothes, shoes, tools, knives, and other things needful to establish a colo-nial holding, none of which he had brought with him.[22] While Henry's decision to become a colonist was certainly impetuous, his parents hoped he would succeed. Margaret wrote that the family at Groton were "very glad to hear such good news of our son Henry," and John recruited some young men who were willing to enter indentures.[23] He bore the costs of supplying Henry, and Emmanuel Downing likewise extended credit for the young man.[24]

But the good news did not continue. Though Henry was named one of the assistants to the colony's governor in September 1628, his tobacco culti-vation was less successful.[25] In late January 1629 John Winthrop wrote to his son questioning the tobacco that had supposedly been sent to cover the debts Henry had run up; some had apparently been sent to others he had bor-rowed from, but little sent to John. Furthermore, John's brother-in-law

Thomas Fones, consulting several members of the Grocers Company, found that what had been sent was "very ill conditioned, foul, full of stalks, and evil colored." As for further help that Henry had requested, his father wrote that "in truth I have no money, and I am so far in debt already to both your uncles, as I am ashamed to borrow any more. I have," he concluded, "disbursed a great deal of money for you more than my estate will bear. . . . Except you send commodity to raise money, I can supply you no further. I have many other children that are unprovided," and as for those uncles and aunts, while they "commend them[selves] to you, . . . they will take none of your tobacco."[26]

Henry came home, possibly even leaving Barbados before his father's discouraging letter reached him. Rather than showing up at Groton, though, he stayed in London with his uncle and aunt Fones. Hoping to keep "my nephew your son from much expense and riotous company," Thomas Fones allowed him to "lodge and diet in my house," but he soon came to regret that decision, as he confessed in a letter to his brother-in-law. Henry regularly brought undesirable friends home with him, including "a papist," treating the Fones "house like an Inn." Furthermore, Fones felt that Henry's "heart . . . is much too big for his estate." Among other extravagances the young man had purchased on credit "a scarlet suit and cloak which is lined through with plush." Worse yet, he had "wooed and won" Fones's daughter Elizabeth, and "both pretend to have proceeded so far that there is no recalling of it" but for them to marry. Fones's consent had not been sought, and he considered it "no fit match for either of them," yet Henry asserted to his uncle that "if he cannot have my good will to have my daughter, he will have her without." When Fones told Henry that he was no longer welcome to stay there, the youth ignored him and "comes and stays at unfitting hours."[27]

The shock waves in the family were considerable. There was nothing to do but consent to the match. John quickly traveled to London, where he found things even worse than he anticipated. Thomas Fones had written that he was "overwhelmed with troubles and afflictions on all sides" and was "so lame I could not feed myself with my hand nor stir out of my chamber."[28] Hardly had John arrived at the Fones residence, at the sign of the Three Fawns near the old Bailey, than Thomas's health became worse. John's trusted brother-in-law and co-owner of Groton Manor died. John was immersed in coping with this new tragedy: buying mourning apparel, food, and drink for the mourners; proving the will; and arranging for the funeral on April 15, including the memorial sermon. He had hardly completed these tasks when he received word from Groton that his mother had passed away and been buried on the nineteenth, six years after the passing of Adam Winthrop.[29] Although beset by these tragedies, John could not ignore the problem that had brought him to London. On the twenty-fifth of the month Henry and Bess were married at the Church of St. Sepulchre at New Gate, London. John, having to stay in London to attend to business, arranged for the couple to travel to Groton, warning Margaret that she would have to "labor to keep my son at home as much as thou can, especially from Hadleigh," the nearest large town in which he might find a way to get into trouble.[30]

Forth Winthrop proved much less of a trial to his parents. Like his oldest brother he showed an aptitude for learning and, after being prepared at Boxford school, was enrolled at the grammar school in Bury St. Edmunds.[31] In many ways Forth shared his father's religious outlook more than any of his siblings. He sent his father verses and a prose piece he had composed on the Gunpowder Plot.[32] Henry Sandes encouraged his godly disposition by giving him books.[33] When his brother John sailed for the Mediterranean, Forth wrote urging him to trust in God "that you and those with you may be safe from every peril, to whose blessing, preservation, and providence, beyond all other felicity, I commit and commend you, for the sake of Jesus Christ our Savior, who is the Way, the Life, and the Truth to all who make him their refuge."[34] In 1626 he began studies at Emmanuel College, Cambridge. He began writing to his brother John and his father in Latin and referred to the "hallowed halls and chapels" of the university.[35] He was attracted to "the science of theology," where those who "may be esteemed as not only lovers of wisdom, but even as already wise men in all other things, are as but infants, tyros, and simpletons, and, when they have done all, only know that they know nothing."[36]

Because Forth was considering a ministerial career, his father was prepared to meet the expenses of a Cambridge education, but it was not easy. On more than one occasion the young man had to remind his father that his quartering fees had not been paid. On other occasions he wrote that he had "need of some clothes, for these are worn out," and to admit that he "stood in need of a cloak, my other being much worse and also a great deal too short."[37] In the summer of 1629 the dream was deferred. Accumulating pressures on the Winthrop finances made Cambridge an expensive luxury—John would write bitterly at the time of "the unsupportable charge of this education" at Oxford and Cambridge[38]—and he expressed to Margaret his reluctance to continue to bear the cost if Forth was not committed to a ministerial career.[39] She wrote that "Forth will go to Cambridge this week and talk with his tutor, I think he is resolved to be no longer there," and indeed that was the case.[40]

Expensive as it was to assist them, these three young men were but the oldest of a growing family. Mary, born in 1612 and named for her mother, was the other surviving child from John's first marriage. Stephen was born to John and Margaret in 1619, followed by Adam—named after his elderly

grandfather—a year later, Deane in 1623, Nathaniel (who died shortly after birth) in 1625, and Samuel in 1627. The lives of these young children
were full of the mishaps that were part of growing up. As he was learning
to walk Stephen tripped and fell into a fireplace, but fortunately he emerged
unscathed.[41] Later, as a young boy, he had another close call. Together
with his brother Adam and their cousin Benjamin Gostlin he was standing
near the stable door while his brother Forth was practicing his archery.
One of the arrows went awry and flew towards the boys. John thought "it
must needs strike into Adam's side, but it pleased God it missed him a very
little and struck into the wall by him."[42]

In addition to their children, in 1621 John had taken into his home the
seventy-six-year-old woman who had nursed him as a child. When his good
friend Henry Sandes died, John became executor of his friend's estate and
took upon himself responsibility for the education of Sandes's ward Thomas Arkisden, who enrolled at Emmanuel at the same time as Forth, becoming the young Winthrop's chamber mate. Arkisden eventually received
his BA and later achieved fame by inventing a shorthand alphabet.

The Winthrop household budget also included the costs of hospitality.
Entertaining guests was an important aspect of gentry life in this period,
critical for reflecting and improving one's status, and it was a responsibility
that the Winthrops shouldered willingly.[43] Kin such as Sir Henry Mildmay
and his wife, Carew Mildmay, the Tyndals, the Dukes, and the Deanes
were often at Groton. Rites of passage such as the baptisms of John and
Margaret's children were special occasions for gatherings of family, friends,
and neighbors. Clergy such as Knewstub, Egerton, and Daniel Rogers were
welcome in John Winthrop's home as they had been in his father's. With
John's appointment to the commission, new guests visited and were visited, including Robert Reyce, Sir Nathaniel Barnardiston, and Sir Robert
Crane. John was a visitor to Shrubland Hall, the home of the prominent
Bacon family. Hospitality extended across other divides, so that the Winthrops visited and exchanged gifts with the Mannock family, prominent
Catholic recusants on the Essex side of the Stour.

The costs of all this made the rent charge paid to his aunt seem more
burdensome, and the sense of grievance against his uncle's failure to settle
her dower claims festered. During the winter of 1621–22 John traveled to
Dublin.[44] On this visit he arranged for his son John to matriculate at Trinity College and initiated two suits against Elizabeth Powlden Winthrop
and her new husband, Thomas Notte. In the Court of Common Pleas
Winthrop sought to gain from his uncle's estate the thousand marks that
the elder John Winthrop had bound himself to pay if he failed to provide
the purchasers of the manor security against the dower claims, and in the
Irish Chancery he sought an equitable payment for the expenses he had
been forced to bear because of his uncle's failure.[45]

The decision to proceed with the suits may very well have been urged on John by Emmanuel Downing, who had wooed John's sister Lucy and who was to marry her in April 1622. The Winthrops had a long-standing connection with the Downings, since that family lived in Ipswich, where Emmanuel's father, George, was schoolmaster from 1589 to 1610. Emmanuel himself had been a student at Trinity Hall when John Winthrop was at Trinity College.[46] Downing had traveled to Ireland with his brother in the early 1610s and settled in the highly puritan parish of St. Werburgh's.[47] Emmanuel obtained a number of government posts, including that of filacer and exigenter in the Court of Common Pleas. In 1614 he married Anne Ware, the daughter of Sir James Ware, who was then auditor-general of Ireland. The next year Downing was admitted as a member of the King's Inns in Dublin, which allowed him to practice law in the kingdom.[48] Following Anne's death in October 1621, he married Lucy Winthrop in April 1622, thus cementing the connection between the families. Downing was certainly well positioned to advise John Winthrop on recovering funds from his uncle's estates, providing advice that had not been available when such remedy had first been considered in 1614. Moreover, Downing's contacts within the legal system in Ireland made the financial costs and risks involved in prosecution seem more bearable.

The Nottes responded to this attack by filing a bill of complaint against John Winthrop and Thomas Fones in the English Court of Chancery in June 1623, attaching Emmanuel Downing to the suit as well. Their filing covered a wide range of issues and told a story that was not complimentary to the Groton Winthrops. Their bill contained three principal charges. According to them the elder John had been driven to leave England by the actions of his wife, Elizabeth Risby, who had "eloped from him and lived a most lewd and wicked life to his great grief and discontent of mind." Ignoring the fact that the elder John had tried this argument in his effort to gain a divorce and failed, they claimed that rather than paying the widow and suing the Nottes, John Winthrop and Thomas Fones could have used the fact that Elizabeth Risby Winthrop had "lived with other men and so adulterously continued and absented herself from her said husband" to have her "barred and excluded all dower." Second, they claimed that Adam Winthrop had tricked the elder John Winthrop into signing the thousand-mark obligation by omitting to include a promised clause in the purchase agreement that would actually discharge the elder John from the need to provide security against any claim of dower rights. The elder John, they complained, had been "ill of grief and distempered of mind" when the sale was concluded and placed "faith and credit [in] the said Adam, his brother, whom he relied on and trusted." John Winthrop and Thomas Fones, as purchasers, were well aware of this promise. The Nottes raised questions as to why the Winthrops had failed to approach the elder John about the security during the last four years of his life and why they subsequently had waited almost another decade before claiming the thousand marks. Finally, they argued, Adam had harried his brother into selling the manor for a price "far under the value of the said manor and premises," taking advantage of the "great trust and confidence" that the elder John had in Adam as "his brother and counselor at law."[49]

A commission, including John Winthrop's friends Sir Robert Crane and Brampton Gurdon, was appointed by the Chancery to take the statements of John Winthrop and his mother, Anne, in Suffolk, which was done in September. The Winthrops rejected all the claims made in the bill of complaint. They denied that they could have barred Elizabeth Risby Winthrop's claim to dower since the guilty party had been the elder John Winthrop, who had "neglected and cast off" his wife because "his affections were set upon other women." They pointed out that the guilt had been established when the ecclesiastical courts had awarded her alimony, and again when she sued her husband for failure to make those payments, leading to his excommunication for failing to obey the court's judgment. They denied that there had ever been a promise to discharge the elder John from his obligation to provide the purchasers security against the dower claims and asserted that they had taken steps to make their claim earlier but had been frustrated by their unfamiliarity with the situation in Ireland, their lack of effective counsel, and the machinations of the Powldens and Nottes.[50] Furthermore, they indicated that they had been led to believe that the elder John had died only after disposing of his estate in ways that protected it but subsequently discovered that he had actually left the bulk of his estate to Elizabeth Powlden as his "wife" and executor. They tried to turn the tables on that Elizabeth, arguing that while Adam Winthrop had long maintained the estate for his brother and provided his brother with funds, "without any recompense," Elizabeth—whom the elder John had "used as his concubine for many years," he "in his old age being carried away by his intemperate affection" for her—had induced that John to force his Groton kin to buy what they would have been entitled to inherit on his death. The purchase price, they asserted, was beyond what anyone else would have paid at the time, forcing John and Mary Winthrop, Adam and Anne Winthrop, and Thomas Fones to sell property of their own to make the purchase. The Winthrops had dutifully paid Elizabeth Risby Winthrop the alimony she was owed during coverture and then the rent charges to satisfy her dower rights, none of which they had anticipated.[51]

Assessing the merits of the case is made difficult by the fact that much of the supporting documentation does not survive, having, according to the formal answer of Anne and John Winthrop, been sent to Ireland to support the Chancery case there. However, the fact that copies of the bill of sale and other documents were available to send to Ireland and that ultimately Irish Chancery entered a judgment in Winthrop's favor makes it appear that the merits were on his side. The Nottes suit in England may have been designed to apply pressure to persuade the Winthrops to drop their Irish cases.

In late September 1623 John wrote to Margaret that he was awaiting a judgment and said, "I pray God for good success, that we may each of us return to our own home with joy and thankful hearts," yet in the same letter he hinted that he had perhaps strayed from the path of perfect rectitude in an attempt to avoid the ruin that losing the case would entail. Combining his assessment of the personal with the societal, he confessed that "we have cause to fear the worst, in regard that things are so far out of order, and the sins of our own, and of the whole land, do call for judgments rather than blessings."[52] The following month he wrote to Margaret that the case in Chancery was proceeding slowly. The following February the initial answers of the defendants were deemed insufficient for summary action and submitted to Sir Richard More for review; he would determine whether additional subpoenas were necessary.

The case dragged on. Early in 1628 Sir Robert Crane wrote to John with indirect references to it, indicating that he would be coming again "upon commission for examining witnesses [and] must be enforced to examine you to some interrogatories," though he assured his friend that he "would not willingly do anything that might prejudice you."[53] Then, an undated letter from John to Margaret refers to his "business, which hath . . . had success beyond our expectation. We must attend at the Court again tomorrow, when I hope we shall know how things will go."[54] And in March 1628 Lucy Downing wrote to her brother that "I rejoice in your and our so gracious deliverances from such perils as we have escaped."[55] This might indicate that the case had finally been dropped by the Nottes, though the case in Ireland clearly continued to grind on.

Regardless of the merits of their case, by carrying the dispute to the English Chancery the Nottes had created enormous problems for John Winthrop.[56] Some of these were financial, as he would bear the costs of prosecuting a suit in Ireland while defending one in England for the remainder of the decade. Much more serious, the Nottes' suit called into question the sale agreement by which he claimed title to Groton Manor. And the charges that his father defrauded his uncle with his connivance, that his aunt was a whore, and that he knowingly was pursuing an unfounded attack on the executors of his uncle's Irish estate all damaged his public standing at precisely the time when his prospects for advancement had seemed in the ascendant.

THESE PERSONAL TRIALS were played out against the background of Winthrop's concerns for the fate of the godly and of England itself, with his worry over his personal fortunes matched by growing fear for the future of the reformed cause in England and abroad. In retrospect, it is easy to see that the tide began to shift against puritans in the aftermath of the Hampton Court conference. James I was more interested in ensuring that no one would challenge his authority than in actually exercising it, and as long as clergy subscribed to the Three Articles—affirming the ecclesiastical supremacy of the king, that the liturgy of the Book of Common Prayer was not contrary to the word of God and that the clergyman would use the Prayer Book, and that the Thirty-nine Articles of the church were rooted in the Bible—he cared less about any mental reservations they made in doing so or whether they actually conformed. Archbishop Bancroft had spearheaded the demand for clerical subscription, which peaked from 1604 to 1606. Many bishops extended a good deal of sympathy to those who claimed to be troubled by the articles, and the overall number of godly clergy driven from the church was small.[57] However, in the years that followed an increasing number of bishops such as William Laud, Richard Neile, and others began to use their own authority to advance a view of the church, its beliefs, and its ceremonies that was far from the ideals that had flourished in the Stour Valley. And it appears that by the mid-1610s King James was deliberately choosing anti-puritan bishops in dioceses such as Norwich.[58] One of these, Samuel Harsnet, installed as bishop of Norwich in 1619, was committed to root out "'conformable Puritans,' who subscribed in order to escape deprivation."[59] His visitation articles for the diocese demanded that every clerical lecturer be in holy orders and licensed as a preacher, read public prayers according to the Prayer Book while wearing the prescribed surplice, and twice each year administer the sacraments according to the prescribed rites.[60] There was no local protection to be found from these articles in the archdeaconry of Sudbury since Theophilus Kent, a protégé of Harsnet, had been placed in the seat once held by John Still. And so, on January 4, 1621, Adam Winthrop recorded in his diary that "the Thursday sermon ceased at Boxford."[61] The combination lectureship, which had long sustained the faith of the Winthrops and others, was no more.[62]

Similar crackdowns threatened reform throughout the godly kingdom of the Stour. The ability of the godly to respond was weakened by the passing of many of the clerical giants who had struggled hard to advance reform. Oliver Pigge had died in 1591, Edmund Chapman in 1602, Robert Welche in 1605, Roger Weston (Adam Winthrop's brother-in-law) in 1605, Miles Mosse in 1614, Richard Rogers in 1618, George Gifford in 1620, Stephen Egerton in 1621, John Chaplin (John's old tutor) in 1623, John Knewstub in 1624, Henry Sandes in 1626. Others, such as William Ames, had been forced into exile. While some of the older generation such as John Rogers and Samuel Fairclough remained, and younger clergy such as John Wilson, Daniel Rogers, and Thomas Hooker were beginning to exert an influence in the region, the passing of the earlier generation weakened the movement immeasurably.

Such clergymen, and lay puritans such as Winthrop, were also troubled by England's failure to offer strong support for the international reformed cause. The election of King James's son-in-law, Frederick of the Palatinate, to be king of Bohemia precipitated in 1618 the outbreak of what became known as the Thirty Years War. The fate of Bohemia and the German Palatinate soon came to involve the security of the Protestant Netherlands. Germany was the heartland of the Reformation and had provided refuge for English reformers as far back as the reign of Queen Mary. Englishmen had fought to help secure the independence of the Netherlands, and it too had been a home to English religious exiles such as William Ames. For many, the early stages of this new struggle assumed the character of Armageddon, with Catholic and Protestant Europe fighting for supremacy. But whereas in her day Queen Elizabeth—the "Protestant Deborah"—had pursued a militantly Protestant foreign policy, James seemed unwilling to adopt such a course. Though English volunteers fought and died at places like Frankenthall, Bergen op Zoom, and Heidelberg, James flirted diplomatically with Spain and ignored his son-in-law's plight. Clergymen, not all of them puritans, organized to raise funds for the support of Protestant refugees and preached that the cause of reform on the continent was God's cause and should be England's as well. "Shall the members of Christ suffer in other countries, and we profess ourselves to be living members, and yet not sympathize with them?" asked Richard Sibbes. William Bridge urged his listeners to "pray for all the Churches, pray for Germany, the first place of reformation, pray for Holland, your hiding place, and in all your prayers forget not England, still pray for England." John Davenport argued that "the distress of our brethren abroad should quicken us to the use of all means whereby we many be enabled to help them."[63] Bishops hostile to these puritans used such criticisms of the country's foreign policy to persuade James that he had been mistaken to tolerate such vipers in his church, and gradually he began to rely more on the advice of bishops such as Laud, Andrews, and Neile and to approve harsher measures against the puritans. John Winthrop followed these developments with concern. As early as 1621 he noted that "the news from Bohemia is very bad."[64] Later in the decade he expressed his belief that God "hath smitten all the other Churches before our eyes, and hath made them drink of the bitter cup of tribulation."[65]

Of even greater concern to the godly was the erosion of the theological foundations of England's church. The tide of anti-Calvinism that had begun in the sixteenth century gained strength during the reign of James. In 1622 James prohibited preaching on controversial matters, but that edict seemed to be enforced more against those who sought to defend predestinarian views than against those who undermined them. This theological reaction appeared linked to the outlook of churchmen such as Laud, who began to talk about restoring the beauty of holiness and reintroduced ceremonies long thought purged from the church. Laudians captured the church establishment after the accession of Charles I in 1625. The tolerance of local diversity that had marked most of James I's reign was not acceptable to King Charles and his bishops. Nonconforming clergymen were increasingly called before ecclesiastical courts, and parish churchwardens were strictly instructed to bring local practice into accordance with the new church order. Much of this even seemed to hint at a return to Catholicism. Such fears of a Catholic plot were only increased when Charles married the French princess Henrietta Maria and allowed Catholic worship in her household.

In the providential view that John Winthrop and other godly Englishmen held, following the path set forth by God would bring peace and prosperity, while turning away from the path of godliness would bring down divine judgments. A growing chorus warned of punishment to come if England did not reverse her recent course. "We have," Winthrop himself wrote, "humbled ourselves not, to turn from our evil ways, but have provoked him more than all the nations round about us; therefore he is turning the cup towards us." "I am verily persuaded," he continued, that "God will bring some heavy affliction upon this land, and that speedily."[66]

GRAPPLING WITH THESE CONCERNS, Winthrop at one point considered emigrating to Ireland. It was not the Ireland of his uncle that attracted him—the border settlements that offered a chance of prosperity—but the kingdom with a church that seemed to him and many others in the early 1620s to represent all that puritans had striven for in England. Even in Elizabethan days the Protestant Church of Ireland had attracted godly Englishmen. Both Thomas Cartwright and Walter Travers had spent time in Ireland, and Cartwright had even been proposed for an Irish bishopric.[67] The Church of Ireland was independent of the Church of England, though the supreme head of each was the monarch of England. Trinity College, Dublin, reflected the same Calvinist commitment found at puritan Cambridge, which was not surprising since Henry Ussher, who had been at Magdalene, Cambridge, in the time of Adam Winthrop, had been the key figure in its founding. In the 1610s and 1620s the unquestioned head of the church in Ireland was James Ussher, a friend and correspondent of many of the godly clergy in England, including Samuel Ward, Ezekiel Culverwell, and John Cotton. By drawing on the anti-Arminian Lambeth Articles, the Irish Articles of 1615 had committed the Irish church to predestinarian Calvinism to a degree that English reformers could only envy as they fought against the rising tide of Arminianism.[68]

This was the Ireland where John Winthrop determined to send his eldest son for his college education. At the time when he had visited Dublin, the senior fellows of Trinity had just voted to name Samuel Ward—the same Ipswich preacher whose sermon at the Bury assizes had riveted John Winthrop—to be the new Professor of Theological Controversies. When Ward declined the post, it was filled by Joshua Hoyle, a younger but well-regarded puritan who would later play a large role in writing the Westminster Confession of Faith. Hoyle was also rector of the Dublin parish of St. Werburgh. He would be the younger Winthrop's tutor at Trinity. There were other students from the Stour Valley at Trinity as well, including Thomas Crooke, a distant relative of the Winthrops whose family also owned land in Munster. Joseph Ware, Emmanuel Downing's nephew, was also a student. At Trinity Calvinism prevailed, and the surplice was not worn.[69]

This staunchly Protestant Ireland was also the Ireland to which John Winthrop's cousins Joshua and Adam had migrated early in the seventeenth century. Those two sons of William Winthrop had settled in the vicinity of the town of Bandon, a stronghold of Protestantism. In 1611 Joshua Winthrop held almost a thousand acres on the seignory of Sir Bernard Grenville, including the farm called Mischells, just to the northwest of Bandon. Ten English tenants were settled on his land. Adam held a smaller property in the same area.[70] Bandon had been founded by the new English settlers by a patent issued in 1588 and by the mid-1610s was the center of a community of over two thousand, most of whom have been characterized by the town's historian as having been puritans.[71] Richard Newman had been the first vicar of the parish of Kilbrogan in Bandon and in 1615 was replaced by Robert Sutton, who possibly came from a Stour Valley family and who also served the parishes of Ballymodan and Desertserges.[72] John would have known both of his cousins from their frequent visits to Groton, and when the younger John Winthrop was at Trinity, Dublin, his father asked to be commended to his little cousins and to his "goddaughter Susan Nutton," suggesting that both John and his son were in touch with the Bandon Winthrops.[73]

Troubled as he was by personal problems and concerns for the state of the faith in England, it was natural for John Winthrop to consider emigrating to Ireland. While in Dublin in 1622 he discussed with Emmanuel Downing the latter's plans to establish a plantation called Mountrath in the Irish midlands. Downing had acquired the land in 1620 along with his brother Joshua, his brother-in-law James Ware Jr., Samuel Mayart, and Jacob Newman. Over the next two years the group used their connections to strengthen their legal title to the land. On Winthrop's visit he and Downing met with Ware, who had Suffolk roots, Mayhart, who was from Ipswich, and Newman. All had puritan sympathies and were close to James Ussher.[74] If Winthrop was to consider migration, this was the type of godly group with which he would have wanted to associate.

In April 1623 Winthrop wrote that "I wish oft God would open a way to settle me in Ireland, if it might be for his glory."[75] As he looked for such a way he did what he could to assist the Mountrath settlement. He encouraged the migration of some tenants from his Groton estate, including his brother-in-law Samuel Gostlin. When Downing sought a godly minister to preach to the settlers and convert the native population, Winthrop helped the Stour Valley clergyman Richard Olmstead to migrate.[76] In Ireland, Olmstead would expand on his reputation as a preacher at the parish church of Clonenagh, next to the Montrath plantation, where he was supported by Emmanuel Downing and other godly Englishmen. Olmstead preached predestination effectively to the English settlers and publicly attacked the local Irish as governed by "the devil and every base lust, a certain sign of the state of reprobation."[77] His two volumes of published sermons were dedicated to Sir Adam Loftus, lord chancellor of Ireland, who at the time would have been hearing the Winthrop case in Irish Chancery. They were published with the encouragement of James Ussher.

Though he continued to be interested in news of the plantation, John abandoned any thoughts of migrating himself. The lawsuits with the Nottes would have made selling Groton Manor difficult, but more likely he was deterred by the fear that the same forces that were undermining the faith in England would soon be operating in Ireland. In the mid-1620s the king began to take steps to curtail the autonomy of Trinity College, Dublin. Christopher Hampton, named archbishop of Armagh by James I, was instructed to tighten up the discipline of the Irish church and to curb the Scots nonconformists in Ulster. In March 1624 John Winthrop wrote to his son, asking about "how things go in Ireland," at Mountrath and elsewhere, and whether there had been any good results from the king's recent proclamation to crack down on the actions of Jesuits and seminary priests.[78] Any hope that such a policy would be pursued was clouded by the granting of concessions that enabled Catholic landlords to gain more secure title to land potential planters such as Winthrop may have sought and, more important, concessions in the actual practice of the Catholic faith in Ireland.[79]

DISCOURAGED FROM EMIGRATION, John Winthrop turned his energies to rebuilding the walls of the godly kingdom in the Stour Valley. He continued to serve on the commission, doing what he could to enforce a culture of discipline. Through his connections with leading county figures he began to assist in drafting bills to be presented to Parliament. A draft statement of "Common Grievances Groaning for Reformation," a catalogue of complaints that the godly of the Stour Valley and elsewhere had about the tendencies of their times written in the mid-1620s, is partially in the handwriting of Robert Reyce of Preston, Winthrop's friend, and partially in Winthrop's own hand. What prosperity remained in the valley at this time was fragile. Pauperism and vagrancy were increasing, charity was strained, theft and crimes of violence were on the rise.[80] Mixed with more specifically economic and political grievances were the following complaints, most of which are found in the portion written by Winthrop. There was a daily increase in the multitude of papists. Clergy and laity were "unjustly traduced" for participating in illegal religious conventicles, even if they were merely private assemblies of devout Christians seeking to further their spiritual health, such as the conference Winthrop had earlier joined in with Knewstub, Sandes, and others. There was an abundance of "scandalous and dumb ministers" despite there being "many godly and painful ministers which do want benefices and are kept out by these." The holding of plural livings by some clergy was a scandal since it deprived worthy ministers of benefices and deprived parishioners of worship. The bishops were condemned for "punishing the subject for going to another parish to hear a sermon when there is none in their own parish" and for the "suspension and silencing of many painful learned ministers for not conformity in some points of ceremonies, and refusing subscription directed by the late canons." Equally damaging to the religious health of the nation was "the strict oath" that churchwardens were required to take in answering questions posed in ecclesiastical visitations. The petition also addressed legal reform, particularly the great delays in the prosecution of lawsuits, a grievance Winthrop could certainly identify with. The petition suggested that no suit should be prolonged beyond four terms in order to "ease the subject of great charge and trouble."[81]

This can almost be read as a platform that John Winthrop would pursue should he have been elected a member of Parliament, an honor he clearly aspired to and almost received. But following the accession of Charles I new commissions of the peace were issued, and in Suffolk Winthrop was left off the bench. This may have been an oversight since his status put him on the fringe of the previous commission, but it might have reflected harm his reputation had suffered from the Chancery cases or suspicion in some quarters of his puritan sympathies. Yet this did not stop him from trying to influence the elections to the first Parliament of the new reign. Winthrop wrote to Sir Robert Crane proposing that Crane lobby their fellow justices at the next sessions to support Sir Robert Naunton, a member of the king's Privy Council, as one of the county members for Parliament.[82]

Naunton had a reputation as being sympathetic to godly reform and a strong opponent of Catholicism. In 1621 he had been removed from his post as secretary of state for having lobbied too energetically for English aid to the Protestant forces in the Thirty Years War. Winthrop knew Naunton and spoke favorably of his former suffering "for the Commonwealth" and his affection for Suffolk. Winthrop further urged Crane to stand himself for the other county seat or, if he was unwilling, to promote the selection of Sir Nathaniel Barnardiston.[83] Crane was unsure of promoting Naunton since some feared his standing as a privy councillor would limit his ability to act independently in the Parliament, but in the end he circulated Winthrop's letter among his fellow justices at a dinner and added his own endorsement to it. At the event Naunton and Crane were chosen to represent the county, as Winthrop had proposed.

Crane then decided to use his personal influence to secure the election of Winthrop and Barnardiston as MPs for the borough of Sudbury. The electorate of the borough consisted of the mayor, who served as the returning officer, six aldermen, and twenty-four burgesses. Crane had become the principal patron of the borough and had himself represented Sudbury in the Parliaments of 1614, 1621, 1624, and 1625.[84] Winthrop was well known in Sudbury, which was but a few miles west of Groton, and he was a friend of the Reverend John Wilson, lecturer at All Saints Church in Sudbury, a godly preacher whose sermons attracted men and women from throughout the Stour Valley. Wilson had been suspended but restored to his pulpit through the intercession of the earl of Warwick.[85]

Yet something went wrong. On the thirtieth of January in 1626 the Sudbury electors met and chose Sir Nathaniel Barnardiston as one of their parliamentary representatives. But instead of choosing Winthrop they filled the other slot with Thomas Smith, a former mayor of the town and at the time of the election one of the aldermen. The decision proved controversial. The freemen of the town, perhaps egged on by Wilson, sent a petition to the new Parliament charging deceit in the conduct of the election.[86] Shortly thereafter Brampton Gurdon wrote to John Winthrop relating that he had "met the mayor of Sudbury on [the previous] Friday at the Lion in Groton [and] he told me that Sir Robert Crane took it very unkindly at his hand that he [had] labored not to choose you a burgess there." The mayor excused himself by saying that Crane had "never made his mind known to him," but this is unlikely.[87] The culture of discipline that had prevailed in Sudbury during Elizabeth's reign—practices such as enactment of a law whereby those convicted of adultery and fornication were to "be set on a cart and carried about the town with papers set on their heads, declaring the matter and cause of offence"—was being opposed in some quarters, and Winthrop's affiliation with John Wilson and the puritan party may have cost him support.[88] His omission from the commission of the peace may have made some leery of hitching the borough's fortunes to what might have been a declining star. The fact that the Winthrop and Risby names were being dragged through the mud as a result of the Chancery cases might also have been a factor. Barring the discovery of new evidence we will never know why the corporation defied Crane and chose Thomas Smith, and we should not discount the possibility that the decision had less to do with Winthrop and more to do with the ambitions of that former mayor and current alderman. Whatever the reasons for this disappointment, the fact is that John Winthrop would never again come so close to being a member of the nation's Parliament.

The summer did see Winthrop restored to the commission of the peace, no doubt due to the intercession of friends such as Naunton.[89] But any rejoicing about his return to the bench was soon dispelled by a lesson in what such prominence could entail in the kingdom of Charles I. Benevolences, as they were referred to, were advances of money requested by Tudor and Stuart monarchs to provide additional revenue in times of emergency when there was no Parliament in session to vote subsidies. But Charles I would establish a reputation among some of his subjects for demanding such loans when no emergency justified them, in order to avoid calling Parliaments that could approve more regular taxation. The Parliament of 1626 protested the drift of England's foreign and religious policy and then brought charges against the king's favorite, the duke of Buckingham, who was accused of influencing the king in dangerous directions. King Charles responded by dissolving the Parliament before it had authorized the subsidies the king needed and by demanding a benevolence and appointing commissions to collect the money in the provinces. John Winthrop was one of the more than sixty commissioners named for Suffolk, a group that included friends such as Robert Naunton, Edmund Bacon, Thomas Jermyn, Robert Crane, William Spring, Nathaniel Barnardiston, and Brampton Gurdon.[90]

Opposition to the loan was considerable, particularly among those who had been frustrated by the defeat of the reform agenda that had resulted from the dissolution of Parliament. Those who resisted were heartened when in November the bench of central court judges, led by the lord chief justice, declined to proclaim the loan's legality. Leading peers spoke out against the benevolence and indicated that they would refuse to pay it.[91] Dedham's Reverend John Rogers and other clergymen encouraged resistance.[92] Essex, where puritan supporters of the earl of Warwick had been removed from the county commission, was a particular hotbed of resistance, and Sir Francis Barrington, Sir William Masham, and Sir Harbottle Grimstone were all imprisoned for refusing the loan.[93] In December John Winthrop and his fellow Suffolk commissioners were called to Bury St. Edmunds to take their oath before members of the Privy Council. Winthrop went anticipating that he would be joining Barrington and the other resisters in a London prison, but, he recorded thankfully, "it hath seemed good to the Lord's most wise providence to dispose otherwise of it." On the other hand, "Sir Nathaniel Barnardiston came not to Bury till Saturday near noon, when all was done, and when I was sent out of the town, the Lords sent for him."[94] Barnardiston had evidently hoped to come late to avoid confrontation, but instead found himself bound over to appear in London for refusing to take the oath. Disconcerted, he initially backed down—thus giving the government a propaganda victory—but later recanted and was imprisoned.[95]

Winthrop's sympathies were certainly clear. He asked his son John, who was then in London, to "go into Southwark to the Marshalsea [prison], and remember my love to Sir Francis Barrington, and acquaint him with how things have gone in our country [i.e., county], but you must do it in private."[96] Thankful for his own escape, he had been made aware of the fact that as an officer of the king he might very well have to choose more than once between his principles on the one hand and his office and his personal freedom on the other. And soon he would be placed in a situation that would demand even harder choices.

ON JANUARY 15, 1627, JOHN WINTHROP JR. wrote to his father that "Mr. Lattimer, one of the Attorneys of the Court of Wards, is yesterday dead, so as now that place is void." Emmanuel Downing, who was already an attorney of the court, saw a chance for his brother-in-law to gain the post, which was at the disposal of Sir Robert Naunton as master of the Court of Wards. Downing, through the younger Winthrop, urged Winthrop to rush to London and then ride out to meet Naunton when he returned to town for the start of the next law term, thus advancing his candidacy before the "King's or Duke's letter may be a means to make it disposed of some other way."[97] The strategy worked, and Winthrop was appointed to the post within a few days of the start of the term. He was granted a special admission to the Inner Temple in order to facilitate his work.[98]

Established by Henry VIII, the Court of Wards was charged with assigning wardships of minor heirs who inherited lands that were held by various forms of feudal tenure. This affected the majority of the gentry. The officers of the court were the master, surveyor, attorneys, receiver-general, and auditors. The court had developed a well-earned reputation for corruption by the early seventeenth century, with its officials amassing fortunes by accepting gifts from rapacious individuals who sought wardships for the opportunities they provided to strip a ward's estate of its assets. To curtail such abuses, new royal instructions were issued in December 1618. Naunton, appointed master in 1624, initially appears to have administered the court fairly in accord with the new policies, but that situation had changed shortly before Winthrop was appointed. The very opposition to court political and religious thinking that had led Winthrop to support Naunton's election to Parliament meant that Naunton was close to losing the king's favor, and he decided to feather his nest while he still could. In the view of his biographer, Naunton had to have had a role in the decision "to turn loose the hidden wardship hunters in earnest."[99] The reforms were undone and a system reintroduced that led to many officials of the court, down to the lowly clerks, amassing great fortunes.[100]

Emmanuel Downing, like Winthrop an attorney of the court, clearly engaged in dubious practices. On at least one occasion in 1628 he purchased a hidden wardship and sold it a month later for a profit to someone who would never have been directly granted it.[101] John Winthrop did not amass a fortune, but his actions do raise some questions about how closely he approached the boundaries of propriety, as when in March 1628 he sent a "present" to Naunton at the latter's Essex home and it was "accepted . . . very thankfully."[102] Temptations did not always come in the form of bribes. Winthrop acknowledged that he sometimes cared too much about what others thought of him, and in this context it is important to note that during his tenure at Wards he was approached for assistance by many friends and kin concerned with business before the court, including Brampton Gurdon, Sir William Masham, William Clopton, Miles Corbet, Sir John Wentworth, Robert Stansby, Miles Burroughes, Arthur Tyndal, and Sir Henry Mildmay.[103] Working in a climate of venality, the temptation to act in such a way as to advance the interests of these men must have been strong. But we know that Brampton Gurdon used inside information to petition for the custody of a Somerset heir who was being raised by a papist mother, and Winthrop could have been the source of that information. Also questionable, at least by modern standards of conflict of interest, was his use of his position to gain for himself the wardship of Samuel Fones, his nephew, after the death of Thomas Fones in 1629. Though the elder Fones had in his will entrusted Samuel to his brother-in-law's care, this did place Winthrop in the position of supervising Samuel's interest in any funds owed him by Winthrop from the purchase of Groton Manor.[104]

John had never learned how to accommodate worldly ambition and godliness and held himself to a higher standard than friends such as Emmanuel Downing. With his strict conscience he found it difficult to negotiate through the corridors of power that he had finally entered. His physical health often reflected his inner turmoil, and it does not take much imagination to see the serious illness he suffered in December 1628 as brought on in part by agonies of conscience. In his spiritual diary he recorded that "at London at the end of Michaelmas term I fell into a dangerous, hot, malignant fever."[105] In a letter to Margaret after the worst was over he admitted that for a time "it was uncertain" if he would live.[106] But the physical trial became an occasion for confronting his sins, for spiritual cleansing, and for rededication, as the Lord "sanctified it unto me, by discovering many corruptions which had prevailed over me, giving me Repentance, and pardon for them, thereby subduing the flesh and giving more strength to the spirit." It pleased God "to reveal his favor and goodness abundantly towards me, so I never had more sweet Communion with him, then in that affliction." When he appeared on the verge of death "it pleased him [God] to restore me to life." And "among the benefits" he reaped, "the greatest of all was the assurance he gave me of my salvation, and grace over some corruptions which had gotten mastery of me, which increased my experience of his truth and faithfulness in disposing the worst condition of his children to his best good."[107]

In the closing years of the decade John was faced with a choice. He had the chance to ally himself with men such as Naunton and seek power, riches, and the acclaim of the nation's leaders. Such success would enable him to shower Margaret and his children with everything they may have desired. On the other hand, the path of godliness seemed increasingly to lead to an uncertain future that might include loss of office, financial ruin, and perhaps even prison. The epitaph he placed on his father's tomb was "Heaven the Country: Christ the Way." John Winthrop came to accept the fact that for him as well the way of Christ was to be followed rather than the way of men. Heaven—not London, not Ireland, not even the Stour Valley—was the country he too aspired to, and it was to be found wherever the way of Christ could best be pursued.

8

The Decision to Migrate

JULY 28, 1629. John Winthrop and Emmanuel Downing were riding toward the Sempringham estate of the earl of Lincoln. They had left the rolling hills of Suffolk a few days before and were traversing the East Anglian fens, twelve hundred square miles of low-lying land that is a mixture of water, bog, and swamp. The underlying peat nourished grasses, sedges, rushes, and wildflowers along the fringes of the open waters. They moved along narrow causeways from village to village, each perched on high ground rising out of the marshy landscape. Some of those primitive roads dated back to the days of the Romans. In the morning the mists rising off the slow-moving, almost stagnant water obscured the path until burned off by the summer sun. In the evening there were brilliant sunsets over the flat terrain.

On this particular day, as they approached the crossing of the River Ouse near Littleport, they could see in the distance the Isle of Eels, where, many years before, Hereward the Wake had held out against the forces of William the Conqueror. On the highest point of that island, the sun was reflecting off the lantern tower of the cathedral of Ely. Riding along, they saw locals fishing for eels, abundant in the surrounding waters and a staple of the local diet.

But the landscape only occasionally drew their attention. They were talking about the commencement at Cambridge earlier in the month. There the gathered clergy had discussed the plan Dorchester's Reverend John White had been promoting for a puritan settlement in New England. White and his friend and parishioner John Humfry had been members of the Dorchester Company of Adventurers, a West Country effort to establish colonial fisheries. Out of the ashes of that venture had arisen the Massachusetts Bay Company, combining some of the original members with new investors from London and East Anglia. An advance party of colonists had been sent out under the leadership of John Endecott and established an outpost at Naumkeag, which they had renamed Salem. Winthrop had been urged by Isaac Johnson and other members of the new company to join the enterprise, and he and Downing were traveling to attend a meeting of the company leadership being hosted by the earl of Lincoln. Though the earl was hosting the meeting, this enterprise was led for the most part by gentry and clergy rather than aristocrats. On the agenda was the suggestion that leaders of the company should migrate to the new England themselves rather than governing its affairs from London or elsewhere in England.

Preoccupied, perhaps, by their discussion, Winthrop was inattentive. His horse stumbled, slipped, and fell into a bog. John found himself immersed in water up to his waist in a life-threatening accident. He struggled to right himself in the foul-smelling fen waters. The footing was treacherous, and he was tangled with his horse. But, as he later wrote, "the Lord preserved me from further danger. Blessed be his name."[1] Once again God had shown him special favor. What did this mean? What message was God sending him?

Ↄ

*J*OHN WINTHROP'S DECISION for New England had many roots. His interest in carrying the gospel and the culture of England to distant lands was first stimulated by Samuel Purchas as he listened to that chronicler's tales of earlier pilgrimages and explorations. When he had pondered moving to Ireland, the mission of aiding in the civilizing of that Catholic land had been part of the appeal. He followed the trials and tribulations of Englishmen in the Chesapeake during the early seventeenth century. But equally important as the draw of foreign mission was the fact, as he would once express it, that God had been weaning him of his affection for England and the Stour Valley. Concern for his family, concern for England, concern for the cause of religious reform—all these began to point to his undertaking an errand into the American wilderness. If he was still wavering on his journey to Sempringham, being saved from danger in the fens was the sort of experience he would have seen as a sign. At last he seemed to sense what God had chosen him for. He was ready to serve.

A YEAR EARLIER THE HOPES of puritans and other Englishmen had been raised by the calling of a new Parliament that was to meet on March 17, 1628. Finally, perhaps, grievances about taxation could be redressed and concerns about changes in the nation's religious course addressed. Elections were held in late February and early March. In Essex Winthrop's cousin Sir Henry Mildmay, whom he often visited, was elected for the borough of Maldon. Mildmay, attacked by one of the king's supporters as "bred a Puritan in blood and education too," had contributed to the school that the Reverend Thomas Hooker had opened at Little Baddow, near Graces.[2] He would be joined in the Parliament by others well known to Winthrop, including Sir Nathaniel Rich and Sir Harbottle Grimstone.

In Suffolk the members sent to Westminster included many of John's fellow justices, but there is no indication that his candidacy was promoted. The failure to secure his election to the previous Parliament may have discouraged any efforts to revive such plans. The fact that in early February he had again been questioned by a commission appointed by Chancery regarding the Notte case may have again raised questions about his character. And his affiliation with the Court of Wards may not have benefited his reputation among the county leadership, particularly if he had not been as helpful as some of them had hoped in promoting their interests before that court. Sir Robert Crane was returned from Sudbury along with Sir William Poley. John Winthrop was present at the choice of the county members, which was held at Ipswich on February 25.[3] In the initial return Sir Nathaniel Barnardiston and the famous jurist Sir Edward Coke were elected as the knights for the county, but neither generated much enthusiasm.[4] Barnardiston's popularity had suffered when he dropped his initial resistance to the king's benevolence in 1627, and his recantation of that surrender had not fully restored his reputation. Coke, though having earned a reputation as a champion of popular liberties in earlier Parliaments, was viewed by some as a court figure and likewise elicited little enthusiasm.[5] After Coke, who had also been chosen to represent Buckinghamshire, declined the Suffolk seat, a by-election was held. The county elite was divided between Sir William Spring and Sir John Rous. We do not know where Winthrop stood on this choice. His friend Sir Francis Barrington wrote to stir another Winthrop ally, Sudbury's John Wilson, to support Rous. But it was Spring, Winthrop's close personal friend, who was chosen for the seat.

Winthrop's friendships with members of Parliament, and especially with Sir William Spring, provided him with opportunities to influence legislation without being a member of the Commons. His strong support for the culture of discipline is reflected in a draft he prepared for a parliamentary bill designed to prevent "the loathsome vice of drunkenness and other disorders in Alehouses." In particular he was concerned with the proliferation of alehouses and the fact that it has become "the common practice for everyone to strive to exceed other in the strength of their beer, that they may draw the more customers to them." This diverted barley from the hungry and encouraged drunkenness, which was a sin that would contribute to the "shame and ruin of our nation."[6]

When the Parliament adjourned in the summer, there was still reason to hope for reform. The king had been pressured to grudgingly accept the Petition of Right, which cited the Magna Carta and a variety of statutes to spell out the restrictions on the exercise of royal prerogative powers. The assassination of the duke of Buckingham in August removed a contentious figure whom many blamed for the distasteful policies of recent years. But

when Parliament reassembled in January 1629 it was clear that the fundamental issues that divided Charles from his subjects still remained. The king
had continued to use questionable means to collect revenues and had promoted various clerics whom puritans branded as "Arminian" to positions of
authority—including William Laud to the see of London and Richard
Montagu to Chichester.[7] The House of Commons created a committee to
examine the condition of the church, and in late February that group condemned the "subtle and pernicious spreading of the Arminian faction" and
proposed that in appointing bishops the king seek the advice of his Privy
Council and confer such posts upon "learned, pious, and orthodox men."[8]
One of those who spoke forcefully against the church's drift toward popery was Winthrop's cousin Sir Henry Mildmay. Fearful that the Speaker
of the House had been instructed to dissolve the Parliament, on March 2
members of the Commons forcibly held the Speaker in his chair while the
House passed resolutions declaring that anyone who advanced "innovation in religion" or paid or collected certain royal levies be considered an
"enemy to this kingdom and commonwealth."[9] Emmanuel Downing communicated the dramatic events to Winthrop, relating how the Speaker "was
by force kept in" and how members had "commanded the Sergeant to lock
the door, ere the [king's] messenger entered."[10] Charles did indeed dissolve the Parliament and imprisoned nine members of the Commons for
their role in the events of March 2. He would not call another Parliament
until forced to in 1640.

These developments bore heavily on Winthrop and others who had
hoped that Parliament might redress the course of church and state in what
he called "these so evil and declining times."[11] Shortly after the dissolution
of the Parliament, Royal Instructions were issued to the two archbishops.
As historian Tom Webster has characterized them, "Afternoon sermons
were to be converted into catechizing by question and answer; every lecturer was to read divine service in his hood and surplice before his lecture;
market-town lectures were 'to be read by a Company of grave and Orthodox Divines [as determined by Laud and his fellow anti-Calvinists]' from
the same diocese; [and] corporation lecturers were not to preach until they
professed a willingness to take a benefice" in which their conformity could
be more carefully regulated.[12]

On the Essex side of the Stour godly clergy began to feel the hot breath
of their new bishop. By 1629 Laud had begun to establish a network of parochial and other informants who would report on those who failed to adhere
to the new instructions or who manifested what he viewed as ceremonial
nonconformity or doctrinal unsoundness. Dedham's roaring John Rogers
was reported for not wearing the surplice and would soon be suspended.[13] In
May 1629 Margaret Winthrop had written to John of "the going of the

young folk to Dedham, where many thanks were given to God."[14] John had made that journey many times himself, often in the company of his father. But the opportunity to be stirred by Rogers's fiery preaching was now threatened. Now, in 1629, Rogers published *A Treatise of Love*, which he addressed to his "loving neighbors of Dedham," who might soon be deprived of his services. He hoped that they would be as a city on a hill, so that "other towns, seeing your well-doing and good order, may be provoked by your example."[15] But he feared for the future, for "when some would bring in the ministry of the Word, and others oppose it, how must not the Devil needs [sic] have his throne in such a place."[16] Rogers was not the only clerical friend of Winthrop to feel such pressure. His son, Daniel Rogers, who had succeeded Richard Rogers at Wethersfield, was another. Thomas Hooker was forced to move. Nathaniel Ward, John Beadle, Thomas Shepard, and Thomas Welde suffered from this new scrutiny as well.[17]

As THE CLOUDS CONTINUED to gather over the godly, and as his own situation worsened, Winthrop again began to consider emigration. This time he turned his eyes to New England. The colony that was to become Massachusetts had humble beginnings in the efforts of a small band of investors from Dorchester, led by the Reverend John White. White was a well-known evangelical Calvinist who had been installed in 1605 as rector of Holy Trinity Church in Dorchester, in the west country of England.[18] A devastating fire in that town in 1613 was seen by many as a "fire from heaven" and fueled a major campaign of the godly to purge Dorchester of sin and make it a model Christian community. Their agenda called for discipline, order, and charity. One element of the campaign involved providing the children of the poor with rudimentary education and vocational training. Funds to support the effort came from many sources, including a contribution from the lottery that had been established to finance some of the costs of the Virginia Colony. In 1622 a municipal brewhouse was founded primarily for the purpose of supporting these efforts from its profits. The Dorchester Company was conceived as a similar profit-making venture.

The company received a patent from the Council for New England in 1623. That council represented a reorganization of the old Virginia Company of Plymouth and had been granted a charter from the king in November 1620. At a time when the geography of the region was still imperfectly understood, the grant gave the council control over a vast territory stretching from the fortieth to the forty-eighth parallel, which overlapped other colonial grants. The council was a board of proprietors rather than a joint stock company and would be an important player in the history of New England during John Winthrop's lifetime. Its members included some of the leading peers of the realm, among them Robert Rich, the second earl of Warwick. The driving force behind the formation of the council was Sir Ferdinando Gorges, who dreamed of establishing a feudal empire in the New World.[19]

The Council for New England was empowered to establish its own colonies and also to grant patents to other groups, which is what it chose to do in the case of the Dorchester Company. That company's first governor was White's friend Sir Walter Earle. Its members included members of the local gentry, prosperous Dorchester townsmen, and some clergy of neighboring parishes. John Humfry, who was to become a key figure in the evolution of the enterprise, was the company treasurer. The goal of the investors was to make money from fishing ventures along the coast of New England, generating profits that would have supplemented the charitable ventures in Dorchester itself. White, like Samuel Purchas, also saw England's mission abroad in terms of creating a bulwark against the spread of Catholicism in the new overseas worlds and of spreading the true Word to the native population. It is likely too that, opposed as he and other puritans were to separatist impulses, White wished to counteract the role of the Pilgrims who had settled along Cape Cod in 1620. The Dorchester Company established a series of year-round fishing settlements sustained by agriculture along Cape Ann on the coast of Massachusetts. But the enterprise failed, in large part because where the fishing was good, the land was unsuitable to farming, though ill management also contributed.[20]

In 1625 Roger Conant was hired to take charge of the Cape Ann outposts. He moved the twenty or thirty settlers to a new location along the coast that bore the native name Naumkeag. Meanwhile, in England the company was being dissolved, the losses greater than the investors wished to bear. Some of its members were not willing to give up on the colony and scrambled to find new support. White and Humfry organized a small group, including some newcomers such as John Endecott, that sought and received a patent in 1628 from the Council for New England, empowering them as "the New England Company" to establish a colony between the rivers Charles and Merrimack. The actual events are shrouded in mystery since the Council for New England was largely moribund at this time, with no surviving records indicating any meetings or decisions. In 1622 and 1623 the council had distributed much of the land it controlled to its prominent members as a way to assuage those who had invested money with no tangible returns. With Gorges occupied with military responsibilities, the president of the council was the earl of Warwick. As a supporter of godly enterprises as well as a colonial promoter, Warwick was likely sympathetic to the request for a patent. The actual document he granted has not survived, and there are questions as to what bounds were specified in the patent and whether it came from the council (at a meeting that has left no record) or was a grant from Warwick himself from the lands he had been awarded in the 1622 distribution of the council's assets.[21]

Whatever the circumstances of the patent, for the enterprise to succeed, new investors were desperately needed, and White and Humfry turned to their contacts in London for support.[22] Prosperous merchants such as Matthew Craddock, Thomas Hewson, and George Foxcroft invested, as did the minister Hugh Peter and the gentleman Sir Richard Saltonstall.[23] A number of the new investors were members of the Inns of Court, which may be where the Winthrops first heard of the venture. One of the first steps taken by the new company was to dispatch John Endecott to New England to take charge of the remaining outposts and to prepare for a larger enterprise.

Troubled perhaps by questions about the adequacy of the patent they had received, Saltonstall, Craddock, the London lawyer John White, and other well-connected members of the company sought a more secure title to the region by petitioning for a royal charter, which was granted to them as the Governor and Company of the Massachusetts Bay in New England on March 4, 1629. This ignored the fact that the 1620 grant of the same land to the Council for New England had never been rescinded. Such awarding of overlapping charters was not uncommon at this time, but Gorges would later challenge the legitimacy of the Massachusetts charter on these grounds as well as questioning the boundaries provided therein.[24]

A month after receiving the royal charter, the Bay Company contracted with the Reverends Francis Higginson, Samuel Skelton, and Francis Bright to journey to New England to "do their true endeavor in their places of the ministry as well as preaching, catechizing . . . [and] teaching, or causing to be taught, the Company's servants and their children, as also the savages and their children."[25] At the end of the month John Endecott, already in the Bay, was given the title of governor of the settlement.[26] Naumkeag was renamed Salem, which in Hebrew means peaceful. In England the company continued to reach out for investors. John Humfry had married Susan Fiennes-Clinton, the daughter of the third earl of Lincoln, which brought him into contact with the godly circles in Lincolnshire that included that family. Many of these men and women would be attracted to the new venture and become important figures in the early history of Massachusetts. Isaac Johnson also married a daughter of the earl, Lady Arabella Fiennes-Clinton. Thomas Dudley had served as steward for Theophilus Clinton, the fourth earl of Lincoln, a position also held by Simon Bradstreet, who would soon marry Dudley's daughter Anne. John Cotton, the minister of St. Botolph's in Boston, Lincolnshire, was friend and religious counselor to the earl's household, to which he was taken to recover when he and his first wife were taken grievously ill. Thomas Leverett, William Coddington, Atherton Hough, and Richard Bellingham were members of Cotton's congregation.

Anne Marbury Hutchinson was but one of many in the surrounding region who gadded to Boston to listen to Cotton preach.

There are a variety of ways in which John Winthrop may have come into contact with the growing number of Bay Company promoters. Spending much of his time in London, mingling with fellow lawyers and attending religious services in the churches of the city, he would have encountered many of the London investors, especially those who were involved in on-going efforts to oppose Laudian initiatives and reform the church. Thirteen of the investors, including the Reverend John Davenport and the lawyer John White, had connections to the feoffees for impropriation, trustees who raised funds and used them to purchase church livings in which godly clergy could be installed.[27] One of them, John White, was Thomas Fones's lawyer and well known to John Winthrop.[28] These godly circles were not the only places where Winthrop would have met Bay Company members. Some of the investors had business before the Court of Wards that Winthrop was involved with. Dr. Lawrence Wright, who tended to John during his serious illness in the winter of 1628–29, was the brother of Nathaniel Wright, who was an assistant of the Massachusetts Bay Company, and he might easily have passed time at his patient's sickbed filling him in on the plans of the adventurers.[29]

Winthrop would also have heard of the company from East Anglian friends. Cicely Chaderton, the wife of Emmanuel's Master Lawrence Chaderton and sister of Winthrop's friend Ezekiel Culverwell, referred to herself as Isaac Johnson's "grandmother" in her correspondence with him.[30] Herbert Pelham, one of the investors, whom Winthrop referred to as his "cousin," had married Jemima Waldegrave, perhaps the Waldegrave daughter who had considered marrying John Winthrop Jr., and lived near Groton at Bures.[31] Pelham's interest in colonization had been nurtured by tales of his uncle, Lord de la Warr, an early governor of Virginia. His father-in-law, Thomas Waldegrave, was also a friend of Winthrop and an investor in the Bay Company by April 1629.

All of this is suggestive, since there is no record of the myriad contacts and conversations that drew Winthrop into the enterprise. He had shared the idea of emigrating to Massachusetts with Deane Tyndal by April 1629.[32] In mid-May he wrote to Margaret bemoaning the state of affairs in England and alluded to the possibility of emigration when he expressed his confidence that "if the Lord seeth it will be good for us, he will provide a shelter and a hiding place for us."[33] Thomas Motte of nearby Stoke was leaning toward migration and wrote to Winthrop about putting him in touch with lawyer White to discuss the matter further.[34] On June 5 John was back in London and wrote to Margaret that he was "still more confirmed in that Course which I propounded to thee, and so are my brother and sister Downing, The good Lord direct and bless us in it."[35] He took steps to surrender his office of attorney at the Court of Wards and around the nineteenth of June wrote that his office was gone, as were his chambers at the Inns.[36] Though he pledged to Margaret that "we shall never part so long again, till we part for a better meeting in heaven," he added that "where we shall spend the rest of our short time I know not. The Lord, I trust, will direct us in mercy. My comfort is that thou art willing to be my companion in what place or condition soever in weal or in woe."[37]

But as John discussed the possible move with his friends, the advice he received was generally negative. Margaret's brother Deane Tyndal bemoaned that if the Winthrops moved to New England, distance would keep them from being as "useful and comfortable one to another as now we are, which makes me still desire your stay here," and added that "Mr. [Daniel] Rogers of Wethersfield is against your going, and would fain meet with you, for your reasons do not satisfy him."[38] Robert Reyce pointed out that there were "a thousand shipwrecks which may betide."[39] Some ships never made it to the New World, and on those that did passenger illness and death were commonplace. Among those who made it to the Virginia colony the mortality rate had been horrendous, with around 80 percent of all arrivals dying during the first fifteen years. And it was not just Virginia. John Carver, the first governor of Plimoth, had died in the plantation's first year along with many other colonists. Furthermore, as Winthrop himself recognized, "those plantations, which have been formerly made, succeeded ill."[40] Life in early America was difficult at best, brutal all too often. The comforts men such as Winthrop were accustomed to in England were absent in the colonies. Diet was meager and starvation a real threat. The climate was difficult for Englishmen to adapt to, and some colonies had proved the breeding ground for virulent diseases against which the newcomers had little resistance. Hostility from the natives was as likely as cooperation. And when colonies struggled, civil order frequently dissolved, since the "authority" of the governor was "not regarded, alleging he had no authority in that place, being not acquired, hereditary, or conquered, settled, or established place, as here at home."[41]

Winthrop's friends, like Winthrop himself, had read their Richard Hakluyt, Samuel Purchas, and John Smith. They knew of Humfry Gilbert's misfortune, the loss of the Roanoke colony, and Virginia's Starving Time and "Great Massacre." For Winthrop, "to adventure your whole family upon so many manifest uncertainties standeth not with your wisdom and long experience," wrote Reyce. Besides, Winthrop was in his forties. "Plantations," Reyce warned him, "are for young men, that can endure all pains and hunger."[42]

WHEN WINTHROP CONSIDERED EMIGRATION to Ireland, he had worried over the ability of the plantations there to protect against the threats to religion that were already undermining the church in England. He was familiar as well with how the success of Jamestown's government had been compromised by the attempt to dictate events in America from London boardrooms. Settling in a new world would be risky if control was exercised by investors three thousand miles away whose needs and objectives might change as time went on. Consequently he would have been encouraged to hear of a plan being suggested by some of the Bay's promoters that the charter and seat of governance of the colony be moved to the New World. At a meeting of the company's General Court on July 28, the governor, Matthew Craddock, proposed "that for the advancement of the plantation, the inducing and encouraging persons of worth and quality [to] transplant themselves and families thither, and for other weighty reasons, ... to transfer the government of the plantation to those that shall inhabit there, and not to continue the same in subordination to the Company here."[43] Among the weighty reasons not explicitly expressed was the fact that the colonists would thereby achieve a semi-autonomy that would give them considerable freedom to shape a society as they would. Those in attendance in London were asked to reflect on the matter pending a later vote. The proposal had been crafted in consultation with those Lincolnshire investors who were planning to meet in Sempringham, with Isaac Johnson serving as the contact between the Lincolnshire and London leaders.[44] The proposal was probably also discussed with the godly ministers gathered at the Cambridge commencement. Isaac Johnson wrote that it was "an excellent time for Mr. Winthrop to have been this commencement at Cambridge, where I hear are many reverend Divines, to consider of Mr. White's call."[45]

It would not have been lost on Winthrop that if this proposal passed, the opportunities for and responsibilities of true leadership in the New World would be greater, since the local authorities would indeed be the government and not just the agents of the English corporation. And men were already suggesting that he would be an ideal person to bear such responsibility, as indicated by Johnson's interest in Winthrop being at the Cambridge commencement.

Thus, together with Emmanuel Downing, he found himself riding through the fens to Lincolnshire. Those who gathered in Sempringham represented a godly faction among the company membership. Joining them in the discussions were the Reverends John Cotton, Thomas Hooker, and Roger Williams.[46] The group was particularly interested in making the erection of a godly commonwealth in New England the company's priority. Transferring the government of the colony to America would be a way of accomplishing that goal if the majority of the company officials who emigrated were themselves members of the faction. Much of the meeting would have been devoted to discussion of how to bring this about without arousing the suspicions of those who would have opposed the plan as involving a separation from or attack on the established church. Subsequent events make it clear that Winthrop not only agreed with this goal but also impressed those assembled as a potential leader of the venture.

On August 8 Lucy Downing wrote to John Winthrop Jr. that Emmanuel and John had been in Lincolnshire for a fortnight, that John urgently wished to see his son John, and that Forth Winthrop was planning on sailing to New England in the spring.[47] Discussions with Margaret and his sons helped Winthrop to make his plans. When he attended the session of the commission of the peace at Bury St. Edmunds on August 12, he presented his fellow justices and others with the arguments for emigration. His friend Robert Reyce, who could not attend the meeting, heard of Winthrop's stance and continued to oppose the plan, stressing his conviction that "the church and commonwealth here at home hath more need of your best ability in these dangerous times than any remote plantation, which may be performed by persons of lesser worth and apprehension."[48] But it was to no avail. By the time of the meeting at Bury Winthrop was emerging as a spokesman for the colonization of Massachusetts. He was the principal author of a document, usually referred to as the "General Observations," that was a list of reasons for the launching of the Massachusetts Bay Company. This was likely prepared for the Bury meeting and then circulated further in godly circles. It survives in multiple, slightly variant copies. Each version sets forth the reasons for colonization, lists objections that had been raised, and proceeds to answer them.[49] There is a duality to the list, and indeed through much of Winthrop's justification of the errand into the wilderness—reasons for going to America, and reasons for leaving England. Winthrop sought to persuade his readers that God had special tasks to be performed by those who received the call to migrate. He combined these with discussion of the troubles facing the godly in England, interpreting these both as warnings of a judgment to come and also as hardships God was employing to wean the chosen from their comfortable homes so that they might more readily embrace the challenge to which they were being called.

In the order he presented them, the reasons were as follows:

- To carry the gospel into America and thus "to raise a bulwark against the kingdom of Antichrist which the Jesuits labor to raise in all parts of the world."
- With the Protestant churches throughout "Europe being brought to desolation it cannot be but that the like judgment is coming upon us, and who knoweth but that God hath prepared this place for a refuge for many whom he meaneth to save."
- England "groaneth under her inhabitants," with many ill consequences of overpopulation. In another version this is explained

more fully: "This land grows weary of her Inhabitants, so as man which is the most precious of all Creatures, is here more vile and base, then the earth they tread upon: so as children, neighbors, and friends (especially if they be poor) are rated the greatest burdens, which if things were right, would be the chiefest earthly blessings."

- Inflation has soared so that "no man's estate will suffice him to keep sail with his equal and he that doeth not must live in contempt," leading many to engage in deceitful and ungodly behavior in order to maintain their status, and making it impossible "for a good upright man to maintain his charge and to live comfortably in his profession."

- Oxford and Cambridge universities, "the fountains of learning and religion, are so corrupted" (and expensive) that "many children of best wits and fairest hopes are perverted, corrupted, and utterly overthrown by the multitude of evil examples and licentious government of those seminaries."

- Since "the earth is the Lord's garden and he hath given it to the sons of men to be tilled and improved," it was foolish to expend enormous labor and expense to hold and improve a few acres in England when the same effort would transform much more of the vast reaches of the land God had prepared for them in the New World. Dismissing, as did most of his fellow Englishmen, the land claims of the native Americans, who did not in a European sense "improve the land," Winthrop felt that it was against God's will that "whole countries as fruitful and convenient for the use of man [be allowed] to lie waste without improvement."

- Nothing could "be a better or more honorable work than to help raise and support a particular church while it is in the bud and infancy of its life"; the timely assistance of Winthrop and his fellow colonists could spell the difference between the success and ruin of the church in New England.

- "If such as are known to be godly and live in wealth and prosperity here," as opposed to less reputable men, "shall forsake all this to join themselves to this [New England] Church, and to run the hazard with them of a hard and mean condition," it would refute the claims of those who dismissed the enterprise as driven by worldly ends, encourage "God's people in their prayers for the plantation, and also . . . encourage others to join the more willingly in it."[50]

These reasons boil down to a view that England was in trouble. Unprecedented population growth and runaway inflation had led men and women to begrudge their obligations to their neighbors. Fearful of the changes they experienced in a new, market-driven world, they compromised their souls to secure their wealth and status. While overpopulation and inflation might be looked upon as God's means to wean affection from England, Winthrop also presented them as causes of sin; he was distressed with how changing circumstances had led men to behave. The nation had turned from the path of righteousness and the social gospel, and God threatened judgment on England, just as he had punished the Israelites when they had turned from him, just as he had punished the backsliding Protestants on the continent in Winthrop's own lifetime. Unstated in Winthrop's reasons, in part because it would have been impolitic and risky, was the belief that punishment was pending for England in large part because the king and bishops had failed to keep the nation on the path of righteousness and, indeed, in recent years had pursued policies that encouraged the drift from God's way. The closest that he did come to acknowledging this was his lament regarding the corruption of Oxford and Cambridge, the fountains of religion.

America offered a fresh start. There a chosen remnant of the godly would be free to follow the path of righteousness while obeying God's command to increase and multiply. They would transform the vast and unimproved lands of the New World into a bulwark against Antichrist. In meetings with those considering joining the enterprise, he began to spell out what that bulwark would look like, setting forth aspects of his vision of the new England on which he would later elaborate.

On August 26 a group of twelve of the leaders of the godly faction, including Winthrop, met at Cambridge, the university that had long nurtured the godly cause. There they signed an agreement whereby "for the better encouragement of ourselves and others that shall join with us in this action, and to the end that every man may without scruple dispose of his estate and affairs as may best fit his preparation for this voyage, . . . [each] doth hereby freely and sincerely promise and bind himself in the word of a Christian and in the presence of God, who is the searcher of all hearts, as by God's assistance we will be ready in our persons, and with such of our several families as are to go with us, and such provisions as we are able to conveniently furnish ourselves with, to embark for the said plantation by the first of March next, . . . to inhabit and continue in New England."[51] And yet this covenant would only have meaning if a General Court of the company agreed to move the government to the New World.

At a meeting of the General Court on August 28 and 29 Sir Richard Saltonstall, Isaac Johnson, and others presented the case for the transfer. Deputy Governor Thomas Goffe put the matter to a vote "where, by the erection of hands, it appeared by the general consent of the Company that the government and patent should be settled in New England."[52] It is at the next General Court, on September 19, that Winthrop first appears in the company records, named along with Johnson, lawyer John White, and the Reverend John Davenport to represent the company's interest on behalf of the colony's governor, John Endecott, in arbitration of a dispute that had arisen in Salem between Endecott and some of the settlers.[53] He soon began to regularly attend the meetings of the company's leadership, participating in decisions regarding the proper steps to be taken in legally transferring the government, providing for the support of the clergy who would be recruited to migrate, and figuring out how the financial interests of the investors who stayed behind would be safeguarded.[54]

Given the plan to move the company's operations, at a meeting on October 20 the General Court proceeded to the election of new officers and, "having received extraordinary great commendations of Mr. John Winthrop, both for his integrity and sufficiency as one being very well fitted and accomplished for the place of Governor, did put in nomination for that place the said Mr. John Winthrop, Sir Richard Saltonstall, Mr. Isaac Johnson, and Mr. John Humfry." And "the said Mr. Winthrop was, with a general vote and full consent of this Court, by erection of hands, chosen to be Governor for the ensuing year, to begin this present day."[55]

WHY JOHN WINTHROP, who was a man of limited means and little fame? A major part of the explanation for the election of an obscure Suffolk gentleman to lead the Massachusetts Bay Company lies in the perceived unimportance of the corporation. The later significance of the colony has misled many as to the way it was viewed by leading puritans in the late 1620s.

Compared to other companies involved in England's overseas expansion, such as the Virginia Company and the East India Company, the Bay Company had a very low profile, even among enterprises promoted by the godly. More prominent puritans directed their attentions elsewhere. The earl of Warwick and his kinsman Sir Nathaniel Rich, both known to Winthrop from the days when they had listened to Samuel Purchas in Rochford, were at the center of overtly Protestant overseas enterprises. They organized fellow members of the puritan gentry in ventures that combined privateering, trade, and the establishment of colonies seen as bulwarks of Protestantism. Both were involved in the Virginia Company before its charter was revoked and the colony made a royal colony. Complementing his colonizing interests, the earl maintained a large privateering fleet, whose activities were directed to attacking Spanish settlements in the Americas. Together with Nathaniel he had been a principal figure in the effort in 1619–20 to establish a colony in Guiana.[56] Early in March 1629, as John Winthrop was perhaps first considering joining the Massachusetts venture, Warwick, along with Lord Saye and Lord Brooke, maneuvered to take control of the East India Company.[57] Both Warwick and Nathaniel Rich were leaders of the Somers Island (Bermuda) Company, and in 1628 the earl had assumed the governorship of that enterprise. As president of the nearly defunct Council for New England in 1628, it was Warwick who granted the patent to the unincorporated New England Company, the entity that bridged the Dorchester Adventurers and the Massachusetts Bay Company, and he aided the latter group's effort to gain a charter. But in the last years of the 1620s his main focus was on bringing fellow puritan peers and their allies, such as Lord Saye, Lord Brooke, Sir Richard Knightly, and John Pym, into the Bermuda Company, which in 1629 spawned the Providence Island Company.[58]

Yet two of the others proposed for governor, Saltonstall and Humfry, were wealthier and more prominent than the lord of Groton Manor.[59] And both were involved in the some of the more visible colonizing ventures. The Saltonstalls had a history of investing in overseas ventures. Sir Richard was the nephew and namesake of one of the founding members of the Spanish Company and the Turkey Company, who had also been a member of the Levant Company.[60] Both he and Humfry were close to the gentry peers and were involved in some of the ventures promoted by the Warwick circle, which was not the case with Winthrop, whose sole focus at the crucial time was Massachusetts.[61] Yet that fact likely worked in favor of Winthrop. Those who were planning to go to Massachusetts were, for the most part, liquidating their English assets and making a permanent move. They demanded leaders who were as committed as themselves, and while Saltonstall and Humfry would both eventually come to Massachusetts, neither remained. The attention of Saltonstall and Humfry was spread among various projects rather than focused on the Bay. Humfry's commitment to the colony in particular was always in doubt. In a letter written in 1630 Humfry expressed reservations about the appropriateness of the Bay as a site of settlement, suggesting that the colony relocate to "a good river and in a less snowy and cold place."[62] Little surprise, then, that investors planning to migrate themselves should have looked to Winthrop as someone as committed as they were and persuaded him that "the welfare of the plantation depends upon my assistance, for the main pillars of it, being eminent gentlemen of high quality and eminent parts both for wisdom and godliness, are determined to sit still if I desert them."[63] More important than the judgment of those eminent men, however, was his conviction that "hereby I have assurance that my charge is of the Lord, and that he hath called me to this work."[64]

HAVING COMMITTED HIMSELF to migrate as well as to an investment of £200 in the company, there was much for John to do. He continued to explain himself to his friends, surprising some of them with his assessment of the precarious financial straits that had entered into his decision. "My means here are so shortened (now my three eldest sons are come to age) as I shall not be able to continue in this place and employment," he wrote.[65] Robert Reyce at least, acknowledging that the full circumstances "was in no ways known to your friends," was one who came around, writing that "your friends do now rather encourage you to proceed, and do entreat the Almighty Lord of Hosts to go with you, to bless and govern you in your ways."[66] Gradually, as the finality of his decision became evident, other friends likewise extended their support and prayers.

John was also concerned with family plans. Though his wife and children supported him, it was not immediately clear how many of them would join him in migrating. On the letter he wrote to Margaret announcing his election as governor, he added a postscript in which he wrote that "I would fain know if thou shalt be like to go with me, for thou shalt never have so good [an] opportunity."[67] He had sent her materials on the colony and discussed his decisions with her. It was not her intention to join him that was in doubt, but the timing. The fact that she was pregnant and due to give birth in April 1630 led to the difficult decision that she would not make the journey with her husband but travel at a later date. Forth seems to have quickly decided to join the colony, though he too postponed departure due to his courtship of Ursula Sherman. As early as August 1629 the younger John had written to his father that "for the business of New England, I can say no other thing but that I believe confidently that the whole disposition thereof is of the Lord" and that he had determined to "dedicate myself . . . to the service of God and the Company."[68] He would take a large part in the preparations but would defer his departure for Massachusetts in order to devote himself to representing his father in both family and colony business. From John's adult family, only Henry would sail in April 1630.

Winthrop also felt obliged to provide for the welfare of those in Groton who would not follow him to New England. After the death of Henry Sandes, who had often preached in Groton as well as Boxford, in 1626, John was concerned about the provision of preaching in Groton church. The rector, Thomas Nicholson, had never been seen as a godly preacher, and his advancing blindness limited his pastoral work even more. Seeking an assistant who could make do with a small income while Nicholson lived, Winthrop consulted neighboring ministers and invited various clergymen to preach in Groton.[69] John meticulously took notes of those sermons and finally settled on one of those preachers to assist and then replace Nicholson.[70] His choice, William Leigh, was regarded as "a zealous, faithful and true hearted minister" of sound doctrine and an effective preacher.[71] Leigh bowed to Winthrop's wishes regarding omitting the use of disputed vestments and agreed to preach on holy days as well as ordinary occasions.

ON WINTHROP'S SHOULDERS now rested the responsibility of properly preparing for a great migration. The first years of a new colony were always arduous, and many settlements had failed in their first year because of inadequate preparations. In the case of Massachusetts a beachhead had been secured by John Endecott, but the magnitude of what was to be attempted in 1630 was immense. A sense of what was entailed can be gathered from a 1629 list of supplies that the company had determined essential to dispatch to the colony. It was headed by "ministers" but was primarily comprised of items more geared to sustain material existence: wheat, barley, oats, beans, and peas for cultivation; the stones of various fruits to plant, including peaches, plums, and cherries; seeds for other fruits such as apples, quince, and pomegranates; currant plants; woad seed and saffron heads; potatoes; hop roots; hemp seed and flax seed; tame turkeys and rabbits; linen and woolen cloth; pewter bottles; brass ladles and spoons; and copper kettles of French manufacture.[72]

Other necessities dispatched were arms for one hundred men. These included eighty muskets with four-foot-long barrels; six long fowling pieces five and a half feet in length; ten full muskets with matchlocks; bandoleers and bullet bags; one hundred swords and belts; sixty cosletts, sixty pikes, and twenty half-pikes; eight pieces of land ordnance (cannon) for the fort; and twelve barrels of powder. Drums, flags, and halberds for the sergeants were also on the list. Added at the bottom was a large fishing net.[73]

To sustain the hundred colonists on the 1629 voyage and in their early days, the *Talbot* was supplied with forty-five tuns (large casks) of beer; a tun each of Mallegra and Canary wines; six tuns of water; "12 m [?]" of bread, twenty-two hogsheads of beef; forty bushels of peas; twenty bushels of oatmeal; candles; beer vinegar; mustard seed; oil; soap; butter; and cheese.[74] All this and more would be required for the 1630 fleet, but on a much larger scale. Looking ahead to the task of feeding hundreds of passengers on their voyage, in mid-November Winthrop ordered 14,700 brown biscuits and 5,300 white biscuits from Thomas Keene of Southwark and ordered thirty hogsheads of beef, six hogsheads of pork, and two hundred tongues from a London butcher, specifying that the "beef is to be of the best steer beef" and the "pork to be of sound and fat hogs."[75]

In addition to providing the colonists with material sustenance, Winthrop was concerned with securing the provision of godly clergy for the colony. Within days of his election he dispatched letters calling for a meeting of puritan leaders in London in early November to discuss the recruitment of ministers.[76] One of those invited as a result of the meeting was William Ames, who wrote to Winthrop in late December of his plans to join the colony.[77] This was a major coup since Ames, who was related through marriage to Winthrop and had preached in Boxford in 1609, was a distinguished theologian and a revered figure among puritans.[78] John Cotton may have attended the London meeting, for a few weeks later Winthrop wrote to his wife that Cotton might stop at Groton on his way back to Lincolnshire and that she should "get him to stay a night if thou canst."[79] But even before that meeting Winthrop's efforts had begun to bear fruit. He received a letter from his kinsman John Maidston that George Phillips, the rector of Boxted and an occasional preacher at Groton, was prepared to emigrate.[80] To further ensure the godly focus of the company it was agreed by the General Court in late November to admit as freemen of the company the London ministers John Archer and Philip Nye and the Essex clergyman Nathaniel Ward.[81]

Clergy were not the only individuals being recruited by the new governor. Winthrop and others who had determined to sail sought to persuade kin, friends, and neighbors to join them. John's "neighbor [Ephraim] Child" of Nayland agreed to come over.[82] Henry Kingsbury of Assington, with his wife and two children, signed up to accompany Winthrop as part of his personal company of servants and friends.[83] Winthrop welcomed the decision of Margaret's brother Arthur Tyndal to settle in the colony.[84] He arranged for a kinsman of Boxford's constable to join Sir Richard Saltonstall's entourage.[85] Recruitment continued into the new year. Francis Borrowes of Colchester wrote to Winthrop of his son's intention to migrate.[86] John Sampson of Kersey, who had married Thomasine Clopton Winthrop's sister Bridget, also announced his son's plan to join the venture.[87] The Reverend Nathaniel Ward wrote from Essex of two families known to him who had committed.[88] Winthrop persuaded William Gager of Little Waldingfield, "a godly man skilled in the art of surgery," to emigrate.[89] Over seventy men, women, and children from Groton and the closely neighboring villages would migrate with Winthrop in 1630, with more of his family and neighbors following over the next five years. In all, almost two hundred of the over seven hundred initial emigrants came from Essex and Suffolk, the counties bordering the Stour River.[90]

Not everyone came for the same reasons. Even those who were driven by religious objectives did not all agree. Some saw their task as an opportunity to create a society in which they could live exemplary lives in total accord with God's ordinances, thus providing a model for Christians everywhere. Others were more concerned with escaping the judgment they feared that God would wreak on England for its failure to perfect its religious reformation. Even with the most godly men and women other factors influenced the decision to migrate. Personal economic concerns such as Winthrop's anxieties about his estate might truly be viewed as God nudging one to embark on this crusade, but they were serious concerns as well. The hope that one would prosper in the New World was not incompatible with religious sentiments. Many who made the trip were more likely to decide because they saw cherished clergymen leave, or because members of their family or close friends planned to emigrate. The communal nature of the migration—congregations, neighbors, relatives journeying together—

has always been seen as one of the striking characteristics of the settlement of New England. But even those whose reasons were essentially economic or social had to recognize from the nature of the company's solicitations that this was to be a colony characterized by the culture of faith and discipline, and it is unlikely that many who resented such control in England would have risked all to subject themselves to a like governance in America.[91]

As GOVERNOR WINTHROP BORE much of the burden for arranging shipping and contracting for supplies that would be needed both for the voyage itself and in order to successfully plant the colony. Unexpected items also demanded attention, such as the question of whether the goods destined for the colony were required to be searched and charged by customs officials.[92] Through correspondence with Isaac Johnson and Sir Nathaniel Rich, permission was obtained to allow John Winthop Jr. to examine and sketch plans of the Landguard Fort at Harwich and to enlist some of the laborers who had built it so that adequate fortifications could be erected in New England.[93] Discussions were also held about the type of ordnance that would be needed to defend the colony, and steps taken to purchase it. In addition to his work at Harwich, the younger Winthrop also examined and drew up plans for windmills that might prove useful in the colony.[94]

At meetings of the General Court of the company, Winthrop worked to negotiate a settlement with those members who had invested or pledged to invest in the enterprise but planned to remain in England. It had been decided that it was best that the "joint stock [be divided], yet to be ordered as every adventurer [i.e., investor] should in time have his own."[95] After the charter and governing bodies were transferred to America, the investors who remained in England would suffer by not being able to participate in decisions over how their funds were used; it was now Winthrop's task to win them over to this proposal by appealing to their shared interest in the godly nature of the venture. Employing themes that he had expressed before and would continue to utilize, he urged the investors to consider that "the eyes of all the godly are upon you. What can be more honorable for this city [i.e., Massachusetts] and the Gospel which you profess than to deny your own profit [so] that we may say Londoners can be willing to lose that the Gospel" might gain. And again, "that being assured of each other's sincerity in our intentions in this work, and duly considering in what relations we stand, we might be knot together in a most firm bond of love and friendship."[96] Though a plan was eventually approved designating ten undertakers, including Winthrop, to manage the joint stock for seven years, not all of the investors were appeased, and this would cause problems when many failed to make good their pledges during the times of the colony's early struggles.[97]

As governor of the company Winthrop was responsible for the settlement at Salem led by John Endecott and for the religious practices being adopted there. Shortly after his arrival Endecott had led an expedition to nearby Mount Wollaston to take action against the Englishman Thomas Morton. An earlier outpost of Morton's had been attacked by the Plymouth colony, whose leaders charged Morton with selling guns to the natives and shipped him back to England. Returned to the region, Morton was still seen as a threat to the peace and moral tone of the area, and Endecott marched on the settlement, cut down a maypole, and put an end to the trading post, sparking a lengthy sequence of complaints from Morton against Massachusetts.[98] Meanwhile, Endecott had written to the company officials deploring the "profane and dissolute living of divers" Englishmen in the region "and their irregular trading with the Indians, prompting the company leaders to appeal to the Privy Council to enforce English proclamations against such activities.[99]

A more serious controversy centered upon the church practices adopted by the Salem church under the leadership of the two clergymen the company had dispatched, Francis Higginson and Samuel Skelton. The founders of the Bay colony wished to create a godly environment but had no clear blueprint in mind when they left England, and it would take time and much debate for a New England way to emerge. Given the variety of local practice in puritan parishes in the various regions of England and the diverse nature of the group that settled in Salem, it was inevitable that whatever these two clergymen did would strike some of the colonists as inappropriate. Perhaps influenced by representatives of the Separatist Plymouth church, Higginson and Skelton organized a congregation that was founded on a written covenant. Those seeking membership made a statement of faith and swore to "covenant with the Lord and one another, and do bind ourselves in the presence of God to walk together in all ways according to how he is pleased to reveal himself unto us in his Blessed word of truth." With no bishops in America to appoint parish ministers, and no lay landholder with the right of naming clergy to livings, the members of the new congregation controlled their own affairs and chose Skelton and Higginson as their pastor and teacher. Any new arrivals who wished to join the congregation would have to be formally admitted by the existing members to receive the sacraments. Not surprisingly, the worship of the Salem congregation departed from the English Prayer Book, though how far is impossible to tell. Some of the settlers found this unacceptable. John Browne, one of the company's assistants and a member of Endecott's council, was, along with his brother Samuel, particularly upset by these developments. When they persisted in their opposition, accusing their fellow colonists of being separatists and even Anabaptists, and holding their own unofficial church meetings for readings from the Prayer Book, Endecott ordered that the two be sent back to England.[100]

Winthrop's involvement in this matter had begun with his selection in September as one of those charged with meeting representatives of the Brownes to resolve their grievances.[101] The dispute continued into the period of Winthrop's governorship, with the company agreeing to reimburse the Brownes for property lost when they were expelled, but leaving consideration of their other grievances for Winthrop to decide once he had reached Massachusetts and could look into the problems himself.[102] The origins and resolution of the dispute reflected the growing predominance in the company of those, like Winthrop and Endecott, who were committed to making Massachusetts a godly commonwealth, as opposed to some of the original investors, such as the Brownes, who had more material objectives. It played out during the same period as the debate over transferring the charter to the Bay, which was intended in part to guarantee the godly faction's dominance. At the same time, it was Winthrop's ability to defuse the situation rather than opt for confrontation that helped earn him a reputation as being "both for his integrity and sufficiency . . . one very well fitted and accomplished for the place of governor."[103]

IN ADDITION TO SUPERVISING the company's business and deflecting adverse scrutiny, Winthrop also had to make preparations for his own departure and for the supply of his own family and entourage. As governor he would be able to live in greater comfort on shipboard and expected to live in a better style in the New World than most of his fellow colonists. He instructed Thomas Hawes, who leased from him the Essex manor house of Stewards, part of John Forth's legacy, to send him the wall hangings and other furnishings.[104] Other items for his new household would come from Groton, providing a reminder of his personal England in the new land in which he was to settle. A bill he paid in February was for the purchase of beds, bolsters, a bed pan, a close stool and pan, and a "french bedstead."[105] There would be no shops on the ships nor in the New World to supply what was not carried with the colonists, and anticipating his family's needs was a constant concern. Reflecting in one of his first letters home from Massachusetts on his own experience, he would urge Margaret when she came to bring for use on the ship warm clothes, fresh provisions, meal, eggs stored in salt or ground malt to keep them from breaking, butter, oatmeal, peas, fruits, and a strong locked chest or two to keep these in. To prepare meals on shipboard she should bring skillets of several sizes, a large frying pan, a small stewing pan, a case to boil puddings in, pewter and drinking vessels, linens, and a quantity of sack (a class of white wine) to "bestow among the sailors." To protect against disease he advised that she bring "a pound of Doctor Wright's electuarium lenitium" and a gallon of "scurvy grass" to drink in the mornings with some saltpeter dissolved in it along with some grated nutmeg. Looking beyond the voyage he urged her to "come well furnished with linen, woolen, some more bedding, brass, pewter, leather bottles, drinking horns, etc." and asked her to have John Jr. "provide 12 axes of several sorts" from "the Braintree smith or some other prime workman, whatever they cost, and some augers great and small."[106]

ONE OF THE MOST TROUBLING MATTERS for Winthrop was the disposal of his English lands, which he needed to sell in order to finance the family emigration. The ongoing dispute with the Nottes was not ended until after Winthrop's departure; the Irish Chancery rendered a judgment in his favor on June 27, ordering Thomas Notte to pay the sum of £460 and costs.[107] But other questions with the title lingered, and it was not until the spring of 1631 that Groton Manor was finally sold and Margaret and the rest of the family freed to come to New England.[108]

For the most part, John had been separated from Margaret since being chosen as the company's governor. For the four months leading to the fleet's departure he spent almost all his time in London, where the merchants and suppliers he needed to deal with were located. About once a month he was able to steal a few days for a visit to Groton, but such interludes were too rare and too short. Correspondence had to suffice, and his letters were testaments both to the heavy burden of work he was bearing and to his constant love for his wife. After a brief visit home in late October 1629 he wrote, "Our business comes so fast upon us here that I cannot yet appoint when I shall return."[109] It would not be until late December. Meanwhile, on November 24 he wrote that while "I have nothing to write thee of, . . . having so fit an opportunity, I could not let it pass without a letter to my best beloved. I know thou wilt consider how it is with me in regard of business, which so takes up my time and thoughts as I can no more but let thee know that I have a desire still to be writing to thee."[110] For her part, Margaret was dealing with family concerns, supervising the estate, entertaining visiting guests involved in the enterprise, and sending on to her husband not only letters but also tangible signs of her affection such as fowl, puddings, and other products of the Groton kitchen.[111]

Following another brief visit home in late January, Winthrop returned to London to "find here so much to do as I doubt I shall not come down these three weeks, but thou mayest be sure I will stay [in London] no longer than my occasions shall enforce me," indicating that he penned the letter at eleven o'clock at night.[112] By February the magnitude of the work still to be done made both wonder if that next visit would ever take place. On February 2 Margaret wrote that "I begin to fear I shall see thee no more before thou goest, which I should be very sorry for, and earnestly entreat thee that thou wilt come once more if it be possible."[113] Receiving her plea, John responded that "[t]he reading of it hath dissolved my head into tears. I can write no more. If I live I will see thee ere I go. I shall part from thee with sorrow enough."[114] Only their trust in God and their belief that they were pursuing God's design sustained them. On the fourteenth he reminded her that "[t]he Lord our God hath oft brought us together with comfort when we have been long absent, and if it be good for us, he will do so still. When I was in Ireland"—a risky journey that had led Winthrop to prepare a will—"he brought us together again. When I was sick here in London he restored us together again. How many dangers near death hast thou been in thyself"—referring to her difficult childbirths—"and yet the Lord granted me to enjoy thee still." Then, remembering the date, in a romantic postscript he added, "Thou must be my valentine, for none hath challenged me."[115] John did return to Groton for one final visit in late February, which was the last time he would see Margaret in England and the last chance to bid farewell to those friends and neighbors he would never see again.

On his February visit John and Margaret agreed on a way that would bring them together though miles apart. Perhaps suggested by Imogen's vow to think regularly of her beloved in Shakespeare's *Cymbeline*, they pledged each other to enter into a dialogue of the spirit each Monday and Friday between the hours of five and six.[116] On his way back to London he wrote to Margaret urging her to "remember Monday and Friday between 5 and 6," and he would continue to do so through the long separation that awaited them.[117] On April 3 he wrote that "when 5 of the clock came I had respite to remember thee (it being Friday) and to parley with thee, and to meet thee in spirit before the Lord."[118] It is likely that at this time he presented her with a small miniature portrait of himself that survives in the collections of the Massachusetts Historical Society. Over the following months, from London and then from his flagship in port, he continued to write to her, informing her of news, reassuring her from on board the *Arbella* that their boys—eleven-year-old Stephen and ten-year-old Adam— were "well and cheerful" and "lie with me and sleep as soundly in a rug (for we have no sheets here) as ever they did in Groton."[119] But the true sense of his loss is to be sensed in the loving salutations by which he addressed her—"mine own, mine only, my best beloved," "my love, my joy, my faithful one."[120]

Other farewells were also painful, for he realized that they might be final. In early February he wrote a parting letter to his closest friend, Sir William Spring. Opening with his wonder at how God had blessed him, "a poor worm, and raised but yesterday out of the dust," with Spring's love and esteem, he stated that he had loved Spring "before I could think you took any notice of me" and now had come to esteem and value their mutual affection, which was such that his "soul is knit to you, as the soul of Jonathan to David." "Were I now with you," he continued, "I should bedew that sweet bosom with the tears of affection," for "[o]h, what a pinch will it be to me, to part with such a friend." Yet though their parting was final in terms of this earth, he was confident that "we shall meet in heaven, and while we live our prayers and affections shall hold an intercourse of friendship."[121] It may have been around this same time that, according to Thomas Hubbard's seventeenth-century account, Winthrop, "at a solemn feast among many friends a little before their last farewell, finding his bowels yearn within him, instead of drinking to them, by breaking into a flood of tears himself, set them all aweeping . . . while they thought of seeing the faces of each other no more in the land of the living."[122]

FOR AS LONG AS HE COULD REMEMBER John Winthrop had been struggling to give shape to his life. Looking ahead as he prepared to depart from England, he recalled that "as a youth I did seriously consecrate my life to the service of the Church (intending the ministry) but was diverted from that course."[123] Opportunity to serve in the magistracy had opened with his acquisition of Groton Manor, but he never rose to the quorum of the bench, remaining always on the fringe of the commission, his influence limited by that circumstance. The door to Parliament had closed almost as quickly as it had opened. His financial difficulties prevented him from contributing to the godly cause as a patron of clergy. Even in his own neighborhood, when Henry Sandes died and Groton's Thomas Nicholson was in his decline, Winthrop was strapped to find funds to support an assistant to the ailing pastor. To a degree these circumstances were the result of outside forces, but they were in part the product of his decisions. Faced with the choice of sacrificing his values to gain the world, he had chosen to serve God, making himself into a puritan.

If Massachusetts had been a larger, more important venture, he would not have been entrusted with the responsibilities now offered to him. Here was a chance to serve the Lord, and it was not surprising that he saw his deliverance from the waters of the fens as a sign. His formal and informal education, his friendships and conversations with godly ministers and godly magistrates, and his life in the Stour Valley had shaped his vision of what a godly society should be. His status as a landowner and member of the commission of the peace had given him some experience of exercising the authority that would be needed in a new colony. When he made the decision to migrate, John Winthrop saw his future, recognized it as what God had chosen him for, and eagerly embraced it. Now he had arrived. The time for self-fashioning was over. The time for him to take his place on the world stage had come.

Interlude

&

Interlude: Christian Charity

THE SALT SMELL OF THE OCEAN was in the room as John Winthrop stood to address those gathered in the Church of the Holy Rood in the port of Southampton on a day in late March 1630. Much had happened since his elevation as governor of the Massachusetts Bay Company the previous October. As calculated by Englishmen, a new year had just begun, and now the new venture of colonizing New England was to be launched. Preparations for the voyage were nearly complete. The fleet of ships was assembled in the port. Soon, God's winds being willing, the *Arbella* and her sister ships would set their sails, raise their anchors, and depart for the New World.

In anticipation of the departure, those who were set to embark, along with many supporters who were to remain in England—including Matthew Craddock and other company officers—had gathered in the Holy Rood to mark the occasion and seek God's blessing on the enterprise. John Cotton had accompanied members of his Lincolnshire flock who would be sailing with Winthrop. He presided over the service at Southampton and earlier in the day had preached on *God's Promise to His Plantation*. Then it was Winthrop's turn to speak. We do not know how often he had been able to prophesy as a lay preacher in the Stour Valley, though it is safe to say that he did, since such efforts were not uncommon in puritan gatherings, and we know that he would assume that responsibility on many occasions in the New World, fulfilling in a minor way the ministerial role that he had reluctantly put aside when he abandoned his studies at Cambridge. Rising in Southampton to address those who were placing their lives and fortunes in his hands, as well as speaking to those who wished them well, he took as his subject the importance of Christian charity. Never before had he commanded a greater stage. Never before had so much been required of him.[1]

As Winthrop rose to speak, those assembled in the nave of the church saw a man of average height and solemn demeanor. His head was of an oval shape, its length accentuated by a long nose and a beard stretching from the line of his mustache and nestling in the ruff. His dark brown hair, parted in the middle, fell to just below his ears. His eyes, also brown, were emphasized by the thick arching eyebrows that framed them. The portrait painted of him at this time of his life shows a man who dressed well, as befitted his station. His upper garment, a silk doublet, was black—a sign not of puritanism but of wealth, since it was a difficult and thus expensive color to achieve with natural dyes. It was accented with an elaborate linen ruff trimmed with lace and with linen cuffs, both the ruff and cuffs likely made from lawn, a particularly fine and expensive form of linen. In his one hand he is holding a silk glove.[2] His overall demeanor seems to be that of a man who is comfortable with who he is and confident in the course he has chosen.

⟶ ⟵

*U*NFORTUNATELY, THIS VIGNETTE represents only a guess at the exact time and place of Winthrop's sermon. We are told by three different sources that Cotton preached to the departing colonists, though none mentions the exact date or location. In Winthrop's case we are on even less certain ground. Despite the relative abundance of source material dealing with the settlement of Massachusetts, not a single individual recorded in letter, diary, or other source having heard Winthrop deliver the sermon. The only contemporary reference to the sermon that survives is the Reverend Henry Jessey's request that John Winthrop Jr. send him copies of a number of papers relating to the colony, including "the Model of Charity."[3] Whereas Cotton's farewell was published soon after it was delivered, "Christian Charity" was not. Indeed, only one contemporary manuscript copy of Winthrop's work survives, and it is not in his handwriting.[4] Though Edward Johnson sailed with Winthrop in 1630, he does not mention the sermon in his history of the *Wonder-Working Providence of Sion's Saviour*.[5] William Hubbard was rewarded by the Massachusetts government in 1682 for his *General History of New England*, an account that drew heavily on the recollections of those who had known the earliest settlers; he tells of the farewell dinner at which Winthrop parted from his friends but says nothing about "Christian Charity."[6] Similarly, though familiar with Winthrop family traditions and having access to many of the family papers, Cotton Mather omits the sermon from his *Magnalia Christi Americana* (1702).

Unremarked upon by contemporaries, Winthrop's lay sermon has been labeled the greatest sermon of the millennium by Harvard's current university preacher, Peter Gomes.[7] While that might seem excessive, the judgment that the address has become "a kind of Ur-text of American literature" is one that few historians or literary scholars would debate.[8] Probably no other work of colonial literature has been as frequently anthologized. How then could it have been ignored by Winthrop's contemporaries? The explanation lies in the fact that the ideas which have struck so many later commentators as original and influential were commonplaces of the time. So, to understand the importance of "Christian Charity" for Winthrop and those who heard it, it is necessary to analyze the text and examine it in the context in which it was delivered.

WHETHER PREACHED JUST PRIOR to the departure of the fleet, during the voyage as some have suggested, or on arrival in the New World, the sermon was primarily intended for those who were going to New England.[9] But it was heard and needs to be read as one of three statements about the purpose of the venture that were made in connection with the fleet's departure, the other two—which were quickly published—being Cotton's *God's Promise* and the *Humble Request*. Together they represent an effort to balance the desire of Winthrop and his supporters to bring forth further fruits of reformation in New England while denying any separation from the Church of England which might either be suspected by those who remained at home or desired by some of those emigrating. Both of these fears were very real. Concerns about separatist practices had been raised by the dispute with the Brownes, and John Cotton himself would, shortly after bidding the colonists farewell, express worries about separatist tendencies among the colonists in a letter to Salem's Reverend Samuel Skelton.[10] On the other hand, Roger Williams, one of the most eminent of those who would go to New England in the next few years, expected more and was disappointed by the inadequate separation that the colonial churches asserted and practiced.[11]

Cotton's sermon stressed the legitimacy of the colonial venture, denied that the colonists were such as "dream of perfection in this world," and asserted that they would continue to consider themselves members of the Church of England, their "dear Mother."[12] The signatories of the *Humble Request* elaborated on this point, insisting that "such hope and part as we have obtained in the common salvation we have received in her bosom and sucked it from her breasts," an image paralleled in Cotton's admonition to the departing colonists to "forget not the womb that bore you and the breasts that gave you suck."[13] Cotton reminded the colonists that they were still part of the English church "though absent in body" from England, and the signers of the *Humble Request* acknowledged that they would be "members of the same body" and beseeched those in England to "pray for us without ceasing."[14]

Winthrop addressed some of the same issues in "Christian Charity" but devoted most of his attention to directing the colonists toward their goals in New England. In doing so he offered no blueprints for particular governmental or ecclesiastical systems but affirmed the importance of the values of community and Christian love which the godly had sought to implement in England—with some success for a time in the Stour Valley—and which should be the foundation of their holy experiment in the New World. The sermon provides insight into the beliefs and values that Winthrop had adopted as a result of his experience in England and thus sets a framework within which to understand his actions in the new England. It should be noted that as used in the sermon "charity" meant more than alms-giving and the like. As Winthrop and his contemporaries used it the word meant love.

The first part of the sermon was a "model" of social order.[15] "God almighty," according to Winthrop, "in his most holy and wise providence hath so disposed of the condition of mankind as in all times some must be rich, some poor; some high and eminent in power and dignity, others mean and in subjection."[16] None of this would have been a surprise to those raised in Winthrop's England. Inequality was a cultural assumption and a socioeconomic reality. There were, Winthrop explained, various reasons for it. The variety and diversity of men was a reflection of God's glory and power. By making everyone different God provided himself with greater opportunities to manifest the power of his Spirit, moderating and restraining the wicked and exercising his graces in the godly. But, most important, God made men different so that "every man might have need of other, and from hence they might all be knit more nearly together in the bond of brotherly affection." Of critical importance here was that "no man is made more honorable than another, more wealthy, etc. out of any particular and singular respect to himself, but for the glory of his creator and the Common good." No one was to take satisfaction from being superior to others. Talents were not reflections of intrinsic superiority but rather gifts from God. Here Winthrop was drawing on elements of traditional Christian religious teachings and English commonwealth ideas as they had recently been modified to emphasize both the hierarchical and communal elements of society.[17] The special seating of the Winthrop family in the church at Groton had not separated them from the parish folk gathered in worship in such a way as to imply their superior worth but rather recognized their specific role in the parish. At a fundamental level all were equally sinners united as creatures of God.

Unlike some of his fellow colonial leaders, Winthrop never lost sight of his own sinfulness, and as a result he was generally able to treat with charity those whose views differed from his, even when he felt compelled to take action against them for the good of the colony as a whole. Believing that each individual had received special gifts from God, he concluded that within the community each had his or her distinct responsibilities in serving the common good of all.

Having rejected any perfectionist claims for equality of power or condition, he proceeded to ask what these differences in condition and talents meant for the functioning of society. He recognized "two rules whereby we are to walk one towards another: Justice and Mercy"; the former derived from the natural law of creation, the latter from the law of grace.[18] Justice requires that every man love his neighbor as himself, doing unto others as he would have done unto him. Mercy requires each man to help others beyond what he could afford—selling all and giving to the poor, doing whatever was necessary to help another even at great cost to oneself. "Community of perils," Winthrop stated, "calls for extraordinary liberality, and so does community in some special service for the church." Those who had in the past been most bountiful to God's children—such as "some of our forefathers in times of persecution here in England"—had been commended and remembered for their charity.

Having raised and answered a series of possible objections to the imperative of caring for others, he used an analogy between the Christian community and the human body. First, "all true Christians are of one body in Christ." Second, "the ligaments" which knit this body together "are love." Third, "no body can be perfect" which lacks its "proper ligaments." Fourth, the various parts of the body, each different and with its own responsibilities, are tied together in the body "as they must needs partake of each other's strength and infirmity, joy and sorrow, weal and woe." And, last, "sensibleness and sympathy of each other's condition will necessarily infuse into each part a native desire and endeavor to strengthen, defend, preserve, and comfort the other." Winthrop drew on a variety of sources to demonstrate the validity of these conclusions. Scriptural examples started with Christ's ultimate sacrifice of his life to heal those who were of his body.

The love that each should bear for others was especially found in those who had been saved by God's grace. It was "the fruit of the new birth" and worked "like the Spirit upon the dry bones," which "gathers together the scattered bones" and "knits them together into one body again." Winthrop expounded on the nature of this love by two examples that he had often written of—the love between husband and wife, and that between David and Jonathan. Using Adam and Eve as the prototypes of a wedded couple, he wrote how, when joined with Adam, Eve must have him one with herself—"this is flesh of my flesh, saith she, and bone of my bone." Expanding, he explained how "she conceives a great delight in it, therefore she desires nearness and familiarity with it." Drawing no doubt on his own relationship with Margaret, he talked of how if a wife hears her love "groan she is with it presently, if she find it sad and disconsolate she sighs and mourns with it. She hath no such joy as to see her beloved merry and thriving." She sets no bounds to her affections. Similarly, in the Old Testament relationship between David and Saul's son Jonathan, Jonathan had "his heart knit to him by this ligament of love, so that it is said he loved him as his own soul." When he saw David in danger, "he spares neither care,

pains, nor peril to divert it." Such love, according to Winthrop, was recip-
rocal. By giving we receive. In sum, "to love and live beloved is the soul's
paradise, both here and in heaven."

In our times, the most familiar parts of the sermon are in the second
part, Winthrop's application of these general principles. Those who were
migrating to New England were "a company professing ourselves fellow
members of Christ." Even though they would be separated by many miles—
for Winthrop understood that the over seven hundred new colonists would
not settle in a single community—"we ought to account ourselves knit together by this bond of love, and live in the exercise of it." Knowing full
well how other colonies had fallen apart, he underscored the importance
of the Massachusetts community. The colonists were undertaking their
task by "mutual consent" as well as God's providence and a "more than ordinary approbation of the Churches of Christ." They were seeking a "place
of cohabitation and consortship." In such a case, "the care of the public
must oversway all private respects," the common wealth take priority over
individual self-interest. But even selfishness pointed to the importance of
sustaining the community, for "it is a true rule that particular estates cannot subsist in the ruin of the public."

The goals of the new commonwealth were "to improve our lives, to do
more service to the Lord," and to "increase . . . the body of Christ whereof
we are members, [so] that ourselves and our posterity may be the better
preserved from the common corruptions of this world" and "serve the Lord
and work out our salvation under the power and purity of his holy ordinances." They must strive as never before to achieve these goals and not
content themselves with an ordinary effort. "Whatsoever we did or ought to
have done when we lived in England," he told the colonists, "the same must
we do and more also where we go. That which most in their churches maintain as a truth in profession only, we must bring into familiar and constant
practice, as in this duty of love." We must, he preached, drawing on the rich
language of Scripture, "love brotherly without dissimulation. We must love
one another with a pure heart, fervently. We must bear one another's burdens," and look not only to private goals but to the good of others.

It was especially important for these men and women to heed these
scriptural counsels since, as was the case with the Israelites, God would not
tolerate from them failings that he would tolerate among others. This was
because of the "near bond of marriage" between the Lord and the colony—
"he hath taken us to be his after a most strict and peculiar manner, which
will make him the more jealous of our love and obedience." "When God
gives a special commission," claimed Winthrop, "he looks to have it strictly
enforced," and this would be the case with Massachusetts. "We are," he
declared, "entered into Covenant with him for this work." The emigrés

had proposed to plant a colony to further God's cause. If the Lord "shall please to hear us, and bring us in peace to the place we desire, then hath he ratified this Covenant . . . and will expect a strict performance of the articles." If they failed, neglected their duties, embraced the things of the world and their own selfish interests, "the Lord will surely break out in wrath against us, be revenged on such a perjured people, and make us know the price of the breach of such a covenant." If, on the other hand, they succeeded in living as they promised God they would, "the Lord will be our God and delight to dwell among us as his own people, and will command a blessing upon us in all our ways, so that we shall see much more of his wisdom, power, goodness and truth than formerly we have been acquainted with." They would find that God was with them "when ten of us shall be able to resist a thousand of our enemies" and when God would "make us a praise and a glory, that men shall say of succeeding plantations, the Lord make it like that of New England." They would be, Winthrop reminded them, "as a City upon a Hill. The eyes of all people are upon us." Reiterating what he had said before, he urged them to follow the counsel of Micah—"to do justly, to love mercy, to walk humbly with our God." They must "be knit together in this work as one man." Each must be willing to give from his excess for the benefit of those who had need. In their dealings with one another they must demonstrate "meekness, gentleness, patience, and liberality." They were to "delight in each other, make others' conditions our own; rejoice together, mourn together, labor and suffer together—always having before our eyes our commission and community in the work, our community as members of the same body."

NONE OF THIS WOULD HAVE SOUNDED exceptional to Winthrop's audience. "Christian Charity" was an exposition of the social gospel that had long been proclaimed in the Stour Valley and elsewhere in England. Numerous clergy preached on the organic nature of society, the difference in men's gifts, and the interdependence of all the parts. Thomas Carew stated that "[t]here hath always been, are, and shall be diversities of estates and degrees in the world, some rich and some poor, and, many times it falls out, though not always, that wicked men have a greater portion of outward things than godly men, . . . [so] no man can say, because I am rich, therefore I am loved of God."[19] John Knewstub preached to Winthrop and others that "the Lord is the author of the diversity in gifts," not men, and that "the envying of others for their gifts given unto them is indeed to pick a quarrel with the Lord." It was a call to humility that Winthrop would never forget, though he, like all sinners, would at times neglect that call. And, as Winthrop would state, because men were "fellow members of one body" they each would "fare the better for the several gifts of others." Because "the Lord hath made such a division of his gifts . . . he hath laid a necessary part of the welfare of every man out of himself [and] in some other." Uniting the members of the social body was love, and "this love doth so join and unite them that there can be nothing taken from the one, but the other taketh himself to be maimed thereby, as if he had lost some limb or joint of his own."[20] George Gifford asserted that "all the true believers are knit together by one spirit and do make one mystical body in Christ Jesus."[21] Nicholas Bownde made the same point when he preached that those "of the same society and fellowship of religion" were united by "a mutual feeling and compassion which they have one of another as the lively members of one and the same mystical body" and that they ought to "rejoice with them that rejoice, and weep with them that weep."[22] The society Bownde was speaking of consisted of individuals united by an awareness of being fellow saints, joined together with those in whom they detected the root of true piety. Winthrop too saw Christian charity as grounded in a mutual apprehension of that of God within each other, and not on consent to specific propositions. While he expected true saints to agree on certain doctrinal fundamentals, he was aware of the fact that different men and women apprehended God's work on their souls differently and might therefore differ on doctrinal non-essentials. Unity rather than uniformity made for a community.

Similar parallels to Winthrop's points can be found in the sermons of other preachers. All, of course, were drawing on the language of Scripture and long traditions of Christian teaching.[23] It is especially important to note this when considering Winthrop's application to the colony of the image of a "city upon a hill." He was not coining a new phrase but drawing upon the gospels, specifically Matthew 5:14–16:

> Ye are the light of the world. A city that is set on a hill cannot be hid. Neither do men light a candle and put it under a bushel, but on a candlestick, and it giveth light unto all that are in the house. Let your light so shine before men, that they see your good works, and glorify your Father who is in heaven.

His use of the word "city" does not mean that he anticipated that all the colonists would settle in a single urban-style community.[24] Nor did his use of the gospel image mean that he saw New England as the only light that could save the world. The distinguished scholar Perry Miller wrote that the early colonists saw their "errand into the wilderness" as "a flank attack on the corruptions of Christendom." "These Puritans," he believed, "did not flee to America; they went in order to work out that complete reformation which was not yet accomplished in England and Europe, but which would quickly be accomplished if only the saints back there had a working model to guide them."[25] While Miller never claimed that the colonists viewed themselves as the *only* hope for religious reform, his work was interpreted that way by many who then proceeded to identify Winthrop's "Christian Charity" as the key text in the development of American exceptionalism, sparking an intense debate over the New England contribution to the sense of American national destiny. Small surprise that more attention has been paid to the sermon by modern scholars than by Winthrop's contemporaries.[26]

Matthew's images of a city on a hill, lights, and candlesticks were widely employed in Winthrop's England. Colchester, in the Stour Valley, had been described as being in Queen Elizabeth's reign a "town [which], for the earnest profession of the gospel, [was] like unto the city upon a hill; and as a candle upon a candlestick."[27] Looking back to the churches of Judea, Samaria, and Galilee, the Essex clergyman Richard Rogers talked of these as "particular churches . . . [that] showed forth as shining lights" and urged England to follow their example.[28] Individuals could be referred to in like terms. William Ames spoke of William Perkins as "a burning and shining light, the sparks whereof did fly abroad into all corners of the land."[29] Nicholas Bownde commended Sir Robert Jermyn for, "as it were, . . . lighting other men's candles at yours."[30] Bezaleel Carter referred to Sir Edward Lewkenor, a godly colleague of Jermyn's on the Suffolk bench, as one who "shined like a light amongst us all."[31] Boston in Lincolnshire and the ministry of John Cotton there were accorded the same image—"in that Candlestick the Father of Lights placed this burning and shining light."[32]

In using the image Winthrop was expressing his belief that it was the task of all, individuals and communities alike, to live exemplary lives and witness to religious truth. New England was not to be the only arrow in the quiver of reform, but it was to be one such weapon in the war against Antichristian forces. For a time, the Stour Valley had been such an exemplary society, but night was closing there and the light of the godly was being put out. Drawing on the models that had influenced him, Winthrop hoped to kindle a gospel light that would shine forth once more in a new England. There he would encourage the colonists to do that which they ought to have persisted in, but failed to do, in England. There, that which in England they had given lip service to would have to be put into everyday practice. With a partnership of ministry and magistracy New England might become not *the* city upon a hill, but *a* city upon a hill.

POISED, AS IT WERE, at this interlude between his life in England and the new life he was embarking on, John Winthrop may well have felt overwhelmed by the challenges facing him. Placed in the broad stream of seventeenth-century migration to British America, the early New Englanders may strike

us as a distinctive group easily differentiated from those who journeyed to
Virginia, Pennsylvania, and other colonies. Looking more closely, however, it is possible to see significant differences among the colonists that
must have given Winthrop pause. The fact that "Christian Charity" offered a call for fellow-feeling rather than a blueprint for institutions and
policies reflects Winthrop's awareness that achieving consensus for the
architecture of the city on a hill would be a daunting task.

The fact is that there was no uniform puritan identity or plan. Men
and women from different parts of England had varied experiences of what
constituted godly communities and how they were to be governed.
Winthrop certainly knew this. The puritanism of southeast Essex where
he had lived with Mary Forth was not the same as that of the Stour Valley.
His contacts with the godly clergy and lawyers of London had offered yet
another perspective on how saints organized and advanced godliness. And,
of course, different though such regions may have been, it is clear that within
each of these and other regional communities there were unique strains of
piety and practice.

The Massachusetts migration brought together many different types
of puritan. On a basic level of piety and character, Winthrop and many
others knew God loved them because of strong, mystical experiences of
the divine caress. Others never achieved such ecstatic evidence of God's
blessing and relied instead on proofs of sanctification to reassure themselves of their transformation into saints. Some, like Winthrop, had emerged
from their conversion experiences with the humility that came from confronting and accepting one's own sinfulness and unworthiness of God's
grace. Others, believing themselves remade by God's grace and given a
special light to discern the divine will, would be arrogant and intolerant of
those who differed from them. On matters of doctrine and practice, different puritans drew the line between what was acceptable and what was not
at different places. In terms of polity, some were drawn toward congregational ways of organizing their communities, while others were more comfortable with hierarchical presbyterian forms. Looking to transform society,
some looked to reform the English church and state, but a growing number of revolutionaries sought to overthrow traditional forms and create a
New Jerusalem modeled on biblical norms. Puritans disagreed on a whole
host of other matters as well, from the celebration of Christmas to the
forms of burial.

Throughout his life John Winthrop had chosen not only between being a magistrate or a minister, a courtier or a man of simplicity, but also
between the different puritan stands he had heard and seen. And while the
time and nature of each of those choices are irrecoverable, the product of
that self-fashioning was the man who delivered "Christian Charity" and

took on the challenge of governing Massachusetts. While zealous, he was not a zealot. Committed to do God's will, he was not as confident as were some other leaders that the will of God was easily discerned. Some beliefs—particularly familism—he had no tolerance for, but his instincts were tolerant. For Winthrop, the apprehension of the spirit of God in an individual always counted for more than doctrinal purity.

Raised in a loving household by caring parents and sisters, he made the connection between the love of family and the message of Christian love. The loving community he spoke of in "Christian Charity" was an extension of the community of mutual aid and comfort he experienced growing up in Groton. And, on a deeper level, he used his intense relationship with Thomasine Clopton and Margaret Tyndal to come to a new appreciation of God's love for his saints, his personal experiences and religious beliefs interacting in such a way as to enrich both. All of this helped to shield him from the excesses of arrogance and sanctimoniousness which darken the reputation of some puritans. He was a man, according to one contemporary, of "sweet temper and disposition in a heart of bounty and goodness."[33] In the years to come it would be his instinct to take a moderate stance, seeking always to maintain the spirit of Christian community in opposition to those who would seek to define orthodoxy in such a way as to write others out of that community.

WINTHROP'S FORM OF PURITAN PIETY was the foundation of his character, but his exercise of authority was also shaped by his memory of the Suffolk magistrates on whom he had tried to model himself. Their success in creating a godly kingdom in the Stour Valley had involved working within traditional English forms. As a youth Winthrop had seen Sir John Higham and Sir Robert Jermyn use their discretionary authority as members of the Suffolk commission to shape local practice in accord with a broadly conceived social gospel. Named to the commission himself, he chose to ally himself with justices such as William Spring and Brampton Gurdon and learned firsthand how to exercise authority. While even men such as Jermyn and Gurdon could and did on occasion use their power in ways others deemed arbitrary and selfish (as Winthrop too would be accused of doing), Winthrop focused on the benefits of discretionary authority exercised by godly men. Other colonists, including some from East Anglia, had come to distrust the exercise of power by royal officials and local magistrates. They were willing to abandon the principles of England's ancient constitution in favor of biblical models of law and government. But Winthrop never lost his confidence in the customary forms of English justice and rule when properly employed.

Though he deferred spelling out the details of his vision when he addressed the gathered colonists in Southampton, the City on a Hill that

Winthrop hoped to build was one in which godly men and women, united by mutual respect and love, labored together to better discern and advance God's will. It was also to be a community in which all were protected by the traditional safeguards of English law and custom. To realize his ambition he would have to confront and overcome New World nature and natives, threats from abroad, and challenges from heretics and zealots within the community.

Part Three
Errand

⸎

9

Passing Through Hell

JULY 1630. "My son Henry, my son Henry, ah my poor child." The words were torn from John Winthrop as he wrote to Margaret about the death of his son.[1] Henry had missed the *Arbella* when she left Cowes and had found passage on one of the other ships of the fleet. Arriving at Salem around the first of July, when John had already moved on to explore the coast to the south, he joined some of the officers of the ship in exploring their new surroundings. The town of Salem itself was unimpressive, consisting of about ten wooden houses along a muddy street stretching uphill from the harbor. Walking along the North River to view a native encampment, the young men spied a canoe on the opposite bank. Henry, the only one of the group who could swim, volunteered to swim over and paddle the canoe back for all to see. But the water was colder than he anticipated, and he cramped and drowned. It is likely that his father did not even know of Henry's arrival in America until he received the news of the youth's death.[2]

The price paid by the English to settle the New World was a steep one—though nothing, of course, compared to that paid by the native inhabitants. Being separated from friends and family left behind was part of that price. But there was a cost in lives lost as well. John Winthrop paid heavily in his first years in Massachusetts, testing his fortitude and his acceptance of God's will. Henry's death was only the first blow he experienced. In England John's son Forth sickened suddenly and died in late November 1630.[3] His father, who had placed great hopes in this pious son, was not there to console him and care for him. In fact, John was ignorant of Forth's passing as late as the following March, when he wrote to his son John expressing surprise that he had not received letters from Forth.[4] While the *Arbella* was crossing the Atlantic, back in Groton Margaret gave birth to a baby girl, christened Anne after John's mother (like two previous daughters who died young) on April 29.[5] John's joy at being reunited with Margaret and his other children in November 1631 would be muted by the news that the toddler Anne had died a week into the voyage and been buried at sea without her father ever getting to see or hold her.[6] Meanwhile the extended family of the colony struggled mightily to survive. Was the settlement of Massachusetts God's will if it exacted such a high cost?

CB

*T*HE VOYAGE TO AMERICA had begun shortly after Winthrop preached his "Christian Charity" sermon. A few days after that day, probably on the twentieth of March, Winthrop boarded his flagship, the *Arbella*, a large vessel of 350 tons with twenty-eight brass cannons on her gun deck, whose name had been changed from the *Eagle* to honor the Lady Arbella Johnson, Isaac Johnson's wife, who was sailing on her.[7] The wind was fair, and the ships crossed from Southampton to the north shore of the Isle of Wight, where they rode anchor off the Cowes, two forts erected by Henry VIII to guard the Medina estuary. On the twenty-third the last meeting in England of the company's assistants was held on board the *Arbella*. John Humfry, who had decided not to embark at that time, was relieved of the post of deputy governor and replaced by Thomas Dudley.[8] The final departure was delayed because some of the ships were not ready. Finally, on March twenty-ninth, the captains of the *Arbella*, the *Talbot*, the *Ambrose*, and the *Jewel* set out on their own.[9] Matthew Craddock, who had been visiting, departed, and the ships weighed anchor, but they soon anchored again, a bit west along the Isle, near Yarmouth. There they remained, beset with rain and contrary winds.

On the seventh Winthrop signed a copy of the "*Humble Request*," a public letter denying any intent to separate from the Church of England, which was carried ashore by the last departing well-wishers and soon published. On the eighth the poor weather abated, and they were able to sail through the Needles (a narrow passage between the western end of the Isle of Wight and the mainland) and into the English Channel. The next day they sighted eight ships gaining on them from the east. Fearing that they might be pirates out of Dunkirk, the crew dismantled the passenger accommodations on the gun deck and prepared to do battle. "Our trust," Winthrop recorded, "was in the Lord of hosts and the courage of our captain."[10] It proved, however, a false alarm. Henry Winthrop, John's son, had been ashore when preparations were made to depart from Cowes and failed to rejoin the *Arbella*. On the tenth the *Arbella* passed Plymouth and entered the western approaches to the Atlantic. John gave up hope that Henry would catch up, assuming he would join one of the later ships. Having recorded this he drew an implicit contrast with Henry's behavior. "I must add here," he wrote, "one observation, that we have many young gentlemen in our ship who behave themselves well and are comfortable to all good orders."[11]

The journey itself was less difficult than that experienced by many voyagers to America. Early on many, including the Reverend George Phillips, were seasick, but they soon adapted to the movement of the ship. While Winthrop and the company officers had makeshift cabins, most of the passengers were merely assigned floor space on the lower decks. Within a week of leaving England Captain Milborne complained that the passengers "were very nasty and slovenly, and that the gun deck where they lodged was so beastly and noisome with their victuals and beastliness as would much endanger the health of the ship." After praying on the matter Winthrop set up a rotation in which every three days a different group of four men would be responsible for keeping the area clean.[12] With the exception of the first Sunday on the open sea, when Phillips was sick, each Sabbath was observed with religious services. Tuesdays and Wednesdays Phillips undertook the catechizing of the children on the voyage.

Cold numbed the voyagers; Winthrop wrote that "the sun did not give so much heat as in England."[13] John observed the shifting position of the polestar, a whale that sailed close to the *Arbella* for a time, and other phenomena. There were a few fights among the passengers and at least one infraction against a settler by one of the ship's officers. In the latter case Winthrop interceded with Captain Milborne to moderate the punishment that Milborne had originally set, an instance of the leniency for which Winthrop would later be both applauded and condemned.[14]

On the sixth of June land was sighted. The voyage was over, the journey about to begin.

WE KNOW MOST OF THE DETAILS of this voyage, and indeed of the early history of Massachusetts, from a journal that Winthrop began as the *Arbella* was riding at anchor at the Cowes on March 29, 1630. The small notebook in which he had recorded his personal spiritual growth and trials was, with one exception, put aside and replaced with what was to be the first of three small notebooks in which he began to record the growth and trials of the colony to which his life was now committed. During the voyage itself he recorded events as they happened, so that the storm encountered on April 15 is reflected in the unsteady hand in which it is described. After arrival in the New World the struggle for the colony's survival left him little time with his journal, and the early months rarely contain more than brief notations, with space left on the pages to expand on them later, though he never did. As the years went on the regularity and length of entries increased until, in the early 1640s, he seems to have put it aside for a time. When he resumed, probably in mid-1648, he went back to the previous years. The later entries therefore are more of a retrospective narrative than a daily journal.[15]

The journal focused on the principal public events and figures in the history of the Bay, and it is largely from its pages that we gain insights into the character of men such as Thomas Dudley, Henry Vane, John Cotton, and the other principal actors of the time. Consequently, to an unknown but necessarily large degree, we see these events and people as Winthrop wished us to see them. But the journal is not merely a record of public events as we understand them. Rarely, but on occasion, his own experiences and those of his family are described. Comments on the weather, the success of crops, and the fortunes of ordinary settlers dot the pages of the journal.

Winthrop copied and sent to England the narrative of the ocean passage, which would have been of interest to Margaret and others intending to follow him. The record of colony affairs may have initially been intended, much as his spiritual diary had been, for his own reflection. Winthrop's view of history was a providential one. New England had entered into a covenant with God, and just as he had found it useful to trace his personal relationship with God in the diary, so too he believed that it was important to trace the course of New England's covenant relationship. The narrative itself and the incorporation of portents and providential signs both reflect this intent. As time went on it became clear that Winthrop viewed the account as one that others would find useful. It is also evident that its composition was known to others. In 1640 the Reverend Thomas Shepard urged Winthrop to persevere in the project, indicating his belief that "the work is of God" and that "the hearts and prayers of many" were behind him.[16]

THE LAND THAT WINTHROP FIRST SAW from the deck of the *Arbella* was a vista of hills and forest, very different from the Stour Valley. As he came to know it better he would understand its varied qualities. The ice sheet that had once covered the entire region did not completely recede until about thirteen thousand years before the arrival of the English, leaving rocky debris and allowing little time (in geological terms) for the accumulation of topsoils. Though early colonists such as William Wood claimed that the natural soil was superior to that of English counties such as "Surrey or Middlesex, which if they were not enriched with continual manurings would be less fertile than the meanest ground in New England," there was actually little land that was well suited for growing crops.[17] In fact, the geography featured several distinct regions. The coastal estuaries were full of shellfish and were resting places for large numbers of waterfowl, while the waters off the coast were rich in deep-sea fish such as cod. The islands off the coast and in the bays would come to be the favored places for gardens, orchards, and pasture free from predatory animals. Along the mouths of the rivers it was possible to harvest eels on their seasonal migrations, especially so on the river the natives called "the Big Eel," which the English renamed the Charles.[18] The tidal salt marshes along the coast and extending up the rivers provided the most nutritious grasses for the livestock brought over by the colonists, especially important in a landscape with few natural meadows. The hardwood forests, reaching down to the shoreline in many places, provided timber for fuel and building; nuts, berries, and other useful plant life; and wildlife ranging from small creatures such as squirrels and rabbits to deer, bear, and wolves. It was only in the river valleys that the colonists found rich, loamy, tillable soils.[19]

Before the arrival of the Europeans the landscape of New England had been home to perhaps as many as one hundred thousand native Americans, organized in various confederated bands. The largest of these in southern New England was the Narragansetts, who lived in what would become known as Rhode Island. To their west lived the Pequots and their kin, the Mohegans, who were rivals of the Narragansetts. On the eastern shore of the Narragansett Bay were the Pokanoket Wampanoags and, farther east along Cape Cod, the Nauset. The Massachusetts Bay was called that after the natives of the same name who lived there. Farther to the north were the Pawtucket and Abenaki.[20]

As with native populations throughout the Americas, contact with Europeans had brought diseases that devastated the Indians. An epidemic that swept the New England coast from 1616 to 1618 all but eliminated the native peoples in many areas. A smallpox epidemic in the early 1630s took a new toll. As Winthrop would write to his friend Sir Simonds D'Ewes, "for the natives in these parts, God's hand hath so pursued them as for 300 miles space the greatest part of them are swept away by the smallpox."[21] Just as a previous generation of Englishmen, including John's uncle and cousins, had used the devastation of Ireland to justify the settlement of Munster, so too would this generation of Englishmen point to the vacant state of the lands of eastern New England as justification for their settlement.[22] The depopulation brought by disease removed any danger that the natives may have posed to the infant settlements. And the abandoned native villages on river sites provided the English with ideal sites for their own towns.

THE *ARBELLA* ANCHORED OFF SALEM on June 12. At two in the afternoon John Endecott and the Reverend Samuel Skelton came on board to invite Winthrop, the assistants, and other gentlemen and their ladies to come ashore and dine. They supped on "a good venison pasty and good beer," which was a feast to those accustomed to ship's fare. Two days later the ship was warped into the inner harbor, and the passengers went ashore as the ship's captain fired a five-gun salute to celebrate.[23]

But the good cheer could not obscure the precarious state of the Salem settlement. As Thomas Dudley recalled a year later, Endecott's outpost was in "a sad and unexpected condition." Eighty of the settlers had died in the previous winter, and "many of those alive [were] weak and sick." Despite the meal provided the new arrivals, "all the corn and bread amongst them all [was] hardly sufficient to feed upon a fortnight."[24] During the brief history of the settlement the English leaders of the enterprise had sent over about 180 servants. Since their indentures had guaranteed them support, those still alive approached Winthrop for food. Unable to provide them their due, he acknowledged that the contract had been broken and set them free.[25]

Salem was never intended as the final destination of the new arrivals. Acting on orders from London, Endecott in the summer of 1629 had supervised the erection of a large home, designed as a place for the new governor to live and conduct business in, as well as other impermanent structures, to the south, on a neck of land protruding into Massachusetts Bay between the Mystic and Charles rivers.[26] On the seventeenth of April Winthrop journeyed to the Bay to examine that site and others, spending a night with Samuel Maverick, who had been living for a number of years on nearby Noddle's Island, before returning to Salem.[27] Over the next few months Winthrop moved back and forth between Salem and the Bay, supervising the settlement of many of the new arrivals at Charlestown, as the site chosen by Endecott came to be called.[28] Winthrop was residing in the Great House in Charlestown by mid-July.

During these early months religious services at Charlestown were held outdoors. One of the colonists, Roger Clap, remembered years later "their Meeting-Place being abroad under a tree, where I have heard Mr. Wilson and Mr. Phillips preach many a good sermon."[29] On July 30 the Charlestown settlers gathered for a day of fast and prayer and, led by Winthrop, Dudley, Isaac Johnson, and John Wilson, swore to a covenant whereby they formed a church, "solemnly and religiously . . . promis[ing] and bind[ing] ourselves to walk in all our ways according to the rule of Gospel and in all sincere conformity to His holy ordinances, and in mutual love and respect each to other, so near God shall give us grace."[30] Two days later others joined these pillars of the church in signing the covenant, bringing the number of members to near one hundred. Increase Nowell was elected an elder and William Aspinwall and William Gager deacons. John Wilson was chosen teacher (one of the two ministerial offices in a church recognized by the colonists). Intent on stressing that they were not separatists, the members of the congregation installed Wilson with an "imposition of hands, but with this protestation by all that it was only as a sign of election and confirmation, not of any intent that Mr. Wilson should renounce his ministry he received in England."[31]

Not everyone chose to locate in Charlestown. About four miles to the west, along the Charles River, Sir Richard Saltonstall and the Reverend George Phillips founded Watertown. Another assistant, William Pynchon, was one of the first settlers of Roxbury. Medford and Lynn were settled between Salem and Charlestown, and Dorchester established to the south of Boston.[32] In all the new settlements, many lived in tents and wigwams as they struggled to build more permanent shelter against the approaching winter. Winthrop's journal, which he had diligently kept on the voyage and which he would continue to write in regularly for the remainder of his life, contained virtually no entries from July 8, when he noted a day of thanksgiving for the arrival of the last of the fleet's ships, until the end of September. Other sources tell of the struggles. William Bradford mentioned a letter in which Winthrop talked of the colonists being "visited . . . with sickness, taking diverse from amongst them, not sparing the righteous."[33] Thomas Dudley said that people were so "sick of fevers and the scurvy" that they struggled to move their goods.[34] The eighteenth-century historian Thomas Prince, using records since lost, wrote that many of the colonists had arrived sick with scurvy and that the lack of housing and the damp conditions, coupled with the lack of fresh food, contributed to the growing death toll.[35] "Pease, puddings, and fish . . . [were their] ordinary diet," according to Winthrop.[36] Toward the end of July Winthrop dispatched Captain Pierce and the *Lyon* to Bristol to secure needed provisions.[37]

The Charlestown settlement seems to have been particularly hard hit. Edward Johnson, who was there, later recalled that "almost in every family lamentation, mourning, and woe was heard." Passing "from one hut to another, . . . [one] beheld the piteous case these people were in, and that which added to their present distress was the lack of fresh water." Only one spring had been found to serve the town, "and that only to be come at . . . when the tide was down."[38] Consequently, despite the difficulties of building new homes at that time of the year, in late September Winthrop and most of the community relocated across the river on the Shawmut peninsula, drawn there by a spring with abundant fresh water. They named their new settlement Boston, and by the end of October it had a population of about 150.[39]

In all, between April and December as many as two hundred colonists died, including the Lady Arbella Johnson and her husband, Isaac; the Reverend Francis Higginson; William Gager, the surgeon of Great Waldingfield whom Winthrop had persuaded to emigrate; and Edward Rossiter, one of the assistants. In September John confided to Margaret that the colony was afflicted with "much mortality, sickness, and trouble" but accepted it as the will of God, who "hath purged out corruptions, and healed the hardness and error of our hearts, and stripped us of our vain confidence in this arm of flesh, that he may have us rely wholly upon himself."

He hoped that "the days of affliction will soon have an end, and that the Lord will do us more good in the end than we could have expected, and will abundantly recompense [us] for all the trouble we have endured. It is enough that we shall have heaven, though we should pass through hell to it."[40]

But heaven would have to wait. Writing two months later he reported that twelve members of his own household had died since June.[41] Troubles and setbacks were means that God used to humble his children and make them aware of their dependence on his graces. Confident that God did support the enterprise, Winthrop accepted these reverses and sought to cooperate with God's grace as best he could. Two separate reports attest to his efforts. One spoke of Winthrop as "a discreet and sober man, giving good example to all the planters, wearing plain apparel such as may well beseem a mean man, drinking ordinary water," and, when not involved in the governing, "putting his hand to any ordinary labor with his servants."[42] The latter point was also made in a report by an unknown author who wrote that, "perceiving what misery was like[ly] to ensue through their idleness, [Winthrop] presently fell to work with his own hands, and thereby so encouraged the rest that there was not an idle person to be found in the whole plantation."[43] At a later date Cotton Mather reported the tradition that Winthrop had been the colony's "Joseph, unto whom the whole body of the people repaired when their corn failed them," supplying them from his own stores.[44]

Just as the colonists had found the summer hot and humid—more like southern Spain than their native land—so they learned that the winters were longer and harsher than they were accustomed to, though the harsh temperatures were mitigated by the fact that there was more winter daylight than they were used to in England.[45] On December 25 Winthrop noted that "the wind came [from the] northwest very strong, and some snow," and that it was "so cold as some had their fingers frozen and in some danger to be lost." The next day "the rivers were frozen and they of Charlestown could not come to the sermon at Boston" since the ferry could not operate.[46] Disease and malnutrition made additional inroads on the colonists. The Charlestown records noted that "[t]he people were compelled to live on clams and mussels, ground nuts and acorns, and these got with much difficulty in the winter time."[47] Little had been done to provide for the wintering of livestock, and the harsh realities of the New World were driven home as wolves attacked the colonists' cattle.[48] Facing a challenge that was unknown in the fields of England, the Assistants enacted a bounty for killing wolves.[49] Struggling to warm themselves, the settlers built roaring fires in their homes, with the result that many houses burned down."[50]

Returning ships had brought news of the colonists' sufferings back home—some carried by settlers who had abandoned the Bay—and support for the colony was threatened. John Humfry was still in England and observed that "as soon as this damp of ill report of the state of things came" to London, "strange it was to see how little brotherly love" was directed to New England. Investors who were pledged to contribute to the colony sought ways to evade their obligations.[51] Emmanuel Downing acknowledged that it was "the judgement of most men here that your colony would this winter be dissolved, partly by death through want of food, housing, and raiment, and the rest to return or flee for refuge to other plantations."[52] Humfry wrote to Winthrop that it was "solicitously agitated by many good and noble friends" that the colonists move to a location farther to the south— a suggestion that would plague Massachusetts throughout its first decades, and that Winthrop would always resist.[53]

Yet Winthrop never lost hope. He was encouraged by reports that not all Englishmen were ready to abandon the settlement. Dedham's Reverend John Rogers was one of many who did contribute funds for the aid of friends and neighbors who had migrated.[54] And Winthrop labored persistently to convince all who would listen that the colony would survive to become an example to all. From the start, his messages to friends such as Sir William Spring and Sir Nathaniel Barnardiston insisted that "these afflictions we have met with need discourage none, for the country is exceeding good."[55] As he became more aware of the region's climate and resources, he offered more detailed advice on things new settlers should bring with them. Rather than warning off his wife and family, he continued to anticipate their arrival. He never considered abandoning or moving the colony, maintaining his faith that he was doing God's will. Yet he would always remember the "good and noble friends" who had been quick to give up on the colony, their lukewarm commitments strengthening his resolve to trust only in God and God's soldiers in New England.

As the situation in the Bay continued to deteriorate, another day of fast was appointed for February. But on "February 5," according to Cotton Mather's history, when Winthrop "was distributing the last handful of the meal in the barrel unto a poor man distressed by the 'wolf at the door,' at that instant they spied a ship arrived at the harbor's mouth, laden with provisions for them all."[56] The arrival of the *Lyon* and the long-awaited supplies led to the day of fast being changed to a day of thanksgiving.[57] The immediate threat to their survival was over, though the colonists' struggles were not.

DURING THESE MONTHS OF TRIAL Winthrop was deeply engaged not only in securing the physical survival of the colony but also in the effort to shape its government and religious practices. He was familiar with the disorder that had contributed to the failures of earlier English efforts at colonization. "Christian Charity" had been an attempt to cement the commitment of the colonists to the principles of order and brotherhood. Transferring the charter and government to the New World provided a legal basis for authority, but it was the way authority was exercised that would be most important in determining how it would be accepted. Not all of those who had signed the Cambridge Agreement had actually joined the 1630 migration to the colony. When Winthrop convened the first Court of Assistants in the colony, in Charlestown on August 23, 1630, he was joined by Deputy Governor Thomas Dudley, Sir Richard Saltonstall, Robert Ludlow, Edward Rossiter, Increase Nowell, Thomas Sharpe, William Pynchon, and Simon Bradstreet.[58] The governing experience of the group was limited. Saltonstall, knighted in 1618, had served as a member of the commission of the peace in the West Riding of Yorkshire and had been lord mayor of Ledsham, Yorkshire. He, however, would return to England shortly after his arrival in Massachusetts. Ludlow appears to have had at least some formal training in the law, while Dudley had clerked for a judge.[59] Some of these men may have had experience of government and a knowledge of the law garnered from service in the institutions of the hundred and the parish or from handbooks of the law. Nonetheless, standing head and shoulders above all his fellow colonists in terms of his background as a member of the Suffolk commission and an attorney at Westminster was John Winthrop. This, as much as anything else, made him the key figure in shaping the way the Bay was governed.

It seems clear that Winthrop's instincts were to bring to the colonists the type of government that they had been familiar with in the old world, with the Court of Assistants in Massachusetts functioning much as the commission of the peace did in England. At its August meeting, the court designated its members and other specified individuals as justices of the peace, "in all things to have the power that Justices of the peace hath in England for reformation of abuses and punishing of offenders, but not [to] inflict any corporal punishment without the presence and consent of some one of the Assistants." In doing so they in essence designated those justices who were assistants to carry the authority which in England was given to those members of the commission who were "of the quorum." The court also set out procedures, again modeled after English precedent, for calling people before the court in civil actions and fixed prices for certain commodities and trades.[60] Years later, William Pynchon would write to Winthrop that he could "remember at our first coming, as soon as ever the people were divided into several plantations, you did presently nominate a constable for each plantation as the most common officers of the king's peace, and gave them their oath in true substance as the constables take it in England. Likewise, all controversies about meum et tuum were tried by juries after the manner of England, and after a while grand juries were appointed for further inquiry into such matters as might tend to the king's peace."[61]

Over the next few years the assistants continued to act like an English commission, empaneling juries, conducting trials, and sentencing offenders to whippings, fines, appearances in stocks and bilboes, and physical disfigurement. Each individual magistrate was granted power to issue warrants, summonses, and attachments. The court also bound individuals to appear before it and to carry out orders of the court, taking sureties to further guarantee compliance. Administratively, the court established prices for labor and goods; appointed militia officers and constables; set dates for musters; required town watchhouses to be built and watches to be kept; appointed days of fast and thanksgiving; regulated the sale of ale and liquor; took responsibility for administration of estates and appointed commissioners to further that task; licensed ferry operators; required and regulated town maintenance of stocks, roads and bridges, and scales and weights; set standards for the care of the poor; and passed orders to regulate what the magistrates conceived as moral behavior, such as prohibitions on the use of tobacco and the wearing of costly apparel.[62]

Winthrop exercised no greater powers than other magistrates, though as governor he did preside over the meetings of the Court of Assistants. In this he acted as did the custos rotulorum of the English commission of the peace, setting the agenda by giving the court its charge. He also exerted a strong personal influence, as many looked to his lead because of his experience and the confidence with which he exercised his authority. Recognizing the new and unique circumstances facing the colonists, he used discretion in determining what matters needed to be dealt with formally and which transgressions could be best handled with a word of warning. He quickly earned a reputation for fairness that was applauded by some, though from the start some of his peers, especially Thomas Dudley, grumbled about his leniency. Just as he set an example for a culture of work by joining his servants in their tasks, so too Winthrop sought to promote godly culture by his example. In England he had been particularly concerned with the scourge of drunkenness, and so in New England, "upon consideration of the inconveniences which had grown in England by drinking one to another," the practice of toasting, Winthrop "restrained it at his own table and wished others to do the like, so as it grew little [by] little to be disused."[63]

IT HAD BEEN THE COOPERATION of godly magistrates and ministers that had made the Stour Valley of his youth a model for the sort of society Winthrop wished to replicate in the new England, and that required him to pay attention to the planting of religion as well. One of the first acts of the assistants had been to provide housing and maintenance for the Reverends Wilson and Phillips.[64] The model of congregational Christians covenanting

together and selecting their ministers had been set forth in Endecott's Salem in 1629 and was followed by Winthrop and those who joined with him
in forming the church at Charlestown. His friend from the Stour Valley,
George Phillips, pursued the same course in organizing the church in
Watertown.[65] At this time proper belief and godly behavior were all that
was required of church members, and the laity were involved not only in
the formation of congregations but in the search for truth. Members were
allowed to speak out to request clarification of doctrine, and lay prophesying could enrich services. When John Wilson sailed to England in March
1631 in order to bring his wife over to the colony, the Boston church was
left for over a year without a formally trained minister. Praying with the
congregation before he departed, Wilson exhorted them "to love and commended to them the exercise of prophesy in his absence," designating
Winthrop as one "most fit for it."[66] Winthrop exercised this gift often in
Wilson's absence, and on at least one other occasion in the following years
he would "exercise by way of prophesy" in one of the other churches in the
colony.[67]

One of the challenges resulting from the adoption of a congregational
polity was how to maintain proper unity between the churches of the Bay.
Left to their own resources in England by the hierarchy's rejection of reform, the godly had turned to informal mechanisms of consultation to determine their practices and seek agreement on matters of faith. Clerical
conferences, such as those in the Stour Valley, were one such form of
association. For a time, clergy there had been able to count on magistrates like Jermyn and Higham to lend their assistance. These experiences
shaped the ways in which the colonists dealt with diversity and strove toward consensus.[68]

The need to employ such mechanisms came early, following the arrival
in Massachusetts of Roger Williams among the passengers on the *Lyon* in
February 1631. A graduate of Pembroke College, Cambridge, and a protégé
of Sir Edward Coke, Williams had served as a chaplain to the Masham family in Essex and was noted by Winthrop as "a godly minister."[69] Knowing
that Wilson was soon to leave, the Boston church had invited Williams to
supply their needs, but he refused to do so because "they would not make a
public declaration of their repentance for having communion with the Churches
of England while they lived there."[70] Moving on to Salem, Williams continued to make it clear that he had left behind the Church of England spiritu-
ally and institutionally as well as physically.

Despite their experimentation with forms and ceremonies that differed from those of their old parishes, Winthrop and the majority of colonists had been serious when they protested their loyalty to the English
church, their "dear Mother," on the eve of their departure.[71] The path of

separatism was one they emphatically rejected. Winthrop wrote notes of "[r]easons to prove a necessity of reformation from the corruptions of Antichrist which hath defiled the Christian Churches, & yet without an absolute separation from them" in response to Williams's arguments and may actually have delivered these arguments in the Boston church.[72] Winthrop criticized those "censurers [of the Church of England who] will not give them leave to distinguish between corrupt Churches & false Churches, as they do term the Congregations. Neither will they put any difference between the Churches as they are technically appointed by man, & as they are particular congregations, & appointed by Christ; for so they are, as they remain particular Congregations, even Churches of Christ's own appointing, although now they be corrupted." In England "particular Congregations were as true Churches in the days of Queen Mary as they were in the days of Queen Elizabeth, only they did differ in doctrine, & were more corrupt in Mary's days than in Elizabeth's, although too much corrupt then & now too. But the corruption of a thing doth not nullify a thing, so long as the thing hath a being in the same nature that it had when it was in the best being. So is it with the particular Congregations."[73] These arguments might have swayed the Boston church, but Salem was prepared to invite Williams to be the congregation's teacher despite his views, leading the Court of Assistants to write a letter to John Endecott questioning the choice. Williams was persuaded to move on to what he anticipated would be the more congenial atmosphere of the Plymouth Plantation, though he would later return to the Bay.[74]

Given the belief of Winthrop and others that truth could persist in the structure of a corrupt church, it was probably no great surprise that Watertown's George Phillips was found to have given that notion a new twist by asserting that the Church of Rome was a true church, though corrupted.[75] This, however, was further than most of the colonists were willing to go, and the Boston church dispatched Winthrop, Thomas Dudley, and Increase Nowell to confer with the Watertown congregation. The issue was debated, and all but the Watertown elder Richard Brown and two others finally agreed that Rome was not a true church.[76] When Brown's continued assertion of the error threatened to be disruptive to the point where the magistrates were taking notice, the Watertown congregation wrote to Winthrop in his private capacity. Once again he, Dudley, and Nowell traveled to the neighboring town, where the issues were debated anew, leading to a day of fast and a reconciliation of the opposing factions.[77]

Both the Watertown dispute and that with Williams touched on the issue of baptism and the legitimacy of baptism received in corrupt churches, a matter that would continue to trouble the congregations of the Bay. But both disputes, either of which could have led to a fracturing of the colony, were handled through nonconfrontational methods that preserved godly harmony. Winthrop's hand is to be seen in both instances. Witnessing the labors of Knewstub, Sandes and others in the conferences of the Stour Valley, he had learned to place his emphasis on the nurturing of godly piety and the encouragement of forms that promoted such godliness. Agreement was to be obtained when possible, but only through conferencing and exchanges of mutual advice, while avoiding efforts to develop precise standards and doctrinal norms that could stifle the spirit and divide the saints. Though some puritans became known as precisionists, where puritanism succeeded it did so because spokesmen such as Winthrop worked with a spirit of humility in trying to discern the mysteries of God's way.

DURING THESE TIMES OF TRIAL and planting, contacts with the native Americans did not command much of Winthrop's attention. Of course, by 1630 the presence of Europeans was a familiar one to the native bands, and the area in which the colonists were planting had been all but abandoned during the waves of epidemic disease that had devastated their lives. Given the crippled nature of Massachusetts native society, their ability to have assisted the colonists (should their help have been sought, and should they have desired to do so) would have been minimal. But it is clear that whatever the promotional literature had said about the goal of converting the natives, the first priority of the colonists for a long time would be crafting their own godly society. In later years contacts between the two peoples would become more important and more complex.

WHILE HIS ATTENTION WAS FOCUSED on leading the colonists through the hell that they were experiencing in the New World, Winthrop's thoughts were never far from Groton. He wrote often to Margaret, and though he acknowledged that "much business hath made me forget Mondays and Fridays," he tried whenever possible to enter into spiritual communion with her at the appointed times. The words of one surviving letter in September 1630 address her as if, indeed, she was with him in spirit to actually hear his words: "I am sorry to part with thee so soon, seeing we meet so seldom. . . . So I kiss my sweet wife and my dear children, and rest thy faithful husband."[78] He does not seem to have fully comprehended how the flawed title to Groton and the delays in the sale of the manor threatened their reunion. In March 1631, expecting that she might already be on her way, he wrote nonetheless, and thanked God, who "hath pleased to preserve us unto this hope of a joyful meeting, that we may see the face of each other again, the faces of our children and sweet babes."[79] Bereft of information on when she would actually sail, through the summer John must have had his hopes rise with the sighting of each ship, only to be dashed when it was confirmed that his family was not among the passengers. Finally, on November 2, Captain Pierce's *Lyon* arrived off the coast carrying Margaret, Mary, and Samuel Winthrop, as well as John Jr. and his wife, Martha Fones Winthrop. Adverse winds kept the ship from landing her passengers until the fourth, at which time the ship finally docked in Boston. The celebration of the governor's family reunion was general. A salute was fired, the trained bands provided an escort, and a crowd gathered to welcome the new arrivals. Well-wishers brought and sent "great store of provisions, as fat hogs, kids, venison, poultry, goose, partridges, &c, so as the like joy and manifestation of Love had never been seen in New England."[80] Never again would John Winthrop think of New England as hell.

10

The Best of Them Was But an Attorney

THE TOWN WHERE MARGARET WINTHROP was reunited with her husband in 1631 was a small diamond-shaped peninsula, the basic topography of which was dramatically different from today's modern city, which has been created by leveling the hills and filling in the bays of Winthrop's Boston.[1] The Charles River bent around the west and north sides of the peninsula, flowing into the Massachusetts Bay, which wrapped around the eastern side of the peninsula until almost rejoining the Charles west of the town. Only a small neck of land a quarter mile wide separated the peninsula from the interior there. At high tide the waters encroached on the neck, and at certain times in the spring, rains made the road along the neck almost impassable. On the northern point of the diamond was a hill on which the colonists would erect a windmill in 1632, moving it from Watertown because there it only ground when the wind was from the west. The southern tip of the peninsula was the neck. The eastern tip was dominated by a large hill where the colonists would build a fort commanding the harbor. On the opposite, western point were three hills which became known as the tri-mount, later corrupted to Tremont. One of these was the tallest hill on the peninsula, which was a sentry point where a beacon would be placed. One of the first inhabitants, Anne Pollard, later remembered the landscape at this time as "very uneven, abounding in small hollows and swamps, covered with blueberries and other bushes."[2]

To the south of the beacon hill and stretching alongside the Charles River marshes was the common grazing land. Fences across the neck protected the townsmen's livestock from wolves. The shoreline from the windmill hill to Fort Hill curved to form a cove, and it was around that cove that the settlers built docks and their first habitations. Each arrival in the town had been allowed to pick a spot suitable to his family needs. Paths shaped by these settlers as they drove cattle to graze by the salt marshes, carried their grain up windmill hill, or moved around the hills and across the uneven landscape became the twisting streets that would remain part of the map of Boston. Slightly inland from the cove, at the base of the western hills, was the spring whose fresh water had attracted the colonists to the peninsula. There townsmen and women met and exchanged news as they gathered water for their homes. Slightly to the north of the spring was the market place. In 1634 Thursday would be appointed the regular market day, which was also set (as had been the practice in England) as the religious lecture day.

On the east side of the marketplace was the Winthrops' first home.[3] Referred to as his "mansion house," this structure was likely the "governor's house," previously erected in Charlestown and now moved to Boston. It would have been similar to the main range of his Groton home. On the ground floor an entry lobby separated a parlor from a hall. A service wing including a kitchen, pantry, buttery, and other workspace extended from one end of this main range, and there was another wing at the opposite end. There were two chimneys, one rising through the parlor and the other through the hall, with one of them also serving the kitchen. The hall was a public space in which meetings of the assistants were held, as were services of the church until a meetinghouse was erected. A second floor contained a sleeping chamber for John and Margaret, as well as other chambers for their children and for the servants. There was room for a study on this floor also. A garret above the chambers was used for storage, as was a cellar.[4]

Other homes were built in a somewhat haphazard fashion along the twisting paths. Two lanes emerged as major thoroughfares. One, winding from the town dock and the home of the merchant and ferryman Edward Bendall, entered the marketplace and then continued south to the common pasturelands. Crossing the marketplace in an east-west direction was the lane on which Winthrop's mansion house stood, along the eastern side, near the cove. On the north side of that lane was the land of John Wilson. Just to the west of Wilson, on the northeast corner of the marketplace, was the home of John Coggan, in which he opened the community's first store. In a few years Robert Keayne, destined to be a controversial figure, would open his own store on land opposite Coggan's, on the southeast corner. Thomas Leverett's home was located to the west of Winthrop, between the governor and the marketplace. John Cotton would settle farther west on that lane, on the slope of one of the three hills, when he arrived in 1633. The first meetinghouse would be erected in 1632 on the south side of the marketplace. A few years later Philemon Pormont came to occupy a lot behind the meetinghouse, where he instructed students in the town's first school. South of the meetinghouse, in the direction of the pastureland, was the first inn in Boston, operated by Samuel Cole. A short distance farther south were the homes of Atherton Hough and Thomas Oliver. Richard Fairbanks settled along the same lane by 1633. In 1638 he would be licensed to sell wines and liquors, and his tavern would be designated as the place to which all letters from overseas would be delivered for collection by the inhabitants. Next to Fairbanks was the lot on which the Hutchinson family would build their home. In all, the population of the town in 1631 was probably under two hundred men, women, and children.

Defensible, blessed with good spring water, and with grazing land easily protected from predatory animals, Boston also had liabilities. Few trees grew on the peninsula, and thus wood for building and for fuel had to be brought to the settlement. There was also little prime land for growing more than small gardens. Winthrop, as befitted his status, was more fortunate than most. Along the east shore of the peninsula, nestled between two creeks just to the southeast of the spring, he owned a tract of arable land referred to as his "green." For most Bostonians, the deficiencies of the peninsula were supplied by the farms on the various islands close by in the Bay. And from as early as 1631 residents of Boston were granted farmlands off the peninsula, to the west along the Muddy River, to the northeast along the Mystic River, and to the south around Mount Wollaston.

The sea air and salt marshes must have reminded John of his days in Great Stambridge, but much of the environment was of a type that was new to him. Mixed with the familiar oak, chestnut, and walnut trees were species of hickory, flowering dogwood, and tulip trees that were unknown in England. Blueberries along the slopes of the hills and cranberries in the marshes complemented the blackberries and gooseberries familiar to the English. Wild turkey were found in large numbers, one contemporary claiming to have seen up to a hundred in a flock. Thomas Morton claimed that geese were so abundant that "I have had often 1000 before the mouth of my gun."[5] A traveler to the region wrote that the smaller shore birds were so numerous that he killed twelve score in two shooting trips.[6] Wild pigeons flew in flocks that seemed like large moving clouds blocking out the sun. Whether the area became a well-appointed hell or something approximating a paradise would depend on the success of Winthrop and his fellow magistrates and the ministers in constructing effective forms of government.

☙

BY THE END OF 1631 the foundations of the colony had been established. The Court of Assistants was functioning like a county commission, and the individual justices of the peace were supervising the growth of the various towns. Churches had been formed and clergymen selected as their officers. But the challenge of building upon those foundations remained, and over the next three years Winthrop would be deeply involved in the efforts to shape and refine colony government, town administration, and the practice of the churches. Complicating these tasks would be the constantly changing population. The colony would grow steadily in the 1630s as the changing conditions of church and state in England persuaded more and more of the godly to emigrate. Those changes in England would produce threats to the colony's autonomy, but they also meant that each wave of immigrants would bring new perspectives shaped by those changes and by the concerns that those changes evoked.

Rather than isolating themselves from their native land, those who came to New England embraced news from home and corresponded with friends and kin there. Many journeyed back and forth between the two Englands. For Winthrop and others, the determination to persevere in New England was only strengthened by the news from England. Parliamentary leaders, including Winthrop's friend Sir John Eliot, who had been imprisoned for standing against royal policies in 1629, remained in prison. Eliot would die in confinement. Fears of Catholic influence were heightened when the Spanish ambassador was welcomed in London with a great feast.[7] In 1631 Winthrop received news that "divers godly lecturers and ministers daily are put by" and that Thomas Welde had been targeted by the bishop of London, William Laud.[8] Early in 1632 the Reverend Henry Jessey wrote to John Winthrop Jr. with news that Laud had "excommunicated Mr. Weld," suspended Dedham's John Rogers and given him a month to conform or suffer excommunication, ordered Thomas Shepard out of his diocese, and threatened Stephen Marshall, Nathaniel Ward, and other Essex clergy.[9] By the following year some English correspondents were fearful of committing detailed news to paper lest their letters be intercepted and used against them. This was far from paranoia. When Laud's agents arrested the puritan clergyman John Stoughton they seized correspondence that included letters to and from Winthrop, John Wilson, other New Englanders, and English divines such as Henry Whitefield and Stephen Marshall. The bishop's agents likewise intercepted a letter from the Reverend Hugh Peter, then in the Netherlands, to his clerical friend John Phillips in Suffolk, copying it before allowing it to be delivered.[10] Thus, when Winthrop's former Groton steward John Bluett wrote to the governor in March 1633, he stated that "as concerning anything in our nation, you may have relation by word of mouth. . . . Neither can I say any good thereof, but may complain of bad times, and great fear of worse."[11]

The news from England became ever more dismal as the decade progressed. Mary Wright, a kinswoman and the wife of Winthrop's physician Lawrence Wright, wrote of living "in the midst of a sinful land."[12] Henry Jessey wrote in June 1633 that "Arminianism doth much spread, especially in York," where "Bishop Neale is now their Archbishop and Dr. Cousin Dean." Furthermore, "popery much increaseth, . . . [and] in Durham County and Northumberland many are known to go as openly to a mass . . . as others to a sermon."[13] William Laud was elevated to archbishop of Canterbury in August 1633, and New Englanders heard that John Davenport, Philip Nye, and other godly London preachers were targeted for episcopal action.[14] In October of that year the controversial Book of Sports, allowing Sunday recreation, was reissued. In 1634 William Prynne was sentenced to be whipped and have his ears cut off for a published attack on stage plays, and Sir Robert Heath, chief justice of common pleas, was dismissed from his office for his opposition to Laudian policies. The king's personal rule without Parliament continued, and new and questionable expedients to raise money were employed, most controversial being the 1635 extension of demands for "ship money"—a tax purportedly for naval construction—to inland counties. Godly clergy continued to come under attack. Henry Jessey was proud of the fact that some of his fellows "stand in the gap as we can, though we be not without some danger for it," and asked for colonial prayers.[15] But those who stood up against the new policies suffered for their stand. Muriel Gurdon, Brampton's wife, wrote to Margaret Winthrop in April 1636 that it "will grieve any Christian heart to hear that in so short time so many of God's faithful ministers should be silenced, and, what is worse, many that seemed to be zealous do yield obedience to the inventions of men."[16] A few months later Lucy Downing wrote from England that the new "Bishop of Norwich, whose name is Wren, doth impose a hundred and thirty-two articles to the clergy in his diocese," threatening the ability of clergy like Groton's William Leigh to hold their livings. The new and offensive ceremonies were enforced on the laity as well, and even so prominent a gentlewoman as "Mrs. Gurdon is questioned for not bowing and kneeling at burial prayers."[17] Outbreaks of plague and famine were interpreted as signs of God's displeasure with the course of English events.[18]

When the Winthrop fleet had sailed from Southampton in 1630, many had felt that the rights of Englishmen and the purity of the church were threatened, but threat was a prospect rather than a reality. Winthrop himself was disappointed by the decline of godliness in the Stour Valley and the slim chances of reversing that trend. Some lectureships had been disbanded and some ministers temporarily suspended. Parliament had been dissolved, but none knew that it would be more than a decade before a new Parliament would be called. None of the clergy emigrating in 1630 had been deprived of their ecclesiastical posts, and none of the laity had lost their pastors or seen them forced to employ hateful ceremonies. Ministers who came later—such as Roger Williams, John Cotton, Thomas Hooker, Thomas Shepard, John Eliot, Thomas Weld, Nathaniel Ward, and John Davenport—had actually felt the hard hand of authority. Lay men and women who came had suffered from the efforts of bishops such as Laud and Wren to impose ceremonial uniformity while reintroducing a Catholic-style "beauty of holiness."[19] Tales told by these newcomers underscored the importance of New England protecting itself against the policies and policymakers of Caroline England. Many of them had been radicalized by their experiences and were less likely than the earlier settlers to have fond memories of the English church and government. The challenge facing the colonists in the early 1630s was to balance their quest for perfection with the need to avoid provoking royal reprisals against the colony. Winthrop needed to draw upon all of his experience and judgment as he sought to shape the institutions and policies of state and church in accord with his model of Christian charity, and to do so in such a way as to ensure the survival of his holy experiment.

IN WORKING TO PERFECT the Massachusetts body politic, Winthrop was guided by lessons that he had learned as a citizen and magistrate in the godly kingdom of the Stour Valley. He had heard from his father and from friends such as Knewstub and Sandes of the success of clerical conferences in bringing together the godly clergy of the Stour Valley so that they were united if not uniform in all their beliefs and practices. He had seen how magistrates like Higham and Jermym had forged a majority which made the Suffolk commission a force for good, and he had tried to emulate them when he was named a justice. He had witnessed the involvement of the parish of Boxford in adopting social orders. Winthrop had learned how to seek consensus through compromises that respected the views of all, and he was suspicious of those who were too quick to claim the wisdom to know what was right and the authority to impose it on others. He believed that the best order was that achieved through persuasion and was one to which individuals consented, rather than one crafted by power and discipline. In every controversy he would face, his initial impulses were in the direction of moderation and reconciliation. He respected the views of those he saw as godly even when he disagreed with them, though he could react harshly to those in whom he saw no holy spark. He believed in the use of discretion to take into account the circumstances of crimes. He favored setting policy by example rather than by laws whenever possible.

Winthrop had shaped his character in the process of making sense of his religious experience. While some puritans took from their spiritual progress an arrogance stemming from their sense of divine election, Winthrop brought to his tasks a humility forged in his long struggle to come to grips with his sinfulness. Like his father, who picked up a drunkard and carried him home, John rarely let his hatred for the sin affect his care for the individual. The one contemporary reference to his service as an English justice recalled his kindliness and respect for others.[20] The reports of him setting an example for other colonists by toiling in the fields reflected this. The call in "Christian Charity" for the colonists to "love brotherly" was something that came naturally to this leader who in the colony's early days of scarcity shared his supplies to help those in want. But not all of his fellow magistrates shared his lenient instincts, and the issue of how justice was to be administered and the colony governed would prove contentious.

In the colony's first months the assistants met in Winthrop's house at eight in the morning on the first Tuesday of each month, and more often as needed. Though it was determined that the General Court should meet the last Wednesday in every legal term (the set times for court sessions in England), there were no freemen who were not assistants, and so the Court of Assistants in effect would have been identical to the General Court. In October a meeting of that General Court—reduced by death and departure to eight freemen/assistants—met in Boston. Believing that it was important for justice not only to be done but to be seen to have been done, Winthrop invited the residents of the towns to attend the court, much as had been the case at the English assizes and quarter sessions. But Winthrop also wished to expand freemanship in order to establish the colony on a consensual basis, and he sought to modify the charter to do so. First the court, with assent of the "general vote of the people" by a show of hands, agreed that in the future the freemen should choose the assistants, the assistants choose the governor and deputy governor from among themselves, and the assistants, governor, and deputy governor have the power to make laws and appoint officers to enforce them.[21] An invitation was then extended to all who desired to be made freemen to petition the court for that status.

At the next General Court, in May 1631, 116 freemen were allowed to vote for the assistants. This was close to all the adult males resident in the colony who were not servants. The assistants then reelected Winthrop as governor and Thomas Dudley as deputy governor. The leaders of the colony had not been required to extend freemanship. By involving the colonists in the selection of leaders, Winthrop sought to engage them in the system of government so as to promote their acceptance of magisterial rule. At that same May General Court, to ensure that those admitted to freemanship be "honest and good men," it was "agreed that for time to come no man shall be admitted to the freedom of this body politic but such as are members of some of the churches within the limits of the same."[22] Though this would come to be restrictive, at the time church membership was probably universal, with all who assented to puritan beliefs allowed to join in covenant. Thus, at the time it was adopted the franchise was left open to a far higher percentage of the male population than would have been able to vote in England.

Under the terms of this charter modification it was the assistants, not the entire General Court that included the freemen, who exercised the powers of government. In practice, therefore, the assistants continued to govern much as they had before the changes. With Winthrop presiding, on September 7, 1630, they set Thomas Morton in the stocks and then sent him to England for illegal trade with the natives. They appointed train band (militia) commanders and ordered that no one could settle in the Bay without the approval of the court. Three weeks later they prohibited sales or gifts of guns to the natives, chose constables for some of the towns, set prices that various craftsmen would be allowed to charge for their services, and empaneled a grand jury that indicted Walter Palmer for beating to death a servant. On November 9 the court set a just price for the sale of beer, established rates for the ferry serving Boston and Charlestown, set a bounty for killing wolves, and empaneled a jury that tried and acquitted Walter Palmer. On November 30 a colonist was whipped for stealing a loaf of bread, and Sir Richard Saltonstall was fined for having two persons whipped without the concurrence of a second magistrate. In March 1631 the court shipped five settlers, including the Catholic Sir Christopher Gardiner, to England as unfit to settle in the colony; an enterprising man named Nichols Klopp was fined for selling plain water as a cure for scurvy; and a surveyor of the colony's cannon and other military supplies was appointed. Over the following months it was ordered that natives might not be taken into English homes as servants without a license from the court; Saltonstall appeared again to offer satisfaction to the natives for one of his servants having burned two Indian wigwams; a servant sent over by Matthew Craddock to manage his interests was whipped for maligning the court; towns were instructed to take steps so that all inhabitants were to be furnished with good and sufficient arms; every captain was required to train his men each Saturday; and town watches were ordered and fines set for those who discharged guns after sunset. John Endecott was charged with battery, tried, convicted and fined, which, like the actions against Saltonstall, his servants, and the servant of Matthew Craddock, attested to the fact that no one was above the law in the colony. In October 1632 the court ordered that a house of correction be built in Boston.[23]

The court also acted to create what scholars of English society have referred to as a culture of discipline. John Baker was whipped for shooting fowl on the Sabbath. Anyone with dice and cards was ordered to get rid of them under pain of punishment. The assistants prohibited William Clark from continuing to board with Samuel Freeman and his wife because of a strong suspicion of sexual impropriety between Clark and Mrs. Freeman. Philip Ratcliffe had his ears cut off (a common sentence in England), and was whipped and fined, and banished for malicious attacks on the government and on the practices of the Salem church. Another critic, Henry Lynn, slandered the execution of justice in the colony and was whipped and banished. John Dawe was severely whipped for seducing a native woman to sleep with him. Actions were taken against those found drunk and those who sold too much spirits to servants and others. Public smoking of tobacco, something Winthrop had himself once enjoyed, was prohibited and power given to the assistants to fine offenders. Though a house of correction was built, many punishments took the form of shaming rituals. Thus, in September 1633 Robert Coles was fined £10 and "enjoined to stand with a white sheet of paper on his back wherein 'a drunkard' shall be written in great letters, and to stand there as long as the Court thinks meet." It was hoped that in a society where all aspired to be seen as godly, such humiliation would be a strong deterrent. This evidently was not the case with Coles, who in March 1634 was again found drunk, disenfranchised, and ordered to "wear about his neck" draped over his outer garments "a 'D' made of red cloth set upon white, to continue this for a year and not to leave it off at any time when he comes among company."[24]

In the early years of the colony the affairs of the various towns were supervised by the colony government. The assistants appointed town constables and militia officers. An effort was made to ensure that there was an assistant from each town who could act as a local magistrate in managing minor matters. Under the English-style system that had been adopted in the Bay, such matters were dealt with by individual magistrates or pairs of magistrates. It is clear that in carrying out his responsibilities as a local justice, Winthrop himself exercised a good deal of discretion and leniency, in sharp contrast to some of his fellow magistrates, most notably Thomas Dudley.

Striking the balance between the authority of the colony government and the liberties of the towns was not always easy. While Winthrop had witnessed and participated in what he viewed as the beneficial exercise of discretionary authority by the Suffolk commission of the peace, others— especially new arrivals in the colony—brought from England more bitter memories of how authority was exercised there and were suspicious of anything that smacked of arbitrary rule. Winthrop was called upon early in 1632 to smooth over jurisdictional differences when Captain Daniel Patrick, who commanded the militia north of the Charles River, continued to call upon Watertown citizens to keep watch near Newtown after he left Watertown to settle in the nearby community.[25]

Watertown would also initiate a more thorough airing of the colony-town relationship in response to a tax rate the assistants levied on the towns in 1632 to raise funds for colony fortifications. Just as the colony government was evolving, so too was local government. The English parish was both a civil and ecclesiastical unit of government, and at least some of the residents of Watertown had lived in parishes where there had been open meetings of the parish to set policies. It was a step in the evolution of the town meeting as the civil equivalent of the congregation when the Reverend George Phillips and the ruling elder of the Watertown congregation,

Richard Brown, called the townsfolk together in the meetinghouse to discuss the tax. They expressed their belief that "it was not sage to pay monies after that sort for fear of bringing themselves and posterity into bondage."[26] Clearly English concerns about arbitrary taxation such as the so-called Forced Loan had been carried to the New World. The Court of Assistants issued warrants calling Phillips, Brown, and others to appear before the court for an airing of the issues. The Watertown protestors explained that they viewed the colony's form of government to be equivalent to that of an English borough, where the aldermen were required to gain popular consent to rates. But, according to Winthrop, the government of Massachusetts was not like that of an English borough, for in those corporations aldermen formed a self-perpetuating body not subject to election. By virtue of the freemen having the right to elect assistants, the Massachusetts "government was rather in the nature of a Parliament," which, as in the case of the English Parliament, was the appropriate body to levy rates and subsidies. The fact that defense was a matter of critical importance to the colony might also have led him to point to the fact that the English commissions of the peace had the power to impose rates in times of crisis. Indeed, as a member of the Suffolk commission Winthrop himself had voted to impose a rate for the relief of the victims of the plague in Sudbury.

Similar challenges to the authority of governors to govern had had catastrophic results in other colonies, a fact well known to Winthrop, and so it was not enough that the Watertown leaders acknowledged the right of the assistants to levy the rate. They were asked to sign a statement retracting their opposition and then required to read the retraction in the Watertown meetinghouse the following Sabbath. Rather than alienate the Watertown protestors, however, the next General Court decided to ask each settlement to send two delegates to Boston to consult with the magistrates on matters of taxation, a step that contributed to the development of a legislative assembly two years later.

Seeking to steer a course that recognized the authority of the magistrates while seeking the consent of the governed, as he had tried to do with the Watertown protest, Winthrop also had to deal with conflict among the magistrates over how authority was to be exercised. Particularly troublesome was a widening gulf between himself and Deputy Governor Thomas Dudley. Each man represented a different side of puritanism. Winthrop was inclined to reach out to all those in whom he detected the spark of godliness. There were limits to what he would tolerate, but the communion of saints he sought was one that recognized that men of good faith might disagree on nonessentials as they grappled to discern and follow God's will. On one occasion he informed a friend that when faced with differences he sought to "improve that which is profitable, and cover the rest with love."[27] That had been the essence of his call for Christian charity as the ligaments of a godly society. The intolerance he occasionally displayed would most often be sparked by the intolerance of others. As a magistrate he was willing to shape penalties to the circumstances of the crime. As a leader he placed consensus over consistency, showing a willingness to compromise details if by doing so he could garner greater support for what he considered essential. Dudley, on the other hand, was hard and inflexible, characteristics which had stood him in good stead in England when, as steward to the earl of Lincoln, he had dug that peer out of a pit of debt by his rigorous management of the earl's estate. While there are few details of Dudley's English career that survive, it is at least suggestive that he worked for Lincoln, whose controversial activities, as one scholar has put it, were "often considered at variance with traditional agrarian paternalism." That same scholar has observed that "if the verses found in Dudley's pocket at his death and his personal testimony at the beginning of his will are a fair indication of his religious interests, then hating heresy was the largest component of his piety."[28] Whereas Winthrop tended to be flexible in his exercise of authority, Dudley was noted for being inflexible.

Friction between the two leaders had been evident from the colony's first days but flared up in 1632 as a result of a disagreement over the location of the Bay's principal settlement. During their first winter in Massachusetts there had been rumors of a French attack on the colony, which prompted concerns about the scattered nature of the settlements.[29] Early in December the magistrates considered building a fortified town on a site between Roxbury and Boston but then rejected it because there was an inadequate supply of spring water. Dudley, however, continued to push for a new town, and his fellow magistrates agreed to erect houses at a chosen site west of Boston and on the north side of the Charles River. In the spring Dudley moved to this new town (hence Newtown) and began building a grand house befitting his position. Winthrop sent servants to work on a home for himself, but none of the other magistrates followed suit, and in all only eight or ten families relocated to Newtown. Residents of Boston beseeched Winthrop not to desert them, and he agreed not to move. Dudley felt betrayed and directed his ire at Winthrop, who made matters worse by suggesting that the deputy governor had set a bad example in difficult times by building a mansion house with excessive wainscoting and other adornments.[30]

Other incidents probably contributed to Dudley's increasing sense of marginalization, and he resented the growing popularity of the governor. At a meeting of the Court of Assistants on April 3, 1632, a lifetime lease of Conant's Island in Boston harbor, which became known as Governor's Island, was awarded to Winthrop. Winthrop recorded in his journal that at the same meeting the assistants defined the powers to be exercised by the colony's governor, secretary, and treasurer. Dudley clearly disagreed with that definition, which was never recorded in the colony's official records. After the meeting he sent the governor a letter resigning as deputy and assistant. Asked to attend an informal meeting of the magistrates in Boston to discuss his reasons, Dudley explained that he was resigning to avoid disturbing the public peace, since as an assistant "he must needs discharge his conscience in speaking freely, and he saw that [this] bred disturbances." Encouraged to share those views nonetheless, Dudley needed little reflection to produce a list of grievances that were for the most part directed at Winthrop. He was upset with Winthrop's failure to move to Newtown as promised. He accused Winthrop of defaming him by suggesting that he had set a bad example by extravagant adornment of his house. And he objected that Winthrop had privately suggested that Dudley's practice in lending poor men grain for the promise of a larger repayment at harvest was no more than usury. Perhaps nothing explains the difference between the two men more than the contrasting images of Winthrop sharing his own meager stores to aid the hungry and Dudley bargaining with poor neighbors over how much they should repay him if he lent them grain. None of these charges was new to Winthrop, who in his own recollection of this meeting "took notice of these speeches and bore them with more patience than he had done upon a like occasion at another time." However his fellow magistrates responded, it was not enough to persuade Dudley to withdraw his resignation.[31]

The May General Court was also the occasion for the annual election of colony officers. On the day before, Winthrop met privately with Dudley and effected a reconciliation. The General Court then judged Dudley's resignation null, and he publicly accepted his position again, following which he was returned to office in the election. As Winthrop put it, "all things were carried very lovingly amongst all, . . . and the people carried themselves with much silence and modesty."[32] The underlying sources of friction between the two leaders had been papered over but had not been erased, and the threat to public unity had merely been deferred.

Dudley was not the only magistrate whose arbitrary dispositions caused Winthrop problems as he sought to negotiate the colony's political evolution. After dinner at the same informal meeting at which Dudley had been allowed to air his complaints, Winthrop shared with his colleagues the news that some of the colonists were planning to propose a greater role for the freemen in the colony's government. Specifically, the freemen wished to vote on all of the assistants every year, not simply when necessary to fill vacancies, and they wished to elect the governor rather than leave that task to the assistants. Winthrop persuaded the majority of the magistrates to accept the proposed changes rather than divide the colony, but Roger Ludlow "grew into a passion, and said that then we should have no government, but there would be an interim wherein every man might do as he pleased." Ludlow refused to be reconciled and threatened to return to England. Despite his opposition, when the General Court met "it was generally agreed by erection of hands that the Governor, Deputy Governor, and Assistants should be chosen by the whole court of Governor, Deputy Governor, Assistants, and freemen and that the Governor shall always be chosen out of the Assistants."[33]

Shortly thereafter Winthrop, having acceded to his neighbors' request to remain in Boston, ordered his servants in Newtown to dismantle and remove the house they had been building there. This rekindled Dudley's anger, and he complained about the matter to John Wilson and the Reverend Thomas Welde of Roxbury, who alerted Winthrop to the new storm. On August 3 the two leaders came together on the neutral site of Charlestown with Wilson, Welde, the Reverend John Warham, the Reverend John Maverick, and Increase Nowell, a magistrate who had been an elder of the Boston church when Dudley was a member. Dudley opened the meeting by stating that while he had a number of other particular grievances about Winthrop, which he had been advised by other magistrates not to raise, he did wish to complain that Winthrop and others had breached a promise they had made to settle at Newtown. Winthrop responded that he had fulfilled his promise by building a home there and had only removed it when it was evident that none of the other assistants planned to do so. Furthermore, he claimed that Dudley himself had discouraged many of the ordinary citizens of Boston from relocating to Newtown and that since he, Winthrop, had promised his fellow Bostonians that he would never desert them, that prior commitment required him to remain there. The ministers met among themselves for an hour and then returned their judgment that Winthrop was at fault for removing the house without first consulting with Dudley and the assistants, but that his fault was somewhat minimized if Dudley had in fact discouraged other Bostonians from moving to Newtown. Winthrop said he was "willing to submit . . . to the judgement of so many wise and godly friends, [and] acknowledged himself faulty."[34]

After dinner Dudley raised further complaints, charging Winthrop with a variety of abuses of power as governor. He started by asking by what right Winthrop claimed his authority as governor, arguing that according to the charter the governor had no more power than any other assistant. Caught off guard by this, Winthrop argued that the office of governor as created by the charter "gave him whatever power belonged to a governor by common law or the statutes," though in point of fact nothing in Winthrop's behavior as governor before or after this clearly indicates that he ever took any action which would have exceeded his authority as a mere magistrate. Dudley "began to be in a passion" and argued that if Winthrop was going to be uncompromising he would be uncompromising too, and

Winthrop responded in kind.[35] At this point "the Deputy rose in great fury and passion, and the Governor grew very hot also, so they both fell into bitterness." With difficulty the mediators restored order, and Dudley offered specific instances in which he believed Winthrop had acted arbitrarily.

Dudley charged that Winthrop had no authority to have moved some of the colony's ordnance and erected a fort at Boston. Winthrop responded that a decision had been made by the assistants to build such a fort; nothing having been done and the ordnance lying rusting on the beach, he and some other assistants had moved it and started a fort as private individuals and without any public expense. Next Dudley accused him of misconduct in having lent twenty-eight pounds of gunpowder to Plymouth. Winthrop responded that this was from his own stock of powder, not the public's, and that he had done so because of their neighboring colony's great need. Dudley then accused him of authorizing a settlement on the Merrimack River, but Winthrop said he only licensed trade there, which was within his power as a magistrate. Dudley further charged that Winthrop had illegally approved the building of a fishing weir at Watertown. Winthrop explained that he specifically told the Watertown citizens that he had no authority to allow them to build a weir but that, given their food shortages, if they did so he would urge the next General Court to give its blessing retroactively. The deputy questioned by what authority Winthrop had deferred the execution of sentences of banishment against two miscreants. Winthrop claimed that the court had given the governor authority to stay the execution of any sentence and, since the individuals may have perished if sent from the colony in the depths of winter, he had exercised that power in charity. Dudley's sixth charge was that Winthrop had been negligent in collecting fines imposed by the court. While Winthrop claimed he had signed any warrants brought to him by the colony secretary, he acknowledged that he had not pressured the secretary to draw up such warrants. In a clear indication of the differences between himself and Dudley, he "confessed that it was his judgement that it were not fit in the infancy of a commonwealth to be too strict in levying fines, though severe in other punishments." Finally, Dudley complained that even when a cause had been decided by the assistants, Winthrop was prone to ask his colleagues to consider additional circumstances and to urge more leniency, which Winthrop admitted and sought to justify.

Having responded to the specific charges, Winthrop acknowledged that while he undoubtedly had made some slips over the years in which he had served, he had always expended his time and private funds to advance what he considered the best interests of the colony. He criticized Dudley for having sprung the charges of autocratic rule without prior warning, charges he believed stemmed from "such jealousy he had conceived that the Governor intended to make himself popular, that he might gain absolute power and bring all the Assistants under his subjection." The meeting broke up without any resolution, but in the following month the ministers evidently succeeded in calming the passions of the two, with Winthrop making a contribution toward establishing a minister in Newtown, which Dudley graciously returned. And, according to Winthrop, "notwithstanding the heat of contention which had been between the Governor and Deputy, yet they usually met about their affairs . . . without any appearance of any breach or discontent."[36] Both men being loving fathers, the marriage around this time of Winthrop's daughter, Mary, to Dudley's son Samuel must have helped to bring the two together, though Winthrop would comment a year later that "some differences fell out still now and then between the Governor and the Deputy," which were always soon healed.[37]

The stability of the colony was still fragile, however. Though resembling the forms of English government, the institutions of the Bay colony were not enhanced by long tradition, and none of the colony's leaders came from the highest levels of English society to which the settlers had been taught to defer. One critic of the Court of Assistants, Thomas Dexter, complained that it was a "captious government [that] will bring all to nought" and further observed, speaking of Winthrop, "that the best of them was but an attorney."[38] Dexter had migrated in 1630 and had a history of challenging authority and suing his neighbors. Controlling such individuals was always a problem. New arrivals, having felt what they considered to be the lash of arbitrary government in England in the early 1630s, and not familiar with the reasons why the Bay government had evolved the way it had, could also be critical of the actions of the magistrates. In order to undergird its authority the Court of Assistants adopted a new oath of loyalty in April 1634 which was to be taken by every non-freeman above the age of twenty, whereby the individual swore that as an inhabitant of Massachusetts he would submit "to the authority of the governor, and all the other magistrates there, and their successors, and to all such laws, orders, sentences and decrees as now or are hereafter shall be lawfully made." A second refusal to take the oath would be cause for banishment.[39] The May meeting of the General Court then approved an oath to be taken when someone was admitted to freemanship. The new freeman would acknowledge himself subject to the government of the colony and pledge to be "true and faithful to the same, and . . . accordingly yield assistance and support thereunto, . . . submitting myself to the wholesome laws and orders made and established by the same."[40]

That May 1634 meeting of the General Court was an important one for the colony and for Winthrop. The balance between magisterial and popular authority was once again adjusted. In April a deputation of representatives from each town had been invited to advise Winthrop on matters to be addressed at the coming court and had asked to see the charter. After reading it they realized that the document granted the freemen meeting in the General Court, not the assistants, the power of making laws. They questioned the readjustment of power made in the colony's first year, before many of them had immigrated. Winthrop explained that while the governance spelled out in the charter might work in a commercial company such as the Bay Company initially had been, the sheer number of freemen made such a practice impractical in the colony itself. And if all freemen could not gather to legislate, delegating others to act on their behalf would still be impractical since it would require more qualified lawmakers than the colony had available at that stage of its history. Furthermore, it would draw such delegates away from their important work on their farms and in their crafts for too long a time. As a compromise he did, however, suggest that he would be willing to call a delegation of town representatives together annually to review the laws and orders of the court and suggest changes.[41]

The fact that the pattern of government had diverged from the charter lent credence to fears that the magistrates posed the same threat to liberty that the new emigrants had fled England to escape. For those harboring such concerns Winthrop's proposal was clearly insufficient. And if the charter was to be upheld as the foundation of the government, then clear divergences from its requirements could not be tolerated. Winthrop and the assistants bowed to the inevitable, and it was entered in the records of the May General Court that "none but the General Court hath power to make and establish laws, nor to elect and appoint officers, [and] . . . to set out the duties and powers of the said officers." It was further declared that the General Court, and not the assistants, had sole authority to admit new freemen, levy taxes, and dispose of lands.[42] It was not clear how the freemen as a whole would exercise these powers in the General Court, but an important step in establishing the consensual basis of Massachusetts government had been established.

DURING THESE YEARS OF POLITICAL EVOLUTION, the religious institutions and practices of the Bay were also taking shape. In Winthrop's vision, the City on a Hill was to be a model of proper cooperation between godly magistrates and godly ministers. A due form of church order was as important as a due form of civil order. While his involvement in this task would not be as great as his efforts in forming the institutions of government, it was greater than his lay status might suggest to us.

With no bishops in New England and no lay patrons to induct pastors, the colonists were thrown upon their own resources, and they learned to employ and formalize the informal methods they had used to achieve unity in England. The process began before Winthrop's arrival with the formation of the Salem church. That precedent had been followed by some settlers from the west country of England who formed a congregation before their departure. The group, including Roger Ludlow, Edward Rossiter, and Roger Clap, "kept a solemn day of fasting in the New Hospital in Plymouth in England, spending it in Preaching and Praying." The Reverend John White of Dorchester was with them and was one of those who preached, and in the afternoon "the people did solemnly make choice of and call" the Reverends John Warham and Samuel Maverick to be their ministers in the New World.[43] The same pattern was followed by Winthrop and those who formed the Charlestown church in August 1630 and by the settlers of other towns, with each forming its own congregation which defined its own purposes and managed its own affairs.

Discussions of this "non-separating congregationalism," to use a phrase employed by Perry Miller, too often ignore the English roots of this practice. Where puritanism had been most successful, as in the Stour Valley, pious lay men and women had joined with godly clergy in informal associations in which they not only prayed together but also discussed and reached agreement on matters of faith and practice. In some English parishes the laity, formally or informally, chose the minister to be presented to the bishop for induction into the parish living. But in all English parishes the true authority of local pastors and lecturers rested not simply on the respect of their peers but on lay acceptance of their role, a role that was defined in everyday exchanges in which godly lay men and women were important players. Sermon gadding was a way in which the godly laity voted with their feet for a given cleric and his preaching. The reputation of a clergyman such as John Rogers was enhanced when people from a broad area made their individual decisions to travel to Dedham to hear him preach. Likewise, the judgment that a pastor was a "dumb dog" was a judgment based on the dissatisfaction of the members of his parish. Thus, when scholars talk about a collective puritan mentality or explore the movement as an example of popular religion, they are discussing phenomena that were shaped by lay as well as clerical activity.[44]

The centripetal and even anarchic implications of this English proto-congregationalism was inhibited by the forging of networks of associated clergy and laity who struggled to achieve agreement on religious essentials. Clergy organized in conferences such as those centered in Dedham, Essex, and Cockfield, Suffolk maintained a united front without achieving precise uniformity. Indeed, their success in achieving unity owed much to their willingness to tolerate differences on matters where they could not agree. Prophesyings, conferences, combination lectureships, and regional fasts were all means of straining toward symmetry. Many of these efforts involved lay participation in one form or another, and the effectiveness of clerical initiatives was enhanced by their willingness to join in conferencing and acts of piety with lay saints. Attacked as conventicles by episcopal critics, these small associations generated a sense of community among the saints. None of this was incompatible with episcopacy, and indeed the goal of most English puritans into the 1640s was the creation of a reformed episcopacy. At the same time, episcopal efforts to control or suppress nonconformity exerted a pressure that brought the godly together, and some feared that the absence of such pressure in the New World might let loose the centripetal forces within congregationalism. Preventing this and maintaining unity was a high priority not only for the clergy but also for John Winthrop and the magistrates.[45]

Winthrop had, of course, been a part of the godly community in the area of Groton. He had joined with fellow laity and with clergy in a small association which some would have called a conventicle. He gadded to sermons and took notes of what he heard. He devoted a part of each morning to prayer and study. He dined with clerical friends and had the chance to discuss teachings and experiences that he found troubling. Though there is no direct evidence for it, it would not be surprising if he exercised his religious gifts in Groton or Boxford church in a period set aside for lay prophesying. This was the background he drew on as he contributed to the task of shaping New England's religious practice.

The Massachusetts churches were founded on written covenants that were drawn up by laymen of particular piety, usually joined by someone who had exercised the ministry in England. In the case of the church at Charlestown, Winthrop, Dudley, Isaac Johnson, and John Wilson had drawn up the covenant, which pledged those who became members and signed the agreement to work together as a community in deciding all matters. The authorization of clergy by lay congregations was formalized by the designation of the congregation as the agency which chose and ordained its ministers. After the first few years of settlement the decision to invite a clergyman was made only after experiencing his preaching. Thus, when John Cotton arrived in Boston in September 1633 he was invited to preach on a topic chosen by the congregation. Having impressed the members, he was propounded for membership, admitted, and then shortly thereafter elected to the ministerial office of teacher.[46] As men with university training and reputations for godliness, the clergy wielded considerable influence in their congregations. The system was once described as one in which a speaking aristocracy spoke to a silent democracy, and there is no denying that during the early decades of settlement ministers such as Cotton, Shepard, Hooker, and Davenport were strong leaders in their congregations and in the broader community. Having chosen a minister because his learning and piety were respected, it was natural for the laity to be inclined to defer to his views, but the laity did take their responsibilities seriously and on occasion asserted their governing responsibilities.[47] The ability of a clergyman to command the support of his congregation depended in part on his constant nurturing of his relationship with them and on his ability to draw upon the support of his fellow ministers.

Accustomed to forming networks of support in England, the early clergy of the Bay continued that practice in Massachusetts. From the earliest days of settlement ministers supplemented their Sabbath preaching with weekday lectures, and colleagues from surrounding towns traveled to hear their peers and to meet afterward to discuss common issues. Initially some lectures began in the morning, with the whole day given to the occasion, so the Court of Assistants, concerned about time lost from work, in October 1633 passed an order that no lectures could begin before one o'clock.[48] In addition to these occasions, according to Winthrop "the ministers in the Bay . . . did meet once a fortnight, where some question of moment was debated." Salem's Samuel Skelton and Roger Williams both criticized this practice for possibly leading to some sort of presbyterian authority over independent congregations, but their concerns were dismissed, with the members of the association agreeing that no person or body could have jurisdiction over individual congregations.[49] Nevertheless these gatherings, like their counterparts back in England, were expected to contribute to keeping the clergy, and through them the congregations, on the same course.

It has been recognized for some time that there was no single "New England mind" or orthodoxy to which all the colonists were expected to slavishly subscribe. Accepting the tentativeness of any formulation of the will of God and always holding themselves open to further light were central to puritanism wherever and whenever it was successful.[50] The fact is that the clergy did not always agree—but as long as those differences were over indifferent matters or slightly different emphases on common doctrines, this was acceptable. Discussion was meant to illuminate issues, achieve consensus when possible, and solidify common ground when it was reached. The goal was, as one scholar has put it, "cohesion through compromise."[51] Just as the members of the Dedham conference in the Stour Valley had been unable to agree on the observation of the Sabbath, so too the clergy of Massachusetts could not always agree. The secret was to tolerate such differences while praying for further light. As John Eliot chided one of his fellow ministers, "brother, learn the meaning of these three little words, bear, forbear, forgive."[52] And when Eliot himself applied a doctrine in one of his sermons in such a way as to imply criticism of the colony's dealings with the natives, the magistrates sent John Cotton, Thomas Hooker, and Thomas Welde to bring "him to acknowledge his error in that he had mistaken the ground of his doctrine."[53]

Congregations formally and informally consulted with one another so as to avoid drifting into dangerous differences. Thus, Winthrop had been one of the lay representatives who traveled to Watertown to debate the beliefs of some members of that congregation that the Church of Rome should be considered a true church. Following the election of Increase Nowell as one of the assistants in 1632, there was concern in the Boston church as to whether he could hold that position in the civil government and also continue as one of the officers of the church. The congregation solicited advice from the churches of Plymouth and Salem, and on a visit to Plymouth Winthrop debated the issue with Roger Williams and other members of that congregation. The outcome was that Nowell resigned as church elder.[54] Another example of the process used to try to reach consensus can be found on that same visit to Plymouth. Following the administration of the sacrament on the Sabbath, Roger Williams had propounded the question of whether it was proper to refer to an unregenerate man as "goodman." The Plymouth pastor, Reverend Ralph Smith, preached on the issue, after which Williams, Plymouth governor William Bradford, and other laymen spoke to the question by way of prophesying. Winthrop and John Wilson, who was also part of the visiting Boston group, were invited to speak. Winthrop argued that "goodman" as commonly employed was used as an English custom of civility and did not imply spiritual goodness.[55] In March 1634, following the lecture in Boston, a question was raised about whether or not Scripture dictated that women should wear veils when they went out in public, and especially in assemblies such as the church. Roger Williams had asserted this belief in Salem, where it evidently became the practice. Earlier, called to preach to the Salem congregation, Cotton had argued that the practice itself was indifferent, not mandated by Scripture, and that in societies where veils were not customary as a sign of women's subjection there was no need for it. Now, the issue was raised again at the Boston lecture. Cotton reiterated his belief that wearing veils was not required, while John Endecott challenged him and argued for the former practice of the Salem church. Winthrop, acting as a member of the Boston congregation, "perceiving it to grow to some earnestness, interposed, and so [the debate] brake off."[56]

Other informal mechanisms also contributed to keeping the separate churches on a common course. Ministers, and sometimes laymen such as Winthrop, occasionally preached to neighboring congregations. Handwritten treatises exploring various religious issues were composed and exchanged. Lay men and women traveled to nearby towns to attend lectures, took notes, and gathered with neighbors in their homes to review and discuss the teachings.[57] Copies of these sermon notes were often shared.[58] Through such means common forms of worship and religious practice began to take shape.

Worship and lectures were held in what Winthrop and his fellow colonists called a meetinghouse, rejecting the term "church" and all connotations that the building was holy territory. The same structure that served for religious gatherings also served a community's need for civic meetings; in the case of Boston, the meetinghouse was large enough to hold meetings of the General Court of the colony. The cruciform structure of English churches was rejected in favor of a simple square or rectangle. There was no internal division of space such as that between the chancel and the nave in the churches the colonists had left behind. There was no religious ornamentation—no wall paintings or statues, no communion rails or crucifixes. Windows were small and of plain glass. Surprisingly, there is no evidence of the placing of commandment boards or painted panels containing the Lord's Prayer and verses of Scripture, innovations of the Reformation in England to which puritans seemed to have no objection. Furnishings were sparse. A table that could be used by clerks at a public meeting could be brought forth to serve as a communion table during worship. In the 1630s most of the congregation would have sat on rough forms, or benches, though the ministers sat in elevated chairs near the pulpit, and beneath them were seats for lay elders and other members of the elite. A pulpit, with the Bible prominently displayed in front of it, was centered on the north wall and facing the south entrance to the meetinghouse; it would have been the focal point of the service.

For John and Margaret Winthrop and their children the Sabbath began on Saturday evening, at which time all nonessential work in the household ceased. Meals could be prepared, but as simply as possible. Travel was similarly limited, and all recreational activities were suspended. Sabbath time not spent in the meetinghouse was to be devoted to activities such as prayer, Scripture reading, and meditation.[59] In the morning, responding to the bell that called them to services in the Boston church, the Winthrops came to participate in a liturgical world that not only differed dramatically from that which his great-grandparents had experienced in pre-Reformation Lavenham but also was far different from what he had known in Groton.[60] Godly clergy in England had gone as far as they could in refusing to wear vestments and in dispensing with those parts of the liturgy they found least acceptable, but there were many undesirable yet fundamentally indifferent practices which they accepted as part of the cost of maintaining their livings so that they could tend to their flocks. In New England even the least offensive elements of the prescribed English worship could be dispensed with.

The morning service on the Sabbath began at nine and opened with prayers of intercession and thanksgiving, which might last a quarter of an hour. Members of the congregation could request that the prayers include their special intentions. Following this either John Wilson or John Cotton would read and expound on a chapter of the Scriptures, which was followed by singing of a psalm, probably from the Sternhold and Hopkins translation. Because they rejected the use of musical instruments in church (though not in the home or in public space), there was no accompaniment to this singing.[61] One of the ministers would then preach a sermon of an hour or longer, which also would be followed by a psalm. A lengthy prayer and a blessing would follow. If the Lord's Supper was to be celebrated, that would come next. On other Sundays the congregation would be dismissed until the afternoon service, which began about two o'clock and followed the same basic pattern. In Boston, if Cotton had preached in the morning Wilson would be in the pulpit in the afternoon. Notes of the proceedings in the Boston church taken by one of Winthrop's contemporaries indicate that following the sermon individuals were allowed to raise questions about points of the doctrine which they found unclear.[62] Afternoon services concluded with baptisms, when appropriate. Contributions for the poor were collected at the end of the afternoon service. Wilson or Cotton might exhort the community to charity, following which Winthrop and the other prominent citizens would lead the members of the congregation one by one to the front of the church, where they would place their donations in a box held by the deacon. Church business would then be conducted. In contentious cases when the congregation dealt with an offending member, the session could last late into the day and even be adjourned until the next Sabbath. Finally came a prayer, a psalm, and a blessing dismissing the congregation and sending them home. Both morning and afternoon services were attended by all members of the community and open to all, including English visitors and native Americans.

Only two sacraments were accepted and administered in New England, and they were available only to church members who had accepted the covenant, though all could witness the ceremonies. As was called for in the Church of England, no one, though otherwise eligible, could receive the Lord's Supper if involved in any breach of peace among the members of the church. Consequently, notice of the Lord's Supper was given a few weeks in advance so that those in need could reconcile themselves with those from whom they were estranged. At the time of the ceremony a table was brought into the center of the church. The ministers and lay elders sat around the table, while others moved their seats or forms as near as they could. One of the ministers repeated the words of Christ spoken at the Last Supper, after which the bread was passed around on a platter for all to partake of. Then the wine, in the silver communion cup donated by Winthrop, was likewise passed around for all to drink.[63] The number of communicants in Boston was so great that all could not see while sitting, so some stood and shifted their positions, though they would resume their seats to eat the bread and drink the wine. A psalm was then sung and the congregation dismissed.

Baptisms were almost invariably performed on the Sabbath, though they could be held anytime the congregation was gathered together. There was no font around which the participants would gather; the ceremony took place at the deacon's seat. The pastor would pray and then preach a brief exhortation to the congregation and the parents. One of the parents held the child, who was then baptized in the "name of the Father, and of the Son, and of the Holy Ghost" by "washing and sprinkling." The sign of the cross and other popish trappings against which puritans had long complained were absent from the ceremony. Godparents were not employed. After Margaret Winthrop gave birth to a boy in the summer of 1632, Winthrop recorded that at the baptism "the Governor himself held the child to baptize, as others in the congregation did use."[64]

Critics of the colony complained to English authorities that in Massachusetts the Lord's Prayer was not used, that ministers did not perform marriages, and "that fellows which keep hogs all week preach on the Sabbath." These are only some of the ways in which the colonists departed from the practices of the English church.[65] The New England puritans were suspicious of set prayers, which they believed tended to be repeated by rote, with no thought or fervor, and clergy preferred to offer extemporaneous prayers. While the Lord's Prayer was well rooted in Scripture and employed by the godly, it was not a regular part of the liturgy as it was in England. Marriage was rejected as a sacrament and became a civil ceremony performed by local magistrates. The use of the ring in marriage, another English church ritual challenged by the puritans, was also dispensed with. Confirmation was another sacramental practice abandoned in the New World.[66] Needless to say, the hated vestments prescribed by the English bishops were eschewed by the New England clergy, who exercised their office wearing the university gowns that were emblems of learning rather than of special sanctification. The charge that farmers preached represents a distortion of the colonial use of prophesying. The colonists insisted on the importance of an educated ministry but did allow laymen to ask questions and preach by way of prophesying. Winthrop recorded in his journal that the Boston church met on Saturday evenings in an "ordinary exercise" that appears to have featured a prophesying directed to a specific question, with significant lay involvement.[67] While clergy were called to deathbeds to pray with those who were dying, there were no religious funerals or funeral sermons per se in Massachusetts, and no church graveyards for burial. Just as they rejected the notion of the church as holy space, so too they rejected the practice of consecrating burial grounds. The bell tolled often to mark the death of colonists in the first years of the settlement, and Winthrop and others accompanied the deceased to a community cemetery a short distance from the church where they were laid to rest.

The churches of New England departed from the traditional liturgical calendar with its commemoration of saints' days and holy days, including Christmas. Many Christians, not only puritans, had long recognized that there was no scriptural basis for locating the birth of Christ on the twenty-fifth of December and that the decision made by the church in the fourth century to celebrate that date was an attempt to Christianize the traditional pagan observations of the winter solstice. The Christian veneer placed on those festivals was notoriously thin, and in the early modern world many marked Christmas with an extended period of "misrule" that included rowdiness, inversions of proper social order, gluttony, drunkenness, and sexual license. Reformers fought to bring an end to these carnival-type activities. Some English puritans believed that eliminating the holy day was the best solution. Others, and this is another example of the godly agreeing to disagree, believed that it would be sufficient to restore a proper observance of Christmas. In Groton, Winthrop attended church on December 25, 1627, and took notes on a sermon preached from Matthew 1:21, "She shall bear a son, etc."[68]

The early observance of Christmas in New England is shrouded in mystery. Though many of the Pilgrims in Plymouth worked on the day in 1620 and 1621, Governor Bradford excused some on the later occasion because they claimed that "it went against their consciences to work on that day," telling them that "if they made it a matter of conscience he would spare them till they were better informed." His anger later in the day was precipitated by their abuse of any religious observance. He found them "in the street at play, openly; some pitching the bar and some at stool ball and such like sports."[69] Bradford's experience may have been the practice in the Bay in the 1630s if those who were used to marking the day with prayer and Scripture reading saw no reason to change that habit. By the mid-seventeenth century, however, the inability to purge the day of its revels led to puritan efforts to ban it on both sides of the Atlantic.[70]

Though Adam Winthrop recorded Ash Wednesday as the first day of Lent in 1620, and an English friend living with Emmanuel Downing wrote to John Winthrop Jr. in 1633 that in the Downing household "we keep the strictest Lent that ever was," that penitential period was also dispensed with in the colonies.[71] Easter was likewise ignored in New England. There is ample evidence that puritans in England, including John Cotton and John Winthrop, accepted at least some of the customs of St. Valentine's Day, but there is no evidence that sheds light on the survival of these practices in the colony.

While normal routines were not broken by religious holy days, there were other occasions on which the colonists abandoned their work and gathered together. Guy Fawkes Day, commemorating the thwarting of the 1605 Gunpowder Plot by Catholics to blow up the king and Parliament, was observed by devout puritans in Massachusetts later in the century, which would suggest that the first settlers carried this over from England.[72] Once freemen had been granted the right to vote for colony offices, election days were an occasion for many to gather in Boston or another delegated location, and almost immediately thereafter it became customary for a leading clergyman to be invited to deliver an election sermon. Muster days were times for socializing as well as for military drill. Later, Harvard commencement, like those at Oxford and Cambridge, would become a major social occasion, attracting more than just students and their families. Public punishments, especially executions, were intended to teach a lesson, and eventually, though not apparently in Winthrop's time, executions would be an occasion for preaching sermons, as had been the practice in England.

In addition to coming together in their meetinghouses for worship and lectures, the colonists gathered there for specially appointed days of fast and thanksgiving. Joining fellow Christians to beseech God for special favors and to thank him for favors received had a long tradition. Fasts were generally called to seek divine aid to ward off epidemic disease, impending famine, or threatened invasion. Days of thanksgiving were observed to acknowledge the gift of an abundant harvest, deliverance from enemies, or other blessings. By nature these were not set to be observed regularly—no one in the seventeenth century would have had the hubris to set an annual day of thanksgiving on the assumption that God would always bless them. In England, beginning in the late sixteenth century, authorities had become concerned about the political use of such occasions and placed strict regulations on them. Fasts, for example, could be called to ask God to spare the people for having failed to reform the church properly, or for failing to pursue a sufficiently protestant foreign policy. Therefore the bishops made it more difficult for local authorities or clergy to call such days.

In New England all such restraint was removed. From the very first days of the colony magistrates and ministers utilized these means to beseech and thank God. On days appointed to seek God's favor, colonists fasted and gathered in their churches to pray and listen to the clergy preach. Individual communities fasted and asked God's aid as they sought to organize a congregation and choose a minister. On days of thanksgiving, prayer and preaching were joined with celebration and feasting. In the 1630s colony-wide days of thanksgiving were called to mark the arrival of new ships with no loss of passengers and to note the successes of the Protestant forces in the Thirty Years War raging on the European continent.[73]

In its first years the Boston church flourished under the ministry of John Wilson, and then, according to Winthrop, "it pleased the Lord to give special testimony of his presence in the Church of Boston after Mr. Cotton was called to office there. More were converted and added to that church than to all the other churches in the Bay."[74] At this time those who wished to enter the covenant had to demonstrate their knowledge of the principles of the faith and had to respond to any questions from the congregants about their lives and actions. There was no narrative of a conversion experience required. When Cotton was called to the ministry of the Boston church in the fall of 1633, there were approximately eighty-eight members. Over the next fifteen months more than a hundred and thirty new members were added. One of these new members was Winthrop's fourteen-year-old son, Stephen. Though he "had been a dutiful child and not given up the lusts of youth," he had not felt sure of his worthiness for membership and the sacraments, due largely to his inability to shake "blasphemous and wicked thoughts." He "went mourning and languishing daily" but continued to attend services, read the Scriptures, and pray. He sought counsel from his father, who remembered his own struggles to find assurance, as well as from others. Stephen "came at length to be freed from his temptations and to find comfort in God's promises" and was "received into the congregation upon good proof of his understanding in the things of God." Stephen's younger brother Adam "was no whit short of him in the knowledge of God's will" but, being only thirteen, hesitated to present himself for membership. John, proud and no doubt relieved to observe the godliness of his sons, recorded a dream that must have confirmed his confidence in the godly society he was seeking to help build. Though noting that there was "no credit nor regard to be had of dreams in these days," he recalled dreaming of "coming into his Chamber, where he found his wife (she was a very gracious woman) in bed & 3 or 4 of her Children lying by her with most sweet & smiling countenances, with Crowns upon their heads & blue ribbons about their necks. When he awoke he told his wife his dream & made this interpretation of it, that God would take of her Children to make them fellow heirs with Christ in his kingdom."[75]

11

Relations with England

THE YEAR IS 1634. The brisk autumn winds were whipping over the Salem common as the men of the town's trained band began to assemble. The colony's enemies had been busy in England, and there were fears that the king might seek to revoke the charter and undo all that the colonists had worked for. Some of the men were talking about the latest rumor, that a governor-general might be appointed by the king and lead a military force to suppress the colony. The colony's leaders were determined to resist any such attempt. John Endecott had worked longer than any of these men to establish a godly commonwealth and was determined that his work would not be dismantled. As he approached the troop his attention was drawn to the ensign whipping in the wind—the white English flag with the red cross of St. George in the upper left quarter. The cross in the ensign had long bothered Endecott. To him it was a papist symbol, an idolatrous emblem. He had discussed the matter on more than one occasion with his friend Roger Williams, but on this day he could not control himself, perhaps because of his anger at the thought of the king's forces coming under the same banner to dismantle the puritan experiment. Drawing his sword, he cut the cross from the flag and tossed the shreds to the ground. Endecott had a reputation for being impulsive, but even so the men of the trained band were shocked. Idolatrous cross or not—and many agreed with their leader on that point—it was the English flag that has been defaced.

Unaware of what was happening in Salem, John Winthrop sat in his Boston study contemplating the English threat to the colony. The threat had been building for two years, ever since Sir Ferdinando Gorges protested to the king's Privy Council that his Council for New England had been granted the land of Massachusetts a decade before the Massachusetts Bay Company had received its charter. Men banished from the colony, such as Thomas Morton and Philip Ratcliffe, added their voices to the growing chorus of complaints. In the previous year William Laud had turned his attention to the puritan colonies. Winthrop's task was to organize English friends of the colony, and work with his brother-in-law Emmanuel Downing to orchestrate a response to the Bay's enemies. As he pondered what other steps he could take, he must have reflected on how the colonial saints could be their own worst enemies, rejecting tact and adopting postures that only made English action more likely. The news from Salem would not be welcome.

CƷ

*A*LONG WITH HIS EFFORTS to shape a godly commonwealth and godly churches, Winthrop labored in the 1630s to steer his colony's course in such a way as to protect it from external threats. In defending his City on a Hill he would use constitutional arguments and political stratagems. He would also be prepared to use armed force if nothing else succeeded. Though he never returned in person to the land of his birth, Winthrop continued to view himself as an Englishman and worked hard to sustain his connections there, for personal as well as public reasons. Throughout his life in New England he would correspond often both with friends and kin in Groton and with men he had known during his public service, including Brampton Gurdon, Sir William Spring, and Sir Nathaniel Barnardiston. Though only a portion of that correspondence survives, the letters we can read refer to far more extensive exchange and reflect feelings of personal love and Christian fellowship. Yet he was always alert to the dangers that English interference could present for the Bay colony and resolved that no royal governor would have a chance to reduce the godly institutions of New England.

FROM THE START WINTHROP claimed that the charter provided Massachusetts the right to order its own affairs, yet at the same time he sought to avoid provoking the English government. Thus, when the colonists found that Robert Wright had fled to New England after having been convicted of treason for clipping some of the king's coins, they apprehended him and sent him back, Winthrop writing to the lord chief justice to explain that the colonists would never knowingly harbor any such criminals.[1] But not all English officials accepted the loyalty of the Bay. The colony had enemies in England and, if Winthrop believed that the eyes of all the faithful would be hopefully focused upon the settlements, as one correspondent wrote from England, there were also "a thousand eyes watching over you to pick a hole in your coats," with many complaining "against the severity of your government, especially Mr. Endecott's."[2] Some of these complaints came in letters to royal officials from disaffected colonists. Others came from disgruntled settlers who returned home. Still others came from visitors to the colonies. In 1632 crew members from a ship that had traded with Boston spread reports that the colonists were "heretics" who aspired to "be more holy than all the world. They would be a peculiar people to God, but go to the devil." Charges circulated that "your preachers in their public prayers pray for the governor before they pray for our king and state," that the Prayer Book liturgy was ignored, that laymen preached, and that "you count all men in England out of your church and in the state of damnation."[3]

Of course, the very reports that aroused the hostility of some were signs of hope for others. Suffolk's Reverend James Hopkins told his friend John Winthrop in 1633, "I like it well that the wicked speak evil of you." Hopkins urged Winthrop to be strong and counseled him that only "weak men weary of your plantation. Send Achans packing, for they will hinder you in your prosperous succeedings."[4] Another friend of the puritan experiment wrote, "I doubt not but that you sing the Songs of Sion in a strange land."[5]

The negative reports encouraged enemies of New England who sought to undermine the enterprise. Late in 1632 Sir Christopher Gardiner, Thomas Morton, and Philip Ratcliffe, encouraged by Sir Ferdinando Gorges, petitioned the Privy Council against the Massachusetts Bay Company. All of these men would be persistent in their efforts to have the charter vacated. In 1620 Gorges was the key figure in obtaining a royal charter for the Council for New England, which was awarded control of the land between the Delaware Bay and the St. Lawrence River. Three years later, Sir Ferdinando's son Robert led an expedition designed to plant the foundations of a feudal principality in New England. After wintering in the area just to the north of the Plymouth colony, which he visited, he deserted his plantation. His chaplain, the Reverend William Morrell, who had ambitions to be the first colonial bishop, left within a year, as did most of the colonists. Over the next few years both Sir Ferdinando and Robert Gorges turned their attentions elsewhere, and in 1628 the council, under the new leadership of the earl of Warwick, bestowed the land grant to the Massachusetts Bay Company, which then obtained its own royal charter.[6] In 1629, with the end of war with France and Spain, Gorges resumed his active involvement with the council, once again convening formal meetings seeking to direct the council's business. In 1630 he sent an expedition to establish a trading post on the Piscataqua River, to the north of Massachusetts.[7] Yet it appears that the leadership of the Massachusetts Bay Company had maintained such a low profile regarding the details of their operations that Gorges may have been ignorant of the royal charter to the Company until John Humfry, a member of this and other colonizing groups, inadvertently revealed it at a council meeting in 1632.[8] The initial reaction of the Council for New England was to demand that Humfry, who had also been one of the members of the New England Company, bring in the patent which that group claimed to have obtained from the council. When he explained that it had been taken to New England, the council called Sir

Richard Saltonstall, John Humfry, Matthew Craddock, and others to provide information, then ordered that "all patents formerly granted should
be called for and perused and afterwards confirmed if the Council shall see
fit."[9] Matters became so contested that the earl of Warwick, who was in
the process of perfecting a new patent to puritan grandees intending to
settle on the north shore of Long Island Sound, ceased to attend council
meetings and gave up his presidency.

　　Because the Bay colony's charter appeared to shield Massachusetts from
the jurisdiction of the Council for New England, Gorges determined to
attack the validity of that grant, and in his efforts to achieve that end he
used disaffected colonists and allies in the English court and church. Christopher Gardiner, who claimed to have been knighted by the pope, had
settled in what would become Boston a year or so before 1630. Gardiner
was viewed suspiciously by Winthrop and his fellow puritans, who believed
him to be a bigamist as well as a papist and a spy. He was called to answer
to the Bay government but fled, only to be captured and returned to the
Bay by Plymouth authorities. Sent back to England, he became part of the
chorus that Gorges orchestrated to complain about Massachusetts. Thomas Morton was another Englishman who had settled in the region before
the arrival of the Winthrop fleet. He dealt arms and alcohol to the natives,
leading to his expulsion from the region by Plymouth in 1628. A year later
he returned, erected a maypole at his settlement at Merrymount, just south
of the Boston peninsula, and resumed his activities. In 1630 John Endecott
led an expedition which cut down the maypole, burned the trading house,
and seized Morton, who this time was sent back to England by the Bay
authorities.[10] Philip Ratcliffe, a servant of Matthew Craddock, had emigrated in 1630. He soon became a vocal critic of the authorities. Brought
before the Court of Assistants for his "most foul scandalous invectives against
our churches and government, [he] was censured to be whipped, and lose
his ears, and be banished from the plantation, which was presently executed."[11] Needless to say, he was eager to join any plan to overthrow the
Bay colony's magistrates.

　　When Gorges brought Gardiner's petition and his own complaints to
the king's Privy Council, that body appointed a special commission to hear
the case in December 1632. The threat posed by this action was regarded
by one of the colony's English friends, not as "a Spanish powder plot, nor
an accounted invincible armada, but . . . a Spanish like French infection,"
and an ill result was feared since the "plantation and planters had often
lately been preached against at Paul's Cross" in London, a pulpit where
invited preachers expounded on what many felt to be court policy.[12] Sir
Richard Saltonstall and Matthew Craddock had been called to testify, and
others came to the support of the colony as well. Emmanuel Downing,
who was still in England, had a close relationship with Sir John Coke, one

of the king's principal secretaries of state, and wrote to him arguing the colony's case. While legally the charter should not have been approved without first vacating the Council for New England's land claim, Downing and others argued that the decision had been justified because the council had, by its long lack of activity, forfeited its claims to the region. It was because "Sir Ferdinand Gorges," he wrote to Coke, "with some others of his co-partners have these many years labored to make a plantation in New England, where having spent their money and travail in vain, [and] being ashamed of their own and envying their neighbor's prosperity, have of late made claim to the very ground where Mr. Winthrop, with a colony, hath built and planted, laboring either to overthrow this patent of incorporation or to have other government established."[13] Help also came from unexpected sources. Captain Thomas Wiggin, who was the governor of Gorges's settlement on the Piscataqua, had written to Coke praising the Massachusetts colony and Winthrop in particular, as "a discreet and sober man . . . ruling with mildness and justice" and denouncing Gardiner, Morton, and Ratcliffe as "all discontented and scandalous characters."[14] Sir Thomas Jermyn, the son of the godly Suffolk magistrate Sir Robert Jermyn, was comptroller of the king's household and a member of the Privy Council. He knew Winthrop well and also "spoke much in the commendation of the Governor both to the Lords and afterwards to his Majesty." Faced with admitting the failure to properly issue the charter and with the fact that the Massachusetts Bay Company had succeeded where Gorges had previously failed in establishing a colony that would contribute to England's prosperity and crown revenue, the Privy Council commission acted quickly, and the Privy Council itself found in favor of the Bay Company. The king not only accepted their finding but went so far as to declare that "he would have them punished who did abuse his governor and the plantation."[15]

Yet such promises were fragile. Gorges would continue to insist on the illegality of the crown's earlier grant of land. He would also continue to seek allies among those who were disturbed by the ecclesiastical practices of the Bay. The danger was clearly recognized by the Bay's friends. One English correspondent, rejoicing in the colony's delivery, warned the colonists against allowing too much free expression, assuring them that "their letters will come to light that write against our state civil or ecclesiastical," and that it would be advisable that the clergy take pains to correct those "of weak judgments."[16] Another friend urged that "praying for our king be not neglected in any of your public meetings, and I desire that you differ not no more from us in Church government than you shall find that we differ from the prescript of God's word."[17]

Such warnings seemingly did not register with all the colonial leaders. Not having anticipated the rapid dismissal of the Gardiner petition, the

Massachusetts magistrates had prepared a response to the complaints lodged against them. All agreed to the answer except Thomas Dudley. In their answer, the majority had referred to the English prelates as "Reverend Bishops," a designation the deputy governor refused to assent to. The majority "professed to believe all the articles of the Christian faith according to the scriptures and the common received tenets of the churches of England," and again Dudley had dissented. And he refused to address the king as his "sacred majesty."[18] This was the type of attitude that frustrated Winthrop, whose strategy toward English critics then and always was to minimize differences that might prove contentious and to obfuscate matters in cases where the colonists' position could provoke English action. In a letter written at this time to his English friend Sir Simonds D'Ewes, he acknowledged that "both our practice and judgment differ from yours" but minimized those differences by suggesting that "we should soon be agreed if you were here to see the state of things as we see them."[19] The difficulty of controlling more zealous colonists such as Dudley, Endecott, and Roger Williams would pose a major challenge to the success of his vision.

In May 1633 the Privy Council was persuaded to revisit the case of Massachusetts. A new committee was appointed that recommended creation of a special Commission for Regulating Plantations that was to be headed by William Laud, the bishop of London who was already well known as an enemy of puritans and who would soon be elevated to archbishop of Canterbury.[20] It was with the knowledge of this renewed English attention being focused on the colony that late in December 1633 the magistrates met to discuss a treatise which Roger Williams had prepared. Williams, whose call for an explicit separation from the English church had led to his removal to Plymouth, had been dissatisfied with the churches there and returned to Salem. This new treatise raised new and equally serious issues. In it Williams questioned any claim to the lands of New England which derived from the royal charter, rejecting the notion that the land had been the king's to grant. Specifically, the treatise accused King Charles of having "told a solemn public lie" because he claimed to be the "first Christian prince that had discovered this land." In addition, he accused the king of blasphemy for calling Europe "Christendom or the Christian world," which Williams clearly thought was a misnomer. And he had implied by references to the Book of Revelation that the king was in league with the forces of the devil.[21]

Winthrop, like virtually all of his contemporaries, believed that there was one truth and one way of God, while acknowledging that discerning the details of that way was difficult for sinful mankind. But he differed from many of his fellow leaders in believing that conferencing with fellow Christians in whom one detected the presence of God's spirit could lead to agreements on matters of faith and practice. Where godly men could not

reach accord, he hoped that they could agree to disagree while still searching their hearts and the Scripture for the truth. Henry Jessey encouraged
this stance when he urged the colonists in 1633 to recognize that "God
Almighty be amongst you, and preserves you that you may be all of one
mind according to truth [and] that you, having salt in yourselves, may be at
peace with one another" but, when there were differences, "that you may
deny yourselves and your own reasonings, in humility condescending one
to another so far as may stand with a good conscience, considering one
another's weakness, to cover it in love, avoiding needless disputes causing
strife rather than edifying."[22] This, of course, required the willingness of
all who held differing opinions to concede that in the absence of agreement
they themselves might be wrong, which is something Roger Williams was
generally loath to do.

As was their policy whenever they dealt with the open advocacy of
beliefs they could not accept, the leaders of the Bay first sought to persuade Williams of his error. Winthrop himself sought to refute the contested opinions and enlisted John Endecott, John Wilson, and John Cotton
in the effort. On this occasion he was successful. Williams responded to
Winthrop "very submissively, professing his intent only to have written
for the private satisfaction" of the Plymouth authorities and to have provided Winthrop a copy because he requested it. Williams denied "any purpose to have stirred further in it" and offered "his book or any part of it to
be burnt."[23] In January the Court of Assistants met to determine a course
of action. After reviewing Williams's submissive stance and consulting with
Wilson and Cotton, the magistrates found "the matters not to be so evil as
at first they seemed, whereupon they agreed that upon his retraction and
taking an oath of allegiance to the king, it should be passed over."[24]

Though the breach had been healed for the time, it was impossible to
prevent reports of such radical views reaching England, where they provided ammunition for Gorges and the Laud Commission. In February 1634
that commission issued instructions to ship captains that all who sought to
embark for New England had to take oaths of allegiance and supremacy
and that religious services on shipboard had to be conducted in accordance
with the Book of Common Prayer.[25] Any restriction on emigration posed
a serious threat to Massachusetts, since at the time the colonists depended
on new arrivals to sustain the economy as they brought new resources and
purchased supplies from the established settlers.[26] The commission further pressured the Bay in December when they instructed the officers of
the port of London not to allow anyone who was a "subsidy man"—wealthy
enough to be assessed in a tax subsidy—to embark without a special license
from the commission, nor anyone beneath that rank to depart without an
affidavit from two justices of the peace and his local minister attesting to

his loyalty to the king and the established church.[27] Neither of these measures was effectively enforced. Twelve ships were temporarily stayed in February, but ship masters protested that the measures hindered their important trade and fishing voyages, and the vessels were released.[28] Emmanuel Downing reported that one of the officials who was to enforce the December order told those thinking of emigrating to "bring him any certificate from minister, churchwardens, or justice that they were honest men and he would give them their pass." As for the license expected of subsidy men, "he answered that he could not tell who were subsidy men and would discharge them" if they had a certificate from a minister or justice.[29] Some ministers traveling from England would use assumed names to avoid official attention, but most emigrants did not have to resort to any subterfuge.

Nevertheless, these were merely the commission's opening salvos against Massachusetts. As the threat to the colony developed Winthrop and his fellow magistrates showed every sign that they would defend their commonwealth against any effort to unseat it by Gorges or the Laud Commission. At their meeting of March 4, 1634, the Court of Assistants discussed plans for a "sea fort," a floating gun platform that would be anchored in Boston harbor. A month later they adopted the oaths whereby freemen and non-freemen were required to assert their loyalty to the colony's government. Notably absent in the oaths was any recognition of the king or the home government.[30] The idea of a floating battery was scrapped, but in May Winthrop noted that cannons had been placed in the fort in Boston. In July Winthrop met with some of the magistrates and ministers at Castle Island in the harbor and laid out a plan for two gun platforms and a small fort to secure the entrance to the harbor. They agreed that a tax should be levied for its construction and appointed Roger Ludlow to supervise the work.[31] In September the General Court discussed the question of erecting further fortifications at Dorchester and Charlestown.[32] The town trained bands, the militia, which had regularly mustered and drilled since the first days of the colony, increased their training.

Plans for self-defense were further stepped up after news was received in July 1634 that the Laud Commission had demanded that the charter be submitted for their inspection. Matthew Craddock, who was charged to deliver it, forwarded the order to the colonial leaders, but the magistrates resolved "not to return any answer or excuse." When Craddock wrote again, the magistrates responded that they were powerless to act without the consent of the General Court, which would not meet until September.[33] In August Winthrop received a copy of a letter from Morton, the twice banished master of Merrymount, in which he predicted a governor-general would be sent over and in which he made "threats against this plantation and Mr. Winthrop in particular."[34] When the court met in September they had received a copy of the Laud Commission's order as well as news that ships and soldiers were being gathered in England to accompany a new governor. This merely led the colonists to levy additional taxes and "hasten our fortifications."[35]

While prepared to fight for his colony's future, Winthrop sought to avoid confrontation as long as possible. Consequently, three incidents at about this time caused him considerable difficulties. The first involved an English ship captain named John Stone. Said to be related to powerful men in England, Stone was a privateer with an unsavory reputation for smuggling and other illegal actions who was also rumored to have indulged in cannibalism following a shipwreck.[36] While transporting a cargo of salt and cattle from Virginia to Massachusetts in the summer of 1633, Stone had interrupted his voyage with a stay in the Dutch settlement of New Amsterdam at the mouth of the Hudson River. There, according to William Bradford, Stone had attempted to seize a Plymouth trading vessel that was also in the harbor. When Stone finally arrived in Boston, the Plymouth authorities sent Miles Standish to apprehend the captain and bring him to Plymouth for trial. Winthrop and his fellow magistrates chose to bind Stone over to be sent to England and tried in the Admiralty Court. After consulting with the Plymouth authorities, and perhaps fearing that Stone, who had complained bitterly about the colonial authorities, would add to the complaints against the colonies in England, they decided to release him.

Stone continued to disturb the peace of the colony, being found drunk in bed with the wife of Boston's John Barcroft. Winthrop bound him over for trial, and when his ship was prevented from leaving the harbor Stone verbally abused the magistrates, including calling Roger Ludlow a "just ass." Winthrop had him placed in irons until he cooled down, and the Court of Assistants prepared an indictment against him for adultery and drunkenness. A grand jury rejected the indictment since conviction of adultery required two witnesses and the authorities could only provide one. Stone was, however, fined one hundred pounds and ordered never to return to the colony without a special license from the court, under pain of death. As Stone sailed from Boston harbor, Winthrop would have recognized that the colony had made another enemy who would be eager to join the chorus of complainants being orchestrated by Gorges. Stone, however, sailed first to trade along the Connecticut River. A trade dispute between the Pequot tribe and the Dutch, who had an outpost on the future site of Hartford, had recently led to the murder by the Dutch of a principal native sachem. Angered, the Pequots took their revenge upon Stone and the seven men sailing with him. Perhaps they failed to distinguish between Europeans, or perhaps they knew that Stone was a friend of the Dutch governor. His death seemed providential to New England's Roger Clap, who recorded that "thus did God destroy him that so proudly threatened to ruin us by complaining against us when he came to England. Thus God destroyed him, and delivered us at that time also."[37]

A second threat developed from an incident on the northern frontier. The Lord Saye and Sele and Lord Brooke had purchased a grant of land in the Piscataqua region of modern New Hampshire and in 1633 appointed to develop their interests the same Captain Thomas Wiggin who had recently defended the Bay in a letter to Sir John Coke.[38] In the spring of 1634 John Hockin, representing the Piscataqua proprietors, infringed on trading grounds that the Plymouth colony claimed along the Kennebec River on the basis of a grant from the Council for New England. In the resulting dispute Hockin and Moses Talbot, one of the Plymouth settlers, were both killed. At the May General Court the magistrates ordered the arrest of Plymouth's John Alden, who had been present when Hockin was killed and who was then in Boston. The Plymouth authorities were notified and asked if they wished to take jurisdiction. The matter was a serious one since it might alienate Saye and Sele and other English supporters as well as provide another excuse for royal intervention in the region. Additionally, as Winthrop wrote, reports of the clash would bring all New Englanders, "and the Gospel, under a common reproach of cutting one another's throats for beaver."[39] In July William Bradford, Edward Winslow, and other Plymouth representatives came to Boston to discuss the matter. After considerable discussion with Winthrop and other Bay leaders, tensions between the two New England colonies were resolved, and Edward Winslow was sent to England carrying letters from Winthrop and Dudley to Lords Saye and Brooke that appear to have been effective in deflecting any trouble.[40]

Hardly was this issue resolved when Winthrop was troubled by the report from Salem in early November 1634 that the English flag used by the town trained band had been mutilated. At this time the flag Englishmen commonly utilized was a white ensign with the red cross of St. George in one of its quarters.[41] John Endecott, believing "that the red cross was given to the king of England by the pope, as an ensign of victory and as a superstitious thing, and a relic of Antichrist," cut it out with his sword.[42] Endecott was more known for his zeal than for his diplomacy, and it was feared that his action "would be taken as an act of rebellion, or of the like measure, in defacing the king's colors." Meeting at Governor Dudley's house, the magistrates requested that Winthrop write Emmanuel Downing to make clear to English authorities that they disapproved of the action and would take steps to punish the offense.

However, the magistrates and the ministers were divided over the issue of the cross, a symbol which in other contexts puritans clearly rejected as idolatrous. For example, in October 1632 Winthrop, on a visit to Plymouth, rode out of the settlement and came to a ford across the North

To Sempringham

KING'S LYNN

Wisbech

NORWICH

Ely

Thetford

Beccles

Framlingham

Newmarket

Bury St.Edmunds

CAMBRIDGE

Cockfield

Thorpe Morieux

Lavenham

Stour River

Groton Hadleigh

Ipswich

Sudbury

Boxford

Great Maplestead

Dedham

COLCHESTER

Braintree

Chelmsford

Maldon

Rochford

To LONDON

Great Stambridge

0 5 10 15 20 Kilometers

0 5 10 15 Miles

John Winthrop's England.
Map by John Watson, Millersville University Geo-Graphics Lab.

Detail of the Groton area, Suffolk.
From John Speed, *Theatrum Imperii Magnae Britannae* (London, 1616).

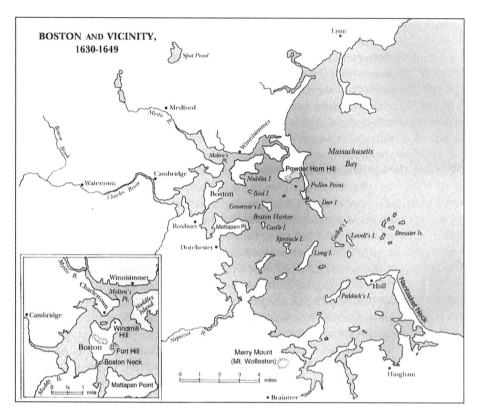

Boston and Vicinity, 1630–1649.
Map by Robert C. Forget. Courtesy of Richard S. Dunn.

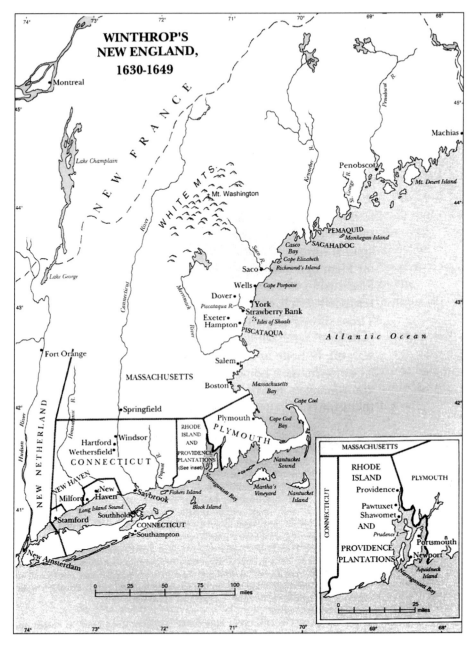

Winthrop's New England, 1630–1649.
Map by Robert C. Forget. Courtesy of Richard S. Dunn.

Adam Winthrop (1498–1562),
Master of the Clothworkers.
Oil painting by Charles Osgood
(1809–1890). Courtesy of the
Massachusetts Historical Society.

Winthrop tomb at Groton Church. Photograph by Francis J. Bremer.

☾ Laſt quarter the 4. day, 35 minutes after eight at night.
● New moone the 12 day, 31 minutes paſt 3 in the aftern.
☽ Second quar. the 20 day, about 7 of the clocke at night.
● Ful moone the 27 day, 50 minuts paſt 3. in the afternoon

1	Kal	we dined at Groton hall.	11	d
2	4		12	e
3	3		13	f
4	Pri	The thursday sermon ceased at least.	14	g
5	No		15	a
6	8		16	b
7	7	A comunion at Groton.	17	C
8	6		18	d
9	5		19	e
10	4		20	f
11	3		21	g
12	Pri	Mr Gurdon fel out of his conche in	22	a
13	Id	Boxforde streete.	23	b
14	19	The quarter sessions at Bury.	24	C
15	18		25	d
16	17		26	e
17	16		27	f
18	15		28	g
19	14	Job Grimwade was hurt with a fal of his horse	29	a
20	13		30	b
21	12		31	C
22	11		1	d
23	10		2	e
24	9		3	f
25	8		4	g
26	7		5	a
27	6		6	b
28	5		7	C
29	4		8	d
30	3	The parlement began.	9	e
31	Pri		10	f

Here and facing page: Selections from *Allestree's Almanac*
for 1620 and 1621, with notations by Adam Winthrop.
Courtesy of the Massachusetts Historical Society.

Da.	Sun riseth	Sun setteth
1	houre 6 and 34 minuts	houre 5 and 26 minuts
14	houre 7 and 0. minuts.	houre 4 and 0. minutes
28	houre 7 and 26 minuts	houre 4 and 34 minuts

1	Kal		11
2	6		12
3	5		13
4	4		14
5	3	Mr Sterne preached at Boxforde . 1.	15
6	Pri		16
7	No		17
8	8	A comunion at Groton.	18
9	7	The quarter sessions at Bury.	19
10	6		20
11	5		21
12	4	Mr webster preached at Boxforde . 9.	22
13	3	my daughter Lucie came to Groton.	23
14	Pri		24
15	Ide		25
16	17		26
17	16		27
18	15	Mr Stansby preached at Groton	28
19	14	Mr Hatrison prech. at Boxford. (4)	29
20	13		30
21	12		31
22	11		No
23	10		2
24	9	The horsemil was finished.	3
25	8	Mr Parson preached at Boxforde . 4	4
26	7		5
27	6		6
28	5	Mr sands began to pr. vpon Jonah	7
29	4	Mr Prime preched in Groton churche.	8
30	3		9
31	Pri		10

The 18 day Judith Ponde died.

Trinity College, Cambridge. King Edward's Gate
from the Great Court, laid out in the time of John Winthrop.
Photograph by Francis J. Bremer.

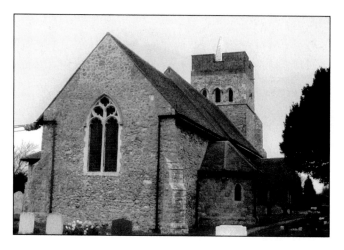

Great Stambridge Church, where Ezekiel Culverwell married
John Winthrop and Mary Forth. Photograph by Francis J. Bremer

Groton Church, with Groton Hall in the background.
Photograph by Francis J. Bremer.

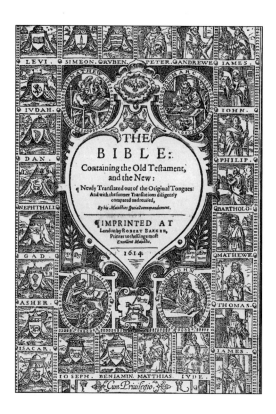

Title page of Bible (King James version) given to John Winthrop by his father, Adam, in 1623. Courtesy of the Massachusetts Historical Society.

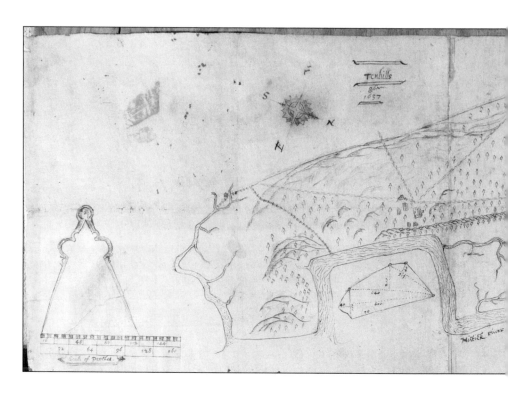

Detail, Massachusetts Bay Colony Charter. Courtesy of Massachusetts Archive.

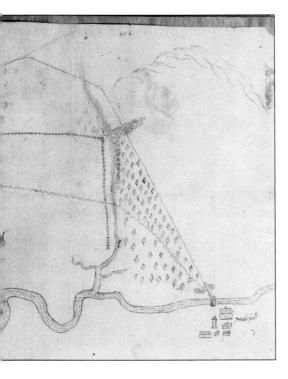

Sketch of the Winthrop farm at
Ten Hills, Charlestown,
Massachusetts, 1637.
Probably by John Winthrop, Jr.
Courtesy of the Massachusetts
Historical Society.

Portrait of Governor John Winthrop. Courtesy of the American Antiquarian Society.

"Mrs. Winthrop." Identity unknown, but possibly Margaret Winthrop. Courtesy of the Massachusetts Historical Society.

John Winthrop, Jr. (1605/6–1676).
Courtesy of the Massachusetts Historical Society.

Stephen Winthrop (1618/9–1658).
Courtesy of the Massachusetts Historical Society.

Facing page: Woodcut engraving of the New Englanders'
attack on the Pequot Village.
From *Newes from America; or a new discoverie
of New England* (London, 1638).

The figure of the Indians fort or Palizado in NEW ENGLAND And the maner of the destroying It by Captayne Underhill And Captayne Mason.

Their enters Captayne Underhill

Their Streets

Their Entters Captayne Mason

The Indians houses

Frederick Winthrop portrays John Winthrop
during the Salem Tercentenary celebrations in 1930.
Photograph courtesy of the Peabody Essex Museum.

River. Informed that the place was named "Hue's Cross"—evidently after Plymouth settler John Hewes, who had crossed the river there—he promptly renamed it "Hue's Folly," not wanting the name of a popish idol on the map of New England.[43] In the Salem case, Winthrop and John Cotton agreed with Endecott that the "cross in the banner" was "the image of an idol, and the greatest idol in the Church of Rome," a position that Roger Williams also subscribed to.[44] Its introduction as a military emblem by the Emperor Constantine was intended to ward off hostile forces, and the superstitious belief that the emblem had power to protect troops made its use unacceptable. Thomas Dudley, John Haynes, and Thomas Hooker, however, spoke for those who believed that the Reformation had succeeded in weaning people from an idolatrous use of such symbols and that the cross in a flag could be accepted as a national emblem.[45] Israel Stoughton wrote to an English friend that the controversy "hath bred some evil in our body" and "caused no little alienation of affection."[46] He felt that the majority favored the use of the ensign but acknowledged that the minority was zealous. An anonymous commentator reported that the citizens who made up the trained bands declared "that they [would] sooner turn heathens and yield to the enemy than follow or fight under a popish idol."[47]

The controversy was being played out against a background of concern regarding the plans of the Laud Commission. In March 1635 the General Court ordered that there should be a beacon set on the sentry hill in Boston, which came to be known as Beacon Hill, to give notice of any danger to the colony. The court also established a military commission of eleven magistrates, including Winthrop, that would be in charge of all military affairs—supervising ongoing training, appointing lesser officers, taking command themselves in either an offensive or defensive war, and "imprison[ing] or confin[ing]" those "that they shall judge to be enemies of the commonwealth."[48] It was still impossible to agree on what to do about Endecott, and so the matter was deferred until the next court. The military commission, however, met and decided to put aside the ensigns with the cross. At the May General Court Endecott was censured and deprived of office for the following year. Winthrop's hand may be detected in the punishment, which was not for doing something wrong but for having acted rashly and without discretion. If Endecott judged the use of the cross in the ensign to be sinful, Winthrop commented, then he should have brought it to the attention of the magistrates so that it might be removed from all the flags and not just Salem's.[49]

In December 1636 the military commissioners rendered their final verdict on the use of the cross by appointing colors for all the trained bands and leaving the cross out of all of them. The king's arms were to fly over the fort on Castle Island, but that was likely the quartered flag adopted by James I and kept by Charles I, with the lilies of France combined with the lions of England in the first and fourth quarters, the red lion of Scotland in the second, and the harp of Ireland in the fourth.[50] While there would be continued grumbling over the matter, the incident had finally been handled in such a way as to deflect royal anger without fracturing colonial unity.

News of Endecott's actions certainly reached England and played into the hands of the colony's enemies. Gorges convened a meeting of the Council for New England at which the land it controlled was divided and a decision made to surrender its authority to the king. With the region reverting to the control of the crown, Gorges hoped to be sent to the region as governor-general. Gorges was also cooperating with the Laud Commission. In May 1635, acting on behalf of that commission, the Privy Council instructed the attorney general to initiate action to recall the Bay charter. A writ of *quo warranto* was issued demanding the surrender of the charter, and Gorges was instructed to serve the writ. The actual legal proceedings before King's Bench dragged on, with Thomas Morton representing the Council for New England and the Bay colony only occasionally defended by Sir Richard Saltonstall and other members of the company who happened to be in England. Finally, in May 1637 a final judgment was entered against the Company and its officers, with orders that the charter should be delivered to the Laud Commission.[51]

But it was one thing to issue orders in England, and another to enforce them in New England. At least one of the colony's enemies was convinced that the colonists were ready "to spend their blood in maintaining their present way and humor," and the building of fortifications and drilling of the trained bands would seem to substantiate that.[52] Reports of a fleet carrying a governor-general circulated widely, and in April 1635 reports of ships hovering off the coast raised an alarm, but they were only fishing vessels. In fact, Mason and Gorges had ordered the construction of a "great ship" to carry them to New England, to seize the charter and take control of what they had always considered their domain, but in June Winthrop heard from Lord Saye and Sele that when the ship had been launched it broke apart. Neither Mason nor Gorges had the resources to build a new ship, and the king's financial troubles certainly precluded him from subsidizing any effort to curb Massachusetts. The Laud Commission would continue to complain about New England, but it was soon evident that the complaints were toothless. The breakup of the "great ship" seemed providential. God was looking out for his New England saints.

12

On the Fringe

MAY 1634. Early in the day the freemen had assembled in Boston to elect the colony's leaders for the coming year. Using paper ballots for the first time, they chose Thomas Dudley as governor and Roger Ludlow as deputy governor. John Winthrop received barely enough votes to be retained as an assistant. For the first time since his election in England in 1629, Winthrop was no longer the governor of Massachusetts. When the new court assembled in the Boston meetinghouse, it was Dudley presiding in the governor's chair, while Winthrop sat with the other magistrates on a lower bench. The court decided that it would henceforth meet four times per year rather than twice, that the freemen of each town could choose to be represented there by two or three deputies, and that sessions of the court could not be ended without the consent of the majority.[1] Magistrates, presumably including Winthrop, were "questioned by the freemen for some errors in their government" and fines imposed on them to make a point. Dudley graciously remitted the fines.[2]

But Winthrop's humiliation was not over. As he had on previous election days, he had made plans to entertain his fellow magistrates in his home. Bitter perhaps, certainly humbled, he brought his colleagues home to dinner nonetheless. As godly English divines had taught him, God afflicted his saints for a purpose. It was not the first time that Winthrop had been brought low by events, nor would it be the last. How one used such reverses was critical. Outwardly he demonstrated grace in bringing Dudley and his colleagues home. It is easy to imagine the joy which Dudley felt at being finally given his due, and he likely did little to hide that joy. When the day was finally over, Winthrop recorded his defeat in his journal and noted that he had in fact entertained his fellow magistrates for dinner. Later, perhaps because the mere mention of the meal evoked too many bitter memories, he would cross that passage out.[3]

A little more than a week after being turned out of the governorship, Winthrop wrote a lengthy letter to his "honorable friend" Sir Nathaniel Rich, surveying the colony and what had, in effect, been accomplished under his watch. The exercise of reflection helped to heal his pain. He noted that the population had grown and the threat of devastating disease was no longer a concern, so that "there hath not died above two or three grown persons and about so many children all the last year." He acknowledged that the colony was being supported in large part by "the yearly access of newcomers, who have supplied all our wants [in return] for cattle and the fruits of our labors, as boards, pales, smiths' work, etc." But if emigration slowed, the colonists hoped to get what they needed by profits from the fishing industry, for "no place in the world exceeds us" in the supply of cod, bass, and herring. The land was suitable for growing hemp, flax, rape, and all sorts of root vegetables, "for which the wholesomeness far exceed those in England." The grapes grown "afford a good hard wine." There were about twenty ploughs, and the soil was suited for rye and oats. Winters were "sharp and long," while the summers "are somewhat more fervent in heat than in England."

As for the colony's institutions, Winthrop wrote that the "civil government is mixed," elaborating that the freemen chose the magistrates every year and that at four courts each year three deputies from each town "do assist the magistrates in making of laws, imposing taxes, and disposing of lands." Juries were chosen by the freemen of each town. The churches were "governed by pastors, teachers, ruling elders and deacons, yet the power lies in the whole Congregation and not in the Presbytery." The natives were nearly all "dead of the smallpox, so as the Lord hath cleared our title to what we possess." In all, surveying the colony, Winthrop was clearly proud of how much had been accomplished.[4]

❧

*W*INTHROP HAD MADE ENEMIES during his tenure as governor during the first years of the colony, not the least of whom was Thomas Dudley. Though letters back to England referred to Winthrop as "a wise, religious governor," and "incomparable in wisdom, godliness, etc.," he was not strict enough to suit the precise puritanism of some, and too strict in the eyes of others.[5] Despite the fact that more than anyone else he had worked to involve the ordinary colonists in the process of government, more than anyone else's his reputation was undermined by the revelation that the system of government was not as spelled out in the charter. A little earlier, in 1633, the Reverend John Eliot had observed that some believed that it was time to change governors lest Winthrop's rule become customary and considered unchangeable.[6] That concern must have been widespread in 1634, since John Cotton's election sermon to the gathered freemen argued "that a magistrate ought not to be turned into the condition of a private man without just cause."[7] But, voting perhaps for the first time with paper ballots, the freemen chose Thomas Dudley as governor and Roger Ludlow as deputy governor, though retaining Winthrop as one of the members of the Court of Assistants. Ironically, in elevating Dudley and Ludlow the freemen had chosen the two men who had been most outspoken against popular participation in government.

The period of Winthrop's relative powerlessness that began with the 1634 election was a time of flux in the governance of the Bay and of the emergence of new leaders. Roger Ludlow had flown into a rage when it had first been suggested that the whole General Court should elect the colony's magistrates, yet he had been elected deputy governor in 1634.[8] The justification for not returning Winthrop to the governorship had been that there should be a rotation in that office, and in 1635 many expected Ludlow to have been chosen governor to replace Dudley. Instead, John Haynes was chosen governor and Richard Bellingham deputy.[9] Ludlow challenged the election, charging that the deputies of the various towns had improperly made up their minds before they came to the court.[10] So furious were the voters at this accusation that Ludlow was not even returned to the Court of Assistants. One who was there reported of Ludlow, "I question whether he will ever be magistrate more, for many have taken great offence at him."[11]

John Haynes, who was chosen instead of Ludlow, had only arrived in Massachusetts in 1633. He was a prosperous member of the Essex gentry; Winthrop called him "a man of great estate."[12] He was a follower of Thomas Hooker and settled in Newtown with that clergyman. His deputy, Richard Bellingham, came from a distinguished Lincolnshire family, had studied at Brasenose College, Oxford, and been a student at Lincoln's Inn. He had served as recorder of Boston, Lincolnshire, in the 1620s. Like Haynes, he was a new arrival, migrating to Massachusetts and settling in Boston in 1634. In the brief time between his arrival in the colony and his election as deputy governor, he had been critical of Winthrop's leniency in the administration of justice.[13] Arrogant and opinionated, he would continue to clash with Winthrop in the years that followed.[14] In the fall of 1635 came another well-connected Englishman who impressed the colonists, though only twenty-two years old: Henry Vane, who was identified by Winthrop as the "son and heir of the Comptroller of the King's Household" and "a young gentleman of excellent parts" who "called to the obedience of the Gospel forsook the honors and preferments of the Court to enjoy the ordinances of Christ in their purity here."[15] At the 1636 elections Vane was chosen the colony's governor.

The best insight into Winthrop's feelings about these developments comes neither from his journal, where his record of events was terse and dispassionate, nor his correspondence, where he avoided personal comments that could be intercepted and used against the Bay, but from a letter of Israel Stoughton to his brother in England, the Reverend John Stoughton. Israel may have migrated in 1632 but was not admitted to membership of the Dorchester church and to freemanship before November 1633. Well educated and very self-confident—he wrote to his brother that as soon as he had been made a freeman he would have been chosen an assistant if there had not already been a sufficient number—Stoughton very quickly became embroiled in a heated exchange with the somewhat marginalized Winthrop.[16]

The General Court was not yet divided in 1634 into separate houses of assistants and deputies, so that all voted in a common assembly. The assistants, however, claimed a negative voice or veto. They asserted that for any proposal to become law it had to receive not only the support of a majority of the General Court as a whole but also the support of a majority of the assistants. As a speaker for the deputies in the September 1634 meeting of the General Court, Stoughton was called upon to oppose the negative voice. After the session Winthrop, according to Stoughton, "had harshly and unadvisedly" attacked one of the other deputies but later came to Stoughton and apologized for his intemperance. He told Stoughton that "though we had opposed him, yet the more he honored us both in his very heart, adding that he saw our aims and ends were good."

In anticipation of the next session of the court, Stoughton prepared a written statement of twelve reasons why he felt that the negative voice was wrong. The statement was discussed at the regular meeting of the area clergy and, according to Stoughton, was passed on to Winthrop by John Cotton. At the General Court in March 1635 Stoughton was accused of asserting that the assistants as a group had no powers of governance but were merely law judges. Claiming that this was not what he had actually meant, Stoughton acknowledged that it was possible to read his arguments the way his opponents did and also conceded that he had phrased some of his attacks in a "very plain English such as to some is offensive." The court determined that "whereas Mr. Israel Stoughton hath written a certain book which occasioned much trouble and offense to the Court, the said Mr. Stoughton did desire of the Court that the said book might forthwith be burnt, as being weak and inoffensive." The court also voted that "Stoughton shall be disenabled for bearing any public office in the commonwealth . . . for the space of three years for affirming the Assistants were no magistrates."[17]

Stoughton identified Winthrop and Roger Ludlow as his principal opponents. He suggested that Ludlow, his fellow Dorchester townsman, "had forsworn himself." And, according to Stoughton, Winthrop had said of him that "'[t]his is the man that had been the troubler of Israel,' and I was a worm . . . and an underminer of the state." Stoughton did accept that previously Winthrop had treated him well and "in truth had done to me above my deserts." But if either Stoughton or one of his supporters had taken advantage of the former governor's reduced political circumstances to blame him in particular for excessive assertions of magisterial authority, Winthrop may well have let his frustrations and anger pour out. And Stoughton did acknowledge in his self-justifying letter to his brother that he had heard that at the next court Winthrop confessed that he "had too much forgot and overshot himself."[18]

Stoughton went on to claim that support for Winthrop had diminished in the colony and that in the 1635 elections there were "very many hands against him for being either governor . . . or assistant." The former governor had "lost much of the applause that he hath had (for indeed he was highly magnified)." He was "indeed a man of men, but he is but a man, and some say they have idolized him and do now confess their error." Some were opposed to his views on the cross in the ensign. Some had complained about his arbitrary exercise of discretionary justice. Some of the new arrivals, who felt themselves his social equals if not his betters, may very well have been jealous of his popularity. And Dudley was not the only one to complain that Winthrop had been too lenient in his administration of justice. Frustrated by the direction of colonial affairs, Winthrop was finding it increasingly difficult to restrain his feelings. And with good reason, for the Christian community which he had envisioned was in serious jeopardy.

The complaints of those who had relegated Winthrop to the fringe of the colony's leadership were aired again in a meeting of ministers and magistrates in January 1636. The newly arrived Hugh Peter and Henry Vane had detected "some distraction in the commonwealth arising from some difference in judgment, and withal some alienation of affection among the magistrates and some other persons of quality," and the development of factions, "some adhering more to the old Governor Mr. Winthrop, and others to the late Governor Mr. Dudley." Vane convened a meeting of key magistrates and ministers in an attempt to heal the divisions. Winthrop and Dudley both stated that any personal quarrels had been resolved, but others spoke up. Governor Haynes mentioned a few occasions when he felt Winthrop had administered justice too leniently. Winthrop responded that he believed that "in the infancy of plantations justice should be administered with more leniency then in a settled state, because people were then more apt to transgress partly of ignorance of new laws and orders." But he received very little support, and when the ministers delivered their advice on the next day they specifically advised that "strict discipline both in criminal offenses and in martial affairs was more needful in plantations than in a settled state, as tending to the honor and safety of the Gospel." Winthrop accepted the rebuke and indicated that he "would endeavor (by God's assistance) to take a more strict course hereafter."[19]

A series of ten articles were then drawn up which well illustrate the course being charted by the new leaders of the colony. The colonists were given their marching orders. More strictness was to be used in civil matters and military discipline. Magistrates should consult privately before rendering decisions so they would appear to speak with one voice. Magistrates should not discuss court business with involved parties outside of the court sessions. Trivial matters should be dealt with at the town level. When differences existed between the magistrates, they should deal with each other decorously and avoid criticizing decisions once they were made. Magistrates should seek to develop closer relations with each other. The governor should be shown honor by submitting to him the main leadership of the court. Assistants should not support anyone who crossed the decisions of another assistant. Efforts should be made to enhance the authority of other colony offices. All contempt of authority was to be severely punished, and more pomp and ceremony should accompany the public appearance of the magistrates.[20]

The new leadership of the colony represented a harder edge of puritanism. In areas where Winthrop tried to lead by example, Dudley sought to legislate. Where Winthrop was willing to shape his judgments by considering the circumstances in which offenses had been committed, Dudley and others sought to spell out specific penalties for specific crimes. After the electoral revolution of 1634, the General Court under the leadership of Dudley and Ludlow passed a series of sumptuary regulations. No tobacco was to be smoked in inns or in public places, nor in an individual's own home. No person in the future was to buy or make any apparel with lace or silver or gold embroidery. Clothes with excessive fashionable slashes (more than one slash in a sleeve, for instance) were prohibited. Gold and silver girdles, hatbands, belts, ruffs, and beaver hats were likewise banned, as were, generally, "new fashions, long hair, or anything of the like nature," though for the time being inhabitants were allowed to wear such clothing they already possessed.[21]

Although Winthrop was a member of the court that passed these decrees, his influence was limited. Not only was he merely an assistant in 1634 and 1635, but the election results indicated that confidence in Winthrop's leadership was not as great as it had been. And the harsher tone revealed in the sumptuary legislation would also be evident in the ways the new leaders dealt with challenges to the colony's orthodoxy and external security.

WITH HIS COLONY RESPONSIBILITIES REDUCED, Winthrop became more involved in the affairs of his town. The early pages of the Boston town records, recording regulations adopted on September 1, 1634, for the common landing place, is in Winthrop's handwriting, and the records for the following years reveal him to have been heavily engaged in town matters.[22] The order dictating the care of the landing place so as to avoid hazards to ships was expressed as being "only a declaration of the Common Law" and was the type of response that Winthrop might have employed when he served on the sewer commission in the Stour Valley. While there is no clear record of the meeting of the community as a civic entity before 1634, by October of that year town meetings of the inhabitants were being held, closely approximating the practices of some English parishes.[23] Initially the citizens met monthly and chose ten selectmen to regulate affairs in the interval. The first settlers had simply claimed and built upon the land that they desired, but by 1634 the community as a whole was recognized as owning the right to land not in the possession of any individual. In December 1634 Winthrop was one of a number of townsmen who were chosen to divide and dispose lands on and off the peninsula, including farmland along the Mystic River, at Mount Wollaston, and at Pullen Point.

Winthrop was the most prominent magistrate in Boston as the town meeting passed orders to regulate local affairs. The decisions it made provide insight into the nature of the infant community as well as into the social consciousness of the settlers. Planting ground was to be fenced in to protect it from cattle. Since wood was scarce, the cutting of trees on the islands was regulated. In November 1635 the town meeting agreed that no newcomers should be allotted land unless they were likely to be church members and that no one could sell a house or allotment without the consent of the land committee. Anyone who had previously been allotted land was to build on it before the following March or lose it. No townsman could sue another without first bringing the case to some of the magistrates for arbitration. The following January the first steps were taken to lay out highways. Reflecting the growth of the community, it was ordered that no one could keep more than two milch cows on the peninsula. Strangers were limited to a stay of fourteen days in the town unless a longer stay was approved by town officers. Bailiffs were appointed to prevent dumping along the waterfront. In October 1636 the town ordered that the site of any new building had to be approved by the town's officers in order to avoid encroachments on the lanes and highways. The General Court, by an act of March 1636, had formally established the legal basis for town government, but, like her sister communities, Boston had already assumed the responsibility of regulating her affairs.[24]

John's absence from the highest level of colony government also allowed him to spend more time with his wife and family. In August 1632 Margaret had given birth to a son, baptized William, which Winthrop recorded "signifies a common man."[25] But the boy died in infancy. In March of the following year his son John, who had lived with his parents since his arrival in 1631, left to join in the settlement of Agawam, later named Ipswich. The younger John's wife, Martha Fones Winthrop, remained for a time with her in-laws in Boston but then traveled to Agawam in the fall. John,

prompted by the news of his daughter-in-law's pregnancy, traveled by foot
to visit the couple in April. Since the town had no minister, John "spent
the sabbath with them and exercised by way of prophesy."[26] Margaret may
have accompanied him, though she herself was pregnant and in June gave
birth to a girl whom they named Sarah. No further record of Sarah survives; she likely died shortly after birth. She was the last child Margaret
would bear. More tragic news followed shortly thereafter when Martha
and her infant child died in Agawam in late August or early September.[27]
Martha's clothes, including a sea-green gown and a silk mantle with gold
lace, were lovingly packed in a large chest that belonged to her mother,
and the bereaved John Winthrop Jr. placed with her clothes the blankets
and clothing they had prepared for their first child.[28]

John and Margaret missed their friends and relatives back home. They
had anticipated that many of their kin would follow them to the New World.
Emmanuel and Lucy Downing were committed to coming and had sent
cattle for Winthrop to tend, but their departure from England was delayed. They did send their son James in 1630 and their daughters Mary
and Susan in 1633, all of whom who lodged with the Winthrops. But Lucy
clearly was reluctant to migrate, writing to her brother in 1636 that "for
old England and London, who that knows them can deny the desirableness
of them" and worried about how one "could enrich oneself in the Bay."[29] At
one point, John accused William Leigh, the minister whom he had selected for the Groton pastorate, of having influenced Lucy to stay.[30] While
the presence of the Downings was missed on a personal level, there was
some consolation in the excellent service Emmanuel was able to provide in
protecting the colony's interests. The Downings would finally come over
in 1638, though they would return to England a few years later. John's
sister Anne and her husband, Thomas Gostlin, had likewise said they would
come, and again it was John's sister who seemed reluctant to leave England, though Thomas later expressed some concerns of his own about the
religious practices of the Bay.[31] There was hope that the Gostlins' daughter Margaret would migrate in 1638, but none of that family ever arrived.
Though deprived of their presence, John was happy to have the news they
were able to send of friends in Groton.

John and Margaret likely spent some of their summers at Ten Hills,
the Winthrop farm on the Mystic River where the town of Somerville now
stands. The property stretched along the west side of the river, part of the
shoreline being an oyster bank.[32] Toward the northern end of the property
two streams flowed into the river from the west, forming a watery U. By
fencing in the open end of the U Winthrop was able to create a protected
meadow for grazing cattle, both his own livestock and those sent over in
advance by friends who intended to emigrate. He planted fruit trees to the
south of the fenced pasture, set back slightly from the river. Next to the

orchard was a cluster formed by the farmhouse and four outbuildings. The farmhouse itself was a substantial structure made of stone with a central chimney.[33] Beyond the fields was still a wilderness, which is well illustrated by a story he recorded in his journal. In the fall of 1631, when staying at the farm, John had taken a walk after supper, carrying a musket with him in case he encountered the wolves that "came daily about the house and killed swine and calves." He lost his way in the woods when it got dark. Finding a small house that he recognized as belonging to one of the local sagamores, he decided to spend the night rather than continue to blunder through the trees. By using the match for his gun, he was able to light a fire. He was content to stay outside the house, using some mats he found to lie on, but he was unable to sleep and "spent the night sometimes walking by the fire, sometimes singing psalms, and sometimes getting wood." Toward morning it began to rain. Not wearing a cloak and already cold, he overcame his scruples about trespassing and entered the house. When a squaw came seeking shelter, he locked her out; she gave up and went away, and he then made his way back to his farm. Presumably he locked her out to avoid the embarrassment of being alone in the small space with a woman, especially a native woman with whom he could not communicate.[34]

Winthrop enjoyed traveling through the countryside. Even as governor he had found time for exploring the interior, and he took pleasure naming features in the landscape. On one such trip he encountered "a great rock upon which stood a high stone" which had been split asunder, and he named the unusual feature "Adam's chair" after his eleven-year-old son, who had accompanied him. He named a rocky hill "Mount Feake" after Robert Feake, who had married his son Henry's widow. On another journey one of his servants had forgotten to pack bread. Relegated to eating only cheese, Winthrop whimsically called the expedition's resting place "Cheese rock."[35] He rode to Plymouth on more than one occasion and indulged himself by naming features in the landscape then as well, and changing "Hue's Cross" to "Hue's Folly." After 1633 he may often have been accompanied by one of the four Irish wolfhounds that Emmanuel Downing shipped to him that year.[36]

WHILE ENGAGING IN TOWN AFFAIRS and spending time with his family, Winthrop closely followed the renewal of controversy swirling around his friend Roger Williams. The Salem preacher had provoked many of his fellow colonists ever since his first arrival in New England, when he refused to join the Boston church unless it renounced its ties to the Church of England. His views on the legitimacy of the charter had created a storm in 1633, but Winthrop's inclinations to leniency, combined with Williams's willingness to retract his views, had avoided a crisis. Williams continued to be controversial, however. Preaching as a lay member of the Salem church, he had strongly supported the view that women should wear veils, had expressed fears that the regular gatherings of the Bay clergy would lead to presbyterian authoritarianism, and was believed by many to have inspired Endecott's attack on the cross in the ensign.

By August 1634, when the Reverend Samuel Skelton died, Williams had built up strong support in the Salem congregation, and there was talk of electing him to fill the vacancy in the congregation's ministry. Given the controversial views Williams had expressed in the past, and rumors that he had broken his promise to avoid speaking about the charter and the Church of England, this was sure to raise the ire of many in the colony. In April 1635 Williams escalated his attack on the established order by teaching "publicly that a magistrate ought not to tender an oath to an unregenerate man, for that we thereby have communion with a wicked man in the worship of God & cause him to take the name of God in vain."[37] This was an attack on the recently established oaths of allegiance which the General Court had required of all inhabitants; persuaded by Williams, some men were refusing to take the oath. Williams was called before the court, where he was allowed to present his views, following which some of his fellow clergy spoke and, in Winthrop's view, "very clearly confuted them."[38] But Williams continued to speak his mind to all who would listen and his supporters in the Salem church secured his election as the congregation's teacher.

Congregationalism allowed the Salem church to act as it pleased, but there were informal pressures that could be brought to bear. In July Williams was summoned before the General Court and accused of asserting, in addition to his views on administering oaths, that it was wrong for the magistrates to enforce breaches of the first table of the Ten Commandments; that it was wrong for a godly individual to join in prayers with any unregenerate person, even a spouse or child; and that it was wrong to give thanks after meals, even the Lord's Supper. He was informed that the "other Churches were about to write to the Church of Salem to admonish him of these errors" and that his views were "adjudged by all magistrates & ministers (who were called to be present) to be erroneous & very dangerous" and that Salem's "[c]alling of him to office at that time was judged a great Contempt of authority." Because it was "professedly declared by the ministers (at the request of the Court to give their advice) that he who should obstinately maintain such opinions (whereby a Church might run into Heresy, Apostasy, or Tyranny) . . . were to be removed, & that the other Churches ought to request the magistrate so to do," Williams and the Salem church were given until the next meeting of the court to repent or suffer the consequences.[39]

Williams's preachings tended to undermine the magistrates at a time when the colony was threatened by English intervention, and they were not likely to be tolerated. John Cotton later recalled having, along with other ministers, spent much of the summer trying to persuade Williams of his errors.[40] Dudley and his fellow magistrates adopted another tactic. Salem had petitioned the General Court for land on Marblehead Neck, which the magistrates rejected because the town had defied the rest of the colony in appointing Williams as teacher. The Salem church complained to the other congregations about what they viewed as an abuse of power. The elders of the Boston church declined to share that letter (which has not survived) with the congregation, and we do not know if it was read elsewhere, though its contents must have been known to all.[41] Citing the contents of the Salem letter, the magistrates refused to seat the Salem deputies at the next General Court.[42]

Support for Williams within the Salem congregation began to wane, the most significant defection being John Endecott. But heavy-handed though his opponents were, Williams was equally intolerant of those who disagreed with him. With his own congregation entertaining second thoughts about the position they found themselves in, Williams informed them in August that he renounced the other churches as Antichristian and "could not communicate with the Churches in the Bay, neither would he communicate with them [the Salem church] except they would refuse Communion with the rest."[43] Few members of the congregation followed Williams into this personal separation.

In October Williams was called before the General Court to answer for the letter he had written to the other churches on behalf of Salem, in which he had charged the magistrates with oppressive policies, and also to answer for the letter to his own church denouncing the other churches as Antichristian. Thomas Hooker sought to persuade him to recant those views, but he persisted, and on the following day he was ordered to leave the colony within six weeks. The Salem church members confessed their errors, apologized for the letter attacking the magistrates, and submitted to the Court.[44] Because Williams was ill, the court deferred execution of the sentence on the condition that he not continue speaking out on the disputed issues. Over the following months, however, Williams not only conducted religious services in his home but also continued to attack the practices of the Bay. In January Dudley convened the assistants, who ordered Williams to be sent to England immediately. They dispatched Captain John Underhill to apprehend Williams and carry him to an England-bound ship.[45] But when Underhill arrived, his quarry had escaped. As Williams himself later recalled the events, "That ever honored Governor Mr. Winthrop privately wrote to me to steer my course to the Narragansett Bay and Indians, for many high and heavenly and public Ends, encouraging me from the Freeness of the place from any English Claims or Patents."[46]

Winthrop had never found a reason to correct his first impression of Williams as "a godly minister." He admired the spirit of godliness in the young clergyman even when he disagreed with his views. Like his famous contemporary Oliver Cromwell, he respected all those, such as Williams, in whom he recognized "the root of the matter," though he was more conservative than Cromwell would be in drawing the line between liberty and license, diversity and heresy. When his views on the charter first brought Williams before the magistrates Winthrop was governor, and he steered the parties to a peaceful resolution. But in 1635 Thomas Dudley was governor and Winthrop merely one of the assistants. He recorded the downfall of his friend with dispassion, always referring to Williams respectfully and never showing the animosity that would slip into his references to Anne Hutchinson at a later date. After Williams's difficult winter journey through the forests of eastern New England and his settlement among the natives on the Narragansett Bay, Winthrop would maintain a friendly correspondence with the exiled cleric, rely on him for advice on Indian relations, and join him in purchasing land. In 1636 he was engaging Williams in religious discussions in his correspondence.[47]

A DIFFERENT THREAT TO THE COLONY came as the colonists began to expand from the coastal settlements. One impetus for expansion was the fur trade, which offered substantial profits to both individuals and the colony. In the 1620s William Bradford and the Plymouth colonists had embarked on fur-trading ventures along the northern New England coast as a means of acquiring the means of paying off their London creditors.[48] The Dutch colony of New Netherlands, with claims to western New England as well as to what would later become New York and New Jersey, was founded on the hopes of profit from furs, and to the north the colonists of New France likewise were heavily engaged in the trade. Initially the Indians expanded their hunting in order to obtain more furs to exchange for the European manufactured goods that enabled them to facilitate their traditional activities. Later they traded furs for wampum. As they sought more furs for the trade, significant changes in Indian society and economy began to occur, and in many cases new friction between tribes developed and older rivalries became more intense.[49]

William Pynchon, who migrated from Essex in 1630, was one of the first Massachusetts settlers to engage himself in the fur trade. As early as 1631 he was engaged in a partnership with a London mercer and owned a ship trading along the northern New England coast.[50] In July 1631 John Winthrop launched a ship of his own, a three-masted bark named *The Blessing of the Bay*, which was designed for coastal exploration and the fur trade.[51] Two years later Winthrop and his son partnered with Pynchon. In 1634

Pynchon's trade was such that he owned ten times as many pelts as any other Massachusetts merchant involved in the trade. The growth of competition in the coastal regions led him to direct his attention to the interior, and in particular to the Connecticut River Valley, where Dutch traders had regularly obtained ten thousand pelts per year.[52] In 1634 Pynchon began to plan a settlement, later named Springfield after his Essex birthplace, just above the highest point of the Connecticut River that was then navigable.[53] This placed him in direct competition with the Dutch, who in 1633 had purchased land from the local tribes and established a trading post on the west side of the Connecticut River at the future site of Hartford.

In 1632 Plymouth's William Bradford and Edward Winslow had sought to persuade the Massachusetts authorities to join in a common trading venture along the Connecticut River, but nothing came of it. The following summer, however, Winthrop dispatched the *Blessing of the Bay* on a voyage of trade and exploration into Long Island Sound and received encouraging reports of the prospects for trade with the tribes along the southern reaches of the Connecticut River. John Oldham, who had been granted land by the Council for New England to engage in the fur trade along the Saco River in northern New England, traveled overland to the Connecticut River in search of furs in late August 1633.[54] But in September the Plymouth colony stole a march on Massachusetts interests by sending William Holmes to establish a trading post north of the Dutch so as to intercept trade coming down the river. Though all of this region was within the general grant of land that had been given to Gorges and the Council for New England, none of it was clearly within the jurisdiction of any of the existing colonies, and thus there was considerable potential for conflict.[55]

Movement into the interior of New England was also fueled by the search for more abundant grazing lands.[56] One of the surprises the colonists had found in the land they settled was the scarcity of good meadowland. This was critical since breeding livestock was one of the surest ways to prosperity. Bostonians had satisfied their immediate needs by claiming lands along the Mystic River and to the south of their peninsula to satisfy their needs. The towns settled inland along the Charles River found themselves in a more difficult situation. At the May 1634 meeting of the General Court "[t]hose of Newtown complained of straitness for want of land, especially meadow, & desired leave of the Court to look out either for enlargement or removal, which was granted."[57] Representatives of the town examined land to the northeast, near Ipswich, but the grazing land there was deemed inadequate.

Some of the Newtown townsmen sailed on the voyage of the *Blessing of the Bay* that explored the Connecticut River that summer. Though some additional meadowland in the Bay was granted to the town by the Court of

Assistants in July, at the September General Court, held at Newtown, representatives of the town requested permission to move instead to the Connecticut River valley. They argued that they desperately needed more pasture if they were to continue to prosper and to welcome friends and family coming from England to join their settlement. Thomas Hooker, recently chosen by the Newtown congregation as their pastor, spoke in favor of the move and argued that the towns of the Bay had been planted too closely together to allow for necessary expansion.[58] While it was Newtown that took the lead in this proposed migration, settlers in Watertown and Dorchester were also casting their eyes on the rich meadowlands of the western valley.

Though Governor Dudley favored the Newtown petition, John Winthrop was among those who opposed it. Foremost among his reasons was that moving from the Bay colony was inappropriate because the settlers were "knit to us in one body and bound by oath to seek the welfare of this commonwealth." Allowing them to depart at that time was particularly dangerous since the colony was facing a potential threat from the English authorities and would need the strength of all to resist any forcible attempt against the Bay. The fact that Hooker was intending to join the migration was further cause for concern, for the "removing of a candlestick" from the Bay would draw others to the new settlements instead, both those already in New England and also those considering emigration from England. And Winthrop pointed out that those who settled in the Connecticut River valley would be in danger from the Dutch, the Indians, and also English authorities.[59]

It is possible that Winthrop was also trying to protect the interests of others who were planning to settle along the river. In March 1632 Winthrop's friend Robert Rich, the second earl of Warwick, president of the Council for New England, had assigned a large tract of land stretching south and southwest of the Narragansett River to William Fiennes, first viscount Saye and Sele; the second Lord Brooke; Warwick's son, Lord Rich; his second cousin, Sir Nathaniel Rich; Sir Richard Saltonstall; John Hampden; John Humfry; Herbert Pelham; Richard Knightley; and John Pym. Humfry and Saltonstall were members of the Massachusetts Bay Company, and some of the others were well-known supporters of that enterprise. What became known as the "Old Patent" was actually a sale of lands which Warwick claimed by an earlier and unrecorded division of lands by the Council for New England.[60] These associates then divided the land they had acquired. In June 1632 Warwick applied to the Council for New England for a separate patent transferring his own rights to his portion of that land to his son and others, possibly as part of a settlement of property subsequent to his son's marriage. There is no evidence that this July petition was granted.

After two years of apparent inactivity, John Humfry arrived in Massachusetts in 1634 representing "some persons of great quality and estate (and of special note for piety)" who intended to settle in the Bay. He also carried a letter from the Reverend John Livingstone, minister of a parish in County Down, Ireland, conveying the interest of Ulster Protestants in migrating, though the connection of these Ulstermen with Lords Saye and Brooke is not clear. As a further indication of the goodwill of those he represented, Humfry brought a good quantity of guns and powder, "much money," and the promise of "yearly pensions."[61] It is likely that Humfry also conveyed proposals made by Lord Saye, Lord Brooke, and the other persons of quality who had purchased land from Warwick, setting out a model for the government of the colony they proposed to establish—which would come to be known as Saybrook—and seeking the advice of the more experienced Bay colonists.[62] They wished to divide authority in their colony as in a parliament, between an upper house of "gentlemen of the country" and a lower house of representatives of the freemen. The governor would be chosen from the members of the upper house. In some respects this was similar to the practice of the Bay. But the authors stipulated that the upper house be hereditary and that "Lord Viscount Saye and Sele, the Lord Brooke, . . . and such other gentlemen of approved sincerity and worth as they, before their personal remove, shall take into their number, should be admitted for them and their heirs, gentlemen of the country." Puritan peers, though willing to recognize lesser men as fellow saints, were not willing to allow such men to determine through annual elections whether they, the peers, should wield the authority they considered theirs by right of birth.[63]

These proposals differed in two ways from the practices of the Bay. Not only were the magistrates to hold office for life, but the peers also chose not to adopt the Massachusetts limitation of the franchise to church members. Such differences in a neighboring colony would not necessarily have worried the Bay leaders. They would have been very aware of the benefits they would derive from the migration of such peers to the region. Their presence would have guaranteed the continued assistance of Warwick and his aristocratic friends in fending off its English enemies, though some may have worried about the new colony of Saybrook drawing future godly emigrants away from the Bay. It is even possible that some of the Bay's new leaders sympathized with the idea of a permanent upper class, since in March 1636 the Massachusetts General Court ordered that the court "from time to time, as occasion shall require, shall elect a certain number of magistrates for term of their lives as a standing council," which would have powers to be determined by the court to act between court sessions.[64] John Cotton was deputed the task of officially responding to the demands of the peers, while Winthrop, though no longer governor, was also enlisted to deal with the English lords and their company.[65] Not only did he know many of the key figures, but his experience dealing with such men on the Suffolk commission of the peace and the Stour Valley sewer commission gave him a better feel for political maneuvering than most of his fellow Bay magistrates. His letter to Sir Nathaniel Rich, spelling out the institutional structure of the Bay, was a way of indicating the colonists' commitment to those forms, indirectly rejecting the suggestion that English peers should have special status if they settled within the jurisdiction of Massachusetts. In the same letter he also addressed the murder of John Hockin on the Kennebec River in the spring of 1634, an incident many feared would alienate the puritan peers. Explaining the "sad accident which lately fell out between our neighbors of Plimoth and some of the Lord Saye his servants at Pascataqua," Winthrop implored his friend to convey to Lords Saye and Brooke the colonists' regret that "such an injury should be offered to those honorable persons who for love of us and for furtherance of our beginnings here had so far engaged themselves with us."[66]

Disagreement over the shape of the Bay's governing institutions and disputes over the northern fur trade did not preclude Lord Saye and his associates from their plans to settle on the lands they had acquired. And the Winthrops, perhaps envisioning a powerful confederation of separate puritan colonies, were willing to assist them. Sometime in October 1634 John Winthrop Jr. and the Reverend John Wilson sailed from Boston for the British Isles. The story of Winthrop Jr.'s activities strongly suggests that the purpose of his journey was to find ways of accommodating the groups considering migration. Claiming bad weather, the ship interrupted its voyage with a stop in Galway. The younger Winthrop disembarked and made his way across the country, possibly stopping to visit his kin in the Bandon area and acquaintances in Dublin. In Ulster, he visited next with Sir John Clotsworthy, a large landowner and an opponent of Charles I's Irish policies. At Clotsworthy's estate Winthrop met with "divers godly persons" who planned to emigrate to New England, providing them with encouragement and advice. Clotsworthy would correspond with Winthrop Jr. in code as the plans of those considering emigration matured over the coming months.[67]

The younger Winthrop then crossed to Scotland and worked his way south through England, visiting Reverend Henry Jessey, a correspondent and friend who had for a time been chaplain to the Gurdons. Jessey had since joined the household of Sir Matthew Boynton in Yorkshire, and Boynton was one of those considering investing in the Saybrook venture. John Clotsworthy was also one of this group, as were Sir William Constable, Henry Darley, George Fenwick, Oliver Cromwell's friend Henry Lawrence, Sir Richard Saltonstall, and the younger Sir Henry Vane. The Reverends Philip Nye and Hugh Peter were also involved in the group's discussions.[68] Many of these men were considering migrating themselves and wanted to hear about the Bay settlements. In February 1635 Henry Jessey wrote Winthrop Jr., asking questions about the way in which ministers were chosen and requesting copies of the "Model of Christian Charity," Higginson's letter describing the countryside, "and the Humble Petition asserting membership in the Church of England."[69]

In July 1635 leaders of the Saybrook Company then in London signed an agreement with Winthrop Jr. whereby, on behalf of all the proprietors, they appointed him "governor of the River Connecticut in New England and of the harbors and places adjoining."[70] The commission was to last for a year, during which time he was expected to establish a foundation for the new colony, much as John Endecott had done for Massachusetts. It is likely that this was the culmination of a plan that had been proposed in correspondence with the Winthrops and matured in the younger Winthrop's meetings with the company directors in Ireland, the north of England, and London. If so it would provide a further explanation for the senior Winthrop's opposition to the plans of the various groups in the Bay to settle along the Connecticut River. Shortly after arriving back in Massachusetts, Winthrop Jr. dispatched an advance party to begin fortifying the mouth of the Connecticut River. The following spring that outpost was strengthened and placed under the command of Lion Gardner, who had fought with English volunteers in the wars in the Netherlands. Meanwhile, Sir Richard Saltonstall had dispatched twenty servants to establish a trading post on his portion of the Saybrook grant near the Plymouth colony trading post.

John Winthrop's opposition had not been sufficient to stop the migration into the valley, which had the support of Thomas Dudley as well as Roger Ludlow and John Haynes. As early as 1634 some residents of Watertown accompanied John Oldham and established a trading post that evolved into the town of Wethersfield. The following year Roger Ludlow and some of the settlers of Dorchester settled on land near Plymouth's trading post on the river. They ignored the land claims of Plymouth when that colony's representative, Jonathan Brewster, protested their settlement, and they likewise obstructed the efforts of Saltonstall's servants to survey the land and build homes. Unable to stem the migration, the Massachusetts General Court gave its approval to the move of Newtown in 1635 and shifted their focus to asserting authority over the far-off settlements. While Massachusetts wished to retain authority over these groups, the lands along the Connecticut River on which they were settling were also claimed by the Saybrook proprietors.

Henry Vane and the Reverend Hugh Peter, both part of the Saybrook enterprise, arrived in Massachusetts in the fall of 1635 and joined the younger Winthrop in challenging the right of the river settlements to the land they had occupied. But their protests had no more impact than those

of Plymouth's Brewster or of Saltonstall. Winthrop Jr. finally joined
Gardner at the town called Saybrook, in April 1636. The rich lands of the
valley were now disputed among Plymouth, the Dutch, the Saybrook proprietors, the Massachusetts Bay Colony, and the new residents who had
moved there from the Bay.

In March 1636 the Massachusetts General Court, with John Haynes
serving as governor, sought to deal with the circumstances of the new settlements and the intentions of the English peers. It was agreed that the new
towns would be governed by an eight-person commission that was empowered to call a General Court for the settlements and that derived its
authority jointly from Massachusetts and the Saybrook proprietors as represented by Winthrop Jr. The compromise avoided dealing with the fundamental issue of whose jurisdiction the river towns fell under. The situation
was further confused by the conflicting roles of many of the key individuals. Winthrop Jr. was the appointed governor of the Saybrook grant but
was still officially an assistant of the Massachusetts Bay Colony. Vane, who
had come to the region as a representative of the Saybrook proprietors,
was elected governor of Massachusetts in May 1636. Haynes, whom he
succeeded, moved to the Connecticut settlements shortly after Vane replaced him. William Pynchon, farther up the river at Springfield, accepted
the authority of Massachusetts and was an assistant of that colony but was
also named one of the Connecticut commissioners.

Everything that had been done through 1636 was provisional. Winthrop Jr.'s appointment as governor had been for one year and expired in
July 1636, though he continued for a time to speak for the proprietors'
interests. The joint commission was appointed for one year. All were waiting for the promised arrival of the peers, who would have been expected to
exert a considerable influence on the resolution of the disputes. And many
of the Saybrook proprietors had been and were actively preparing to migrate. Robert Barrington, a good friend of the Winthrops, sent over servants in September 1635 to be used on colony projects.[71] While John Jr.
was still en route from England to Massachusetts two of the proprietors,
Arthur Heselrige and George Fenwick, had written to him expressing their
support and urging him to make sure that houses were built for the anticipated arrival of the peers.[72] Heselrige sought to purchase John Endecott's
original Salem house and to have it moved to the river.[73] Edward Hopkins
sent over servants and supplies.[74] Henry Lawrence, one of the proprietors,
also wrote to Winthrop Jr. that fall. He underlined his faith in the young
man's ability but reminded him that the peers were so determined to settle
on the Connecticut that "nothing but a plain impossibility could divert us
from that place," where their settlement would prove "most advantageous
for the securing of our friends at the Bay and our own personal accommodations." Like Heselrige and Fenwick, Lawrence urged that work proceed

on the erection of "convenient buildings for the receipt of gentlemen," and he indicated that they were "like to come over next Summer," which Winthrop was not yet aware of.[75] It is at least possible that Oliver Cromwell, a friend of Lawrence, was one of those considering emigration at this time.[76]

Yet the anticipated migration did not materialize. According to Philip Nye, a number of the "gentlemen of the North," presumably including Matthew Boynton, had been selling off their estates and had moved to London preparatory to sailing for New England. Restrictions on emigration to New England were still in place, and when their hope of sailing without attracting government attention was thwarted, they desisted for the time. Boynton himself asked the Winthrops to take great care in writing to him lest letters be intercepted, even by friends.[77] The authorities made it difficult for them to settle their affairs, though in February 1636 Boynton still expressed a determination to migrate and hoped that he would be so well furnished that he "might have beavers to kill as soon as I come"!

George Fenwick did arrive in Boston in May of 1636 and evidently assumed the watching brief over the Saybrook enterprise, which Henry Vane gave up following his election as governor of Massachusetts.[78] Fenwick journeyed to Saybrook the following month to examine the progress that had been made and then returned to Boston in July along with Winthrop Jr. before sailing for England to report to his fellow proprietors. Though he returned the following year to settle at Saybrook, Fenwick's report could not have been encouraging. Hugh Peter had settled in Salem rather than at Saybrook. At about this time, suspecting that the interest of the peers was waning, he wrote to Winthrop Jr. warning him to be careful about advancing any more of his own funds in the venture.[79]

The commission jointly appointed by Massachusetts and John Winthrop Jr. assumed the authority to call a General Court for Connecticut, which met in April 1636 and issued orders, passed regulations, and swore in local constables. Roger Ludlow seems to have been the commissioner who took the lead in the meetings. John Winthrop Jr. was neither consulted nor invited. Courts were held again in June, September, and November, and with each session the magistrates expanded their authority without concern for the pretensions of Massachusetts or the Saybrook proprietors, neither of which was able to do more than protest.[80] A new colony, with an independent government, was in the process of taking shape.

The role of John Winthrop himself in all this is hidden in shadows, but not totally obscure. He clearly was in contact with the godly peers and gentlemen behind the Saybrook venture. He recognized the benefits of their proposed migration for Massachusetts, though he may have had doubts about the autocratic style that was implied in the proposals for government they had sent over. He was closely involved in his son's efforts, from the younger Winthrop's travels through Ireland and England to his assumption of the governorship of Saybrook. Matthew Boynton wrote to John Jr. that he "desired not to communicate with any but yourself and your worthy father, nor that any other should have any intelligence from you of anything that concerns my own particulars."[81] On his Ten Hills farm Winthrop grazed cattle for some of those planning to emigrate. He argued against the migration of Bay colonists to the Connecticut River, but his reduced influence in the Massachusetts General Court meant that he was unable to prevent it. Gauging what he learned from English sources, in June 1636 he was able to write to his son that "the gentlemen seem to be discouraged in their design here."[82]

A new Privy Council proclamation issued in April 1637 and reissued the following year prohibited emigration to New England without a license. This may have been a direct response to the rumored migration of the peers. It certainly made their departure next to impossible and sealed the fate of the "Saybrook Colony."[83] But seeds of confusion had been sown along the Connecticut River, and they would soon produce a bitter harvest.

13

War

As he walked from his home to the town dock near Edward Bendal's home on the morning of April 10, 1637, John Winthrop received a lukewarm reception. Though his reputation had risen in the colony as a whole—he had recently been elected deputy governor—divisions in Boston had cost him much of his popularity. But that was far from his mind on this April day that had a touch of winter still in the air. As commander of one of the colony's militia regiments, he was going to the dock to see the departure of twenty soldiers for the relief of the Connecticut settlements. The situation in that region had steadily deteriorated, and a previous military expedition led by John Endecott precipitated war rather than imposing peace. Lion Gardner, commanding the fort at Saybrook, felt that his settlement was vulnerable and had implored John Winthrop Jr. for further assistance. Governor Vane, as well as the two Winthrops, had links to the Saybrook colony and agreed to send a small relief force while making plans for a greater Massachusetts contribution to the war.

A crowd was gathering to bid farewell to the troops. Friends and family offered prayers for their success. The commander of the expedition was Captain John Underhill, who was aggrieved at a recent reorganization of the militia which named Winthrop, Endecott, and John Haynes as commanders of the Bay's three regiments under the overall command of Governor Vane. As a veteran of European wars hired by the colonists as a military expert, Underhill had protested being placed in a post no better than that of a muster master, and under the command of a civilian. His resentment toward Winthrop made their meeting at the dock frosty.[1] But Winthrop was convinced of the need to send help to Saybrook and had confidence in Underhill as a commander, while Underhill himself welcomed the chance to engage in military action away from civilian control. In all, it was a somber occasion, with the colonists hoping that the small force might deflect the clouds of war that threatened English New England.

❧

*I*T HAD BEEN EXPANSION of the fur trade and the establishment of settlements along the Connecticut River that had brought the colonists to
war. Whereas the eastern coastal tribes had been virtually wiped out
before 1630, native tribes in southern New England, such as the Narragansetts and the Pequots, had been relatively unaffected by European diseases. The leaders of the Bay had tried to negotiate a path through the
intricacies of rivalries between those and other tribes, while at the same
time dealing with the claims of other colonies and the Saybrook proprietors to the interior expanse of New England. Those conflicting English
claims added to the region's instability and contributed to conflict with the
Pequots.

To make sense of that war it is necessary to understand English attitudes toward the native population. Englishmen in John Winthrop's time
did not subscribe to a view of the native inhabitants as noble savages. Anyone who had read his Hakluyt, Purchas, or John Smith—as Winthrop did—
recognized how dangerous the Indians could be. The self-identity of Englishmen at that time depended significantly upon how they defined themselves
in relationship to others whom they encountered in the outside world. In
reading their Hakluyt and Purchas, and George Abbot's *A Brief Description
of the Whole Worlde* (1599), they discovered their uniqueness by contrasting
their own physical appearance, material goods, folkways, and religion to
those of Africans, native Americans, and peoples of the Mediterranean.
Closer to home they focused on characteristics that distinguished them
from their neighbors in Scotland and Ireland.[2]

The "wild Irish" in particular were described in much the same way
that native Americans would come to be understood. They possessed fertile land but failed to make it fruitful. They lived in primitive huts. Their
language was alien. They were "by nature extremely given to idleness."[3]
They "lurked and lay in wait to do mischief."[4] Though they were raised as
Roman Catholics, the faith was said to have degenerated to a level where
the native Irish were depicted as "superstitious and given to use [of] witchcraft."[5] The killings and depredations of the Munster uprising and the Nine
Years War reinforced the image of the Irish as barbarous, brutish, treacherous, and superstitious—everything that the English were not and rejected.
In colonizing Ireland the English would gradually move from a policy of
civilizing the natives to a policy of displacing them. The parallel with North
America is striking.

Englishmen were no different from others of their time in being unable
to appreciate other cultures from the perspectives of the host societies, and
viewing things from their own perspective, they inevitably misunderstood
and misjudged. The later appellation of "redmen" is not found in the records
of Winthrop's time. Though the natives were of a darker hue than Englishmen, their complexion was believed to have been white at birth, then

darkened by exposure to the sun or other factors.[6] As in the case of the native Irish, the native Americans were seen as culturally different from Englishmen, not racially apart. Yet they were neither Christian nor civilized.[7] Natives were often depicted as devil worshipers and their shamans as witches. They had no settled habitations, failed to till the soil as effectively as they could have, and governed themselves in ways the English found hard to comprehend. Like the Irish, the men were perceived as lazy and shiftless. Even so, they were potentially threatening. Any Englishman who migrated to America in the 1630s would have been familiar with tales of Indian attacks on English colonists in the Chesapeake and elsewhere. Yet the English were capable of overcoming cultural stereotypes in dealing with individuals. John's cousins Joshua and Adam would have shared the English disdain for and suspicion of the native Irish, yet accepted them as tenants on their Irish lands; individual New Englanders made the effort to treat native Americans with the same consideration they gave fellow Englishmen.

It is difficult to determine John Winthrop's personal attitudes toward natives. His writings contain few generalizations about Indians, so for the most part his views must be deduced from his recorded behavior. His first encounter with a member of the local tribes came when Masconomo, sagamore of the Agawam band, came aboard the *Arbella* and spent the day. In his role as governor Winthrop frequently entertained native leaders in his Boston home. His comment that because Chickabot, sagamore of the Massachusetts tribe, was "in English clothes, the governor set him at his own table, where he behaved himself as soberly, etc. as an Englishman" is instructive.[8] He was willing to treat Chickabot as an equal, but only because the native leader conformed to English standards of civility. To the degree that natives accepted those standards, they could expect to be treated fairly, but the English, including Winthrop, neither sought nor found any merit in native customs and values.

Over the following years, though wary of the natives, the colonists sought to treat them in a way that reflected English concepts of fairness. When some of the Pawtucket tribe complained of being cheated by a visiting fur trader, Winthrop directed Emmanuel Downing in England to investigate the charges. The General Court sought to protect the natives from unscrupulous colonists or visitors by ordering that no strong drinks were to be sold to Indians, that no one was to trade with them without license from the court, and that any natives who had been forced into servitude were to be released. The court carefully regulated land sales and extended to the natives the protection of English justice. One Englishman was severely whipped for "enticing an Indian woman" into sex. Others were punished for theft from Indians. Sir Richard Saltonstall, an assistant himself, was ordered to make restitution for Indian property destroyed by his servants and his cattle. The town of Agawam was ordered to compensate the sagamore of the Agawam band when the town cattle damaged his crops.

Though Winthrop had listed the conversion of the natives as one of the reasons for the colonization of Massachusetts, albeit the seventh of his "particular considerations," there was little direct effort to share the benefits of Christianity in the early years of the colony. A sagamore of a band in the area of Marblehead showed some interest in conversion but died along with most of his band in the 1632 smallpox epidemic. In that year the Englishman Edward Howes wrote to John Winthrop Jr. that he was glad to hear that it appeared that John Sagamore was becoming "civilized and a christian."[9] And when John Sagamore died in December 1633 he left his son to be raised by the Reverend John Wilson. This is the extent of the evidence for early conversions. Puritan congregationalism, in which clerical office was bestowed on an individual by a congregation for the purpose of ministering to that congregation alone, was not well suited to missionary activities.

A few examples of fair treatment did not mean that the colonists were without fear and prejudice. After all, in cases where punishment was meted out for crimes against Indians, the offense often stemmed from individual Englishmen treating natives in ways they would not have treated fellow English men or women. These darker emotions were most likely to come to the fore than when the restraints of law and civilization disappeared under the conditions of war.

THE EXPANSION INTO THE CONNECTICUT RIVER VALLEY created an extremely volatile situation. Not only was European control of the area disputed by the Dutch, the Plymouth colony, Massachusetts, the Saybrook proprietors, and the settlers of the new towns themselves, but native society was also in a state of flux as the Pequot tribe's hold on the region was eroding. In the spring of 1631 sachems from several villages along the river sought to escape Pequot hegemony by seeking an alliance with the Massachusetts and Plymouth authorities. Around the same time, Uncas, a Mohegan sachem whose village was around the site of modern Norwich, began to assert his right to be sachem of the Pequots as well, leading to clashes between the two groups. In 1634 the Pequots and Narragansetts fell into conflict over a twenty-mile tract of land along the border of present-day Connecticut and Rhode Island.[10] Various native leaders sought English support against their enemies, offering inducements to trade with them and stimulating fear of their enemies. Neither Englishmen nor natives were quite sure who spoke for the other side.

The conflicts in the Connecticut Valley first came to the attention of the English in April 1631 when Wahginnacut, a sachem from the area, came to Boston accompanied by an Indian called Jack Straw, a native who had been taken to England, where he had served Sir Walter Earle before returning to America.[11] Wahginnacut "was very desirous to have some Englishmen to come plant in his country, and offered to find them corn and give them yearly eighty skins of beaver." Winthrop was suspicious and declined the offer, later deciding that the sachem had been seeking to enlist the colonists on his side in a land conflict with the Pequots.[12] The Bay next took notice of the region when the colonists heard of the murder of John Stone, but their history with Stone made it easy to conclude that he had likely brought his death upon himself, and Winthrop as governor saw no need to inquire further into the episode beyond informing the Virginia authorities.[13]

In October 1634 the Pequots, engaged in conflict with both the Dutch and the Narragansetts, sent an envoy to Massachusetts seeking an alliance with the English. The Bay leaders exchanged gifts with the envoy and indicated that they were willing to negotiate with appropriate representatives of Sassacus, the Pequot sachem. However, the clergy advised the magistrates that in their view it would be inappropriate to enter into an alliance with people who had killed Englishmen (no matter how reprehensible) unless they surrendered the murderers, and this the native envoys agreed to, indicating that only two of the perpetrators were still alive. The two sides entered into a treaty of peace and friendship. The Pequots agreed to welcome the Bay colonists as trading partners and to cede land to them if they decided to settle along the Connecticut River. The Massachusetts leaders agreed to mediate between the Pequots and the Narragansetts, handing over to the Narragansetts wampum that the Pequots would provide, for the latter "stood so much on their honor as they would not be seen to give anything of themselves."[14] The colonists did not, however, pledge themselves to fight with the Pequots against their enemies. The colonists quickly sent out a pinnace under John Oldham to initiate the trade, but the result was disappointing, and in early March 1635 Winthrop wrote to Plymouth's William Bradford that the experience of the Bay traders led the magistrates to conclude that the Pequots were "a very false people, so as they mean to have no more to do with them."[15]

It is possible that the terms agreed to by his envoys were too steep for Sassacus, especially as the threat from the Dutch seemed to be diminishing. At any rate, not only was Oldham disappointed by the trading opportunities, but the Pequots delivered neither Stone's murderers nor the remainder of the wampum the envoys had agreed to. While contact between the natives and the Bay leaders virtually ceased for a time, the Massachusetts authorities still believed that their treaty with the Pequots was binding. Meanwhile, native enemies of the Pequots took advantage of the situation to sow suspicions of the tribe. In June 1636 Jonathan Brewster wrote from Plymouth's trading post to John Winthrop Jr., warning the

Saybrook governor of reports that the Pequots were planning to attack the English along the river. Brewster also claimed to have learned that the murder of Stone had been plotted by the Pequots and that Sassacus himself was involved. This news had come from Uncas, who was plotting to replace Sassacus, but Brewster seems to have been unaware that he was being used.[16]

Brewster's report also included information he had gathered from the captain of a Dutch ship on the river. According to him two Englishmen had journeyed to Long Island to salvage material from an English shipwreck along that coast. They had been set upon by natives, and one of them was killed. This had followed the murder of two other Englishmen on Long Island, and according to the Dutchman the Pequots were incriminated in these events. Brewster felt that this added credence to the rumors of projected Pequot attacks on his own trading post and other English settlements on the river.[17]

Though William Pynchon, who was trading with the tribes farther up the river, did not take the rumors of Pequot aggression seriously, in July 1636 Massachusetts Governor Henry Vane and Deputy Governor John Winthrop commissioned John Winthrop Jr., who was still a Bay colony assistant, to act on their behalf in calling the Pequots to answer to their failure to fulfill the terms of the 1634 treaty as well as to the charges that they were implicated in the recent killings on Long Island. He was to "demand a solemn meeting for conference" with the Pequots "in a friendly manner," during which conference he was to discuss the concerns of the Bay. He was to ask for immediate fulfillment of the long-standing promise to surrender the murderers of John Stone, and he was to confront the sachem with the failure to complete the promised payment of wampum called for in the treaty. He was also to raise with the Pequots the charges made by Brewster, assuring them that "it is not the manner of the English to take revenge of injuries until the parties that are guilty have been called to answer fairly for themselves." If they failed to grant him a meeting, Winthrop Jr. was to return the gifts given by the natives in 1634, signifying thereby that the colonists considered themselves "free from any peace or league with them as a people guilty of English blood" and "shall revenge the blood of our countrymen as occasion shall serve."[18] The skins received from the Pequots were sent to Saybrook, and Winthrop Jr. was asked to advance the wampum from his own supplies if a return of gifts became necessary, the Bay promising to reimburse him. At the same time, while divesting himself of responsibility for acting on behalf of the Saybrook proprietors, Vane indicated that George Fenwick and Hugh Peter would be arriving to assist the younger Winthrop in making decisions that would "be for the benefit of the Gentlemen."[19]

Lion Gardner was evidently disturbed by the idea of confronting the Pequots, recognizing that it could lead the tribe to advance plans for war if they had any, or provoke a conflict where none was being contemplated. There is no evidence that the Pequots agreed to a conference, but the younger Winthrop did return the skins and wampum, thus signaling the English belief that they were no longer bound by the treaty of 1634.[20] Almost immediately thereafter Winthrop left Saybrook and returned to the Bay. He had not formally been renewed as governor of the colony, was owed money by the proprietors, with little hope of repayment, and by this time had come to realize that whatever society he had hoped would emerge along the Connecticut was not going to come to pass.

At about the same time, the trader John Oldham's ship was discovered along the coast of Block Island with the Englishman's dead and mutilated body. The Block Island tribe was a tributary of the Narragansetts, but that tribe intervened quickly to deflect suspicion from themselves, returning to the English two of Oldham's servants who had been captured as well as much of the seized cargo. The Narragansett sachems also sought to deflect English anger to their own enemies by claiming that the renegade Block Islanders who had killed Oldham had subsequently sought refuge among the Pequots.[21]

The English colonists in New England certainly had reason to feel uneasy in the summer of 1636. In addition to Stone and Oldham, the total number of English killed in the preceding few years was a dozen or more, and none of the murderers had been turned over or punished.[22] This alone was reason to worry about rumored plans for other attacks on the settlements. Stephen Winthrop had taken a shallop from Saybrook to trade with the Pequots but had withdrawn when threatened by the natives. Fears were heightened by recollections of the "Great Massacre" of February 1622 in which Powhattans had launched an unexpected attack on the English settlements in Virginia, killing 347 colonists—a third of the population.[23] As the English prepared for military action, Roger Williams wrote to John Winthrop of Pequot preparations and of their boast that "a witch among them will sink the [English] pinnaces by diving under water and making holes" and that they sought to "enrich themselves with store of guns."[24]

The leaders of the Bay decided on a show of force in an attempt to deter further native attacks. In late August Governor Vane and the Standing Council of the Bay, which included John Winthrop, assembled the colony's magistrates and ministers. They decided to punish the murderers of Oldham by sending a force of ninety men under John Endecott to put to death the native men of Block Island—sparing the women and children— and then to proceed to the main Pequot village. There they were to demand the surrender of the murderers of Stone and the other English as well as a large payment of wampum for damages.[25]

Endecott's force sailed from Boston on the twenty-fourth of August. Struggling waist deep through a high surf to land on Block Island, they found themselves under attack from about forty natives. The Indian arrows glanced off the body armor of the English, and only two of the soldiers received wounds. Once the English gained the beach, the natives dispersed and evidently fled the island. Endecott's forces spent two days moving through the hilly, overgrown terrain without encountering any hostile forces. They burned sixty native wigwams in the two villages they found and destroyed seven canoes and close to two hundred acres of native corn. They then moved on to the main Pequot village.

Endecott demanded to speak to Sassacus, the chief sachem, but was told that he was away on Long Island. While the English waited for his return or the arrival of other sachems, and messengers went back and forth between the two sides, over three hundred Pequots took up positions to ready themselves to attack Endecott's force. Finally, after a four-hour standoff, Endecott set forth to an Indian messenger the English demands for the surrender of those who had murdered colonists and for the wampum payment. He instructed the messenger to tell his sachem "that if he would not come to him nor yield to these demands, he would fight with them." When the messenger returned and indicated that the sachem would only come to speak if the English laid down their arms, Endecott rejected the proposal and indicated that the time had come to fight. As the Pequots dispersed, the English pursued them in hopes of forcing them into an engagement. Though they killed some natives in a running fight, they were unsuccessful in forcing a decisive clash. As they had done on Block Island, they then proceeded to burn the native wigwams and attempted to destroy the cornfields.[26] The English force returned to Boston by way of the Narragansett territory to show their erstwhile allies their strength.

Historians have agreed that Endecott had some European military experience, and the nature of this campaign suggests that he may have fought in England's Irish wars. The tactic of laying waste the land of their enemies is something that strongly recalls the practice of the English forces in crushing the Desmond rebellion of 1579 in Munster as well as the subsequent campaigns there of Essex and others.[27] Both in Ireland and in New England, the English found themselves often frustrated by enemies who would not engage in set battles. And in both cases they responded by laying waste the land both to intimidate their foes and to deprive them of their ability to support themselves in the field. In the case of the Block Island Indians, this seemed to work, for they subsequently submitted to English oversight and made annual wampum payments to Massachusetts.[28] In the case of the Pequots, those goals were not realized. Endecott had merely poked a stick into a hornet's nest and returned to Boston. Those English who remained in the valley were soon to be stung.

Lion Gardner, in charge of Saybrook's defense, was highly critical of Endecott's actions, as were Plymouth's William Bradford and the settlers in the river towns. Bradford wrote not to Vane but to Winthrop, who was then deputy governor. It is hard to discover Winthrop's views on the turmoil in the Connecticut River Valley in the years leading up to this point, and it is important to remember that during the period from May 1634 to May 1636 he was on the periphery of power, having been rejected for the governorship and deputy governorship two elections in a row. When approached by Wahginnacut and Jack Straw in 1631, when he was governor, he had shied away from getting involved in the native rivalries in the valley. But he had then worked with the Saybrook proprietors and his son in trying to stake their claim to the region while opposing as long as he could the Massachusetts migration to the river. There is no reason to think that he would not have been troubled by the murder of Englishmen, and particularly by the deaths that occurred after the Stone incident. And he was aware as anyone of the sudden nature and devastating effects of Irish uprisings and the Virginia massacre. He signed the instructions for dealing with the Pequots sent to his son, and he was a member of the Standing Council that drew up Endecott's instructions.

In responding to Bradford, Winthrop acknowledged that there was some reason for Plymouth's concerns but defended his friend Endecott's conduct. The troops had been sent "not to make war upon them, but to do justice." Yet, given that the Pequots had refused to surrender those accused of murdering Englishmen, Winthrop appeared to admit that it would have been better if Endecott had been able to inflict damage on the natives rather than just their homes. He offered excuses—the Pequots had fled and Endecott had no scouts familiar with the terrain, and even if the English had killed many of the Indians, those who survived would have been as likely to attack the colonies as the entire tribe. And he felt that the actions of the expedition should have taught the Pequots to fear the English, as it had in the case of the Block Islanders. Taking "notice of our advantage against them," they "would have sit still, or have sought peace, if God had not deprived them of common reason."[29]

When rumors reached Boston that the Pequots were not just preparing for war but seeking to enlist the far more powerful Narragansetts as allies, the true danger of the situation became clear. Winthrop, who had remained friends with Roger Williams, recognized that Williams had developed strong relations with the Narragansetts and sought his aid. The Standing Council requested Williams to try to "break the league labored for by the Pequots . . . against the English." Years later, Williams wrote that "the Lord helped me immediately to put my life into my hand, and scarce acquainting my wife [of his plans], to ship myself alone in a poor canoe, and to cut through a stormy wind thirty miles in great seas, every

minute in hazard of my life, to the sachem's house." There he found himself "having to lodge and mix with the bloody Pequot ambassadors, whose
hands and arms (me thought) reeked with the blood of my countrymen."[30]
The Narragansetts might not have allied themselves with a declining native power against the powerful English colonies with whom they conducted a valuable trade, but Williams's intervention was credited with
deciding the issue, and the Rhode Islander continued to serve as a media-
tor in the negotiations that led to a formal alliance between the Narragansetts and the Bay colony in October 1636.[31]

Almost immediately after Endecott's departure from the region,
Saybrook settlers were attacked by Pequots as they tried to gather their
harvest from the fields surrounding the fort. Frustrated by the younger
Winthrop's decision not to return to Saybrook, Gardner complained about
the situation he had been left in and warned that all vessels intended to
navigate the Connecticut River needed to be well armed. Calling upon
Massachusetts Governor Vane, Winthrop Jr. did arrange for twenty Bay
troops under Captain John Underhill to reinforce the garrison, the expense to be borne by the Saybrook proprietors. Meanwhile the river towns
refused to accept Gardner's authority or guidance. In April Wethersfield
was attacked. Three women and two men were killed, two women were
carried off, and some of the settlement's cattle were slaughtered.[32] Rumors
that Pynchon's settlement at Springfield had been wiped out were false but
spurred the English preparations to take the offensive. In April the Massachusetts General Court authorized the call-up of 160 men and called upon
Plymouth to support the war. Friction with Plymouth had been growing,
and that colony's authorities rejected Governor Vane's appeal, though later,
after John Winthrop was elected governor of Massachusetts in May, Plymouth did contribute fifty men to the common cause. Also in May 1637,
representatives from Hartford, Wethersfield, and Windsor gathered in a
General Court, declared war on the Pequots, and levied military quotas on
each town. This force was placed under the command of Captain John
Mason, a veteran who had served with English volunteers in the Netherlands in the 1620s. Uncas offered the English the help of his Mohegans,
and, after he proved his allegiance by bringing to Gardner the heads of
four Pequots as well as a live captive, he and his warriors would participate
in the campaigns.

Mason and Gardner decided to launch an attack on the Pequots from
the east. In late May a force of ninety English soldiers under Mason and
seventy Mohegans landed along the Narragansett Bay. Adding some
Narragansetts, they crossed the Pawcatcuk River into Pequot country.
There were two fortified Pequot villages, one at Mystic and the other at
Weinshauks. Though Sassacus was believed to be at the latter site, Mason
decided to strike at Mystic, which was the closest. Despite the fact that he

was unsure of his native allies and his own men were weary from a difficult march in extreme heat, Mason launched an attack on the village in the early morning of May 26. Part of the English force, under Mason, fought their way into one of the two entrances while the other part, under John Underhill, forced their way into the village from the other side. The Pequots put up a fierce resistance but moved from place to place as they sought to inflict casualties without presenting clear targets themselves. Greatly outnumbered, and finding negotiating the maze of wigwams dangerous, Mason pulled his troops out and set fire to the village. The English surrounded the palisade and killed all who tried to escape as the Mystic fort went up in flames. As many as six or seven hundred Pequots were killed. Many were warriors, but women, children, and the elderly made up a significant portion of the death toll. Two Englishmen were killed, but another twenty were wounded, a substantial casualty rate for an attacking force believed to have been seventy-seven. His force seriously weakened and low on powder, shot, and food, Mason abandoned for the time any thought of attacking Sassacus's main encampment. As they made for the coast the English forces fought off a shadowing force of about three hundred Pequots, inflicting what some native informants said were about a hundred casualties in a series of brief but vicious skirmishes.

The spirit of the Pequots and their allies was broken by the horrendous losses at Mystic. Some of the smaller groups who had allied themselves to the tribe sued for peace with the English. Various groups within the Pequot tribe deserted Sassacus, some migrating to Long Island and others surrendering to the Narragansetts. The sachem himself, with several hundred followers, crossed the Connecticut River—killing the three-man crew of an English trading shallop they encountered—as they sought to find refuge with the Mohawks to the west. A new expeditionary force from the Bay colony, commanded by Israel Stoughton, arrived to crush the last elements of resistance. The English force caught up to the retreating Pequots and won a victory in the "Great Swamp Fight" near the future site of New Haven. Many Pequots were killed, and close to two hundred surrendered. Sassacus and some of his chief undersachems escaped, but their hope of refuge among the Mohawk was an illusion. That tribe, understanding English power, attacked and killed the Pequot leaders, then sent Sassacus's scalp to the Boston authorities as proof of their friendship with the English. Pequots captured during the war were often executed if they were men and enslaved if they were women or children. Some of those slaves were given to Englishmen or their Indian allies in New England. Others were shipped to the British island colonies in the Caribbean.

The brutality with which the English crushed the Pequots horrifies modern sensibilities, but the events can be placed in context without condoning them.[33] When Shakespeare has Henry V warn the citizens of

Harfleur that if their city does not yield, the English will grant no quarter, "mowing like grass your fair fresh virgins and your flowering infants," "your fathers taken by the silver beards and their most reverend heads dashed to the walls," and "your naked infants spitted upon pikes," this is not just literary hyperbole. The Peasants' War of 1524–26 in the German states left as many as one hundred thousand dead. The Spanish efforts to suppress the Dutch revolt in the 1570s included numerous instances of cities sacked, civilians killed, and women raped. More relevant to the experience and knowledge of the English colonists in New England were the wars in Ireland and Virginia. Humfry Gilbert suppressed an Irish uprising in 1569 by slaughtering men, women, and children. Five years later the earl of Essex seized over two hundred men and women at a banquet and had them all executed. The same earl sent Sir Francis Drake "to the island of Rathlin, a base for incoming Scottish mercenaries. Drake killed every one of the 600 men, women, and children who lived there." The actions of Cromwell's troops in Ireland in the 1650s have been deemed excessive by later generations but were accepted at the time.

The New Englanders were well versed in tales of the "Great Massacre" of 1622 in Virginia, when English women and children had been killed along with men by the Powhattan warriors. The English there responded with the same ferocity and failure to distinguish between combatants and noncombatants. Philip Vincent pointed to the relevance of that episode in his contemporary narrative of the Pequot War, writing that "[t]he long forbearance and too much lenity of the English towards the Virginian savages had like to have been the destruction of the whole plantation."[34] In his own account of the campaign the Massachusetts commander John Underhill asked rhetorically, "Should not Christians have more mercy and compassion?" In answer he referred readers to the Scriptures, and particularly to the wars of King David. According to Underhill the lesson was that "[w]hen a people is grown to such a height of blood, and sin against God and man," God's forces must have "no respect to persons, but harrow them, and saw them, and put them to the sword and the most terriblest death that may be. Sometimes the Scripture declareth women and children must perish with their parents. . . . We had sufficient light from the word of God for our proceedings."[35] All such brutal excesses were intended to terrorize and cow enemies into submission. From the perspective of Boston in 1637, the lesson of the Mystic fort fight was the surrender of many Pequots and the abandonment of that tribe by their allies. Even the powerful Mohawks declined to challenge the English at this point.

And what of John Winthrop in all this? His direct involvement in the events leading up to the conflict had been minimal, but once war appeared imminent he did all that he could to ensure victory. He used Roger Williams to gain the neutrality of the Narragansetts. He smoothed the ruffled feelings of William Bradford and secured a commitment of Plymouth troops to the war. There is no reason to think that he had any objections to the conduct of the campaign. He was governor again when the war ended, and October 12, 1637, was appointed a day of thanksgiving. After the sermon that day, "the captains and soldiers who had been in the late service were feasted," Winthrop and his fellow magistrates escorting them from the meetinghouse to where they were to dine.[36]

In the aftermath of the fighting the captive women and children were sent to Boston, where Winthrop supervised their disposition. Some were sent as slaves to Barbados. Israel Stoughton asked for one to be reserved for him, as did other officers.[37] Roger Williams wrote to Winthrop "to request the keeping and bringing up one of the children," noting that he had "fixed mine eye on this little one with the red about his neck."[38] Winthrop retained some to serve as servants in his household. Included among them were "Mononotto, a woman of a very modest countenance and behavior," and her children. According to Winthrop she had been responsible for saving the lives of the two Wethersfield women who had been captured by the Pequots at the outset of the war.[39] She had requested that her body not be abused and her children not be taken from her.

It is not clear what slavery meant in these cases. Roger Williams suggested that if it could be done safely the Pequot captives ought, "after a due time of training up to labor and restraint," be set free. They appear to have been incorporated into households such as Winthrop's as servants, with the heads of household bearing the same responsibilities they had toward all their servants. Williams himself is believed to have educated the boy he was given.[40]

The cloud of Indian war had passed, and it would be almost four decades before a similar conflict broke out. But even while the conflict in Connecticut had been raging, another, greater threat to Winthrop's hopes for New England had arisen. This danger arose not just within the colony of Massachusetts but in Winthrop's own Boston church.

14

Struggling to Hold the Center

THE SUN HAD YET TO BURN the morning mists off the marshes along the Charles River as the first colonists began to gather on Newtown's grazing common. The occasion was the election meeting of the freemen of Massachusetts Bay on May 17, 1637, which had been moved to Newtown from Boston by the March General Court. Some had crossed the Charles on ferries and walked north along creek lane until crossing a bridge near the town spring. Passing the burying ground, they came to the common and its ancient oak. Others traveled by road the entire way from Charlestown to the east and Watertown to the west. All who came overland entered through gates in the wooden palisade that surrounded most of the town. John Endecott had sailed from Salem to Boston, and then up the Charles to the Newtown dock, bringing with him some of his townsmen.

As in elections for county members of Parliament in England, the size of the expected electorate made it essential that the vote be conducted outdoors. The cows and goats moved to the further stretches of the common as the number of men began to grow. Some freemen stretched out on the grass; others sheltered from the sun under the oak or other trees which still dotted the grassland. More than a few gathered around the public house recently opened by Thomas Chesholme as they waited for the election to be called.[1] Most freemen tended to cluster with neighbors who had traveled with them. It was a lengthy journey for many, but the important issues facing the colony seemed to require it. Some were talking about the Pequots and the threat of the Indian war about to erupt. Some discussed the weather and the progress of their crops. But the primary topic of conversation was the coming election and what it might mean for the future of the colony, for the religious unity of the Bay, cherished by all, had fragmented in the past year.

When Thomas Hooker and others had migrated to the Connecticut River, they sold their property in Newtown to new arrivals, among them the young clergyman Thomas Shepard, who had organized a new church there early in 1636. Shortly thereafter Shepard had begun to raise questions about the beliefs of lay members of the Boston church, and then about the teachings of the Reverend John Cotton. Saints who had accepted one another's different ways of understanding the workings of God were now demanding precision in doctrine, and the colony had become polarized. A spiritist emphasis on the centrality of free grace was being promoted by Governor Henry Vane, the well-respected laywoman Anne Hutchinson, and another newly arrived clergyman, John Wheelwright, Hutchinson's brother-in-law. Zealous promoters of that viewpoint had taken to accusing those who disagreed with them of Arminianism, the teaching that man's works help shape his salvation. In response to Shepard's lead most of the Bay's clergymen had banded together in an attempt to write the Boston proponents of free grace out of the orthodoxy consensus. Chosen to preach a healing fast-day sermon, John Wheelwright had recently driven a deeper wedge between the two sides. In March the General Court called Wheelwright before them and, over the objection of most of the Boston representatives, found him guilty of sedition, deferring sentencing until the next court, scheduled to assemble on this day, after the election.

As the election morning advanced, Thomas Dudley left his home near the town wharf to make his way to the commons. Dudley was a strong opponent of the faction, which he saw as centered on the brash laywoman Anne Hutchinson. He viewed them as secret familists or antinomians, and he lobbied those he met in the gathering crowd to do their duty for God and commonwealth. Thomas Shepard was engaged in the same sort of discussions as he walked from his home, westward past Watch House Hill toward the commons. Shepard had staked his reputation on the defeat of the radicals. Also making his way to the scene of the election was John Winthrop, who had spent the previous night with his daughter, Mary, and her husband, Samuel Dudley, in their house next to the Newtown meetinghouse. At the previous election Winthrop had emerged from his position on the margins of the colony's government, being elected deputy governor. On this day he hoped to regain the governorship. Certainly, he knew, many saw him as the only man who could keep the colony from fragmenting.

Most of those intending to vote were gathered on the common by one o'clock, when Governor Henry Vane, escorted by four colonists bearing halberds, entered the field. The honor guard was a recent innovation, introduced by Vane to underline the importance of his office. With his arrival the election could begin. However, a Boston freeman interrupted to demand the right to present the General Court with a petition challenging how Wheelwright had been treated. The gathering was thrown into an uproar by the unexpected maneuver. Speaking above the clamor, Winthrop asserted that the court itself could only be constituted after the elections and that any petitions would have to wait until that time. Vane, closely allied to the petitioners, disagreed and argued that until the petition was read there would be no election. The dispute spread to the freemen, and sharp words and blows were exchanged. As the tumult grew, John Wilson climbed into the lower branches of the large oak tree at the corner of the commons and harangued the assembly. He urged them to remember the charter and their hopes in coming to New England. He reminded them that they had come great distances that day to elect the colony's officers. His intervention turned the tide. Many called out, "Election! Election!" The issue was put to a vote, with those in favor of the election moving to one side of the common, and those opposed to the other side. Though a clear majority supported proceeding, Vane and his supporters remained adamant until it was clear that the election would proceed with them or without them. When the votes were tallied it was announced that Winthrop had been chosen governor with Dudley deputy governor. John Endecott was added to the Standing Council and Israel Stoughton and Richard Saltonstall (son of Sir Richard) chosen assistants for the first time. Vane and two of his key supporters on the Court of Assistants were not voted to any office.

With the new officers chosen, the magistrates and deputies prepared to make their way to the Newtown meetinghouse, where the court would convene and address its business. But there was one more bit of drama. The members of Vane's honor guard laid down their halberds to protest the result, leaving Winthrop to proceed to the meetinghouse without escort. Angered though he was by this sign of disrespect, that was the least of his worries. Though his supporters had regained control of the holy experiment, they still had to deal with the strongly disaffected element in the colony.[2]

 જી

*P*URITAN COMMUNITIES MAINTAINED their cohesion by glossing difficult doctrines in a way that allowed for some disagreement and continuing discussion. Religious bodies were to be held together by the ligaments of love. Charity underlay the achievement of unity. But all those who migrated to New England knew how fragile unity could be. Even in areas such as the Stour Valley, where restraint and informal mechanisms of consultation generally succeeded in maintaining cohesion, there had occasionally been fractures in the unity of the godly. The expulsion of Thomas Rogers from the Bury lectureship after he had criticized the teachings of the revered Lawrence Chaderton was one such example.[3] More recently many New Englanders knew of the division in the London puritan community in the 1620s, which centered on the clergyman Stephen Dennison's accusations of familism and other heresies against John Etherington. The bitterness engendered was very similar to what would erupt in Massachusetts in the mid-1630s.[4]

Peace and unity were maintained through a variety of strategies. Informal associational methods of achieving consensus were employed when possible. The process of extreme inversion whereby one emphasized those elements of an individual's thinking that could be presented as totally heterodox and outside the pale of truth was employed against those regarded as outside the community of saints, but never against those within that communion. And individuals learned to refrain from advancing views which they thought would be controversial.[5] Where the fundamental godliness of an individual was beyond question, such tensions were not allowed to disrupt the unity of the faithful.

During the first years of New England settlement the exercise of charity had generally served to establish and maintain a unified religious order. Differences that came to the surface in later years were there from the beginning, but ministers were willing to categorize the disputed matters as nonessentials. Most potential disputes never became significant enough for a record of them to have been left behind. Those that we do know about actually testify to the importance placed on agreement. When George Phillips suggested that the Church of Rome was a true but corrupted church, John Winthrop and other members of the Boston church were able to persuade the majority that they were in error. Hooker and Cotton disagreed over the appropriate use of the cross. When differences over the need for women to be veiled became too heated, discussion was ended and the matter removed from public debate.[6] Subsequent events would make it clear that William Pynchon, the magistrate and Winthrop's partner in the fur trade, held controversial views, but no one made anything of them until the 1640s.[7] Unity, rather than uniformity, was the hallmark of the New England struggle for godliness.

This all began to change in 1634, as a result of new arrivals then and in the following year. Whereas older colonists were moving from experimentation toward consolidation by 1634, the newcomers were still involved in the search for a better understanding of God's will. And many of them had been influenced by radical tendencies that had been developing in English puritanism. The issue of man's involvement in the process of salvation, which had long troubled Protestants, continued to do so in the Atlantic community of the 1630s. Reacting against the danger that pastoral guidance on moral behavior might slide toward a form of legalism that would deny the efficacy of God's grace, some individuals sought to emphasize the experience of grace as the sole validation of salvation.

THE ROOTS OF THIS STRUGGLE can be traced back to the arrival in the colony of a number of key figures in 1634 and 1635. Some men and women who migrated to Massachusetts felt that the religious atmosphere of the Bay did not live up to their expectations, but it is hard to imagine that any puritan could have found fault with the vitality of the godly community in Boston. The heightened piety of the Boston church at this time had as much to do with new arrivals such as Henry Vane, the Hutchinsons, and the Dyers as it did with John Cotton. Yet it was precisely these individuals who would be at the heart of the dispute that would threaten the future of Winthrop's City on a Hill.

The name that was to become most closely identified with that controversy was Anne Hutchinson, who, along with her husband, William, was admitted to the Boston church in the fall of 1634. She was the daughter of Francis Marbury, a godly clergyman who had written one of the commendatory epistles for Richard Rogers's massive guide to the moral life, the *Seven Treatises*. She was literate, well versed in Scripture and religious argument, and deeply pious. Her spiritual progress was not very different from that of many other puritans, including John Winthrop. At some point in the early 1630s she had a conversion experience which assured her of God's love. When her sense of God's caress faded, she looked to recapture her assurance by works. Then, recognizing that she was relying on herself rather than God, and troubled about the state of the English church, she observed a personal fast during which she opened herself to the words of Scripture, assuming that the verses that came to mind were placed there by the Holy Spirit. After recovering her assurance, she continued to work out her faith by relying on this form of scriptural free association. This means of seeking spiritual guidance was popular in the Lincolnshire circles that she seems to have been associated with, and she became adept at it. Drawing on Scripture in this manner, she came to believe that the teachings of most clergy were incorrect and that few in that region of England, aside from John Cotton and her brother-in-law Wheelwright, were worth hearing. What distinguished those two in her estimation was that they disdained a legalist approach to salvation and preached assurance of salvation gained though the seal of the Spirit. Another scriptural revelation persuaded her and her family to follow Cotton to the New World.

William and Mary Dyer were typical of those who were attracted to Hutchinson's form of spirituality. They had been admitted to the Boston church in 1635. Before coming to New England, they had lived in the London parish of St. Michael's Crooked Lane at a time when Peter Shaw regularly preached a form of antinomian doctrine there.[8] This is not to say that the Dyers were antinomians but that they came from a background where anti-legalist expressions of puritanism were not exceptional. Like Anne Hutchinson, they would have been exposed to preaching that stressed the importance of the saint's direct encounter with God's love.[9]

Henry Vane, who would also play a large role in the controversy, was also admitted to the Boston church in 1635, at the age of twenty-two. His

father was an orthodox member of the Church of England and a prominent member of the king's household. Young Henry was converted in his
mid-teens by a strong personal experience of God's transforming love. He
too embarked on a religious pilgrimage. In his enthusiastic pursuit of his
new faith he encountered unorthodox as well as mainstream views circulating in the English puritan community. After his stay in Massachusetts
his route would ultimately lead to support of England's Puritan Revolution, a role as an outspoken advocate of religious toleration, and execution
in 1660 as one of those bearing large responsibility for the decision to execute Charles I in 1649. While Vane left ample evidence of his mature religious thought, it is difficult to know how many of those ideas he had adopted
when he came to New England. It is clear that when he arrived in Massachusetts he impressed all with his faith and piety, appearing to be another candle
to make the City on a Hill shine brighter. He might well have reminded
Winthrop of Roger Williams in his youthful enthusiasm and quest for purity. Seeking further spiritual growth, he became a member of John Cotton's
household, building an addition onto the clergyman's home. This eager,
pious, well connected young man made such an impression on his fellow
colonists that he was elected governor not long after his arrival.[10]

Another key player in the controversy was John Wheelwright, Anne
Hutchinson's brother-in-law, who arrived in the Bay and was admitted to
the Boston church in 1636. A classmate of Oliver Cromwell at Sidney Sussex, Cambridge, he had ministered to the church in Bilsby, Lincolnshire,
prior to his emigration. Wheelwright had a reputation as a charismatic
preacher who believed in direct inspiration from the Holy Spirit.

The Boston congregation which welcomed these men and women
seemed to Winthrop and others to be a vital center for their spiritual lives.
Laymen actively questioned and prophesied at services, shared their religious experiences with their fellow church members, and organized prayer
groups and religious study groups in their homes. The weekly lecture was
well attended, and John Wilson would lead members of the congregation,
likely including his friend John Winthrop, to hear lectures in neighboring
towns. Though Cotton and Wilson differed over whether the first stirrings
of sanctification could provide assurance of salvation, they were able to
work effectively in harness together, shaping the faith of their congregants
and seeking to steer them from errors.[11]

One of the things that contributed to the vitality of the Boston church
was that its lay and clerical leaders, including Winthrop, Cotton, and Wilson, recognized that religious seekers might adopt and express errors.
However, they exercised charity and sought to wean them toward the broad
orthodox center rather than challenge them and push them further into
error. And this moderation and indulgence was not limited to Boston. Hugh
Peter, for a time the pastor at Salem, where he faced the task of reuniting a

congregation that had been divided by the views of Roger Williams, on a later occasion expressed a moderate stance in asserting, "I am no tolerator, but a peacemaker I would be."[12] John Endecott, a member of that Salem church and himself an early supporter of Williams, certainly deserved the reputation he would later earn for intolerance for those beyond the orthodox pale. But he also wrote that "God's people are marked with one and the same mark" and that "where this is, there can be no discord." This belief underlay toleration of differences among those who regarded each other as godly, though compromise required tolerance on both sides. The same stance, of course, could also lead to rejecting those with whom one could not compromise as ungodly.[13]

The fact is that not everyone exercised charity. It is difficult to capture the nuances of belief in John Winthrop's Boston, and efforts to do so run the risk of drawing clear distinctions where the reality was cloudy. Yet just as there were different forms of puritan piety and different opinions on the exercise of discretion by magistrates, so too—and in some ways connected to these other differences—there were different views of the nature of religious communities, whether those communities be clerical associations or religious congregations. At one end of the spectrum, some welcomed discussions of faith and the sharing of religious experiences as useful in achieving a clearer understanding of God's designs. Such men and women valued inclusive communities encompassing all who agreed on the essentials of faith, and exercised the judgment of charity in admitting newcomers to their congregations. At the other end of the spectrum were those who sought to define the faith precisely, to weed out all errors from their religious gardens, and to build walls to protect their fragile flowers from outside threats. Which end of the spectrum any given community leaned toward was always relative to what other community it was being compared to. In the early years of Massachusetts only those whose views challenged a clear majoritarian consensus were plucked and discarded, and then only after attempts to redeem them. But by 1636 new voices were demanding a more rigorous care of the garden.

One of those who would advocate greater vigilance in searching out, warning against, and removing error may have been Anne Hutchinson. Someone whom that description definitely fits was Thomas Shepard. A graduate of Emmanuel College, Cambridge, he had been silenced by Bishop Laud in 1630 but preached unofficially in the puritan underground until his emigration and settlement in Newtown in 1635. Having been tempted by familist ideas when he was a young man, he committed himself to stamping out all such radical views. Shepard never experienced the presence of God with the intensity of John Winthrop. Devoid of any sense of the seal of the Spirit, he was highly suspicious of those who claimed assurance on that basis and aggressive in searching others for signs of the spiritist beliefs he had himself been tempted by. It has been argued that it was Shepard who worked at this time to require personal narratives of their conversion experiences from all who sought full church membership, a means whereby the quality of each believer's experience could be judged.[14]

Having come to Massachusetts in the expectation of joining Thomas Hooker and other English friends in a truly reformed society, Shepard was disappointed to hear of Hooker's impending departure for the Connecticut River and disillusioned by reports on the Bay's imperfections which he heard from Hooker and from Newtown's Thomas Dudley. He soon had personal evidence that all was not perfect in the puritan commonwealth. Gadding to lectures meant that residents in the colony became familiar with one another and the goings-on in the various churches. By the beginning of 1636 Shepard was concerned about some of the opinions being expressed by members of the Boston church, and these concerns became more serious after he heard John Cotton deliver a lecture in which the Boston clergyman preached doctrines that Shepard felt were indistinguishable from familism. Denying that he "thus writ to begin or breed a quarrel," he wrote to Cotton raising questions about those doctrines and urging that the Boston minister "give us satisfaction by way of writing rather than speech." He asked a number of questions designed to draw out what he clearly believed were Cotton's suspect beliefs and deigned to lecture the older clergyman on the dangers of familism.[15] If this was intended merely as an invitation to brotherly dialogue, the questions would have been posed to Cotton face-to-face at one of the regular meetings of the area clergy. But Shepard's intent was different.

Cotton thanked Shepard "for this labor of your love" in acquainting him with passages in his preaching that might have been in error or misinterpreted but assured him that he needed no instruction on the dangers of familism or any other heresy and that he did not believe that he had misled any believers either in old Boston or in New England. "As for differences and jars, it is," he wrote, "my unfeigned desire to avoid them with all men, especially with Brethren. But I do not know, I assure you, any difference, much less jars, between me and any of my Brethren in our public ministry, or otherwise, to any offense."[16] Cotton was not being disingenuous. Whatever differences in understanding of essential doctrines existed within the Boston congregation had not caused concern to Cotton, Wilson, or any other member of the church, nor had any such differences caused a recorded breach between Cotton and his ministerial colleagues. There were a variety of ways in which individuals expressed their understanding of grace. Some found assurance through a process of self-scrutiny; others derived it from a spiritual experience of God's union with their soul. But until this time the various emphases were kept in a creative tension that did not rend the fabric of the society.

While it is most likely that Shepard was challenging what others had previously tolerated, it is also possible that the enthusiasts in the Boston congregation were becoming more intolerant of the traditional emphasis the majority of the clergy placed on human activities that were believed to prepare one for God's call. Hutchinson hosted meetings at her home which energized those who shared her spiritist approach to faith and spurred them on to evangelize others. Edward Johnson, returning to New England in October 1636, encountered "a little nimble tongued woman . . . who said she could bring me acquainted with one of her own sex that would show me a way, if I could attain it, even revelations, full of such ravishing joy that I should never have cause to be sorry for sin, so long as I live, and as for her part she has attained it already."[17] This is the first such encounter of which we have knowledge, but it is likely that lay men and women who felt the seal of the Spirit had been sharing their good news for quite some time. It is equally likely that such enthusiasm further stirred the concerns of Shepard and perhaps others.

By the early summer of 1636 Shepard had begun preaching an extended sermon sequence on the parable of the wise and foolish virgins. He had two concerns to warn against. One was a lack of zeal which he found in his congregation in particular and in New England in general. While it was something of a commonplace to complain that in a world without opposition puritan fervor had abated, it is difficult to judge how widespread this lukewarmness actually was and how much complaints about it were merely rhetorical prods to get believers to guard against complacency. The other thrust of Shepard's sermon sequence was a warning against those who would seek a mystical-style assurance of salvation and neglect the normal means of grace. In this Shepard was attacking what he saw as the false religion flourishing in the Boston church. Few who gadded to Cambridge to hear these lectures would have any doubt that the Boston church, and by implication John Cotton, were being singled out for attack.[18]

It is difficult to know how to refer to those who became associated with the views of Anne Hutchinson and her allies. Most of the terms generally employed—such as "antinomian" and "familist"—were coined by their enemies and were inaccurate, at least in terms of what we know of most of the supporters of Hutchinson in the Boston church and elsewhere. I have chosen to call them "enthusiasts" because it was the heightened spiritual excitement that they brought to their evangelizing that appears to have first struck others, like Edward Johnson, when they first encountered them. I also hope it conveys something of the arrogance of those who felt that their encounter with the Spirit gave them superior insight into God's way. In using the word I am aware of the fact that in many respects the religious experiences of John Winthrop himself could have led others to label him "enthusiast." That is intentional, for I believe that many who tried to hold the center did have such experiences themselves, and appreciated them in others, but were unwilling to accept that this was the only way to apprehend God's grace.

In seeking to understand the dynamics of conversion, individual men and women in the Bay had emphasized two different ways of measuring one's inner state without denying the reality of the other. Some favored looking for signs of grace in one's actions, while others relied on a sense of personal union with the Spirit. Now some individuals who favored one understanding were beginning to reject the validity of the other. During 1636 the intolerance of Shepard would be matched by that of Anne Hutchinson and her more extreme followers. The enthusiast who confronted Edward Johnson in October 1636 warned him of the clergy he would encounter in most churches, "a company of legal professors . . . pouring on the law which Christ hath abolished."[19] The effort the extremists on each side made to write the other side out of the communion of true saints polarized the colony, eroded the consensual middle ground that had characterized the churches, and threatened the very survival of the holy experiment.

Since the clergy of the Bay kept no record of their regular meetings and deliberations, there is no way of knowing if they ever used these gatherings to discuss with Wilson and Cotton Shepard's concerns about the activities in the Boston church. Nor do we have any sense of the lobbying that may well have been going on behind the scenes. Given his concerns it is likely that Shepard shared his fears with his fellow clergymen, and particularly with ministers such as Thomas Welde and John Eliot, with whom he had been closely connected in England.

When the magistrates and ministers gathered in Boston for the October 1636 session of the General Court, some of the colony's clerical leaders took that opportunity to heal the developing breach by meeting with Cotton at his home. Assembled there were seven clergy in addition to Cotton, Wilson, and Wheelwright. What evidently concerned the visiting clergy was reports that members of Cotton's church were publicly disparaging them for preaching doctrines that were not validated by Scripture. It appears that Shepard and his friends Eliot and Welde were there and took a leading role. Winthrop and Wilson's old Suffolk neighbor, George Phillips of Watertown, was present, though he claimed that he had not been told the reason for the meeting. Also there was Hugh Peter, who, as minister at Salem, had been sensitized to the dangers of radical theology by his ongoing struggle to heal the wounds that Roger Williams's teachings had left in that community. Richard Mather and Nathaniel Ward may have been there as well. After the concerns of the visiting ministers were expressed, it was decided to call Anne Hutchinson, Boston's lay elder Thomas Leverett, and the church deacon John Coggeshall to answer questions.[20]

According to Winthrop's account, Cotton and Wheelwright gave satisfaction to their colleagues "so as they all did hold that sanctification did help to evidence justification." Cotton acknowledged that he had preached that the Holy Spirit dwelled within the saints but that the union he spoke of did not amount to a personal union such as maintained by familists and similar heretics.[21] At a later date others would remember the session as being more confrontational. Peter claimed that Hutchinson asserted that "there was a wide and broad difference between our brother Cotton and ourselves" in that, according to her, "he preaches the covenant of grace and you the covenant of works, and that you are not able ministers of the new testament and know no more than the apostles did before the resurrection of Christ." Welde likewise remembered that she claimed that "Mr. Cotton did preach a covenant of grace and we a covenant of works" and that those clergy could do nothing else "because we were not sealed, and we were not able ministers of the new testament." Shepard and Eliot had similar recollections, though Leverett and Coggeshall thought that all of these clergymen exaggerated Hutchinson's distinction between them and Cotton, Leverett recalling that she merely said that the other ministers "did not preach a covenant of grace as clearly as Mr. Cotton did."[22] While Cotton and the ministers may have found a common ground, the questioning of Anne Hutchinson made it clear that the division was not going to fade away easily. And because Hutchinson was claiming that her ideas went no further than the teachings of Cotton and Wheelwright, Shepard and perhaps other clergymen remained suspicious of Cotton's orthodoxy, regardless of what he claimed at their meeting.

Because John Wheelwright had been identified by his sister-in-law as one of the two true spiritual shepherds in the Bay, the group of enthusiasts in the Boston church had welcomed his presence, and some of them proposed that he be called as co-teacher of the congregation. This may have been so that Wilson could administer the sacraments at nearby Mount Wollaston, where he already preached to some Bostonians who also held land there, but it may have been proposed so that Wheelwright could play a major role in the Boston congregation itself. In any event Wheelwright's identification with the enthusiasts had led to suspicions that he was a familist, suspicions that had not been put entirely to rest at the meeting in Cotton's home. Winthrop, who had learned much of his faith from John Knewstub, had never doubted that Suffolk clergyman's warnings against the Family of Love, and he would consistently show less tolerance toward anyone suspected of that heresy than he did toward those who maintained other errors. Concerned that Wheelwright might be an exponent of familism, Winthrop single-handedly prevented the Boston church from proceeding to call him to a ministerial post.[23]

Winthrop had been slow to identify the coming storm. Nowhere in his journal or his correspondence prior to October 1636 is there a hint of awareness that the Boston church was dividing. Nor is there any evaluation of Anne Hutchinson. Years later he would write of Hutchinson that initially she appeared to rest the foundation of her beliefs on Christ and free grace, that the "rule she pretended to walk by was only the Scripture," that "the persons she conversed with were (for the most part) Christians in Church Covenant," that "her ordinary talk was about the things of the Kingdom of God," and that she conducted herself "in the way of righteousness and kindness."[24] In short, she seemed like an ideal citizen of the City on a Hill. Winthrop clearly knew the Hutchinsons, and it is likely that Margaret, who was a pious woman, attended some of the meetings for women in the Hutchinson home. It is also possible that she attended a few and then ceased. It would tell us a lot if we knew if Margaret found in Anne Hutchinson a kindred spirit or if she found the other woman's enthusiasm off-putting, but there is no record whatsoever of her feelings.

In November Winthrop joined with Wilson and others within the Boston church in another attempt to save the moderate center. Vane, whom Winthrop categorized as "a wise and godly gentleman," "held, with Mr. Cotton and many others, the indwelling of the person of the Holy Ghost in a believer" but "went so far beyond the rest as to maintain a personal union with the Holy Ghost." This was one of the beliefs identified with Hutchinson, and Vane was known to admire her and to have encouraged her to hold the religious gatherings that seemed to be the center of the dissension. Winthrop, Wilson, Vane, and Cotton exchanged views on the issue—"in writing, for the peace sake of the church, which all were tender of"—until all agreed that "the Holy Ghost is God, and that he doth dwell in the believers (as the Father and Son both are said to), but whether by his gifts and power only, or by some other manner of presence, seeing the scripture does not declare it—it was earnestly desired that the word person might be forborne, being a term of human invention, and tending to doubtful disputation in this case."[25] If they thought that Vane would be able to moderate Hutchinson and her other followers they were mistaken. It was too late for the controversy to be dampened by any such means.

The practices of New England puritanism, which had served to maintain consensus in the past, now contributed to division when employed by those committed to asserting the correctness of their own views rather than to maintaining unity. In the first years of the colony, inviting lay questions during services allowed ministers to correct misapprehensions before they became the basis for heterodox opinions. Now, according to Johnson, the enthusiasts "grow bold, and dare question the sound and wholesome truths delivered in public by the Ministers of Christ," so that "church meetings are full of disputes."[26] Wilson not only had his teaching questioned, but, as Winthrop later recalled, it became common for "many of the opinionists, rising up and contemptuously turning their backs upon the faithful Pastor of that Church, [to] go forth from the Assembly when he began to pray or preach."[27]

At the December 1636 meeting of the General Court, the religious dispute finally spilled out into the political sphere. It was a struggle for those involved in the dispute to maintain their civility and continue to trust those who seemed to be attacking them. John Wilson, invited to preach to the court, "made a very sad speech of the condition of our churches, and the inevitable danger of separation if these differences and alienations among brethren were not speedily remedied," and "laid the blame upon these new opinions risen up amongst us." All the magistrates except for Vane and two other unidentified assistants agreed, and a fast day was appointed for the purpose of healing the divisions. Cotton had just preached a sermon on sanctification which had been questioned by some, and he felt that Wilson's court lecture was an attack on him. On the last day of December the Boston congregation called Wilson to task for having implicitly attacked their church. Vane "pressed it violently against him, and all the congregation," except for Winthrop and a few others, agreed. Wilson "answered them with words of truth and soberness, and with marvelous wisdom." If he had any doubts before this, Winthrop recognized the intensity of the factionalism as he witnessed those "that had known" Wilson "so long, and what good he had done for that church . . . fall upon him with such bitterness." Having defended Wilson publicly, Winthrop also worked behind the scenes, lobbying Cotton and the lay elders in an attempt to limit the damage.[28]

At this stage Winthrop was striving both to understand the issues at stake and to reconcile the contesting parties. On the eve of his forty-ninth birthday he pulled out his spiritual diary. His previous entry had been the notation of his deliverance from the waters of the Fens when he and Emmanuel Downing were journeying to Sempringham for the meeting of the Massachusetts Bay Company. Now, almost a decade later, he made what would be his last entry in the diary, writing that "[u]pon some differences in our Church about the way of the Spirit of God in the work of Justification, myself dissenting from the rest of the brethren, I had occasion to examine mine own estate." Reviewing his spiritual pilgrimage in light of the conflicting arguments in the Bay over how man was saved and received assurance of salvation, he once again felt the presence of God:

> The Lord wrought marvelously upon my heart, reviving my former peace & consolation with much increase & better assurance than formerly. And in the midst of it (for it continued many days) he did one time dart a beam of wrath into my soul which struck me to the heart. But then the Lord Jesus showed himself, & stood between that wrath & my soul. Oh how sweet was Christ then to my soul. I thought I never prized him

before, I am sure never more, nor ever felt more need of him. Then I
kept him close to my heart & could not part with him. Oh, how my heart
opened to let him in. Oh, how was I ravished with his love! My prayers
could breathe nothing but Christ, & Love, & mercy, which continued
with melting & tears, night & day.[29]

Just as his experience of deliverance in 1629 had convinced him that it was
God's will to shape a holy experiment in the American wilderness, so did
this new experience lift him from any self-pity over his reduced political
circumstances and motivate him to try to save the colony he had done so
much to create.

Following this renewal of his sense of election, Winthrop composed
an abbreviated relation of his Christian experience. In some respects this
was similar to the types of narratives beginning to be asked of candidates
for church admission at this time. Winthrop, one of the founding pillars of
the Boston church, hardly needed to offer such an account, and there is no
evidence showing whether he delivered this orally, circulated it widely in
manuscript, or shared it only with a few. But his intent was clearly to use
his own experience to speak to the issues of the day. In many ways the
account went far toward acknowledging the concerns of the enthusiasts.
He told how at one time he had placed false confidence in his outward
works as evidence of his communion with God, only to have that assurance
shattered. Though he had earned a reputation as a great professor of the
gospel, he felt himself to be a hypocrite. Every time he tried to gain assurance by strict observance of religious duties he failed. Only when God had
humbled him and made him see what a vile wretch he was did "the good
spirit of the Lord breathe upon my soul, and said I should live." In years to
come he would find that his "comfort and joy slackened a while," yet he
had "grown familiar with the Lord Jesus Christ," so that "he would oft tell
me he loved me" and "I did not doubt to believe him." "If I went abroad he
went with me, when I returned he came home with me. I talked with him
upon the way. He lay down with me, and usually I did awake with him."
He would continue to experience spells of lukewarmness and admitted that
the proclaiming of God's free grace by the Boston enthusiasts "took me in
as drowsy a condition as I had been in (to my remembrance) these twenty
years, and brought me as low (in my own apprehension) as if the whole
work had to begin anew." But the voice of Christ spoke to him, "though it
did not speak so loud, nor in that measure of joy that I had felt sometimes."
He realized that he had "defiled the white garments of the Lord Jesus" in
undervaluing the work of Christ in his justification, but that he had also
defiled "the other garment of sanctification" by acting in ways that contradicted his inner holiness.[30] In shaping his own religious experience this
way, Winthrop was carefully trying to steer a middle course, asserting the
importance in his own life of the experience of the spirit of God in a way

that few of the enthusiasts would object to, while also accepting that sanctification was not only a sign of the inner transformation of the soul but an obligation placed on the saints by God.

At about the same time, Winthrop prepared two theological position papers, which John Wilson passed on to Thomas Shepard. Neither survives, though we can get a sense of them from Shepard's response. The papers were also clearly designed to bridge the gulf between the positions represented by Shepard and the enthusiasts in the Boston church. It is not too strong a characterization to say that Shepard was horrified at what Winthrop had written, believing that "some passages . . . seem to me to be doubtful and some others to swerve from the truth." He questioned "whether it will be most safe for you to enter into the conflict with your pen," though he tried to take some of the sting away by acknowledging that "the Lord hath made you very able and fit for it." The Newtown minister then went on to provide a lengthy critique of Winthrop's views. While he thought that one of Winthrop's points "bears a color of Arminianism, which I believe your soul abhors," for the most part he felt that Winthrop was conceding too much to the enthusiasts, blaming this leniency on the "sweetness of your spirit inclining and desiring for peace and truth if possible." For Shepard, at this point, peace and truth appeared irreconcilable. It is worth speculating as to why Shepard was shown Winthrop's treatises. Surely if they contained serious errors Wilson would have corrected his friend rather than pass them on to the man who was earning a reputation as the colony's foremost heresy hunter. But if the views expressed were acceptable within a broad understanding of orthodoxy (though likely unacceptable to Shepard), sharing them might have been a way of moving the Newton minister toward a middle ground lest he wish to add Winthrop and Wilson to his targets.[31]

Cotton also was trying to dampen the fires of discord. Addressing a group of colonists returning to England, according to Winthrop he "willed them to tell our countrymen that all the strife amongst us was about magnifying the grace of God; one party seeking to advance the grace of God within us, and the other to advance the grace of God toward us (meaning by the one justification, and by the other sanctification)." John Wilson also spoke to the passengers, asserting that in his view "none of the elders or brethren of the churches did but labor to advance the free grace of God in justification, so far as the word of God required."[32]

ON THE MORNING OF JANUARY 19, 1637, John and Margaret Winthrop joined the other members of the Boston church in the meetinghouse for observation of the court-appointed fast day. John Cotton took the pulpit and preached on the need for peace and reconciliation. In other congregations similar messages were delivered. When the Boston congregation reassembled for the afternoon sermon, Wheelwright rather than Wilson preached. Given that Winthrop at least suspected Wheelwright of familism, and that the church had declined to call Wheelwright to a ministerial office, this was a curious decision, for which there is no provable explanation. Perhaps with Cotton having urged reconciliation, Winthrop and the moderates anticipated that having Wheelwright deliver a similar message would isolate the enthusiasts from all clerical support. Or perhaps the enthusiasts, who represented a majority of the congregation, insisted upon it.

With John Winthrop and Henry Vane sharing the honorific magistrates' bench at the front of the meetinghouse, Wheelwright opened by examining the reason for a fast, stating that there was cause to fast only if Christ was absent from a people. The cause of his absence in Massachusetts was the presence of Antichristian spirits who advanced a covenant of works. If Christ was to be kept in Massachusetts, all who had the true spirit of godliness "must prepare for a spiritual combat, . . . put on the armor of God," and "show themselves valiant. They should have their swords ready, they must fight and fight with spiritual weapons." They must identify their Antichristian enemies and "kill them with the word of the Lord," but "be willing to be killed like sheep" themselves if that was God's will. In addressing the concern that his sermon was promoting division rather than reconciliation, he stated that "I confess and acknowledge it will do so, but what then?" Warning that the saints were to take care that they "give not occasion to others to say we are libertines or Antinomians," he branded the opposition "the greatest enemies to the state that can be."[33]

The Boston church did contain many enthusiasts, but that does not mean that they all agreed among themselves. If anything united them it was their resentment about the way they had been categorized by Shepard and others. Wheelwright's sermon inspired many, but it achieved that result in part because it was devoid of details and specifically rejected charges that the congregation was filled with heretics. Yet some who had once encouraged the almost Pentecostal fervor that characterized their congregation had perhaps begun to wonder where this was taking them.

Henry Vane, who was seen by most as the protector of the enthusiasts, might well have been reconsidering his position in Massachusetts and his reputation in England. In November he had reached common ground on one disputed point with Winthrop, Wilson, and Cotton. And in December he announced his plan to leave the colony, telling a special meeting of the General Court that disturbing letters from England demanded his return. Urged by many to stay, he asserted that the business at home involved possible financial ruin, but he also expressed his fear of divine judgments that would come on the Bay as a result of the religious divisions, as well as his resentment that some felt that he was the cause of the uproar.

The impending collapse of the Saybrook venture may have been an undisclosed additional reason. Plans were made for a special court of elections to be held in less than a week. Members of the Boston church intervened to persuade Vane to change his mind, and he decided that, not having the permission of the church to depart, he would stay. Though he would remain anxious to preserve his standing in the colony and was bitter when he was later turned from office, he did not go out of his way to protect or defend those enthusiasts who were soon to be hauled into court.

It was evident at the March 1637 General Court that the tide had begun to turn against the enthusiasts. Winthrop noted that "when any matter about these new opinions was mentioned, the court was divided, yet the greater number [by] far were sound."[34] The majority took note of the Boston congregation's criticism of Wilson's sermon to the previous court and "declared it to have been a seasonable advice" with no blame deserved. The ministers were brought in to express their judgment that no congregation should call someone to task for something said at a meeting of the court, unless the court approved such an inquiry. Wheelwright was called to answer for his fast-day sermon. He was charged with having "inveighed against all that walked in a covenant of works as he described it," namely "such as maintain sanctification as evidence of justification, . . . and called them antichrists, and stirred up the people against them with much bitterness and vehemency." Answering the court, Wheelwright acknowledged that that was what he said and meant. The other ministers were then called to testify and acknowledged that they indeed did preach that a godly life could be seen as proof of one's salvation. The court thereupon judged Wheelwright guilty of sedition for having sought to inflame the people against their spiritual leaders and also guilty of contempt of the court, since they "had appointed the fast as a means of reconciliation of the differences, etc., and he purposely set himself to kindle and increase them." Vane and a few others protested this action, and the Boston church submitted a petition challenging the judgment. Since the court's judicial proceedings were open to all freemen, the uproar in the Boston meetinghouse, where the court met, must have been considerable. Deciding to defer the sentencing of Wheelwright until its next session, the court set that meeting—as well as the election of magistrates—to be held in Newtown. In a related matter the majority sent a message by fining the Boston merchant Stephen Greensmith £40 for saying that all the ministers but a few taught a covenant of works. In addition to the fine he was ordered to acknowledge his error in each of the churches of the Bay.[35]

The heated court of elections at Newtown saw opponents of the Boston enthusiasts rally behind the moderate Winthrop, who was returned to the governorship while Vane was left out of the magistracy entirely. The

election completed, the General Court assembled in the Newtown meetinghouse and proceeded to address the crises facing the colony. Israel
Stoughton was appointed to command the military expedition against the
Pequots; John Wilson was chosen by lot to accompany the forces as chaplain. Another day of fast and humiliation was set. All the churches were
called to send representatives to a synod to discuss the theological issues
disturbing the colony and to define dangerous errors. Fearing an increase
in the ranks of the enthusiasts through immigration, the court passed an
order preventing any person or town from offering accommodation to any
new arrival for more than three weeks without the approval of a member
of the council or two of the magistrates. Similar to the measures that Boxford
and other English towns had taken to bar vagrants who might become a
charge on the community, this step was designed to keep out those who
would threaten religious rather than financial well-being. The sentencing
of Wheelwright was deferred yet again in the hope that he would acknowledge his errors.[36]

In the previous months many Bostonians had subscribed to a remonstrance seeking to exonerate Wheelwright. Wheelwright himself had circulated a written justification of his position, which Winthrop believed
altered the argument of the fast-day sermon. In addition, Winthrop indicated, "divers writings were now published about these differences."[37] In
December a group of ministers had sent a list of sixteen questions to Cotton, which he answered in the same month. In January the clergy responded
to Cotton's answers, prompting a lengthy rejoinder from the Boston
teacher.[38] In March Peter Bulkeley, soon to be ordained as pastor of the
Concord church, wrote separately to Cotton, agreeing with the Boston
clergyman's "complaint of the want of brotherly love" evident within the
ministerial community at the time and seeking further insight into Cotton's
understanding of the theological issues being debated.[39] Winthrop, overly
optimistic, believed that these exchanges, as well as Shepard's election-day
sermon, brought the clergy closer to an agreement, with the remaining
differences appearing to nontheologians as being "so small as (if men's
affections had not been formerly alienated, when the differences were formerly stated as fundamental) they might easily have come to reconciliation."[40] Finally the clerical community was reverting to the practice that
had served it well in the past—setting forth articles of belief phrased in
such a way that everyone could accept them, and leaving considerable latitude for each to interpret the nuances of those beliefs. Evidence that
Winthrop was closely involved in the process is found in the fact that he
tucked a copy of the ministers' sixteen questions in the second manuscript
volume of his journal.[41]

Winthrop also prepared his own manuscript response to the Bostonians
who had remonstrated about the conviction of Wheelwright. As he had in

response to Winthrop's earlier contributions to the dispute, Shepard faulted him for being too lenient. He blamed Winthrop for depicting Wheelwright "as a good man in zeal of a conceived good cause," rather than a major architect of all the recent disturbances, as Shepard believed him to be. He could not believe that Winthrop displayed "admiration of persons you know hath carried on great stroke in this cause." As far as Shepard was concerned, what Winthrop should be doing was "to make their wickedness and guile manifest to all men that they may go no farther and then will sink of themselves."[42] But this was characteristic of Winthrop's approach. Rather than define and proscribe error, Winthrop was struggling to hold a moderate common ground where most if not all could unite.

Despite his efforts for reconciliation, Winthrop felt the hostility of many of his fellow townsmen in the months that followed his election. This had first been expressed when the Boston men who served as the governor's escort under Vane put down their halberds and refused to serve Winthrop. At services in the Boston meetinghouse Vane ostentatiously refused to sit with Winthrop on the magistrate's bench, though he was still entitled to do so. At least one member of the congregation addressed him disrespectfully during a discussion in the church. Neighbors shunned him and criticized his conduct behind his back. The brotherly love which he saw as the foundation of all society was no longer being extended to him and his family. Bostonians were reluctant to volunteer for the expedition against the Pequots, in large part because those who were enthusiasts were unwilling to serve with John Wilson as chaplain, though some may have refused because Winthrop was the nominal commander.[43]

Winthrop took up his pen again that summer to defend the Court order requiring immigrants to be accepted by magistrates. In July a group of Lincolnshire immigrants arrived in Boston and were questioned by magistrates—we don't know by whom—about whether or not they knew Wheelwright and what they thought of his doctrines. When they refused to disavow the controversial cleric's teachings, they were given only four months to remain in the colony. Some of those excluded had relatives in Boston, which led to renewed protest about the court order. Winthrop prepared "A Declaration in Defense of an Order of Court," in which he justified the action not in terms of the needs of a religious community but as a reasonable step for a civil society. Whereas "Christian Charity" was an expression of a social gospel, the "Defense," perhaps because there was no longer a consensus on who the saints were, was crafted around the needs of the civil sphere, though there were clear parallels between the two. It was fundamental, he believed, that "no commonweal can be founded but by free consent" and that "the persons so incorporating have a public and relative interest each in other." In forming a commonwealth every member commits himself "to seek out and entertain all means that may conduce to the welfare of the

body and to keep off whatsoever doth appear to tend to their damage."
Thus, it was within the rights of the Massachusetts magistrates, selected by
the freemen, to "refuse to receive such whose dispositions suit not with
ours and whose society (we know) will be hurtful to us. . . . No man has
[the] right to come unto us without our consent." To those who questioned this specific law by saying that it "was made to purpose to keep away
such as are of Mr. Wheelwright his judgment, . . . where is the evil of it? . . .
If we find his opinions such as will cause divisions, and make people look at
their magistrates, ministers, and brethren as enemies to Christ and Antichrist, etc., were it not sin and unfaithfulness in us to receive more of those
opinion, which we already find the evil fruit of?" Indeed, many of those
who now objected to this policy had been involved "in expelling Mr. Williams for the like, though less dangerous."[44]

Winthrop's defense was attacked in a circulated manuscript that has
often been attributed to Vane, necessitating Winthrop's "A Reply in Further Defense of an Order of Court" in August.[45] In this he again defended
the restriction of immigration as proper to any government, including those
of the Turks and pagans. He then proceeded to respond point by point to
the objections that had been raised. In the process he connected his arguments with the religious basis of this particular society, arguing that the
"civil state must be raised out of the churches" and that the freemen as well
as the magistrates were expected "to direct all their ways by the rule of the
gospel." It was the practice in New England to exclude from the churches
those who did not meet the requirements for membership, and the practice of townspeople to exclude those whose values and beliefs would challenge the harmony of the town. The court's order simply extended that
practice to the colony as a whole.[46]

Henry Vane departed Massachusetts on August 3. Some of his supporters gathered to see him off and fired a volley of shots to honor him,
"but the governor [Winthrop] was not come from the court."[47] There is
no question that relations between the two men were strained at the time.
The enthusiasts hoped that Vane would use his influence in England to be
appointed governor-general and return to raise them to power.[48] And Thomas Shepard both likened Vane to Abimelech, the Old Testament figure
who tried to usurp power, and also depicted him as the point man of a
Catholic conspiracy to topple the Bible commonwealths.[49] But there is some
indication that Winthrop viewed Vane much as he did Roger Williams—
young, overzealous, in error on some matters, but someone who carried
the mark of God's election. There is no record of any attempt on Winthrop's
part to banish Vane or to include him on the list of those who were to be
brought up on charges before the General Court. When Winthrop wrote
his account of the events, he minimized Vane's role in the disturbances.
Some of this may have been simple pragmatism on Winthrop's part, seek-

ing to avoid stirring Vane to join the enemies of the colony in England. If so, the strategy worked, for in the years after his departure Vane did assist the colony whenever he was asked. But there would have been no such reason for Winthrop referring to Vane in his journal in 1645 as one "who had sometime lived at Boston, & though he might have taken occasion against us for some dishonor which he apprehended to have been unjustly put upon him here, yet both now and at other times he showed himself a true friend to New England and a man of noble and generous mind."[50]

Meanwhile Winthrop favored efforts to persuade the remaining enthusiasts of their errors. "We spent much time and strength in conference with them," Winthrop later recalled, "sometimes in private before the elders only, sometimes in our public congregation for all comers. Many, very many hours and half days together we spent therein to see if any means might prevail." The enthusiasts were invited to defend their views, which were then discussed and—from the orthodox point of view—sufficiently refuted by "clear arguments from evident scriptures." This may have had some success, but for the most part "such was the pride and hardness of heart" of the enthusiasts that "they would not yield to the truth." Over time the gap between the orthodox and some of the enthusiasts actually began to widen, "so that our hopes began to languish of reducing them by private means."[51]

In addition to meetings with the lay enthusiasts, extensive meetings were held by Cotton and his fellow ministers in the months leading up to the synod. There were those, likely including Shepard and Dudley, who blamed Cotton for the troubles of the times and wished to force him to acknowledge his errors. But Winthrop worked hard to restore Cotton's standing. It was Winthrop who healed the important breach between Cotton and John Wilson that had resulted from Wilson's sermon to the court. John Davenport, one of the more respected English puritan clergymen and a friend of Cotton, arrived in the Bay at this time and also helped to reconcile the Boston teacher with his clerical colleagues. Having been a leading London clergyman, Davenport had experienced the similar conflict that had divided that puritan community, which helped him to help resolve the Boston controversy. During that summer Cotton and his colleagues reduced the areas of friction between them to five points, then to three, and then statements were devised regarding those three that all could accept. By the time the synod met at the end of August, Cotton had in effect been drawn away from the lay enthusiasts who claimed to have been pursuing the implications of his teachings.[52]

On August 30, 1637, the region's clergy finally assembled in Newtown. The synod drew clergymen from Plymouth and the Connecticut settlements as well as from Massachusetts. Lay representatives of Boston and other churches came as well. Winthrop followed the deliberations closely and was likely in attendance at some of the sessions. Following prayer and the selection of Thomas Hooker as moderator, the synod listened to a list of eighty-two errors that had been drawn up in advance and began to deliberate the issues. Cotton later recounted his surprise that "some of the members and messengers of our church were ready to rise up and plead in defense of sundry corrupt opinions, which I verily thought had been far from them." Challenged, the Bostonians claimed that they did not necessarily accept the doctrines being attacked but were merely opposed to them being condemned; in effect they wished to preserve the freedom to explore various doctrines, which was characteristic of the Boston church. Their contribution to the synod's debates gave Cotton an opportunity to distance himself from those who had been claiming him as the source of their religious beliefs. Speaking of the list of eighty-two, Cotton declared to the synod that "I esteemed some of the opinions to be blasphemous, some of them heretical, many of them erroneous, and almost all of them incommodiously expressed."[53] It is likely that there were no proponents of some of the listed doctrines, and certainly no one maintained all of them, but what the synod accomplished in condemning them all before the conclusion of its work in late September was to set the bounds for acceptable interpretations of a variety of doctrines.

The work of the synod was also intended to pressure those who held erroneous opinions to give them up. The intent of the General Court that assembled at Newtown in November 1637 was to deal with those whose religious radicalism had led them to actions that threatened the unity and security of the colony.[54] John Wheelwright, rejecting all opportunities to retract the incendiary remarks made in his fast-day sermon, was banished and given two weeks to leave the colony. Next, the court called before it those who had petitioned them in favor of Wheelwright and attacked the actions of the court. William Aspinwall, a prominent Bostonian and a deputy to the court, was judged for having signed the petition to be "a seditious libel, and justifying the same, . . . and for his insolent and turbulent carriage" was disenfranchised and banished. William Coggeshall stood up and protested this action and "for disturbing the public peace was disenfranchised and enjoined not to speak anything to disturb the public peace" further under pain of banishment. While some wished to banish Coggeshall immediately, Winthrop evidently persuaded the court to adopt the more moderate sentence.[55]

Next came the trial of Anne Hutchinson. The conduct of the proceedings was very different from what we would expect in the twenty-first century but not that different from what was customary in English quarter sessions and in the court proceedings of Massachusetts in the seventeenth century. The task of the magistrates was to inquire as well as to judge, and other members of the court could interject questions and statements.

Though Hutchinson had neither preached publicly to stir up divisions as had Wheelwright, nor signed any petitions or other documents against the leadership of the Bay as had Aspinwall, Winthrop led off her examination by noting that she was "known to be a woman that hath had a great share in the promoting and divulging of those opinions that are the causes of this trouble, and to be nearly joined not only in affinity and affection with some of those the court had taken notice of and passed censure on." Furthermore, she had "spoken divers things, as we have been informed, very prejudicial to the honor of the churches and ministers thereof." The purpose of bringing her before the court was, he concluded, to bring her to reject her errors so that she "may become a profitable member here among us," or, "if you be obstinate in your course, that then the court may take such course that you may trouble us no further."[56] At the heart of the proceedings was Hutchinson's presumed denigration of the clergy as no true ministers because they preached a covenant of works. It was a charge that threatened to overthrow the foundations of the society, because Anne Hutchinson and those who agreed with her were no more willing to tolerate the teachings of the established clergy than those ministers were willing to grant her liberty for her views.

The trial lasted two days. Winthrop and the other magistrates questioned Hutchinson in efforts to get her to incriminate herself, while until the end she deftly avoided providing them with such grounds. She questioned the charges against her and justified her behavior by placing it solidly within orthodox practice. When clergymen came forth to testify to their recollections of her statements during the meeting in Cotton's home, she demanded that they swear to their accounts under oath, knowing full well that they might be reluctant to do so given how seriously oaths were taken and the length of time that had passed since their conversations. There were times when the trial seemed poised to move in pursuit of others. At one point, when Cotton was offering his recollections, Thomas Dudley and a deputy from Dorchester seemed eager to question the complicity of the Boston teacher in the divisions, but Winthrop quickly intervened to point out that "Mr. Cotton is not called to answer anything, but we are here to deal with the party standing here before us."[57]

Finally, Hutchinson gave the magistrates what they had been looking for. She claimed to know "which was the clear ministry and which the wrong" by "an immediate revelation," asserting that by such revelation she also knew that she would be delivered from the efforts of the court by the Lord's providence. She further stated that it had been revealed to her that if the court and colony proceeded in their current course "you will bring a curse upon you and your posterity, and the mouth of the Lord hath spoken it."[58] Her statements were taken to indicate that she rested her beliefs on the claim of direct revelation from God apart from the inspiration of Scripture. The court, by a show of hands with only three dissenters, voted that "for traducing the ministers and their ministry in this country, [for which] she declared voluntarily her revelations for her ground, and that she should be delivered and the Court ruined, with their posterity," she be banished.[59]

This did not bring an end to the controversy. Following Hutchinson's sentencing, the court continued to call before it those who had taken a lead in criticizing Wheelwright's treatment. William Balston and Edward Hutchinson, sergeants who had been part of Vane's honor guard, were first. Though "the Court"—presumably Winthrop—"reasoned a good while with them both, . . . they were peremptory, and would acknowledge no failing."[60] Because of their contemptuous speeches and earlier offenses offered to the magistrates (presumably their refusal to escort Winthrop after his election), they were disenfranchised and fined. Those called the next day were more moderate in their responses and were merely disenfranchised and removed from any offices they held. Others who had signed the controversial petition began to appear and retract their support of it. On November 20 the court ordered the colony's munitions removed from Boston (where most of the dissidents lived) to Newtown and Roxbury and followed this by ordering that any signers of the Wheelwright petition who did not recant were to hand in their "guns, pistols, swords, powder, shot, and match" and desist from drilling with the trained bands.[61] With the civil proceedings against her completed, in March 1638 Anne Hutchinson was brought before the Boston church on charges of heresy. As a member of the congregation Winthrop was involved in the proceedings, and he attempted to use them as a means of healing the open wounds among his brethren, though without much success. The trial ended with Hutchinson's excommunication.[62]

WINTHROP WAS CONDEMNED BY THE ENTHUSIASTS who were banished by the court. He has also been criticized by those historians who believe that he should have led the Bay colony to a modern system of religious freedom and toleration that no one at the time—including Vane, Wheelwright, and Hutchinson—would have accepted. Equally unhappy were Shepard and Dudley, who desired to use the controversy to impose a more rigid definition of orthodoxy and to rid the colony of others beyond those actually banished, perhaps even John Cotton. For them, the settlement Winthrop guided them to allowed too much diversity within the bounds of orthodoxy.

Winthrop himself likely regretted the outcome since the proceedings had failed to reclaim most of the enthusiasts, which was his objective. He had managed events to avoid any branding of Vane as a heretic, despite Shepard's frustration. He conceded that Wheelwright might have been godly but regretted that the clergyman had not been convinced of the dangerous consequences of some of his teachings.[63] Remaining in Newtown during the November court sessions, John exchanged letters with Margaret in which she expressed views which may not have been far from his own. Writing from "Sad Boston" on November 15, she admitted that "[s]ad thoughts possess my spirits, and I cannot repulse them, which makes me unfit for anything, wondering what the Lord means by all these troubles among us. Sure I am that all shall work to the best to them that love God, or rather are loved of him. I know he will bring light out of obscurity and make his righteousness shine forth as clear as the noon day, yet I find myself in an adverse spirit, and a trembling heart, not so willing to submit to the will of God as I desire. There is a time to plant and a time to pull up that which is planted, which I could desire might not be yet, but the Lord knoweth what is best and his will be done."[64] In response John admitted that the news she would hear "may be some[what] grievous to thee, but be not troubled. I assure thee things go well, and they must needs do so, for God is with us and thou shalt see a happy issue."[65] Like her, he would regret some of the uprooting that was in process. William Coddington, who had once wooed Winthrop's daughter, would be one of those who followed Anne Hutchinson to Rhode Island.

However much he may have struggled to recover many of the enthusiasts from their errors, Winthrop's charity did not then nor would it ever extend to Anne Hutchinson. In large part this was due to the fact that she never admitted that she might be in error either in her views or in her expression of those views. The fact that she was uncompromising in her negative judgment of clergymen he respected, John Wilson most particularly, angered him. For such challenges to come from a woman might have stoked that anger, because although like most of his contemporaries Winthrop admired piety in women—one thinks of his respect for the faith of his mother, his wife Thomasine, and his wife Margaret—that admiration did not extend to women asserting religious leadership outside the home. Some of his anger may have arisen from the humiliation he felt because this threat had arisen in his own church, and his embarrassment over not having seen it developing. Her adroit deflection of his efforts to get her to incriminate herself before the General Court was infuriating, and her ultimate refusal to accept the correction of the court or the Boston church drew him to conclude that she was indeed an "American Jezabel" and an agent of the devil. This anger was clearly evident when he came to write an account of the divisions for an English audience, where by focusing the blame on Hutchinson he was also able to serve the interests of his colony by deflecting blame from Vane and Cotton. When he learned that Mrs. Hutchinson had given birth to a deformed fetus in 1638, he took this as a providential sign that he and his colleagues had been on God's side;

the monstrous human birth was a reflection of the monstrous heresies Hutchinson had given birth to.[66]

Though some of his fellow colonists might not have been satisfied with the outcome of the free-grace controversy, Winthrop's English correspondents complimented him on the success of the Bay in dealing with this serious threat. Before news of the final banishment of the leaders was known, Emmanuel Downing wrote that "[h]ere hath been great joy for your great victories, but far more for vanquishing your erroneous opinions than for conquering the Pequots. Our best and worthiest men do much marvel you did not banish Wheelwright and Hutchinson's wife, but suffer them to sow sedition among you. Mr. Vane's ill behavior there hath lost all his reputation here."[67] In order to make sure that English puritans understood what the dispute was all about, Winthrop penned a manuscript collection of the relevant documents and a history of the controversy, all of which was later published as *A Short Story of the Rise, Reign, and Ruin of the Antinomians, Familists and Libertines* (1644). In March 1638, after that account and others had begun to circulate among the colony's friends, Downing wrote to John Winthrop that "[a]ll things stand well in the eye of our state concerning your plantation. No word of any murmuring against it. Your new upstart opinions are here generally cried down."[68] While the episode would be used against the New England way by both Presbyterian and sectarian critics during English religious debates of the 1640s, at the time no one seemed to speak for the enthusiasts. The center had held. There was no reason for observers to curse the inhabitants of the City on a Hill for abandoning their covenant promises.

15

New Trials and Disappointments

MAY 1640. It was a cool evening, such as one often experiences in a New England spring, and John and Margaret Winthrop sat by the fire in their Boston hall discussing the new tests God had delivered. While his judgment and leadership were valued when the colony was threatened, in normal times old jealousies resurfaced. Recently a delegation had urged him not to stand for the governorship in the 1640 election. Probably the freemen would have returned Winthrop to office, but some deputies and assistants had again raised concerns that he was becoming too powerful, and the delegation had expressed fears that if he was elected again the breach would widen. John had bowed to their wishes. Now, the election was over and Thomas Dudley had been chosen governor, with Richard Bellingham as deputy governor.

John's willingness to relinquish power stemmed from his concern for the good of the commonwealth, but it may have also been influenced by his need to devote attention to his personal affairs. Preoccupied with serving the public, John had entrusted the management of his private estate in Massachusetts to James Luxford. That steward's gross and fraudulent mismanagement of Winthrop's affairs left the governor deeply in debt. Having migrated to America with the expectation that in addition to serving God he would be able to better provide for his family, John now found that expectation threatened. Margaret and four of his children were still to be provided for. Now, in order to do so, he would have to sell various property, including his Boston mansion. In the aftermath of this, he would be further humiliated when William Hathorne, a deputy from Salem, suggested that Winthrop be excluded from the magistracy entirely because he had become poor.

But if God tests, God also reassures. Toward the end of 1640 Winthrop would record a remarkable providence. His son John Winthrop Jr. had "above a thousand" books stored in a chamber where he also kept corn. These included copies of the Greek New Testament, a collection of the psalms, and a copy of the Book of Common Prayer which had been bound together. Happening to pick this up, he found "the common prayer eaten with mice, every leaf of it, and not any of the two other touched, nor any of his other books."[1] The words of God were spared. The words of Thomas Cranmer, author of the Book of Common Prayer, were mutilated. No clearer sign could be found that God approved the puritan rejection of the English liturgy. Such signs were reassuring to Winthrop. He would add a codicil to the will he had made before his estate had suffered, entrusting his fate and that of his family "to the most wise and gracious providence of the Lord, who hath promised not to fail or forsake me, but will be an husband to my wife and a father to our children, as he hath hitherto been in all our struggles. Blessed be his holy name."[2]

இ

*T*HE LATE 1630S AND EARLY 1640S were a time of continuity mingled with change in the affairs of the colony, and in Winthrop's own circumstances. Massachusetts had continued to grow, and with that growth came new challenges and institutions and also the renewal of old clashes over how the colony was to be governed and how the colonists could be induced to live together in brotherly love. Deeply involved with these developments, Winthrop also had to respond to the maturing of his children and the disruption of his personal finances. But at the center of his domestic life, steadying him when he was buffeted by public and personal setbacks, were two constants—his relationship with Margaret, and his relationship with God.

WITH THE EXCOMMUNICATION OF ANNE HUTCHINSON, the security of the godly commonwealth seemed assured. While clearly Winthrop deserved most of the credit for that accomplishment, the end of the crisis saw him once again the target of both those who felt that he was too lenient in dealing with offenders, on one extreme, and those on the other extreme who sought greater freedoms. Nevertheless, he was chosen governor again in 1638. The colony still faced serious problems that made Winthrop's leadership seem essential. The threat of an English governor-general was still present, though the outbreak of conflict between the king and his Scottish subjects suggested that the English authorities would be too preoccupied to follow up on plans to seize the Massachusetts charter. The departure of those who were banished or chose to follow Wheelwright and Hutchinson into exile may have guaranteed the peace of the colony, but it came at a price as friends and kin bade each other farewell and the fabric of the society was strained.

The colony seemed further diminished by the departure of John Davenport and members of his London congregation, only recently arrived in the Bay, who chose this time to move to the northern shore of Long Island Sound, founding the town and colony of New Haven on the site of the Pequot War's "Great Swamp Fight." Davenport made it clear that he found Massachusetts orthodox and congenial; he explained the need for the move in terms of the desire of his London followers to found a seaport of their own where they could employ their skills in trade. Reading between the lines, it may have been that Davenport wanted to distance himself from Boston's troubles, which were too reminiscent of the divided London community he had left, or that he and his supporters feared English actions against the Bay. Whatever the reasons, the departure of the Davenport group was another loss for Winthrop and Massachusetts. The loss was particularly worrisome because no one knew whether the struggle between the king and the Scots would stifle emigration and make it difficult to replace departing colonists.

Other events contributed to unease among the colonists. Anne Hutchinson's prophecy that God would inflict a harsh punishment on her persecutors was easy to dismiss when she made it, but not quite so easy in 1638. A "very hard winter," with snow lying eighteen inches deep until the end of March, was followed by a "backward Spring" that included a late April snowfall setting back the crops. Then, on June 1, "between three and four in the afternoon, being clear, warm weather, the wind westerly, there was a great earthquake. It came with a noise like a continued thunder or the rattlings of London coaches." It was felt in the Bay, in Connecticut, and in the Narragansett region. According to Winthrop, "It shook the ships, which rose in the harbor," and "the earth was unquiet twenty days" with aftershocks.[3]

Some likely viewed these events as signs that God had turned his back on the colonists—but why would they be subject to God's displeasure? Lacking any contemporary sources, we can only imagine the debates. Had God been angered because the free-grace heresies had not been rooted out quickly enough? Was he chastising the colony for following Winthrop's lead and not dealing more firmly with the heretics? Were any so bold as to openly suggest that Hutchinson was right and God was striking out at the Bay for persecuting those who were truly saints? Whatever the debate, reassurance came by July. The crops had finally taken hold, and threats of famine dissipated. Shiploads of new, and acceptably orthodox, immigrants had arrived with promises of more to come. Their need to buy food and livestock would bolster the regional economy. The future once again looked bright.

A sense of security allowed the renewal of debates over the distribution and exercise of power, the need for a law code, and related issues. In March 1639 the General Court had responded to the increase of towns to

seventeen by limiting each community to two deputies at future courts. This
was justified as an effort to keep the size of the General Court reasonable,
but some feared that the "magistrates intended to make themselves stronger
and the deputies weaker," and Winthrop was blamed for it. When an effort
was made at the court of elections to add Winthrop's newly arrived brother-
in-law to the Court of Assistants, some objected that Winthrop was behind
this as a means "to strengthen his party," particularly since John Winthrop
Jr. already sat with his father on the bench. Once again critics charged that
Winthrop was becoming too powerful. Such concerns seemed justified when,
just before the May 1639 election, one of the clergy indeed proposed that "a
governor ought to be for life." Responding to this, others sought to replace
Winthrop as governor, though the effort failed.[4]

Though Winthrop was returned to the governorship in 1639, fears of
too much power being concentrated in the hands of a few continued. At
that May's General Court these concerns prompted a new attack on the
Standing Council. The origins of the dispute went back to the creation of
the council in March 1636. As established, that body of life members presided over by the current governor was to "have such further power out of
Court as the General Court shall from time [to time] indue them with,"
but specific powers were not spelled out. At the May 1636 elections, when
Henry Vane was chosen governor, Thomas Dudley and John Winthrop
were named to the council, and the court granted the body broad but unspecified authority over general matters and specific charge of all military
affairs between sessions of the court. Winthrop was merely an assistant at
the time but recorded in his journal that the reason advanced for the council had been "that it was showed from the word of God, etc., that the principal magistracy ought to be for life."[5] The proposal for the life council had,
of course, come at the time when the English grandees had raised the question of exercising hereditary and lifetime authority, and Vane, who was
associated with them, was later said to have been behind the idea.[6] In July
1636 John Cotton suggested that as members of the council Winthrop and
Dudley had the power to decide that the king's ensign should be flown
over Castle Island, and it appears that the council took a lead in directing
the Bay's involvement in the events that led to the Pequot War.[7] In May
1637 John Endecott had been added to the council.[8]

The fact that no official records of the council survive and that Winthrop in his journal also used the term "council" to refer to the Court of
Assistants meeting in a nonjudicial capacity makes it difficult to establish
exactly how that body functioned. At the May 1639 General Court some
of the deputies complained that Endecott, a member of the council but not
an assistant at the time, was exercising magisterial powers, which they believed to be in clear violation of the charter. Recognizing the validity of the

argument, the court stipulated that a member of the council not currently a magistrate was not to exercise such authority. This dealt with the immediate problem but did not allay fears of an evolving oligarchy. The debate over the council would be resumed at later courts.

The issue of how power was exercised was also at the heart of the development of a code of law. Some advocates of a code, such as Thomas Dudley, maintained that precise definition of specific crimes and the penalties for violating them would secure the stability of the new colony. Others saw the enactment of a law code as an opportunity to bring the legal practices of the Bay into closer congruence with biblical mandates. Winthrop, on the other hand, consistently argued against codification, explaining that it was important for magistrates to have the ability to exercise discretion to take into account the circumstances of crime. In taking this position he was not simply trying to rule free of restraint. He was also reflecting his background in the common law, the proper administration of which was, to Englishmen like himself, the essence of the "ancient constitution," which at this time was seen as a framework setting forth the obligations and responsibilities of the subject more than as a guarantee of rights.[9]

This too was an issue with roots going back to the colony's earlier years. In May 1635, during the first period when Winthrop's authority had been reduced, the General Court had appointed Haynes, Ludlow, Dudley, and Winthrop "to make a draft of such laws as they shall judge needful for the well ordering of this plantation."[10] This became a long and protracted process which Winthrop did everything he could to stall. A year later the court appointed Vane, Winthrop, Dudley, Haynes, and Bellingham, as well as the clergymen John Cotton, Hugh Peter, and Thomas Shepard, to "make a draft of laws agreeable to the word of God, which may be the fundamentals of this commonwealth."[11] As a member of these committees Winthrop was able to prevent them from reaching any conclusions. In October 1636 Cotton presented his own adaptation of the Mosaic law code for the court's consideration, though again nothing came of it.[12]

Frustrated by these false starts, the General Court tried again in March 1638. Claiming that "the want of written laws have put the Court into many doubts and much trouble in many particular cases," they ordered the freemen of each town to assemble in their communities and "collect the heads of such necessary and fundamental laws as may be suitable to the times and places where God by his providence hath cast us." The town deputies would then deliver those compilations to a committee of eleven magistrates, ministers, and deputies who were charged with making "a compendious abridgement of the same."[13] This effort also foundered. Finally, according to Winthrop, Cotton and Nathaniel Ward were each requested to draw upon all the previous discussions and frame a model, both of which were presented to the General Court and referred to various officials to consider.[14]

Though no longer governor at the time when the Body of Liberties was considered by the General Court in 1640, Winthrop set forth yet again his reasons for opposing such codification. He explained that because the colonists did not have "sufficient experience of the nature and disposition of the people, considered with the condition of the country and other circumstances" it was a mistake to adopt an inflexible code. He expressed a preference for judging cases according to circumstances and allowing the law to develop through the accumulation of such precedents. This was, he stated, the way "the laws of England and other states grew, and therefore the fundamental laws of England are called customs"—in short, a common-law tradition. But, recognizing that his stand was unpopular, he tried to deflect adoption of the code by arguing that such laws were prohibited by the charter, which required that the colonists make "no laws repugnant to the laws of England." Much of what was done in New England was, indeed, repugnant to the laws of England, but as long as that practice was customary and not mandated by statute, the letter of the charter provision was not violated. His arguments were to no avail, however, and the code was adopted in May 1641.[15]

WHILE THE DEBATE OVER THE ADOPTION of a law code progressed through the 1630s, Winthrop and his fellow magistrates continued to administer justice as they had since the first days of the settlement. Winthrop heard complaints, examined witnesses, and bound individuals over for trial. He witnessed depositions. He administered estates.[16] No one had thought that by emigrating the colonists would leave crime behind, and the record of the colony's courts reflected the same human failings that Winthrop had encountered in the Stour Valley and that continue to be found today. Cases of fornication, swearing, and drunkenness were always on the court docket. Mixed in were more tragic cases. Henry Seawall was indicted for abusing his wife. Thomas Ewar was fined for leaving his well uncovered; a child fell in and drowned.[17] A particularly difficult case involved the abuse and rape of two young daughters of the magistrate John Humfry, who had left them in charge of some of his servants, three of whom engaged in the repeated rape of his eight-year-old daughter. Believing that the offenders should be put to death and yet not finding any biblical precedent or Massachusetts law to compel that penalty, the magistrates and elders debated how they could justify such a sentence; Winthrop himself prepared a paper on the crimes of fornication and rape. Without a clear justification, the court settled for imposing upon the men a severe whipping and threat of death upon any future offense.[18]

The story of Dorothy Talby in 1638 was also tragic. A member of the Salem church and "of good esteem for godliness," her marriage began to show signs of strain and she became melancholy. She had "spiritual delusions" and revelations, which, coming in the aftermath of the colony's experience with Anne Hutchinson, was particularly worrisome. She attempted to kill her husband and children. When she rejected the correction of the congregation she was excommunicated. Her behavior became worse, and she was ordered to be whipped. But "soon after she was so possessed with Satan that he persuaded her (by his delusions, which she listened to as revelations from God) to break the neck of her own child, that she might free it from future misery." Convicted, she was sentenced to be hanged. She showed no repentance and fought the hangman, pulling off the cloth that covered her head and slipping it under the noose. "After a swing or two, she catched at the ladder," though to no avail.[19]

Equally tragic, though no criminal liability was assessed, was an incident in Weymouth. Richard Sylvester and his wife went to church services and left their three sons at home. The oldest was outside tending the cattle. The middle son, five years old, picked up his father's fowling piece, "laid it upon a stool, as he had seen his father do," cocked it, "then went to the other end and blowed in the mouth of the piece, as he had seen his father also do." The spring being weak, "with that stirring the piece, being charged, went off and shot the child into the mouth and through his head."[20]

THE DEBATES OVER THE STANDING COUNCIL and the legal code illuminated an important difference between Winthrop and some of the other leaders of the Bay. The goal of many of the colony's clergy and magistrates was to create a unique society shaped by biblical norms. From the mid-sixteenth century some puritan clergy such as Thomas Cartwright had called for reforming the laws and practices of England in accord with biblical standards. John Cotton had quoted the English puritan theologian William Perkins as asserting that "the scriptures of God do contain a short platform not only of theology, but also of other sacred sciences . . . which he makes ethics, economics, politics, church-government, prophesy, academy." In keeping with this, Cotton's proposed legal code was based heavily on Old Testament law. The unnamed minister who suggested magistrates should hold office for life cited biblical precedent. In the 1650s John Eliot would organize communities of Christian Indians according to the political patterns of ancient Israel and then offer that as a model for the creation of other Christian commonwealths. The Reverend Thomas Cobbett's *The Civil Magistrates' Power in Matters of Religion Modestly Debated* (1653) likewise drew heavily upon the Bible.[21]

Winthrop himself employed biblical references to buttress his political positions whenever possible, and he certainly believed that the colony was engaged in a covenant with God. He frequently looked to the Scriptures for guidance in his public as well as his private life. Yet in dealing with the shaping of civil institutions he sought to model the practices of Massachusetts on those of England rather than ancient Israel, though allowing for some reform of those English practices. In defending the authority of the assistants against the 1632 Watertown tax protest, he had argued that the court was a form of parliament. Later that same year he defended his actions as governor by claiming that he had those powers which the common law customarily extended to chief magistrates. More recently, his initial defense of the court's order restricting immigration had been based on the right of any society, not simply a Christian community, to exclude those whose presence might undermine the goals of the society.[22] Throughout his career he continued to draw on English history, law, and custom to justify the practices of the colony and to disregard arguments from Scripture when they were advanced for policies he did not support. Despite the fact that the creation of a Standing Council with life tenure was justified by scriptural precedent, Winthrop himself later claimed that "for the office of Councillor I am no more in love with the honor, or power of it, than with an old friese coat in a summer's day."[23] In arguing against law codes he expressed his preference for the organic growth of customs into law as "the laws of England and other states grew." These stands angered some who wished the City on a Hill to be a new Jerusalem modeled on biblical patterns.[24]

If his positions on issues such as codification can be labeled "moderate," Winthrop also demonstrated a moderate puritan stance in two efforts to define the separate spheres of church and state. At the end of 1637 members of the Boston church, offended with his proceedings against Anne Hutchinson, had approached Cotton and Wilson about calling Winthrop to account before the congregation. Seeking to "prevent such a public disorder" as might result, he "took occasion to speak to the congregation." He explained the reasons for the actions the court had taken but devoted most of his time to arguing that "the church could not inquire into the justice and proceedings of the court." The oath taken by magistrates included (inserted on Winthrop's advice) the statement that "you are to give your vote as in your judgment and conscience you shall see to be most for the public good." While a congregation could examine and act against any of their number for the conduct of their private affairs, they could not censure a magistrate for acting in accordance with his understanding of the common good.[25] There was clearly self-interest involved here, but Winthrop considered the independence of the magistrate so important to the commonwealth that in addition to addressing the church he also prepared and circulated a manuscript essay setting forth the reasons why "a church hath not power to call any civil magistrate to give account of his judicial proceedings in any court of civil justice." Rejecting the views of those who would have tried to turn the colony into a theocracy, he explained that if this were allowed "the church should become the supreme court in the jurisdiction, and capable of all appeals, and so in truth merely Antichrist by being exalted above all, that is called God." Believing in the importance of a proper alliance between magistracy and ministry, as advocated by Samuel Ward and other puritan preachers he had listened to in England, he rejected making the civil magistrates subordinate to the church, for such a "power would confound those jurisdictions, which Christ hath made distinct."[26]

In December 1639 Winthrop took the lead in a new effort to control religious lecture days. These had again become so numerous that some colonists gadded to two or three per week, neglecting their ordinary business. In addition, some of the lectures went on into the night, leading to physical danger for those who had to travel great distances in their return home. Concerned about this, the magistrates ordered the church leaders to meet with them to discuss the matter. If Winthrop had been concerned that allowing a church to censure a magistrate might subordinate the state to the church, many ministers reacted to this order as "a precedent [that] might enthral them to the civil power," as well as casting a blemish on their reputation by implying that they needed to be regulated. It took a good deal of effort to smooth the ruffled feathers of the clergy and bring about a resolution. The clergy agreed to arrange the lectures so that anyone living within a few miles could get home by sunset, and the magistrates agreed to remove the discussion of the matter from the colony's records.[27] Winthrop's intervention could be used by his enemies as further evidence that he was not zealous enough in promoting a godly society.

Stands such as these set him apart from those who sought a more theocratic system and may have been important factors in the successful effort to deny him the governorship in 1640, but lesser points of friction also contributed to that election result. In February 1638 a group of colonists had petitioned the court for the right to incorporate themselves as a military company along the lines of the London Artillery Company. Coming shortly after the General Court had ordered the disarming of Wheelwright's supporters, it is not surprising that "the Council, considering (from the example of the Praetorian band among the Romans, the Templars in Europe) how dangerous it might be to erect a standing authority of military men, which might easily, in time, overthrow the civil power, thought fit to stop it betimes." Though allowed to organize without corporate protections, some of the petitioners found in their rebuff a further reason to dislike Winthrop's leadership.[28]

The extent to which the tensions between Winthrop and his detractors had undermined his authority was evident at the December 1639 session of the General Court. The court was hearing a case between Nicholas Trerice, the master of a local ship, and William Hibbins, a Bostonian and brother-in-law of Assistant Richard Bellingham. Winthrop tried to move the proceedings on when he felt that Bellingham was returning to a question that had already been adequately asked and answered. Bellingham challenged Winthrop's intervention, snapping at the governor. Winthrop "replied, that it was his place to manage the proceedings of the court," to which Bellingham responded, "You have no more to do in managing the business here than I." Taking this as an attack on his office, Winthrop appealed to the entire court "whether he might not enjoin any of the magistrates silence if he saw cause." There was no rush to support him, and when his colleagues did eventually agree with him, their support was lukewarm. In the end, he "pressed it no further, yet expected that the court would not have suffered such a public affront to the governor to have passed without due reproof."[29] If he saw this as actually a reproof to him, he must have regarded the 1640 election of Dudley as governor with Bellingham as deputy governor as even more of one.

While Winthrop likely found many of the developments of the late 1630s distressing, there were accomplishments in which he took great pride, notably the laying down of an educational foundation in the colony. Puritans stressed the importance of reading and writing because they believed that each person should be able to encounter God's word through Bible reading, advised the reading of printed sermons and religious treatises, encouraged the taking and review of sermon notes, and valued keeping a spiritual diary. The majority of the Massachusetts immigrants were literate—a much higher percentage than to be found in the England population as a whole—and it was expected that parents would teach their children and servants basic skills. When too many seemed to neglect their responsibility "in training up their children in learning and labor," the General Court would legislate in 1642 that each town must see to it that all children and servants were taught to "read and understand the principles of religion and the capital laws of the country."[30] As early as 1635 an effort had been made to establish grammar schools that would provide more advanced education. In that year Winthrop's Boston voted that "our brother Philemon Pormont shall be entreated to become schoolmaster for the teaching and nurturing of children with us."[31] Expanding on this, Winthrop reported that "they made an order to allow forever £50 to the master, and an house, and £30 to an usher, who should also teach to read and write, & cipher, and Indian children were to be taught freely."[32] The example was quickly followed by Charlestown, Dorchester, Salem, and other towns. Eventually, in 1647, the General Court would legislate that every town of fifty or more heads of household employ a reading and writing instructor and towns of a hundred or more households support a grammar school.

By 1635 plans were also under way for the creation of a college, which was essential if the colony was to raise its own generations of educated clergy. There were other reasons as well. Though disenchanted with the English universities, some English puritans were disinclined to emigrate to Massachusetts so long as the colony had no college where their sons could be educated. Thus, in a letter she wrote to her brother, Lucy Downing expressed concern about bringing her son George to Massachusetts since "you have yet no societies nor means in that kind for the education of youths in learning."[33] Emmanuel Downing contributed his own opinion that such an enterprise would be welcomed among English puritans "considering the present distaste against our universities" and advised that even before buildings were erected to lodge scholars it should be possible to "make a combination of some few able men, ministers or others, to read certain lectures"; he argued that it should not be a great burden for "a minister for the present (till you have means and be better supplied with scholars) once a week for a month in every quarter to read a logic, Greek, or Hebrew lecture or the like."[34]

At the end of its business on October 28, 1636, even before Downing's letter was written, the General Court had "agreed to give £400 towards a school or college, whereof £200 to be paid the next year, and £200 when the work is finished, and the next Court to appoint where and what building."[35] This represented a substantial portion of the colony's annual tax revenue. Although distracted from plans for the college while dealing with John Wheelwright, Anne Hutchinson, and their followers, in November 1637 the court passed an order for the college to be established at Newtown, perhaps in recognition of Thomas Shepard's role in defeating the free-grace heretics. Winthrop, Dudley, Bellingham, and eight others were appointed overseers. The following May the court renamed Newtown "Cambridge," evoking the name of the English town where many of the colony leaders had studied.[36]

Nathaniel Eaton, a graduate of Trinity College, Cambridge, was appointed the first master of the college but abused his authority. He admitted to beating the staff and scholars excessively. His wife served the scholars "nothing but porridge and pudding" though their fees should have assured them of a more ample diet. Brought before the General Court, Eaton was censured, fined, and "debarred teaching of children in our jurisdiction." After he left the colony it was discovered that he had run up large debts.[37] But the college was able to survive the harm done by Eaton. The bequest of half of his estate by John Harvard in 1638 was a major boost to the college. Other individuals came forth with money and books. Winthrop donated forty volumes to the college, books of his and his father's which he had brought over with him from England. Henry Dunster was engaged to head the college in 1640, and the first class graduated in 1642.

In March 1639 a printing press was established at Cambridge. Winthrop noted that the first item printed was the freeman's oath, followed by an almanac prepared by the mariner William Peirce. In 1640 the press issued *The Whole Book of Psalmes Faithfully Translated into English Meter*, which was the work of Richard Mather, John Cotton, and other ministers.[38] In the decades to come the press would continue to serve the needs of the colony, although the major religious treatises authored by New England's clergy were sent to England for publication.

ANOTHER INSTITUTION THAT WAS EVOLVING in the late 1630s was slavery. The men and women who came to Massachusetts from England in the 1630s were certainly familiar with the imposition of service and control on the poor, and this was particularly true of men like Winthrop who had studied and administered the law. Though villeinage—an unfree status of subjection of individuals to others, defined by some medieval lawyers in terms of Roman laws of slavery—had actually disappeared in England by the sixteenth century, the idea of subjecting the poor and vagrants to the total control of individuals or parishes had not.[39] Henry VIII had approved the use of enforced servitude as a criminal penalty when, in 1545, he ordered that vagabonds, "ruffians," and "evil-disposed persons" be sent to the galleys. In 1547 Parliament had passed a statute that imposed slavery as a punishment for vagrants who refused to work. As envisioned by this act, the courts would impose this sentence for two years, awarding the vagrant to the individual who had brought the matter to the attention of the authorities. The master was entitled to beat or chain the slave and could sell or lease him as he could any other property. Slaves who absconded and were caught were sentenced to lifetime slavery. That act was repealed two years later, and there is no evidence of its application. In the reign of Queen Elizabeth the crown experimented with the use of conditional pardons for those sentenced to death, on occasion offering the felon the option of becoming a galley slave.[40]

While the common-law tradition that the colonists brought to New England was evolving in ways that would have discouraged the general enslavement of Englishmen, the concept of penal servitude still did exist in the common law and may have been seen by some as a solution short of execution where other measures to control criminals had failed.[41] Looking to biblical precedents, those who wished to bring English law into closer congruence with the laws of ancient Israel may have been more likely to explore the use of slavery as a criminal penalty, and punishing crime with servitude seems to have been the practice in early Massachusetts. A step in this direction was taken in 1633 when the Court of Assistants convicted John Sayle of stealing corn, fish, and clapboards from his fellow settlers. His estate was seized and sold to pay double restitution to those he had wronged; Sayle was sentenced to be whipped and bound as a servant for at least three years; his daughter was bound as a servant for fourteen years.[42] In December 1638 William Andrews, convicted of assault, attempted murder, and conspiring against the peace of the commonwealth, was sentenced "to be severely whipped, and delivered up as a slave to whom the Court shall appoint." On the same day Giles Player, "found guilty of several thefts, and breaking into houses, was censured to be severely whipped and delivered up for a slave to whom the Court shall appoint."[43] In December 1639 Thomas Dickerson "was censured to be severely whipped and condemned to slavery."[44] In June 1640 Thomas Savory, for breaking into a house during religious services, received the same sentence of a whipping and enslavement.[45] Also in that year Jonathan Hatch was "censured to be severely whipped and for the present is committed for a slave to Lieutenant Davenport."[46] In each of these cases it was an Englishman who was enslaved. In each of these cases, as in the Edwardian vagrancy law, enslavement was not anticipated as being lifelong. In each of these cases John Winthrop was a member of the court.

The enslavement of strangers—non-Englishmen—was a different matter. Regarding enemies captured in war, the famous English jurist Sir Edward Coke wrote in his *Institutes of the Lawes of England* that an individual "taken in Battle should remain bound to his taker for ever, and he to do with him, [and] all that should come of him, his will and pleasure, as with his beast or any other cattle, to give, or to sell, or to kill."[47] Englishmen knew of compatriots captured and enslaved by the Spanish and Turks. They themselves enslaved Irish and Scots in the wars of the sixteenth and seventeenth centuries. They were familiar with the enslavement of Africans by other Africans and by the Portuguese, Spaniards, and Dutch. Well-known English seafarers such as John Hawkins were involved in slave trading with Spanish colonies during Elizabeth's reign. And, following the example of other European colonizers, the English adopted the use of African slaves in colonies such as St. Kitts, Barbados, Nevis, Providence Island, and Virginia.[48] Writing to his father from Barbados in February 1627, Henry Winthrop had described the population of the island as "three score of Christians and forty slaves of negroes and Indians."[49]

It is possible that Samuel Maverick, an agent of Gorges who lived in Boston harbor before the coming of the Winthrop fleet, owned Negro slaves at the time the colony was settled.[50] But the first step taken by the Bay colonists to enslave non-Englishmen was the decision to enslave Indian captives in the Pequot War. Some of them were claimed by colonial leaders such as Winthrop and Roger Williams. Others were shipped to the West Indies, where they were exchanged for African Americans. Winthrop reported in his journal that on February 26, 1638, "Mr. Peirce, in the Salem ship *Desire*, returned from the West Indies after seven months. He had been at Providence [Island] and brought some cotton, and tobacco, and negroes."[51] This is the first reference to African Americans being brought to New England. It is assumed that they were sold as slaves.

There is no evidence that Winthrop himself owned African-American slaves, but that is not conclusive.[52] He did use Indian slaves, and it is known that his son Deane later used African-American slaves on his farm at Pullen Point, across the harbor from Boston. Certainly there was no puritan objection to the practice. Indeed, the English island colonies on which the institution flourished were all controlled by or dominated by puritans. Emmanuel Downing advocated the employment of African-American slaves in New England, writing to Winthrop that "I do not see how we can thrive until we get a stock of slaves sufficient to do all our business, for our children's children will hardly see this great continent filled with people, so that our servants will still desire freedom to plant for themselves and not stay but for very great wages. And I suppose you know very well how we shall maintain 20 Moors cheaper than one English servant."[53] But slavery played a very small part in the seventeenth-century history of New England, compared to other colonies.

The Body of Liberties adopted in 1641 stated that:

> There shall never be any bond slavery, villeinage, or captivity among us unless it be lawful captives taken in just wars, and such strangers as willingly sell themselves to us or are sold to us. And these shall have all the liberties and Christian usages which the law of God established in Israel concerning such persons doth morally require. This exempts none from servitude who shall be judged thereto by authority.[54]

This law did not specify whether slavery was for life or, as in the case of English criminals, for a period of time, and there is no evidence to answer that question. By designating slaves as "strangers," this law did not pass the status of slavery on to children born in the colony. Though the law would have allowed for the enslavement of Englishmen as a criminal penalty, the practice of doing so stopped at this time, likely because of the increasing identification of slavery with Indians and African Americans.[55]

Those African Americans who were slaves in New England appear for the most part to have been treated like white servants. Some slaves were employed on farms in the planting and cultivation of crops and the tending of livestock. Others were employed in lumbering, shipbuilding, and other trades, and still others as domestic servants. The requirement that heads of household were to educate their children and servants applied to slaves as well as English servants.[56] Servants and slaves were also expected to attend religious services. In April 1641 Winthrop recorded with approval that "[a] negro maid, servant to Mr. Stoughton of Dorchester, being well approved by divers years' experience, for sound knowledge and true godliness was received into the church and baptized."[57]

JUST AS THE COLONY'S GROWTH WAS REFLECTED in the development of new institutions, so too was it reflected in the emergence of a more complex and diverse economy. And economic development was accompanied by controversy. A dispute that affords us a chance to examine one aspect of the resultant debate reached a climax when the Boston merchant Robert Keayne was brought up on charges before the General Court in November 1639. There had been complaints for some time that merchants were overcharging for imported necessities, but Keayne had been singled out. This may have been due to his prominence as the colony's foremost merchant, but it may also have been due to the fact that he had further alienated some of his fellow Bostonians by opposing Anne Hutchinson. Keayne was John Wilson's brother-in-law and a friend of Winthrop. His notebook reveals that as a resident of London and member of the Merchant Tailors Company in the 1620s he had been an inveterate sermon gadder, traveling around the city to listen to the preaching of Richard Sibbes, John Davenport, Thomas Taylor, and John Cotton (when he preached to the New England Company), among others.[58] He had migrated to Massachusetts in the mid-1630s and become a respected member of the Boston congregation until that church began to divide under the strains of the free-grace controversy. In 1639 the General Court was asked to investigate charges of price gouging against Keayne. Among the specific charges, he was accused of paying sixpence for a bag of nails and selling it for eightpence, and of similarly seeking excessive profits in the sale of buttons, thread, and other items. Seeking to send a message, the General Court found Keayne guilty of oppression and fined him the large sum of £200, though later reducing it to £80.

The England in which these men had been born was undergoing vast economic changes that had forced reconsideration of traditional economic practices. More and more local interests were tied to distant markets in ways that undermined communal values. Many puritan spokesmen accepted the new forms of exchange but expected them to be conducted in accord with Christian moral values.[59] The failure of many to maintain those values while adapting to the new economic world was chronicled in some of the reasons given by Winthrop and others for their decision to migrate.

Winthrop's "Christian Charity" set forth some of the general principles that the colonists were expected to live by in their dealings with one another in the New World, but applying those principles was difficult.

The nature of a colonial society meant that goods and labor would be scarcer than the colonists were used to, producing upward pressure on prices. In the first years of the colony efforts were made to regulate the economy in accord with the practices of the English commissions of the peace, but micromanagement of all economic affairs was neither practical nor desired. Individuals had to make their own decisions. Failing to understand why goods in New England should cost so much more than what they were accustomed to paying in England, many began to complain about the practices of merchants. Winthrop observed that Keayne was targeted because he "was wealthy and sold dearer than most other tradesmen," and furthermore because there were reports that he had been guilty of "the like covetous practice in England." He had been "admonished both by private friends and also by some of the magistrates and elders" and promised to reform but failed to satisfy his critics. The fact that Keayne was "a member of a church and commonwealth now in their infancy, and under the curious observation of all churches and civil states in the world," made his crime worse. If, as Winthrop had asserted in "Christian Charity," the eyes of all people were upon Massachusetts, it was imperative that un-Christian conduct not be tolerated.[60]

Following the General Court's decision to fine Keayne, the Boston church called its erring member to account. Cotton preached on the essence of godly behavior in the marketplace. He rejected the notion that an individual could take advantage of scarcity by charging a price as high as the market would bear or by taking advantage of those who knew no better. He asserted that if a man suffered a loss because of his own mistake or lack of skill, he must absorb the loss and not pass it on to his customers. Similarly, if goods were lost at sea or in like manner, the individual should accept the loss as an act of providence and not seek to recoup it by raising prices on other goods. Those with goods to sell might raise their prices under certain circumstances, but they should nevertheless sell their goods at a just price, that is, one that was usual for the time and place.[61]

Some members of the Boston church sought to excommunicate Keayne, but Winthrop defended the merchant against such a severe penalty. He explained that there was no law preventing Keayne from charging as he had, and, however inappropriate, his practice was common in most countries of the world and in Massachusetts itself. As Winthrop expressed it on a different occasion, it was, unfortunately, "the common rule that most men walked by in all their commerce, to buy as cheap as they could, and to sell as dear."[62] Though he accepted the principle of the just price, "a certain rule could not be found out for an equal rate between buyer and seller, though much labor had been bestowed in it." In the end the Boston church consented to the lesser penalty of admonition.[63]

WINTHROP'S MODERATION IS REMARKABLE given the fact that as the complaints against Keayne were being brought forth to the General Court, he had become aware of how his own steward had engaged in business practices that threatened Winthrop with ruin. James Luxford was engaged by Winthrop to manage his Ten Hills Farm sometime around 1633. Over the following years he engaged in a number of practices which led to disaster. He borrowed money on Winthrop's name but without Winthrop's knowledge, agreed to excessive interest rates, and accepted below-market valuations of the goods with which he would pay the loans back. As the full details of Luxford's dealings emerged, Winthrop wrote that "something that troubles me a little [is] that some of my Christian friends should have taken advantage of my servant's unfaithfulness to get such bargains as some of them have."[64] Luxford also forged Winthrop's name to bills of exchange. The result was that Winthrop, thinking that he had financial obligations of about £300, found that he was in debt over £2,600.[65] Luxford's personal life was as disordered as his management of Winthrop's affairs. In December 1639 the steward was accused of bigamy. The Quarter Court at Boston found him guilty, dissolved his second marriage, fined him £100, and set him in stocks for an hour the next meeting day. Then, in May 1640, he was presented for "forgery, lying, and other foul offenses" relating to defrauding Winthrop. He was sentenced to be bound to the whipping post on Boston's lecture day until the lecture began and then, "after the lecture, to have his ears cut off," after which he was to be banished from the colony.[66]

Luxford had few resources, so his prosecution did nothing to help Winthrop. But if Winthrop was distressed to see how some of the "Christian friends" who had taken advantage of Luxford's mismanagement were unwilling to adjust the debts he owed them, he was gratified with the responses of his true friends. Despite the strife that had divided Winthrop from many of his fellow Bostonians in recent years, the Boston church gave him £200.[67] Friends on both sides of the Atlantic rallied with material aid and comfort. His sister Lucy wrote to say "how sadly affected" she was by the news and urged him to follow the example of Job "and to take the stem of bitter as willingly as the stem of prosperity because from God."[68] Remembering that Isaac Johnson had said that "he was resolved to spend and be spent in this business" of colonization and that Winthrop had indeed done so, Emmanuel Downing gave his brother-in-law a calf.[69] Edward Winslow, John's friend from the Plymouth colony, reassured him that God would "sanctify his hand unto you," reminding him that "He that brought Job so low, blessed his later days more than his former."[70] As the news reached England kinsmen such as Benjamin Gostlin and Deane Tyndal offered their help, as did various friends. Sir Francis Bacon, whom Winthrop had known from his days at Gray's Inn, wrote to let "his worthy and much esteemed friend" know that he was prepared to buy an English farm that Deane Tyndal had acquired for Winthrop. Though money was scarce and the farm was not that valuable, he would do so because he realized Winthrop's need.[71] Brampton Gurdon expressed his sorrow at his friend's misfortune and indicated that he and Sir Nathaniel Barnardiston had both agreed to lend money to Winthrop on easy terms to help him overcome his difficulties, or even give him the funds outright.[72]

In October 1639, just before he had discovered his losses, Winthrop had prepared a will in which he had sought to give direction to his executors in providing for his family. At that time he made arrangements for Margaret, "his dear wife who hath been a faithful help to me," to be "maintained in a comfortable and honorable condition," granting her half of the Ten Hills farm and other bequests. He left the other half of Ten Hills to his son John, "who had cheerfully departed with all his interest both in his mother's inheritance and mine to a great value" in order to finance the purchase of Groton and the move to Massachusetts, with the remainder of Ten Hills to pass to him after Margaret's passing. His son Adam was designated to receive Governor's Island and the Indian slaves who labored there. Stephen was to receive Winthrop's interest in Prudence Island in Narragansett Bay, which John had purchased with Roger Williams. Deane was willed lands on Pullen Point. His youngest son, Samuel, was to inherit lands in Concord. John Jr. and Margaret were named executors and were to divide all his books and other possessions.[73]

The will soon had to be revoked when the extent of Luxford's mismanagement became evident. Writing in 1641, John noted that his estate had become "much decayed through the unfaithfulness of my servant Luxford, so as I have been forced to sell some of my lands already, and must sell more for satisfaction of £2600 debts."[74] Much of his land across the harbor north of Pullen Point was sold. His Boston mansion house, where he had entertained his fellow magistrates on election days, was sold and he moved into a smaller home built across from where Anne Hutchinson had lived and held her meetings. To ensure a legacy for his sons, he sold some of the lands he had intended to leave them in his will.[75] Though news of his distress prompted sympathy and charitable outpourings, once again Winthrop had been humbled by events. Some even argued that "because the Lord hath so sadly afflicted the founders" of New England "in their estates, . . . it was not a way of God to forsake our Country" and settle New England.[76] And William Hathorne urged the colonists to see Winthrop's reverses as a judgment from God and to turn from his leadership. Yet if some doubted the errand into the wilderness and Winthrop's own worthiness, he remained confident of God's love and Christ's promise not to forsake him.

UNFORTUNATELY THE RECORDS FOR THIS PERIOD provide few glimpses of the more ordinary patterns of Winthrop's private life, since once John and Margaret were reunited in America there were few occasions for them to write to one another. Therefore we are deprived of the window their correspondence offers us onto their domestic affairs in the 1620s. The few letters they did write to one another during their brief separations during the New England years attest to the continuing strength of their mutual affection. Their epistles continued to include tokens of their affection, as when John closed a letter from Salem by telling Margaret "I kiss thee, and rest thy faithful husband."[77] John's letters to his children also demonstrate strong family feelings. He rejoiced and blessed the Lord "for his faithful providence in delivering" John Jr.'s wife from a domestic accident and, assured that she was well, indulged in some whimsy by expressing his "hope it will teach my daughter and other women to take heed of putting pins in the mouth, which was never seasonable to be fed such morsels."[78] He took great pleasure in the marriage of his son Adam in February 1642 and in the successes of Samuel and Stephen as they embarked on careers abroad. But the strongest expression of his parental love is to be found in a letter to his eldest son, John Jr., in 1643. "I had, by your mother, three sons and three daughters," he recalled, "and I had with her a large portion of outward estate. They are now all gone," he wrote, remembering his own sorrow and commiserating with his son. "Mother gone. Brethren and sisters gone. You only are alive to see the vanity of these temporal things and learn wisdom thereby, which may be of more use to you, through the Lord's blessing, than all that inheritance which might have befallen you. . . . My son," he continued, "the Lord knows how dear thou art to me, and that my care has been more for thee than for myself."[79]

We know little of Margaret's life apart from her husband, though a letter from Lucy Downing tells us that she embroidered: Lucy comments that a piece Margaret had produced was "worthy of all praise and imitation."[80] We also know that Margaret sought to surround herself with memories of her English home, asking her son Stephen to arrange the shipment of some goods from Cheyney House when he traveled to England.[81] Over the years Margaret received various tokens of friendship from friends in the colonies. Roger Williams sent chestnuts for her enjoyment.[82] On another occasion their friend Thomas James sent Margaret "a tame creature" for a pet.[83] John Endecott sent fruit trees to be planted in the Winthrops' garden on Governor's Island.[84]

The Winthrops remained close to kin and friends. There is evidence of contact with the families of John's Irish cousins Joshua and Adam.[85] John's nephew Samuel Fones wrote from Oxford University asking his uncle's advice on whether to study divinity or medicine. In the same letter, he wrote of Groton, where "the house that I had so often made my home looked sadly, as if it mourned for the absence of its master."[86] Mary Cole, a former neighbor in Groton, wrote thanking John and Margaret for their kindnesses over the years and asked John for spiritual advice. She also confessed herself troubled by her "son's condition."[87] There is no indication of what disability her son suffered, but he was likely the "lame man" whom John's old physician and friend Lawrence Wright arranged, at Winthrop's request, to place first in St. Bartholomew's hospital and then in "an hospital at the Bath where he hath hope of further cure."[88]

John also called upon English friends on behalf of colonists traveling to England. He provided Benjamin Hubbard with introductions that enabled him to meet with leading Congregational clergy such as Philip Nye and Thomas Goodwin.[89] Edward Bendall had invented a "tub to dive in," which he used to raise the wreck of the *Mary Rose* from the bottom of Boston harbor. John provided a reference for him to the earl of Warwick, whom Bendall wished to interest in his diving bell.[90]

Missing from the record of Winthrop's private concerns are any details about his relationship with his daughters. Four of the six died within days of their birth, another at less than a year old but before John had seen her. Only one, Mary, who married Samuel Dudley, lived to adulthood, and she died in 1643. No letters between her and her father survive to compare to the extensive correspondence he conducted with his sons. This may reflect what fortune and later family members decided worth preserving, but the explanation more likely lies with the conventions of the early modern period, by which mothers took primary responsibility for raising and counseling their daughters and fathers oversaw their sons. Yet the absence of any insight into John's relationship with Mary prompts questions about Winthrop's attitudes toward women in general. This is especially important given the conflicting ways in which Winthrop has been portrayed—on the one hand a loving partner to Margaret who treated her with respect, and on the other hand a bitter misogynist who persecuted Anne Hutchinson.[91]

John was an only son raised in a petticoat household, his views on women influenced by his mother and three sisters. There is ample evidence that he grew up respecting female intelligence. His mother could at least read Latin and could both read and write French. She managed the household capably during Adam's frequent absences. John's relationship with his younger sister, Lucy, was one of give and take that testifies to their love and mutual respect, and he was also close to his older sisters, Jane and Anne. Similar conclusions regarding his respect for female intelligence can be drawn from his marriages. Initially infatuated by Mary Forth, he was soon disenchanted with her shallow learning, though he sought to educate her and undoubtedly loved her. We know few details of his brief but intense relationship with Thomasine Clopton. But his marriage to Margaret

Tyndal was a match of equals, both of them well read, both of them capable, both of them pious. Mary Winthrop Dudley's letters to her mother attest to the fact that John and Margaret made sure that their daughter was educated.[92]

John took women's religious views seriously, as demonstrated by his correspondence with Margaret and with Mary Cole. But whatever counsel he may have taken privately from his wife or other women, like most men of his time John would not accept a woman publicly correcting or seeking to instruct a man. This, as well as his being repulsed by her ideas and her own intolerance, explains his animosity toward Anne Hutchinson. In contrast, because everything took place behind the scenes, he dealt charitably—too charitably in the eyes of some—with Lady Deborah Moody, who left the Bay to settle on Long Island because of her Anabaptist views.[93]

He was slightly involved in the church proceedings against Anne Hibbens, who was accused of slandering John Crabtree when she was dissatisfied with what he charged her for making a bed and other items, and then slandering Boston's other joiners when they asserted the fairness of Crabtree's fee. The Boston church debated the matter for three full days spread over a period of three months before eventually excommunicating Hibbens in the hope of bringing her to acknowledge her offense. Winthrop intervened rarely. In a characteristic effort to resolve the dispute privately, it was Winthrop who proposed that the first meeting be adjourned because of the lateness of the hour, hoping to allow time for Hibbens to reconsider. His account at the third meeting about her effort to solicit his support against Crabtree displays nothing more than his patience with her importuning.[94]

All of this makes it hard to explain Winthrop's comments regarding the wife of Connecticut's Governor Edward Hopkins. In 1645 Hopkins brought his wife, Ann, to Boston in an attempt to seek help for her. She was, according to Winthrop, "a godly young woman, and of special parts," but she had "fallen into a sad infirmity, the loss of her understanding and reason, which had been growing upon her divers years." Unfortunately, nothing could be done for her, and she continued in a serious mental illness for many years before her death. But it is Winthrop's explanation for her malady that has provided ample fuel for all who would condemn his views on women. Her breakdown, he believed, had resulted "by occasion of her giving herself wholly to reading and writing." Indeed, she had "written many books," and "her husband, being very loving and tender of her, was loath to grieve her." In Winthrop's view, "if she had attended her household affairs and such things as belong to women, and not gone out of her way and calling to meddle in such things as are proper to men, whose minds are stronger, etc., she had kept her wits and might have improved them usefully and honorably in the place God set her."[95] All puritans believed that there was danger in overdoing anything, no mater how good it was in itself, and Winthrop's primary indictment of Mrs. Hopkins was that she read and wrote to the neglect of her other duties. He saw nothing wrong with his mother's spiritual reading, nor with Margaret's religious devotions, because neither allowed such activities to overwhelm her life. But in the end, John Winthrop was a man of his times, and there were things that were proper for men and things proper for women. Like Anne Hutchinson, Ann Hopkins had crossed that line. Both women suffered the consequences. And yet, while he had no sympathy for Hutchinson, he continued to sympathize with and offer advice to Hopkins.

In the aftermath of the 1640 election, Winthrop may well have believed that his time of public service was drawing to an end. But as their native land became embroiled in the turmoil of civil war, his fellow colonists would once again turn to Winthrop to direct their affairs.

16

War Clouds and Concerns

IT IS A FINE JUNE DAY IN 1643. John and Margaret, their sons Samuel and Adam, and Adam's wife were enjoying the day in their orchard on Governor's Island. From the high point on which they stood they could see the town of Boston, which John had done so much to develop. Closer, to the north, was Charlestown, where he and the early settlers had first lived. Toward the mouth of the harbor was Castle Island, whose fortifications had recently been abandoned by order of the General Court. The threat from Charles I had subsided, and because no one wanted to pay the taxes, the defensive works in the harbor had been abandoned. Winthrop and his fellow Bostonians disagreed with the decision and had been trying to find a way to reestablish the fort on Castle Island without openly defying the wishes of the court, but so far they had failed.

The Winthrops saw Margaret Gibbons, one of their Boston neighbors, and her children, sailing to their farm on Deer Island, near the entrance to the harbor. Suddenly, the Gibbonses reversed course, making toward Governor's Island. Following them into the harbor were a ship of 140 tons and a small shallop, both of which approached the coast undetected, flying the French flag. Others soon noticed the pursuit and the approach of the French vessel to the island where the Winthrops were known to be relaxing. There was general confusion in Boston and Charlestown, and fears that the governor would be captured. Townsmen hastily armed themselves, and when the French shallop left the island and sailed toward Boston, three vessels of armed men pushed off from that town and Charlestown. Encountering the French ship they found the Winthrops talking amiably with Charles de La Tour, a Frenchman who had come to seek the Bay's help against his rival in Acadia. The colonial ships provided an escort as all made their way to the town. There had been no real threat. However, as Winthrop noted, "if La Tour had been ill minded towards us, he had such an opportunity as we hope neither he nor any other shall ever have the like again; for coming by our castle and saluting it, there was none to answer him." Had he wanted to, "having the governor and his family, and Captain Gibbons' wife, in his power, he might have gone and spoiled Boston."[1]

A lesson had been learned. Danger need not only come from internal dissenters and from Indians. The world beyond New England continued to contain threats. Dealing with these had been an important part of Winthrop's life and would continue so in the 1640s.

𝒞𝒷

*T*HOUGH THE FIRST DECADE of settlement had seen struggles against nature, natives, and dissenters, compared to other English colonies, the settlements in New England had flourished. Massachusetts in particular had grown. By 1640 the population of the colony was over twelve thousand.[2] The number of towns had swelled to more than twenty, leading in the early 1640s to the creation of separate counties and regional quarter sessions of the courts. Recalling the colonists' places of origin, these were named Suffolk (which included Boston, Dedham, Dorchester, Roxbury, Braintree, Hingham, and Weymouth), Essex (including Salem, Ipswich, Newbury, Rowley, Gloucester, Wenham, and Andover), Middlesex (Watertown, Charlestown, Cambridge, Sudbury, Concord, Woburn, and Reading), and Norfolk (containing the northern settlements of Hampton, Salisbury, and Haverhill).[3]

In addition, the Bay colony had spawned offspring. Hartford and the other towns along the Connecticut River were functioning as a separate colony and had absorbed the Saybrook settlement. Exiled dissidents had created towns along the Narragansett Bay. In March 1638 John Davenport and those who had followed him to Massachusetts from London had departed Boston to establish the town and colony of New Haven. Furthermore, Winthrop, who favored the expansion of New England, offered advice to settlements such as that at Acomenticus, on the coast of what would become Maine, and Dover, in what would become New Hampshire.[4] And, of course, there was the Plymouth colony that had been established in 1620.

Although the growth had not occurred as he had expected when cooperating with the plans of the Saybrook group, Winthrop had seen the raising of many candlesticks of reform throughout the region. For a time it seemed as if the eyes of all people were on New England. The Bible Commonwealths were sought out for prayers and advice by colonists outside of New England. Virginia's Philip Bennet arrived in Boston in 1642 seeking "a supply of faithful ministers" to sustain the faith of some of his fellow colonists of puritan leanings. The Bay's William Tompson and John Knowles responded to the call and were joined by Thomas James from New Haven. Over the following years these clergy were able to organize congregations and introduce elements of the New England way to the southern colony, until Virginia's Governor William Berkeley persuaded the Virginia Assembly to ban all nonconformists in March 1643. Within a year Virginia suffered another Indian massacre, and Winthrop noted that "it was very observable that this massacre came upon them soon after they had driven out the godly ministers we had sent to them."[5] Lord Baltimore invited New Englanders to settle in Maryland in 1643 "with free exercise of religion and all other privileges which the place afforded," but none took him up on the offer.[6] In that same year Governor Philip Bell of Barbados wrote to Winthrop about the difficult circumstances he faced on the island and requested the dispatch of ministers and godly settlers, but none were willing to go.[7]

The proliferation of colonies led to questions about boundaries and jurisdictions, and, after the Pequot War, the need to maintain a common front toward the Indians. In May 1638 Roger Ludlow had written to the Massachusetts authorities on behalf of the General Assembly of Connecticut suggesting cooperation. The Connecticut settlers were "desirous to retain that old love and familiarity which formerly we enjoyed" with their Massachusetts neighbors, being confident that "your ends of coming into these western parts were and so remain the same with ourselves, which was to establish the Lord Jesus in his kingly throne as much as in us lies." In order "to maintain the common cause of his gospel," Ludlow suggested discussion of arrangements for ensuring the cooperation of the colonies.[8] Winthrop responded by taking the lead in the effort to bring about a political union of the orthodox colonies. The heretical Narragansett Bay towns were excluded from such plans from the first. As an initial step, Winthrop wrote that summer to Thomas Hooker reflecting on some of the points of friction existing between Massachusetts and Connecticut, including a dispute over control of Pynchon's Springfield.[9] Hooker complained about people in Massachusetts spreading ill reports about Connecticut to keep people from moving there, which Winthrop discounted, claiming it "makes me a little merry." Responding in 1639, the Massachusetts governor stressed that "we all profess Christianity" and "are now put upon some trial for the practice of it," urging that differences be put aside for the common good. "We are brethren," he wrote, "one in consociation, in the same work of God, in the same community of peril, under the same envious observation [from common enemies], in the same relation for mutual succor and encouragement. . . . We must," he continued, "live in peace and love, and blessed be God that hath fixed us in one mind in the truth." He suggested, among other proposals, "that you should yield in some things and we in the rest."[10]

Progress on the union ground to a halt during 1640 and 1641 while Dudley and Bellingham served as governor of Massachusetts but resumed in the fall of 1642 when rumors of a new Indian attack on the colonies began to circulate. The specter of the Virginia massacre of 1622 was evoked again with reports from Connecticut that "Indians all over the country had combined themselves to cut off all the English" by going after the harvest "to the chief men's houses by way of trading, etc., and should kill them in their houses and seize their weapons, and that others should be at hand to prosecute the massacre." Winthrop was governor of Massachusetts at this time, which he had not been when the Pequot War broke out. He called a special meeting of the General Court, which agreed with his recommendation to "strike some terror into the Indians" by disarming those within the Bay jurisdiction. Some favored launching a preemptive attack, but Winthrop urged restraint, suggesting that the rumors might have been planted by rival tribes as a way of drawing the English to attack their enemies. Preparations for war were advanced, and an emissary was sent to Miantonomi, the chief of the Narragansetts, demanding that he appear before the court to discuss the rumors. In the end there was no war, but in the process the need for regular forms of cooperation between the various colonies was again underlined.[11]

In September 1642 the General Court appointed a committee to consider a draft of articles of confederation that had been sent by Connecticut and to deal with representatives of the other colonies in the matter.[12] Things then moved quickly. The May 1643 General Court appointed a committee headed by Winthrop "to treat with our friends of Connecticut, New Haven, and Plymouth about a confederacy between us."[13] The delegates quickly agreed to Articles of Confederation, which Winthrop proudly copied into his journal. The preamble set out the purpose of the confederation, opening with the statement that "we all came into these parts of America with one and the same end and aim, namely, to advance the kingdom of our Lord Jesus Christ, and to enjoy the liberties of the gospel in purity with peace." Because they were "further dispersed upon the seacoasts and rivers than was at first intended, so that we cannot, according to our desire, with convenience communicate in one government and jurisdiction," and surrounded with "people of several nations and strange languages, which hereafter may prove injurious to us or our posterity"—not to mention the natives who had "formerly committed sundry insolences and outrages upon several plantations of the English"—they were entering into a "consociation amongst ourselves for mutual help and strength in all future concernments, that, as in nation and religion so in other respects, we be and continue one."[14]

The United Colonies of New England, as the confederation was called, was an alliance among four independent colonies and was envisioned as not only providing for defense but also allowing for arbitration of disputes, facilitating the return of criminals and runaway servants, and adopting united stands on matters of common concern such as the best way to preserve and propagate the true faith. Each colony would send two delegates fully empowered by their respective governments to an annual September meeting of the confederation, which would rotate among the various colonies, with Massachusetts having two slots in the rotation and the others one each. Emergency meetings could be called by three magistrates of any one of the colonies. Decisions required a three-quarter majority.

Winthrop took great pride in the confederation and was critical in later years when Massachusetts chose younger, inexperienced magistrates as commissioners and failed to provide powder when requested by Plymouth under the terms of confederation.[15] He must have appreciated a congratulatory letter he received from Thomas Hooker a few months after the ratification of the articles, particularly because the two men had had their differences in the past and still failed to see eye to eye on matters such as magisterial discretion in the administration of justice. "Though the appearance of flattery (if I know myself and be known to you) be not only cross to my conscience but to my disposition," the Connecticut clergyman wrote, "yet my heart would not suffer me but as unfeignedly to acknowledge the Lord's goodness, so affectionately to remember your candid and cordial carriage in a matter of so great consequence, laboring by your special prudence to settle a foundation of safety and prosperity in succeeding ages." "It is," he concluded, "the greatest good that can befall a man in this world to be an instrument under God to do a great deal of good."[16]

IN CREATING THE UNITED COLONIES the leaders of the Bible Commonwealths asserted their commitment to advancing God's kingdom. Because of that determination they were also looking closely at events occurring in England. The threats posed in the 1630s by the efforts of Sir Ferdinando Gorges and Archbishop William Laud to control New England had foundered not only on considerations of cost but also on Charles I's preoccupation with turmoil in his northern kingdom of Scotland. Charles was determined to impose conformity to the religious system crafted by William Laud throughout his domains, in Scotland and Ireland as well as England. As a step toward achieving this he imposed a new Prayer Book on Scotland in 1637. This precipitated riots in Glasgow and Edinburgh. Opponents of the book drafted and circulated a National Covenant that called on all Scots to reject the new forms. A General Assembly in Scotland overthrew the royal supremacy, abolished bishops, and restored a full presbyterian system. Scotland was in revolt, and Charles had more serious concerns than New England.[17]

Winthrop and his fellow colonists followed the news from England avidly. They heard of the king's invasion of Scotland in 1639, in what became known as the First Bishops' War, and his failure to subdue the Scots.[18] They learned that the fighting ceased but threatened to resume because the Scots demanded the king pay for their costs in resisting him.[19] After over a decade of personal rule, Charles was finally forced to call a Parliament. Winthrop's good friend Sir Nathaniel Barnardiston wrote to him to let him know that he had been chosen to sit in the Parliament, where he hoped to advance the reforms for which the puritan party had long labored. He referred to "this great work, which if it succeed not well is like to prove exceeding perilous and dangerous to this church and kingdom," and regretted the absence of Winthrop and others who, had they not left England, "should have stood in the gap and have wrought and wrestled mightily in this great business."[20] But the hopes of the godly were thwarted, for, as Brampton Gurdon informed Winthrop, "we are here in very hard condition in regard our parliament is dissolved," though it "comforteth the hearts of the honest men of both houses that they yielded not to give a pence to the King in his intended war against the Scots."[21] Edward Payne wrote that with hopes of reform dashed by the brief life of what became known as the Short Parliament, "here hath been great stir. The [London] apprentices did rise and would have pulled down the [arch]bishop of Canterbury's house." Like Gurdon, Payne pointed with pride to Parliament's resistance to the king and reported that "the lower house of Parliament stood very strongly for the privileges of the subject and for reestablishing of religion."[22]

With one eye cast on England, many colonists felt that they received a providential sign in the summer of 1640 that God was on their side and, by implication, on that of their English co-religionists. The *Mary Rose*, an English merchant ship trading with the colonies, had berthed in Charlestown harbor. The crew quickly became notorious for their "atheistical passages and hellish profanations of the Sabbath and deridings of the people and ways of God." On their journey to New England "they would constantly jeer at the holy brethren of New England and would in a scoff ask when they should come to the holy land." They spent the Sabbath "drinking aboard with singing and music in times of public exercise [i.e., worship]."[23] The twenty-third of July was set as a day of fast on behalf of English reform, but the captain and crew remained on board and pointedly read from the Book of Common Prayer. Four days later the gunpowder on the ship "took fire (no man knows how) and blew all up"; "the captain and nine or ten of his men as well as four or five strangers" were killed.[24] John Endecott felt that this "extraordinary judgment" showed God's displeasure with those who opposed his way.[25]

The news during the rest of the year was mixed, and the leaders of New England puzzled over how to interpret it. William Bradford thanked Winthrop for acquainting him with the news from England and prayed that "the Lord be merciful to them, and us."[26] Reacting to the dissolution of the Short Parliament, Roger Williams feared that "the issue . . . will be general and grievous persecution of all saints."[27] Toward the end of December fishing vessels brought news "of the Scots entering England, and the calling of a [new] parliament, and the hope of a thorough reformation."[28] Faced with a renewal of fighting, called the Second Bishops' War, Charles desperately needed funds, but before even addressing the king's needs the new Parliament would extract a guarantee that it could not be dissolved without its consent. Its power assured, that Long Parliament began presenting long-deferred demands for reform.

Sensing the dawn of a better day, some New Englanders "began to think of returning back to England."[29] More serious, Englishmen no longer had any incentive to come to New England. The first signs of this came in February 1640 when John Tinker, writing from London, informed Winthrop that it was "like to be a year (so far as I can see for the present) there are like to come but a small quantity of passengers over, in comparison of what hath been formerly, and the reason I conceive to be the hopes of some reformation in England by the intended parliament," a judgment that was shared by Winthrop's nephew Benjamin Gostlin, a sea captain.[30] No immigrants meant no market for New England goods and no money from expected sales of cattle and other commodities to new arrivals. By October Winthrop recorded that "the scarcity of money made a great change in all commerce. Merchants would sell no wares but for ready money, men could not pay their debts though they had enough, prices of land and cattle soon fell to the one half and less, yea to a third, and after to one fourth."[31] Winthrop, struggling over the debts run up by his steward, was among those hit hard by these developments. Within a few years the colonies would also begin to suffer a severe servant shortage.[32]

Promoters of other colonies, also faced with English emigration drying up, sought to dissuade possible emigrants from choosing New England and tried to attract New Englanders to their own ventures. This was part of the explanation for the solicitation of colonists by the leaders of Maryland and Barbados. As the New England colony struggled, some settlers were tempted by promises of a better life elsewhere. The puritan proprietors of Providence Island in the Caribbean were particularly aggressive in trying to draw New Englanders to their colony, appointing John Humfry as governor of Providence and charging him with soliciting Bay colonists to join him there. Humfry, one of the first leaders of the original Massachusetts Bay Company, had previously been involved in the efforts of the Saybrook proprietors to create a colony along the Connecticut River.

Winthrop responded to the effort to draw colonists to Providence Island with rare and sustained anger. He ridiculed the very idea that there was a better life to be found in that southern clime, recording in his journal that over the past years that colony had begged cloths and other necessities from the Bay and that, without encouragement, some families had deserted "Providence and other Caribee Islands" and had come to New England with "meager, unhealthy countenances." He was clearly dissatisfied with Humfry, whom he criticized for seeking settlers for the new enterprise by disparaging New England and claiming that it would be impossible to continue to subsist there.[33] Humfry was called before the General Court, where Winthrop and others criticized him on three grounds. Defending their own colony, they asserted that it was "dangerous to bring up an ill report upon this good land, which God had found out and given to his people, and so to discourage the hearts of their brethren." They questioned why Humfry would try to induce men to "leave a place of rest and safety to expose themselves, their wives, and children to the danger of a potent enemy, the Spanish," who had a strong presence in the area. Finally, they wondered why anyone who lived in Massachusetts and was able to choose his governing officials would settle in a colony where the governor and chief officers were appointed by English proprietors.[34] Winthrop saw it as a providential judgment on Humfry when the latter's barn burned, destroying all of his grain and hay.[35]

Winthrop was not satisfied with criticizing Humfry and his efforts before the General Court. He also wrote a sharp letter to Lord Saye and Sele, one of the leading proprietors of the island colony, accusing him of spreading harmful reports about Massachusetts and diverting men from New England to Providence Island. It is likely that his relationship with that peer had been damaged by the outcome of the Saybrook venture, particularly because he felt that the Saybrook proprietors had left John Winthrop Jr. in an untenable situation. Though Winthrop's letter does not survive, Saye and Sele's lengthy response does, and from it we can follow Winthrop's argument and sense his anger. The peer accused the Massachusetts leader of misusing Scripture by assuming "that there is the like call from God for your going to that part of America and fixing there, that there was for the Israelites going to the land of promise." He did not deny that God had inspired the migration but did contend that God had brought them to New England to prepare them for greater things—like the settlement of Providence. Since the New Englanders "find it but a wilderness (which causeth many of you to struggle)," they should recognize that when a better opportunity was offered to them—by Lord Saye and Sele and John Humfry—"you might not neglect it, but see yourselves called to it, as you have been here sheltered by a gracious providence until you were fit and able to undertake it." To reject this chance was to defy God's providence. Saye and Sele defended the governance of the island against Winthrop, asserting that the Bay colonists practiced a mere democracy "where every man is a master," and did not understand "what true government is, and desirable liberty." Finally, he asserted the superior promise of Providence Island, with its warmer climate, more fruitful soil, and greater opportunities.[36]

It is possible that the English peer had been misled by some of the reports of New England's situation that he received from Humfry, who had been discontented with the climate and soil of New England and had advised a southern move as early as 1630, but that did not deflect Winthrop's anger at Saye and Sele. Despite new economic concerns, Massachusetts remained a flourishing enterprise compared to Providence Island, where the settlers had struggled and failed to achieve anything. Winthrop had his own friends in the Providence Island Company and knew something about the extent of its failure. In a memorandum he wrote on the back of Saye and Sele's letter, he shot back that those who had invested in that venture found that "their estates were gone already. Ask Mr. Gurdon. Ask Mr. Darley, etc., what became of their adventures? What content those have who be there? What conveniences they return with? What staple commodities [they have] for livelihood? What is become of their £120,000?"[37]

Although Humfry told his English supporters that there were at least two or three hundred New Englanders willing to move with him to Providence, only thirty men, five women, and eight children eventually sailed for the island in June 1641. Winthrop grimly noted that on their arrival the emigrants discovered that the colony had been captured by the Spanish the previous month.[38]

WHILE OPPOSED TO EFFORTS to draw New Englanders to more southerly colonies, Winthrop was well attuned to the value of trade with those settlements as a way of boosting the faltering Massachusetts economy. The first step in developing trade was to build ships to carry cattle and grain. In Salem the Reverend Hugh Peter stirred up citizens to invest in the building of a ship of 300 tons. Bostonians made plans for a ship of 150 tons.[39] By the end of 1643 Winthrop could report the departure of five ships from Boston harbor, three of which had been built in New England. Directed by George Story and other Bostonians, the greatest initial success was found in exporting timber and other supplies to Spain, the Azores, and the Canaries.[40] And just as the Winthrops had been among the first to engage in the early fur trade, so now John and his sons would work to establish trade links with other colonies. In 1645 John's son Stephen shipped a cargo of grain, fish, beef, and timber to the Canary Islands. Another son, Samuel, joined Stephen in this enterprise and settled for a time at Tenerife, where he worked for an English merchant hoping to develop trade with New England.

Eventually a more profitable trade developed with the West Indies. Cultivated land in those colonies was almost exclusively devoted to the production of export crops such as sugar, tobacco, and indigo, leaving the colonists dependent on imported foodstuffs and other necessities. In 1639 Stephen Winthrop sailed on a trading voyage to Bermuda. Samuel left

Tenerife and relocated in Antigua, where he succeeded as a merchant, became one of the prominent citizens of that island, and bought and settled
on a plantation he named Groton Hall.[41] The Winthrops were not the
only colonists interested in such ventures. In fact, the trade came to be
dominated by other families such as the Hutchinsons as it gradually became a central pillar of the New England economy. By the end of the
decade Winthrop could record with pride that "it pleased the Lord to open
us a trade with Barbados and other islands in the West Indies, which . . .
proved gainful."[42]

Efforts were also undertaken to free the colonies of their dependence
on English manufactures. John Winthrop Jr. had experimented with a salt-
works near Ipswich and by the summer of 1641 was convinced that iron
goods could be produced in the region. He was probably instrumental in
the decision of the Massachusetts General Court to encourage prospecting
by exempting those who expended funds in developing mines from public
levies for twenty-one years. For much of the 1640s, the younger Winthrop
would labor to establish the profitability of an ironworks he established in
the Bay.[43] The costs involved in starting to manufacture cloth in the New
World had discouraged efforts to do so, despite the fact that this had been
the key industry in the East Anglian region from which most immigrants
had come. Faced with new economic realities, the Massachusetts General
Court offered a bounty for the production of woolen, linen, and cotton
cloth. A fulling (cloth-processing) mill was built in Rowley in 1643. However, there were insufficient skilled workers and tools to satisfy local needs,
much less make cloth a major export item.[44]

EVENTS IN ENGLAND WERE NOT just watched for their implications for the
New England economy. The colonists hoped and prayed for reformation
in their native land and sought opportunities to further that cause. Early in
1641 it was reported that Archbishop Laud was "fast in the tower, and . . .
is like to cool his shins ere he gets out in this cold weather, for we speak
only of his confusion and unpardonable sins."[45] This was followed by other
welcome news—the king's chief advisor "the Earl of Strafford . . . beheaded,
and the archbishop (our great enemy) and many others of the great officers
and judges, bishops and others, imprisoned and called to account"—and
there was discussion in Massachusetts of sending "some chosen men into
England to congratulate the happy success there," to satisfy the colony's
creditors, "and to be ready to make use of any opportunity God should
offer for the good of the country here, as also to give advice, as it should be
required, for the settling the right form of church discipline there."[46]

Not everyone approved the idea of sending agents to England in 1641.
John Endecott, for one, wrote to Winthrop to express his view that doing
so might prove more harmful than helpful. His main concern was that it

would appear to be a begging mission that would confirm all that Saye and Sele and others were saying about the inability of the colony to survive on its own.[47] It was also feared that sending a formal delegation to approach Parliament might make it appear that "we should put ourselves under the protection of the parliament, [and] we must then be subject to all such laws as they should make, or at least such as they might impose on us." Despite these concerns, agents were sent. The clergymen Hugh Peter of Salem and Thomas Welde of Roxbury were chosen, along with the merchant William Hibbins of Boston.[48] Although John Winthrop Jr. accompanied them when they sailed in August 1641, he was not considered part of the mission. Hibbins contributed little to the agency, but Welde and Peter were successful on a number of fronts. They reassured the colony's creditors. They succeeded in gaining donations for the recently founded Harvard College, raised money in support of missionary work among the Indians, and obtained needed supplies for the colony. They also received approval to raise funds to send orphaned children of Irish Protestants to New England as servants.[49] Furthermore, they defended the New England way against its critics and encouraged the colony's friends in Parliament.[50] Winthrop Jr., meanwhile, gathered financial support for a colonial ironworks and engaged the skilled workers he would need for the project.

Emmanuel Downing had provided Peter with careful legal instructions on how to respond if he was told that a judgment had previously been entered against the Bay charter as a result of the proceedings of the Laud Commission in the 1630s, but the need did not arise.[51] Before the agents arrived, friends of New England had petitioned the House of Lords to remove the restraint that the Privy Council had placed on ships bound for New England. The Lords appointed a committee to meet with the king, and on March 31, 1641, the Privy Council removed the previous restraints and ordered that the colonies should enjoy all their liberties. "Thus," as Winthrop saw it, "our patent, which had been condemned and called in upon an erroneous judgment in quo warranto, was now implicitly revived and confirmed."[52]

In December 1640, the same month Laud was imprisoned, Parliament had entertained a petition calling for the reform of the Church of England "root and branch." In the succeeding months New Englanders followed with approval the abolition of the ecclesiastical Court of High Commission, the removal of church images, and orders for the return of communion tables to the approved Protestant position. In November Parliament presented the king with a "Grand Remonstrance," an itemized list of grievances that had accumulated since the beginning of his reign. Many of these dealt with religious matters. Charles was accused of condoning Jesuit activities and being a tool of the papist party. He was blamed for the deprivation of godly clergy by the bishops and for condoning the persecution of the godly so that "great numbers to avoid their miseries departed out of the kingdom, some unto New England and other parts of America, others unto Holland."[53] News of these developments was soon followed by word of the Triennial Act, which guaranteed that Parliament would be called at least every three years, and news of the enforcement of the laws against Roman Catholics. The Massachusetts General Court responded by appointing September 2, 1641, as a public day of thanksgiving "for the good success of the Parliament in England."[54]

Late in 1641 an uprising in Ireland added to the turmoil in the British kingdoms. Many in New England, including the Winthrops, had relatives in Ireland and were fearful for them. It was the Irish revolt that led to an irreconcilable breach between the king and Parliament in England. All recognized the need to suppress the Irish revolt, but Parliament, having extracted so many reforms from the king, would not trust him with command of an army, and the king would not surrender his right to have such control. When the king's attempt to seize the ringleaders of the opposition failed, he left London and the country began to divide. In August 1642 the king raised his standard and declared Parliament in revolt. The English Civil Wars had begun.

The colonists were saddened by the outbreak of fighting. As William Hooke preached in a fast-day sermon in the Plymouth colony, "If you should but see war described to you in a map, especially in a country well known to you, nay dearly beloved of you, where lately you dwelt, where you have received ten thousand mercies, and have many a country-man and kinsman abiding, how could you but lament and mourn?"[55] Yet their sympathies were clear. Hooke himself saw the war as an act of God that would "purge the land of this filth." Plymouth's Bradford rejoiced that "the tyrannous Bishops are ejected, . . . their plots for popery prevented," while Thomas Shepard regarded the civil wars as a "blessed work of public reformation."[56] On April 14, 1642, Massachusetts observed a day of fast and thanksgiving for the troubles in England and Ireland. In the eyes of the colonists, prayer was one of the most potent weapons they had to aid the reform of their native land. As Lynn's Reverend Thomas Cobbet put it, "Churches of praying believers are terrible as so many armies with banners, as so many thundering legions."[57] Englishmen solicited the prayers of Winthrop and his fellow colonists, and the New Englanders responded enthusiastically. At the 1642 fast, Hooke exhorted his congregation to join the fight against the king and the enemies of reform: "Let us pray against them, and sing against them, and live against them." The role of the colonists, he stated, was to "lie in wait in the wilderness, to come upon the backs of God's enemies with deadly fasting and prayer, murderers that will kill point blank from one end of the world to the other." If the colonists exerted themselves "thousands shall fall, and never know who hurt them."[58]

New Englanders supported the cause of English reform in other ways as well. Concluding that "great pity were it that they should want any light which might possibly be afforded them," John Cotton began to send treatises explaining the New England way to be published in England.[59] Other clergymen did the same, counting on allies in England to see their works published. William Hooke's two fast-day sermons were published with the aid of the rising parliamentary leader and general Oliver Cromwell, who was a kinsman. Peter and Welde would assist in such efforts as well. It was Welde who prepared Winthrop's manuscript treatise on the Anne Hutchinson controversy for the press. Over the next decade and beyond, other New Englanders returned to their native land to aid the cause. Ten colonists would rise to the rank of major general or higher in the parliamentary armies. Others would serve in Parliament or hold other government offices. Some clergy, such as John Phillips and Robert Peck, returned to minister to the English parishes which they had been forced to leave. Seven of the ten members of Harvard's first graduating class (1642) went to England to join those trying to introduce the New England way of church organization and worship. Other Harvard graduates would follow.[60]

In 1642 the English Parliament signed a Solemn League and Covenant with the Scots, both sides uniting to pursue the objectives of advancing religious reform. The English negotiators, who included a number of men with New England connections—Henry Vane, Philip Nye, and Sir Henry Darley—committed themselves to preserve the newly reformed Church of Scotland and to reform the Church of England "according to the Word of God and the example of the best Reformed Churches." Hearing this news, William Pynchon wrote to Winthrop that he saw the alliance as "the highway of God for their deliverance. I hope it is now the day of Antichrist's great overthrow at Armageddon."[61] Pursuant to this, Parliament prepared to create an assembly to recommend a new English church settlement. A group of parliamentary leaders including the earl of Warwick, Lord Saye and Sele, Thomas Barrington, Arthur Heselrige, Nathaniel Barnardiston, Henry Darley, and Oliver Cromwell wrote inviting John Cotton, John Davenport, and Thomas Hooker to join that body. Winthrop noted that "such of the magistrates and elders as were at hand met together and were most of them of opinion that it was a call of God." Hooker and Davenport were reluctant, however, and soon letters were received from religious allies in England who recommended against the journey. As the composition of the Westminster Assembly had become known, it was evident that by far the largest number of delegates were sympathetic to the Scottish presbyterian model of reform, with only a minority—led by Nye, Thomas Goodwin, and other friends of New England—advocating the congregational model that had become known as "the New England way." Under these circumstances it was thought that the principal colonial clergy could better serve the cause by their written advocacy of congregationalism.[62]

NEW ENGLAND'S SUPPORT WAS APPRECIATED by Parliament, which in March 1643 issued an order freeing New Englanders from paying any customs duties until the Parliament should decide differently.[63] Not only was this a generous waiver for an English government straining to pay the costs of war, and a welcome benefit to the struggling colonial economy, but it was also seen by Winthrop and the colonial leaders as recognizing their semi-autonomy since it referred to the Bay as a "kingdom."[64] The colonists recorded their thanks to Parliament.

There were risks in identifying too closely with a Parliament at war with the king, even if that Parliament was controlled by fellow puritans. Under these circumstances the freemen evidently felt that Winthrop's continued leadership was necessary, and he was reelected governor in May 1643. Under his leadership the General Court then proceeded to omit from the oath taken by the governor and magistrates the phrase "You shall bear true faith and allegiance to our sovereign Lord King Charles," justifying that action by the fact that the king "had violated the privileges of parliament, and made war upon them, and thereby lost much of his kingdom and many of his subjects."[65] This was the strongest sign yet of the Bay's commitment to the parliamentary cause.

In November 1643 Winthrop was encouraged when Parliament named his friend the earl of Warwick to head the committee appointed to regulate colonial affairs.[66] During the following spring Winthrop reported that there were in Massachusetts "some malignant spirits beginning to stir, and declare themselves for the king."[67] Following the election of John Endecott as governor in 1644, with Winthrop as deputy, the General Court adopted an order that any person who shall "by word, writing, or action endeavor to disturb our peace, directly or indirectly, by drawing a party under pretense that he is for the King of England and such as adjoin with him against the Parliament, shall be accounted as an offender of an high nature against this commonwealth, to be proceeded with either capitally or otherwise, according to the quality and degree of his offense."[68] In keeping with this, the court summoned William Jennison of Watertown, who had been heard to have questioned the lawfulness of Parliament's proceedings. Jennison confessed that "if he were in England he should be doubtful whether he might take their part against their prince, yet if the king or any party from him should attempt anything against this commonwealth, he should make no scruple to spend estate and life and all in our defense against them." Then, after further persuasion, he stated that "he was now satisfied that the Parliament's cause was good, and if he were in England he would assist in defense of it."[69]

The magistrates faced a more complex situation that summer when Captain Thomas Stagg, a Virginia merchant with a privateering license issued by the earl of Warwick as lord high admiral of England, demanded the surrender of a Bristol-based ship berthed in Charlestown harbor. Stagg considered the ship a legitimate prize since Bristol was loyal to the king. As the confrontation developed, a crowd of Bostonians gathered on Windmill Hill. When the captain of the Bristol ship surrendered its vessel and cargo, and Stagg had them rowed to Boston, one of the merchants who had an interest in the cargo, "a bold malignant person" according to Winthrop, stirred up some of the crowd against Stagg and his crew. Because Governor Endecott was in Salem, Winthrop took control of the situation. He committed the merchant and some of the rioters who were not Bostonians to a room in a tavern with a guard watching over them, sent troublemakers who were townsmen to the Boston prison, and dispatched the constable to disperse the rest of the crowd. He then asked to see Stagg's commission and, having examined it, requested the captain appear with it at the next meeting of the Court of Assistants at Salem.[70]

Before the court convened, some of the clergy preached against Stagg's action, asserting that it represented an interference with the colony's liberty. Together with some of the magistrates they argued that a commission from the earl of Warwick was not valid within the Bay jurisdiction unless the magistrates granted it that status. Those who took this stand urged that the ship and its cargo be restored to its original captain and crew. Winthrop took the opposite position, upholding Stagg's authority. Having been taught by Parliament that the welfare of the people is the supreme law, the colony could reject commissions from other agencies or foreign powers if it felt they were called for. Each case should be decided on the merits. In the present circumstances, since "the king of England was enraged against us [Massachusetts], and all the popish states in Europe" as well, if the colony "should now, by opposing the parliament, cause them to forsake us, we could have no protection or countenance from any, but should lie open as a prey to all men." In Winthrop's opinion "we might not deny the parliament's power in this case, unless we should deny the foundation of our government by our patent." Furthermore, if Massachusetts, which had "so openly declared our affection to the cause of the parliament by our prayers, fastings, etc., should now oppose their authority," it would encourage opposition to Parliament in other colonies and "would grieve all our godly friends in England." Some insisted that Massachusetts was a "perfecta republica and not subject to appeals, and consequently to no other power but among ourselves." Winthrop responded that while the

charter did free the colony from judicial appeals, it did not make Massachusetts free in matters of state, since neither the king nor parliament could
create an independent state. A majority sided with Winthrop, and Stagg
kept his prize. As a concession to the other side a petition was sent to Parliament seeking compensation for goods thus lost by Massachusetts merchants.[71]

AS THE DEBATE OVER THE REFORMATION of the English church continued,
divisions emerged between those puritans who favored a system tending
toward congregational autonomy, such as predominated in New England,
and those who preferred the greater central authority found in a presbyterian
system, such as Scotland's. In light of this, representatives of the colonial
churches gathered at Cambridge in September 1643 in an effort to
strengthen the New England voice in those debates by bringing all the
colonial churches into agreement. About fifty of the clergy and some lay
elders tried to strike a balance between the two positions. They endorsed
monthly, quarterly, and yearly conferences of clergy to maintain uniformity, and emphasized the importance of congregational clergy having significant authority, but concluded that the lay members of each church should
determine admissions and excommunications. These findings were only
advisory, as befitted a congregational polity, and the Reverends Thomas
Parker and James Noyse of Newbury, whose governing practices were more
presbyterian, merely took the recommendations under advisement.[72]

This was not the only way in which English events prodded the colonists to reconsider their religious positions. With the outbreak of the English Civil Wars censorship effectively ceased, and various controversial
religious opinions were sent abroad in sermons and print. As sectarian views
spread in England, the debate between presbyterians and congregationalists there focused in part on how well each system could sustain religious
truth and control error. Presbyterian apologists, such as the Scot Robert
Baillie, pointed to the free-grace controversy in Massachusetts as a sign of
how congregationalism spawned sectarian views. The publication of Winthrop's *Short Story* was intended to make the counter-argument that such
errors could be suppressed in a society of congregational churches. There
were, of course, those in Massachusetts who themselves felt that Winthrop's
treatment of Wheelwright and Hutchinson's supporters had been too lenient. They would not have been pleased when Wheelwright sought to
make peace with the Bay, writing to Winthrop in September 1643 to say
that he was "unfeignedly sorry that I had such an hand in those sharp and
vehement contentions"; he blamed his role on ideas "presented to me in
the false glass of Satan's temptations and mine own distempered passions."[73]
Winthrop, who was well aware that Wheelwright had gone north to New
Hampshire rather than with the other exiles to Narragansett Bay, pro-

vided the clergyman with letters of safe conduct and brought his case to the General Court, which in June 1644 lifted his banishment.[74]

Among the doctrines and practices that were called into question in England at this time was the validity of infant baptism. This had long been a sensitive point with some puritans, who maintained that baptism was not a saving ordinance even though they continued to baptize their children. In New England and in some of the independent congregations being organized in England, the fact that baptism did not bring admission to full church membership raised even more questions as to why it should not be limited to adults who were determined to be of the elect. Those who adopted these views were called Anabaptists. Roger Williams took such a position briefly in the late 1630s, though he later abandoned it. John Cotton claimed that he knew New Englanders who denied the validity of infant baptism but kept their views to themselves. In fact, Henry Dunster, the highly successful president of Harvard, had doubts about infant baptism that would eventually lead him to resign from the college in 1654.[75]

Anabaptists, however, came in many varieties. Some were indistinguishable from clergy like Cotton and Hooker on every score except their rejection of infant baptism. Others maintained positions that raised further reasons for orthodox opposition, such as Arminianism and rejection of the need for an educated clergy. In the last case in particular, such Baptists posed a challenge not only to religious truth but also to social order. Most colonial leaders had been willing to tolerate the scruples of Englishmen and colonists who were orthodox on all other fronts, so long as they did not openly challenge the practice of infant baptism or leave their existing churches to form Baptist congregations.

In the summer of 1644, "Anabaptistry increased and spread in the country [New England], which occasioned the magistrates, at the last court, to draw an order for banishing such as continued obstinate after due conviction."[76] This was a victory for those who wished to prove that Massachusetts was tough on errors, but it was not universally applauded. In England Calvinist Baptists were working closely with Congregationalists such as Thomas Goodwin and Philip Nye to fend off a national Presbyterian establishment, and they found the colonial exclusion of Baptists from the circle of acceptable opinion to be excessive and counterproductive. By March of 1645 Stephen Winthrop wrote to his father from London that there was "great complaint against us for our severity against Baptists."[77] George Downing, Emmanuel and Lucy's son, wrote of "the law of banishment for conscience which makes us stink everywhere."[78] There was opposition to the laws from within Massachusetts as well, culminating in an October 1645 petition by various merchants and others, citing English concerns, to repeal both the law against Anabaptists and the 1630s law limiting the stay of new arrivals without the approval of magistrates.[79]

Endecott had been elected governor in 1644 and was succeeded by Thomas Dudley in 1645; neither was sympathetic to the petitioners. A close reading of Winthrop's papers reveal that he may have been, though he was likely reluctant to come out forcefully for the Anabaptists. At about this time he prepared a memorandum on baptism, either to persuade others of the validity of infant baptism or to satisfy his own concerns. Winthrop's brother-in-law, Emmanuel Downing, a close ally, was one of the petitioners. In his journal Winthrop indicated that "many of the court"— a phrase that often includes him—were inclined to suspend the laws for a season. But some of the clergy opposed the petition, and the court denied it.[80] To ensure their position the clergy encouraged a counter-petition to keep the laws, which was signed by over seventy colonists and presented to the General Court in May 1646.[81]

Complicating the dispute over Anabaptism was the climaxing of a dispute with a different set of heretics led by Samuel Gorton. A self-educated London clothier, Gorton had arrived in Boston at the height of the free-grace controversy but moved on to the Plymouth colony without having become involved in the Massachusetts dispute. Gorton, however, was far more radical in his religious views than Anne Hutchinson. Like Hutchinson he believed in immediate inspiration and revelation, but he went beyond her in attacking book learning and the need for an educated ministry. He advocated full fraternal equality, rejecting deferential relations between rulers and ruled, masters and servants, husbands and wives, and all others, which would explain his being labeled a familist. He appears to have rejected predestination and infant baptism.[82]

It did not take long for the Plymouth authorities to expel Gorton for his heretical views. He settled next in Rhode Island, where he joined Anne Hutchinson in a quarrel with her former supporter William Coddington.[83] Gorton kept stirring up trouble as he moved from Providence to Pawtucket to Shawomet. In March 1641 the generally tolerant Roger Williams had written to Winthrop that "Master Gorton, having foully abused high and low at Aquidneck, is now bewitching and bemadding poor Providence, both with his unclean and foul censures of all the ministers of this country (for which myself have in Christ's name withstood him) and also denying all visible and external ordinances in depth of Familism, against which I have a little disputed and written, and shall (the most High assisting) to death. . . . All suck in his poison."[84] By November 1641 Gorton had so factionalized Providence that thirteen of the town's inhabitants petitioned Massachusetts to lend them "a neighborlike helping hand" to quell the turmoil. The Bay authorities were not about to intervene in the affairs of Providence, and it turned out not to be necessary since Gorton moved on yet again. In Pawtucket, where he next settled, he so offended some of his neighbors that four of them, led by William Arnold, petitioned the Bay colony to have their settlement taken under the jurisdiction of Massachusetts, which the General Court consented to in September 1642.[85] Winthrop was governor at the time, and part of his motivation was a concern that Gorton was stirring up trouble not only among the English but also with the Indians in the vicinity.

In November of that year Gorton wrote an arrogant and vitriolic letter to the Bay authorities. He challenged their right to annex land beyond the bounds of their charter but went on to attack Massachusetts as a colony of hypocrites led by a false clergy. Having dispatched his letter, Gorton and his close followers settled on land slightly to the south of Pawtucket, which they claimed to have purchased from the local Indians. Soon Punham, the local sachem who was said to have sold the land, and Socononoco, one of his fellow sachems, complained to Massachusetts that Punham had been forced to sell by Gorton and the chief sachem of the Narragansetts, Miantonomo, with whom Gorton had established friendly relations and who was trying to dominate the local tribes. The English colonies were suspicious of the Narragansetts at this time and thus inclined to take the complaint seriously, if only as an opportunity to curb Miantonomo. The United Colonies delegated the matter to Massachusetts to handle, and that colony instructed Miantonomo and Gorton to come to Boston to answer the charges against them. Miantonomo came but Gorton refused. When Miantonomo could not satisfy the Bay authorities of his overlordship in the area, the colony took the bands of Punham and Socononoco under their protection.

A second warrant was sent to Gorton, demanding he come to Boston to answer charges of mistreatment from Punham and Socononoco. Gorton's associate, Randall Holden, responded with an insulting letter addressed to "the great and honored Idol general, now set up in the Massachusetts." He rejected any claims of Massachusetts jurisdiction, dismissed the charges of "heathen, thieving Indians," charged that the Bay followed principles of the Kingdom of Darkness, ridiculed the idea that in the Lord's Supper "the juice of a poor, silly grape" was transformed "into the blood of our Lord Jesus Christ by the cunning skill of your magicians," referred to the clergy as necromancers, and warned that if challenged the settlers of Shawomet would resist.[86] They soon got their chance. A force of forty men crossed the border, overcame the brief resistance of the settlers, and brought Gorton and his followers back to Boston.

On October 17, 1643, Gorton was brought before the General Court to go on trial for heresy and for refusing to obey the ordinances and commands of the magistrates. The incendiary nature of many of the comments of Gorton and Holden had many clergy preaching against the heretics.

John Wilson was said to have called for the death penalty. As the trial progressed the magistrates became frustrated over Gorton's moderate responses. Though it was pointed out that it was accepted practice for familists to lie in order to save themselves, the fact was that Gorton was not willing to admit to the heresies he was accused of and found ways of reinterpreting his written statements to make them seem less offensive. While most of the magistrates wished to execute him nonetheless, a majority of the deputies opposed the death penalty. In the end Gorton, Holden, and five of their followers were fined, set in chains, and put to work in various towns to pay off the fines. If they preached heresy in the future they were to be tried by a jury and, if found guilty, executed.[87]

A divisive force wherever he went, Gorton always had the ability to attract support. Soon Winthrop was being warned that the Gortonists were gaining sympathy among the townsmen where they had been sent to labor. It was decided that they were a greater danger within the Bay than they had been in Shawomet, so they were released and banished from the colony, defined to include Pawtucket and Shawomet. In the summer of 1644 Gorton, Holden, and another of their supporters, John Greene, traveled to Rhode Island and then on to the New Netherland colony, where they boarded a ship for England. There they capitalized on the criticisms of New England intolerance, befriended religious and political leaders who were fighting to maintain religious independence against a threatened Presbyterian establishment, and published a sensationalized account of their treatment in Massachusetts.[88] They then approached the Warwick Commission to overthrow the Bay's claim to Shawomet and their banishment. No one was prepared to represent the Massachusetts side of the case, and so in May 1646 the commission ordered that Gorton and his followers be allowed to return to their lands and that they further be allowed to land at any port in New England in order to travel to their lands. Holden made a point of sailing to Boston immediately. While some magistrates and clergy wanted to defy the order, Winthrop's cooler head prevailed, and Holden was allowed to proceed.[89]

The full order of the Warwick Commission did not reach Winthrop until November 1646. The commissioners noted that they had been hamstrung by the fact that no one could present the Massachusetts case and that it would have been a hardship to Gorton and the petitioners if they were asked to wait in England until the Bay did respond. Their judgment, therefore, was "not grounded upon an admittance of the truth of what is charged." In fact, the commission knew "well how much God hath honored your government" and believed that "your spirits and affairs are acted by principles of justice, prudence, and zeal." Without judging the events of the past, the commission had granted the Gortonists the right to return to the land they claimed because it did not appear to be within the Bay's legal jurisdiction. Winthrop had to know that the Bay's claim to jurisdiction was flimsy and would have gained some comfort from the kind words about Massachusetts. But he was concerned that the commission had accepted an appeal from colonial jurisdiction, something he and his fellow leaders had always claimed was not allowed under the charter. They had been caught by surprise by Gorton's tactics. Winthrop would see that that would not happen again.

WHILE THE COLONISTS WERE SUPPORTING the parliamentary forces and grappling with the issues posed by the religious debates in England, Winthrop and Massachusetts had become involved in quite a different conflict. The origins lay in a dispute between Charles de Saint Etienne de La Tour and Charles de Menon, Sieur d'Aulnay de Charnise, both of whom claimed to be the legitimate governor of French Acadia. Each had been appointed by Louis XIII at different times and without any clarification of their respective powers. Their struggle spilled over to the coastal regions of northern New England, where English fishing settlements were sometimes caught in the crossfire. In 1635 each had attacked Plymouth trading posts in that area. In September 1641 La Tour sent an envoy to the Bay, judiciously choosing a French Protestant. He proposed free trade between the French and English, which was agreed to. But he also wanted Massachusetts to support him against d'Aulnay and to use Bay merchants to obtain goods from England. Since he could produce no official commission from La Tour, Governor Bellingham and his fellow magistrates declined to enter into an agreement on those points.[90]

Almost a year later "came in a French shallop with some fourteen men," one of whom was La Tour's lieutenant carrying letters from his superior. The Frenchmen stayed about a week; they were "kindly entertained, and though they were papists, yet they came to our church meetings." One of the Bay clergy gave the lieutenant a French Protestant biblical commentary.[91] Following this, Boston merchants sent a pinnace to trade with La Tour on the St. John's River in modern New Brunswick. But on their way home they stopped at Pemaquid, where d'Aulnay warned them from further trade with his enemy, sending on to the Massachusetts authorities a copy of an order he had received from the French government in 1640 authorizing him to arrest La Tour and seize his goods.[92]

It was against this background that La Tour himself arrived in Boston harbor in June 1643, scaring Mrs. Gibbons and the townsmen of Boston and Charlestown. Landing on Governor's Island, La Tour explained to Winthrop that d'Aulnay had blocked his return to Acadia and he had come to Massachusetts for assistance. The two men had talked, with Winthrop inviting the Frenchman to Boston so that the other leaders of the colony could be called together and consulted. The next day La Tour showed an official commission signed by the vice admiral of France, as well as a letter of support from the Company of New France, to those magistrates and deputies whom Winthrop had been able to assemble. It was decided that Massachusetts could not grant official aid to La Tour without the approval of the United Colonies but that they could allow him to hire any ships and men to advance his ends.[93]

Staying in Boston to recruit supporters, La Tour's men drilled on the town training ground the following week. Forty French troops were escorted onto the field by the 150-man Boston trained band. In the morning everyone watched the colonists drill. La Tour and his officers dined with the Boston officers, and the French soldiers went home with local citizens to eat. Then, in the afternoon, the Frenchmen went through their military exercises. At one point they threw down their muskets and bandoliers, drew their swords, and appeared to charge the crowd, spreading momentary fear among the women and children. Winthrop commented drily that "they were very expert in all their postures and motions."

As he continued to recruit men and ships, La Tour and his officers were entertained by Winthrop and other town leaders. On the Sabbath and lecture days La Tour and Winthrop walked together to the meeting-house, the Massachusetts governor accompanied by "a good guard of halberts and musketeers"—which he must have reflected was in sharp contrast to his situation following the 1637 election in which he had defeated Vane. But with "rumor of these things soon spreading through the country," questions were raised and opposition began to develop. Some of the clergy were particularly incensed that Catholics were being entertained in the capital of the new Israel. One, who was generally considered "a judicious minister, hearing that leave was granted to them to exercise their men in Boston, out of his fear of popish leagues and care of our safety, spake as in way of prediction that before that day were ended store of blood would be spilled in Boston."

Many wrote to Winthrop raising doubts about the aid given the Frenchmen; some even charged that his policies were sinful. Thomas Gorges, a kinsman of Sir Ferdinando who had come to New England to govern the only surviving remnant of that Englishman's colonial dream, had established a relationship of mutual trust with Winthrop. From his northern vantage point of Piscataway, where he had been a close observer of the struggle in Acadia, he warned of the dangers of getting involved, stating that "all New England will find d'Aulnay a scourge . . . if all his hopes be frustrated through your aid."[94] Winthrop's friend and ally John Endecott also raised concerns, arguing that it was in the interest of New England to allow the French to occupy themselves fighting each other. Endecott was not convinced that "these idolatrous French" could be trusted and was worried that they had been allowed to stay in Boston and observe the state of the colony's defenses.[95] But the sharpest criticism came in the form of a letter signed by Richard Saltonstall, Simon Bradstreet, Samuel Symonds, and the clergymen Nathaniel Ward, Ezekiel Rogers, Nathaniel Rogers, and John Norton. These leaders, all living in Essex county, which, being north of Boston, was closer to the scene of fighting and more vulnerable, raised five serious objections to helping La Tour. In the first place they did not believe that there was sufficient evidence to indicate that the struggle between La Tour and d'Aulnay was a just war, and if it was not, New Englanders should not engage in it in any way. Second, if English colonists were to engage in a war against the colonists of a foreign nation, they should do so only with the approval of the English government. The third objection was that "the ends of war ought to be religious, [and] what glory is intended hereby to God we see not, and how our peace shall hereby be settled we foresee not, but suspect it will rather be a beginning than an end of our troubles and fears." Fourth, they felt that those going to war ought to have an expectation of success, whereas all that they had heard from the north indicated that La Tour's cause was already lost. Finally, if the Bay was to go to war—indirectly as well as directly—they should have challenged d'Aulnay to first show them the justice of his cause and considered his response.[96]

The Essex protest was received the same day that La Tour sailed from Boston harbor with four colonial ships and seventy Massachusetts recruits. Though the horse had, in effect, already left the barn, Winthrop convened a meeting of magistrates, deputies, and clergy to discuss the issues that were being raised. He also wrote a lengthy response to the Essex protestors.[97] While he marshaled numerous arguments to justify what he had approved, this episode was unquestionably his most serious political blunder and would haunt him for some years to come. The fact that he had not convened the General Court, nor even, evidently, the Standing Council, but merely involved magistrates and deputies available in Boston in the original decision to allow La Tour to recruit, gave credence in the eyes of many to the charges of arbitrary rule that had long been leveled against him.

Perhaps his biggest miscalculation, however, was in underestimating the extent to which many of his fellow colonists would be offended by the idea of any cooperation with Roman Catholics. His family background probably had something to do with this. His father had continued to meet with and counsel John's cousin William Alabaster when that promising clergyman became one of the most notorious converts to Rome. Adam Winthrop had also maintained cordial relations with leading Catholic families in the Stour Valley, particularly the Mannocks, with whom the Winthrops exchanged seasonal gifts. John thus grew up in a household where Catholicism was seen as a threat, but individual Catholics as men

whom one could deal with.[98] Consequently, faced with a French gentleman who was duly respectful of the Massachusetts authorities, politely attended their religious services, and complimented the drill of their trained
bands, Winthrop focused only on the practical considerations involved in
aiding La Tour and neglected to pay sufficient attention to the religious
dimension.

Winthrop was angered at being publicly challenged by the Essex protestors about a decision already made, but his defense did little to calm
fears. In addition to underestimating the anti-Catholic zeal of many of his
fellow colonists, as a Bostonian he had not taken into account the fears of
those whose proximity to the conflict would make them the first to suffer
the retaliation of d'Aulnay. He might well split hairs in distinguishing between allying openly with La Tour and allowing the Frenchman to recruit
in the Bay, but this ignored the basic concerns of his opponents. Simon
Bradstreet was quick to explain that he had not meant to "cast any dishonor on yourself" in signing the Essex protest and hoped to meet with
the governor and discuss matters further, but he was the only one of the
signers known to have apologized, and even Bradstreet remained concerned
about the decision to help La Tour.[99] The clearest indication of how much
this incident hurt Winthrop's standing came in a letter from John Endecott,
who wrote in late July that he found "your troubles are many, and especially about this French business. The Lord in mercy support you. I am
much grieved to hear what I hear." He bemoaned the spread of ill reports
about Winthrop, noting that "the rumors of the country you know they
rise out of ignorance principally, and much out of fears." Though he had
his own doubts about the wisdom of supporting La Tour, he urged his
friend to "be of good comfort. I doubt not but our God that is in heaven
will carry you above the injuries of men. For I know you would not permit
anything, much less act in anything that might tend to the least damage of
this people."[100]

Disapproval of his handling of this episode played into the hands of
Winthrop's opponents and contributed to his being kept out of the governorship in 1644 and 1645. In the end, d'Aulnay defeated La Tour. La Tour
turned pirate, prompting Winthrop to note sardonically in his journal
"whereby it appeared (as the scripture sayeth) that there is no confidence
in an unfaithful or carnal man, though tied with many strong bonds of
courtesy, etc."[101] Negotiations were opened with the victorious d'Aulnay,
who did not in the end seem interested in retaliating against the New Englanders. The story ended somewhat as it had begun. On September 20,
1646, as people were getting ready to go to the afternoon Sabbath services,
a pinnace flying the French flag was seen entering the harbor. It was
d'Aulnay himself, and after services the French were escorted to Winthrop's
house (for Winthrop was again the governor), where they were entertained

with wine and sweetmeats. The next day they officially presented their credentials and negotiations were begun. D'Aulnay initially demanded payments for damage done by the Massachusetts volunteers who had assisted La Tour. D'Aulnay and his officers did not choose to attend puritan services but spent the next Sabbath privately at Winthrop's home, reading "such books [in] Latin and French as he had" in his library and taking "a private walk in his garden." When it was evident that some colonists felt strongly about the flying of a French flag in the harbor, it was taken down from the ship. Finally, on September 28, articles of agreement were concluded. As a token of the peace Winthrop presented d'Aulnay with a large sedan chair that had been ordered by the viceroy of Mexico for his sister, captured by an English privateer in the West Indies, and previously presented by him to Winthrop.[102]

FACED WITH NEW FORMS of foreign challenges to his City on a Hill, Winthrop's touch at the helm of the ship of state had not been perfect. He came to regret being persuaded by La Tour to get involved in the Acadian conflict, though he was pleased with a final settlement that protected the colony's interests. He had shown far better judgment in helping his fellow colonists mobilize to support the cause of their English friends.

17

Under Attack

MAY 1645. The heat was oppressive for the crowd gathered in and around the Boston meetinghouse. Men and women who were unable to find places inside were jostling for position by the door and windows in the hope that they would be able to hear the proceedings within. There was a mix of tension and excitement in the crowd, because of the word that charges were to be brought against the colony's deputy governor, John Winthrop, for abusing his authority and trampling the rights of citizens.

As the court was brought to order the magistrates were sitting at the bench facing the deputies and those freemen opposite the bar who had managed to squeeze into the room. Governor Dudley prepared to open the proceedings, but Winthrop, with a flair for the dramatic, rose from his seat among the magistrates, stepped down from the bench, and crossed to the other side of the bar. As he stood there like a common criminal, many, both on the bench and in the crowd, protested and urged him to return to his place of office. Winthrop responded that "being criminally accused, he might not sit as a judge in that case." Furthermore, if he were upon the bench "it would be a great disadvantage to him, for he could not take that liberty to plead the cause, which he ought to be allowed at the bar."[1]

The trial that followed involved not only charges of abuse of power but also the question of the proper authority of the magistrates. It was one of many incidents in the 1640s in which Winthrop would be called upon to defend his vision of how Massachusetts should be governed and how its people should treat one another.

♋

THE EXPANSION OF NEW ENGLAND that led to the formation of the United Colonies had many implications within the colony of Massachusetts. While it can be argued that some of the residents of the first towns had been jealous of the preeminence of Boston, the formation of new towns and then counties heightened regional jealousies.

Essex County, surrounding Salem, seemed particularly resentful of the influence of Boston at this time, as seen in some of the reactions to Winthrop's decision to aid La Tour. But this was only one way in which the social body of the colony was strained. Some prosperous men of social standing who had come to the Bay in the late 1630s resented the greater status accorded founders such as Winthrop, Dudley, and Endecott, pointing to a gap of sorts between the new gentry and the established gentry. Some towns were themselves divided as settlers from different parts of England failed to come together in a true sense of community. In Hingham, for example, a group of families that emigrated from the English county of Norfolk formed an oligarchy whose influence was not always accepted by townsmen from other English backgrounds.[2] Each of these strains, and others as well, influenced the course of elections and political development in the 1640s. Just as it required great skill for Winthrop to negotiate the waters of foreign relations, it called upon all of his experience to cope with the legal and governmental challenges of the time. In seeking to deal with these, he would apply the lessons of his English experience to attempt to uphold the societal ideals he had set forth in "Christian Charity."

The Standing Council had always been a bone of contention, used by those who felt cheated of their proper share of authority to attack the established leaders as potential tyrants. In May 1642 the issue was raised again when Thomas Dudley brought to the attention of the General Court a manuscript treatise criticizing the council as a sinful innovation. The manuscript had evidently been circulating for well over a year among those who were dissatisfied with the exercise of power by Winthrop and his colleagues. It set forth that in a religiously constituted commonwealth such as Massachusetts there should be no power or office not commanded and ordained by God, that such powers as had been ordained by God and given a particular form through his providential direction (such as the charter) might not be lightly changed, and that God would never approve of any change so long as the commonwealth could be run effectively without it. Having laid a foundation that was sure to appeal to those with theocratic leanings, the author went on to argue that the charter represented God's plan and that the Standing Council deviated from the charter and was thus sinful.[3]

Many members of the court, if not all, knew that the author of the treatise was Richard Saltonstall, the son of Sir Richard Saltonstall, an original member of the Massachusetts Bay Company and one of the founders of Watertown. Sir Richard had left the Bay in 1631 and never returned. Twenty years old when his father departed, the young Richard soon followed him to England, studied briefly at the Inner Temple, and returned to the Bay after 1635, settling in Ipswich. Though regularly chosen one of the assistants, he did not wield the influence that his father had. This was due in part to his location in one of the outlying towns but likely was also due to his age. Winthrop's references to Saltonstall in his journal imply that the older man viewed Saltonstall much as he might a talented nephew. Saltonstall had become associated with others, such as Richard Bellingham, Israel Stoughton, and William Hathorne, who also felt deprived of their proper roles in the colony.

Bellingham, of course, had served as deputy governor twice and been elected governor in 1641, but he had failed to achieve the stature of Winthrop or Dudley and resented that other magistrates were more popular.[4] He was particularly aggrieved by the fact that he had not been elected to the council. His confrontations with Winthrop would be frequent and heated, starting with Bellingham's challenge to Winthrop's authority during the 1639 trial of Nicholas Trerice. The most recent clash had occurred after Bellingham ignored the betrothal of Penelope Pelham to a close friend of his and persuaded her to marry him in November 1641. He compounded his offense by ignoring a court order that marriages had to be announced in advance, then performed the ceremony himself, claiming authority as a magistrate. Legal proceedings had begun at the time when the General Court took up Saltonstall's attack on the Standing Council. In the end, Bellingham rejected Winthrop's argument that he should leave the bench to answer the charges, and the court decided to drop the issue.[5]

Israel Stoughton had assumed that he was ready for leadership when he wrote to his brother in 1635 that as soon as he had been made a freeman he would have been chosen an assistant had there not already been a sufficient number. He had, of course, been engaged in a dispute with Winthrop at that time. Though he had risen to assistant, he was never accepted into the inner circle of leaders.[6] Hathorne was a deputy representing Salem and assumed a leadership role among his fellow representatives, seeking to enlarge their authority and often irritating the magistrates in the process. Saltonstall had discussed his views with Bellingham and Hathorne and very likely with Stoughton and other members of the lesser gentry.

When Dudley brought the treatise to the attention of the court, Winthrop moved to have the contents of the book examined and then for the author to be called to answer for his views. Saltonstall's supporters put it about that if the book was condemned first, the magistrates would seek to deal with Saltonstall the way they had with John Wheelwright. Some even went so far as to suggest that Saltonstall's life might be in danger. They insisted that criticism of the Standing Council was covered by a standing order for freemen to consider and deliver their judgments on the colony's fundamental laws and that Saltonstall therefore should be given immunity from any form of censure before the court took up the nature of his comments. After a few days of debate they got their way.[7] Writing in the aftermath of the dispute, Winthrop protested that he had no problems with Saltonstall—"he hath ever been and is still dear to me, and many friendly affairs have passed between us, both former and later, and so we are like to continue"—and that he personally did not care about the continuation of the council one way or another. In suggesting that the book be dealt with first he was only seeking that things be "done in an orderly way," with the court to have "first determined of the matter in it before they meddled with the author." However, "finding the Court to be bent the contrary way, I drew up an order for his clearing as full and safe for him as himself could have drawn."[8]

The court then agreed to send the book to the clergy for their advice on the issues. That verdict, rendered in October, found that while Saltonstall's principles were sound, his application of them had been faulty, since a council to make decisions between meetings of the court was in fact essential for the security of the commonwealth. The clergy specifically rejected Saltonstall's argument that such a group would invariably be "of dangerous consequence for disunion among the magistrates, or factions among the people." They argued that "all magistrates, by their calling and office, together with the care of judicature, are to consult for the provision, protection, and universal welfare of the commonwealth." Yet a smaller group, such as the Standing Council, distinct from but not superior to the Court of Assistants, was needed for cases of "instant danger." The ministers did suggest, however, that it might include not only some of the assistants but some of the freemen as well.[9]

The debate over the Standing Council was still being agitated when a new cause for dispute between the magistrates and the deputies came to the fore in June 1642. This became a perfect example of how small-town jealousies can have great consequences. Its origins dated back six years, when a stray sow was brought to the merchant Robert Keayne. Cattle and pigs and other livestock were still kept by townsmen, and though there were fencing regulations, it was not uncommon for animals to stray. Keayne had his servants spread news of the sow through the town, and several individuals came to see the sow but found that it wasn't theirs. About a year later Keayne, according to his testimony, killed one of his own sows. Elizabeth Sherman, the wife of merchant Richard Sherman, then came to Keayne's house to see if the sow he had taken in was the one she was missing. After she determined that the sow she was shown had different marks than hers, she charged that the sow Keayne had butchered was actually hers.[10]

Sherman's accusation came at the time when the Boston community was divided over the free-grace controversy and when Keayne himself was being attacked for his business practices, culminating in his being called before both the church and General Court in 1639. Under the circumstances, many of the townsmen were quick to believe the worst of the merchant. Elizabeth Sherman may have been urged on to attack Keayne by George Story, a young London merchant who was boarding with her at this time. Since Robert Sherman was in England, Keayne had brought suspicions about the relationship between Story and Mrs. Sherman to John Winthrop in his capacity as the local magistrate. Nothing came of that presentment, but it clearly heightened the animosity between Keayne and Mrs. Sherman, as well as fueling Story's bitterness toward his fellow merchant. When the charges regarding the sow did not die down, the elders of the Boston church intervened, "many witnesses were examined, and Captain Keayne was cleared."[11]

Not satisfied with the church's findings, in 1640 Mrs. Sherman brought her cause before the Suffolk Quarter Court that met at Boston, "where, after a full hearing, Captain Keayne was again cleared, and the jury gave him £3 for his costs." Keayne then brought an action against Story and Mrs. Sherman for spreading the report that he had stolen her sow and was awarded damages by the court.[12] Furious, Story tried to dig up further evidence and got one of Keayne's witnesses to swear before the Salem Quarter Court that he had perjured himself. On that basis Story petitioned the General Court on Mrs. Sherman's behalf, asking them to investigate the case, perhaps counting on the aid of some deputies who were accustomed to boarding with the Shermans during court sessions.

And so the case of Mrs. Sherman's sow came before the General Court of the Colony of Massachusetts Bay in June 1642, where it precipitated a constitutional crisis. After seven days of questioning witnesses and examining the evidence, the court could not agree on a verdict. Two magistrates and fifteen deputies found in favor of Sherman, seven magistrates and eight deputies for Keayne, and the remaining seven deputies remained undecided.[13] The two magistrates who broke with their colleagues were likely Saltonstall and Bellingham.[14] Since in March 1636 it had been agreed that decisions required not a simple majority of all present but a majority of the magistrates and a majority of the deputies, the result was a stalemate.

Given Keayne's general reputation, it had been easy for Mrs. Sherman's partisans to stir up popular support in her favor and to present the failure to find for her as an abuse of magisterial authority. Winthrop noted that the unresolved case "gave occasion to many to speak irreverently of the court, especially of the magistrates, and the report went that their negative voice had hindered the course of justice, and that these magistrates must be put out, that the power of the negative voice might be taken away." Winthrop used his legal expertise to present and evaluate the evidence in the case and concluded that the testimony for Keayne clearly appeared to exonerate him. Nevertheless, he indicated that since there was disagreement the case could have been heard again or dispatched to a committee for review, options opposed by Sherman's supporters. He attested to this summary and had it circulated in order to explain the thinking of the magistrates.[15] In an attempt to heal some of the hard feelings Winthrop tried to get the court to agree to "a declaration in nature of pacification, whereby it might have appeared that, howsoever the members of the court dissented in judgment, yet they were the same in affection, and had a charitable opinion of each other," but this was rejected.[16]

The sow case had reopened the question of whether the approval of a majority of the assistants was necessary for decisions, commonly phrased as whether they had a "negative voice" in the deliberations of the court. Following the adjournment of the court, Winthrop prepared a manuscript defending the importance of that practice, and in the fall he presented his arguments to the meeting of the clergy who were debating the matter of the Standing Council. He argued that nothing could be "more dishonorable and dangerous to our state" than to remove that authority from the Court of Assistants. The charter placed governing power in the governor and assistants, and to change that would be to "erect a new frame of government upon a new foundation." In essence, Winthrop sought to use the charter to defend the authority of the assistants, just as his opponents in the 1630s had appealed to the charter to expand the roles of the freemen and their deputies. As for fears of the negative voice expressed by some, he answered that the possibility of the assistants making mistakes or committing injustices was no greater than the chance of error on the part of the General Court voting as a single entity. In fact, under the existing system there was a check of sorts in that the deputies could suggest to the magistrates that they were wrong, giving them a chance to correct their mistakes. And, if they still did not heed that advice, at the next election those magistrates "may be turned out and better put in their places."[17]

Richard Bellingham, for one, rejected these arguments, prompting Winthrop to expand his points further in a manuscript "Reply to the Answer Made to the Discourse About the Negative Voice."[18] In this reply Winthrop first quoted directly from the charter and examined the document to support his argument that the consent of seven magistrates was necessary for the passage of any law or order. He supported his interpretation of the language in the charter by referring to the operation of similar provisos used in England in "commissions or patents where a negative voice is granted" to a portion of a larger body. Thus, for example, in Commissions of Oyer and Terminer, though "there be usually above twenty joined with the judges of Assize, . . . yet they all can do nothing in the Court without the judges' consent." And, "so it is in the Commissions of the Peace, where, upon twenty years' experience, I never knew any cause carried by vote against such as were of the quorum."[19] Yet, having made this point, he also clarified his use of English precedent in an important way. He rejected Bellingham's use of an English statute from the reign of Henry VIII to argue against the negative voice on two grounds. On the one hand, the statute in question was inapplicable to courts in corporations and to parliaments (with regard to which Winthrop cited a recent argument in England by William Prynne). He then went on to state that "besides, the statutes of England do not bind in any other parts of that kingdom," so that even if Bellingham was correct in his understanding of the meaning of the particular law for England, the statute was not applicable to the colonies. Here, and throughout his career as Massachusetts governor, Winthrop was trying to replicate the forms of English life that made up the ancient constitution while at the same time maintaining that New England was a parallel but not subordinate form of England itself.

Having established to his satisfaction that the negative voice was required by the charter, Winthrop then spelled out why he believed it was fundamental to the forms of Massachusetts government. The separate authority of the magistrates made the Bay's government a desirable mixture of aristocracy and democracy, whereas "if the negative voice was taken away, our government would be a mere democracy," something the overwhelming majority of colonists would have instinctively rejected. To change to such a form would have had no warrant in Scripture, a point he makes without elaborating on it, and furthermore would lead to the colonists abasing themselves and depriving themselves of the dignity "which the providence of God hath put upon us." "A democracy," he explained, "is, among most civil nations, accounted the meanest and worst of all forms of government," branded by most political writers with epithets such as "monster," and "histories do record that it hath been always of least continuance and fullest troubles."

After addressing the legality of the negative voice, Winthrop proceeded to explain what he saw as the proper place and role of the freemen and deputies. The deputies, as perceived by Winthrop, "have the same place and power which the freemen assembled in General Court ought to have. . . . These, joined with the magistrates in any General Court, have (together with them) all the power legislative, and the chief power judicial of this body politic." Neither the magistrates nor the deputies had any power in the General Court without the consent of the other. In essence, the magistrates and deputies exerted a check on each other.

While Winthrop's defense was enough to blunt any effort to overthrow the negative voice at the time, he provided fodder for Bellingham and others who wished to depict him as a potential tyrant by pointing to Winthrop's statement that the colony would "incur scandal by undervaluing the gifts of God, as wisdom, learning, etc., and the ordinances of magistracy, if the judgment and authority of any one of the common rank of people should have equal weight with that of the wisest and chiefest magistrate." Bellingham had pounced on this elitist passage and called it scandalous. Winthrop spent considerable effort in his answer explaining that this had not been meant the way it sounded, that he had "intended . . . not

to extol the gifts of the magistrates, nor to debase those of the deputies."
He acknowledged that it was his "duty to honor the gifts of God wherever
I find them" and expressed his "hope [that] my ordinary practice hath not
been different." Yet despite the efforts of Bellingham to use this against
him, most colonists had learned to trust Winthrop. Francis Williams in
Portsmouth was probably voicing a common sentiment when he claimed
that Winthrop was a man of such "known worth and inward candor" that
neither "frown nor flattery could ever force" him from pursuing "the general good. . . . Your constant zeal for the things of God and man may truly
entitle you to be the Father and first founder of this flourishing colony,
and will have the happiness to leave behind you a lasting memory."[20]

Distracted for a time by the issue of the negative voice, the General
Court returned to the case of the missing sow in the summer of 1643. Sherman's supporters had prepared a very partial digest of the case which they
presented to the clergy, and some of the ministers wavered from their earlier support of Keayne (who had, after all, been found innocent of any
wrongdoing by the Boston church). Confused by this, the clergy met with
the magistrates and some of the deputies and declared that "notwithstanding their former opinions, yet, upon examination of all the testimonies, . . .
they did not see any ground for the court to proceed further with the case,
and therefore earnestly desired the court might never more be troubled by
it." According to Winthrop, all agreed to this "except Mr. Bellingham,
who still maintained his former position and would have the magistrates
lay down their negative voice, and so the cause to be heard again." The
clergy "labored also to make a perfect reconciliation" between Winthrop
and Bellingham, but while Winthrop was ready to cooperate, Bellingham
spurned the idea. Nonetheless, there appeared to be a chance to make the
Keayne-Sherman dispute go away. Since the deputies present had agreed
to abandon the case, the clergy went home to work on local deputies who
had not been party to the meeting.

When the General Court next convened, Winthrop apologized for
certain expressions in his manuscript summary of the sow case that he had
been told had offended some of the deputies. Maintaining that the substance of his presentation of the case had been accurate, he explained that
when he wrote it he was laboring under "great provocation by some of the
adverse party," but "that was no sufficient warrant for me to break out into
any distemper." He might, he acknowledged, "have obtained the cause I
had in hand without casting such blemish upon others as I did." Although
he had been led astray by "the pride of mine own spirit," the Lord had led
him to see his errors, "wherein I acknowledge my failings, and humbly
entreat you will pardon and pass them by. If you please to accept my request, your silence shall be sufficient testimony thereof, and I hope I shall
be more wise and watchful hereafter."[21] Characteristically, he was willing

to humble himself to advance the public peace. With Winthrop's apology and the behind-the-scenes efforts of the clergy, the Keayne case effectively came to an end. In the process the controversy over the negative voice was temporarily stilled. Secured in that right, in March 1644 the magistrates agreed to a proposal for the physical separation of the assistants and deputies into two legislative houses, each meeting in a separate chamber during sessions of the court.[22]

When the court of elections met in May 1644, John Endecott was chosen governor, with Winthrop deputy governor. Some who voted for Endecott undoubtedly feared that a creeping tyranny might evolve if the same person was always entrusted with power, as Ezekiel Rogers had warned in the previous year's election-day sermon. The defeat of those who had fought to dismantle the Standing Council and abolish the negative voice provided them with grievances against Winthrop. Unable to secure the election of Bellingham, they saw Endecott as a compromise. But perhaps the most potent factor was the growing concern among many colonists that Boston and its leaders had lost touch with the needs of the other towns. Endecott, still residing in Salem, was an established leader and friend of Winthrop without being a Bostonian. Evidence that this was a major factor in the vote can be found in the effort following the election to shift the center of government. A caucus of Essex County deputies met in Salem before the following General Court and proposed to hold the next court of elections at Salem and to shift the colony's military supplies to that location. But the magistrates rejected both proposals and, in a conference between the two houses, persuaded deputies from the other counties that this was simply an effort to advance the local interests of Essex County and Salem itself.[23]

At the same session the deputies proposed the election of a new commission comprised of seven magistrates, three deputies, and Nathaniel Ward to administer all government between sessions of the General Court, in essence superseding both the Court of Assistants and the Standing Council. The magistrates rejected this as well, arguing that it changed the nature of the colony's government as established by the charter, and in so doing would actually curtail the liberties of the freemen. This brought about another conference. In arguing against the new commission, Winthrop began by pointing out that there was no provision in the charter for such a body appointed by the General Court. But he also stressed that the proposal violated the spirit as well as the letter of the charter. As he had argued only recently, he emphasized that the authority of the assistants was established by the charter, which also required that it be the freemen, by their annual vote, who chose who was to exercise that authority. Similarly, when certain magistrates were chosen to sit on the Standing Council, it was the

freemen who exercised that choice at the annual court of elections. Freemen in their towns chose the deputies who would act on their behalf. Thus,
all who wielded authority in the colony were elected by the freemen. The
proposed commission would deny the freemen that power because it was
to be chosen and instructed by the General Court. Furthermore, since not
all the assistants would serve on the commission, the proposal would deny
power to some of those the freemen had elected. While Winthrop had
been forced over the years to yield to the freemen and their deputies greater
powers than he had thought desirable when he had initially led the migration to the Bay, he had consistently maintained not only a broad interpretation of magisterial authority but also the need for those magistrates to
derive their authority from the direct vote of the freemen.

Led by their speaker, William Hathorne, the deputies answered that
there was precedent for the court acting in this way since they had appointed a similar commission to deal with military affairs at the time of the
Pequot conflict. Winthrop responded that such "examples, which were
against rules or common rights[,] were errors and no precedents." Hathorne
also maintained that "the governor and assistants had no power" between
sessions of the court other than that granted them specifically by the court.
This clearly flew in the face of the colony's brief history, but the deputies
appeared adamant. As the stalemated court prepared to adjourn, John
Endecott stated that should the need arise before the next session the magistrates would respond as they saw necessary. Hathorne declared, "You will
not be obeyed."[24]

The deputies had only just returned to their homes when Endecott
called the court back into session a week later, on June 28. The question of
the magistrates' authority was center stage, and a majority of the assistants
forced the issue by signing a declaration maintaining their authority between court sessions and threatening to publish it. Unsurprisingly, the only
two assistants present who refused to sign the declaration were Bellingham
and Saltonstall. Not wanting the declaration published, the deputies agreed,
without prejudicing their claims, "that the governor and assistants shall
take order for the welfare of the commonwealth in all sudden cases that
may happen in our jurisdiction, until the next session of this court, when
we desire this question may be determined."[25]

Although he was not governor, Winthrop found himself at the center
of the storm, called upon once again to defend his vision of how the Bay
colony should be governed. He prepared a long manuscript entitled "Discourse on Arbitrary Government" for the consideration of his fellow magistrates and the deputies.[26] At the center of this effort was his definition
(though he later called it merely a description) that "arbitrary government
is where a people have men set over them without their choice, or allow-
ance, who have power to govern them and judge their causes without a

rule." On the other hand, "where the people have liberty to admit or reject their governors, and to require the rule by which they should be governed and judged, this is not arbitrary government." The existing forms of government in Massachusetts were not arbitrary, because the rulers were chosen by the people as required by the charter and by the colony's own laws and customary practice. Once again, Winthrop presented his understanding that the charter called for authority to be vested in the governor and assistants, while the liberty of choosing those rulers, offering counsel, and approving laws and taxes was vested in the freemen, acting through their deputies with the assistants. On this occasion he provided a lengthy examination of the wording of the charter. He reminded the colonists that their counterparts in Virginia, Bermuda, and the West Indies were subject to arbitrary rule by companies based in England and that the clause which would have similarly required the Massachusetts Bay Company to be headquartered in London had "with much difficulty" been "abscinded" from their charter, thus allowing the free government that they enjoyed.

Those charging that the magistrates exercised arbitrary power to the detriment of the subjects' liberty had again cited as evidence the discretionary authority of the magistrates in the exercise of justice. Winthrop acknowledged that the colony was in general bound to the rule of God, but he denied that this required, as his opponents asserted, that there be prescribed penalties for all crimes. He pointed out that in the Body of Liberties, which the same men had pushed for, there were at least forty crimes for which no sentence was mandated, and he believed that this was as it should be. Mandatory sentences were inadvisable because "justice ought to render to every man according to his deserving." Judges had to be allowed to consider the circumstances of the crime. What if, for example, the law required that every lie be punished with the same penalty? In that case "a youth of honest conversation, never known to lie before," who, surprised and fearing some dishonor, had told a lie which posed "no danger to any other" would be punished the same as an "old notorious liar" who lied on purpose "for a pernicious end." This, argued Winthrop, was "not just." Furthermore, punishment required what the word implied, that the offender suffer. But if a set fine was established for a particular offense, this would be unjust; "if the same penalty hits a rich man, it pains him not, . . . but if it lights upon a poor man, it breaks his back." God worked through those upon whom he bestowed the gift of justice, and to deny them the chance to exercise those gifts was to offend God. All men were imperfect, and judges could make mistakes, but such errors affected few. The errors of legislators in setting an inappropriate mandatory sentence would affect all.

Winthrop used scriptural grounds for his arguments (and also turned to the writings of Thomas Aquinas, though not explicitly referring to that Catholic theologian). He again drew the colonists' attention to England, where many of them had sat on juries which, as in Massachusetts, were free to assess damages and impose fines as they saw fit. While England had statutes that specified penalties for offenders, the common law allowed judicial discretion, and, he asserted, it was "the Common Laws of England which are the ancient laws and of far more esteem for their wisdom and equity than the statute laws."

A committee of the deputies reviewed the "Discourse" and challenged it, but Winthrop quickly dismissed their objections as being based on a hasty reading. "There is no such sentence in the book" as one they took objection to. Elsewhere, what they quoted "is not truly recited," and on another point, "this is also misrecited." Turning politic again, he told them that "I will not justify every passage in my book," since there were "two or three words that offense has been taken at," and "I must now confess they do not now please me," but the "matter is good and the intention of the writer honest," and "if these be questioned I would stand and fall with them."

Winthrop felt confident in taking a strong stand because he believed that the majority of the non-freemen and many, if not most, of the free-men preferred the system they had to the more rigid one being proposed. They would rather have Winthrop's discretion than the rule of the theo-crats. He was confident that in any public confrontation with Hathorne and Bellingham his arguments and popularity would prevail. That proved to be the case in this instance. In July Endecott called together all the magistrates and many of the clergy and spoke of his concerns about the recent divisions in the court. He blamed the clergy for not adequately sup-porting the colony's leadership and for frequent criticisms of whoever sat in the governor's chair. Over Bellingham and Saltonstall's protests, the ministers agreed to lend their services to reconcile the magistrates and deputies.[27] In the end, the authority of the assistants was upheld, as was the legitimacy of the Standing Council and the need for some discretion in administering justice. The findings were accepted by both houses, "with most deputies . . . now well satisfied concerning the authority of the mag-istrates, etc.," though "some leading men (who had drawn on the rest) were still fixed upon their opinions, so hard it is to draw men (even wise and godly) from the love of the fruit of their own inventions."[28]

IN THE SPRING OF 1645 YET ANOTHER CONTROVERSY, this time in the town of Hingham, divided the Bay. There the Reverend Peter Hobart was the pastor of the church and exercised an authority that was more suited to presbyterian than congregational practice. His nephew Joshua Hobart was frequently returned to the General Court as one of the town's deputies. The Hobarts, the town's dominant family, and most of the other leading men of the town came from the country of Norfolk, forming a clique that controlled most offices. Outside the Hobart faction, Anthony Eames, an immigrant from the West Country of England, had arrived in 1636 and was admitted to freemanship in the following year. He commanded the local militia band with the rank of lieutenant, and when it was raised to the status of a company the troops chose him to be their commander and submitted his name to the magistrates. The next time the company assembled, however, an effort was made to replace Eames with one of the Hobarts' close allies, Bozoan Allen.

Though the magistrates had not yet formally approved the selection of Eames, they refused to approve the change. At a meeting of the Standing Council, noting that Eames had served well in the past, they instructed the townsmen to go back to Hingham and await the court's further deliberations, with Eames continuing to drill the militia until then. Bellingham, however, had pulled Eames aside and told him that he should lay down his authority. Either this was overheard, or Bellingham expressed his disagreement with his colleagues to others, for Joshua Hobart soon claimed that those in authority had instructed Eames to resign. Hobart then called a meeting of the trained band without informing Eames. When he arrived, Eames found that the troops were unwilling to obey his commands; some had been persuaded that he had been told to resign, while others asserted that the choice of Allen was a local matter that the magistrates could not override. Yet another election was held by the trained band, and Allen was again installed by the majority, though a third walked off the field along with Eames.

The following Sunday Peter Hobart accused Eames of lying when he denied that the Standing Council had instructed him to resign. One of the parishioners—who later refused to repeat the charge under oath—testified that Winthrop and Dudley had told Eames not to train the company. Hobart called upon Eames to repent and indicated that he was prepared to excommunicate him, though the pastor was prevailed upon to delay that judgment. Eames appealed his case to the magistrates; when it became evident that Hobart would proceed to the sentence of excommunication, Eames and a dozen of his friends withdrew from fellowship with the congregation. Sitting as a petit court, the magistrates Winthrop, Endecott, William Hibbins, and Increase Nowell summoned to Boston some of those felt to be behind the ouster of Eames, including Joshua Hobart and his brothers Thomas and Edmund. Peter Hobart accompanied them and ranted at the magistrates for sending for his brothers as if they were criminals. He was "so provoking, as some of the magistrates told him that were it not for respect to his ministry they would commit him" to prison. The Hinghamites were then questioned and bound over to the next Court of Assistants. The magistrates summoned five individuals who had testified in the Hingham church that the Standing Council had supported Allen's position. Instead of coming before the magistrates at the petit court sessions, these men

approached Winthrop in his home, demanding the reasons for their sum-
mons and refusing to post bond for their appearance before the Court of
Assistants. Winthrop "labored to let them see their error" in refusing to
post bond "and gave them time to consider of it," but they continued to
defy his authority. About two weeks later, noticing two of them in the
court on other business, he had them arrested and committed to the prison.[29]

The General Court met in May 1645, following the colony election at
which Thomas Dudley was elected governor and Winthrop deputy governor, and before the next meeting of the Court of Assistants before which
the Hinghamites were to appear. Joshua Hobart and Bozoan Allen,
Hingham's deputies, presented a petition signed by eighty-one townsmen,
demanding that the court investigate the reasons for which some of them
had been bound over and others imprisoned.[30] The deputies quickly agreed,
and the magistrates indicated that they would listen to the complaint if the
petitioners would identify the magistrates against whom they were making
a complaint. Hobart and Allen, acting as agents for the larger group, singled
out Winthrop and proceeded to make the case against him. They claimed
that the magistrates had interfered with their liberty in choosing a militia
captain and that those summoned before the Court of Assistants were being persecuted for having questioned the authority of the magistrates and
raising questions about Eames in a church meeting. To allow the magistrates to get away with this was to deprive the Hinghamites of their rights
as freeborn Englishmen. In essence they were reopening the charge that
the magistrates—and Winthrop in particular—acted in arbitrary and ty-
rannical fashion, while also asserting local rights against the intervention
of the Standing Council. They may very well have been advised in their
course by William Vassall, who had been one of the original assistants of
the Bay, had returned to England for a time, and was living near Hingham
in the Plymouth colony, where he was working to undermine the established order of both that colony and Massachusetts.[31] Edward Winslow,
Winthrop's friend and sometimes Massachusetts agent to England, wrote
that during the prosecution of the Hingham case Vassall took a room in
Boston, where the Hingham leaders "had recourse to him many days, yea
many times a day for advice, and followed it to the utmost."[32]

And so John Winthrop found himself standing in front of the bar for a
trial that would determine not only his future but also the direction in
which the government of the colony would develop. Of course, the petitioners had overreached themselves by singling out Winthrop for criminal
charges, and he had trumped them by assuming the mantle of an ordinary
defendant. The fact that he was willing to submit to the law, whereas a few
years earlier Richard Bellingham, one of his strongest critics, had refused
to leave the bench to answer charges that his marriage had violated court
orders, could not have been lost on anyone present.

Allen and Hobart presented their case, accusing Winthrop of having acted illegally in binding the Hingham leaders over for trial and for ordering the imprisonment of the townsmen who refused to post bond. There was a question as to why the other magistrates of the petit court, who had acted along with Winthrop in questioning the Hinghamites and binding them over, were not charged. Winthrop turned this to his advantage, asserting that "he accounted it no disgrace, but rather an honor put upon him to be so singled out from his brethren in the defense of a cause so just." He reviewed the reasons why he could have called for the case to simply be dismissed—"there is nothing laid to his charge that is either criminal or unjust," judges were not criminally liable in England or Massachusetts for mistakes (even assuming one had been made in this case), and it was improper to single out one member of a court for what all had agreed on—but he preferred to address the complaints. He then reviewed the events and called witnesses to support the view that there had been a serious rift in the Hingham community and that complaints made to the magistrates had to be examined. Everything that was done, including binding individuals over to appear in court, was "according to the equity of laws here established and the customs and laws of England, and our constant practice here these fifteen years." Two days were spent in presenting arguments and examining witnesses, the process being compromised by the prejudices of those who opposed Winthrop and those who supported him. As Winthrop perceived the division, "two of the magistrates and many of the deputies were of the opinion that the magistrates exercised too much power, and that the people's liberty was thereby in danger; and the other deputies (being about half) and all the rest of the magistrates were of a different judgment, that authority was overmuch slighted, which if not timely remedied would endanger the commonwealth and bring us to a mere democracy." Each side tried to force the evidence to support its own view. When the pleadings were finished, a committee of both houses drew up a summary of the salient points, and each house entered into its own deliberations.[33]

The deputies proved no more willing to find Winthrop guilty than the magistrates, but negotiations between the two houses dragged on through June and into July as they sought to agree on how the Hinghamites should be dealt with. Finally, on July 3, "after the lecture, the magistrates and deputies took their places in the meeting house, and the people being come togther, and the Deputy Governor placing himself within the bar, as at the time of the hearing, the Governor read the sentence of the Court, without speaking any more, for the deputies (by importunity) obtained a promise of silence from the magistrates."[34] In a solemn voice Thomas Dudley announced that "the General Court, having very largely heard and debated a complaint brought against John Winthrop, Esquire, Deputy Governor, by certain persons of Hingham, do judge that the Deputy Governor is legally acquitted of those things that have been complained of, or laid to his charge, and have therefore, and for their other offenses, punished the said complainants by several fines to be paid to the country."[35] Winthrop was invited to resume his place on the bench.

Before the court concluded its business, Winthrop rose again and requested permission to speak. What followed was one of his most significant speeches. He began by expressing his thanks that the "troublesome business" had come to an end. "I was publicly charged," he said, "and I am publicly and legally acquitted, which is all I did expect or desire." Yet to have been "criminally charged in this Court is [a] matter of humiliation," and he hoped to learn from it. But perhaps others could learn as well, and though he was unwilling to keep those assembled from their affairs, he hoped that he might be able to "inform and rectify the judgments of some of the people, and . . . prevent such distempers as have arisen among us." The colony was still struggling to define the authority of the magistrates and the liberties of the people, and Winthrop wished to once again address these issues.

The magistrates had been called to office by the people, and "being called by you, we have our authority from God." In making the choice the freemen were picking men like themselves, "men subject to like passions as you are. Therefore, when you see infirmities in us you should reflect upon your own, and that would make you bear the more with us, and not be severe censurers of the failings of your magistrates." The freemen should insist that magistrates do their best to advance the commonwealth, and it was that effort that magistrates should be judged on. If magistrates were unfaithful to that trust they could be censured or replaced at the next election, but if they exercised their best efforts they were to be obeyed and respected.

As to the liberties of the people, Winthrop asserted that there were two liberties that needed to be distinguished. The first was natural liberty, which men shared with beasts and other creatures. This was a liberty to do whatever a person wanted, "a liberty to evil as to good," and the "exercise and maintaining of this liberty makes men grow more evil, and in time to be worse than brute beasts." The other kind of liberty Winthrop called "civil or federal" and said it might also be called "moral." Maintaining this "liberty is the proper end and object of authority, and cannot subsist without it, and it is liberty to that only which is good, just, and honest." It is "maintained and exercised in a way of subjection to authority," just as those who have accepted the rule of Christ say that God has made them free. Years before, in his "Christian Charity," Winthrop had warned that if the colonists "embrace this present world and prosecute our carnal intentions, seeking great things for our selves and our posterity, the Lord will surely break out in wrath against us, be revenged of such a perjured people, and make us know the price of the breach of such a Covenant." "Even so brethren," he now concluded, "it will be between you and your magistrates. If you stand for your natural corrupt liberties and will do what is good in your own eyes, you will not endure the weight of authority, but will murmur, and oppose, and be always striving to shake off that yoke" of godly authority. "But if you will be satisfied to enjoy such civil and lawful liberties as Christ allows you, then you will quietly and cheerfully submit unto that authority which is set over you, in all the administrations of it, for your good." With that he sat down, and the court adjourned.

AT THE MAY 1646 COURT OF ELECTIONS John Winthrop was returned to the governor's office, with Thomas Dudley as deputy. The General Court session that followed lasted three weeks, and Winthrop was pleased to record that everything "was carried on with much peace and good correspondency" and that near the end of the session the magistrates and deputies met together and "departed in much love." But shortly before the adjournment Robert Child, Thomas Fowle, Samuel Maverick, and other freemen submitted to the deputies a "Remonstrance and Humble Petition" calling for fundamental changes in the colony. Behind the petition Winthrop recognized the hand of Samuel Vassall, "a man of a busy and factious spirit, and always opposite to the civil governments of this country."[36] Presenting their demands at the end of the session, the petitioners could hardly have expected them to be acted on, and in fact the deputies postponed consideration of the petition till their next meeting.

The petition began by referring to recent troubles which had afflicted Massachusetts, alluding to the effects of the slumping economy and an outbreak of syphilis in Boston, and arguing that these were afflictions sent by God for the colony's practices. The colonists were being punished because the settlers' traditional rights as Englishmen were being violated. They were being punished because there was no comprehensive body of laws for the colony. They were being punished because arbitrary judges were guilty of illegal commitments, unjust imprisonments (both clearly referring to Winthrop's actions in the Hingham case), and similar abuses of authority. They were being punished because of the negative voice exercised by the magistrates. They were being punished because many thousands were debarred from officeholding and could not vote for those who did govern them. They were being punished because godly New Englanders who were members of the Church of England and supported the recent reformation in their native land were nonetheless denied full membership and receipt of the sacraments. The petitioners called for sweeping reforms of the colony's system, including adopting a presbyterian-style parish system in which all inhabitants would be church members, the consequent extension of freemanship to virtually all adult males, the restriction of magisterial authority, and the publication of a law code. If these changes were implemented God would restore his blessings to New England. If the General Court failed to make these reforms, the petitioners would appeal to the English Parliament.[37]

Winthrop and his colleagues were surprised by the identity of the principal organizers of the petition. Vassall, whose hand Winthrop saw in it, had previously demanded that the Plymouth colony adopt religious toleration. He was not, however, a freeman of the Bay and thus could not sign the document. Robert Child, the man who became most closely identified with the petition, was a good friend of John Winthrop Jr., with whom he shared various alchemical and scientific interests. The two had corresponded frequently and joined together in business ventures. He was a doctor of medicine with degrees from both Cambridge and the University of Padua. Child had been in Massachusetts between 1638 and 1641 and had seemed to accept the New England way. Returning in 1645, he may have been interested in introducing some of the reforms he had witnessed and ideas he had read about in England.

Another petitioner, Thomas Fowle, was a Boston merchant who was well known to Winthrop. He evidently had little objection to the colony's congregational church system but had earlier signed the petition to relax the laws against strangers and Anabaptists. If Fowle was an unexpected critic, Samuel Maverick certainly was not. He had lived in Boston since before the puritan colonization and had been admitted a freeman before church membership qualifications were established. A persistent troubler of the godly commonwealth, he had been fined for sheltering accused adulterers who had escaped from prison, appalled his neighbors by seeking to force his black slaves to breed, and constantly found fault with the established authorities.

Less is known of the other petitioners. Thomas Burton was a lawyer who had settled in Hingham in the late 1630s. Some believed that he had been persuaded by others to sign the petition by playing upon his dissatisfaction with the recent treatment of his fellow townsmen. John Smith lived in Boston but was not a resident and thus technically should not have been allowed to petition the court. David Yale was a Welshman who had migrated with John Davenport, settled in New Haven, and then relocated in Boston in 1641. His mother was harshly dealt with by the New Haven church in 1644 for suspected Anabaptist beliefs, and this likely influenced Yale toward toleration. The last signer was John Dand, an elderly Boston grocer whom the authorities dismissed because of advanced age and infirmities.[38]

Winthrop hoped to avoid a confrontation. With the exception of Maverick, the signers were for the most part men he knew and respected. He himself had hoped to repeal the laws against strangers and Anabaptists and had supported a measure introduced into the court prior to the petition which would have allowed non-freemen equal power with freemen in town affairs and allowed some extension of the right to vote for magistrates. As he later explained to his son John, he "thought we should only have declared our apprehensions concerning the petition without questioning the petitioners."[39] But the recess of the court, which its supporters may have hoped would allow popular support for their petition to mobilize, actually worked against them. The clergy for the most part used the summer to attack the petitioners and their proposals, and various magistrates and deputies likewise lobbied the public against the petition and its signers.

When the General Court convened in November, any hopes that Winthrop had to deal with the petition unofficially were quickly dashed. The deputies brought the petition to the floor and called upon Fowle and the other signers to post bond to answer to their conduct. Whether or not the petitioners initially believed that the General Court would make some of the reforms, it was soon clear that there was no chance of such a victory, so the signers announced that they would petition the English Parliament for redress of their grievances. The Bay authorities had recently received the Warwick Commission's safe-conduct for the Gortonists and clearly took the petitioners' intent seriously. They called a secret meeting with the ministers to discuss strategies. Before they began someone complained that Peter Hobart, who was in attendance, had himself had a hand in the drafting of the petition. Hobart claimed to know nothing about the petition—this was hardly credible—and Winthrop suggested that since the Hingham clergyman "had so much opposed authority and offered such contempt for it " it would be appropriate if he withdrew from the deliberations. Winthrop made the reasons for removing him clear when, following Hobart's departure, he spoke to the court and clergy about "a great miscarriage, in that our secretest counsels were presently known abroad, which could not be but by some among ourselves, and desired them to look at it as a matter of great unfaithfulness." He urged that the "present consultations might be kept in the breast of the Court, and not divulged abroad as others had been."[40]

The court determined to send an able man to England to represent their concerns to the Warwick Commission before any appeal from the colony could reach that body or the Parliament. Before discussing the instructions to be drawn up for the agent, Winthrop undertook to review the colony's relationship to the mother country. All were agreed that the charter was the foundation of the colony's government, but there was disagreement over the nature of the Bay's ties to England. Some "thought that we were so subordinate to Parliament as they might countermand our orders and judgments" and suggested that the colony's agent should petition the

ERRAND

Parliament for an enlargement of powers. Others, Winthrop included, accepted that the colonists owed allegiance to England, citing the facts that "our commonwealth was founded upon the power of that state," that they had received their tenure to the land from the king, that they "depended upon them for protection" as well as for advice and counsel when the colonists sought it; they considered themselves Englishmen. However, they believed that by virtue of its charter the Massachusetts government "had absolute power of government, for thereby we have power to make laws, to erect all sorts of magistracy, to correct, punish, pardon, govern and rule the people absolutely." Winthrop drew an analogy to the medieval states such as Normandy and Gascony; these paid homage to the king of France as well as to the English king, but "in point of government they were not dependent on France." Consequently, there could be no legitimate appeal by colonists beyond the General Court.

Winthrop argued that the colonists should rest upon the rights granted them by the charter rather than, as some wished, seek any clarification of their authority from Parliament. Pointing to a charter that Parliament had recently bestowed upon Roger Williams for the organization of the Narragansett Bay settlements into the colony of Rhode Island, he noted that the grant specifically reserved supreme power over all things to Parliament. Such a grant to the Bay would reduce the authority they already had. The clergy addressed the court and in essence agreed with the positions set forth by Winthrop, though suggesting that if the agent sent found the earl of Warwick and his fellow commissioners amenable, he should seek a mere confirmation from the commission of the colony's existing charter rights.

Next the court turned to the question of whom to send on the mission. One of the clergy suggested that Winthrop himself be dispatched, along with the Reverend John Norton, and the consensus seemed to favor the proposal. Winthrop indicated in his journal that he "was very averse to a voyage into England, yet he declared himself ready to accept the service if he should be called to it, though he were then fifty-nine years of age wanting one month." It is not clear whether he shared his reluctance, but the court soon reconsidered, fearing that "if he were there he might be called into the Parliament and so detained" or that his departure might prompt others to leave the Bay; there was also concern about "what changes his absence might produce." It was decided to send Edward Winslow instead. Winthrop "was very glad when he saw the mind of the Lord to be otherwise."

In its open session the court then proceeded against the petitioners, charging them "with divers false and scandalous passages in a certain paper, entitled a remonstrance and petition, . . . against the churches of Christ and the civil government here established, derogating from the honor and authority of the same, and tending to sedition," citing twelve particulars.[41]

The response of the petitioners did not win them any support, since they labeled the colony "an ill compacted vessel" while continuing to maintain their criticisms of it.[42] The court rejected their petition and levied fines on them, with Saltonstall, Simon Bradstreet, Bellingham, and five deputies (including Bozoan Allen and Joshua Hobart) dissenting. When Child prepared to sail for England, the magistrates ordered a search of his papers and of the study of one of the lesser petitioners, John Dand. When the officers entered that study they found another petitioner, John Smith, gathering papers, which they seized. Among the papers found were petitions to Parliament seeking the imposition on the colonies of the presbyterian system recently approved in England, the extension of all English laws to New England, the appointment of a governor-general for the colonies, and similar provocative proposals. Child was brought before Winthrop and the council, which decided to hold him until the ships sailed, thus ensuring that no appeal to Parliament would be made until Winslow had reached England and lobbied the colony's friends there.[43] In March 1647 he was still under guard, though as he wrote to Winthrop Jr., "your father (I thank him)" had seen to it that he was lodged comfortably in a private house rather than in the prison. He expected to be there till the General Court or the Parliament ordered his release.[44] The final resolution of his case, and of the affair in general, awaited decisions being made in England.

Winthrop had disapproved of the confrontational stance toward the petitioners taken by the deputies and most of the clergy. Of course, it was not unusual for him to strive for moderation and conciliation while others tried to draw sharp lines and prosecute those on the other side. During the first half of the decade of the 1640s Winthrop had faced numerous challenges to his vision of how Massachusetts should be governed, and in each case he had triumphed. Now he waited to see if Parliament would sustain his accomplishment or overthrow all that he had accomplished.

18

Last Years

MAY 1647. Edward Winslow had done his work well, and a new letter had been received from the Warwick Commission, granting the colonial authorities the virtual autonomy they had sought. Having learned from Winslow that the Child petitioners were prepared to follow Gorton's example in appealing to Parliament, the commissioners wrote that they "thought it necessary (for preventing further inconveniences of this kind) hereby to declare that we intended not thereby to encourage any appeals from your justice, nor to restrain the bounds of your jurisdiction to a narrower compass than is held forth by your letters patent, but to leave you all that freedom and latitude that may in any respect be duly claimed by you, knowing that the limiting of you in that kind may be very prejudicial (if not destructive) to the government and public peace of the colony."[1]

The day after receiving this welcome news, the court of elections met, and though the supporters of the "Remonstrance" tried to get someone sympathetic to their cause elected governor, "the mind of the country appeared clearly, for the old governor was chosen again with two or three hundred votes more than any other."[2] Nearby, in Cambridge, a synod was convening to provide a formal statement of the New England congregational way. Winthrop was riding a wave of solidarity, and he could clearly see a bright future opening up for the colony he had labored so hard for.

Then the foundations of his personal life were struck a devastating blow. Margaret, his wife of twenty-nine years, his confidant, and his valentine, took gravely ill. There was no long and lingering death watch such as he had kept with Thomasine. There was no time for the children to gather. John Jr. was in Connecticut, Samuel in the West Indies, Stephen in England. There was not time for Anne, Adam, or Deane to arrive. John, alone of her family, was there to comfort her, joined no doubt by John Wilson and John Cotton. Turning to his journal he entered next to the date of June 14 that "the Governor's wife, daughter of Sir John Tyndal, knight, left this world for a better, being about 56 years of age. A woman of singular virtue, prudence, modesty, and piety, and especially beloved and honored of all the country.["3] For the third time in his life John accompanied a wife to the grave. There were no funeral services in puritan New England, no sermons preached over the body of the deceased, no consecrated cemeteries, and no marble tombs to mark one's last resting place. Margaret was carried to the burial ground below the three hills, where so many of her neighbors had gone before. Friends joined the sad procession and extended their condolences to John, who was comforted only by his confidence that she had truly gone to a better world.

CB

*T*HE LAST YEARS of John Winthrop's life were bittersweet. There were no major new threats to his City on a Hill, and he was able to preside over the consolidation of the civil and religious order. Relations with England were stronger than ever. Trade with Barbados and the West Indies was beginning to flourish, offering the prospect of a revival of the region's economy. He was able to take pride in his children, though his daughter, Mary, had died in 1643. John Jr. had established a home in New London and would soon emerge as a major leader in the colony of Connecticut. Stephen, who had returned to England, was making a name for himself in the parliamentary army. Samuel seemed poised to succeed in the Leeward Islands. Richard Vines wrote John of having seen Samuel and noted that "[h]e is a very hopeful gentleman."[4] Adam and Deane had reached maturity, and Adam had married. John himself was reelected governor each year until his death, his reputation being such that it overcame fears of him becoming a tyrant or abusing in any way the authority he wielded.

Yet at the same time, this most loving man found himself alone with his servants in his home. The success of his children had led them to households of their own, some of them in distant lands. Memories of Margaret were brought back when he packed her ring and Bible to send to Stephen, her oldest son. As news of Winthrop's loss spread slowly around the Atlantic world, letters of condolence from family and old friends appeared unexpectedly to reopen the wounds. In September he received a letter from Samuel, writing from the island of St. Kitts, devastated by the news, remembering his mother with warmth until he finished by saying, "Grief cuts me off that I cannot write either what nor as I would."[5] Stephen thanked his father for the gift of his mother's things and wrote that her passing "was very sad tidings to me, and my loss was as much in it as any son's could be in a mother."[6] He was still receiving letters remembering Margaret in the following spring. Herbert Pelham wrote to sympathize on "the loss of your dear yolk fellow, whom the Lord hath taken to himself," and offering the consolation that "though your own and the country's loss therein be very great, yet our comfort is when the streams fail we may go to the fountain."[7]

In December 1647 John sought to fill the gap in his life by marrying again. His bride was Martha Nowell Cotymore, the widow for three years of Thomas Cotymore of Charlestown, and a kinswoman of the colony's longtime treasurer Increase Nowell. With the assistance of Winthrop and Nowell, Martha established a trust whereby half of her deceased husband's estate was put aside for her young son, Thomas Cotymore.[8] Some may have been surprised by the marriage, but at least one old friend wrote that "I do rejoice in the Lord's mercy, grace and favor to you in bestowing on you a meet helper."[9] Though fifty-nine years old, John married for more than simple companionship. From the time he was a teenager, he saw his sexuality as a gift of God and, like most puritans, believed that intercourse was an important element of married life. About a year following their union the couple rejoiced in the birth of a son. Emmanuel Downing and John's son Adam had shared the anxious hours of Martha's confinement with the governor, and from her husband Lucy Downing learned that "much rejoicing there was." Following the delivery the midwives rejoiced "with special good cheer, and sack and claret."[10] On December 17, 1648, John presented the infant to the Boston church to be baptized and given the name Joshua, in memory of his cousin.

John continued to follow events in England with interest. The first civil war had ended in 1646 with the king's surrender to the parliamentary army. The Westminster Assembly of Divines agreed on a statement of faith and doctrine which all New Englanders could approve, and while the Assembly recommended a presbyterian national church, congregational dissenters had forged an alliance with others seeking the independence of individual churches and prevented the successful implementation of presbyterianism. The influence of the New England way in England continued to grow, promoted by Harvard graduates who instituted New England practices in their English churches and fostered by the writings of colonial divines.[11] Negotiations between the king and Parliament collapsed, and Charles I escaped his confinement in 1648, joining with Scottish supporters to challenge Parliament in the Second Civil War. Oliver Cromwell began to emerge as a military genius as he played a key role in the campaigns that quickly led to the defeat and surrender of the king and his allies.

Although some such as his friend William Pynchon looked upon their native land as being in "the saddest posture that ever they were for danger of ruin," Winthrop never expressed such pessimism.[12] He heard promising news of the military exploits of Oliver Cromwell from Thomas Peter,

whose brother Hugh was serving as the general's chaplain.[13] While saddened by the reports of the war, his connections with those fighting in
Parliament and the army probably contributed to his essential hopeful-
ness. His long friendship with the earl of Warwick had continued, and he
looked after some of the peer's interests in the New World.[14] He continued to correspond with Brampton Gurdon and other supporters of the
parliamentary cause. He wrote proudly to his son John that Stephen Winthrop was also campaigning in Wales under Cromwell, who "hath subdued all persons and places that made resistance," and noted that his
brother-in-law Deane Tyndal was a lieutenant colonel serving in one of
the regiments under Thomas Fairfax that had besieged royalist forces in
Colchester.[15] In his last surviving letter, written in early February 1649 to
John Jr., he rejoiced that "the Army hath prospered beyond all expectations in Wales, in Kent, at Colchester, and especially against the Scots
(where your brother Stephen was in the van)." A father's pride was evident
when he went on to note that "Sowlby was taken by a strategem by your
brother (who hath done very good service through the Lord's assistance,
to whom he ascribes all)."[16]

THE FIGHTING IN ENGLAND had given rise not only to an explosion of sectarian heresies but also to a dramatic increase in witchcraft accusations,
trials, and executions, especially in the county of Essex, which John knew
so well. News of these perhaps contributed to the first noted cases of witchcraft in New England.

   The Winthrops were skeptics when it came to witchcraft. John's uncle
John Cotta had written a moderate treatise, *The Triall of Witchcraft* (1616),
which Adam Winthrop had in his library and which John brought to New
England. Another English author of a moderate work on witchcraft, the
Reverend George Gifford, was well known to the Winthrops and other
puritans in the Stour Valley.[17] As a member of the commission of the peace
in Suffolk, John had likely heard charges of witchcraft brought against individuals, but there is no evidence that he was involved in any actual trials.
His influence was likely part of the reason why there were no witchcraft
trials in the Bay until 1648. Likewise, his son John Jr. played a major role
in bringing to a halt a spate of witchcraft trials in Connecticut in the 1650s.[18]
This does not mean that the Winthrops did not believe in the existence of
witches and their ability to use demonic powers to inflict harm on others.
Such beliefs were almost universal at the time. What distinguished moderates such as Cotta, Gifford, and the Winthrops was the care with which
they examined accusations and the standards of evidence they required for
conviction.

   In June 1648 John recorded in his journal that "one Margaret Jones of
Charlestown was indicted and found guilty of witchcraft and hanged for

it." If John was not familiar with her history, his new wife, Martha, as a former resident of Charlestown, would have been. The evidence against Jones included claims that men, women, and children whom she touched with any displeasure were "taken with deafness, or vomiting, or other violent pains or sickness"; that medicines that were normally safe prevented healing when she administered them; that she had preternatural knowledge of future events and private conversations; and that on physical examination she had been found to possess what was believed to be a "witch's teat" on which familiars would suck. After she was charged the General Court ordered that "the same course which hath been taken in England for the discovery of witches, by watching, may also be taken here with the witch now in question, and therefore do order that a strict watch be set about her every night." On two occasions the appointed watchers at the prison claimed to see an unknown child sitting on her lap which, when approached, disappeared. Jones did nothing to dispel suspicions when "her behavior at her trial was very intemperate, lying notoriously, and railing upon the jury and witnesses."[19]

DURING HIS LAST YEARS John continued to pursue his interest in theology, discussing such matters with Thomas Dudley as well as with clerical friends. He approved the calling of the Cambridge synod in 1646, agreeing with those who saw the value in defining the New England way, both as a blueprint for the formation of future churches and as a way of ensuring that Parliament would be less likely to impose a settlement of its own on the colonies. The Boston church was suspicious that such a synod was a violation of congregational principles, and as a member of that church as well as governor he helped to ease those concerns and gain approval for the congregation's clergy to join in the deliberations at Cambridge. Laymen as well as clergy were able to attend, and it is easy to imagine Winthrop sitting in on some of the sessions and then discussing matters of faith and polity with the clergy as they took their meals at Harvard. He might well have been there when the assembly was disrupted on August 15, 1648, as the Reverend John Allen of Dedham was preaching an "excellent sermon." As Allen addressed those who had assembled for the session "there came a snake into the seat where many of the elders sat behind the preacher. It came in the door where the people stood thick upon the stairs. Divers of the elders shifted from it, but Mr. Tompson, one of the elders of Braintree (a man of much faith) trod upon the head of it" and killed it. As always, John saw the hand of providence: "[T]he serpent is the devil, the synod the regeneration of the churches of Christ in New England. The devil had formerly and lately attempted their disturbance and dissolution, but their faith in the seed of the woman overcame him and crushed his head."[20] The deliberations proceeded, and the resulting Cambridge Platform of 1648 endorsed the Westminster Assembly's Confession of Faith but recommended a congregational system of church government and association.[21]

JUST AS THE CAMBRIDGE PLATFORM institutionalized the religious system as it had developed during Winthrop's years as the region's foremost leader, the Laws and Liberties of 1648 codified the colony's civil and criminal procedures. In answering the Remonstrants in 1646 the General Court commissioned Winthrop, Dudley, Bellingham, and Nathaniel Duncan to prepare a declaration in which they sought to demonstrate the conformity of colonial laws with those of England. The result, presented in parallel columns, compared the colony's practice and that of England in such a way as to minimize differences.[22] This gave further impetus to efforts to publish a permanent code that would build on the 1641 Body of Liberties.[23] Though he still had reservations about codification, Winthrop cooperated in the enterprise, exchanging views with his fellow magistrates on the contents, and with John Cotton on the preface to the collection.[24]

IN HIS LAST YEARS, Winthrop also took great satisfaction from John Eliot's efforts to Christianize the Indians. Though this had been one of the stated objectives of the movement to colonize, little had been done to advance it. There was no provision for missionaries in a congregational system that ordained ministers to serve established congregations only. But in September 1646 Roxbury's John Eliot had gone with an interpreter to preach to Indians near Dorchester. Eliot himself worked to master the native language and soon was preaching and catechizing. The General Court agreed to provide land for Indians who converted and wished to live among the English, as well as funds for ministers to carry on this effort. Winthrop recorded some of the early developments with interest and approval.[25]

JOHN'S HEALTH DETERIORATED in the summer of 1648, but though he had "been ill of a fever these six weeks," he wrote to his son John at the end of September that "yet (I praise God) I have been able to go abroad every day." He was more concerned with his son Adam, whose wife had died on Governor's Island a short time before.[26] John had been seriously ill, thought to be near death, in 1628. Ten years later, in 1638, on the night following the court of elections that had chosen him governor, "he was taken with a sharp fever, which brought him near death," though "many prayers were put up to the Lord for him, and he was restored after one month."[27] He hoped for the same good fortune again in 1648. Ignoring his health, he traveled to attend a court at Ipswich because other magistrates were unavailable. In December he brought his son Joshua to be baptized, but his health was clearly failing. In February he wrote his last surviving letter, to John Jr., expressing his pride at Stephen's successes in England.[28] On March 1 his old friend and ally John Endecott wrote to Winthrop expressing concerns for his health. While Endecott hoped that the Lord would grant John a recovery, he evoked Winthrop's famous words in "Christian Charity" in urging that they "labor to love one another and harbor the best thoughts one of another. We have not long to live in this life, yet we shall here remain as long as our appointed times are set."[29]

John did not improve, and on March 14 Adam Winthrop wrote to his brother John in Connecticut that their father was

> very ill, and has been so about a month. He hath kept his bed almost all the time. He hath still upon him a feverish distemper and a cough, and is brought very low, weaker than I ever knew him. The Lord only knows the event. We should be very glad if you could be here. My father, not being able to write himself, desired me to remember his love to you, my sister, and the children.[30]

Addressing the Boston church, John Cotton called for the congregation's prayers for Winthrop, referring to him as a governor "who has been to us as a friend in his counsel for all things, an help for our bodies by physic, for our estates by law, and of whom there was no fear of his becoming an enemy, like the friends of David." He was, Cotton continued, "a governor who has been unto us as a brother, not usurping authority over the church, often speaking his advice . . . often contradicted, even by young men and some of low degree, yet not replying, but offering satisfaction also when any supposed offenses have arisen." He had also "been unto us as a mother, parent-like distributing his goods to brethren and neighbors at his first coming, and gently bearing our infirmities without taking notice of them."[31]

Cotton and Wilson prayed with him, friends visited him, Bostonians and people throughout the Bay prayed for him. Winthrop turned his thoughts to God and how he might "be found faithful when [he] was called for." Although Thomas Dudley came and urged him to sign an order for the banishment of someone judged to be a heretic, "he refused, saying that 'he had done too much of that work already.'"[32] On the twenty-sixth of March he passed away. While there is no evidentiary basis for Nathaniel Hawthorne's statement in *The Scarlet Letter* that men saw portents in the sky that they interpreted to mean that their beloved governor had become an angel, it is not unlikely that such tales were told and handed down to the nineteenth-century descendant of Winthrop's old foe William Hathorne.

In the parlor of Winthrop's house his son Adam, John Wilson, John Cotton, and others consulted and decided to wait until April 3 for the funeral so that proper preparations could be made and John Jr. might be there. They sent the fastest Indian messenger they knew to carry their letter to the younger John. A barrel and a half of powder was given to the artillery company for salutes that would "acknowledge Boston's great, worthy, due love and respects to the late honored governor."[33] On the day appointed he was carried to the burial ground and laid beside his beloved Margaret. He had served God and country well. It was finally time to rest.

Epilogue

⟊

Epilogue

THERE IS A BRILLIANT blue high sky over Groton on this June morning, as John Winthrop walks down the hill from Groton to Boxford. He has been a frequent visitor to the region, but this time is special. He has journeyed from his Charleston, South Carolina, home with his wife and youngest son in order to celebrate the life of the most famous John Winthrop on the 350th anniversary of that worthy's death. It is June 26, 1999, and there is a remarkable gathering in this normally sleepy area of the Stour Valley. Under the supervision of Mr. Martin Wood a group of scholars from England and the United States are talking to gathered townsfolk and others interested in local history about John Winthrop and the world he had left when he migrated to America in 1630.[1]

Among those in attendance is the U.S. ambassador to the United Kingdom, the Honorable Phil Lader, who has come from London to mark the event. Following the talks, Winthrop and his wife, Libby, join Ambassador Lader and Ron Partridge, the prosperous local farmer who is the new "lord of Groton Manor," and Ron's wife, Gladys, for a horse-drawn carriage ride to Groton Croft. Land that once belonged to the manor, the croft has been purchased by the community of Groton as a place of recreation and remembrance. There is to be found the "Winthrop Mulberry," a remnant of the trees Adam Winthrop planted in response to the initiative of King James in 1609. On this day the croft is a place for rides and refreshment.

Ↄ

GROTON AND THE NEARBY TOWNS of Boxford and Edwardstone have embraced Winthrop and the American connection that he gives them. There is a warm welcome for the determined tourists who find their way to this sleepy part of Suffolk. Once there, visitors go to Groton's Church of St. Bartholomew and pay their respects at the family tomb, which rests hard against the outer wall, next to the chancel door. In it are buried John's father, Adam, and his mother, Anne. The original marble slab ordered by Lucy Winthrop Downing has been replaced with a more recent cover and inscription. Unmarked, but close by, on his instructions to be buried next to his friend Adam Winthrop, is the resting place of Henry Sandes. John's grandfather Adam, the first Winthrop lord of the manor, and John's wives Mary Forth and Thomasine Clopton are buried under the chancel, a privilege given to the manor lords and their spouses. The monuments marking their graves were taken up when the chancel was raised in Victorian times. The brass memorial that once marked the grave of Adam the clothworker and lord of the manor is now installed on a wall of the church. No markers survive for John's wives.

The visitor to Groton will notice stained glass installed in the nineteenth century through the generosity of the American Winthrop family, as well as a side chapel with the Winthrop arms and the arms of the Commonwealth of Massachusetts. The basic structure of the church is little changed since John Winthrop kept his notes of the sermons of various clergy in the late 1620s. At the apex of a window on the west side of the church, next to the bell tower, is a small stained glass Winthrop coat of arms, perhaps placed there by the Winthrops.

Today's residents of Groton are proud of their town's American connection. Townspeople like Mary Every and Martin Wood (and Jenny Robinson in Boxford, which has its own Winthrop connections) have labored to popularize the Winthrop story. The places where the family lived have been identified, the extent of the manor mapped out. It is not uncommon for the town to celebrate America's birthday with its own Fourth of July celebration. On one recent Independence Day a visitor could have observed townspeople and their guests line dancing to a country-western band on Groton Croft. But local knowledge of the Winthrops is, in historical terms, a relatively recent event.

When Robert C. Winthrop, Speaker of the U.S. House of Representatives and gatherer of the family papers, visited Groton in 1847, memories of the Winthrop family were scant and confused. Seeking to be helpful, locals suggested that a crumbled foundation might have been all that remained of the Winthrops' Groton Hall, unwittingly walking him past the large Georgianized house that was the true Elizabethan Winthrop mansion house. They knew little of the family's story, though some opined that the Winthrops had been regicides who fled England in the 1660s, leaving treasure buried behind. Some thought that the American visitor had come in search of that hoard.[2] Winthrop's history had been lost in England in the centuries following his departure. Now it has been found.

In America, the Winthrop story fared better, but only for a time. While the Paul Revere house in Boston's North End has survived as the only remaining seventeenth-century structure in that city, none of the places that Winthrop lived, worked, or worshiped in were deemed worthy of being preserved against the nineteenth-century march of urban development. So imperfect was the communal recollection of Winthrop that not until 1895 did anyone establish where his first Boston home was located. Indeed, in 1879 there was talk of removing the graves of Winthrop, Cotton, and the other colonists in what had become the King's Chapel Burial Ground in order to make better use of the site.[3]

WHAT ACCOUNTS FOR HISTORICAL REPUTATION? What makes us commemorate John Adams more than his cousin Samuel, or remember Patrick Henry more vividly than his fellow Virginia patriot George Mason? Why are the names of Miles Standish and John Smith more familiar than that of John Winthrop? Though a prominent historian referred to Winthrop as "America's first great man" in the *New York Review of Books* in 1997, and presidents and politicians have long quoted from his "Christian Charity" sermon, for the public at large John Winthrop is the forgotten founding father.[4]

To a large degree this has been the result of changing historical fashion as it has affected the story of the puritan founders of New England. Until the late nineteenth century the public had willingly received the judgments of popular historians—most of them New Englanders—that the puritans and their Pilgrim religious cousins were the true architects of what made America what it was, and Winthrop proudly held his place among the other stalwarts held up for Americans to emulate. The characterization of the puritans evolved over that period. Cotton Mather and his contemporaries depicted them as the new chosen people and Winthrop as the "American Nehemiah" of the new Jerusalem. By the time of the American Revolution the colonists were being refashioned as apostles of liberty rather than of godliness. A generation later, Nathaniel Hawthorne offered in his novels and tales a nuanced puritan view of the puritan past, but most of his contemporaries preferred to extol the settlers as an "iron race" of "uncompromising," "straight-forward" Yankees. By the end of the century this puritan character was seen as the plant which had produced the business and political leaders of Victorian America. Over the course of the century the New England town had come to be identified as the seedbed of American democracy and the Pilgrims' thanksgiving as a symbol of the nation's providential destiny.[5]

Late in the nineteenth century and on into the first part of the twentieth, this all began to change. If most previous writers had praised Winthrop's New England as the source of all that was good in America, a new generation blamed it for all that was bad, making it responsible for prudery, bigotry, and opposition to fun and drink. Charles Francis Adams wrote of the seventeenth-century land of his forebears as a "glacial age" and pointed more effectively than others had to episodes in which the puritans had displayed intolerance. Vernon Louis Parrington had no sympathy for the religion of Winthrop and Cotton and portrayed the New England mind of the colonial period as harsh and reactionary. H. L. Mencken most famously captured this negative attitude toward the puritans when he described them as a people "haunted by the fear that someone, somewhere may be happy."[6]

Celebration of the three hundredth anniversary of the first settlements caught the public imagination in New England. A new *Arbella* sailed into Salem harbor with Frederick Winthrop dressed as his famous ancestor standing proudly on the deck, accompanied by his son, Frederick Jr., attired as the young Deane Winthrop.[7] The commemorations failed to attract national attention, however. Americans in general preferred to hold on to the stereotype of sour, steeple-hatted persecutors that had been popularized by Mencken and others. A new wave of Harvard-based scholars that included Kenneth Murdock, Samuel Eliot Morison, and Perry Miller revolutionized the study of puritanism in the academy. But history was increasingly being written by and for scholars rather than the public, and so these efforts likewise failed to unseat popular stereotypes.

Along with the general displacement of the puritans from the halls of American memory, awareness of the life and career of John Winthrop similarly faded. This was true even within the scholarly community. In the decades since the publication of Edmund Morgan's brilliant short biography of Winthrop, *The Puritan Dilemma* (1958), historians have been more interested in the lives of ordinary people than the role of great men. In the 1960s town studies examined the ordinary patterns of life at the local level. Students of native American life have tapped archaeological findings to help them appreciate New England before the *Mayflower* and the meeting of cultures that followed. Studies of the family, of women, and of childhood have enriched our understanding of the rhythms of everyday life. Books have been written to examine aspects of education, attitudes toward death, and various components of puritan theology. What biographies were written tended to focus on Anne Hutchinson or clergymen such as Roger Williams and Thomas Hooker. Those nonacademics who did pick up books on early New England may have had their preconceptions about the puritans challenged, but they rarely encountered Winthrop, even when the authors relied heavily on his writings.

WHILE IT IS IMPORTANT TO RECOVER the everyday lives of ordinary Americans, it is also important to recognize the role that exceptional men and women can play in directing the course of events. Individuals such as John Adams, Abraham Lincoln, Susan B. Anthony, and Martin Luther King do make a difference. And the case can be made that no one made a greater difference in making New England what it became than John Winthrop. By striving toward what he saw as a radically better world while insisting on moderate and traditional measures to progress toward that goal, he helped to prevent his colony from being blown off course by the winds of extremism and from being wrecked on the rocks of fanaticism. He envisioned a City on a Hill that would inspire others, but his vision was rooted in traditional forms and patterns of the England in which he had been raised. Zealous, but not a zealot, he strove always to include as many as possible in his journey toward a better world, and to teach them to love one another. Perhaps no better tribute can be paid to him than that which came from one of those banished from Massachusetts—Roger Williams's judgment that he was "a counselor of peace."

Certainly John Winthrop was not perfect. No hero is without blemish, and Winthrop's own introspective writings reveal to us his failings. He had made the decision to be active in the world, and he knew that to serve his colony meant that at times he had to forgo the ideal to achieve the possible. He is not as democratic as later times would like, yet when he sought to preserve his authority as a magistrate he did so in order to exercise discretion in ways that helped ordinary colonists. In the process he frustrated those who sought a radically reformed society. In the end, however, most came to acknowledge that it was his vision and determination that had preserved the holy experiment and prevented the type of internecine conflicts that brought about the collapse of the English puritan regime of the 1650s. He was a man of piety who was willing to acknowledge his imperfections. He was also a man of great personal integrity, something always to be prized in leaders. He was humble, attributing to God what successes he achieved and taking the blame for his failures. A man of his times, he did not rise above his times in his views on race, gender, and many other matters.

John Winthrop's most enduring message has proven to lie not in the peculiarly puritan nature of his beliefs but in the inspirational message of his sermon "Christian Charity"—that we "we must love one another with a pure heart, fervently," so that we "delight in each other, mourn together, labor and suffer together." Though our understanding of community has become broader than he could have envisioned, the message has continued to resonate through the centuries. It is this message and Winthrop's qualities that the modern citizens of the Stour Valley see as the meaning of John Winthrop's life and that they identify as the best that America stands for in the modern world. Perhaps that message, and the story of Winthrop's attempt to realize it, will inspire future generations to dream of new worlds just as the tales of Samuel Purchas opened the horizons of the young John Winthrop on the cold winter nights in Rochford Hall in the early years of the seventeenth century.

Notes

Frequently Cited Sources

CA   *Records of the Court of Assistants of the Colony of the Massachusetts Bay, 1630–1692*, comp. John Noble, 3 vols. (1901).

RMB *Records of the Governor and Company of the Massachusetts Bay*, ed. Nathaniel B. Shurtleff, 5 vols. (1853).

WJ   *The Journal of John Winthrop, 1630–1649*, ed. Richard S. Dunn, James Savage, and Laetitia Yeandle (Cambridge: Harvard University Press, 1996).

WP   *Winthrop Papers*, various eds., 6 vols. to date (1928–).

Prologue

1. See Adam Fox, *Oral and Literate Culture in England, 1500–1700* (Oxford: Clarendon Press, 2000), 30.
2. T. W. Davids, *Annals of Evangelical Nonconformity in the County of Essex from the Time of Wycliffe to the Restoration* (London, 1863), 40–41.
3. Charges quoted in Davids, *Annals*, 71. At the time when this volume was in copy-editing Christopher Thompson shared the information, derived from British Library Landsdowne MS 108 f. 46r, that John Forth, whose daughter John Winthrop would marry, was a member of this congregation.
4. A new and anticipated biography of Richard Hakluyt is being prepared by Peter Mancall. A biography of Purchas is much needed.
5. Samuel Purchas, *Purchas His Pilgrimage; or, Relations of the World and the Religions Observed in All Ages and Places discovered, from the creation unto this present* (1617), 907.
6. Purchas, *Pilgrimage*, 915.
7. Purchas, *Pilgrimage*, 920.
8. Purchas, *Pilgrimage*, 921.
9. David Armitage, *The Ideological Origins of the British Empire* (Cambridge: Cambridge University Press, 2000), 83–85.
10. See esp. Stephen Greenblatt, *Renaissance Self-fashioning: From More to Shakespeare* (Chicago: University of Chicago Press, 1980).
11. See Margo Todd, "Puritan Self-fashioning," in Francis J. Bremer, ed., *Puritanism: Transatlantic Perspectives on a Seventeenth-Century Anglo-American Faith* (Boston: Massachusetts Historical Society, 1993), 57–87.

Chapter 1. Lavenham to London

1. Isaac Appleton Jewett, comp., *Memorial of Samuel Appleton with Genealogical Notices of His Descendants* (Boston, 1850), 70.
2. Eamon Duffy, *The Stripping of the Altars: Traditional Religion in England, 1400–1580* (New Haven: Yale University Press, 1992), 302 and passim.
3. D. P. Mortlock, *The Popular Guide to Suffolk Churches: No. 1, West Suffolk* (Bury St. Edmunds: St. Edmundsbury Press, 1988), 132–138, for a description of the church of SS. Peter and Paul, Lavenham.
4. David Cressy, *Birth, Marriage and Death: Ritual, Religion, and the Life-Cycle in Tudor and Stuart England* (Oxford: Oxford University Press, 1997), 150.
5. Cressy, *Birth, Marriage and Death*, 97–232, deals with the rituals of baptism and the disputes over the sacrament between Catholics and Protestants and among English Protestants. There is an excellent evocation of the sacrament at the time when young Adam Winthrop would have been baptized in Peter Ackroyd, *The Life of Thomas More* (London: Chatto and Windus, 1998), 1–3.
6. Ackroyd, *Life of More*, 1.
7. David Dymond and Alec Betterton, *Lavenham: 700 Years of Textile Making* (Woodbridge, Suffolk: Boydell, 1982), 21–22.
8. For the functions of the guilds see Duffy, *Stripping the Altars*, 141–154.
9. The home, with "the largest oriel window of any house in the town," is carefully described in F. Lingard Ranson, *Lavenham, Past and Present* (Suffolk: n.p., 1930), and in Evelyn Hardy, "Three Suffolk Ancestors," *Contemporary Review* (June 1972), 311–312. I would like to thank Alec Betterton for a private communication confirming the local tradition that this was the Winthrop home. In 1991 the then occupants allowed me to inspect the home in the company of Mr. Martin Wood.
10. Dymond and Betterton, *Lavenham*, 79; Mortloke, *Suffolk Churches 1*, 136.
11. Ranson, *Lavenham, Past and Present*, 46.
12. Barbara Hanawalt, *Growing Up in Medieval London* (New York: Oxford University Press, 1993), 139–141.
13. Steven Rappaport, *World Within Worlds: The Structure of Life in Sixteenth-Century London* (Cambridge: Cambridge University Press, 1988), 81–82.
14. Susan Brigden, *New Worlds, Lost Worlds* (London: Allen Lane, 2000), 12, 295.
15. Dymond and Betterton, *Lavenham*, 40–41.
16. John Schofield, *Medieval London Houses* (New Haven: Yale University Press, 1994), 9.
17. Hanawalt, *Growing Up*, 31–32.
18. See Hanawalt, *Growing Up*, chaps. 8 and 9, for insight into the lives of apprentices.
19. Rappaport, *World Within Worlds*, 311–312.
20. Rappaport, *World Within Worlds*, 233–234.
21. Clarence Hopper, ed., *A London Chronicle During the Reigns of Henry VII and Henry VIII* (Westminster, 1859), 7.
22. This paragraph relies on Bruce R. Smith, *The Acoustic World of Early Modern England: Attending to the O-Factor* (Chicago: University of Chicago Press, 1999), chap. 3, "The Soundscapes of Early Modern England."
23. W. R. Cooper, "Richard Hunne," *Reformation 1* (1996), 221–251.
24. The Fullers had taken up temporary residence on Fenchurch Street in 1520; Schofield, *London Houses*, 47.

25. Robert C. Winthrop, *Life and Letters of John Winthrop*, 2d ed., 2 vols. (Boston, 1869), I, 15.
26. James Muskett, *Evidences of the Winthrops of Groton* (Exeter, 1896), 25. The evidence for Alice's parentage is circumstantial but persuasive. W. R. Cooper, Hunne's most recent biographer, agrees with this identification. I thank Mr. Cooper for his input. Stefan Smart's "John Foxe and 'The Story of Richard Hun, Martyr,'" *Journal of Ecclesiastical History* 37 (1986), 1–14, argues that Foxe's account of Hunne was largely based on hearsay and oral sources. A likely source was William Winthrop, the surviving son of Adam Winthrop and Alice Hunne, who, as will be seen in the following chapter, provided Foxe with various information for the *Acts and Monuments*.
27. William Herbert, *History of the Twelve Great Livery Companies* (London, 1836), II, 644.
28. Clothworkers Company, Court Orders, 1536–1558, CM I and CM II, manuscripts in the Archives of the Clothworkers Company. I would like to thank Mr. David Wickham for granting me access to the records and to Dr. Steven Rappaport for sharing his own research into the Clothworkers.
29. For feasts see Ian Archer, "Governors and Governed in Late Sixteenth-Century London, c. 1560–1603: Studies in the Achievement of Stability" (Oxford University, Ph.D., 1988), 132.
30. Clothworkers Company, Court Orders, CM II, and Renter Warden Accounts, RWA, manuscript books in Archives of Clothworkers; Schofield, *London Homes*, 49. The Clothworkers had used the old Shearsmen's Hall, which had been built in around 1472. This was demolished in 1548 and replaced on the site by a new hall.
31. Schofield, *London Homes*, 51.
32. Adam was a merchant member of the company as opposed to an artificer. For a discussion of these groups and their occasional conflicts see G. D. Ramsay, *The City of London in International Politics at the Accession of Elizabeth Tudor* (Manchester: Manchester University Press, 1975), 43–46; and Ramsay, "Industrial Discontent in Early Elizabethan London," *London Journal* 1 (1975), 227–239.
33. James Williamson, *Maritime Enterprise, 1485–1558* (Oxford: Clarendon Press, 1913), 187.
34. British Library, Cotton MS, Galba X.
35. Public Record Office (PRO), High Court of Admiralty (HCA) 3/3 f. 180–184, 231; HCA 2/4 f. 133–136, 160, 162, 167, 171–172, 175, 177, 189, 194, 198, 201, 205, 209–210, 213, 228–229; HCA 24/11 f. 20, 23; HCA 38/1 f. 51, 52, 56, 74, 111, 116; HCA 38/2 f. 15, 173. While there are few surviving records of imports and exports from this early period, there is evidence of Adam's shipments of cloth in the Customs Records of 1546–1547; PRO E122/1676/1 f. 16v, 19r, 150v. His willingness to cut corners resulted in his being briefly imprisoned in the Fleet prison in 1543, evidently for negotiating with foreigners for prohibited sales of cloth. He was released on payment of the substantial sum of £600; *Acts of the Privy Council*, I, 92, 102. I would like to thank Steve Gunn for discussing this incident with me.
36. R. G. Lang, ed., *Two Tudor Subsidy Rolls: For the City of London: 1541 and 1582*, London Record Society Publications 29 (1993), 22.
37. Adam was also involved in other legal disputes, one of which became a cause célèbre at the time and of interest to historians because of the conflicting jurisdictions it crossed. In 1546 he sued Thomas Combes in the common

court of the City of London in a dispute over payment for goods Combes had purchased from Winthrop. Combes, "by the sinister labor of the French ambassador and also by other crafty means," as Winthrop subsequently complained, managed to have the suit delayed and Winthrop arrested by process of the High Court of the Admiralty. The intervention of the Admiralty Court in a common-law matter led the Privy Council, in 1558, to stay all action. But Combes ignored this and again secured an Admiralty process for Winthrop's arrest. The Court of King's Bench responded by issuing a warrant for the arrest of the judge of the Admiralty. This brought the Privy Council back into the dispute. The council called both the chief justice and the judge of the Admiralty before them to argue the issue of jurisdiction, and in response to a petition of Winthrop appointed a panel of London citizens to arbitrate the original dispute. Still later, Winthrop would take the arbitration decision to the Court of Chancery in an effort to improve on the settlement he had received. See Reginald Marsden, ed., *Select Pleas in the Court of Admiralty, Vol. I: The Court of the Admiralty in the West (A.D. 1390–1404) and the High Court of Admiralty (A.D. 1527–1545)*, Publications of the Selden Society 6 (1894), no. 37.

38. Grenville W.G.L. Gower, ed., "Registers of Christenings . . . with the Parish of St. Peter's Cornhill," *Harleian Society Register, I* (1977).

39. The Winthrops owned property on Finkes Lane in the Cornhill Ward that William Winthrop eventually sold in 1577 (*WP*, I, 24–28), which was likely at one point a family residence. John Schofield kindly reviewed the description of that home in the deed of sale and suggests that it was like that at 16 Cornhill, which is described in Schofield, *London Houses*, 178. I thank Dr. Schofield for his assistance. The conjectural description of the Winthrop London home that follows derives from an analysis of the 1577 deed and the description we have of the home at 16 Cornhill.

40. Schofield, *London Houses*, 115–116.

41. Schofield, *London Houses*, 91–92.

42. Smith, *Acoustic World*, 70–71.

43. For the fashion of the flat cap see John Stowe, *A Survey of London Written in the Year 1598*, ed. Antonia Fraser (Stroud: Alan Sutton, 1994), 445.

Chapter 2.   Reformation

1. John Stowe, *A Survey of London*, rpt. from the text of 1603, ed. by Charles Kingford, 2 vols. (Oxford: Clarendon Press, 1908), I, 195–196.

2. For the German tale and its early English popularity see Ian Green, *Print and Protestantism in Early Modern England* (Oxford: Oxford University Press, 2000), 431–432.

3. The literature on the supernatural in early modern England is vast. Those interested should start with Keith Thomas, *Religion and the Decline of Magic* (New York: Scribner's, 1971), but also consult James Sharpe, *Instruments of Darkness* (Philadelphia: University of Pennsylvania Press, 1996); and Stuart Clark, *Thinking with Demons* (New York: Oxford University Press, 1997).

4. In the early days of the Reformation the pace of reform varied from parish to parish, and it is impossible to know just how the sacrament of baptism was performed in St. Peter's Cornhill in 1548. The possibilities outlined and other disputes over baptism are thoroughly discussed in David Cressy, *Birth,*

Marriage and Death: Ritual, Religion, and the Life-Cycle in Tudor and Stuart England (Oxford: Oxford University Press, 1997), 97–196.

5. The following discussion of the Reformation and its unfolding in England is based upon a variety of studies. Among the numerous treatments of the early English Reformation, the most valuable is Diarmaid MacCulloch's *Thomas Cranmer: A Life* (New Haven: Yale University Press, 1996). But see also A. G. Dickens, *The English Reformation* (New York: Shocken Books, 1964); Eamon Duffy, *The Stripping of the Altars: Traditional Religion in England c.1400–c.1580* (New Haven: Yale University Press, 1992); Christopher Haigh, *English Reformations: Religion, Politics, and Society Under the Tudors* (Oxford: Clarendon Press, 1993); and MacCulloch, *Tudor Church Militant: Edward VI and the Protestant Reformation* (London: Alan Lane, 1999). A valuable analysis of how the new worship compared to the older forms is found in Christopher Marsh, *Popular Religion in Sixteenth-Century England: Holding Their Peace* (Basingstoke: Macmillan, 1998). Eamon Duffy offers a striking history of religious change in one parish in *The Voices of Morebath: Reformation and Rebellion in an English Village* (New Haven: Yale University Press, 2001).

6. H. B. Walters, *London Churches at the Reformation with an Account of Their Contents* (New York: Macmillan,1939), 572–586; Susan Brigden, *London and the Reformation* (Oxford: Clarendon Press, 1989), 11–12.

7. Brigden, *London*, 288–292; see also Margaret Aston, *England's Iconoclasts* (Oxford: Clarendon Press, 1988).

8. The documents regarding the purchase of the manor are to be found in PRO, E 3/18, 23/1271. See also *Calendar of Patent Rolls, Edward VI, 1553* (1971), 132.

9. PRO, E 334/3 f. 111r. I owe this reference and the comment to Mr. Brett Usher.

10. Walters, *London Churches*, 574, where he prints an inventory of all the goods and ornaments of the parish church of St. Peter's Cornhill, "Adam Wyntrop and Thomas Laws then being church wardens."

11. Walters, *London Churches*, 584.

12. Information on Pulleyne here and in the next paragraphs is drawn from E.L.C. Mullins, "The Effects of the Marian and Elizabethan Settlements upon the clergy of London, 1553–1564," (University of London, MA, 1948), 400–401; Christina H. Garrett, *The Marian Exiles* (Cambridge: Cambridge University Press, 1938), 1263; Barrett L. Beer, "London Parish Clergy and the Protestant Reformation, 1547–1559," *Albion* 18 (1986), 386–387; Dickens, *English Reformation*, 274–275; Brigden, *London and the Reformation*, 561–562; and John Fines, *A Biographical Register of Early English Protestants and Others Opposed to the Roman Catholic Church*, pt. 2 (typescript, 1985), P-23. I would like to thank Dr. Fines for providing me with a copy of this typescript.

13. Lawrence Shaw Mayo, *The Winthrop Family in America* (Boston: Massachusetts Historical Society, 1948), 4.

14. Mullins, "Effects," 365. For Bonner's visitation see Meriel Jagger, "Bonner's Episcopal Visitation of London, 1554," *Bulletin of the Institute of Historical Research* 45 (1972), 306–311.

15. This school had been one of the four parish grammar schools created by parliamentary order in the reign of Edward VI. The selection of St. Peter's may well have been due to the presence of a well-furnished parish library. See John Stowe, *A Survey of London Written in the Year 1598*, ed. Antonia Fraser (Stroud: Alan Sutton, 1994), 205–206.

16. The story of the underground churches in London is examined in J. W. Martin, "The Protestant Underground Congregations of Mary's Reign," *Journal of Ecclesiastical History* 35 (1984), 319–338, and Dickens, *Reformation*, 272–277. For the story of Protestant responses to Mary Tudor in general, with attention to those who remained in England, see Andrew Pettegree, *Marian Protestantism* (Aldershot: Scholar Press, 1996).

17. I have examined William Winthrop's efforts more fully in "William Winthrop and Religious Reform in London, 1529–1582," *London Journal* 24 (1999), 1–17.

18. "Autobiographical Anecdotes of Edward Underhill," in John Gough Nichols, ed., *Narratives of the Days of the Reformation, Chiefly from the Manuscripts of John Foxe*, Camden Society, o.s. 77 (1859), 149, 171.

19. Foxe, *Acts and Monuments*, VI, 672. The manuscript is in the Foxe collections at Emmanuel College and has Winthrop's name on the reverse. According to Dr. Tom Freeman of the John Foxe Project, Foxe generally wrote the name to indicate whom the original was to be returned to, almost always the original recipient.

20. Diarmaid MacCulloch, "The Impact of the Reformation on Suffolk Parish Life," *Suffolk Review*, n.s. 15 (1990), 7.

21. Diarmaid MacCulloch, "Catholic and Puritan in Elizabethan Suffolk: A County Community Polarizes," *Archiv für Reformationsgeschichte* 72 (1981), 263–264.

22. Joseph L. Chester, ed., *The Parish Records of St. Michael, Cornhill, London, 1546 to 1754*, Publications of the Harleian Society, *Registers, Vol. VII* (1882). I thank Diarmaid MacCulloch for suggesting the significance of the choice of name, for which there is no family basis.

23. Thomas Wood to Sir William Cecil, 29 March 1566, in Patrick Collinson, "Letters of Thomas Wood, Puritan, 1566–1577," in Collinson, *Godly People: Essays on English Protestantism and Puritanism* (London: Hambledon, 1983), 83.

24. Collinson, *Godly People*, 54.

25. Stowe (Fraser ed.), 204–205.

26. William H. Overall and Alfred Waterlow, eds., *The Accounts of the Churchwardens of the Parish of St. Michael, Cornhill in the City of London, from 1456 to 1608* (London, 1883); Guildhall Library, St. Michael upon Cornhill Vestry Minutes, MS 4072/1.

27. H. Gareth Owen, "The London Parish Clergy in the Reign of Elizabeth I" (University of London, Ph.D., 1957), 478.

28. Stowe's account of the quarrel with his brother and of Winthrop's intervention is to be found in British Library, Harleian MS 367, f. 6–7; an excerpt was published by Charles Kingsford in his introduction to Stowe's *Survey*.

29. See John Strype, *The History of the Life and Acts of . . . Edmund Grindal* (Oxford, 1821). When Stowe's study was raided, various "old fantastical Popish books" were discovered; see Ian Archer, "The Nostalgia of John Stowe," in David L. Smith, Richard Strier, and David Bevington, eds., *The Theatrical City: Culture, Theatre, and Politics in London, 1576–1649* (Cambridge: Cambridge University Press, 1995), 29.

30. Overall and Waterlow, *Churchwardens of St. Michael's*, 1576.

31. Cotton Mather, *Magnalia Christi Americana* (London, 1702). The Foxe Papers at Emmanuel College provide evidence of Winthrop's role in passing material to Foxe beyond what Mather wrote of. A notation in Foxe's hand

indicates that he received some of Philpott's letters from Winthrop. I would like to thank Dr. Tom Freeman for guiding me to the relevant manuscripts in this collection.

32. William Winthrop to John Foxe, 18 November 1560, *WP*, I, 15–16. The phrase used by Winthrop echoes that of Edward Underhill, another Londoner who evaded the authorities during the London persecution and who wrote that at that time "[s]ome were moved by his spirit to flee over seas; some were preserved still in London, that in all the time of persecution never bowed their knees unto Baal"; "Anecdotes of Underhill" in Nichols, *Narratives*, 149.

33. Yonge, like Winthrop himself, would be active in the French stranger church and a supporter of the so-called presbyterian movement led by John Field and Thomas Wilcox in the 1570s. Bull had lost his fellowship at Magdalen College, Oxford early in Mary's reign when, along with Thomas Bentham, he had snatched a censer from a priest during mass and denounced him for idolatry. Bull had been active in the London Protestant underground for the rest of Mary's reign and then was linked with Foxe in the 1560s. In the same letter, Winthrop urged Foxe to use his influence to find a living for Robert Cole, who had served as an intermediary between the exiles, the prisoners, and the underground congregations.

34. For Upcher see Fine, *Biographical Register*, pt. 2, U-1; Garrett, *Marian Exiles*, 316–317; J. E. Oxley, *The Reformation in Essex* (Manchester: Manchester University Press, 1965), 165; Champlin Burrage, *The Early English Dissenters in the Light of Recent Research, 1550–1641*, 2 vols. (Cambridge: Cambridge University Press, 1912), I, 51–53. Upcher's Elizabethan career is traced in part in Mark Byford, "The Price of Protestantism: Assessing the Impact of Religious Change on Elizabethan Essex: the Cases of Heydon and Colchester, 1558–1594," (Oxford University, Ph.D., 1988). I would like to thank Dr. Byford for additional discussions of Upcher.

35. Collinson, *Godly People*, 468.

36. For information on the Spanish church see Paul Hauber, *Three Spanish Heretics and the Reformation* (Geneva: Droz, 1967), and A. Gordon Kinder, *Casiodora de Reina: Spanish Reformer of the Sixteenth Century* (London: Tamesis, 1975). I thank Brett Usher for the suggestion that Winthrop may have been one of those who helped negotiate Grindal's gift of the church's use to the Spanish. William would have been familiar with St. Mary Axe, a formerly redundant church which the queen gave to Grindal to use as he willed, from when he was there to attend the retroactive ordination of his friend Thomas Simpson, one of the ministers of the underground congregations, by Grindal.

37. Owe Boersma, *Vluchtig Voorbeeld: de nederlanse, franse en italiaanse vluchtelingenkerken in londen, 1568–1585* (1994). I wish to thank Dr. Andrew Pettegree for directing me to Dr. Boersma's work and making his copy of Boersma's thesis available to me.

38. *Actes du Consistoire de L'Eglise Francaise de Threadneedle Street, Londres, Vol. I, 1560–1565*, Publications of the Huguenot Society of London 38 (1937), 57, 60; Library of the French Protestant Church, Soho Square, MS 194, f. 3v. I would like to thank Mr. Charles Littleton for sharing with me his paper, "Competing Communities? The French Church of London, Its Congregation, and the London Parishes, 1560–1625," delivered at the North American Conference for British Studies, October 1995; those interested in the subject should also consult Dr. Littleton's thesis, "Geneva on Threadneedle

Street: The French Church of London and Its Congregation, 1560–1625"
(University of Michigan, Ph.D., 1996).

39. Minutes of the Italian Congregation, British Library, Add. MS 48096. Owe
Boersma and A. Jelsa have published a transcription of the manuscript as
part of *Unity in Multiformity: The Minutes of the Coetus of London, 1575, and
the Consistory Minutes of the Italian Church of London, 1570–1591*, Publications of the Huguenot Society of Great Britain and Ireland 59 (1997).

40. Adam Winthrop copied some of the letters into a commonplace book; his
copies are published in *Massachusetts Historical Society Proceedings* 12 (1871–
1873), 285–287.

41. G. D. Ramsay, "Clothworkers, Merchant Adventurers, and Richard Hakluyt,"
English Historical Review 92 (1977), 515.

42. Albert Peel, ed., *The Seconde parte of a Register, Being a Calendar of Manuscripts . . . by the Puritans About 1593*, 2 vols. (Cambridge: Cambridge University Press, 1915), I, 105; Foxe is quoted by Patrick Collinson in *Archbishop
Grindal, 1519–1583* (London: Cape, 1980), 137.

43. The general patterns of this support are discussed in Usher, "Backing Protestantism."

44. Not all who stood surety did so for such reasons. It is clear that some chose
to do so as an investment with a promised financial reward. But among the
godly laity such as Winthrop the commitment to promote reform is clear.

45. PRO E 334/7 f. 136v, 185r; E 334/8 f. 150v; E 334/9 f. 31r.

46. *Calendar of Patent Rolls, Elizabeth, 1577–1578* (1976), 2256 for the patent for
the Spanish Company; heading the list of members is the earl of Leicester,
who would recommend William's brother Adam for admission to the bar of
the Inner Temple. See also Theodore K. Rabb, *Enterprise and Empire: Merchant and Gentry Investment in the Expansion of England, 1575–1630* (Cambridge, Mass.: Harvard University Press, 1967), 406, where Winthrop is listed
as a member of the company; V. M. Shillington and Wallis Chapman, *The
Commercial Relations of England and Portugal* (London: G. Routledge, 1907);
and Pauline Croft, *The Spanish Company*, London Record Society, vol. 9
(1973).

47. Clothworkers Company Archives, CL II f. 188r.

48. Guildhall Library, Cornhill Ward Mote Inquest, MS 4069/1.

49. *WP*, I, 24–29.

50. Guildhall Library, St. Michael's Vestry Minutes, MS 4072/1 f. 21, 22.

51. Adam Winthrop's Diary, *WP*, I, 159.

Chapter 3. John and Adam

1. Bruce R. Smith, *The Acoustic World of Early Modern England: Attending to the
O-Factor* (Chicago: University of Chicago Press, 1999), 74–80.

2. William Dugdale, *Monasticon Anglicanum* (London, 1846), 126, has a record
of the lease from the abbot's register. An abstract of the "First Minister's
Account" for the Abbey of St. Edmund returned to the Court of Augmentations shows a payment by Gooche and a reference to the lease; *Proceedings of
the Suffolk Institute of Archaeology and Natural History* 12 (1907), 311–366. I
thank Mr. Martin Wood for providing me these references. It has been suggested by various scholars that as the turmoil in Henry VIII's church grew,
abbeys began to lease properties under longer terms.

3. The report of the lease is to be found in the Norwich Diocesan Records, Faculty Book 1, Norfolk Record Office (NRO), DN/FCB/1, f. 65.

4. Norwich Diocesan Records, Faculty Book 1, NRO: DN/FCB/1, f. 65. Examination of the existing Groton Place, reports by county archaeologist Sylvia Colman, and photographs of a 1970s renovation of the structure provided me by Mr. and Mrs. Edgar Elliot of Groton make it clear that the existing Groton Place was what Adam and his heirs referred to as their "mansion house," generally the principal family residence on the manor. The existing north wing includes the remains of the original fifteenth-century parsonage. Winthrop expanded this as well as a separate structure to the south, then connected them with a central hall. For more on this, including illustrations, see Francis J. Bremer, "Winthrop Residences in England and Ireland," privately printed and to be placed on the Winthrop Papers website, muweb.millersville.edu/~winthrop.

5. See Bremer, "Winthrop Residences."

6. The induction is recorded in the Suffolk Record Office at Bury St. Edmunds (SRO/B) E 14/5/1; the guarantors for first fruits are recorded in PRO E 334/3 f. 111r. Ponder replaced William Chamberlin, who had died. The parish church had originally been dedicated to St. Margaret, but at the Reformation such identifications were abandoned in many places. In the nineteenth century it was rededicated to St. Bartholomew.

7. Lord Francis Hervey, ed., *Suffolk in the Seventeenth Century: The Breviary of Suffolk by Robert Reyce, 1618* (London: J. Murray, 1902), 25; hereafter cited as Reyce, *Breviary*.

8. The general description of the soil and the farm use is drawn from David Dymond and Edward Martin, eds., *An Historical Atlas of Suffolk*, rev. ed. (Ipswich: Suffolk County Archaeological Service, 1999), and Joan Thirsk, ed., *The Agrarian History of England and Wales, Vol. IV: 1500–1640* (Cambridge: Cambridge University Press, 1967).

9. Diarmaid MacCulloch, ed., *The Chorography of Suffolk*, Suffolk Record Society 19 (1976), 19.

10. Reyce, *Breviary*, 53.

11. Reyce, *Breviary*, 52–53.

12. Reyce, *Breviary*, 25.

13. SRO/B E 14/5/1.

14. SRO/B E 14/5/1.

15. License to Alienate, Patent Rolls: 4 & 5 Philip and Mary, pt. 11, n. 8. This is published in its original Latin in James Muskett, *Evidences of the Winthrops of Groton, co. Suffolk, England and of families in and near that county with whom they intermarried* (London, 1894–1896), 16. I would like to thank Dr. Carol Miller for her translation of the document and Dr. J. H. Baker for his correspondence guiding my understanding of the procedures. Since the manor was held in chief of the king, Winthrop would have needed this to ensure that the manor did not pass to his eldest son, William, whom he had already provided for. Adam named Simon and John Ponder as his nominees in the license.

16. Jenny Robinson, *Boxford: A Miscellany* (Boxford: privately printed, 1998), 40, notes the evidences of a school in the period before the 1595 chartering of the free grammar school.

17. For a perceptive study of Adam Winthrop (1548–1623) see Martin Wood, "Adam Winthrop of Groton, Suffolk, 1548–1623" (University of Essex, MA, 1998).

18. Alice Cely was the stepsister of Adam Winthrop's first wife, Alice Hunne. Her marriage to John Cely of Bury St. Edmunds was her second marriage. Her stepdaughter, Marion Cely, married Richard Byrd of Ipswich. A son, William Cely, is believed to have been the William Cely who married Mary Winthrop, the daughter of Adam and Agnes Winthrop, about 1564; Muskett, *Evidences*, 166. For insight into the religious climate of Ipswich at this time see Diarmaid MacCulloch and John Blatchly, "Pastoral Provision in the Parishes of Tudor Ipswich," *Sixteenth-Century Journal* 22 (1991), 457–474.

19. Some of the details of Dawes's life, and particularly his being master of a private school before the chartering of the Ipswich grammar school, are to be found in Adam Winthrop's handwritten "A true narrative of the lyfe and deathe of Mr John Daus, the translator of this booke, written by a scholler of his," on a flyleaf of his copy of Dawes's translation of Henry Bullinger's *A Hundred Sermons upon the Apocalypse* (1561), which is in the Harvard University Library.

20. *The Institution of Christian Religion, wrytten in Latine by maister Jhon Calvin, and translated into Englysh according to the authors last edition* (1561). On the back page the printers indicated that Dawes had submitted a manuscript a year earlier but that for various reasons it had to be reworked by Norton. Among the possible reasons may have been the loss or destruction of Dawes's effort.

21. See the notice of Dawes's effort and Bullinger's preface in John Strype, *Annals of the Reformation* (London, 1709), 245. Dawes also published a translation of John Sleidan's *Reign of Charles V, a Fameuse Cronicle of oure time called Sleidanes Commentaries* (1560).

22. The will is printed in *WP*, I, 17–23.

23. The payments to Alice and Bridget were to be made by William Winthrop, who had entered into a bond with his father for this purpose.

24. SRO/B E 14/5/1.

25. PRO E 334/7 f. 185r.

26. Copy of Groton parish register. The original is in SRO/B. This was the second marriage for both.

27. The story of the Mildmays of Essex is deserving of further study. Though containing some clear errors, the best existing guide is Herbert A. St. John Mildmay, *A Brief Memoir of the Mildmay Family* (London: John Lane, 1913).

28. The procedure called for the prospective grantee to obtain from the auditor a detailed statement of the value of the property, after which the paperwork would go to the commissioners and the sale would be perfected. For the story of the dissolution of the monasteries see David Knowles, *Bare Ruined Choirs: The Dissolution of the English Monasteries* (Cambridge: Cambridge University Press, 1976), and Joyce Youings, *The Dissolution of the Monasteries* (London: Allen & Unwin, 1971).

29. Groton parish register.

30. SRO/B microfilm of parish registers of Thorpe Morieux.

31. Will of Robert Risby, 1551, in Muskett, *Evidences*, 68–69.

32. W. A. Copinger, *The Manors of Suffolk: The Hundreds of Babergh and Blackbourn* (London: Unwin, 1905), 28–29.

33. Will of Robert Risby, in Muskett, *Evidences*, 70.

34. Will of John Wincoll, 1576, in Muskett, *Evidences*, 70. Wincoll bequeathed to Elizabeth a taffeta gown that had belonged to her mother in consideration of these services to his daughter, Amy.

35. From the depositions in Notte c. Winthrop, PRO C 33/145/526.

36. Record of Christenings, St. Andrew Undershaft Parish, London, 23 July 1582, Family Search International Genealogical Index, accessed through www.familysearch.org.

37. The actual indenture does not survive, but the details are spelled out in Elizabeth's Chancery suit undertaken three years later to enforce the agreement; for technical reasons the suit was brought against Robert Munning of Nedging, whom John had engaged as co-signer: PRO C 2/JasI/230/91.

38. Laura Gowing, *Domestic Dangers: Women, Words, and Sex in Early Modern London* (Oxford: Clarendon Press, 1996), 180–182. See also Martin Ingram, *Church Courts, Sex and Marriage in England, 1570–1640* (Cambridge: Cambridge University Press, 1987), chap. 5, Matrimonial Causes: (1) The Breakdown of Marriage," and Ralph Houlbrooke, *Church Courts and People During the English Reformation* (Oxford: Oxford University Press, 1979). It is likely that one of the Winthrops sued for separation in the church courts, but the appropriate records for the consistory court of the diocese of Norwich are incomplete, and those of the archbishop's Court of Arches (where some gentry could initiate such suits and which John later claimed to have sued in) were lost to fire in 1666. Without a legally granted separation it is unlikely that Elizabeth would have been able to bring her suit in Chancery.

39. PRO C 2/JasI/230/91. I would like to thank Tim Wales for advice on this matter and Ralph Houlbrooke for suggestions on searching the Norwich records.

40. Kelke had been one of the Marian exiles and had been ordained by Bishop Grindal on his return to England. He was master of Magdalene College, Cambridge in addition to being Ispwich town preacher; see Christina H. Garrett, *The Marian Exiles* (Cambridge: Cambridge University Press, 1938), 202–203. Winthrop's kinsman Richard Byrd was one of the Ipswich justices, and Richard Cely, another kinsman, was an alderman when the town voted to hire a town preacher and chose Roger Kelke; Nathaniel Bacon, *The Annalls of Ipswich . . . Collected out of the Records Bookes and Writings of That Town (1654)*, ed. William Richardson (Ipswich, 1884), 254–256. When Kelke was accused of being "a preacher of no trew doctrine" they were there to acquit him of the charges; Bacon, *Annalls*, 263.

41. I have discussed life at Cambridge, albeit a generation later, in my *Congregational Communion: Clerical Friendship in the Anglo-American Puritan Community, 1610–1692* (Boston: Northeastern University Press, 1994), chap. 1, "The Cambridge Connection." The following discussion is based on that and also V.I.H. Green, *Religion at Oxford and Cambridge* (London: SCM Press, 1964); Mark Curtis, *Oxford and Cambridge in Transition, 1558–1642* (Oxford: Clarendon Press, 1959); Hugh Kearney, *Scholars and Gentlemen* (London: Faber, 1970); and H. C. Porter, *Reformation and Reaction at Tudor Cambridge* (Cambridge: Cambridge University Press, 1958).

42. C. H. Cooper, *Annals of Cambridge* (Cambridge, 1843), II, 206, 315–316.

43. John Evelyn, quoted in Bremer, *Congregational Communion*, 24.

44. Thomas Fuller, *The History of the University of Cambridge* (London, 1840), 171. The most complete discussion of Magdalene is to be found in Peter Cunich, David Hoyle, Eamon Duffy, and Ronald Hyan, *A History of Magdalene College, Cambridge 1428–1988* (Cambridge: Magdalene College, 1994). David Hoyle is the author of the relevant section, pt. 2, "Mid-Sixteenth Century to Mid-Seventeenth Century." Though providing much useful detail, Hoyle has little sympathy with Roger Kelke's reformist views and focuses more on his admitted mismanagement of the college finances.

45. Cooper, *Annals*, II, 217.
46. Edward Purnell, *Magdalene College* (London: F. E. Robinson, 1904), 58.
47. Cunich et al., *Magdalene*, 74.
48. Cunich et al., *Magdalene*, 72.
49. Information in this paragraph is drawn from John Venn, *Alumni Cantabrigiensis: A biographical list of all known students, graduates and holders of office at the University of Cambridge from the earliest times to 1900* (Cambridge: Cambridge University Press, 1927).
50. Fuller, *History*, 197.
51. Thomas Baker, *History of the College of St. John the Evangelist, Cambridge*, 2 vols. (Cambridge, 1869), II, 583.
52. Baker, *St. John*, II, 590.
53. Sarah Bendall, Christopher Brooke, and Patrick Collinson, *A History of Emmanuel College, Cambridge* (Woodbridge, Suffolk: Boydell, 1999), 36.
54. Bendall et al., *Emmanuel*, 51–52.
55. "Adam Winthrop's Library: An Annotated List," muweb.millersville.edu/~winthrop.
56. St. John's College Archives, Thin Black Book, C7.14, 65–66. I would like to thank M. G. Underwood of St. John's for providing me with a copy of this document and Mr. Lawrence Woodlock for assistance in translating it.
57. PRO E 334/8 f. 150v.
58. PRO E 334/9 f. 31r.
59. For the rise of the legal profession see Wilfrid R. Prest, *The Inns of Court Under Elizabeth and the Early Stuarts* (London: Longman, 1972), and Prest, *The Rise of the Barristers* (Oxford: Clarendon Press, 1986).
60. Aspects of the educational process are dealt with in the works of Prest, above, and also in Louis A. Knafla, "The Law Studies of an Elizabethan Student," *Huntington Library Quarterly* 32 (1969), 221–240; and Prest, "The Learning Exercises at the Inns of Court, 1590–1640," *Journal of the Society of Public Teachers of Law*, n.s., 9 (1966–67), 301–313.
61. *WP*, I, 178.
62. *WP*, I, 5. See also Bremer, "Winthrop Residences."
63. F. A. Inderwick, ed., *A Calendar of the Inner Temple Records, Vol. I: 21 Henry VII (1505)–43 Elizabeth (1603)* (London, 1896), 329.
64. Simon Adams, "Puritanism and the Elizabethan Court: The 'Puritan Faction' Anatomised," paper delivered at Millersville University conference, "Puritanism in Old and New England." 1991. See also Adams, "A Godly Peer? Leicester and Puritans," *History Today* (January 1990), 14–19.
65. Eleanor Rosenberg, *Leicester, Patron of Letters* (New York: Columbia University Press, 1955), 42. John Harington, *Nugae Antiquae: Collection of Original Papers Written During the Reigns of Henry VIII, Edward VI, Queen Mary, Elizabeth, and King James* (London, 1804), II, 268. I would like to thank Dr. Simon Adams for advice on the connections that may have led to Leicester's sponsorship of Winthrop and for the transcript of a letter of Still to Leicester (1577) which he made from the manuscript in the British Library.
66. Letter from Robert Dudley, Earl of Leicester, to the Court, 8 May 1583, Inner Temple Archives, Misc. MS no. 30, item 9. In the letter Dudley refers to having previously sent other letters, which do not survive, regarding Winthrop's admission to the bar.
67. Inner Temple, Misc. MS no. 172. The printed *Catalogue of Manuscripts in the Library of the Honourable Society of the Inner Temple* (London: Oxford Univer-

sity Press for the Masters of the Bench, 1972) lists his name as "Andrew Winthrop," which might account for why others have not noted Adam's involvement, but this is a transcription error, as an examination of the manuscript itself makes clear.

68. See Geoffrey de C. Parmiter, "Elizabethan Popish Recusancy in the Inns of Court," *Bulletin of the Institute of Historical Research*, Special Suppl. no. 11 (1976).

69. Inderwick, *Calendar of Inner Temple*, 405–406.

70. George Gifford, prefatory letter to William Fulke, *Praelections upon the Sacred and Holy Revelation of St. John, translated into English by George Gifford* (1573).

71. Phyllis Hembry, *The Bishops of Bath and Wells, 1540–1640* (London: Athlone, 1967), 183.

72. SRO/B E 14/5/1, f. 20v, 21r. Interestingly, John Wincoll, a stepcousin of Elizabeth Risby Winthrop, was one of the guarantors of first fruits for Knewstub.

73. Patrick Collinson, "Magistracy and Ministry: A Suffolk Miniature," in Collinson, *Godly People: Essays on English Protestantism and Puritanism* (London: Hambledon, 1983), 448. While Collinson is specifically discussing Suffolk, the judgment seems to apply equally to north Essex south of the Stour. I wish to thank Professor Collinson for his views on this, exchanged in conversation and correspondence.

74. Ralph Houlbrooke, ed., *The Letter Book of John Parkhurst, Bishop of Norwich* (Norwich: Norfolk Record Society, 1975), 44.

75. In London, Grindal (1559–1570) was replaced by Edwin Sandys (1570–1577), John Aylmer (1577–1594), Richard Fletcher (1594–1596), Richard Bancroft (1597–1604), Richard Vaughan (1604–1607), Thomas Ravis (1607–1609), George Abbot (1610–1611), John King (1611–1621), and George Montaigne (1621–1627) before the appointment of William Laud to that see. John Le Neve, *Fasti Ecclesiae Anglicanae, 1541–1857: I, St. Paul's, London*, comp. Joyce M. Horn (London: Athlone, 1969). In Norwich, Parkhurst (1560–1575) was replaced by Edmund Freake (1575–1584), Edmund Scambler (1585–1594), William Redman (1595–1602), John Jegon (1603–1618), John Overall (1618–1619), Samuel Harsnett (1619–1628), and Francis White (1629–1631). John Le Neve, *Fasti Ecclesiae Anglicanae, 1541–1857: VII, Ely, Norwich, Westminster, and Worcester Dioceses*, comp. Joyce M. Horn (London: Athlone, 1992).

76. Jay Anglin, "The Court of the Archdeacon of Essex, 1571–1609: An Institutional and Social Study" (UCLA, Ph.D., 1965), has demonstrated that in Essex during this period "efforts to enforce conformity . . . were seriously hampered by the bishops themselves, whose own treatment of the puritans was lenient and ineffective" (274).

77. Nathaniel Ward's preface to Samuel Ward, *Jethro's Justice of the Peace. A Sermon Preached at a General Assises held at Bury St. Edmunds, for the Countie of Suffolk* (1618).

78. See Diarmaid MacCulloch, *Suffolk and the Tudors: Politics and Religion in an English County, 1500–1600* (Oxford: Clarendon Press, 1986). Adam Winthrop's tribute to Jermyn is in *WP*, I, 176.

79. John Knewstub, *Answeare unto Certaine Assertions* (1579), epistle.

80. Sandys to the Privy Council, 13 July 1576, in Stanford Lehmberg, "Archbishop Grindal and the Prophesyings," *Magazine of the Protestant Episcopal Church* 34 (1965), 99.

81. Walker to Sandys, July 1576, in Lehmberg, "Prophesyings," 107.

82. Houlbrooke, *Parkhurst*, 46.

83. Those orders are included in Leonard J. Trinterud, ed., *Elizabethan Puritanism* (New York: Oxford University Press, 1971).

84. PRO STAC 5 C 81/23, quoted in Mark Byfield, "The Price of Protestantism: Assessing the Impact of Religious Change on Elizabethan Essex: The Cases of Heydon and Colchester, 1558–1594" (Oxford University, Ph.D., 1988), 218.

85. Oliver Pigge to John Field, quoted in Patrick Collinson, *The Elizabethan Puritan Movement* (Berkeley: University of California Press, 1967), 218–219. Pigge wrote that this "meeting was appointed to be kept very secretly," but this likely means secret from the archbishop since it is unlikely that sixty ministers could have convened in Cockfield without attracting local notice.

86. John Rylands MS 874, f. 10r. I have been guided in my reading of that manuscript by a transcript that John Craig has been kind enough to share with me. Dr. Craig, along with Patrick Collinson and Brett Usher, is editing a new edition of that manuscript, which will greatly aid our understanding of the conference movement.

87. John Rylands MS 874, f. 10v.

88. John Rylands MS 874, f. 29v.

89. John Rylands MS 874, f. 7v.

90. John Rylands MS 874, f. 2v.

91. The best study of these events remains Collinson's *Elizabethan Puritan Movement*. See also Christopher Marsh, *Popular Religion in Sixteenth-Century England* (London: Macmillan, 1998).

92. See Robin Clifton, "Fear of Popery," in Conrad Russell, ed., *The Origins of the English Civil War* (London: Macmillan, 1973); John Bossy, "The Character of Elizabethan Catholicism," in T. Aston, ed., *Crisis in Europe, 1560–1660* (London: Routledge & Keegan Paul, 1965); and Patrick McGrath, "Elizabethan Catholicism: A Reconsideration," *Journal of Ecclesiastical History* 35 (1984).

93. For discussions of Catholicism and anti-Catholicism see Michael Questier, *Conversion, Politics, and Religion in England, 1580–1625* (Cambridge: Cambridge University Press, 1996) and Peter Lake and Michael Questier, *The Antichrist's Lewd Hat* (New Haven: Yale University Press, 2002).

94. References to Mannock in Adam Winthrop's Diary, *WP*, I, 73, 75, 81, 86, 87, 88, 90, 93, 94, 99, 101, 102.

95. Henry Sandes to John Winthrop, 1622, *WP*, I, 270.

96. William's cousin Joshua Winthrop was one of the guarantors for the first fruits of the living. PRO E 334/12 f. 60v.

97. Adam Winthrop's Diary, *WP*, I, 71.

98. English College at Rome, Archives, Scriptura 24.1.1. The original is in Latin. I thank the staff of the English College for allowing me to have access to the manuscripts.

99. See the essay on Alabaster in the *New Dictionary of National Biography*.

100. For the general efforts of the puritans to distance themselves from the separatists see Stephen Brachlow, *The Communion of Saints: Radical Puritan and Separatist Ecclesiology* (Oxford: Oxford University Press, 1988). For the Family of Love and Knewstub's attacks on it see Christopher W. Marsh, *The Family of Love in English Society, 1550–1630* (Cambridge: Cambridge University Press, 1994).

101. See Stuart Barton Babbage, *Puritanism and Richard Bancroft* (London: SPCK, 1962); and Collinson, *Elizabethan Puritan Movement*, pt. 8.

102. I would also like to acknowledge that in light of the consensual process whereby reformers in the Stour Valley had come to decide on religious matters, Bancroft's claims for the divine authority of bishops in his 1589 St. Paul's sermon would have made for inevitable conflict.

103. From "The Life of Father William Weston," in John Morris, ed., *The Troubles of Our Catholic Forefathers Related by Themselves* (London, 1875), 241.

104. I have borrowed the use of the term "holy fair" from Patrick Collinson, who had borrowed it from Leigh Eric Schmidt. Patrick Collinson, "Elizabethan and Jacobean Puritanism as Forms of Popular Religious Culture," in Christopher Durston and Jacqueline Eales, eds. *The Culture of English Puritanism, 1560–1700* (Basingstoke: Macmillan, 1996), 53–54. Collinson has written of one part of the godly kingdom what I would argue can be extended to the whole of the Stour Valley: "The Suffolk clergy were indeed a remarkable society, one of the first groups of the English clergy to have realized the reformed ideal of the pastoral ministry, *and to have achieved it in concert* [italics added], as 'brethren and fellow ministers,' 'the reverend, wise and godly learned fathers and brethren.'" Collinson, "Magistracy and Ministry: A Suffolk Miniature," in R. Buick Knox, ed., *Reformation Conformity and Dissent: Essays in Honour of Geoffrey Nuttall* (London: Epworth, 1977), 76.

105. Richard Rogers Diary in M. M. Knappen, ed., *Two Elizabethan Puritan Diaries* (Chicago: American Society of Church History, 1933), 56, 59. Knappen's edition is not complete. Omitted from it are further instances of collegiality and conferencing. The manuscript is in Dr. Williams's Library.

106. Giles Firmin, *The Real Christian* (1670), 67–68.

107. Richard Rogers, *Seven Treatises* (1603), 490. I am preparing a modernized edition of the *Seven Treatises* in conjunction with Susan Ortmann for publication by Soli Deo Gloria Press.

108. Rogers quoted in Bremer, *Congregational Communion*, 50.

109. Diarmaid MacCulloch, *The Later Reformation in England, 1547–1603* (Basingstoke: Macmillan, 1990), 158, where he discusses these and other examples of what Collinson has called "an idiosyncratic congregationalism."

110. I would like to thank Michael Winship for sharing with me his essay "Weak Christians, Backsliders, and Carnal Gospellers: Assurance of Salvation and the Pastoral Origins of Puritan Practical Divinity," prior to its publication in *Church History* 70 (2000), 462–481. In that essay Winship writes: "George Gifford, contentious minister at Maldon, Essex, complained in 1582 of the 'very many carnall professors and beastly abusers for christianity, which doe seeme very willingly and gladly to embrace the promises of the Gospell, concerninge redemption and eternall life purchased in Christe Jesus: and they make great boast that they looke for their parte in the same as well as any other, and yet they look nothing at all to the this godliness and vertue.' The ministers called these people, quick to accept the good news of the Reformed gospel, but reluctant to accept the burdens that accompanied it, 'carnall gospellers.' Their appearance in sermons demonstrates that already by the turn of the 1580s a pastoral tension existed between the new Reformed message that assurance of salvation was self-evidencing and the old Christian imperative of a holy life." The ministers whom Winship identifies as troubled by and responding to this seem to have been largely from the Stour Valley.

111. For Rogers and Still see John Craig, "The 'Cambridge Boies': Thomas Rogers and the 'Brethren' in Bury St. Edmunds," in Susan Wabuda and Caroline Litzenberger, eds., *Belief and Practice in Reformation England: A Tribute to Patrick Collinson* (Aldershot: Ashgate, 1998), 154–176. I thank John Craig for sharing with me his transcript of the manuscript detailing Rogers's complaint, which he is editing for publication.

112. F. G. Emmison, *Early Essex Town Meetings* (London: Phillmore, 1970). Once again one finds many isolated studies of towns and parishes in the region that deal with the reformation of manners. Among them are Mark Byford's "The Price of Protestantism: Assessing the Impact of Religious Change on Elizabethan Essex: The Cases of Heydon and Colchester, 1558–1594" (Oxford University, Ph.D., 1988), and K. Wrightson and D. Levine, *Poverty and Piety in an English Village: Terling, 1525–1700*, 2d ed. (Oxford: Clarendon Press, 1995). An excellent overview of some of the issues involved in the effect of reformed ideas on social policy can be found in Steve Hindle, *The State and Social Change in Early Modern England, c. 1550–1640* (Basingstoke: Macmillan, 2000). Similar reformation was pursued in Dorchester, a community which would have strong links with the settlement of Massachusetts; see David Underdown, *Fire from Heaven: Life in an English Town in the Seventeenth Century* (New Haven: Yale University Press, 1993).

113. In R. G. Usher, ed., *The Presbyterian Movement in the Reign of Queen Elizabeth*, Camden Society, 3d ser. 8 (1905). See also A. R. Pennie, "The Evolution of Puritan Mentality in an Essex Cloth Town: Dedham and the Stour Valley, 1560–1640" (University of Sheffield, Ph.D., 1989).

114. SRO/B, Boxford Churchwarden Accounts, 28 March 1608.

115. Keith Wrightson, *English Society, 1580–1680* (London: Hutchinson, 1982), 212; for details see Wrightson and Levine, *Poverty and Piety*.

116. Reyce, *Breviary*, 55–56.

117. The grant of land by Adam Winthrop is to be found in SRO/Ipswich/T4/58/1 and SRO/Ipswich/T4/58/3; a brief early history of the school is to be found in Robinson, *Boxford*; the list of overseers is in *WP*, I, 145–146.

118. I owe these references to Mr. Martin Wood, who pointed out to me the importance of schools in shaping the region's culture. Mr. Wood is currently working on a study of the free schools in the area.

119. Nicholas Bownde, *The Holy Exercise of Fasting* (1604), dedicatory letter to Bishop John Jegon.

120. John Craig, "Reformation, Politics, and Polemics in Sixteenth-Century East Anglian Market Towns" (Cambridge University, Ph.D., 1992), a revised edition of which is soon to be published by Ashgate; MacCulloch, *Suffolk and the Tudors*, 323–325.

121. Patrick Collinson, "Christian Socialism in Elizabethan Suffolk: Thomas Carew and his *Caveat for Clothiers*," in Carol Rawcliffe, Roger Virgoe, and Richard Wilson, eds., *Counties and Communities: Essays in East Anglian History Presented to Hassell Smith* (Norwich: Centre of East Anglican Studies, 1996), 161–178, where Collinson also discusses and quotes from Carter's sermon.

122. The fact that there were divisions in New England over matters such as the popular balance between magisterial authority and popular liberty, and the fact there were dissidents such as Morton, Gardiner, and Child, do not prevent us from labeling the region "puritan New England," nor should the existence of some dissidence in the Stour Valley undermine its identification

as a godly kingdom. This goes back to a point I raised earlier about not expecting uniformity of all within any movement or society.

123. Reyce, *Breviary*, 21.

124. Richard Sibbes, dedication to Ezekiel Culverwell, *Time Well Spent in Sacred Meditations* (1634). I should acknowledge that it is not entirely clear that Sibbes is referring to the Felsted area. Brett Usher and others have contended that the reference to the unhealthy air makes it more likely that the reference is to the marshes of southeast Essex and Culverwell's ministry in Great Stambridge. But Culverwell's stay at Great Stambridge was very short and not likely to have coincided with Mrs. More's youth. Furthermore, William Gouge's letter to the reader prefaced to Culverwell's *A Treatise of Faith* (1623) has comparable praise for Culverwell's ministry which he knew, he wrote, "from my infancy," since "under his Ministry was I trained up in my younger yeares." Gouge was part of the circle of friends based in London that included Sibbes, Mrs. More, and James Ussher, and he is clearly making reference to Felsted since he had attended school there at the time when Culverwell was exercising his ministry in Felsted.

125. Quoted in Bremer, *Congregational Communion*, 51. Other examples are scattered through chap. 3 of that work and in Tom Webster, *Godly Clergy in Early Stuart England: The Caroline Puritan Movement, c. 1620–1643* (Cambridge: Cambridge University Press, 1997).

126. Quoted in Bremer, *Congregational Communion*, 52. Jessey left Cambridge in 1624, when, as we will see, the foundations of the godly kingdom were being eroded. But it still remained the region of the country most compatible with evangelical clergy.

Chapter 4. Youth

1. Adam's first three surviving children, Anne, John, and Jane, were all born in Edwardstone rather than Groton, though the baptisms of John and Jane were entered into the Groton parish register. (Jane's baptism, however, was also included on the Edwardstone register bill report to the archdeacon of Sudbury; SRO/B J 502, microfilm of parish register reports, reel 7.) In 1596 Adam recorded that Thomas Mildmay "came to Edwardstone my home," and in August of that month that he had the great pond dragged. For more on this see Bremer, "Winthrop Residences in England and Ireland," privately printed and to be placed on the Winthrop Papers website, muweb.millersville.edu/~winthrop.

2. There are scraps of surviving evidence that attest to some of Adam's landholdings. An indenture that involved Adam and his father-in-law Henry Browne, in 1583 referred to lands Adam held in Groton, Edwardstone, Lindsey, and Milding (SRO/B FL 506/11/2). In 1585 he purchased land in Polstead from Sir William Waldegrave for £435 (SRO/B Ac 680/9).

3. Adam Winthrop's Diary, *WP*, I, 41, 72 indicate his loaning of Googe to others.

4. Adam Winthrop's Diary, where there are references throughout to crops, as *WP*, I, 117. For a general treatment of agriculture in Winthrop's East Anglia see Joan Thirsk, ed., *The Agrarian History of England and Wales, Vol. IV: 1500–1640* (Cambridge: Cambridge University Press, 1967), esp. 40–48.

5. *WP*, I, 56.

6. *WP*, I, 81.

7. *WP*, I, 53–54.

8. *WP*, I, 55.

9. Income from this was recorded in 1596 and 1597; *WP*, I, 120–121, 129.

10. In Adam's library were two copies of Janus Dubravius's *A New Booke of Good Husbandry . . . conteining the order and maner of making fish ponds, with the breeding, preserving and multiplying of the Carpe, Tench, Pike and Trout* (1599). One of the copies has the last printed page missing, replaced by a handwritten copy in Adam Winthrop's writing.

11. Thirsk, *Agrarian History, IV*, 167.

12. *WP*, I, 68.

13. *WP*, I, 123.

14. *WP*, I, 135.

15. An example of this is found in a letter of Adam's on 29 January 1595 to Hugh Sexey in Whitecross Street, asking him for assistance in securing a repayment of a loan granted the queen in June 1591 (PRO SP 46/39 f. 3).

16. *WP*, I, 53–54.

17. Adam Winthrop's Library, muweb.millersville.edu/~winthrop/awl.html.

18. This analysis is based primarily on identification of books surviving in American collections that were the property of Adam Winthrop. Fortunately, Adam generally subscribed his name on the flyleaf of books. This has been supplemented by the titles of books that Adam records in his diary and elsewhere. The majority of the books that survive in American collections are in the collections of the Massachusetts Historical Society, the New York Society Library, and Allegheny College. I would like to thank the librarians of these institutions for permission to examine the likely Winthrop titles. The earliest library of Harvard University was destroyed, but a donation of books from John Winthrop identifies some additional volumes. The compiled list of "The Library of Adam Winthrop" can be seen at muweb.millersville.edu/~winthrop/awl.html. The limitation of this list is that it essentially only contains those books of his father's which John Winthrop chose to bring with him to New England. Furthermore, the list is relatively light on titles that would be part of a working lawyer's library. Such works would have been brought to New England but were probably so heavily used by John and his fellow magistrates that they have not survived.

19. Browne was inducted as rector on April 5, 1563, at the instruction of Agnes Winthrop, who had inherited the manor and its entitlements on the death of her husband, Adam the Clothworker, the previous year; SRO/B E 14/5/1. William Winthrop was one of the guarantors of first fruits for Browne, which can be taken as evidence of his evangelical stance; PRO E 334/7 f. 185r. While Browne was clearly learned and zealous, there is no evidence of his holding any later church livings. He might have been the Henry Browne who is listed as being beneficed in Felsham in 1558, which might indicate that he was one of the capable but nonordained laymen who were occasionally placed in church livings at this time due to the shortage of other candidates. Lack of ordination might account for the fact that V. B. Redstone's notes on the Induction Books of the Archdeaconry of Sudbury indicate that Browne was later deprived. No date is given for that action, but it was prior to 1568 when Thomas Howlett was inducted into the living.

20. Henry Browne's notes are found scattered through the manuscript identified as Adam Winthrop's Diary, now in the British Library. Adam evidently

took a largely unused commonplace book of his father-in-law and used it for his own diary notes. While the diary entries and notes of Adam Winthrop have been published in *WP*, I, Browne's jottings were not published. They were, however, transcribed, and Browne's identity established, by Lilian Redstone when she transcribed the manuscript for the Massachusetts Historical Society. Redstone's notes are in the Winthrop Papers at the MHS.

21. The will of Henry Browne, 1593, is published in *WP*, I, 37–38.
22. A copy of this volume with the signature of "Anna Wintropp" and that of her son "John Winthrop" is no. 161 in the Winthrop Collection of the New York Society Library.
23. Anne Winthrop to Adam Winthrop, c. 1581, *WP*, I, 29.
24. Anne Winthrop to Adam Winthrop, c. 1581, *WP*, I, 29.
25. Adam Winthrop's Diary, *WP*, I, 136.
26. *WP*, I, 105–106, contains Adam's "Memorandum of my Cousin Josua Winthrop his wife Anne's behavior."
27. Anne was named not only after her mother but after the couple's first child, who had died shortly after childbirth. Naming a child after a deceased sibling was not uncommon at this time.
28. Adam Winthrop's Diary, *WP*, I, 43–44.
29. Adam Winthrop's Diary, *WP*, I, 136.
30. Adam Winthrop's Diary, *WP*, I, 41.
31. Sir Humphrey was the first cousin of Sir Thomas Mildmay, who had married Adam's sister Alice.
32. But on April 22, 1597, Adam sadly recorded that "Grymble my great mastiffe was hanged, a gentle dog in the house but egrotavit of blindness."
33. For the events leading to this settlement and its character see Michael McCarthy-Morrogh, *The Munster Plantation: English Migration to Southern Ireland, 1583–1641* (Oxford: Clarendon Press, 1986).
34. Pauline Henley, *Spenser in Ireland* (Dublin: Cork University Press, 1928), 77. Spenser was at Pembroke College, Cambridge, during Adam Winthrop's stay at the university, but there is no evidence that they ever met. Spenser did befriend John Still as an undergraduate, and it was through Still that he met Alabaster on this visit to Cambridge. Alabaster showed Spenser his unpublished work, which caused Spenser to praise the young man's poetry in his own *Colin Clouts*.
35. F. F. Covington argues that Spenser had difficulty in gaining tenants for his Irish estate and that recruitment therefore became one of the reasons for his visits to England; "Spenser in Ireland" (Yale University, Ph.D., 1924), 114–115, 132.
36. Adam Winthrop's Diary, *WP*, I, 65.
37. Thomas Kedbye and John Stockton, churchwardens of Groton, c. John Winthrop, Adam Winthrop, and Edward Stowe in the Court of Requests (PRO REQ 2/231/4).
38. Act quoted in McCarthy-Morrogh, *Munster*, 209.
39. F. A. Inderwick, ed., *A Calendar of the Inner Temple Records: I, 21 Hen. VII to 45 Eliz.* (London, 1896), 405–406.
40. I would like to thank Mr. John Taylor, who farms in Groton, for an enlightening and enjoyable discussion of farming and the farm landscape in the region.
41. *WP*, I, 76 and elsewhere.
42. Adam simply recorded, "The 23 of December I felt an Earthquake." *WP*, I, 75 and n.

43. *WP*, I, 65.
44. *WP*, I, 137.
45. *WP*, I, 66.
46. Adam Cely was about ten years older than John, born about 1578.
47. *WP*, I, 70.
48. *WP*, I, 88. This was a sensational case that attracted wide attention and popular published accounts, including *A sorrowfull ballad made by Mistris Browne who for the consenting to the killinge of her husband was burned* (1605).
49. *WP*, I, 140.
50. *WP*, I, 83.
51. *WP*, I, 86.
52. *WP*, I, 216. This early version of football, what Americans call soccer, was played with great intensity. See David H. Fischer, *Albion's Seed: Four British Folkways in America* (New York: Oxford University Press, 1989), 147ff., for a discussion. A game that resulted in death, a divided community, and accusations of witchcraft is described in James Sharpe, *The Bewitching of Anne Gunter: A Horrible and True Story of Football, Witchcraft, Murder, and the King of England* (London: Profile, 2000).
53. The manuscript "Principles of the Christian Religion" was composed by Adam in a commonplace book catalogued in the Winthrop Papers of the Massachusetts Historical Society as "Medical Recipes." It will be published as part of *Winthrop Papers: Religious Manuscripts, 1560s to 1630s* (forthcoming from the Massachusetts Historical Society). Ian Green has discussed the catechisms of the period in *The Christian's ABC: Catechisms and Catechizing in England, c. 1530–1740* (Oxford: Oxford University Press, 1996). Green has pointed out that catechizing was employed by clergymen across the religious spectrum of the English church, reformers as well as supporters of the establishment. Adam Winthrop's friend Henry Sandes of Boxford promoted catechisms in the meetings of the Dedham conference.
54. This paragraph is based on the general experience of families such as the Winthrops and hints found in Adam Winthrop's diary and in John Winthrop's spiritual diary.
55. The overseers of the grammar school represented a cross-section of the keepers of the godly kingdom, including Brampton Gurdon, John Knewstub, Thomas Lovell, Henry Sandes, and Sir William Waldegrave. The charter is in SRO/Ipswich T4/58/6.
56. SRO/Ipswich T4/58/7.
57. Adam Winthrop's Diary, *WP*, I, 73.
58. Sarah Bendall, Christopher Brooke, and Patrick Collinson, *A History of Emmanuel College, Cambridge* (Woodbridge, Suffolk: Boydell, 1999), 222.
59. For more on the school see S.H.A. Hervey, *King Edward VI Free Grammar School, Bury St. Edmunds* (Bury St. Edmunds: Paul & Mathew, 1908). The master of the school in the early 1580s was John Forth. This was possibly the John Forth who became rector of Hawkwell in Essex in 1586 and was the author of *Apocalypsis Jesu Christi, Revelata per Angelum Domini* (1597), which Adam Winthrop owned, and on which he inscribed "Johannis de vado alias," indicating perhaps that Forth was known to him.
60. Information on the school is drawn from R. W. Elliott, *The Story of King Edward VI School Bury St. Edmunds* (Bury St. Edmunds: Foundation Governors, 1963). The quotes are from the 1583 statutes, which are published therein (159–170).

61. Perhaps this is where John Winthrop learned not to mark his books! One of the striking facts in examining books clearly belonging to the Winthrops is that whereas Adam inscribed his name and scribbled numerous notes on the flyleaves and in the margins of his books, his son John appears to have never done so.

62. A new edition of John Winthrop's "Experiencia," or spiritual diary, is to be published in *Winthrop Papers: Religious Manuscripts*. Citations here are to the older, scattered version in the *WP*, vols. I and II. *WP*, I, 193.

63. A new edition of John Winthrop's "Christian Experience," will be published in *Winthrop Papers: Religious Manuscripts*. This quote is from the version in *WP*, 154–155.

64. For the history of Emmanuel and its puritan character see Bendall et al., *Emmanuel College*.

65. The description of Trinity as it existed in John Winthrop's time—much of which remains unchanged—is drawn from Robert Willis and John Willis Clark, *The Architectural History of the University of Cambridge* (Cambridge, 1886), II, chap. 14.

66. While in their essential character the Great Court and the buildings on its four sides remain as they were or were being constructed in Winthrop's time, the appearance of what was then the library has changed. After it was damaged by a fire in 1666 the old library was converted to chambers, and a new, larger library was built along the river on the west side of what was called Nevill's Court.

67. John Twigg, *The University of Cambridge and the English Revolution, 1625–1688* (Woodbridge, Suffolk: Boydell, 1990), 16, 38.

68. Quoted in Francis J. Bremer, *Congregational Communion: Clerical Friendship in the Anglo-American Puritan Community, 1610–1692* (Boston: Northeastern University Press, 1994). Much of the detail on Cambridge life in this and following paragraphs is derived from chap. 1 of that work, "The Cambridge Connection."

69. Quoted in Bremer, *Congregational Communion*, 25.

70. Quoted in Bremer, *Congregational Communion*, 26–27.

71. Nicholas Tyacke, *Anti-Calvinists: The Rise of English Arminianism, c. 1590–1640* (New York: Oxford University Press, 1987), 35–38.

72. William Haller, *The Rise of Puritanism* (New York: Columbia University Press, 1938), 64–65.

73. Willis and Clark, *Architectural History*, II, 635–638.

74. Bremer, *Congregational Communion*, 28.

75. Thomas Shepard's Autobiography, in Michael McGiffert, ed., *God's Plot: Puritan Spirituality in Thomas Shepard's Cambridge*, rev. ed. (Amherst: University of Massachusetts Press, 1994), 42–43.

76. Samuel Ward's Diary, quoted in Bremer, *Congregational Communion*, 29.

77. Among the useful studies for understanding issues of sexuality and gender in early modern England and New England see Susan Dwyer Amussen, "'The Part of a Christian Man': The Cultural Politics of Manhood in Early Modern England," in Amussen and Mark A. Kishlansky, eds., *Political Culture and Cultural Politics in Early Modern England: Essays Presented to David Underdown* (Manchester: Manchester University Press, 1995), 213–233; Lisa Jardine, "Companionate Marriage versus Male Friendship: Anxiety for the Lineal Family in Jacobean Drama," in Amussen and Kishlansky, *Political Culture*, 234–254; Richard Godbeer, "'The Cry of Sodom': Discourse, Intercourse,

and Desire in Colonial New England," *William and Mary Quarterly* 52 (1995), 259–286; Jane Kamensky, "Talk Like a Man: Speech, Power, and Masculinity in Early New England," in Laura McCall and Donald Yacovone, eds., *A Shared Experience: Men, Women, and the History of Gender* (New York: New York University Press, 1998), 19–50; and the papers on gender by Frances Dolan and Richard Godbeer at the 1999 at Millersville University conference "The Worlds of John Winthrop: England and New England, 1588–1649"; an expansion of Dr. Godbeer's paper will be published in Francis J. Bremer and Lynn Botelho, eds., *The World of John Winthrop: England and New England, 1588–1649* (forthcoming from the Massachusetts Historical Society). See also Richard Godbeer, *Sexual Revolutions in Early America* (Baltimore: Johns Hopkins University Press, 2002). I would like to thank Donald Yacovone for discussing this topic with me.

78. Donald Yacovone, "'Surpassing the Love of Women,'" in McCall and Yacovone, *A Shared Experience*, 196.
79. John Winthrop to William Spring, 8 February 1630, *WP*, II, 203–206.
80. Patrick Collinson has written of the relationship at Emmanuel College, Cambridge, in the early 1630s between two students who "became chamber fellows, who read and studied together and became friends in a manner of friendship familiar to both young men from its models in Ovid and other pieces of classical literature," but also warns that "we must make a deliberate effort to understand and interpret" such relationships "as the seventeenth century would have interpreted them and not anachronistically." Bendall et al., *Emmanuel College*, 61, 60.
81. Winthrop, "Christian Experience," *WP*, I, 154; "Experiencia," *WP*, I, 163–164.
82. "The Millenary Petition, 1603," in Henry Gee and William John Hardy, eds., *Documents Illustrative of English Church History* (London: Macmillan, 1896), 508–511.
83. Adam Winthrop's Diary, *WP*, I, 79.
84. Roland G. Usher, *The Reconstruction of the English Church* (London: Appleton, 1910), 298ff.
85. William Hunt, *The Puritan Moment: The Coming of Revolution in an English County* (Cambridge: Harvard University Press, 1983), 105–106. Some of the results are published in Albert Peel, ed., *The Seconde Parte of a Register, Being a Calendar of Manuscripts . . . by the Puritans About 1593*, 2 vols. (Cambridge: Cambridge University Press, 1915). Unfortunately the results of the Suffolk survey do not survive.
86. These events are recorded in Adam Winthrop's Diary, *WP*, I, 79–84.
87. British Library, Add. MS 38492, Townsend Papers re: Puritan Cause, 1584–1604, f. 99.
88. John Spurr, *English Puritanism, 1603–1689* (Basingstoke: Macmillan, 1988), 59–60. The best account of the Hampton Court conference is Patrick Collinson, "The Jacobean Religious Settlement: The Hampton Court Conference," in H. Tomlinson, ed., *Before the English Civil War* (London: Macmillan, 1983). Whitgift's articles are reprinted in Gerald Bray, ed., *The Anglican Canons, 1529–1947*, Church of England Record Society, vol. 6 (1998), 770–772.
89. Canon 36 in the Canons of 1603 (1604), in Bray, *Canons*, 319–321.
90. "Archbishop Richard Bancroft's Letter to His Commissioners for His Metropolitan Visitation, 1605," in Kenneth Fincham, ed., *Visitation Articles and*

Injunctions of the Early Stuart Church, Vol. I, Church of England Record Society, vol. 1 (1994), 4–5.

91. Knewstub's efforts were the subject of correspondence between William Bedell and Samuel Ward which is quoted in Usher, *Reconstruction*, II, 9–10.

92. Norwich diocesan records quoted by Usher in *Reconstruction*, I, 269, 267.

93. Adam Winthrop's Diary, *WP*, I, 80.

94. Powle c. Winthrop, PRO REQ 2/254/72, has six documents relating to the dispute.

95. Adam Winthrop's notes in almanac, *WP*, I, 257.

96. Guildhall Library, Records of the Grocers Company, II, f. 191.

97. Guildhall Library, Merchant Taylor Records, Court Minutes, II, 1574–1595, f. 213v.

98. Joshua and Thomas Palmer stood surety for their kinsman William Alabaster when he was presented to the living of Landulf, in Cornwall, by the earl of Essex in 1596 (PRO E 334/12 f. 60v); Joshua and Adam, listed as a haberdasher, stood surety for Munning when he was inducted rector of Thornham Magna, Suffolk, in 1597 (PRO E 334/12 f. 77r); and the two guaranteed Munning's payment of first fruits for Brettenham in the same year (PRO E 334/12 f. 87r).

99. Powle c. Winthrop, PRO REQ 2/254/72.

100. Adam Winthrop's Diary, *WP*, I, 81, 87.

Chapter 5. Turning Points

1. F. G. Emmison, ed., *Feet of Fines for Essex: Vol. VI, 1581–1603* (Oxford: Leopard's Head Press, 1993), 89. I would like to thank Christopher Thompson for directing me to this reference.

2. William Forth of Hadleigh was a prosperous landowner and justice in Suffolk who had profited greatly from the sale of monastic lands. One of those properties was Coddenham Manor in Boxford, which he sold to William Risby of Lavenham. Forth's commitment to religious reform had been demonstrated in a series of suits against the Catholic Walter Clerke, and he had paid for his religious stance by being removed from the county commission of the peace at the start of Mary's reign. When he died in 1559 he divided his estate among his six sons. His eldest son, Robert, inherited Butley Abbey. He was high sheriff of Suffolk in 1569 and subsequently a prominent member of the commission of the peace till his death in 1600. In 1583 he was one of ten signatories of a petition to the Privy Council protesting actions taken at the recently held assizes against some of the godly clergy of the region, including Oliver Pigge. William's third son, also named William, inherited land in Hadleigh and also served on the commission of the peace from the late 1580s. Israel, the fourth son, settled in the Groton area, having inherited pasturelands in Whatfield and married into the Mannock family. He was later described as being "of Kersey." The youngest son of the elder William was John Forth, who inherited his father's copyhold lands in Hadleigh. He married Thomasine Hilles, who was the widow of George Crymble and Thomas Bode. Presumably Thomasine was related to John Hilles, who was a citizen of London and member of the Skinners Company. His nephew William married Joanne Browne, the sister of Adam Winthrop's wife. Their daughter (Adam's niece) Joan married Adam Winthrop of London, William's son (and Adam of

Groton's nephew). Thomasine brought property in Great Stambridge to her marriage, and that is where the couple settled. Forth became bailiff for some of the Essex estates of the Rich family.

In addition to the links through the Hilles connection, there were other connections between the Winthrops and Forths in the late sixteenth century. The first William Forth of Hadleigh had named his cousin Thomas Alabaster as one of the executors of his will. Thomas Alabaster was the father of Roger Alabaster, who married Adam Winthrop's sister Bridget. William Forth's third son, also named William, sold property on Angel Street in Hadleigh to Adam Winthrop in 1592. Adam had other dealings with him as well and in 1596 recorded that William owed him £100, a very considerable sum.

3. Ralph A. Houlbrooke, *The English Family, 1450–1700* (London: Longman, 1984), 63.
4. John Winthrop's Spiritual Diary, or "Experiencia," *WP*, I, 162–163.
5. "Experiencia," *WP*, I, 162.
6. "Experiencia," *WP*, I, 162.
7. On September 6 Adam recorded in his diary that John took an estate, presumably in Rochford Hundred. Then, on September 12, John Forth transferred his deed to Lucas Farm in Kersey to John Winthrop and his wife, Mary, in the presence of Adam Winthrop, Henry Sandes, and Thomas Laister. Two days later another parcel of land was transferred to John and Mary. Memorandum in Adam Winthrop's Diary, *WP*, I, 106.
8. Philip Benton, *The History of Rochford Hundred* (Rochford, 1867), 785.
9. Joan Thirsk, *The Agrarian History of England and Wales, Vol. IV: 1500–1640* (Cambridge: Cambridge University Press, 1967), 53; William Hunt, *The Puritan Moment: The Coming of Revolution in an English County* (Cambridge: Harvard University Press, 1983), 6, 8.
10. The identification of Stewards as the Forth home is based upon later correspondence between John Winthrop and Thomas Hawes, who rented the farm after the Winthrops removed to Groton. Originally called Le Hide, Stewards had been acquired by Thomasine Hilles in 1578 prior to her marriage to John Forth (ERO/Southend D/DB 463/9). From a Hawes letter (*WP*, I, 396–399) and one of John Winthrop to Hawes (*WP*, II, 172–173) it is evident that the Winthrops had lived at Stewards, that they had left some of their furnishings there when they left Great Stambridge, and that it had fallen into a state of disrepair after their departure. Hawes's description of a leaking roof and a flooding cellar reminds us of the poor weather and high water table of the region.
11. I wish to thank Christopher Thompson for guiding me around Rochford Hall and other sites in the hundred and for discussing the history of the region with me.
12. John Winthrop, "A Model of Christian Charity," *WP*, II, 282.
13. J. S. Cockburn, ed., *Calendar of Assize Records: Essex Indictments, James I* (London: HMSO, 1982), 121–122.
14. For a discussion of the religious disputes centering on the Rich family and Rochford Hall see Hunt, *Puritan Moment*, 102–104. Forth's imprisonment and release is contained in British Library, Landsdowne MS 108 f. 46r. I wish to thank Christopher Thompson for providing me with this information. Collinson uses the phrase "retreat from the vision of a city set on a hill into a holy huddle" in Patrick Collinson, "The Shearmen's Tree and the Preacher: The Strange Death of Merry England in Shrewsbury and Beyond,"

in Collinson and John Craig, eds., *The Reformation in English Towns, 1500–1640* (Basingstoke: Macmillan, 1998), 219.

15. See entries in his spiritual diary for this period in *WP*, I.

16. "Experiencia," *WP*, I, 167.

17. "Experiencia," *WP*, I, 166.

18. Lobb quoted in Francis J. Bremer, *Congregational Communion: Clerical Friendship in the Anglo-American Puritan Community, 1610–1692* (Boston: Northeastern University Press, 1994), 251.

19. For the Family of Love and Knewstub's opposition see Christopher Marsh, *The Family of Love in English Society, 1550–1630* (Cambridge: Cambridge University Press, 1994).

20. The struggle over English theology is best examined in Nicholas Tyacke, *Anti-Calvinists: The Rise of English Arminianism, c. 1590–1640* (New York: Oxford University Press, 1987), and Anthony Milton, *Catholic and Reformed: The Roman and Protestant Churches in English Protestant Thought, 1600–1640* (Cambridge: Cambridge University Press, 1995). But see also opposition to Tyacke from Peter White, *Predestination, Policy, and Polemic: Conflict and Consensus in the English Church from the Reformation to the Civil War* (Cambridge: Cambridge University Press, 1992), and Julian Davies, *The Caroline Captivity of the Church: Charles I and the Remoulding of Anglicanism* (Oxford: Clarendon Press, 1992). I believe Tyacke has persuasively met the challenge of his critics. See Nicholas Tyacke, *Aspects of English Protestantism, c. 1530–1700* (Manchester: Manchester University Press, 2001).

21. An excellent treatment of the range of views on grace and works and the variously nuanced treatments that existed in the puritan community will be found in the early chapters of Michael Winship's *Making Heretics: Militant Protestantism and Free Grace in Massachusetts, 1636–1641* (Princeton: Princeton University Press, 2002)

22. This was William Twisse's read on a manuscript of Cotton's that was circulating in England in the mid-1620s; Twisse quoted in Sargent Bush Jr., ed., *The Correspondence of John Cotton* (Chapel Hill: University of North Carolina Press, 2001), 110. Cotton's views at that time are also to be found in a letter he wrote to James Ussher, archbishop of Armagh and a respected Calvinist theologian, in 1626; Cotton to Ussher, 31 May 1626, in Bush, *Cotton Correspondence*, 109–112.

23. "Experiencia," *WP*, I, 161–169.

24. "Experiencia," *WP*, I, 166.

25. See Richard Godbeer, "'Love Raptures': Marital, Romantic, and Erotic Images of Jesus Christ in Puritan New England," in Laura McCall and Donald Yacovone, eds., *A Shared Experience: Men, Women, and the History of Gender* (New York: New York University Press, 1998). I have also profited from Tom Webster's "'Kiss Me with the Kisses of his Lips': Blurred Masculinity in Early Modern Spirituality," an unpublished essay which Dr. Webster let me read.

26. "Experiencia," *WP*, I, 163.

27. For discussion of the purposes of marriage and relations between husbands and wives see Houlbrooke, *The English Family*, chap. 5.

28. Henry was born at Great Stambridge on January 10; Adam rode there on the thirteenth and returned with John and the baby on the nineteenth, when the christening occurred at Groton with Henry Sandes and John Gostling as godfathers. This probably indicates Adam's hopes that he would come to

inherit the manor after his brother and that it would then pass to John and his offspring. Forth was also born at Great Stambridge and probably baptized there. Great Stambridge Parish Register, ERO/S D/P 218/1/1.

29. Mary Winthrop to John Winthrop, n.d., *WP*, I, 161. The editor of that volume of the *WP* places the letter in early 1607, which would have been early in their marriage.

30. "Experiencia," *WP*, I, 202.

31. "Experiencia," *WP*, I, 165.

32. Winthrop c. Munning, PRO C 2/JasI/230/91.

33. PRO REQ 2/231/4. John and his brother Adam responded to the suit by charging that the dwelling had been built in the past by the cellarer of the Abbey of St. Edmund at Bury for use of the inhabitant of the manor house, Groton Hall, and that it was thus their property to hold. While it appears that Winthrop won the case, the dispute could have only further harmed his local reputation.

34. National Library of Ireland, Lismore Castle MS, box of uncatalogued manuscripts, no. 8, Copy of Deed of Bargain and Sale from rolls of Irish Chancery re: sale of Raleigh lands to Boyle, 7 December 1602. Much of what is here presented about the Winthrops in Ireland is based on interpretation of very scant evidence. A significant portion of the Irish records, including those of Chancery, were lost in the destruction of the Four Courts building in 1916 during the Irish civil war. Fortunately, copies of some of the materials existed elsewhere, including some Chancery records that had been copied in the nineteenth century at the request of Robert C. Winthrop and included in the Winthrop Papers donated to the Massachusetts Historical Society.

35. Anthony Sheehan, "The Overthrow of the Plantation of Munster in October, 1598, *Irish Sword* 15 (1982), 11–18, which distills some of the findings in Sheehan, "Provincial Grievance and National Revolt: Munster in the Nine Years War" (University College, Dublin, MA, 1981). The best account of the rebellion throughout Ireland is Hiram Morgan, *Tyrone's Rebellion: The Outbreak of the Nine Years War in Tudor Ireland* (Woodbridge, Suffolk: Boydell, 1993).

36. "The supplication of the blood of the English," quoted in Sheehan, "Overthrow," 18.

37. A tradition among the Irish descendants of the Winthrops claims that John commanded a regiment of dragoons under the command of the earl of Essex, who was dispatched from England to crush the rebellion; *Burke's Landed Gentry of Ireland*, 4th ed. This account, written by Mark Bence-Jones, is uncritically accepted by McCarthy-Morrogh in his treatment of the Munster settlement, but no documents have been found to sustain the claim.

38. Adam Winthrop's Diary, *WP*, I, 76.

39. Nicholas Canny, *Making Ireland British, 1580–1650* (Oxford: Oxford University Press, 2001), 150–151.

40. In 1618 James Spenser and other surviving planters in Carberry petitioned the Privy Council for aid, citing the efforts of Walter Coppinger and other Catholic landowners attempting to frustrate their plans. The petition listed those who had initiated the plantation scheme, including John Winthrop. *Calendar State Papers Ireland: James I, 1615–1625*, no. 407.

41. The elder Adam Winthrop's 1562 will is in *WP*, I, 17–22. To avoid what would have in effect been inheritance fees, Adam had also received a license to alienate the property in 1557, arranging the settlement of the estate on

his son John and, John dying without issue, young Adam (*WP*, I, 12–13). The latter document is in Latin, and I would like to thank Dr. Carol Miller for assistance in translating it and Professor J. H. Baker for answering some of my questions about the legal device being employed.

42. Rpt. in *WP*, I, 38–39. Again I would like to thank Drs. Miller and Baker for their assistance. The fact that John sought this when he did probably has to do with his consideration of settling in Ireland.

43. While such waivers were not uncommon, it is surprising that Adam did not insist on seeing the legal documentation of this waiver. One possibility is that he doubted its existence but would not have been able to find the additional funds to obtain such a waiver himself, thus postponing the day when Elizabeth's interests would have to be taken into account. All this would be aired in court cases involving the title to the estate in the 1620s that will be dealt with in a later chapter.

44. I have not found a copy of that license to alienate, but it is described in Davy's Suffolk Collections, British Library, Add. MS 19.077 f. 329r&v, as well as in Coppinger's *Suffolk Manors*.

45. For example, SRO/B FB 391/21 indicates his sale of lands in Edwardstone for £200.

46. Adam Winthrop's Diary, *WP*, I, 103. He received £20 for his Trinity auditorship.

47. The absence of the license to alienate and the actual documents of the sale makes the details murky. This assessment is drawn from court documents in a Chancery case, to be discussed in a later chapter, in which the title was called into question.

48. Adam Winthrop's Diary, *WP*, I, 103. This reference is responsible for the error that appears in some accounts that Winthrop was a justice of the peace at the age of twenty-one.

49. Gray's Inn, MS Admittance Book. I would like to thank Theresa Thom, librarian of Gray's Inn, for giving me access to this manuscript. There is no evidence that speaks to why John chose Gray's Inn as opposed to the Inner Temple, where his father had studied, though the fact that Nathaniel Rich, whom he would have encountered at Rochford Hall, was admitted to Gray's in 1610 may have influenced him.

50. "Experiencia," *WP*, I, 168.

51. A letter from Thomas Fones to Adam's daughter Anne was addressed to her as being at Groton Hall in 1603 (*WP*, I, 149–150); a 1627 letter from Margaret Winthrop to John indicates that John's mother was living at the Hall, Adam being by then deceased (*WP*, I, 369–370). This would seem to indicate that Adam's residence was the Hall. The "mansion house," presumably the larger and more "modern" structure, would have been the residence of the "lord of the manor."

52. Translation of the entry in Adam Winthrop's Diary, *WP*, I, 177.

53. "Experiencia," *WP*, I, 169.

54. Richard Rogers, *Seven Treatises, containing such direction as is gathered out of the Holie Scriptures, leading and guiding to true happiness* (1603). The quotes are taken from a modernized edition I am editing along with Mrs. Susan Ortmann, which will be published in 2003.

55. "Experiencia," *WP*, I, 169.

56. "Experiencia," *WP*, I, 169.

57. Baptized August 8, buried August 16.

58. Groton parish register, copy at Groton Church.
59. "Experiencia," *WP*, I, 190.
60. SRO/B FL 506/11/8.
61. "Experiencia," *WP*, I, 169.
62. "Experiencia," *WP*, I, 182–190. Winthrop's lengthy account, merely summarized here, is one of the most detailed and moving accounts of a puritan death scene. For a discussion of attitudes toward death and other examples of deathbed narratives see Ralph Houlbrooke, *Death, Religion and the Family in England, 1480–1750* (Oxford: Oxford University Press, 1998).

Chapter 6. A Godly Magistrate

1. PRO C 231/4v, Crown Office Docquet Book entry "A Commission of peace in the Countie of Suffolk for placing of John Winthrop Esquire therein."
2. Unfortunately we do not have detailed records of the assize meetings in Suffolk, or of other court sessions. This account is derived from secondary treatments of sessions such as Conyers Read, ed., *William Lambarde and Local Government* (Ithaca: Cornell University Press, 1962), and Cynthia Herrup, *The Common Peace: Participation and the Criminal Law in Seventeenth-Century England* (Cambridge: Cambridge University Press, 1987), as well as from descriptions of assizes held elsewhere such as Ernest Axon, ed., *Manchester Sessions* (Manchester: Record Society, 1901) and Louis Knafla, *Kent at Law, 1602: The County Jurisdiction: Assizes and Sessions of the Peace* (London: HMSO, 1994).
3. Michael Braddick, *State Formation in Early Modern England, c. 1550–1700* (Cambridge: Cambridge University Press, 2000), 37–38.
4. Diarmaid MacCulloch, *Suffolk and the Tudors: Politics and Religion in an English County, 1500–1600* (Oxford: Clarendon Press, 1986), 122–123.
5. The subject of the grand jury has been ignored by most historians. The best treatment of the subject is John Morrill, *The Cheshire Grand Jury, 1625–1659: A Social and Administrative Study* (Leicester: Leicester University Press, 1976).
6. There are very few records of the Suffolk commission of the peace for this period. Fortunately, a record exists for this first session attended by John Winthrop. Bodleian Library, Tanner MS 284 f. 62r&v.
7. Adam Winthrop's tribute to Jermyn is in *WP*, I, 176; for Jermyn as custos rotulorum see Diarmaid MacCulloch, "Power, Privilege, and the County Community: County Politics in Elizabethan Suffolk," (Cambridge University, Ph.D., 1977), 227.
8. MacCulloch, *Suffolk*, 22–23.
9. The best discussion of the commission of the peace remains Sidney and Beatrice Webb, *English Local Government, Volume I: The Parish and the County* (London: Oxford University Press, 1963 rpt.).
10. For the development of petty sessions, a practice that would be adopted in New England, see Frederick A. Youngs Jr., "Towards Petty Sessions: Tudor JPs and Divisions of Counties," in Delloyd Guth and John McKenna, eds., *Tudor Rule and Revolution: Essays for G. R. Elton* (Cambridge: Cambridge University Press, 1982), 201–216.
11. Because John presided over the Groton Court Baron in 1609, some historians have assumed that he was a justice of the peace at that time, which is incorrect. He was then substituting for his father in presiding as steward on behalf of his uncle. For the role of manor courts at this time see Christopher

Harrison, "Manor Courts and the Governance of Tudor England," in Christopher Brooks and Michael Lobban, eds., *Communities and Courts in Britain, 1150–1900* (London: Hambledon, 1997), 43–59.

12. Bezaleel Carter, *Christ His Last Will and John His Legacy* (1621), 58. Among those mentioned in the margin as godly men who had recently died were Sir Edward Lewkenor, Sir Calthorp Parker, and Sir Edward Bacon. Carter's 1618 *The Wise King and the Learned Judge* was a funeral remembrance of Lewkenor.

13. Samuel Ward, *Jethro's Justice of the Peace. A Sermon Preached at a General Assises held at Bury St. Edmunds, for the Countie of Suffolk* (1618), 60.

14. John Carter, *The Tombstone as a Broken and Imperfect Monument* (1653).

15. Ward, *Jethro's Justice of the Peace*, 34.

16. Ward, *Jethro's Justice of the Peace*, 20–22.

17. Ward, *Jethro's Justice of the Peace*, 23–24.

18. Ward, *Jethro's Justice of the Peace*, 25.

19. Ward, *Jethro's Justice of the Peace*, 39.

20. Ward, *Jethro's Justice of the Peace*, 35.

21. Ward, *Jethro's Justice of the Peace*, 51–52.

22. Ward, *Jethro's Justice of the Peace*, 49, 60.

23. John Winthrop's Spiritual Diary, or "Experiencia," *WP*, I, 195–196.

24. Richard Rogers, *Certaine Sermons Preached and Penned by Richard Rogers* (1612), 189.

25. Thomas Carew, *Four Godlie and Profitable Sermons* (1605), third lecture, n.p.

26. "Experiencia," *WP*, I, 197–198.

27. "Experiencia," *WP*, I, 198–199.

28. "Experiencia," *WP*, I, 204.

29. "Experiencia," *WP*, I, 207.

30. "Experiencia," *WP*, I, 209.

31. PRO E 334/9 f. 45r.

32. The list of school governors is published in *WP*, I, 145–146.

33. John Winthrop to William Spring, 8 February 1630, *WP*, II, 203–206.

34. "Experiencia," *WP*, I, 202.

35. I would like to thank the staff of the History of Parliament Trust, and especially Simon Healey, for allowing me to review their files and take notes on Crane and other members of Parliament whose careers crossed with that of Winthrop.

36. Francis Bacon to the duke of Buckingham in Bacon's *Works* (London, 1824), V, 452, as quoted in Robert C. Winthrop, *The Life and Letters of John Winthrop*, 2d ed. (Boston, 1869), I, 123.

37. The most complete biography of Margaret Tyndal Winthrop is Alice Morse Earle, *Margaret Winthrop* (New York, 1895), which can be supplemented by Mary Ann Groves, *Most Sweet Friend: A Brief Biography of Margaret Tyndal Winthrop* (Greenville, Ill.: Colonial Daughters of Seventeenth Century, 1977).

38. Culverwell's support is to be found in Ezekiel Culverwell to John Winthrop, [1618], *WP*, I, 229–230; John Winthrop to Margaret Tyndal, n.d., *WP*, I, 221–225.

39. Adam Winthrop to Margaret Tyndal, 31 March 1618, *WP*, I, 220–221.

40. John Winthrop to Margaret Tyndal, n.d., *WP*, I, 222.

41. John Winthrop to Margaret Tyndal, 4 April 1618, *WP*, I, 226–229.

42. John Winthrop to Margaret Tyndal, 4 April 1618, *WP*, I, 226–227.

43. "Experiencia," *WP*, I, 235.

44. Adam Winthrop's note on Adam and Stephen Winthrop, *WP*, I, 256.
45. "Experiencia," *WP*, I, 235.
46. The literature on marriage in the Tudor-Stuart period is vast. Scholarship has moved beyond the rather rigid interpretations offered by Lawrence Stone in *The Family, Sex, and Marriage in England, 1500–1800* (London: Weidenfeld & Nicolson, 1977). The literature to the date of its publication is well summarized in Ralph Houlbrooke, *The English Family, 1450–1700* (London: Longman, 1984). Important studies since that date include Anne Laurence, *Women in England, 1500–1760: A Social History* (London: Weidenfeld & Nicolson, 1994), and Anthony Fletcher, "The Protestant Idea of Marriage in Early Modern England," in Fletcher and Peter Roberts, eds., *Religion, Culture and Society in Early Modern Britain: Essays in Honor of Patrick Collinson* (Cambridge: Cambridge University Press, 1994), 161–181. On Puritan marriage in particular see William and Malleville Haller, "The Puritan Art of Love," *Huntington Library Quarterly* 5 (1941–1942), 235–272; Edmund Leites, "The Duty to Desire: Love, Friendship, and Sexuality in Some Puritan Theories of Marriage," *Comparative Civilizations Review* 3 (1979), 40–82; and Lane Belden, "Two Schools of Desire: Nature and Marriage in Seventeenth-Century Puritanism," *Church History* 69 (2000), 372–403. Studies of New England puritan practice that have relevance include Edmund S. Morgan, *The Puritan Family* (New York: Harper & Row, 1966); Amanda Porterfield, "Bridal Passion and New England Puritanism," in *Feminine Spirituality in America* (Philadelphia: Temple University Press, 1980), 19–50; and Michael Winship, "Behold the Bridegroom Cometh! Marital Imagery in Massachusetts Preaching, 1630–1730," *Early American Literature* 27 (1992), 170–184.
47. Margaret Winthrop to John Winthrop, 18 May 1629, *WP*, II, 92.
48. These expressions are drawn from a variety of letters printed in *WP*, I and II.
49. Margaret Winthrop to John Winthrop, 10 April 1627, *WP*, I, 343.
50. Margaret Winthrop to John Winthrop, [1627], *WP*, I, 353.
51. Margaret Winthrop to John Winthrop, [22 November1627], *WP*, I, 369; Margaret Winthrop to John Winthrop, 18 May 1629, *WP*, II, 92.
52. Margaret Winthrop to John Winthrop, [1627], *WP*, I, 355.
53. John Winthrop to Margaret Winthrop, 15 June 1627, *WP*, I, 355.
54. This summary is drawn from a variety of sources that describe the nature of household tasks, including those in n. 46. See also Linda Pollock, *With Faith and Physic: The Life of a Tudor Gentlewoman* (London: Collins & Brown, 1993), which deals with a Winthrop kinswoman, Lady Grace Mildmay; Felicity Heal and Clive Holmes, *The Gentry in England and Wales, 1500–1700* (Basingstoke: Macmillan, 1994); Lena Cowen Orlin, *Elizabethan Households: An Anthology* (Washington, D.C.: Folger Library, 1995); Felicity Heal, *Hospitality in Early Modern England* (Oxford: Clarendon Press, 1990); and contemporary works, including Gervase Markham, *The English Housewife (1615)*, ed. Michael Best (Kingston: McGill University Press, 1986). Earle, *Margaret Winthrop*, offers a view that focuses on Margaret.
55. His father, Adam, seems to have owned more property in Boxford than in Groton, and the churchwardens' accounts there suggest that he was more involved in the Boxford parish than was his son; SRO/B FB77 E 2/2.
56. Queen Elizabeth to Archbishop Parker, 22 January 1560, in *Correspondence of Matthew Parker* (Cambridge, Eng., 1853), 132ff. See Margaret Aston, *England's Iconoclasts, Vol. I: Laws Against Images* (Oxford: Clarendon Press, 1988), 361–362. I would like to thank Professor Ian Green for an exchange

of views on this subject. A fine set of such boards that was donated by Winthrop's friend Robert Reyce can be seen in the church at Preston. Though puritans seem to have had no objection to these aids, there is no evidence that any such boards were placed in New England churches.

57. We have no seating plans for any of the churches John Winthrop attended. This interpretation is derived from Amanda Flather, *The Politics of Place: A Study of Church Seating in Essex, c. 1580–1640* (Leicester: Leicester University Press, 1999), and Kevin Dillow, "The Social and Ecclesiastical Significance of Church Seating Arrangements and Pew Disputes, 1500–1740" (Oxford University, Ph.D., 1990).

58. That sermon notebook will be published for the first time in *Winthrop Papers: Religious Manuscripts*, forthcoming from the Massachusetts Historical Society.

59. In 1578 the first of what have been called "Puritan Prayer Books" was published. This and later versions combined in a single volume an edition of the Bible (in 1578 it was the Geneva translation) along with an edition of the Book of Common Prayer which omitted certain services objected to by puritans, such as those for private confession and the churching of women. Certain rubrics in the communion service and the word "priest" were also omitted. A. Elliott Peaston, *The Prayer Book Tradition in the Free Churches* (London: J. Clarke, 1964), emphasizes the distinctive nature of these editions, which he assumes would have been used in godly parishes such as those in the Stour Valley, and it is true that Adam Winthrop owned one such edition, now in the Massachusetts Historical Society. Ian Green, in "'Puritan Prayer Books' and 'Geneva Bibles': An Episode in Elizabethan Publishing," *Transactions of the Cambridge Bibliographical Society* 11 (1998), 313–349, and in his *Print and Protestantism in Early Modern England* (Oxford: Oxford University Press, 2000), 247–248, argues that these editions were not designed by puritans but were edited by publishers seeking to reach a larger market among the godly. In 1584 the same publisher who printed the *Marprelate Tracts* published a new liturgy entitled *A booke of the forme of common prayer . . . agreeable to Gods word, and the use of the reformed Churches*, which stripped the service of prescribed prayers and recommended the extemporaneous formulation of prayers by the clergyman; see Ramie Targoff, *Common Prayer: The Language of Public Devotion in Early Modern England* (Chicago: University of Chicago Press, 2001), 45. Again, there is no evidence as to how extensively this book was used. Of course, what we would most like to know is how clergy actually used the Prayer Book they owned, and for this there is very little evidence.

60. The following discussion of the services is based on *The Book of Common Prayer, 1559: The Elizabethan Prayer Book*, ed. John E. Booty (Charlottesville: University of Virginia Press, 1976); Adam Winthrop's copy of the Book of Common Prayer (1615) in the collections of the Massachusetts Historical Society; contemporary accounts of the services including that of William Harrison, *The Description of England*, ed. Georges Edelen (Washington, D.C.: Folger Library, 1968); and secondary works including Christopher Marsh, *Popular Religion in Sixteenth-Century England* (Basingstoke: Macmillan, 1998), and Marsh, "'Common Prayer' in England, 1560–1640: The View from the Pew," *Past & Present* (2001), 66–94.

61. This can be traced in the published accounts (Peter Northeast, ed., *Boxford Churchwardens' Accounts, 1530–1561* [Woodbridge, Suffolk: Boydell, 1982])

and for the remainder of the sixteenth century and the early seventeenth century in the manuscript record in SRO/B.

62. *Book of Common Prayer 1559*, 247.
63. A photograph of the cup and a discussion of it are contained in *New England Begins: The Seventeenth Century*, ed. Jonathan Fairbanks and Robert Trent (Boston: Museum of Fine Arts, 1982), III, 282–383. Robert Trent suggests that the cup may have been purchased by Adam Winthrop from the plate of Trinity College during the time when he was college auditor. For a further discussion of communion silver see Mark Peterson, "Puritanism and Refinement in Early New England: Reflections on Communion Silver," *William and Mary Quarterly*, 3d ser. 58 (2001), 307–346.
64. See Targoff, *Common Prayer*, 28–35. My belief that this made an important point for Winthrop is based upon the passage in his "Christian Charity" where he says that "whatsoever we did or ought to have done when we lived in England, the same must we do and more also where we go."
65. Marsh, "'Common Prayer,'" esp. 74–75.
66. For a discussion of the general strains on England's economy and society and the challenge they posed to order see Keith Wrightson, *Earthly Necessities: Economic Lives in Early Modern England* (New Haven: Yale University Press, 2002); Steve Hindle, *The State and Social Change in Early Modern England, c. 1550–1640* (Basingstoke: Macmillan, 2002); and Paul Slack, *From Reformation to Improvement: Public Welfare in Early Modern England* (Oxford: Clarendon Press, 1999).
67. Insight into the work of the Suffolk commission is to be found in the "Letterbook of the Suffolk JPs," British Library, Add. MS 39245.
68. See above, p. 103.
69. "Letterbook," f. 55r.
70. "Letterbook," f. 127v. The order is reprinted in *WP*, I, 331ff.
71. Copy of order entered by John in the manuscript commonplace book in which his father kept his diary; *WP*, I, 142–143.
72. "Experiencia," *WP*, I, 237.
73. He first appears on a list of the commission for 1616; PRO C 181/2. On this list he is listed as being of the quorum, as opposed to his service on the commission of the peace, where he never was of the quorum.
74. "Experiencia," *WP*, I, 236.
75. "Experiencia," WP, I, 237.

Chapter 7.   The Godly Embattled

1. Lucy Downing to John Winthrop, [March 1627–1628], *WP*, I, 380–381.
2. *WP*, II, 114.
3. John Winthrop to John Winthrop Jr., 26 June 1623, *WP*, I, 282–283.
4. Robert C. Winthrop, *Life and Letters of John Winthrop*, 2d ed., 2 vols. (Boston, 1869), I, 4, where Robert C. Winthrop tells of his visit to Groton in 1847 and how he was able to barely decipher the faded inscription on the tomb.
5. Answer of Anne Winthrop and John Winthrop to the Bill of Complaint of Thomas Notte and Elizabeth his Wife, PRO C 2/Jas1/N1/23.
6. Further Answer of Thomas Fones to the Complaint of Thomas and Elizabeth Notte, PRO C2/Jas1/N1/23.

7. The hood was the emblem of receiving a degree; John Winthrop to John Winthrop Jr., 3 October 1623, *WP*, I, 288–289.

8. For a fuller treatment of the youth of John Winthrop Jr., see Robert C. Black III, *The Younger John Winthrop* (New York: Columbia University Press, 1966).

9. The almanac with Adam's notations for his grandson is part of the Winthrop Papers collection of the Massachusetts Historical Society. Adam's entries in the name of the younger John are included in *WP*, I, 243–247.

10. John Winthrop to John Winthrop Jr., 16 October 1622, *WP*, I, 275–277.

11. John Winthrop to John Winthrop Jr., 22 February 1624/5, *WP*, I, 318.

12. John Winthrop to John Winthrop Jr., 21 November 1626, *WP*, I, 335.

13. John Winthrop to John Winthrop Jr., 21 November 1626, *WP*, I, 335.

14. Joshua Downing, Emmanuel's brother, was one of the commissioners of the navy at this time and was instrumental in getting this post for the young man; Joshua Downing to John Winthrop, *WP*, I, 347–348.

15. John Winthrop to John Winthrop Jr., 11 April 1628, *WP*, I, 387.

16. John Winthrop to John Winthrop Jr., 28 July 1629, *WP*, II, 103–104.

17. In May 1628 he and his father had sold lands which had belonged to John Forth to Henry Fetherstone for £590; *WP*, II, 59–61 contains the deed of sale.

18. This possibility is raised by a letter Henry sent to his brother in October 1626 from Keddington; *WP*, I, 332–333.

19. Henry Winthrop to Emmanuel Downing, 22 August 1627, *WP*, I, 356–357.

20. Henry Winthrop to John Winthrop, 15 October 1627, *WP*, I, 361–362.

21. Henry Winthrop to Emmanuel Downing, 22 August 1627, *WP*, I, 356–357.

22. Henry Winthrop to John Winthrop, 15 October 1627, *WP*, I, 361–362.

23. Margaret Winthrop to John Winthrop, 22 November 1627, *WP*, I, 369; John Winthrop to John Winthrop Jr., *WP*, I, 381–382.

24. "Receipts," July 1628, *WP*, I, 403–404.

25. "Appointment of Assistants, Barbados," 4 September 1628, printed in *WP*, I, 405–406.

26. John Winthrop to Henry Winthrop, 30 January 1628/9, *WP*, II, 67–69.

27. Thomas Fones to John Winthrop, 2 April 1629, *WP*, II, 78–79.

28. Thomas Fones to John Winthrop, 2 April 1629, *WP*, II, 78.

29. John's notes of his efforts to arrange the funeral and settle the estate are printed in *WP*, I, 143–144.

30. John Winthrop to Margaret Winthrop, 28 April 1629, *WP*, II, 84–85.

31. In a letter to John Jr., 16 October 1622, John indicated that Forth was enrolled at Bury but that, falling between two forms in his preparation, there had been a thought of sending him back to Boxford; *WP*, I, 276.

32. Forth Winthrop to John Winthrop, 13 February 1627, *WP*, I, 342.

33. Forth Winthrop to John Winthrop Jr., 7 April 1628, *WP*, I, 386.

34. Forth Winthrop to John Winthrop Jr., [1628], *WP*, I, 392–394.

35. Forth Winthrop to John Winthrop Jr., [1628], *WP*, I, 392–394.

36. Forth Winthrop to John Winthrop Jr., [1628], *WP*, I, 392–394.

37. Forth Winthrop to John Winthrop, 1 May 1627, *WP*, I, 348–349; Forth Winthrop to John Winthrop, 4 May 1627, *WP*, I, 350–351; Forth Winthrop to John Winthrop, 15 December 1628, *WP*, I, 416.

38. John Winthrop, "General Observations," *WP*, II, 118.

39. John Winthrop to Margaret Winthrop, 5 June 1629, *WP*, II, 94–95.

40. Margaret Winthrop to John Winthrop, 14 June 1629, *WP*, II, 98.

41. *WP*, I, 259.

42. John Winthrop's Spiritual Diary, or "Experiencia," *WP*, I, 405.
43. See Felicity Heal, *Hospitality in Early Modern England* (Oxford: Clarendon Press, 1990).
44. The strongest evidence for Winthrop's presence in Dublin at this time is his signature as a witness to Emmanuel Downing's signature on a land transaction (National Library of Ireland, MS 114, f. 1, 17v–19) which was discovered by Rolf Loeber. I thank Dr. Loeber for bringing this to my attention. Dr. Loeber also points out that Winthrop's presence would have been required to initiate the suits referred to.
45. The records of the Irish Court of Common Pleas for this period have not survived, and all that remains of the Winthrop case in Irish Chancery is the final judgment issued in 1630 in John's favor. The existence of these suits and the few details provided are from references in the pleadings in the parallel case filed in English Chancery by the Nottes.
46. Frederick Johnson Simmons, *Emanuel Downing* (Montclair, N.J.: n.p., 1958).
47. I would like to thank Dr. Rolf Loeber for generously sharing his information on St. Werburgh's parish and on other aspects of the English presence in Ireland at this period.
48. Rolf Loeber, "Preliminaries to the Massachusetts Bay Colony: The Irish ventures of Emmanuel Downing and John Winthrop Sr.," in Toby Bernard, Daibhi O'Croinin, and Katerine Simms, eds., *"A Miracle of Learning"*: *Studies in Manuscripts and Irish learning. Essays in honour of William O'Sullivan* (Aldershot: Ashgate, 1998),165.
49. Bill of Complaint of Thomas Notte and Elizabeth Notte, PRO C 2 Jas1/N1/23.
50. In connection with this it is interesting to note that the will of John Winthrop of Aghadown was apparently not proved in the Irish Prerogative Court until 1623, ten years after his death and shortly after the initiation of the legal proceedings. Letter from the Deputy Keeper of the Public Record Office of Ireland to Captain J. E. Fitzgerald, 24 December 1630, loose MS in the Winthrop Papers, Massachusetts Historical Society.
51. Answer of Anne Winthrop and John Winthrop, PRO C 2 Jas1/N1/23. An abridged form of the will of John Winthrop of Aghadowne is printed in *WP*, I, 172–173; the original has been lost.
52. John Winthrop to Margaret Winthrop, 27 September 1623, *WP*, I, 286–287.
53. Sir Robert Crane to John Winthrop, 28 January 1627/8, *WP*, I, 376.
54. John Winthrop to Margaret Winthrop, n.d., *WP*, I, 344–345; the editor of vol. I, without indicating a reason, slotted this letter in among papers from 1627.
55. Lucy Downing to John Winthrop, [March 1627/8], *WP*, I, 380–381.
56. For the full story of this case and the difficulties it presented for the Winthrops see chap. 8, n. 108.
57. For this period see Patrick Collinson, *The Birthpangs of Protestant England* (Basington: Macmillan, 1988); Collinson, *The Religion of Protestants: The Church in English Society, 1559–1625* (Oxford: Clarendon Press, 1982); and Kenneth Fincham, *Prelate as Pastor: The Episcopate of James I* (Oxford: Clarendon Press, 1990).
58. Fincham, *Prelate as Pastor*, 19.
59. Fincham, *Prelate as Pastor*, 237.

60. Kenneth Fincham, ed., *Visitation Articles and Injunctions of the Early Stuart Church, I* (Woodbridge, Suffolk: Boydell, 1994), 216.

61. *WP*, I, 257.

62. For the Boxford lectureship see Francis J. Bremer and Martin Wood, "The Boxford Lecture in 1620," *Suffolk Review*, n.s. (1998).

63. See Francis J. Bremer, *Congregational Communion: Clerical Friendship in the Anglo-American Puritan Community, 1610–1692* (Boston: Northeastern University Press, 1994), 66–72, from which these quotes are taken.

64. John Winthrop to Margaret Winthrop, 23 January 1621, *WP*, I, 260–261.

65. John Winthrop to Margaret Winthrop, 15 May 1629, *WP*, II, 91–92.

66. For a discussion of these events see Caroline Hibbard, *Charles I and the Popish Plot* (Chapel Hill: University of North Carolina Press, 1983). The statement by Winthrop is from John Winthrop to Margaret Winthrop, 15 May 1629, *WP*, II, 91–92.

67. Our understanding of the "Puritan Church of Ireland" has been greatly advanced by the work of Alan Ford. Discussion of this topic is based on Ford, *The Protestant Reformation in Ireland, 1590–1641* (Frankfurt am Main: Lang, 1985); Ford, "The Church of Ireland, 1558–1634: A Puritan Church?" in Ford, James McGuire, and Kenneth Milne, eds., *As by Law Established: The Church of Ireland Since the Reformation* (Dublin: Lilliput Press, 1995); and Ford, "Dependent or Independent? The Church of Ireland and Its Colonial Context, 1536–1649," *Seventeenth Century* 10 (1995). Ford's promised biography of James Ussher will be a major contribution to our understanding of these topics.

68. Ford, *Protestant Reformation in Ireland*, 198ff.

69. This paragraph is based on Rolf Loeber, "John Winthrop Jr. and His Fellow Students at Trinity College, Dublin," an unpublished paper which includes an analysis of Trinity MS MUN P/1/144 f. 126–126v, which indicates the housing arrangements in the college in May 1624.

70. National Archives of Ireland, MS RC 4/2/17. A 1617 Chancery Bill also refers to Joshua's holdings (National Archives of Ireland, Chancery Bill P-104). A 1622 report on the plantations in Ireland in 1622 indicated that Joshua held "3 ploughlands, wanting 140 acres, making about 1000 acres for the term of 99 years upon which are planted 10 English families;" British Library, Add. MS 4756. A later rent roll for the land, by then acquired by Robert Boyle, showed that Joshua Winthrop's holdings had increased; National Library of Ireland, Lismore Castle MS, MS 6239, 94. I wish to thank Nicholas Canny for directing me to this last source and for discussions of the Winthrop holdings in Ireland.

71. George Bennett, *The History of Bandon and the Principal Towns in the West Riding of Cork*, enlarged ed. (Cork, 1869), 7, 62. See also Seamas O'Saothrai, "Presbyterians in Bandon," *Bandon Historical Journal* 3 (1987), 48–60.

72. W. M. Brady, *Clerical and Parochial Records of Cork, Cloyne, and Ross: Taken from the diocesan and parish registries, mss in the principal libraries and public offices of Oxford, Dublin, and London, and from private and family papers*, 3 vols. (Dublin, 1864), I, 139.

73. John Winthrop to John Winthrop Jr., 20 April 1623, *WP*, I, 280–281. When Anne Winthrop, Joshua's wife, had left her husband and, quarreling with Adam's wife, Anne, moved out of Groton Manor, she had stayed with John Nutton. Some of the Nutton family, including John Winthrop's goddaughter Susan, had settled with Joshua and Anne Winthrop in Ireland, and John

Nutton on his visits back and forth between Groton and Ireland often carried goods between the Suffolk families and their Irish kin.
74. This paragraph and the next are based on Loeber, "Irish Ventures of Downing and Winthrop."
75. John Winthrop to John Winthrop Jr., 20 April 1623, *WP*, I, 280–281.
76. A graduate of Emmanuel College, Olmstead was rector of Erwarton, Suffolk,
and was related to the Reverend John Rogers through his wife. In August
1623 Winthrop noted Olmstead's plans to emigrate and, after his migration,
often inquired as to his success; *WP*, I, 272, 276, 281.
77. Richard Olmstead, *Treatise of the Union between Christ and the Church* (1627),
256, as quoted in Loeber, "Irish Ventrues of Downing and Winthrop," 175.
78. John Winthrop to John Winthrop Jr., 7 March 1623/4, *WP*, I, 311. Winthrop
referred to the plantation as "mont wealy"; Rolf Loeber has established that
this is in fact a reference to the Downing plantation at Mountrath.
79. See Nicholas Canny, *Making Ireland British, 1580–1650* (Oxford: Oxford
University Press, 2001), esp. chap. 5.
80. Roger Thompson, *Divided We Stand: Watertown, Massachusetts, 1630–1680*
(Amherst; University of Massachusetts Press, 2001) has an excellent account
of the situation in chap. 3, "The View from the Stour."
81. "Common Grievances Groaning for Reformation," *WP*, I, 295–310. Some
of the other grievances, such as better repair of highways, an upsurge in
horse-stealing, need to reform licensing of marriages, and excessive hawking
that led to the decline in the population of partridges and pheasants (!), were
the types of issues that not only would have concerned him as a member of
the commission but also would engage his attention in New England.
82. This last possibility is raised by the fact that the growing division between
the earl of Warwick and the new king's favorite, the duke of Buckingham,
had resulted in prominent Essex puritans affiliated with Warwick being left
off the commission in that county.
83. John Winthrop to Sir Robert Crane, 14 January 1626, *WP*, I, 324–325. The
best treatment of Naunton is Roy E. Schrieber, *The Political Career of Sir
Robert Naunton* (London: Royal Historical Society, 1981). Winthrop could
have befriended the privy councillor in a number of ways, a review of which
reinforces our sense of how small the world Winthrop moved in actually
was. Naunton was a graduate of Trinity, Cambridge, and held a fellowship
there at the time when Adam Winthrop was college auditor. He was recruited into the service of the earl of Essex at a time when William Alabaster, Winthrop's first cousin and a frequent visitor to Groton, was one of the
earl's chaplains. Naunton returned to Cambridge to assume a fellowship at
Trinity Hall at the time when Emmanuel Downing was a student there, and
the two of them became closely bound.
84. The information in this paragraph and the following is largely derived from
the files of the History of Parliament Trust. I wish to thank Dr. Pauline
Croft facilitating my visit to the Trust offices and to express my appreciation
to Dr. Valerie Cromwell, then director of the Trust, and the staff, especially
Simon Healey, for making this material available to me.
85. William Walter Hodson, *The Meeting House and the Manse* (London, 1893),
20–21. I would like to thank Mr. John Webb for directing me to this source
and for sharing his views on Sudbury at this time.
86. "Calendar of the Muniments of the Borough of Sudbury," *Proceedings of
the Suffolk Institute of Archaeology and History* 13, 290. The corporation paid

for a response to be drawn up and submitted to the Parliament. However, there is no record of the freemen's petition having been entertained by the Parliament.

87. Brampton Gurdon to John Winthrop, 19 February 1626, *WP*, I, 317–318.
88. "Calendar of the Muniments of the Borough of Sudbury," 280.
89. PRO C 23 1/4/203v. A letter from John's mother, Anne Winthrop, to Emmanuel Downing urging her son-in-law to use his influence with prominent men to get John restored to the commission is printed in *WP*, I, 294, where it is erroneously dated 1623.
90. PRO C 193 12/2 is the list of the Suffolk commissioners. For the controversy over what historians have come to refer to as the "Forced Loan" see Richard Cust, *The Forced Loan and English Politics, 1626–1628* (Oxford: Clarendon Press, 1987).
91. Cust, *Forced Loan*, 3.
92. Kenneth Shipps, "Lay Patronage of East Anglian Puritan Clerics in Pre-Revolutionary England" (Yale University, Ph.D., 1972), 119.
93. Cust, *Forced Loan*, 199. The development of these political divisions, which would have a role to play in the coming of the English Civil Wars, is explored in Christopher Thompson, "The Origins of the Parliamentary Middle Group, 1625–1629," *Transactions of the Royal Historical Society*, 5th ser. 22 (1972). Mr. Thompson's forthcoming study of the earl of Warwick and his supporters is eagerly awaited.
94. John Winthrop to John Winthrop Jr., 18 December 1626, *WP*, I, 336–337.
95. Cust, *Forced Loan*, 144–145.
96. John Winthrop to John Winthrop Jr., 18 December 1626, *WP*, I, 337.
97. John Winthrop Jr. to John Winthrop, 15 January 1627, *WP*, I, 341.
98. For information on the court see H. E. Bell, *An Introduction to the History and Records of the Court of Wards and Liveries* (Cambridge: Cambridge University Press, 1953); *Calendar of Inner Temple Records*, II, 169.
99. Schreiber, *Naunton*, 104–105.
100. Schreiber, *Naunton*, 104–105.
101. PRO Wards 0/163/1 and PRO Wards 9/543/99. The incident is described by Schrieber, *Naunton*, 101.
102. Lucy Downing to John Winthrop, *WP*, I, 380.
103. These letters are scattered through the first two volumes of *WP*. In addition, vol. II contains a case book indicating cases that Winthrop handled that involved Sir Henry Jermingham, John Popham, Isaac Appleton, Edmund Hampden, Sir Robert Lewkenor, Sir William Monson, and Sir James Altham.
104. "Notebook of Cases Before the Court of Wards and Liveries," *WP*, II, 42–43. See also George W. Robinson, ed., *John Winthrop as Attorney: Extracts from the Order Books of Wards and Liveries, 1627–1629* (Cambridge, Mass., n.p., 1930).
105. "Experiencia," *WP*, I, 412–413.
106. John Winthrop to Margaret Winthrop, 11 December 1628, *WP*, I 413–414.
107. "Experiencia," *WP*, I, 413.

Chapter 8. The Decision to Migrate

1. John Winthrop's Spiritual Diary, or "Experiencia," *WP*, II, 103.
2. J. T. Cliffe, *The Puritan Gentry: The Great Puritan Families of Early Stuart England* (London: Routledge & Keegan Paul, 1984), 81, 93.

3. John Winthrop to John Winthrop Jr., 25 February 1628, *WP*, I, 379.

4. *Return of Members of Parliament: Part I. Parliaments of England, 1213–1702* (London: HMSO, 1989).

5. The election is treated in Christopher Thompson, "New Light on the Suffolk Elections to the Parliament of 1628," *Suffolk Review*, n.s. 10 (1988), 218–244.

6. Draft bill "For Preventing Drunkenness," *WP*, I, 371–374.

7. David L. Smith, *The Stuart Parliaments, 1603–1689* (London: Arnold, 1999), esp. 113–120.

8. Quoted in Smith, *Stuart Parliaments*, 118.

9. Quoted in Smith, *Stuart Parliaments*, 120.

10. Emmanuel Downing to John Winthrop, 6 March 1629, *WP*, II, 74–75.

11. John Winthrop to Margaret Winthrop, 15 May 1629, *WP*, II, 91–92.

12. Tom Webster, *Godly Clergy in Early Stuart England: The Caroline Puritan Movement, c. 1620–1643* (Cambridge: Cambridge University Press, 1997), 187.

13. Kenneth Shipps, "Lay Patronage of East Anglian Puritan Clerics in Pre-Revolutionary England" (Yale University, Ph.D., 1972), 119.

14. Margaret Winthrop to John Winthrop, [c. 25 May 1629], *WP*, II, 93.

15. John Rogers, *A Treatise of Love* (1629), dedicatory letter.

16. Rogers, *A Treatise of Love*, 45.

17. Webster, *Godly Clergy*, chap. 9.

18. White's ministry at Dorchester is best followed in David Underdown, *Fire from Heaven: Life in an English Town in the Seventeenth Century* (New Haven: Yale University Press, 1992).

19. The complex role of the Council of New England in the colonization of New England is surprisingly overlooked by most students of the period. The best treatment of the story remains that to be found throughout Charles M. Andrews, *The Colonial Period of American History: The Settlements*, I (New Haven: Yale University Press, 1934), on which I have drawn in this discussion.

20. Underdown, *Fire from Heaven*, 131–133; see also Frances Rose-Troup, *The Massachusetts Bay Company and its Predecessors* (New York: Grafton Press, 1930).

21. Andrews, *Settlements*, I, 355–356. Andrews makes the important point that the 1620 charter of the council required a majority of members be present for a land grant to be made and that it would have been virtually impossible to assemble a majority at this time.

22. Samuel Eliot Morison, *Builders of the Bay Colony* (Boston: Houghton Mifflin, 1930), chap. 2.

23. A full list of the investors is included in Rose-Troup, *Predecessors*, 19–20.

24. Andrews, *Settlements*, I, chap. 17 takes the reader through all the intricacies. As he points out, a full understanding of what was being done is precluded by the absence of any copy of the council's 1622 distribution of land to Warwick, a transfer of that title to the New England Company, and a council patent to that body.

25. *RMB*, I, 37e–37f.

26. *RMB*, I, 37j.

27. Francis J. Bremer, *Congregational Communion: Clerical Friendship in the Anglo-American Puritan Community, 1610–1692* (Boston: Northeastern University Press, 1994), 75–79.

28. *WP*, II, 82.

29. Wright had married Mary Duke, the daughter of Winthrop's cousin John Duke, who had tended Thomasine Winthrop in her illness. He would later

negotiate to purchase Groton Manor when Winthrop decided to emigrate, though in the end he did not buy the estate. In an interesting coincidence, he would later be the physician to Oliver Cromwell.

30. Cicely Chaderton to Isaac Johnson, 24 August 1625, *WP*, I, 323–324.
31. *WP*, II, 274.
32. Anne Gibson to John Winthrop, 9 April 1629, *WP*, II, 81.
33. John Winthrop to Margaret Winthrop, 15 May 1629, *WP*, II, 91–92.
34. Thomas Motte to John Winthrop, [ca. 13 June 1629], *WP*, II, 97.
35. John Winthrop to Margaret Winthrop, 5 June 1629, *WP*, II, 94–95.
36. John Winthrop to Margaret Winthrop, 19 June 1629, *WP*, II, 99–100.
37. John Winthrop to Margaret Winthrop, 22 June 1629, *WP*, II, 100–101.
38. Deane Tyndal to John Winthrop, 23 October 1629, *WP*, II, 162–163. I am presenting some of the arguments and Winthrop's responses out of the strict chronological order of the surviving letters in order to give a sense of the give-and-take Winthrop engaged in. I feel justified in doing so where the surviving material indicates reiterations of earlier, unpreserved exchanges.
39. Robert Reyce to John Winthrop, 12 August 1629, *WP*, II, 105.
40. John Winthrop, "General Observations," *WP*, II, 117.
41. Robert Reyce, "Response to John Winthrop's Observations," *WP*, II, 131.
42. Robert Reyce to John Winthrop, 12 August 1629, *WP*, II, 106.
43. *RMB*, I, 49.
44. In a letter to Emmanuel Downing on July 8, Isaac Johnson indicates that he had just returned to Sempringham from London and mentions having met with Downing, and possibly Winthrop, to induce them to attend the coming meeting in Lincolnshire. The timing of this trip to London suggests an effort to finalize the proposal that Craddock was to make at the General Court; *WP*, II, 102–103.
45. Isaac Johnson to Emmanuel Downing, 8 July 1629, *WP*, II, 102–103.
46. For the involvement of these clergymen at the meeting see George H. Williams, Norman Pettit, and Sargent Bush, eds., *Thomas Hooker: Writings in England and Holland, 1626–1633* (Cambridge: Harvard University Press, 1975), 17.
47. Lucy Downing to John Winthrop Jr., 8 August 1629, *WP*, II, 104–105.
48. Robert Reyce to John Winthrop, 12 August 1629, *WP*, II, 105–106.
49. For an excellent discussion of the sequence of these drafts, all of which are published in *WP*, II, see Christopher Thompson, "John Winthrop of Groton's Decision to Emigrate to Massachusetts: A Reconsideration of his 'General Conclusions and Particular Considerations,'" *Suffolk Review* (Fall 1996), 19–22.
50. The quotes in this list of reasons are all from "General Observations," *WP*, II, 111–115.
51. "The Agreement at Cambridge," *WP*, II, 151–152.
52. *RMB*, I, 50.
53. *RMB*, I, 51.
54. *RMB*, I, 51–58.
55. *RMB*, I, 59.
56. Robert Brenner, *Merchants and Revolution: Commercial Change, Political Conflict, and London's Overseas Traders, 1550–1653* (Princeton: Princeton University Press, 1993), 100, 111.
57. Brenner, *Merchants and Revolution*, 273.
58. Brenner, *Merchants and Revolution*, 269, 276; Karen Kupperman, *Providence Island, 1630–1641: The Other Puritan Colony* (Cambridge: Cambridge University Press, 1993), 17.

59. Historian Darrett Rutman has suggested that with each of the other candidates representing one of the three key investor groups—Humfry the Dorchester members, Johnson the Lincolnshire element, and Saltonstall the London city interests—Winthrop was a compromise choice. Darrett Rutman, *John Winthrop's Decision for America: 1629* (Philadelphia: Lippincott, 1975), 46. It is possible that along these lines the nomination of the others was a means of recognizing the different investor groups, but Winthrop's selection makes more sense in terms of the relative commitment each of the candidates appeared willing to make.

60. Brenner, *Merchants and Revolution*, 16n, 18n, 74n.

61. The Warwick circle was also heavily involved in political maneuvers at the time. See Christopher Thompson, "The Origins of the Parliamentary Middle Group, 1625–1629," *Transactions of the Royal Historical Society*, 5th ser. 22 (1972), 71–86.

62. John Humfry to Isaac Johnson, 9 December 1630, *WP*, II, 327–329.

63. "General Conclusions and Particular Considerations," *WP*, II, 125.

64. John Winthrop to Margaret Winthrop, 20 October 1629, *WP*, II, 160–161.

65. "General Conclusions and Particular Considerations," *WP*, II, 126.

66. Robert Reyce to John Winthrop, n.d., *WP*, II, 128–129.

67. John Winthrop to Margaret Winthrop, 20 October 1629, *WP*, II, 160–161.

68. John Winthrop Jr. to John Winthrop, 21 August 1629, *WP*, II, 150–151.

69. John Winthrop to John Winthrop Jr., 13 November, 1626, *WP*, I, 333–334.

70. That sermon notebook is included in *Winthrop Papers: Religious Manuscripts*, forthcoming from the Massachusetts Historical Society.

71. William Leigh to John Winthrop, 20 September 1636, recounts his appointment and Winthrop's expectations; *WP*, III, 310–314.

72. *RMB*, I, 24–25.

73. *RMB*, I, 26.

74. *RMB*, I, 26–27.

75. *WP*, II, 171–172

76. John Winthrop and Others to ____, 27 October 1629, *WP*, II, 163–164.

77. William Ames to John Winthrop, 29 December 1629, *WP*, II, 180.

78. For Ames see Keith Sprunger, *The Learned Doctor William Ames* (Urbana: University of Illinois Press, 1972). Adam Winthrop noted that Ames preached in Boxford on the last day of December 1607; Adam Winthrop's Diary, *WP*, I, 96.

79. John Winthrop to Margaret Winthrop, 24 November 1629, *WP*, II, 174.

80. John Maidstone to John Winthrop, 4 November 1629, *WP*, II, 164–165.

81. *RMB*, I, 63.

82. *WP*, II, 157 and 157n. Robert Charles Anderson, *The Great Migration Begins: Immigrants to New England, 1620–1633, Volume I: A–F* (Boston: New England Historical and Genealogical Society, 1995), 349ff.

83. *WP*, II, 169. Kingsbury would be one of Winthrop's trusted servants in the early years of the settlement; Robert Charles Anderson, *The Great Migration Begins: Immigrants to New England, 1620–1633, Volume II: G–O* (Boston: New England Historical and Genealogical Society, 1995), 1131–1133.

84. Arthur Tyndal to John Winthrop, 10 November 1629, *WP*, II, 166–167.

85. John Winthrop to Margaret Winthrop, 12 November 1629, *WP*, II, 168.

86. Francis Borrowes to John Winthrop, 6 January 1630, *WP*, II, 183.

87. John Sampson to John Winthrop, 12 January 1630, *WP*, II, 185.

88. Nathaniel Ward to John Winthrop, 16 January 1630, *WP*, II, 192.

89. *WP*, II, 199. In that letter to his "loving friend Mr. Gager," Winthrop wrote of having "sufficient assurance of your godliness and abilities in the art of surgery to be of much use to us in this work." He was admitted the eighth member of the Boston church in late August 1630 and chosen deacon, but died soon after. Anderson, *Great Migration*, II, 722–724.

90. Compiled from N.C.P. Tyack, "Migration from East Anglia to New England Before 1660" (University of London, Ph.D., 1951).

91. The literature on the migration is vast. I have summarized some of the reasons for migration in *The Puritan Experiment: New England Society from Bradford to Edwards*, rev. ed. (Hanover, N.J.: University Press of New England, 1995), 41–46. For a recent study of those who settled one Massachusetts town see Roger Thompson, *Divided We Stand: Watertown, Massachusetts, 1630–1680* (Amherst: University of Massachusetts Press, 2001).

92. Forth Winthrop to John Winthrop, 2 February 1630, *WP*, II, 200–201.

93. Isaac Johnson to John Winthrop, 17 December 1629, *WP*, II, 177–179.

94. John Winthrop Jr. to John Winthrop, 18 January 1630, *WP*, II, 193–194.

95. Address of John Winthrop to the Company, *WP*, II, 175.

96. Address of John Winthrop to the Company, *WP*, II, 176.

97. *RMB*, I, 65.

98. See Bremer, *Puritan Experiment*, 55–56.

99. *RMB*, I, 48.

100. Bremer, *Puritan Experiment*, 56–57.

101. *RMB*, I, 51, 52–53. One of the steps taken to defuse the situation was the seizure of letters that the Brownes had sent back in the company ships.

102. *RMB*, I, 60–61, 69.

103. *RMB*, I, 59. Accusations that the Salem church had indeed adopted separatist practices, fed no doubt by Morton and the Brownes, continued to spread in England, causing concern among the colony's friends as well as offering ammunition to its enemies then and later. John Cotton would feel impelled to address some of the issues in a letter to Samuel Skelton in October 1630; see John Cotton to Samuel Skelton, 2 October 1630, in Sargent Bush Jr., ed., *The Correspondence of John Cotton* (Chapel Hill: University of North Carolina Press, 2001), a brilliant and definitive edition of all Cotton's known correspondence. The controversies over the practices of the Salem church are reflected in a vast literature, the most important contributions to which are Perry Miller, *Orthodoxy in Massachusetts, 1630–1650* (Cambridge: Harvard University Press, 1933); Larzer Ziff, "The Salem Puritans in the 'Free Aire of a New World,'" *Huntington Library Quarterly* 20 (1957), 373–384; David D. Hall's introduction to his edition of "John Cotton's Letter to Samuel Skelton," *William and Mary Quarterly*, 3d ser. 22 (1965), 478–480; and Stephen Foster, *The Long Argument: English Puritanism and the Shaping of New England Culture, 1570–1700* (Chapel Hill: University of North Carolina Press, 1991).

104. John Winthrop to Thomas Hawes, 20 November 1629, *WP*, II, 172–173.

105. John Winthrop to Margaret Winthrop, 14 February 1630, *WP*, II, 208–209.

106. John Winthrop to Margaret Winthrop, 23 July 1630, *WP*, II, 303–304.

107. National Archives of Ireland, MS RC 6/2/187.

108. Though the story of the sale of Winthrop's English properties is important and has never been told, it is too complex to include in the text. In the first place, there were complications involving the Essex lands that had been inherited from John Forth, particularly those held by his sons. The purchasers

needed a certificate verifying Henry Winthrop's age and that of his young
wife to be assured that they were of legal age to assent to the sale (see correspondence in *WP*, II, 181–182, 182, and the deed of sale, *WP*, II, 186ff.).
But the greatest difficulty Winthrop faced concerned the sale of his Groton
lands, which were still the subject of the dispute with the Nottes in Chancery. Until that dispute was settled the possibility of claims on the title made
it difficult to sell the property at anything like its true value. A related com-
plication was Winthrop's inability to afford a settlement whereby Elizabeth
Risby Winthrop, now married to Reynold Branch, would agree to waive her
dower rights. Until she did agree to waive them, Winthrop was obliged to
make the quarterly payments of £10 to "Aunt Braunch." (A receipt for one
such payment signed by her new husband in January 1630 demonstrates that
the obligation continued to be expected and was being met; *WP*, II, 185. In
a list of 1630–31 "Accounts of JW Jr." is record of £60 paid to "my aunt
Branch for 6 quarters" [*WP*, III, 3], and on 2 November 1631 Emmanuel
Downing wrote to to John Winthrop Jr. that he had "paid my Aunt Branch
£10 for her last quartering" [*WP*, III, 50].) The difficulties involved in selling the lands would deprive Winthrop of his oldest son's presence and aid in
Massachusetts during the colony's first year, as the younger Winthrop was
forced to remain in England working along with his stepmother and his
uncle Emmanuel Downing to effect the sale of the Groton lands. Ironically,
two months after Winthrop's sailing, on June 27 the Court of Chancery in
Ireland entered a judgment in Winthrop's favor and ordering Thomas Notte
to pay the sum of £460 and costs (National Archives of Ireland, MS RC 6/2/
187). It is not clear if Notte ever paid; it is suggestive that at about that time
Notte is recorded in the Irish Statute Staple Books as involved in borrowing
and soon repaying a comparable sum of money, though perhaps for other
reasons. I would like to thank Jane Olhmeyer for discussions of this point.
Whether or not the Nottes paid the award, the decision cleared much of the
uncertainty regarding Winthrop's title to the manor and his obligations. At
one point it appeared that Lawrence Wright, the physician who had treated
Winthrop during his serious illness in 1628, might be interested in purchasing the manor. In July 1629 he had asked Winthrop to check on some houses
in Boxford which his wife had an interest in (Lawrence Wright to John
Winthrop, 3 July 1629, *WP*, II, 102). Certainly by the following spring Wright
was interested in the Groton property. On July 2, 1630, Emmanuel Downing wrote to John Winthrop Jr. that he had reached an agreement with Wright
to purchase the manor for £4600. An £850-portion of that price would come
from the assignment to the Winthrops of Wright's manor of Foulton Hall
in Ramsey, Essex, said to be worth £50 per annum (Emmanuel Downing to
John Winthrop Jr., 2 July 1630, *WP*, II, 299). Margaret asked Thomas
Arkisden, Forth's Cambridge chambermate, who had become a family friend,
to investigate the Ramsey property. He reported that the house was small
and needed repair but that the land was said to be good. However, he also
indicated that Wright was reportedly willing to sell it to others for £50 less
than the value he discussed as part of the Groton purchase. He also wrote
that if the purchase went through, Wright would allow Margaret to keep her
residence at Groton till the following Lady's Day (March 25) (Thomas
Arkisden to John Winthrop Jr., July 1630, *WP*, II, 300). While not perfect,
since the new property would in turn have to be sold, it appeared for a time
that the sale would be completed. Wright's attorney was drawing up a con-

veyance, and Downing found that the offer was probably £200 more than they would get from anyone else. But there were still problems regarding the title since evidently John had forgotten or not been able to provide all the relevant papers prior to leaving for New England. Downing complained that he had been given "only the last conveyance and the parson's lease" and urged John Jr. to bring to him "all the writings concerning the purchase except your Court rolls," specifying his need for the grant from the king; the 1557 license to alienate obtained by Adam the Clothworker, that being the conveyance whereby the John Winthrop who ended in Ireland had obtained the manor; "then the deeds from [that] John W to your father and my brother Fones and what other deeds you have concerning your woods, for this deed you sent me up mentions but 40 acres of wood so its supposed that the rest of the woods were bought of some private men and not from the king." He also asked for a letter approving the sale from Deane Tyndal, who was charged with looking after Margaret's dower interests according to an agreement John had agreed to prior to leaving England (Emmanuel Downing to John Winthrop Jr., 2 July 1630, *WP*, II, 299). John had entered into an £800-bond to Deane Tyndal guaranteeing money for Margaret to use for her and the children following his departure and for protection of her right to the lands. A copy was recorded in the manuscript book that Adam Winthrop had used for his diary. John Bradinge, a lawyer of the Temple to whom Winthrop had entrusted some of his business, wrote to the Massachusetts governor in November informing him that he had perfected the "revocation and settling of your estate," sending him a conveyance to seal and send back, along with the missing deeds (*WP*, II, 319–320). But the problems with the conveyance continued. The next month Emmanuel Downing sent a "dedimus potestatem to acknowledge another fine of Groton & a deed to lead the use thereof because the fine you acknowledged before you went was not well drawn nor sufficient for us to sell your land." He emphasized that Margaret "must stay here until the dedimus be returned back," and he feared that this might delay her departure another year (Emmanuel Downing to John Winthrop, 8 December 1630, *WP*, II, 324–325). John Jr. made the same point in a letter to his father on December 9, and elaborated on the difficulty. The feoffees to whom John had alienated the estate in order to sell it "had power to convey only the manor, which by the writings appears to be little above one hundred acres because all that which hath been laid out in jointure is severed from the manor and cannot now pass by the name of Manerium." This had only been discovered at the end of the law term by the attorney used by Winthrop's friend Brampton Gurdon, who was one of the feoffees. Multiple copies of the new agreement, giving the feoffees possession of the whole, had been dispatched to New England and it was imperative that Winthrop have them sealed and returned (John Winthrop Jr. to John Winthrop, 9 December 1631, *WP*, II, 325–327). The problems with the sale were not only delaying the departure of the rest of the Winthrops but were depriving John Jr. of the funds he needed to pay for the goods his father was requesting from Massachusetts. As the process dragged on, Wright gave up his interest in the estate. Three or four other potential buyers were also leery of the imperfection of the documentation, so that in April 1631 Margaret wrote about the most recent prospective buyer, Thomas Waring, that "I fear Mr. Warren [*sic*] will do as the rest have done when he hath conferred with his counsel," though she added that in her "conceit he is the most likely many of any yet" (Margaret Winthrop to John Winthrop Jr., 29 April 1631, *WP*, III, 29). And she was proven correct. Waring, a London alderman, agreed to pay £4,200 with half of the sum to be paid at midsummer and the rest in two installments at six-month intervals (John Winthrop Jr. to John Winthrop, 16 April 1631, *WP*, III, 27). It appears that a license to sell the land to John Gurdon had been granted. Gurdon petitioned the King's Council to verify the title. John (through the documents he returned), Margaret, John Jr., Emmanuel Downing (representing Lucy Winthrop Downing), Thomas Gostlin (representing Jane Winthrop Gostlin), Dru Deane, and Deane Tyndal (representing Margaret's interest) all attested to the court that though documents had been lost there were no claims on the property that would affect the title. By then Gurdon had backed off and Waring had appeared as the buyer, but the verification of the title was, as John Jr. informed his father, "as good though now we sell it to another." The council published this finding four times, thus validating the claims on 6 June 1631. (The document, in Latin, is in the Suffolk Feet of Fines, Charles I. A transcript by Lillian Redstone is in the unpublished WP at the Massachusetts Historical Society. I wish to acknowledge the assistance of Lawrence Woodlock in translating the document.) Meanwhile, at the end of April the feoffees all gathered in London and the deal with Waring was sealed (John Winthrop Jr. to John Winthrop, 30 April 1631, *WP*, III, 32). Finally Margaret would be freed to join her husband.

109. John Winthrop to Margaret Winthrop, 12 November 1629, *WP*, II, 168.
110. John Winthrop to Margaret Winthrop, 24 November 1629, *WP*, II, 174.
111. John Winthrop to Margaret Winthrop, 15 January 1630, *WP*, II, 191–192.
112. John Winthrop to Margaret Winthrop, 31 January 1630, *WP*, II, 197–198.
113. Margaret Winthrop to John Winthrop, 2 February 1630, *WP*, II, 200.
114. John Winthrop to Margaret Winthrop, 5 February 1630, *WP*, II, 201–202.
115. John Winthrop to Margaret Winthrop, 14 February 1630, *WP*, II, 208–209.
116. Robert C. Winthrop first noted the similarity of this to Imogen's speech in his *Life and Letters of John Winthrop*, 2d ed. (1869), I, 378. Shakespeare's play had first been performed in 1609 and was printed in the first folio edition of 1623, so that it is certainly possible that the Winthrops were familiar with it. His agreement with Margaret also is reminiscent of the agreement that he had made on September 17, 1613, when "Mr. Sandes, Mr. Knewstub, Mr. Bird and his wife, Mr. Chambers and his wife, John Garrold & wife, John Warner & wife, Mr. Stebbin, and Barker of the priory" as well as "I with my company" agreed to meet in person the next year on the Friday closest to September 17 and in spirit on every Friday till then, to recollect each other and ask God to grant everyone's petitions (*WP*, I, 152).
117. John Winthrop to Margaret Winthrop, 26 February 1630, *WP*, II, 211.
118. John Winthrop to Margaret Winthrop, 3 April 1630, *WP*, II, 228.
119. John Winthrop to Margaret Winthrop, 28 March 1630, *WP*, II, 226.
120. John Winthrop to Margaret Winthrop, 10 March 1630, *WP*, II, 218; John Winthrop to Margaret Winthrop, 3 April 1630, *WP*, II, 228.
121. John Winthrop to Sir William Spring, 8 February 1630, *WP*, II, 203–206.
122. William Hubbard, *A General History of New England*, Collections of the Massachusetts Historical Society, 2d ser. 5 (1815), 125.
123. "General Conclusions and Particular Considerations," *WP*, II, 126.

Interlude: Christian Charity

1. John Cotton, *God's Promise to His Plantation* (1630). A number of individuals have shared with me their knowledge of Southampton at this time, and I have drawn upon their work and suggestions to hypothesize that any addresses to the departing colonists would likely have been preached in the Church of the Holy Rood in that city. There was a Thursday lecture at Holy Rood, and Cotton and Winthrop might have been guests on such an occasion, or the church might have been made available on a different day. I would particularly like to thank Andrew Thomson and Peter Abraham for sharing their views of the religious scene in Southampton.

2. There are two portraits likely to have been painted of Winthrop at this time. One was a small miniature that exists in the collections of the Massachusetts Historical Society and which all agree was painted from life. I agree with a number of experts that the portrait now in the possession of the American Antiquarian Society was also painted then. See Ernest J. Moyne, "The Reverend William Bentley and the Portraits of Governor Winthrop," *Essex Institute Historical Collections* 110 (1974), 49–56. It may be that John had the portrait painted to be left with Margaret, who would have brought it to New England when it became possible for her to rejoin him. If this is the case it is at least possible that the painting of an unidentified "Winthrop Woman" of this period might have been of Margaret Winthrop and that on the days they sought to commune with each other each was able to use a portrait of the other to enrich their memories.

3. Henry Jacie [Jessey] to John Winthrop Jr., [ca. February 1635], *WP*, III, 188–189.

4. The copy exists in the collections of the New-York Historical Society. Going back to the time of his "General Considerations" for emigrating, Winthrop regularly had materials hand-copied for distribution, often by his son Forth. It is likely that his original of the "Christian Charity" was copied in England, the surviving manuscript being one of these.

5. One scholar has suggested that Johnson's reference to the colony as being a "light on a hill" suggests that he had heard Winthrop and was adapting the governor's reference to the Bay as a "city on a hill." It is far more likely that both were merely drawing on the biblical images that were part of their shared heritage.

6. William Hubbard, *A General History of New England*, Collections of the Massachusetts Historical Society, 2d ser. 5 (1815).

7. Peter Gomes, "Best Sermon: A Pilgrim's Progress," *New York Times*, 18 April, 1999, late ed., sec. 6, 102.

8. Andrew Delbanco, *The Puritan Ordeal* (Cambridge: Harvard University Press, 1989), 72.

9. Hugh Dawson has argued strongly that "Christian Charity" was preached in England, indeed in Southampton on the same occasion that John Cotton preached, which he specifies as Sunday, March 21; Hugh Dawson, "John Winthrop's Rite of Passage: The Origins of the 'Christian Charity' Discourse," *Early American Literature* 26 (1991), 219–231, and Dawson, "'Christian Charitie' as Colonial Discourse: Reading Winthrop's Sermon in Its English Context," *Early American Literature* 33 (1998), 117–148. The date claimed by Dawson is improbable, since in letters to both Margaret and his son John dated the twenty-second he indicated that the *Arbella* had sailed from

Southampton and was anchored off Cowes. Nevertheless, Dawson has provided an important service in raising the issue of where the sermon was preached. I agree that it was not delivered on board the *Arbella*, but not for Dawson's reasons. If delivered on shipboard it would only have been heard by that portion of the emigrants who were on the *Arbella* and thus had a smaller impact. Dawson relies on internal evidence of the text, but that should always be done with great care when not dealing with a manuscript in the author's hand, since changes in tense and phrasing could easily occur in copying. Furthermore, the text as we have it contains phrases that can be read as meaning that it was delivered in England—"the times of persecution here in England"—and others that indicate the listeners had left England, such as "whatsoever we did or ought to have done when we lived in England, the same must we do and more also where we go." Reading too much into any such turn of phrase should be approached with great care. That both sermons were preached at Southampton and on the same day is plausible. If so, as I have suggested in the opening to this interlude, it may very well have been in Holy Rood Church and on a lecture day rather than the Sabbath. I do believe, contrary to Dawson, that even if others were present, the audience to which Winthrop was appealing was the group of colonists. Edmund S. Morgan has also added to our understanding of the sermon in "John Winthrop's 'Model of Christian Charity' in a Wider Context," *Huntington Library Quarterly* 50 (1987), 145–151.

10. For the Browne dispute see above, chap. 8. For Cotton see his letter to Samuel Skelton in October 1630 and the editorial commentary in Sargent Bush Jr., ed., *The Correspondence of John Cotton* (Chapel Hill: University of North Carolina Press, 2001), 141–149.

11. For Williams's concerns see Edmund S. Morgan, *Roger Williams: The Church and the State* (New York: Harcourt, Brace & World, 1967), and Edwin Gaustad, *Liberty of Conscience: Roger Williams in America* (Grand Rapids, Mich.: Erdmans, 1991).

12. *Humble Request, WP*, II, 232.

13. *Humble Request*, 232; Cotton, *God's Promise*, 18–19.

14. Cotton, *God's Promise*, 18; *Humble Request*, 232.

15. In his careful examination of the manuscript Dawson points out, correctly, that "a model thereof" was not part of the title but would have been the heading for the first part of the sermon, the second part being the "application hereof."

16. John Winthrop, "A Model of Christian Charity," *WP*, II, 282. All quotes from the "Christian Charity" have been modernized in accord with the principles followed in the edition of the sermon that will appear in *Winthrop Papers: Religious Manuscripts*, forthcoming from the Massachusetts Historical Society.

17. See the discussion in Steve Hindle, *The State and Social Change in Early Modern England, c. 1550–1640* (Basingstoke: Macmillan, 2000), esp. 25–26.

18. See the discussion of this in Stephen Innes, *Creating the Commonwealth: The Economic Culture of Puritan New England* (New York: Norton, 1995), 165ff.

19. Thomas Carew, *Four Godlie and Profitable Sermons* (1605), sixth lecture, n.p.

20. Knewstub, *Lectures on Exodus* (1577), 178, 77; Knewstub, *A Sermon Preached at Paule's Crosse* (1579), 22, 28. For more on this see Francis J. Bremer, "The Heritage of John Winthrop: Religion Along the Stour Valley, 1548–1630," *New England Quarterly* 70 (1997), 536ff.

21. George Gifford, *Fifteen Sermons upon the Song of Solomon* (1612), 151.

22. Nicholas Bownde, *The Holy Exercise of Fasting* (1604), 334–335.
23. A good deal of foolish interpretation of "Christian Charity" has resulted from the failure of the interpreters to understand the Christian tradition as it shaped all aspects of English culture at this time. While some of the language employed by Winthrop derives from legal teachings and works of political theory, *those* ideas were shaped in large part by the teaching of the church in medieval and early modern times. To wrench those ideas out of that broader context is to abandon any chance of understanding what they meant to Winthrop.
24. This is a mistake that Darrett Rutman made in his otherwise valuable study of *Winthrop's Boston: Portrait of a Puritan Town* (New York: Norton, 1965). Using that literal reading of the "Christian Charity," Rutman then argued that Winthrop's plan was undermined with the settlement of each and every town in the Bay. Unfortunately, others who also seem to have ignored the "city" as the scriptural image that it was have accepted Rutman's argument that Winthrop's language was a blueprint for a single, unified town or city.
25. Perry Miller, "Errand into the Wilderness," in Miller, *Errand into the Wilderness* (Cambridge, Mass.: Belknap Press,1956), 3–4, 11, 12.
26. Among key works in this debate are Loren Baritz, *City on a Hill* (New York: Wiley, 1964); Sacvan Bercovitch, *The Puritan Origins of the American Self* (New Haven: Yale University Press, 1975); Bercovitch, *The American Jeremiad* (Madison: University of Wisconsin Press, 1978); David Scobey, "Revising the Errand: New England's Ways and the Puritan Sense of the Past," *William and Mary Quarterly*, 3d ser 41 (1965); Andrew Delbanco, *The Puritan Ordeal* (Cambridge: Harvard University Press, 1985); Theodore Dwight Bozeman, "The Puritans' 'Errand into the Wilderness' Reconsidered," *New England Quarterly* 59 (1986); and Theodore Dwight Bozeman, *To Live Ancient Lives: The Primitivist Dimension in Puritanism* (Chapel Hill: University of North Carolina Press, 1988). I have criticized these readings in Francis J. Bremer, "To Live Exemplary Lives: Puritans and Puritan Communities as Lofty Lights," *Seventeenth Century* 7 (1992), upon which my discussion in this chapter is partially based.
27. William Wilkinson, quoted in William Hunt, *The Puritan Moment: The Coming of Revolution in an English County* (Cambridge: Harvard University Press, 1983), 87.
28. Richard Rogers, *Certaine Sermons Preached and Penned by Richard Rogers* (1612), letter "To the Christian Reader."
29. William Ames, preface to Paul Baynes, *The Diocesan's Tryall* (1621), n.p.
30. Nicholas Bownde, prefatory letter in John More, *Three Godly and Fruitful Sermons* (1594).
31. Bezaleel Carter, *The Wise King and Learned Judge* (1618), 73.
32. Samuel Clarke, *Lives of Sundry Eminent Persons* (1683), 106.
33. Thomas James to John Winthrop, c. 1639, *WP*, IV, 90.

Chapter 9. Passing Through Hell

1. John Winthrop to Margaret Winthrop, 16 July 1630, *WP*, II, 301–302.
2. The details were passed down within the family and recorded by John Winthrop, F.R.S., in a manuscript commonplace book that is in the Winthrop Papers collection of the Massachusetts Historical Society. It is also possible that John did not learn of Henry's death for a week, since there is no men-

tion of it in a letter to Margaret dated 8 July and the grief that spills forth in his letter of eight days later seems fresh.

3. Margaret described Forth's death in a letter to John Jr. at the end of November 1630, *WP*, II, 321. He was buried on November 28; Groton Parish Register.

4. John Winthrop to John Winthrop Jr., 28 March 1631, *WP*, III, 21–22. His ignorance is explained by the fact that the most recently arrived ship that had reached New England at this time had departed London on December 1, 1630, only days after Forth's death.

5. Groton parish register, parish copy.

6. *WJ*, 59.

7. All accounts of the voyage are based on the journal which Winthrop began as the journey commenced. A good narrative of it is to be found in John Adair, *Puritans: Religion and Politics in Seventeenth-Century England and America* (Stroud, Gloucestershire: Sutton, 1998), 1–11.

8. *RMB*, I, 70.

9. *WJ*, 2.

10. *WJ*, 7.

11. *WJ*, 9.

12. *WJ*, 13.

13. *WJ*, 19.

14. *WJ*, 18, 20.

15. This account of Winthrop's Journal is based on Richard S. Dunn's introduction to *The Journal of John Winthrop 1630–1649*, ed. Dunn, James Savage, and Laetitia Yeandle (Cambridge: Harvard University Press, 1996), xi–xxxvii; and Dunn's "John Winthrop Writes His Journal, *William and Mary Quarterly* 41 (1984), 185–212. See also James G. Moseley, *John Winthrop's World: History as a Story, the Story as History* (Madison: University of Wisconsin Press, 1992).

16. Thomas Shepard to John Winthrop, 27 January 1640, *WP*, IV, 182–183.

17. William Wood, *New England's Prospect (1634)*, ed. Alden T. Vaughan (Amherst: University of Massachusetts Press, 1977), 35; Gloria L. Main, *Peoples of a Spacious Land* (Cambridge: Harvard University Press, 2001), 2–3. Chap. 1 of Main's book provides an excellent survey of the land and its native peoples.

18. Roger Thompson, *Divided We Stand: Watertown, Massachusetts, 1630–1680* (Amherst: University of Massachusetts Press, 2001), 9.

19. Main, *Spacious Land*, 6–7, 38.

20. This paragraph and the following are based on information drawn from Main, *Spacious Land*; Neal Salisbury, *Manitou and Providence: Indians, Europeans, and the Making of New England, 1500–1643* (New York: Oxford University Press, 1982); Daniel K. Richter, *Facing East from Indian Country: A Native History of Early America* (Cambridge: Harvard University Press, 2001); Kathleen Bragdon, *Native People of Southern New England, 1500–1650* (Norman: University of Oklahoma Press, 1996); and Alden T. Vaughan, *New England Frontier: Puritans and Indians, 1620–1675*, 3d ed. (Norman: University of Oklahoma Press, 1995).

21. John Winthrop to Sir Simonds D'Ewes, 21 July 1634, *WP*, III, 171–172. He made the same point to Sir Nathaniel Rich, writing that "for the natives, they are near all dead of the small pox, so the Lord hath cleared out title to what we possess"; John Winthrop to Sir Nathaniel Rich, 22 May 1634, *WP*, III, 167.

22. See Nicholas Canny, *Making Ireland British, 1580–1650* (New York: Oxford University Press, 2001), 133–134, 204.

23. *WJ*, 35.

24. Thomas Dudley to the Lady Bridget, Countess of Lincoln, 12 and 28 March 1631, in Everett Emerson, ed., *Letters from New England: The Massachusetts Bay Colony, 1629–1638* (Amherst: University of Massachusetts Press, 1976), 71.

25. Ibid.

26. Joan Gallagher, Laurie Boros, Neill DePaoli, K. Ann Turner, and Joyce Fitzgerald, *Archaeological Data Recovery, City Square Archaeological District, Central Artery North Reconstruction Project, Charlestown, Massachusetts, Vol. VII* (Pawtucket: Public Archaeological Laboratory, 1994), 33.

27. *WJ*, 36.

28. Darrett Rutman argued in *Winthrop's Boston: A Portrait of a Puritan Town, 1630–1649* (New York: Norton, 1965) that the colonists planned to settle in a single site, in essence *a* city on a hill. He supported this by a literal reading of records that refer to searching for "a" site for the settlement. The impossibility of a group as large as that which had set sail being able to establish a single farming community casts doubt on this interpretation. While unsupervised dispersal into the wilderness would not be encouraged by Winthrop, nothing in his writings suggests his interest in confining the large migrating group to a single town (which would have also involved relocating the Salem settlement), nor his disapproval of the almost immediate creation of a number of embryo towns clustered near each other. Furthermore, Rutman's analysis of the process, including a statement that the original plan was for everyone to settle at Salem, ignores the fact that the "Governor's Great House" had been erected at Charlestown on the orders of the Massachusetts Bay Company.

29. *Memoirs of Roger Clap*, Collection of the Dorchester Antiquarian and Historical Society, no. 1 (1844), 42.

30. Richard D. Pierce, ed., *The Records of the First Church in Boston, 1630–1868*, Publications of the Colonial Society of Massachusetts, vol. 39 (1961), xviii.

31. *WJ*, 38–39.

32. John Adair, *Puritans: Religion and Politics in Seventeenth-Century England and America* (Stroud: Gloucestershire, 1998), 17.

33. William Bradford, *History of Plymouth Plantation, 1620–1647* (Boston: Massachusetts Historical Society, 1912), II, 112–113.

34. Dudley to countess of Lincoln in Everett, *Letters*, 71.

35. Thomas Prince, *New England Chronology* (Boston, 1736), I, 242.

36. John Winthrop to Margaret Winthrop, 23 July 1630, *WP*, II, 303–304.

37. John Winthrop to John Winthrop Jr., 23 July 1630, *WP*, II, 305–307.

38. J. Franklin Jameson, ed., *Johnson's Wonder-Working Providence, 1628–1651* (New York: Scribner's, 1910), 66.

39. Rutman, *Winthrop's Boston*, 29.

40. John Winthrop to Margaret Winthrop, 9 September 1630, *WP*, II, 312–313.

41. John Winthrop to Margaret Winthrop, 29 November 1630, *WP*, II, 319–320.

42. Thomas Wiggin to Sir John Cooke, 19 November 1632, quoted in Robert C. Winthrop, *Life and Letters of John Winthrop*, 3d ed. (Boston, 1895), II, 31.

43. Quoted in R. C. Winthrop, *Life and Letters*, II, 30.

44. Cotton Mather, *Magnalia Christi Americana* (Boston, 1855), I, 122; the story is also contained in the Charlestown Records, in Alexander Young, ed., *Chronicles of the First Planters of the Colony of Massachusetts Bay from 1623 to 1636* (Boston, 1846), 385.

45. The best discussion of the colonial adaptation to North American climate is Karen Ordahl Kupperman, "The Puzzle of the American Climate in the Early Colonial Period," *American Historical Review* 87 (1982), 1262–1289.
46. *WJ*, 42.
47. Charlestown Records, 385.
48. *WJ*, 39 and passim.
49. *CA*, 8–9.
50. John Winthrop to John Winthrop Jr., 28 March 1631, *WP*, III, 21–22.
51. John Humfry to Isaac Johnson, 9 December 1630, *WP*, II, 328.
52. Emmanuel Downing to John Winthrop, 30 April 1631, *WP*, III, 30–31.
53. John Humfry to John Winthrop, 12 December 1630, *WP*, II, 331–333.
54. John Rogers to John Winthrop Jr., *WP*, II, 316.
55. John Winthrop to John Winthrop Jr., 23 July 1630, *WP*, II, 305–307.
56. Mather, *Magnalia*, I, 122.
57. *WJ*, 44, 46.
58. *CA*, 1.
59. George Haskins asserted in *Law and Authority in Early Massachusetts* (New York: Macmillan, 1960) that John Humfry had been a member of Lincoln's Inn, but Wall's research does not support this. Haskins also followed Samuel Eliot Morison's lead in *Builders of the Bay Colony* (Boston: Houghton Mifflin, 1930) in claiming that William Pynchon was a justice of the peace, but Joseph Smith's examination of the Essex commissions for the peace for this period refute that claim; Smith, *Colonial Justice in Western Massachusetts, 1639–1702* (Cambridge: Harvard University Press, 1961), 7. Smith also discounts the claim that Pynchon presided over manorial courts; his only public office seemed to be that of churchwarden.
60. Court of Assistants, 23 August 1623, in *CA*, 1–3.
61. William Pynchon to John Winthrop, 16 March 1647, *WP*, V, 134–137.
62. This paragraph is based on Michael Braddick and Francis J. Bremer, "English Seeds Transplanted: The Formation of Governance in the Massachusetts Bay Colony, 1630–1636," in Bremer and Lynn A. Botelho, eds., *The World of John Winthrop*, forthcoming from the Massachusetts Historical Society.
63. *WJ*, 40.
64. Court of Assistants, 23 August 1630, *CA*, 1–2.
65. For Phillips and Watertown see Thompson, *Divided We Stand*, chap. 6.
66. *WJ*, 48.
67. The occasion was in the spring of 1634, when he was visiting the new settlement at Agawam, lately renamed Ipswich; *WJ*, 114.
68. I have focused on the transfer of conferencing and other forms of clerical association and consociation to New England in *Congregational Communion: Clerical Friendship in the Anglo-American Puritan Community, 1610–1690* (Boston: Northeastern University Press, 1994).
69. *WJ*, 44. There are many studies of Roger Williams, but he lacks a full modern biography. The best place to approach him is through *The Complete Writings of Roger Williams*, 7 vols. (New York: Russell and Russell Reprint, 1963), and Glenn W. LaFantasie's edition of *The Correspondence of Roger Williams*, 2 vols. (Hanover: Brown University Press, 1988). Edmund Morgan's *Roger Williams: The Church and the State* (New York: Harcourt, Brace & World, 1967) provides an analysis of many of the points that would divide Winthrop and Williams.
70. *WJ*, 50.

71. *Humble Request*, *WP*, II, 232.
72. "Reformation Without Separation," *WP*, III, 10ff. A modernized text will be part of Francis J. Bremer, ed., *Winthrop Papers: Religious Manuscripts* (2003).
73. Selections from *Religious Manuscripts*.
74. *WJ*, 50.
75. For a full discussion of this dispute see Timothy Wood, "'A Church Still by her First Covenant': George Philips and a Puritan View of Roman Catholicism," *New England Quarterly* 72 (1999), 25–41. James F. Cooper Jr. deals with it in terms of the involvement of godly laymen in determining such disputes in *Tenacious of their Liberties: The Congregationalists in Colonial Massachusetts* (New York: Oxford University Press, 1999), chap. 2.
76. *WJ*, 54.
77. *WJ*, 60–61.
78. John Winthrop to Margaret Winthrop, 9 September 1630, *WP*, II, 312–313.
79. John Winthrop to Margaret Winthrop, 28 March 1631, *WP*, III, 21–22.
80. *WJ*, 60.

Chapter 10. The Best of Them Was But an Attorney

1. The following description of Boston is based, except where otherwise noted on the following sources: Justin Winsor, *The Memorial History of Boston* (Boston, 1880); John Gorham Palfrey, *History of New England, Vol. I* (Boston, 1858); Darret Rutman, *Winthrop's Boston: A Portrait of a Puritan Town, 1630–1649* (New York: Norton, 1965); and Annie Haven Thwing, *The Crooked and Narrow Streets of the Town of Boston* (Boston: Marshall Jone, 1920).
2. Anne Pollard quoted in Winsor, *Memorial History*, 521.
3. The location of Winthrop's first home was initially established by Frederick Lewis Gay in a communication in the *Proceedings of the Colonial Society of Massachusetts* (1895), 86–90.
4. The description of Winthrop's first Boston home is based in part on the arguments presented by Robert St. George in his "Appendix O: Architectural Report—The Great House," in *Archaeological Data Recovery. City Square Archaeological District: Central Artery North Reconstruction Project, Charlestown, Massachusetts*, vol. 7 (Pawtucket: Public Archaeological Laboratory, 1994). I have also drawn upon the inventory of Winthrop's second, and smaller, home following his death; *WP*, V, 333–337.
5. Thomas Morton quoted in Winsor, *Memorial History*, 13.
6. Thomas Wood, quoted in Winsor, *Memorial History*, 13.
7. B. G. to Isaac Johnson, 6 December 1630, *WP*, II, 322–323.
8. John Humfry to John Winthrop, 18 December 1630, *WP*, II, 336.
9. Henry Jacie [Jessey] to John Winthrop Jr., 9 January 1632, *WP*, III, 57–61.
10. Francis J. Bremer, *Congregational Communion: Clerical Friendship in the Anglo-American Puritan Community, 1610–1692* (Boston: Northeastern University Press, 1994), 54, 92.
11. John Bluett to John Winthrop, 14 March 1633, *WP*, III, 108. Fears that letters might be intercepted increased as time went on. In 1636 Winthrop's friend Sir William Spring wrote that "neither is the time with us here so free and sure to us that I dare write you what I think" (*WP*, III, 249–251); and Robert Reyce would resort to pseudonyms to protect his identity should his letters be intercepted.

12. Mary Wright to John Winthrop, 15 May 1633, *WP*, III, 197.

13. Henry Jacie [Jessey] to John Winthrop Jr., 12 June 1633, *WP*, III, 126–128.

14. Francis Kirby to John Winthrop Jr., 6 August 1633, *WP*, III, 135–136.

15. Henry Jacie [Jessey] to John Winthrop Jr., 17 December 1633, *WP*, III, 142–143.

16. Muriel Gurdon to Margaret Winthrop, 4 April 1636, *WP*, III, 243–244.

17. Lucy Downing to Margaret Winthrop, 19 May 1636, *WP*, III, 261.

18. Edward Howes to John Winthrop Jr., 4 August 1636, *WP*, III, 290–293; Robert Reyce [writing under the pseudonym Laurence Browne] to John Winthrop, 9 September 1636, *WP*, III, 298–306.

19. Historians are divided over how to characterize the policies of the Caroline Church and over how extensively the bishops suppressed lectureships, deprived clergy, and imposed a new order. But it is hard to overstate how dangerous these policies seemed to those in New England. However slanted their views were by the facts of who wrote to them and who emigrated, the result was a growing despair over the religious scene in their native land. For insight into the Caroline religious scene see Tom Webster, *Godly Clergy in Early Stuart England: The Caroline Puritan Movement, c. 1620–1643* (Cambridge: Cambridge University Press, 1997). The New England perception of events is also dealt with in Bremer, *Congregational Communion*, chap. 5.

20. Edward Revell to John Winthrop, 20 April 1635, *WP*, III, 251–253.

21. *RMB*, I, 79.

22. *RMB*, I, 87.

23. *CA*, 3–32.

24. *CA*, 33–50.

25. *RMB*, I, 79, 91, 96; *WJ*, 67; see also Roger Thompson, *Divided We Stand: Watertown, Massachusetts, 1630–1680* (Amherst: University of Massachusetts Press, 2001), 40–41.

26. *WJ*, 63.

27. Richard Vines to John Winthrop, 25 January 1641, *WP*, IV, 307–309, in which Vines states his intention to "follow the counsel you gave me in your letter, to improve that which is profitable to them, and cover the rest with love."

28. Michael Winship, *Making Heretics: Militant Protestantism and Free Grace in Massachusetts, 1636–1641* (Princeton: Princeton University Press, 2002), 292 n. 15; 137.

29. Thomas Dudley to the Lady Bridget, countess of Lincoln, 12 and 28 March 1631, in Emerson, *Letters*, 71.

30. Darrett B. Rutman, *Winthrop's Boston: A Portrait of a Puritan Town, 1630–1649* (New York: Norton, 1965), 29–32. Rutman believed that Newtown was to be the single "city on a hill" envisioned by Winthrop. I have found no evidence that convinces me that Winthrop ever hoped to concentrate the colonists in a single settlement. Winthrop likely built a home in Newtown in an attempt to avoid a clash with his colleague but changed his mind when none of the other magistrates followed suit and the residents of Boston implored him to stay.

31. *CA*, 22; *WJ*, 64–67.

32. *WJ*, 68.

33. *RMB*, I, 95.

34. This account is derived from *WJ*, 72–77.

35. The language used by Winthrop is that Dudley "told the Governor that if he were so round, he would be round too." "Uncompromising" is the mean-

ing of "round" in the *Oxford English Dictionary* that comes closest to the sense of the exchange.

36. *WJ*, 79–80.
37. *WJ*, 102.
38. *CA*, 30–31.
39. *CA*, 42–44.
40. *RMB*, I, 117.
41. *WJ*, I, 113–114.
42. *RMB*, I, 117.
43. *Memoirs of Roger Clap, 1630*, Collections of the Dorchester Antiquarian and Historical Society (1844), 39. This formation of a congregation *prior* to leaving England has not been sufficiently recognized by historians.
44. Perry Miller's treatment of nonseparating congregationalism is principally found in his study *Orthodoxy in Massachusetts* (Cambridge: Harvard University Press, 1933). There is a vast literature that emphasizes the role of the laity in shaping popular Protestantism in sixteenth- and seventeenth-century England. The works of Patrick Collinson are indispensable to understanding the subject, most particularly recent publications such as *The Religion of Protestants: The Church in English Society, 1559–1625* (Oxford: Clarendon Press, 1982); *The Birthpangs of Protestant England: Religious and Cultural Changes in the Sixteenth and Seventeenth Centuries* (New York: St. Martin's Press, 1988); and *The Puritan Character* (Los Angeles: University of California Press, 1989). But my first sense of the importance of lay shaping of puritanism came from reading a photocopy that Stephen Foster was kind enough to share with me of Collinson's paper "The Godly: Aspects of Popular Protestantism," which was later published in his *Godly People: Essays on English Protestantism and Puritanism* (London: Hambledon, 1983). I would also like to thank Professor Collinson for sharing with me some of his recent unpublished work, especially his 2001 Dudley White Local History Lecture at the University of Essex, "The Cuckoo in the Nest: Elizabethan Puritanism in Dedham and the Stour Valley." Christopher Marsh has contributed an excellent study of lay involvement across the religious spectrum in *Popular Religion in Sixteenth-Century England* (Basingstoke: Macmillan, 1998). Recent works by Peter Lake and David Como, individually and as co-authors, have also illuminated the lay involvement in the shaping of puritanism. Stephen Foster's neglected *Notes from the Caroline Underground: Alexander Leighton, the Puritan Triumvirate, and the Laudian Reaction to Nonconformity* (Hamden: Archon, 1978) was an early contribution to the study of lay and clerical interaction. James F. Cooper Jr.'s *Tenacious of Their Liberties: The Congregationalists in Colonial Massachusetts* (New York: Oxford University Press, 1999) offers the most detailed study yet of the lay involvement in the churches of the Bay, though he fails to connect the subject to its English roots. David Hall's attention to "lived religion" is setting an important new direction for studies of American religion, including colonial religion.
45. Again, the works of Patrick Collinson, and particularly his treatment of prophesyings, conferences, and lectureships, are essential to understanding the efforts of the puritan clergy to maintain consensus. I have dealt in great detail with the formal and informal networking that was employed for that purpose in *Congregational Communion*.
46. *WJ*, 95–96.
47. See Cooper, *Tenacious of Their Liberties*.

48. *CA*, 36–37.
49. *WJ*, 102.
50. The notion of a monolithic colonial orthodoxy emerged from an overly simplistic reading of Perry Miller's *The New England Mind: The Seventeenth Century* (New York: Macmillan, 1939) and *The New England Mind: From Colony to Province* (Cambridge: Harvard University Press, 1953). Studies that explored the diversity within New England teachings included Philip Gura's *A Glimpse of Sion's Glory: Puritan Radicalism in New England, 1620–1660* (Middletown, Conn.: Wesleyan University Press, 1984); Stephen Foster's "New England and the Challenge of Heresy, 1630–1660: The Puritan Crisis in Trans-Atlantic Perspective," *William and Mary Quarterly*, 3rd ser. 38 (1981), 624–660, and *The Long Argument: English Puritanism and the Shaping of New England Culture, 1570–1700* (Chapel Hill: University of North Carolina Press, 1991); and Bremer, *Congregational Communion*. Recently Darren Staloff has argued that a narrow clique did in fact impose a single orthodoxy in his *The Making of an American Thinking Class* (New York: Oxford University Press, 1998), a work that ignores both the diversity of puritan views and the role of the laity in shaping puritanism. In seeking to replace the idea of a single New England mind with an equally simplistic division of colonial religious beliefs into two "orthodoxies" advanced by two coherent schools of thinkers, Janice Knight's *Orthodoxies in Massachusetts: Rereading American Puritanism* (Cambridge: Harvard University Press, 1994) ignores the many more nuanced studies that have come to characterize New England puritan studies. The most sophisticated and persuasive account of the range of early Massachusetts religious ideas and how the unity was shattered by a few individuals more concerned with precise definitions than Christian charity is to be found in Winship's *Making Heretics*.
51. Winship, *Making Heretics*, 10.
52. Eliot quoted in Bremer, *Congregational Communion*, 111.
53. *WJ*, 136–137.
54. *WJ*, 71; Roger Williams to John Winthrop, 1632, in Glenn LaFantasie, *Correspondence of Roger Williams* (Hanover: Brown University Press, 1988), I, 8–12.
55. *WJ*, 82; LaFantasie adds details from an account by Cotton Mather in *Correspondence of Roger Williams*, I, 9–10.
56. *WJ*, 111; the earlier debate at Salem is related in William Hubbard, *History of New England, Collections of the Massachusetts Historical Society*, 2d ser. 5 (1815), 204–205. See also Donald R. Come, "John Cotton, Guide of the Chosen People," (Princeton University, Ph.D., 1949), 196.
57. For the importance of handwritten treatises, "scribal publications," see David Hall and Alexandra Walsham, "Communications in the Anglo-American World of John Winthrop," in Francis J. Bremer and Lynn Botelho, eds., *The World of John Winthrop*, forthcoming from the Massachusetts Historical Society. The sermon gadding of Roger Clap, a layman who came over on the Winthrop fleet, is described in "A Short Account of the Author . . . written by one that was acquainted therewith," in *Memoirs of Clap*, 57.
58. See Hall and Walsham, "Communications," for scribal publication.
59. For the observation of the Sabbath see Horton Davies, *The Worship of the American Puritans, 1629–1730* (New York: Peter Land, 1990), esp. 52–58, and Winton Solberg, *Redeem the Time: The Puritan Sabbath in Early America* (Cambridge: Harvard University Press, 1977). The best contemporary ex-

positions of these views were the Suffolk clergyman Nicholas Bownde's *The Doctrine of the Sabbath* (1595) and the American Thomas Shepard's *Theses Sabbaticae; or, The Doctrine of the Sabbath* (1649).

60. The following discussion of the church practices of the Bay is based largely on the contemporary account given by Thomas Lechford in *Plain Dealing; or, News from New England*, ed. Darrett B. Rutman (New York: Johnson Reprint Corp., 1969), supplemented by Davies, *Worship*; Richard D. Pierce, ed., *The Records of the First Church in Boston, 1630–1868*, Publications of the Colonial Society of Massachusetts, vol. 39 (1961); and the Sermon Notebooks of Robert Keayne, manuscript, Massachusetts Historical Society. It is Lechford who tells us that Bostonians were called to worship by a bell, though he does not specify whether it was a handheld bell or a more traditional hanging church bell. In most of the towns of the Bay a bell was not available, and Christ's soldiers were mustered to the meetinghouse by drumbeat.

61. Laypeople and clergy owned musical instruments in the colonies—the Reverend Nathaniel Rogers of Ipswich owned a "treble viol," for example; Davies, *Worship*, 128. Oliver Cromwell's fondness for music has often been noted. There is no direct or indirect evidence pointing to Winthrop's enjoyment of music or lack thereof. See also Percy Scholes, *The Puritans and Music in England and New England* (Oxford: Oxford University Press, 1934); and Lowell Beveridge, "Music in New England from John Cotton to Cotton Mather," *Historical Magazine of the Protestant Episcopal Church* 48 (1979), 145–165; and Donald P. Campbell, "Puritan Belief and Musical Practices in the Sixteenth, Seventeenth, and Eighteenth Centuries" (Southwestern Baptist Theological Seminary, Ph.D., 1994).

62. The Notebooks of Robert Keayne, manuscript, Massachusetts Historical Society. I would like to thank Helle Alpert for providing me with a transcript of the non-sermon portions of Keayne's notebooks, which reveal a large amount of lay participation in the church.

63. See above, p. 120, for a description of the cup. Further indication that it was used is found in Lechford, *Plain Dealing*, 49, where he refers to "a fair gilt cup with a cover, offered there by one, which is still used at Communion."

64. *WJ*, 79.

65. Edwards Howes to John Winthrop Jr., 28 November 1632, *WP*, III, 100–101.

66. Confirmation has been little studied by students of English religion in this period, and it is not clear that objection to it was ever a major issue for the godly, though it seems as if they denied it to be a sacrament. But however willing they may have been to submit their children to be confirmed in England, since the ceremony was performed by the bishop it would have been impossible to perform in the colonies.

67. This comes in his description of the first occasion on which John Cotton, not yet called to the ministry of the congregation, first addressed the church members; *WJ*, 95–96.

68. Winthrop's sermon notebook, including his notes on that particular sermon, will be published in Francis J. Bremer, ed., *Winthrop Papers: Religious Manuscripts* (2003).

69. William Bradford, *History of Plymoth Plantation*, 2 vols. (Boston: Massachusetts Historical Society, 1912), I, 244–245.

70. For England see Chris Durston, "Lords of Misrule: The Puritan War on Christmas, 1642–60," *History Today* 35 (December 1985), 7–14; David Underdown, *Revel, Riot, and Rebellion: Popular Politics and Culture in England*,

1603–1660 (Oxford: Clarendon Press, 1985), 256–268; Ronald Hutton, *The Rise and Fall of Merry England: The Ritual Year, 1400–1700* (Oxford: Oxford University Press, 1994), chap. 6; and for New England the best treatment by far is Stephen W. Nissenbaum, "Christmas in Early New England, 1620–1800: Puritanism, Popular Culture, and the Printed Word," *Proceedings of the American Antiquarian Society* 106 (1996), 79–164.

71. Edward Howes to John Winthrop Jr., 18 March 1633, *WP*, III, 113–114. An excellent discussion of these matters is to be found in James P. Walsh, "Holy Time and Sacred Space in Puritan New England," *American Quarterly* 32 (1980), 79–95.

72. Horton, *Worship*, 52.

73. The most complete study is William DeLoss Love, *The Fast and Thanksgiving Days of New England* (New York, 1895), but that needs to be supplemented by Richard Gildrie, "The Ceremonial Puritan Days of Humiliation and Thanksgiving," *New England Historical and Genealogical Register* 136 (1982).

74. *WJ*, 106.

75. *WJ*, 111–112.

Chapter 11.   Relations with England

1. John Winthrop to the lord chief justice, [March] 1631, *WP*, III, 15.

2. Edward Howes to John Winthrop Jr., June 1632, *WP*, III, 76.

3. *WP*, III, 100–101.

4. James Hopkins to John Winthrop, 25 February 1635, *WP*, III, 105–107.

5. Thomas Ashley to John Winthrop, 6 March 1635, *WP*, III, 107.

6. Charles M. Andrews, *The Colonial Period of American History: The Settlements, I* (New Haven: Yale University Press, 1934), 338–342.

7. *WJ*, 42.

8. Andrews, *Settlements*, I, 403.

9. Quoted in Andrews, *Settlements*, I, 403.

10. For Morton see Charles Francis Adams, *Three Episodes of Massachusetts History*, 2 vols. (New York, 1903) and Michael Zuckerman, "Pilgrims in the Wilderness: Community, Modernity, and the Maypole of Merry Mount," *New England Quarterly* 50 (1977), 255–277. Morton's own account of his story is *New English Canaan* (1637).

11. *WJ*, 52.

12. Edward Howes to John Winthrop Jr., 18 March 1633, *WP*, III, 110–114.

13. Emmanuel Downing to Sir John Coke, 12 December 1633, Historical Manuscripts Commission, *Twelfth Report, Appendix II*, 38, as quoted in Andrews, *Settlements*, I, 403 n. 1.

14. Quoted in Andrews, *Settlements*, I, 409.

15. Quotes from *WJ*, 90. See Andrews, *Settlements*, I, 409–410.

16. Edward Howes to John Winthrop Jr., 18 March 1633, *WP*, III, 110–114.

17. Francis Kirby to John Winthrop Jr., received in June 1633, *WP*, III, 116–118.

18. *WJ*, 94.

19. John Winthrop to Sir Simonds D'Ewes, 26 September 1633, *WP*, III, 139.

20. Andrews, *Settlements*, I, 410–411. Andrews argues that Laud was likely the chairman of the Privy Council committee whose recommendations led to the creation of the commission. If so, his dislike of puritanism would have predisposed him to lend an ear to Gorges's complaints.

21. I am quoting Winthrop's summary of the points the magistrates found objectionable from *WJ*, 107–108.
22. Henry Jacie [Jessey] to John Winthrop Jr., 17 December 1633, *WP*, III, 142–143.
23. *WJ*, 107–108; and John Winthrop to John Endecott, 3 January 1634, *WP*, III, 146–149, in which Winthrop shares his refutation of the arguments.
24. *WJ*, 109.
25. Andrews, *Settlements*, I, 410–411.
26. For a discussion of the economic importance of immigration see Bernard Bailyn, *The New England Merchants in the Seventeenth Century* (Cambridge: Harvard University Press, 1955), 46–47.
27. Copy in *WP*, III, 180–181.
28. *Acts of the Privy Council, Charles I*, 199–201; *Calendar of State Papers, Domestic, 1633–1634*, 450–451.
29. Emmanuel Downing to John Winthrop Jr., 25 March 1635," *WP*, III, 194–195.
30. *WJ*, 113; *RMB*, I, 115–116.
31. *WJ*, 123.
32. *WJ*, 125–126.
33. *WJ*, 120–121, 123.
34. *WJ*, 124.
35. *WJ*, 128–129.
36. The best treatment of Stone is to be found in Alfred A. Cave, *The Pequot War* (Amherst: University of Massachusetts Press, 1996), 72–77.
37. Clap, *Memoir*, 36–37.
38. Christopher Thompson, "The Saybrook Company and the Significance of Its Colonizing Venture," paper delivered at the Institute of Historical Research in 1999. For this incident see also Charles E. Clark, *The Eastern Frontier: The Settlement of Northern New England, 1610–1763* (New York: Knopf, 1970), 40.
39. *WJ*, 115.
40. *WJ*, 122–123; for Bradford's account of this episode see William Bradford, *History of Plymouth Plantation, 1620–1647* (Boston: Massachusetts Historical Society, 1912), II, 175–189.
41. The now familiar Union Jack was not to become the British flag until the union of England, Scotland, and Ireland in the eighteenth century.
42. *WJ*, 142, 144–145. I have dealt with this incident more fully in "Endecott and the Red Cross: Puritan Iconoclasm in the New World," *Journal of American Studies* 24 (1990), 5–22, upon which these paragraphs are based.
43. *WJ*, 83. See the discussion of the incident in James P. Walsh, "Holy Time and Sacred Space in Puritan New England," *American Quarterly* 32 (1980), 85.
44. British Library, Harley MS 4888, copy in Massachusetts Historical Society.
45. Thomas Hooker, "Touchinge the Crosse in the Banner," *Massachusetts Historical Society Proceedings* 62 (1909), 271–280; Hooker, "Miscellanae," transcribed and printed in Andrew T. Denholm, "Thomas Hooker: 1586–1647" (Hartford Seminary, Ph.D., 1961), 372ff.
46. Israel Stoughton to John Stoughton, 1635, in Everett Emerson, ed., *Letters from New England: The Massachusetts Bay Colony, 1629–1638* (Amherst: University of Massachusetts Press, 1976), 144–145.
47. British Library, Harley MS 4888, copy in Massachusetts Historical Society.
48. *RMB*, I, 136–138.
49. *RMB*, I, 146; *WJ*, 144–145.

50. Jonathan Morris, *The British Flag: Its Origin and History. Incidents in Its Use in America* (Hartford, 1889), 4.
51. Andrews, *Settlements*, I, 420–421.
52. Reverend George Burdett to Archbishop William Laud, quoted in Andrews, *Settlements*, I, 426.

Chapter 12. On the Fringe

1. *RMB*, 117–121.
2. *WJ*, 116.
3. *WJ*, 116.
4. John Winthrop to Sir Nathaniel Rich, 22 May 1634, *WP*, III, 166–167.
5. William Hammond to Sir Simonds D'Ewes, 26 September 1633, in Everett Emerson, ed., *Letters from New England: The Massachusetts Bay Colony, 1629–1638* (Amherst: University of Massachusetts Press, 1976), 111; John Eliot to Sir Simonds D'Ewes, 18 September 1633, in Emerson, *Letters*, 105.
6. Eliot to D'Ewes, 18 September 1633, in Emerson, *Letters*, 105.
7. *WJ*, 116.
8. *RMB*, I, 95.
9. The anticipation of Ludlow's election is reported in Israel Stoughton to John Stoughton, 1635, in Emerson, *Letters*, 151.
10. *WJ*, 144.
11. Israel Stoughton to John Stoughton, in Emerson, *Letters*, 151.
12. *WJ*, 95. See entry by James Walsh in the *New Dictionary of National Biography*, forthcoming.
13. Robert J. Taylor, *Colonial Connecticut* (Millwood, N.Y.: KTO, 1979), 6.
14. Robert Charles Anderson, *The Great Migration: Immigrants to New England, 1634–1635, Vol. I: A–B* (Boston: New England Historical and Genealogical Society, 1999), 243–250.
15. *WJ*, 157.
16. Unless otherwise noted the following description and quotes are from Israel Stoughton to John Stoughton, 1635, in Emerson, *Letters*, 144–155.
17. *RMB*, I, 135, 136.
18. Winthrop's account of the episode in his journal was brief and dispassionate and does not reveal his specific role in the events.
19. *WJ*, 165–168.
20. *WJ*, 165–168.
21. *RMB*, I, 126.
22. The page is reproduced in Justin Winsor, *Memorial History of Boston* (Boston, 1880), facing p. 122. *Second Report of the Record Commissions of the City of Boston: Boston Records, 1634–1660, and the Book of Possessions* (1902), 1.
23. The Boxford parish records show agreements that are suggestive of New England practice, but the English precedent is most clearly found in the records of the Stour Valley towns of Braintree and Finchingfield, presented and discussed in F. G. Emmison, ed., *Early Essex Town Meetings: Braintree, 1619–1636; Finchingfield, 1626–1634* (Chicester: Phillimore, 1970).
24. Town decisions from *Boston Records*, 1–13.
25. *WJ*, 79.
26. *WJ*, 114.

27. There is no surviving official record of the child's birth or of their deaths. Lawrence Shaw Mayo, *The Winthrop Family in America* (Boston: Massachusetts Historical Society, 1948), 39, cites a local history of Ipswich for the approximate date.

28. The manuscript inventory is owned by the Ipswich Historical Society. I would like to thank Pat Tyler of that society for sending me a copy.

29. Lucy Downing to John Winthrop, c. July 1636, *WP*, III, 278–280.

30. William Leigh to John Winthrop, 20 September 1636, *WP*, III, 310–314.

31. Thomas Gostlin to John Winthrop, 2 March 1640, *WP* IV, 211–212.

32. Some of the details of the Ten Hills property are found in a Deed of John Winthrop to John Winthrop Jr., 22 September 1643, *WP*, IV, 416. There is a foldout duplication of a map of Ten Hills sketched by one of the Winthrops in 1637 between pp. 416 and 417 of that volume.

33. *WJ*, 59, where Winthrop records that the first effort to build the house had failed when heavy rains washed two sides of it to the ground since it had not been finished and the workers had used clay between the stones in the absence of lime.

34. *WJ*, 57–58. It is also possible that he was technically trespassing, in a house belonging to Sagamore John. Again, whatever his concern, it would have been compounded by his inability to communicate with the native woman. I wish to thank Alden Vaughan for sharing his views on this issue.

35. *WJ*, 61–63.

36. *WJ*, 101.

37. *WJ*, 144.

38. Glenn W. LaFantasie, ed., *The Correspondence of Roger Williams* (Hanover: Brown University Press, 1988), I, 19; *WJ*, 144.

39. *WJ*, 149–154.

40. John Cotton, *Reply to Mr. Williams* (1647) as rpt. in *The Complete Writings of Roger Williams*, 7 vols. (New York: Russell & Russell Reprint, 1963), II, 76.

41. The refusal of the Boston elders is alluded to in a letter signed by Williams from "The Church at Salem to the Elders of the Church at Boston, after 22 July 1635," in LaFantasie, *Correspondence of Williams*, 23–27.

42. *WJ*, 151.

43. *WJ*, 153.

44. *RMB*, I, 160–161.

45. *WJ*, 163–164.

46. LaFantasie, *Correspondence of Williams*, II, 610.

47. Roger Williams to John Winthrop, 24 October 1636, *WP*, III, 314–315.

48. Bernard Bailyn, *The New England Merchants in the Seventeenth Century* (Cambridge: Harvard University Press, 1955), 23–26.

49. Given the importance of the fur trade to the colonial economies and to the story of relations with the natives, it is surprising that there have been few modern studies of the topic beyond Calvin Martin's controversial *Keepers of the Game* (Berkeley: University of California Press, 1978). William Cronon discusses the ways that the fur trade contributed to the transformation of the region in *Changes in the Land: Indians, Colonists, and the Ecology of New England* (New York: Hill & Wang, 1983), chap. 5.

50. Stephen Innes, *Labor in a New Land: Economy and Society in Seventeenth-Centruy Springfield* (Princeton: Princeton University Press, 1983), 4–5.

51. *WJ*, 53.

52. Innes, *Labor*, 4–5.

53. John Frederick Martin, *Profits in the Wilderness: Entrepreneurship and the Founding of New England Towns in the Seventeenth Century* (Chapel Hill: University of North Carolina Press, 1991), 47–48.

54. Francis X. Moloney, *The Fur Trade in New England, 1620–1676* (Cambridge: Harvard University Press, 1931), 36, 48.

55. Alfred Cave, *The Pequot War* (Amherst: University of Massachusetts Press, 1996), 57–58, 80–85.

56. Some historians have suggested that the migration may have been triggered by differences in how puritanism was interpreted between clergy such as Boston's John Cotton, who stayed, and Newtown's Thomas Hooker, who left. But these differences were no greater than those between Cotton and many of the ministers of the Bay who never left. Differences within a general unity were not cause for departure. Connecticut's Hooker and New Haven's Davenport would cooperate with their Bay colleagues in the decades to come. The notion, advanced by others, that those who left feared the arrival of a royal governor is likewise not very persuasive, since any royal initiative that would have subdued the Bay would easily have extended to isolated towns in the region.

57. *WJ*, 115. It is interesting that this was not recorded in the official records of the General Court.

58. *WJ*, 126.

59. *WJ*, 126–127.

60. The earliest record of this document is when John Winthrop Jr. produced a copy in 1661 as validation of the legitimacy of the colony of Connecticut, of which he was then governor. Most historians have doubted the legitimacy of that copy and have questioned whether any such legal grant was ever made. However, Christopher Thompson has argued persuasively for the document on the basis of being able to match the names of the witnesses to individuals who can be discovered in the estate records of the earl of Warwick. I would like to thank Mr. Thompson for allowing me to read a copy of his paper "The Saybrook Company and the Significance of Its Colonizing Venture," delivered at the Institute of Historical Research in 1999.

61. *WJ*, 120–121.

62. It has generally been assumed that the proposals were conditions for the puritan peers to settle in Massachusetts, but that is not clear from the surviving documents. Given that they had already acquired land to the south of the Bay and had made preparations to establish a settlement there, I find convincing the suggestion of Hugh Engstrom that the proposals were designed for Saybrook. See Hugh R. Engstrom, Jr., "Sir Arthur Heselrige and the Saybrook Company," *Albion* 5 (1973), 161–162.

63. "Certain Proposals made by Lord Saye, Lord Brooke, and other Persons of Quality as conditions of their removing to New England, with the answers thereto," in Thomas Hutchinson, *The History of the Colony and Province of Massachusetts Bay* (Cambridge: Harvard University Press, 1936), I, 410–413.

64. *RMB*, I, 167.

65. John Cotton to William Fiennes, Lord Saye and Sele [after March 1636], in Sargent Bush Jr., ed., *The Correspondence of John Cotton* (Chapel Hill: University of North Carolina Press, 2001), 243–249.

66. John Winthrop to Sir Nathaniel Rich, 22 May 1634, *WP*, III, 166–167.

67. For this journey see Robert Black, *The Younger John Winthrop* (New York: Columbia University Press, 1966), 77–81.

68. Christopher Thompson, "Saybrook Company."
69. Henry Jessey to John Winthrop Jr., c. February 1635, *WP*, III, 188–189.
70. Agreement of the Saybrook Company with John Winthrop Jr., *WP*, III, 198–199. This was the agreement which Philip Nye conveyed to Winthrop for his signature and return in late July; Philip Nye to John Winthrop Jr., 28 July 1635, *WP*, III, 201.
71. Robert Barrington to John Winthrop Jr., 4 September 1635, *WP*, III, 208. Barrington, who referred to John Jr. as "my very good friend," was the second son of Sir Francis Barrington and his wife, Joan, who was herself the daughter of Sir Henry Cromwell of Hinchinbrooke; Robert had married Dorothy, the daughter of Sir Thomas Eden, who had been a member of the Suffolk commission well known to Adam Winthrop.
72. Sir Arthur Heselrige and George Fenwick to John Winthrop Jr., 18 September 1635, *WP*, III, 209.
73. Emmanuel Downing to John Winthrop Jr., 1 March 1636, *WP*, III, 232–233. The negotiations broke down when some of the Massachusetts Bay Company members still in England and trying to recoup their investment claimed the house as company property.
74. Edward Hopkins to John Winthrop Jr., 21 September 1635, *WP*, III, 209–210.
75. Henry Lawrence to John Winthrop Jr., 22 September 1635, *WP*, III, 212–213.
76. In his paper "The Decision to Stay: Oliver Cromwell," at the 1999 Millersville University conference "The Worlds of John Winthrop: England and New England, 1588–1649," John Morrill made a persuasive case for taking seriously the possibility that Cromwell considered emigration to New England. Professor Morrill is currently engaged in further research on this period of Cromwell's life that will demonstrate additional connections with those interested in New England.
77. Sir Matthew Boynton to John Winthrop Jr., 23 February 1636, *WP*, III, 226–227.
78. Sir Henry Vane to John Winthrop Jr., 1 July 1636, *WP*, III, 282.
79. Hugh Peter to John Winthrop Jr., about March 1636 according to the editors, but possibly later, *WP*, III, 231–232.
80. Mary Jeanne Anderson Jones, *Congregational Commonwealth: Connecticut, 1636–1662* (Middletown, Conn.: Wesleyan University Press, 1968), 64–66.
81. Sir Matthew Boynton to John Winthrop Jr., 23 February 1636, *WP*, III, 226–227. Few letters directly to or from John Winthrop and the Saybrook investors survive, but a number of letters to the younger Winthrop, such as this one, allude to his father's involvement.
82. John Winthrop to John Winthrop Jr., 10 June 1636, *WP*, III, 268.
83. Engstrom, "Heselrige," 166. John Morrill, in "The Decision to Stay," has reopened the possibility that there is some basis for the traditional story that Heselrige, Hampden, and Oliver Cromwell were on a ship bound for New England in 1638 when the license for them to depart was withdrawn.

Chapter 13.   War

1. Underhill's resentment is expressed in his letter to Winthrop later that year, in *WP*, III, 460–463. Underhill's background is summarized by Louise Breen in *Transgressing the Bounds: Subversive Enterprises Among the Puritan Elite in Massachusetts, 1630–1692* (New York: Oxford University Press, 2001), 63–66, though I believe her interpretation of Underhill is seriously flawed.

2. Much of the following analysis is drawn from the important essay "England and Its 'Others' in the Old World and the New," by Alden T. Vaughan and Virginia Mason Vaughan, which will appear in Francis J. Bremer and Lynn A. Botelho, eds. *The World of John Winthrop*, forthcoming from the Massachusetts Historical Society.

3. Fynes Moryson, "The Commonwealth of Ireland," quoted in Vaughan and Vaughan, "Others."

4. John Davies, *A Discovery of the True Causes Why Ireland Was Never Entirely Subdued* (1612), quoted in Vaughan and Vaughan, "Others."

5. Moryson, "Commonwealth," quoted in Vaughan and Vaughan, "Others." For a discussion of the actual state of religious belief in Ireland at this time see Raymond Gillespie, *Devoted People: Belief and Religion in Early Modern Ireland* (New York: Manchester University Press, 1997).

6. See Alden T. Vaughan, "From White Man to Redskin: Changing Anglo-American Perceptions of the American Indian," *American Historical Review* 86 (1982), 917–953, rpt. in Alden T. Vaughan, ed., *Roots of American Racism: Essays on the Colonial Experience* (New York: Oxford University Press, 1995), 3–33.

7. For English perceptions of native Americans see the works of Alden Vaughan, cited above; Alfred Cave, *The Pequot War* (Amherst: University of Massachusetts Press, 1996); and Karen Ordahl Kupperman, *Indians and English: Facing Off in Early America* (Ithaca: Cornell University Press, 2000).

8. *WJ*, 47.

9. Edward Howes to John Winthrop Jr., 1632, *WP*, III, 74.

10. Cave, *Pequot War*, 63–68.

11. *WJ*, 49–50.

12. *WJ*, 49.

13. *WJ*, 108.

14. This summary is drawn from a letter of John Winthrop to William Bradford which was written shortly after the events and presented by Bradford in his *History of Plymouth Plantation, 1620–1647* (Boston: Massachusetts Historical Society, 1912), II, 233–234. This letter, ignored by many historians and curiously not published in the *WP*, is more useful than the similar account Winthrop gives in his journal since it was written at the time and not subsequent to the events. The wampum that the Pequots were to pay the English was a considerable amount—equivalent to half the colony's tax income in 1634—and some historians have argued that this exorbitant demand was a major reason for the deterioration of relations over the next few years; see Francis Jennings, *The Invasion of America: Indians, Colonialism, and the Cant of Conquest* (New York: Norton, 1976), 191–196. But Winthrop's letter to Bradford clearly indicates that much of the payment was intended for the Narragansetts as the price the Pequots were willing to pay for peace with their eastern neighbors, though not willing to appear to be paying tribute. The only scholar who seems to have recognized the implications of Winthrop's letter to Bradford is Alden Vaughan; see Vaughan's revised "Pequots and Puritans," in Vaughan, *Roots of American Racism*, 180–181, and the discussion in n. 12.

15. John Winthrop to William Bradford, 12 March 1635, in Bradford, *History of Plymouth*, II, 234.

16. Jonathan Brewster to John Winthrop Jr., 18 June 1636, *WP*, III, 270–271. Brewster reiterated the warnings in a second letter to Winthrop Jr. dated the same day; *WP*, III, 271–272.

17. Jonathan Brewster to John Winthrop Jr., 18 June 1636, *WP*, III, 270–271.

18. William Pynchon to John Winthrop Jr., 2 June 1636, *WP*, III, 267; "Commission and Instructions from the Colony of Massachusetts Bay to John Winthrop Jr. for Treating with the Pequots," *WP*, III, 284–285.

19. Henry Vane to John Winthrop Jr., 1 July 1636, *WP*, III, 282–283.

20. Francis Jennings offers a story of a supposed conference, but there is no evidence for any meeting having taken place; see Vaughan, "Pequots and Puritans," 318 n.15.

21. See Vaughan, "Pequots and Puritans," 181–182; Cave, *Pequot War*, 104–107.

22. Vaughan, "Pequots and Puritans," 193, discusses the reluctance of many historians to take the English deaths seriously and reviews the evidence for the number of murders.

23. Warren Billings, John Selby, and Thad Tate, *Colonial Virginia: A History* (Milwood, N.Y.: KTO, 1986), 44.

24. Roger Williams to John Winthrop, August 1636, in Glenn W. LaFantasie, ed., *The Correspondence of Roger Williams*, 2 vols. (Hanover: Brown University Press, 1988), I, 54–55.

25. *WJ*, 183. Richard Dunn's note states that "this action by the MBC is unrecorded in the court minutes," but that is because Winthrop's account makes clear that this was a decision made by the Standing Council and merely approved by the magistrates and ministers called to advise them.

26. This account is based on *WJ*, 185–186.

27. See Nicholas Canny, *Making Ireland British, 1580–1650* (New York: Oxford University Press, 2001), 50 and passim.

28. Cave, *Pequot War*, 113.

29. No copy of either Bradford's letter or Winthrop's response has survived, but Winthrop summarizes his letter in *WJ*, 192.

30. Roger Williams to John Mason and Thomas Prence, 22 June 1670, in LaFantasie, *Correspondence*, II, 611–612.

31. The text of the treaty is presented in *WJ*, 191–192.

32. Cave, *Pequot War*, chap. 4 provides the most detailed description of the fighting throughout the war.

33. The following is based closely on Ronald Dale Karr, "'Why Should You Be So Furious?': The Violence of the Pequot War," *Journal of American History* 85 (1998), 876–909. The quote regarding Drake is on p. 887.

34. Philip Vincent, *A True Relation of the Late Battell Fought in New England* (1638), rpt. in Charles Orr, *History of the Pequot War: The Contemporary Accounts of Mason, Underhill, Vincent, and Gardener* (Cleveland, 1897), 103.

35. John Underhill, *News from America* (1638), rpt. in Orr, *Pequot War*, 81.

36. *WJ*, 238.

37. Israel Stoughton to John Winthrop, c. 28 June 1637, *WP*, III, 435.

38. Roger Williams to John Winthrop, 30 June 1637, in LaFantasie, *Correspondence*, I, 88.

39. John Winthrop to William Bradford, 28 July 1637, *WP*, III, 457.

40. Roger Williams to John Winthrop, 31 July 1637, in LaFantasie, *Correspondence*, I, 108–110.

Chapter 14.   Struggling to Hold the Center

1. I would like to thank Roger Thompson for the information on the first public house in Newtown, licensed in September 1636.

2. The description of Newtown, including the location of the various homes, is derived from Samuel Eliot Morison, *The Founding of Harvard College* (Cambridge: Harvard University Press, 1935), esp. 183–193. Winthrop discusses the election in *WJ*, 214–215. John Wilson's intervention was first described by Thomas Hutchinson, *The History of the Colony and Province of Massachusetts-Bay*, ed. Lawrence Shaw Mayo (Cambridge: Harvard University Press, 1936), I, 54, where he draws on a manuscript life of John Wilson which has not survived. I have also profited from the scene setting in Emery Battis, *Saints and Sectaries: Anne Hutchinson and the Antinomian Controversy in the Massachusetts Bay Colony* (Chapel Hill: University of North Carolina Press, 1962), 151–153.

3. For Rogers and Still see John Craig, "The 'Cambridge Boies': Thomas Rogers and the 'Brethren' in Bury St. Edmunds," in Susan Wabuda and Caroline Litzinberger, eds., *Belief and Practice in Reformation England: A Tribute to Patrick Collinson from His Students*, (Aldershot: Ashgate, 1998), 154–176. I thank John Craig for sharing with me his transcript of the manuscript detailing Rogers's complaint, which he is editing for publication.

4. The divisions in the London puritan community have been brilliantly dissected by Peter Lake in *The Boxmaker's Revenge: "Orthodoxy," "Heterodoxy," and the Politics of the Parish in Early Stuart London* (Stanford: Stanford University Press, 2001).

5. Back in England in 1625, John Cotton had circulated a manuscript in which he expressed views on the complex issues of predestination and preparation for salvation that the clergyman William Twisse criticized as embracing "the sour leaven of Arminianism." Cotton subsequently avoided touching on the matters that had aroused controversy, earning a reputation instead as an enemy of Arminian. Cotton was not alone in having his views on the thorny matter of predestination challenged, sharing that distinction with Ezekiel Culverwell, among others. Indeed, so complex was that doctrine that there were numerous very different positions that were all accepted as "orthodox" within the broad Calvinist community. These strategies, and in particular their employment in constructing an acceptably orthodox umbrella under which various predestinarian emphases could coexist, are examined in David Como's "Puritans, Predestination and the Construction of Orthodoxy in Early Seventeenth Century England," in Peter Lake and Michael Questier, eds., *Conformity and Orthodoxy in the English Church, c. 1560–1660* (Cambridge: Cambridge University Press, 2000), 64–87. Como takes particular note of the questions concerning the views of Culverwell and Cotton.

6. Any orthodoxy in Massachusetts covered many nuanced differences between individual clergymen and between clergymen and laity. The dynamics of this living and evolving faith community before 1636 have never been captured as well as by Michael Winship in *Making Heretics: Militant Protestantism and Free Grace in Massachusetts, 1636–1641* (Princeton: Princeton University Press, 2002). Efforts to replace the notion of a single orthodoxy with two opposing tendencies or schools of New England thought, such as Janice Knight's *Orthodoxies in Massachusetts: Rereading American Puritanism* (Cambridge: Harvard University Press, 1994) and Louise Breen's *Transgressing the Bounds: Subversive Enterprises Among the Puritan Elite in Massachusetts, 1630–1692* (New York: Oxford University Press, 2001), run the risk of oversimplifying the complex religious scene.

7. For Pynchon see Michael Winship's "Conesting Control of Orthodoxy Among the Godly: William Pynchon Reexamined," *William and Mary Quarterly*, 3rd ser. 54 (1997), and "William Pynchon's *The Jewes Synagogue*," *New England Quarterly* 71 (1998), 290–297; and Philip Gura, *A Glimpse of Sion's Glory: Purian Radicalism in New England, 1620–1660* (Middletown, Conn.: Wesleyan University Press, 1984), 304–322.

8. For Shaw and his radical views see David Como and Peter Lake, "Puritans, Antinomians, and Laudians in Caroline London: The Strange Case of Peter Shaw and Its Contexts," *Journal of Ecclesiastical History* 50 (1999), 684–715.

9. For the Dyers see Johann Winsser, "From Dissenting Puritan to Quaker 'Troubler,'" *New England Historical and Genealogical Register* 155 (2001), 91–104.

10. For Vane see David Parnham, *Sir Henry Vane, Theologian* (Madison: Fairleigh Dickinson University Press, 1997), and J. H. Adamson, *Sir Harry Vane: His Life and Times* (Boston: Gambit, 1973). The most effective depiction of Vane's involvement in the religious controversies of the Bay is to be found in Winship, *Making Heretics.*

11. An excellent overview of the Boston church at this time is Michael Winship's "'The Most Glorious Church in the World': The Unity of the Godly in Boston, Massachusetts, in the 1630s," *Journal of British Studies* 39 (2000), 71–98.

12. Hugh Peter to John Winthrop, April 1647, *WP*, V, 146–147.

13. John Endecott quoted in Winship, "Pynchon Reexamined," 797. In that essay Winship quotes Endecott in support of the position that "[t]ruth was unitary; the saints were not supposed to have serious doctrinal differences," but I believe it is open to another reading. Endecott, after all, was threatened with penalties for his support of Roger Williams, in whom he saw the mark of one of God's saints.

14. Shepard's responsibility for this innovation in church practice has been persuasively argued in Michael Ditmore, "Preparation and Confession: Reconsidering Edmund S. Morgan's *Visible Saints*," *New England Quarterly* 67 (1994), 298–313.

15. Thomas Shepard to John Cotton, between 1 February and 1 June 1636, in Sargent Bush Jr., ed., *The Correspondence of John Cotton* (Chapel Hill: University of North Carolina Press, 2001), 225–229.

16. John Cotton to Thomas Shepard, between 1 February and 1 June 1636, in Bush, *Correspondence of John Cotton*, 230–233.

17. Edward Johnson, *Johnson's Wonder-Working Providence, 1628–1651*, ed. J. Franklin Jameson (New York: Scribner's, 1910), 134.

18. Winship, *Making Heretics*, 72–76, 84–85.

19. Johnson, *Wonder-Working Providence*, 134.

20. I am following Michael Winship's analysis of the time of this meeting between Anne Hutchinson and the lay leaders of the Boston church. Winship believes that this was the meeting that became a focus of attention at the General Court's subsequent trial of Hutchinson.

21. *WJ*, 194–195.

22. Quotes are from the "Examination of Mrs. Anne Hutchinson," in David D. Hall, *The Antinomian Controversy, 1636–1638*, 2d ed. (Durham: Duke University Press, 1990), 319–336.

23. Winship, *Making Heretics*, 92–93.

24. [John Winthrop], *A Short Story of the Rise, Reign, and Ruin of the Antinomians, Familists, and Libertines* (1644), in Hall, *Antinomian Controversy*, 308.

25. *WJ*, 201.
26. Johnson, *Wonder-Working Providence*, 131–132.
27. Winthrop, *Short Story*, 210.
28. *WJ*, 203–205.
29. This entry was published in R. C. Winthrop's *Life and Letters* (II, 161), but not in the *WP*. R. C. Winthrop indicates that this was the last entry in the notebook. It will be published along with the rest of the spiritual diary as a single document in *Winthrop Papers: Religious Manuscripts* (forthcoming, Massachusetts Historical Society).
30. The only surviving copy of this is in the manuscript notebook of Henry Dunster in the Massachusetts Historical Society. A new edition will be printed in *Winthrop Papers: Religious Manuscripts*.
31. Thomas Shepard to John Winthrop, c. December 1636, *WP*, III, 326–332.
32. *WJ*, 208. Michael Winship discusses these sermons in *Making Heretics*, 114–115, and notes that William Coddington's recollection of Cotton's sermon (recorded years later) had the Boston teacher taking a more hostile, polarizing position. However, Coddington, who would be exiled for his support of Wheelwright, is likely to have interpreted Cotton's words from his own perspective at the time he heard the sermon or in retrospect after he had been exiled. But even if he was correct it is clear, which is my point, that Winthrop was trying to minimize the significance of the divisions.
33. Wheelwright as quoted in Winship, *Making Heretics*, 111–113.
34. *WJ*, 209.
35. *WJ*, 210–211.
36. *WJ*, 216–219; *RMB*, 195–197.
37. *WJ*, 216.
38. The texts of these are to be found in Hall, *Antinomian Controversy*.
39. Peter Bulkeley to John Cotton, 31 March 1637, Bush, *Cotton Correspondence*, 253–257.
40. *WJ*, 216.
41. *WJ*, 206, n. 58.
42. Thomas Shepard to John Winthrop, c. 20 May 1637, *WP*, III, 415–416.
43. Edmund S. Morgan, *The Puritan Dilemma: The Story of John Winthrop*, 2d ed. (New York: Longman, 1999), 129–130; Winship, *Making Heretics*, 138–139.
44. John Winthrop, "A Declaration in Defense of an Order of Court Made in May 1637," *WP*, III, 422–426.
45. Though most scholars have attributed this to Vane, I am not entirely sure that he was the author of the response, though he might very well have shared some of the views expressed. Vane was about to leave the Bay and did not necessarily wish to remain involved with the enthusiasts.
46. John Winthrop, "A Reply in Further Defense of an Order of Court Made in May 1637," *WP*, III, 463–476.
47. *WJ*, 228–229.
48. Roger Williams alludes to this longing by the exiled supporters of Wheelwright and Hutchinson in a letter to Winthrop, 16 April 1638, *WP*, IV, 25–26.
49. See Winship, *Making Heretics*, 146–147. I agree with Winship that Vane played a crucial and generally unappreciated role in the controversy. He encouraged Hutchinson, and his own radical doctrinal beliefs—different in some respects from Hutchinson's—circulated among the enthusiasts and were adopted by some. But I believe it is likely that, like Cotton, Vane eventually wished to disassociate himself from the more extreme ideas circulating in

the Boston community, and I do not believe that there is sufficient evidence to indicate that he himself wished to return to reunite with the enthusiasts.

50. *WJ*, 608.

51. Winthrop, *Short Story*, 212.

52. John Cotton, *A Conference Held at Boston*, in Hall, *Antinomian Controversy*, 173–198; John Cotton, *The Way of the Congregational Churches Cleared* (1648), in Hall, *Antinomian Controversy*, 400–407; *WJ*, 233–234. Winthrop seems to indicate that the disputed issues between Cotton and his colleagues were resolved during the synod, but David Hall makes a good case for the conference in question coming before the end of August.

53. Cotton, *Way of the Congregational Churches*, 408.

54. For unknown reasons a special election for members of the court was held in October. The findings of the synod might have influenced the choice of the freemen, since a substantial number of the members of the court that gathered in November were new. See Winship, *Making Heretics*, 167.

55. *RMB*, 207. See Winship, *Making Heretics*, 167–169.

56. "Examination of Mrs. Anne Hutchinson," in Hall, *Antinomian Controversy*, 312.

57. "Examination of Hutchinson," 342–342.

58. "Examination of Hutchinson," 336–343.

59. *RMB*, II, 207.

60. Winthrop, *Short Story*, 261–262.

61. *RMB*, 211–212.

62. A transcript of the trial appears in Hall, *Antinomian Controversy*, 349–388.

63. Winthrop, *Short Story*, 278–279.

64. Margaret Winthrop to John Winthrop, 15 November 1637, *WP*, III, 510.

65. John Winthrop to Margaret Winthrop, 15 November 1637, *WP*, III, 510–511.

66. John Clarke, a Rhode Island physician, described the birth as consisting of twenty-six lumps of flesh, the largest of which was about the size of a fist. Clarke's detailed account is printed in Battis, *Saints and Sectaries*, 347–348. Battis offers the suggestion of a modern physician that she had expelled a hydatiform mole. Winthrop wrote and sent to England a number of accounts of this event, seeing it as justifying his opposition to Hutchinson. For one of these see Valerie and Morris Pearl, "Governor John Winthrop on the Birth of the Antinomians' 'Monster': The Earliest Reports to Reach England and the Making of a Myth," *Proceedings of the Massachusetts Historical Society* 102 (1990), 27–37.

67. Emmanuel Downing to John Winthrop, 21 November 1637, *WP*, III, 512–513.

68. Emmanuel Downing to John Winthrop Jr., 13 March 1638, *WP*, IV, 20–21.

Chapter 15. New Trials and Disappointments

1. *WJ*, 340–341.

2. *WP*, IV, 147.

3. *WJ*, 257–258.

4. *WJ*, 292–294.

5. *WJ*, 174.

6. The charge that Vane was behind it was made by Richard Saltonstall in a later debate over the council; *WJ*, 391.

7. *RMB*, I, 175. Edmund S. Morgan, *The Puritan Dilemma: The Story of John Winthrop*, 2d ed. (New York: Longman, 1999), 143, states that a month (actually two months) after its establishment the council was "empowered to run the colony in the intervals between meetings of the General Court," but this seems somewhat broader and more definite than the actual court order. The initial grant of military authority between court sessions was temporary, but made permanent in October 1636; *RMB*, I, 183.

8. *RMB*, I, 167, 174, 195.

9. For a good summary of the prevalent views of the "ancient constitution" at this time see James S. Hart and Richard J. Ross, "The Ancient Constitution in the Old World and the New," in Lynn A. Botelho and Francis J. Bremer, *The World of John Winthrop* (forthcoming, 2003). Ironically, given the implicit attack on the common-law tradition by the colonial proponents of a code, it was the Stuart monarchs, whom the settlers were so suspicious of, who posed the principal challenge to that tradition in England.

10. *RMB*, I, 147.

11. *RMB*, I, 174.

12. *WJ*, 195.

13. *RMB*, I, 222.

14. *WJ*, 314.

15. *WJ*, 314–315. The Body of Liberties is to be found in William Whitmore, *Introduction to the Reprint of the Colonial Laws of 1660, Containing the Body of Liberties* (Boston, 1888).

16. Examples of these activities can be found in *WP*, IV. A list of complaints is printed on 128–129; an examination conducted by him on 165–166; depositions on 127, 131.

17. *RMB*, I, 133.

18. *WJ*, 370–374. Winthrop's paper on the issue was shared with John Wilson and Thomas Shepard; it does not survive but is referred to in Thomas Shepard to John Winthrop, c. 1642, in *WP*, IV, 345–346. Richard Godbeer discusses this case in *Sexual Revolution in Early America* (Baltimore: Johns Hopkins University Press, 2002), 107–108.

19. *WJ*, 271–272.

20. *WJ*, 404.

21. The importance of this effort to recreate the ways and ordinances of biblical times has been brilliantly explored by Theodore Dwight Bozeman in *To Live Ancient Lives: The Primitivist Dimension in Puritanism* (Chapel Hill: University of North Carolina Press, 1988), with the political aspects in chap. 5. Bozeman identifies Winthrop as an exponent of this primitivism. I believe that he used biblical precedents but was more influenced by his understanding of English legal and social traditions. Cotton's quote is from John Cotton to William Fiennes, Lord Saye and Sele, after March 1636, in Sargent Bush Jr., ed., *The Correspondence of John Cotton* (Chapel Hill: University of North Carolina Press, 2001), 244.

22. Only when Henry Vane took him to task for the fact that "in describing a commonwealth (such as ours is), I do not describe it as it is Christian," and based his own arguments firmly on the Bible, was Winthrop forced to prepare a further defense in which he employed biblical justifications liberally.

23. John Winthrop to _____, c. May 1642, *WP*, IV, 347.

24. In the eighteenth century Thomas Hutchinson examined a draft of Cotton's code on which Winthrop had marked changes. That copy no longer exists.

See Thomas Hutchinson, *The History of the Colony and Province of Massachu-setts-Bay*, ed. Lawrence Shaw Mayo (Cambridge: Harvard University Press, 1936), I, 373n.

25. *WJ*, 242–244.
26. "John Winthrop's Essay Against the Power of the Church to Sit in Judge-ment on the Civil Magistrate," *WP*, III, 505–507.
27. *WJ*, 316–318.
28. *WJ*, 246. Louise Breen tells the story of the formation of the Boston Artil-lery Company in *Transgressing the Bounds: Subversive Enterprises Among the Puritan Elite in Massachusetts, 1630–1692* (New York: Oxford University Press, 2001), 3–4.
29. *WJ*, 312.
30. *RMB*, II, 8–9.
31. *Boston Records, 1634–1660, and the Book of Possessions*, Second Report of the Record Commissioners of the City of Boston (Boston, 1902), 5. This is gen-erally credited with being the beginning of the Boston Latin School, which exists to this day.
32. *WJ*, 569.
33. Lucy Downing to John Winthrop, 4 March 1637, *WP*, III, 368. In May 1636 John Endecott and others proposed in the Salem town meeting that a tract of coastal land there be reserved as the site for a college, though noth-ing came from it. Samuel Eliot Morison, *The Founding of Harvard College* (Cambridge: Harvard University Press, 1935), 162–164. Morison's work remains the definitive study of the subject.
34. Emmanuel Downing to John Winthrop, 6 March 1637, *WP*, III, 370.
35. *RMB*, I, 183.
36. *RMB*, I, 208, 217, 228.
37. *WJ*, 302–305.
38. *WJ*, 283.
39. Though villeinage had disappeared, the discussion of "villein" in John Cowell's *The Interpreter, a booke containing the significance of Words . . . men-tioned in the Lawe Writers or Statutes* (1607) gave the impression to readers that the institution did still exist. Winthrop Jordan, *White over Black: Ameri-can Attitudes Toward the Negro, 1550–1812* (Chapel Hill: University of North Carolina Press, 1968), 50.
40. C.L.S. Davies, "Slavery and Protector Somerset; the Vagrancy Act of 1547," *Economic History Review*, 2d ser. 19 (1966), 533–549. I would like to thank John Thornton, Marjorie McIntosh, John Morrill, David Dean, J. H. Baker, and Steve Hindle for discussion of the meaning of "slavery" in England at this time and the transfer of those attitudes to Massachusetts.
41. While excellent in other respects, I believe that Betty Wood's *The Origins of American Slavery: Freedom and Bondage in the English Colonies* (New York: Oxford University Press, 1997) overstates the degree to which Englishmen found it inconceivable to enslave a fellow Englishman.
42. *CA*, 32. This and the following cases are noted by Richard B. Morris, *Gov-ernment and Labor in Early America* (New York: Columbia University Press, 1946), 346–347.
43. *CA*, 79.
44. *CA*, 90.
45. *CA*, 94.
46. *CA*, 97.

47. Coke quoted in Jordan, *White over Black*, 55.
48. See Wood, *Origins*, chap. 3.
49. Henry Winthrop to John Winthrop, 15 October 1627, *WP*, I, 361–362.
50. For a discussion of whether Maverick owned slaves before 1630 see Lorenzo Greene, *The Negro in Colonial New England* (New York: Atheneum, 1969), 16.
51. *WJ*, 246.
52. Lorenzo Greene argues that Winthrop did not own African-American slaves (*Negro in Colonial New England*, 109, but bases that claim on an inventory of Winthrop's estate following his death. No Indian slaves appeared on that inventory either, and it is not clear that slave property would have been included.
53. Emmanuel Downing to John Winthrop, c. August 1645, *WP*, V, 38.
54. This is number 91 in the Body of Liberties.
55. This was changed with a 1670 correction of the law. See Greene, *Negro in Colonial New England*, 65.
56. Greene, *Negro in Colonial New England*, chap. 4.
57. *WJ*, 347.
58. One of the three surviving manuscript volumes of Keayne's sermon notebook contains sermons heard in London in the late 1620s. The other two volumes consist of sermons heard in Boston, Massachusetts. Sargent Bush Jr. and I are working on an edition of the Keayne Sermon Notebooks, which are in the collections of the Massachusetts Historical Society.
59. For a summary of recent historical views and discussion of English and New England views see Mark Valeri, "Puritans in the Marketplace," in Lynn A. Botelho and Francis J. Bremer, eds., *The World of John Winthrop: England and New England, 1588–1649* (forthcoming, 2003).
60. *WJ*, 306.
61. *WJ*, 307–309. For an excellent discussion of these events and issues see Stephen Innes, *Creating the Commonwealth: The Economic Culture of Puritan New England* (New York: Norton, 1995), and in particular chap. 4, "The Ethics of Exchange, Price Controls, and the Case of Robert Keayne."
62. *WJ*, 342.
63. *WJ*, 307–309.
64. John Winthrop to Ezekiel Rogers, c. March 1640, *WP*, IV, 208–210.
65. Codicil to Will of John Winthrop, *WP*, IV, 147.
66. *RMB*, I, 283, 295.
67. *WJ*, 315.
68. Lucy Downing to John Winthrop, c. January 1640, *WP*, IV, 171–172.
69. Emmanuel Downing to John Winthrop, c. January 1640, *WP*, IV, 173–174.
70. Edward Winslow to John Winthrop, 17 February 1640, *WP*, IV, 192–193.
71. Sir Francis Bacon to John Winthrop, 16 April 1640, *WP*, IV, 228.
72. Brampton Gurdon to John Winthrop, 13 May 1640, *WP*, IV, 243–244. It is important to note that not all of the Winthrop correspondence survived, and so caution should be exercised in reaching conclusions about those friends not mentioned in this regard.
73. Will of John Winthrop, October 1639, *WP*, IV, 146–147.
74. Revocation of Will, *WP*, IV, 147.
75. The best discussion of this is found in Mellen Chamberlain, "Governor Winthrop's Estate," *Massachusetts Historical Society Proceedings*, 2d ser. 7 (1891, 1892), 127–143.
76. Report by Giles Firmin in Giles Firmin to John Winthrop, 12 February 1640, *WP*, IV, 188–189.

77. John Winthrop to Margaret Winthrop, 8 November 1638, *WP*, IV, 73.
78. John Winthrop to John Winthrop Jr., 22 January 1638, *WP*, IV, 9–10.
79. John Winthrop to John Winthrop Jr., c. 1643, *WP*, IV, 366–367.
80. Lucy Downing to Margaret Winthrop, c. 20 January 1641, *WP*, IV, 306–307.
81. Stephen Winthrop to Margaret Winthrop, 20 March 1638, *WP*, IV, 21.
82. Roger Williams to John Winthrop, c. October 1638, *WP*, IV, 65–66.
83. Thomas James to John Winthrop, c. 1639, *WP*, IV, 89–90.
84. John Endecott to John Winthrop, 19 March 1646, *WP*, V, 68.
85. See, for example, Anne Hoskins to John Winthrop Jr., 13 January 1638, *WP*, IV, 7–8.
86. Samuel Fones to John Winthrop, 21 February 1640, *WP*, IV, 198–199.
87. Mary Cole to John Winthrop, 2 May 1640, *WP*, IV, 235–236.
88. Lawrence Wright to John Winthrop, 26 May 1640, *WP*, IV, 220.
89. Benjamin Hubbard to John Winthrop, 25 February 1645, *WP*, V, 10.
90. John Winthrop to the earl of Warwick, c. 1646, *WP*, V, 58.
91. For a different view on Winthrop and women see Laurel Thatcher Ulrich, "John Winthrop's City of Women," *Massachusetts Historical Review* 3 (2001), 19–48.
92. See letters of Mary Winthrop Dudley to Margaret Winthrop, *WP*, 221, 222, 239, 242, 257, 263.
93. See John Endecott to John Winthrop, 22 April 1644, *WP*, 455–456, in which Endecott warns Winthrop about this "dangerous woman."
94. The full account of the Hibbens case, with a transcript that includes Winthrop's statements, is in the notebooks of Robert Keayne, three manuscript volumes in the collections of the Massachusetts Historical Society. Sargent Bush Jr. and I will be preparing an edition of the sermon notes in these notebooks. Dr. Helle Alpert is working on an edition of the non-sermon portions of the notebooks, which include the Hibbens case. I would like to thank Dr. Alpert for lending me a copy of her transcript. Mary Beth Norton includes a discussion of the Hibbens case in *Founding Mothers and Fathers: Gendered Power and the Forming of American Society* (New York: Knopf, 1996), 81–83, 161–164.
95. *WJ*, 570.

Chapter 16. War Clouds and Concerns

1. *WJ*, 440–441.
2. Darrett Rutman, *Winthrop's Boston: A Portrait of a Puritan Town* (New York: Norton, 1965), 179.
3. Robert Emmet Wall Jr., *Massachusetts Bay: The Crucial Decade, 1640–1650* (New Haven: Yale University Press, 1972), 39–40 provides a list of the counties, towns, and population as of 1647.
4. Reverend William Tompson in Acomenticus to John Winthrop, 15 May 1638, *WP*, IV, 31–34; Hanserd Knollys in Dover to John Winthrop, 21 January 1640, *WP*, IV, 176ff.
5. *WJ*, 405–406, 426–427, 508. Thomas Harrison managed to defy the Virginia authorities and sustain a congregation of over a hundred Congregationalists in Nansemond County until 1648.
6. *WJ*, 488–489.
7. *WJ*, 480–481.

8. Roger Ludlow to the governor and assistants of Massachusetts, 29 May 1638, *WP*, IV, 36–37. The full story of the New England Confederation is told in Harry M. Ward, *The United Colonies of New England, 1643–1690* (New York: Vantage, 1961).

9. John Winthrop's summary of his letter to Thomas Hooker, *WP*, IV, 53–54.

10. John Winthrop to Thomas Hooker, c. March 1639, *WP*, IV, 99–100.

11. *WJ*, 406–412.

12. *RMB*, II, 31.

13. *RMB*, II, 35.

14. *WJ*, 432–440.

15. *WJ*, 515.

16. Thomas Hooker to John Winthrop, 15 July 1643, *WP*, IV, 401–402.

17. There are many excellent accounts of the coming of the English Civil Wars. A good starting place for putting the events in context are the essays in John Morrill, ed., *The Oxford Illustrated History of Tudor and Stuart England* (Oxford: Oxford University Press, 1996). The most detailed study of the events leading to the conflict is Conrad Russell, *The Fall of the British Monarchies, 1637–1642* (Oxford: Clarendon Press, 1991). Valuable insights are to be found in John Morrill, *The Nature of the English Revolution* (London: Longman, 1993). Among the works of Christopher Hill consult *God's Englishman: Oliver Cromwell and the English Revolution* (London: Weidenfeld & Nicolson, 1970) and *Puritanism and Revolution* (London: Panther, 1968). William Haller's *The Rise of Puritanism* (New York: Columbia University Press, 1938) still has useful insight into the impact of religion on the coming of the wars. A view more sympathetic to the king is Kevin Sharpe, *The Personal Rule of Charles I* (New Haven: Yale University Press, 1995). Oliver Cromwell offers an interesting parallel to John Winthrop. Those wishing to view the coming of the English conflict, the wars, and the resulting puritan regime through a biographical perspective should consult John Morrill, ed., *Oliver Cromwell and the English Revolution* (London: Longman, 1990), and J. C. Davis, *Oliver Cromwell* (London: Arnold, 2001). I have dealt with the broader issues involved in New England's engagement with the English Civil Wars and their aftermath in *Puritan Crisis: New England and the English Civil Wars, 1630–1670* (Westport, Conn.: Greenwood, 1989), and *Congregational Communion: Clerical Friendship in the Anglo-American Puritan Community, 1610–1692* (Boston: Northeastern University Press, 1994), chaps. 6 through 8.

18. John Harrison Jr. to John Winthrop, 11 August 1639, *WP*, IV, 138.

19. Nehemiah Bourne to John Winthrop, 14 November 1639, *WP*, IV, 153–155.

20. Sir Nathaniel Barnardiston to John Winthrop, 15 March 1640, *WP*, IV, 217–218.

21. Brampton Gurdon to John Winthrop, 13 May 1640, *WP*, IV, 243–244.

22. Edward Payne to John Winthrop, 28 May 1640, *WP*, IV, 248–249.

23. John Endecott's account in a letter to Winthrop, 28 July 1640, *WP*, IV, 270–271.

24. *WJ*, 331–332.

25. Endecott to Winthrop, 28 July 1640, *WP*, IV, 270.

26. William Bradford to John Winthrop, 16 August 1640, *WP*, IV, 275.

27. Roger Williams to John Winthrop, 7 August 1640, *WP*, IV, 273.

28. *WJ*, 341.

29. *WJ*, 341.

30. John Tinker to John Winthrop, 26 February 1640, *WP*, IV, 205–206; Benjamin Gostlin to John Winthrop, 6 March 1640, *WP*, IV, 216–217.

31. *WJ*, 339.
32. The best analysis of the region's economy at this time remains Bernard Bailyn's *The New England Merchants in the Seventeenth Century* (Cambridge: Harvard University Press, 1955), chap. 3.
33. *WJ*, 323; Winthrop's anger with Humfry can be inferred from John Humfry to John Winthrop, c. 1640, *WP*, IV, 166–167
34. *WJ*, 323–324; there is no report of this in the official *RMB*.
35. *WJ*, 334.
36. Lord Saye and Sele to John Winthrop, 9 July 1640, *WP*, IV, 263–267.
37. *WP*, IV, 268.
38. For a different view on the effort to get Bay colonists to relocate see Karen Ordahl Kupperman, *Providence Island, 1630–1641: The Other Puritan Colony* (Cambridge: Cambridge University Press, 1993), chap. 11.
39. *WJ*, 345.
40. See Rutman, *Winthrop's Boston*, 184–185
41. See Larry D. Gragg, "A Puritan in the West Indies: The Career of Samuel Winthrop," *William and Mary Quarterly*, 3d ser. 50 (1993), 768–786.
42. *WJ*, 692–693.
43. Robert C. Black III, *The Younger John Winthrop* (New York: Columbia University Press, 1966), 110, 116–123.
44. Bailyn, *New England Merchants*, 71–74.
45. Lucy Downing to John Winthrop Jr., 28 January 1641, *WP*, IV, 311.
46. *WJ*, 353.
47. John Endecott to John Winthrop, c. February 1641, *WP*, IV, 317–319.
48. *WJ*, 345–346.
49. Bremer, *Congregational Communion*, 145.
50. For the story of the Welde-Peter mission see Raymond Phineas Stearns, "The Weld-Peter Mission to England," *Colonial Society of Massachusetts Publications* 32 (1937), 188–246.
51. Emmanuel Downing to Hugh Peter, 29 July 1641, *WP*, IV, 340–341.
52. *WJ*, 365; Richard Dunn's note on that page provides further details.
53. "The Grand Remonstrance," in Samuel Rawson Gardiner, ed., *The Constitutional Documents of the Puritan Revolution, 1625–1660* (Oxford: Clarendon Press, 1962), 202–231.
54. Bremer, *Puritan Crisis*, 101.
55. William Hooke, *New Englands Teares for Old Englands Feares* (1641), rpt. in Samuel Emery, *The Ministry of Taunton* (Boston, 1853), 87.
56. Hooke, Bradford, and Shepard as quoted in Bremer, *Puritan Crisis*, 101.
57. Thomas Cobbet, *A Practical Discourse of Prayer* (1657), to the reader.
58. William Hooke, *New England Sence of Old England and Irelands Sorrows* (1645), in Emery, *Taunton*, 116–117, 125–126, 116, 117.
59. John Cotton quoted in Bremer, *Puritan Crisis*, 110.
60. Francis J. Bremer, *The Puritan Experiment: New England Society from Bradford to Edwards*, rev. ed. (Hanover, N.H.: University Press of New England, 1995), 125.
61. William Pynchon to John Winthrop, 19 February 1644, *WP*, IV, 443–444.
62. *WJ*, 403. See Bremer, *Congregational Communion*, chap. 6, for a full discussion of the relationship between colonial and English congregationalists at this time.
63. A copy of the order is entered in *RMB*, II, 34; Winthrop records the order in *WJ*, 429.

64. *WJ*, 429. In his note Richard Dunn points out that when Parliament reissued the order in 1644 it substituted the word "country" for "kingdom" in referring to New England.
65. *WJ*, 432.
66. *WJ*, 502.
67. *WJ*, 510.
68. *RMB*, II, 69.
69. *WJ*, 518–519.
70. *WJ*, 524ff.
71. *WJ*, 524ff.
72. *WJ*, 476. See also Williston Walker, *The Creeds and Platforms of Congregationalism* (n.p., 1893), 137–139.
73. John Wheelwright to John Winthrop, 10 September 1643, *WP*, IV, 414–415.
74. John Wheelwright to John Winthrop, 1 March 1644, *WP*, IV, 449–450; *RMB*, III, 6.
75. For a discussion of Baptist views in early New England see William G. McLoughlin, *New England Dissent, 1630–1833: The Baptists and the Separation of Church and State, I* (Cambridge: Harvard University Press, 1971) and Carla Gardina Pestana, *Quakers and Baptists in Colonial Massachusetts* (New York: Oxford University Press, 1991), though my account differs in substantial respects from Pestana.
76. *WJ*, 517.
77. Stephen Winthrop to John Winthrop, 1 March 1645, *WP*, V, 13.
78. George Downing to John Winthrop Jr., 26 August 1645, *WP*, V, 43–45.
79. *RMB*, III, 51.
80. "Memorandum on Baptism," *WP*, V, 32, and will be published in a new transcription in Francis J. Bremer, ed., *Winthrop Papers: Religious Manuscripts* (2003); *WJ*, 611–612. In his note Richard Dunn suggests that the petition was prompted by a letter to Winthrop from prominent English congregationalists protesting against the treatment of Baptists, dated at this time in *WP*, V, 23–25. However, that letter was misdated. It was actually sent in 1669. See Francis J. Bremer, "When? Who? Why? Reevaluating a Seventeenth-Century Source," *Massachusetts Historical Society Proceedings* 99 (1987), 63–75.
81. *RMB*, III, 64.
82. Gorton features throughout Philip Gura's *A Glimpse of Sion's Glory: Puritan Radicalism in New England, 1620–1660* (1984).
83. Coddington, incidentally, was soon writing to John Winthrop in the hope of restoring good relations with his former friend and with the Boston church.
84. Roger Williams to John Winthrop, 8 March 1641, *The Correspondence of Roger Williams*, ed. Glenn LaFantasie, 2 vols. (Hanover: Brown University Press, 1988), I, 215.
85. *RMB*, II, 26.
86. Holden as quoted in Wall, *Crucial Decade*, 131–134.
87. *RMB*, II, 51–52.
88. Samuel Gorton, *Simplicities Defence Against Seven-Headed Policy* (1646).
89. *WJ*, 638–641, which includes the text of the Warwick Commission's order.
90. *WJ*, 366–367.
91. *WJ*, 417.
92. *WJ*, 420.
93. This and the following paragraphs are drawn primarily from *WJ*, 440–450.
94. Thomas Gorges to John Winthrop, 28 June 1643, *WP*, IV, 396.

95. John Endecott to John Winthrop, 19 June 1643, *WP*, IV, 394–395.

96. Richard Saltonstall and others to the governor, deputy governor, assistants, and elders, 14 July 1643, *WP*, IV, 397–401.

97. Winthrop's account of the meeting is in *WJ*, 443–450; John Winthrop to Richard Saltonstall and others, c. 21 July 1643, *WP*, IV, 402–410.

98. Knowing that John's own relationship with the Mannocks was a good one, in 1622 Henry Sandes had asked John to use his influence with that family to have them appoint a godly preacher to the living they controlled at Stoke-by-Nayland. Henry Sandes to John Winthrop, 1622, *WP*, I, 270.

99. Simon Bradstreet to John Winthrop, 21 August 1643, *WP*, IV, 412–413.

100. John Endecott to John Winthrop, 26 July 1643, *WP*, IV, 411–412.

101. *WJ*, 630.

102. *WJ*, 641–643.

Chapter 17.   Under Attack

1. *WJ*, 579.

2. Robert Emmett Wall Jr. discusses some of these strains in *Massachusetts Bay: The Crucial Decade, 1640–1650* (New Haven: Yale University Press, 1972), though I believe he places too much emphasis on class division. For Hingham see John J. Waters, "Hingham, Massachusetts, 1631–1661: An East Anglian Oligarchy in the New World," *Journal of Social History* 1 (1968), 351–370.

3. Wall, *Crucial Decade*, 43–44.

4. See Robert Charles Anderson, *The Great Migration: Immigrants to New England, 1634–1635. I: A–B* (Boston: New England Historical and Genealogical Society, 1999), 248–250.

5. *WJ*, 367.

6. Israel Stoughton to John Stoughton, 1635, in Everett Emerson, ed., *Letters from New England: The Massachusetts Bay Colony, 1629–1638* (Amherst: University of Massachusetts Press, 1976), 144–155.

7. *WJ*, 390; see also Wall, *Crucial Decade*, 44–46.

8. John Winthrop to _____, c. May 1642, *WP*, IV, 347–348.

9. *WJ*, 418–420.

10. *WJ*, 395–396.

11. *WJ*, 396.

12. *WJ*, 396.

13. *RMB*, II, 12.

14. This is the opinion of Wall, *Crucial Decade*, 54.

15. "John Winthrop's Summary of the Case Between Richard Sherman and Robert Keayne," 15 July 1642, *WP*, 349–352.

16. *WJ*, 398.

17. John Winthrop to the elders of the Massachusetts churches, 14 October 1642, *WP*, IV, 359–361. This fragment contains what is in all likelihood Winthrop's statement on the negative voice.

18. Richard Dunn (*WJ*, 456n.) suggests that the author of the answer, which does not survive, was Bellingham, and I agree with him.

19. These and the following quotes are from "John Winthrop's Defense of the Negative Voice," *WP*, IV, 380–391.

20. Francis Williams to John Winthrop, 9 May 1643, *WP*, IV, 375–376.

21. *WJ*, 451–456.

22. *WJ*, 503; *RMB*, II, 58–59.
23. *WJ*, 509ff.; Wall, *Crucial Decade*, 75–76.
24. *WJ*, 509ff.
25. *WJ*, 513–515. A copy of the declaration is in *WP*, IV, 467.
26. "John Winthrop's Discourse on Arbitrary Government," *WP*, IV, 468–488, from which the quotes that follow are taken.
27. Wall, *Crucial Decade*, 83–84.
28. *WJ*, 561.
29. *WJ*, 575–578; Wall, *Crucial Decade*, chap. 3 deals with the Hingham militia case.
30. The petition is quoted in its entirety in Wall, *Crucial Decade*, 100–101.
31. Wall, *Crucial Decade*, 102–103.
32. Edward Winslow, *New England's Salamander, Discovered* (London, 1647), as quoted in Wall, *Crucial Decade*, 104.
33. *WJ*, 579ff.; *RMB*, III, 19–26.
34. *WJ*, 534.
35. *RMB*, II, 114.
36. *WJ*, 624. Vassall had first challenged the Plymouth system. In November of 1645 Edward Winslow wrote to Winthrop about a proposal Vassall made to that colony's General Court that would have granted liberty of conscience to all except Jews, Turks, Catholics, Arians, Socinians, and familists. Many of the deputies supported it—Winthrop would have been surprised "to have seen how sweet this carrion relished to the palate of most of the deputies"— but Governor Bradford refused to put it to a vote as threatening the godliness of the colony. "By these things," wrote Winslow, "you may see that all the troubles of new England are not at the Massachusetts." *WP*, V, 55–56. Then Vassall advised the Hinghamites in their protest.
37. Wall, *Crucial Decade*, 166–169. The petition itself is published in Thomas Hutchinson, *Collection of Original Papers* (1769).
38. Profiles of all the petitioners are included in the appendix to Wall, *Crucial Decade*.
39. John Winthrop to John Winthrop Jr., 16 November 1646, *WP*, V, 119–120.
40. These quotes and those that follow come from *WJ*, 647–655.
41. *RMB*, III, 90–91.
42. *WJ*, 659–665.
43. *WJ*, 665–670.
44. Robert Child to John Winthrop Jr., 15 March 1647, *WP*, V, 140–141.

Chapter 18. Last Years

1. *WJ*, 702–704.
2. *WJ*, 687.
3. *WJ*, 691.
4. Richard Vines in Barbados to John Winthrop, 29 April 1648, *WP*, V, 219–220.
5. Samuel Winthrop to John Winthrop, 30 August 1647, *WP*, V, 180–181.
6. Stephen Winthrop to John Winthrop, 1 March 1648, *WP*, V, 203–205, and see his letter to his brother John in the same volume, 205–206.
7. Herbert Pelham to John Winthrop, 3 April 1648, *WP*, V, 216–219.
8. The witnessed trust agreement was submitted to the General Court for approval; *RMB*, II, 232–233.

9. William Coddington to John Winthrop, 25 May 1648, *WP*, V, 224.

10. Lucy Downing to John Winthrop Jr., 17 December 1648, *WP*, V, 290–291.

11. For a detailed discussion of this see Francis J. Bremer, *Congregational Communion: Clerical Friendship in the Anglo-American Puritan Community, 1610–1692* (Boston: Northeastern University Press, 1994), 152–174.

12. William Pynchon to John Winthrop, 19 October 1648, *WP*, V, 271.

13. Thomas Peter to John Winthrop Jr., 26 June 1648, *WP*, V, 233–234.

14. See a letter from Thomas Turnor, an agent of Warwick, to John Winthrop, 10 June 1648, *WP*, V, 228–229.

15. John Winthrop to John Winthrop Jr., 6 October 1648, *WP*, V, 265–266; he had expressed his sadness about the war in a previous letter to John Jr., 30 September 1648, *WP*, V, 261–262.

16. John Winthrop to John Winthrop Jr., 3 February 1649, *WP*, V, 311–312.

17. For Gifford and witchcraft see Alan Macfarlane, "A Tudor Anthropologist: George Gifford's *Discourse and Dialogue*," in S. Anglo, ed., *The Damned Art: Essays in the Literature of Witchcraft* (London: Routledge & Keegan Paul, 1977), 140–155.

18. There is little direct evidence regarding John Winthrop's views, other than his references to the case of Margaret Jones noted below. John Jr.'s efforts are treated by Walt Woodward in "Prospero's America: John Winthrop Jr., Alchemy, and the Creation of New England Culture (1606–1676)" (University of Connecticut, Ph.D., 2001), which will be published by the Omohundro Institute of Early American History and Culture. John's grandson, John Jr.'s son Wait Still Winthrop, was a member of the Court of Oyer and Terminer in Salem in 1692. No direct evidence of his role on the court exists, though it is suggestive that there is a gap in his ample correspondence for that year.

19. *WJ*, 711–712. The court order is in *RMB*, III, 126.

20. *WJ*, 715.

21. See Williston Walker, *The Creeds and Platforms of Congregationalism* (n.p., 1893).

22. A discussion of this work is to be found in Richard B. Morris, "Massachusetts and the Common Law: The Declaration of 1646," in David H. Flaherty, ed., *Essays in the History of Early American Law* (Chapel Hill: University of North Carolina Press, 1969), 135–146.

23. See Thorp L. Wolford, "The Laws and Liberties of 1648," in Flaherty, *Early American Law*, 147–185.

24. John Cotton to John Winthrop, late March or April 1648, in Sargent Bush Jr., ed., *The Correspondence of John Cotton* (Chapel Hill: University of North Carolina Press, 2002), 400–404.

25. *WJ*, 682–684. For some of the difficulties of converting the native peoples see Charles L. Cohen, "Conversion Among Puritans and Amerindians: A Theological and Cultural Perspective," in Francis J. Bremer, ed., *Puritanism: Transatlantic Perspectives on a Seventeenth-Century Anglo-American Faith* (Boston: Massachusetts Historical Society, 1993), 233–256.

26. John Winthrop to John Winthrop Jr., 30 September 1648, *WP*, V, 261–262.

27. *WJ*, 257.

28. John Winthrop to John Winthrop Jr., 3 February 1649, *WP*, V, 311–312.

29. John Endecott to John Winthrop, 1 March 1649, *WP*, V, 316–317.

30. Adam Winthrop to John Winthrop Jr., 14 March 1649, *WP*, V, 319.

31. Cotton Mather, *Magnalia Christi Americana, Books I and II*, ed. Kenneth B. Murdock (Cambridge, Mass.: Belknap, 1977), 228.

32. Robert C. Winthrop, *The Life and Letters of John Winthrop*, 3d ed. (Boston, 1895), 50.
33. *RMB*, III, 162.

Epilogue

1. The full program of speakers included John Morrill of Cambridge University, Roger Thompson of the University of East Anglia, John Walter of the University of Essex, Francis Bremer of Millersville University of Pennsylvania, and prominent local historians such as David Dymond and Peter Northeast.
2. Robert C. Winthrop, *Life and Letters of John Winthrop* (Boston, 1864), 1–5.
3. *Massachusetts Historical Society Proceedings*, 2d ser. 17, 130.
4. Edmund S. Morgan, "America's First Great Man," *New York Review of Books*, 12 June 1997, 42–44.
5. For a more detailed discussion of how Winthrop has been perceived over time see James G. Moseley, *John Winthrop's World: History as a Story, the Story as History* (Madison: University of Wisconsin Press, 1992), chaps. 7 and 8. For a fuller discussion of the broader theme of how Americans have shaped and used the early history of New England see John Seelye, *Memory's Nation: The Place of Plymouth Rock* (Chapel Hill: University of North Carolina Press, 1998).
6. H. L. Mencken, *A Mencken Chrestomathy* (New York: Knopf, 1949), 624.
7. Lawrence Shaw Mayo, *The Winthrop Family in America* (Boston: Massachusetts Historical Society, 1948), 433. Mayo suggests that Mr. Winthrop, who hated the limelight, had to be persuaded to play the role of his ancestor.

Index

Index